Lecture Notes in Computer Science
Edited by G. Goos, J. Hartmanis, and J. van Leeuw

Springer
Berlin
Heidelberg
New York
Barcelona
Hong Kong
London
Milan
Paris
Tokyo

Tony Field Peter G. Harrison
Jeremy Bradley Uli Harder (Eds.)

Computer Performance Evaluation

Modelling Techniques and Tools

12th International Conference, TOOLS 2002
London, UK, April 14-17, 2002
Proceedings

Volume Editors

Tony Field
Peter G. Harrison
Jeremy Bradley
Uli Harder
Imperial College of Science, Technology, and Medicine, Department of Computing
Huxley Building, 180 Queen's Gate, London SW7 2BZ, UK
E-mail: {ajf/pgh/jb/uh}@doc.ic.ac.uk

Cataloging-in-Publication Data applied for

Die Deutsche Bibliothek - CIP-Einheitsaufnahme

Computer performance evaluation : modelling techniques and tools ; ...
international conference ... ; proceedings. - 7 (1994) [?]-. - Berlin ;
Heidelberg ; New York ; Barcelona ; Hong Kong ; London ; Milan ;
Paris ; Singapore ; Tokyo : Springer, 1994 [?]-
(Lecture notes in computer science ; ...)
12. Tools 2002 : London, UK, April 14-17, 2002. - 2002
(Lecture notes in computer science ; Vol. 2324)
ISBN 3-540-43539-5

CR Subject Classification (1998): C.4, D.2.8, D.2.2, I.6

ISSN 0302-9743
ISBN 3-540-43539-5 Springer-Verlag Berlin Heidelberg New York

Springer-Verlag Berlin Heidelberg New York
a member of BertelsmannSpringer Science+Business Media GmbH

http://www.springer.de

Typesetting: Camera-ready by author, data conversion by PTP-Berlin, Stefan Sossna e.K.
Printed on acid-free paper SPIN: 10846709 06/3142 5 4 3 2 1 0

Preface

The argument for performance engineering methods to be employed in computer-communication systems has always been that such systems cannot be designed or modified efficiently without recourse to some form of predictive model, just as in other fields of engineering. This argument has never been more valid than it is with today's highly complex combination of communication and computer technologies. These have created the internet, the grid, and diverse types of parallel and distributed computer systems. To be practical, performance engineering relies on tools to render its use accessible to the non-performance specialist, and in turn these depend on sound techniques that include analytical methods, stochastic models, and simulation. Tools and techniques also need to be parameterised and validated against real world observations, requiring sophisticated measurement techniques in the picosecond cyber-world. The series of "International Conferences on Modelling Techniques and Tools for Computer Performance Evaluation" (TOOLS) has provided a forum for this community of performance engineers with all their diverse interests. TOOLS 2002, held in London in April 2002, was the continuation of this series, which comprises:

1984 Paris
1985 Sophia Antipolis
1987 Paris
1988 Palma
1991 Torino
1992 Edinburgh
1994 Wien
1995 Heidelberg
1997 Saint Malo
1998 Palma
2000 Chicago
2002 London

This year we were fortunate to have two prominent invited speakers, Onno Boxma, Eindhoven University of Technology, and Peter Key of Microsoft Research, Cambridge. In addition, an invited tutorial was given by Erol Gelenbe, University of Central Florida, one of the leading researchers in Performance Modelling. A total of 57 papers were submitted, including 9 tools proposals. At the Programme Committee meeting in January, 18 excellent papers were considered to be of high enough quality to be accepted, along with 6 tools presentations. The number of tools presentations was somewhat lower than at previous conferences in the series, probably due to the new constraints imposed requiring open source software. These were introduced to facilitate greater ease of dissemination and collaboration. All of the accepted papers have been included in this volume, 10 of them in extended form, up to 20 pages long.

The conference was organised into a single track comprising eight sessions of mixed topics. Some of the papers addressed generic techniques, for example related to Stochastic Process Algebra and the analysis of Petri Nets and Markov Chains. Others concerned the development and practical application of tools in areas such as the Internet, Software Performance Engineering, Parallel and Real-time Systems, and Transaction Processing.

In addition to the 18 main papers, the volume also includes a reduced (up to 6-page) paper for each tool presented.

It is a pleasure for the Program Chairs to acknowledge the staunch efforts made by many to make this conference possible and ensure its success. The whole Program Committee worked tirelessly on a very tight timescale to produce sufficient reviews in time for the meeting in mid-January, only seven weeks after the final submission deadline. There were at least three reviews for every submission and some even had five. Moreover, the large majority gave a careful, in-depth opinion. The same applies to several external referees that supported committee members.

In particular, we wish to thank the following for their administrative, organisational, and IT contributions, without which the schedule could not have been implemented, there would have been nowhere for participants to stay, and we would not have had the superb social events arranged at the *London Eye* and *Bistro 190*:

- Dave Nichol for writing WIMPE and advising us
- Dave Thornley for local arrangements
- Imperial College and the Department of Computing in particular, for hosting the conference and providing technical support
- Denise Grant for helping us to organise the finances

February 2002

Tony Field
Peter Harrison
Jeremy Bradley
Uli Harder

Organisation

Tools 2002 was organised by the AESOP group of the Department of Computer Science, Imperial College, London.

Executive Committee

Conference Chair:	Rob Pooley (Heriot-Watt University, Edinburgh)
Programme Co-chairs:	Tony Field & Peter Harrison (Imperial College, London)
Web Chair:	Jeremy Bradley (Imperial College, London)
Tutorial Chair:	William Knottenbelt (Imperial College, London)
Tools Chair:	Uli Harder (Imperial College, London)
Local Organising Chair:	David Thornley (Imperial College, London)
Local Secretary:	Harf Zatschler (Imperial College, London)

Programme Committee

Vladimir Anisimov (TR)
Heinz Beilner (DE)
Henrik Bohnenkamp (NL)
Jeremy Bradley (UK)
Peter Buchholz (DE)
Rick Bunt (CA)
Maria Calzarossa (IT)
Giovanni Chiola (IT)
Gianfranco Ciardo (US)
Tony Field (UK)
Reinhard German (DE)
Peter Harrison (DE)
Boudewijn Haverkort (DE)
Jane Hillston (UK)
Peter Hughes (UK)
Joost-Pieter Katoen (NL)
William Knottenbelt (NL)
Pieter Kritzinger (SA)
Christoph Lindemann (DE)
Raymond Marie (FR)
Daniel A. Menascé (US)
Brigitte Plateau (FR)
Rob Pooley (UK)
Ramon Puigjaner (ES)
Dan Reed (US)
Martin Reiser (DE)
Gerardo Rubino (FR)
William Sanders (US)
Connie Smith (US)
Edmundo A. de Souza e Silva (BR)
William J. Stewart (US)
Hideaki Takagi (JP)
Nigel Thomas (UK)
Murray Woodside (CA)

Referees

Falko Bause
Olav Beckmann
Marco Bernardo
Nadia Busi
Dan Chalmers
Susanna Donatelli

Derek Eager
Felix Engelhard
Stephen Gilmore
Uli Harder
Holger Hermanns
Kai-Steffen Hielscher
Pierre G. Jansen
Peter Kemper
Alexander Klemm
Marco Lohmann
Dwight Makaroff
Julie McCann
Ken McDonell
Louis-Marie Le Ny
Johannes Lüthi
Isi Mitrani
M. Molnar
Dorina Petriu
Alma Riska
Nunzio Savino-Vazquez
Kevin Schneider
Yussuf Abu Shaaban
Radu I. Siminiceanu
Daniele Tessera
David Thornley
Chris Tofts
Jeroen Voeten
Oliver Waldhorst
Lourens Walters
Wenguang Wang
Carey Williamson

Table of Contents

Heavy Tails: The Effect of the Service Discipline

S.C. Borst[1,2,3], O.J. Boxma[1,2], and R. Núñez-Queija[1,2]

[1] CWI
P.O. Box 94079, 1090 GB Amsterdam, The Netherlands
{sem,sindo}@cwi.nl
[2] Department of Mathematics & Computer Science
Eindhoven University of Technology
P.O. Box 513, 5600 MB Eindhoven, The Netherlands
boxma@win.tue.nl
[3] Bell Laboratories, Lucent Technologies
P.O. Box 636, Murray Hill, NJ 07974, USA

Abstract. This paper considers the $M/G/1$ queue with regularly varying service requirement distribution. It studies the effect of the service discipline on the tail behavior of the waiting- or sojourn time distribution, demonstrating that different disciplines may lead to quite different tail behavior. The orientation of the paper is methodological: We outline three different methods of determining tail behavior, illustrating them for service disciplines like FCFS, Processor Sharing and LCFS.

This paper is dedicated to the memory of Vincent Dumas, a dear friend and gifted young mathematician.

1 Introduction

Measurements indicate that traffic in high-speed networks exhibits burstiness on a wide range of time scales, manifesting itself in long-range dependence and self-similarity, see for instance Leland *et al.* [29], Paxson & Floyd [38]. The occurrence of these phenomena is commonly attributed to extreme variability and long-tailed characteristics in the underlying activity patterns (connection times, file sizes, scene lengths), see for instance Beran *et al.* [5], Crovella & Bestavros [20], Willinger *et al.* [43]. This has triggered a lively interest in queueing models with long-tailed traffic characteristics.

Although the presence of long-tailed traffic characteristics is widely acknowledged, the practical implications for network performance and traffic engineering remain to be fully resolved. An interesting aspect is the role of scheduling and priority mechanisms in controlling the effect of long-tailed traffic characteristics on network performance. In a fundamental paper, Anantharam [3] considered a single-server queue fed by a Poisson arrival process of sessions, with each session lasting for an independent integer time T for which holds: $\mathbf{P}\{T = k\} \sim \alpha k^{-(\alpha+1)} L(k)$, where $1 < \alpha < 2$ and $L(\cdot)$ is a slowly varying function (see Definition 1). Each session brings in work at unit rate while it

T. Field et al. (Eds.): TOOLS 2002, LNCS 2324, pp. 1–30, 2002.

is active. Hence, the work brought in by each arrival is regularly varying and, because $1 < \alpha < 2$, the arrival process of work is long-range dependent, but $\mathbf{E}T < \infty$. Anantharam shows that, in the steady-state case, for *any* stationary Non-Preemptive service policy at the queue, the stationary sojourn time of a typical session must stochastically dominate a regularly varying random variable having infinite mean. Non-preemption means that once service on a session has begun, it is continued until all the work associated with it has been completed. Anantharam does not make any assumptions as to whether the service policy is work-conserving, or whether the length of a session is known at the time of arrival. In marked contrast to the above, Anantharam also shows that there exist causal stationary *preemptive* policies, which do not need information about the session durations at the time of their arrival, for which the stationary sojourn time of a session is stochastically dominated by a regularly varying random variable with finite mean.

The results of Anantharam raise several questions, like (i) are there (preemptive) service disciplines for which the tail of the sojourn time distribution is not heavier than the tail of the service requirement distribution, and (ii) what is the effect of various well-known scheduling disciplines on the tail behavior of the waiting- or sojourn time distribution?

A related issue arises when there are *several classes* of customers, which may be treated in different ways by the server (e.g., using fixed priorities, or according to a polling discipline). Then it is important to understand under what conditions, or to what extent, the tail behavior of the service requirements of one class affects the performance of other classes. The above issues have recently been investigated by the present authors and some of their colleagues. This paper summarizes the results. We focus on the classical $M/G/1$ queue and its multi-class generalizations (although some of the recently obtained results allow a general renewal arrival process, or a fluid input).

The orientation of the paper is methodological. After introducing the model and reviewing the main results for various basic disciplines in Section 2, we discuss three different methods of obtaining the tail behavior of waiting- or sojourn time distributions for $M/G/1$-type queues with regularly varying service requirement distribution(s): (i) an analytical one, which relies on Tauberian theorems relating the tail behavior of a probability distribution to the behavior of its Laplace-Stieltjes transform near the origin; (ii) a probabilistic one, which exploits a Markov-type inequality, relating an extremely large sojourn (or waiting) time with a single extremely large service requirement; and (iii) a probabilistic one, which is based on sample-path arguments which lead to lower and upper bounds for probability tails. These three approaches are the topics of Sections 3, 4 and 5, respectively. Sections 3 and 5 also discuss the multi-class case.

2 Model Description and Main Results

In this section, we formally describe the model, introduce some concepts and notation, and give an overview of the main results.

As stated before, we focus on the $M/G/1$ queue. In this system, customers arrive according to a Poisson process, with rate λ, at a single server who works at unit rate. Their service requirements $B_1, B_2, \ldots$ are independent and identically distributed, with distribution $B(\cdot)$ with mean β and Laplace-Stieltjes Transform (LST) $\beta\{\cdot\}$. A generic service requirement is denoted by B. There is no restriction on the number of customers in the system. We assume that the offered traffic load $\rho := \lambda\beta < 1$, so that the system reaches steady state. We study the stationary sojourn time S of a customer, and in some cases also the stationary waiting time W until service begins.

Before surveying the tail asymptotics of the waiting-time and sojourn time distributions for various service disciplines, we first introduce some useful notation and terminology. For any two real functions $g(\cdot)$ and $h(\cdot)$, we use the notational convention $g(x) \sim h(x)$ to denote $\lim_{x\to\infty} g(x)/h(x) = 1$, or equivalently, $g(x) = h(x)(1+o(1))$ as $x \to \infty$. For any stochastic variable X with distribution function $F(\cdot)$, with $\mathbf{E}X < \infty$, denote by $F^r(\cdot)$ the distribution function of the residual lifetime of X, i.e., $F^r(x) = \frac{1}{\mathbf{E}X} \int_0^x (1 - F(y))\mathrm{d}y$, and by X^r a stochastic variable with distribution $F^r(\cdot)$.

Throughout this paper, we focus on the class $\mathcal{R}$ of *regularly-varying* distributions (which contains the Pareto distribution). This class is a subset of the class of subexponential distributions [27], that contains, a.o., the lognormal and Weibull distributions.

Definition 1. *A distribution function $F(\cdot)$ on $[0, \infty)$ is called regularly varying of index $-\nu$ ($F(\cdot) \in \mathcal{R}_{-\nu}$) if*

$$1 - F(x) = x^{-\nu} L(x), \quad \nu \geq 0,$$

where $L : \mathbb{R}_+ \to \mathbb{R}_+$ is a function of slow variation, i.e., $\lim_{x\to\infty} L(\eta x)/L(x) = 1$, $\eta > 1$.

The class of regularly varying functions was introduced by Karamata [25], and its potential for probability theory was extensively discussed in Feller [23]. A key reference is Bingham *et al.* [7].

In the remainder of this section, we present an overview of the tail asymptotics of the waiting-time and sojourn time distributions in the $M/G/1$ queue for six key disciplines: (i) First-Come-First Served (FCFS); (ii) Processor Sharing (PS); (iii) Last-Come-First-Served Preemptive-Resume (LCFS-PR); (iv) Last-Come-First-Served Non-Preemptive Priority (LCFS-NP); (v) Foreground-Background Processor Sharing (FBPS); (vi) Shortest Remaining Processing Time First (SRPTF).

(i) The $M/G/1$ FCFS queue

The next theorem characterizes the tail asymptotics of the distribution of the steady-state waiting time W for the FCFS service discipline.

Theorem 1. *In the case of regular variation, i.e.,* $\mathbf{P}\{B > \cdot\} \in \mathcal{R}_{-\nu}$,

$$\mathbf{P}\{W > x\} \sim \frac{\rho}{1-\rho}\mathbf{P}\{B^r > x\}, \quad x \to \infty. \tag{1}$$

Remark 1. The waiting-time tail in the $M/G/1$ FCFS queue appears to be one degree heavier than the service requirement tail, in the regularly varying case. This is explained by the fact that an arriving customer has a positive probability of arriving during a service time. His waiting time then is at least equal to the residual duration of the ongoing service – which is regularly varying of index $1-\nu$ (cf. [7]).

Theorem 1 was first proved by Cohen [17] (who in fact considered the $GI/G/1$ case), and subsequently extended by several authors. In particular, Pakes [36] has proven that $\mathbf{P}\{W > x\} \sim \frac{\rho}{1-\rho}\mathbf{P}\{B^r > x\}$ even holds for the $GI/G/1$ queue, for the larger class of service requirement distributions for which the residual service requirement distribution is subexponential.

The fact that the sojourn time of a customer in the $M/G/1$ FCFS queue equals the sum of his waiting time and his lighter-tailed service requirement, the two quantities being independent, implies that the tail behavior of the sojourn time distribution is also given by the righthand side of (1).

(ii) The $M/G/1$ PS queue
The PS (processor sharing) service discipline operates as follows. If there are $n \geq 1$ customers present, then they are all served simultaneously, at a rate of $1/n$. At the ITC conference in 1997, J.W. Roberts raised the question whether the tail of the distribution of the steady-state sojourn time S_{PS} in the $M/G/1$ PS system might be just as heavy as the tail of the service requirement distribution. This question was motivated by the following observations: (i) in a PS system short jobs can overtake long jobs, so the influence of long jobs on the sojourn time of short jobs is limited, and (ii) the mean sojourn time in the $M/G/1$ PS queue only involves the *first* moment of the service requirement, whereas in the $M/G/1$ FCFS queue it involves the first moment of the *residual* service requirement (see also (8) below), and hence the *second* moment of the service requirement. In fact, if $\mathbf{P}\{B > \cdot\} \in \mathcal{R}_{-\nu}$ with $1 < \nu < 2$, then the second moment of the service requirement does not exist, and neither does the first moment of the waiting time in the $M/G/1$ FCFS case. Roberts' question can be answered affirmatively, as shown by the next theorem proven in [51].

Theorem 2. *If* $\mathbf{P}\{B > \cdot\} \in \mathcal{R}_{-\nu}$,

$$\mathbf{P}\{S_{PS} > x\} \sim \mathbf{P}\{B > (1-\rho)x\}, \quad x \to \infty. \tag{2}$$

Apparently, in the $M/G/1$ PS queue the sojourn time tail is just as heavy as the service requirement tail.

Remark 2. Formula (2) allows the following interpretation. When a tagged customer has been in the system for a time period of length x, with x large, then the distribution of the number of other customers present has approximately become the steady-state distribution of the number of customers in the $M/G/1$ PS queue. Hence, on average, the server devotes ρ amount of time per time unit to those other customers. Therefore he will, on average, devote a fraction $1-\rho$ of the time to the tagged customer. Consequently, the amount of service received by that customer during x is approximately $(1-\rho)x$.

(iii) The $M/G/1$ LCFS-PR queue
In the LCFS Preemptive-Resume discipline, an arriving customer K is immediately taken into service. However, this service is interrupted when another customer arrives, and it is only resumed when all customers who have arrived after K have left the system.

The fact that no customer has to wait for the completion of a residual service requirement, suggests that the tail of the sojourn time distribution is just as heavy as the tail of the service requirement distribution. This was indeed proven in [13], using the following observation: The sojourn time of K has exactly the same distribution as the busy period of this $M/G/1$ queue. The busy period obviously has the same distribution for LCFS-PR as for FCFS. The tail behavior of the busy-period distribution in the $M/G/1$ queue has been studied by De Meyer and Teugels [30] for the case of a regularly varying service requirement distribution. This yields the next theorem (S_{LPR} denoting the steady-state sojourn time).

Theorem 3. *If* $\mathbf{P}\{B > \cdot\} \in \mathcal{R}_{-\nu}$,

$$\mathbf{P}\{S_{LPR} > x\} \sim \frac{1}{1-\rho}\mathbf{P}\{B > (1-\rho)x\}, \quad x \to \infty. \tag{3}$$

(iv) The $M/G/1$ LCFS-NP queue
Let W_{LNP} denote the steady-state waiting time in the $M/G/1$ LCFS-NP queue. The possibility of preemption suggests that the tail of W_{LNP} will be determined by the tail of a residual service time. Indeed, in this paper we prove the following result, which in fact also holds for the sojourn time $S_{LNP} = W_{LNP} + B$, as is shown in Section 4.

Theorem 4. *If* $\mathbf{P}\{B > \cdot\} \in \mathcal{R}_{-\nu}$,

$$\mathbf{P}\{W_{LNP} > x\} \sim \rho\mathbf{P}\{B^r > (1-\rho)x\}, \quad x \to \infty. \tag{4}$$

(v) The $M/G/1$ FBPS queue
The Foreground-Background Processor Sharing discipline allocates an equal share of the service capacity to the customers which so far have received the least amount of service, see Kleinrock [26] or Yashkov [46]. We will show (only for the case $1 < \nu < 2$) that the tail of the distribution of the sojourn time S_{FB} is the same as that for the ordinary PS discipline:

Theorem 5. *If* $\mathbf{P}\{B > \cdot\} \in \mathcal{R}_{-\nu}$ *with* $1 < \nu < 2$,

$$\mathbf{P}\{S_{FB} > x\} \sim \mathbf{P}\{B > (1-\rho)x\}, \quad x \to \infty. \tag{5}$$

Although not proven here, it can be shown that the result remains true for $\nu \geq 2$.

(vi) The $M/G/1$ SRPTF queue
With this service discipline the total service capacity is always allocated to the customer(s) with the shortest remaining processing time (Shortest Remaining Processing Time First). Assuming that $B(x)$ is a continuous function, with probability 1, no two customers in the system have the same remaining service requirement [41]. The service of a customer is preempted when a new customer arrives with a service requirement smaller than the remaining service requirement of the customer being served. The service of the customer that is preempted is resumed as soon as there are no other customers with a smaller amount of work in the system. For the sojourn time S_{SR} we will prove the following theorem:

Theorem 6. *If* $\mathbf{P}\{B > \cdot\} \in \mathcal{R}_{-\nu}$ *with* $1 < \nu < 2$,

$$\mathbf{P}\{S_{SR} > x\} \sim \mathbf{P}\{B > (1-\rho)x\}, \quad x \to \infty. \tag{6}$$

Note that the tail of the service requirement distribution behaves as those of the PS and FBPS disciplines. Again, we remark (without proof) that the result is also valid for $\nu \geq 2$.

In the sequel we prove these theorems using different methods. This serves as a demonstration of the methods and allows us to compare them. Theorems 2 and 4 shall be proven in each of the Sections 3, 4 and 5, Theorems 1 and 3 are proven in Sections 3 and 5, and Theorems 5 and 6 are proven in Section 4.

3 Transform Approach

In this section we demonstrate an LST approach to the study of tails of waiting-time and sojourn time distributions in the $M/G/1$ queue and some of its generalizations. In Subsection 3.1 we consider the single-class $M/G/1$ queue, with as service discipline either FCFS, PS, LCFS-PR, or LCFS-NP. In Subsection 3.2 we consider the multi-class $M/G/1$ queue, in which the classes are served according to some scheduling mechanism.

For several of the above-mentioned cases, an expression for the LST of the waiting- and/or sojourn time distribution can be found in the literature. In exceptional cases, this expression is sufficiently simple to allow explicit inversion of the LST, thus possibly enabling one to determine the tail behavior of the corresponding distribution. An example is the $M/G/1$ queue with the FCFS discipline, which will first be considered in Subsection 3.1. But usually such an explicit inversion is not viable. Fortunately, there exists a very useful relation between the tail behavior of a regularly varying probability distribution and the behavior of its LST near the origin. That relation often enables one to conclude from the form of the LST of the waiting- and/or sojourn time distribution, that the distribution itself is regularly varying at infinity. We present this relation in Lemma 1 below.

Let $F(\cdot)$ be the distribution of a non-negative random variable, with LST $\phi\{s\}$ and finite first n moments $\mu_1, \ldots, \mu_n$ (and $\mu_0 = 1$). Define

$$\phi_n\{s\} := (-1)^{n+1}[\phi\{s\} - \sum_{j=0}^{n} \mu_j \frac{(-s)^j}{j!}].$$

Lemma 1. *Let $n < \nu < n+1$, $C \geq 0$. The following statements are equivalent:*

$$\phi_n\{s\} = (C + o(1))s^\nu L(1/s), \quad s \downarrow 0, \quad s \text{ real},$$

$$1 - F(x) = (C + o(1))\frac{(-1)^n}{\Gamma(1-\nu)} x^{-\nu} L(x), \quad x \to \infty.$$

The case $C > 0$ is due to Bingham and Doney [6]. The case $C = 0$ was first obtained by Vincent Dumas, and is treated in [16], Lemma 2.2. The case of an integer ν is more complicated; see Theorem 8.1.6 and Chapter 3 of [7].

3.1 The Single-Class Case

(i) The $M/G/1$ FCFS queue
In the $M/G/1$ FCFS queue, the LST of the steady-state waiting-time distribution is given by the Pollaczek-Khintchine formula [18]:

$$\mathbf{E}[\mathrm{e}^{-sW}] = \frac{1-\rho}{1-\rho\beta^r\{s\}}, \quad \mathrm{Re}\, s \geq 0, \tag{7}$$

where $\beta^r\{s\} = (1 - \beta\{s\})/\beta s$ is the LST of the residual service requirement distribution $B^r(x)$. The geometric structure of this LST enables one to invert it, yielding (with B_i^r a random variable with distribution a residual service requirement distribution):

$$\mathbf{P}\{W < x\} = \sum_{n=0}^{\infty}(1-\rho)\rho^n \mathbf{P}\{B_1^r + \ldots + B_n^r < x\}, \quad x \geq 0. \tag{8}$$

A Karamata theorem (cf. Section 1.5 of [7]) implies that if $\mathbf{P}\{B > \cdot\} \in \mathcal{R}_{-\nu}$, then the integrated tail $\mathrm{P}(B^r > \cdot) \in \mathcal{R}_{1-\nu}$. More precisely, if

$$\mathbf{P}\{B > x\} \sim x^{-\nu} L(x), \quad \nu > 1, \quad x \to \infty, \tag{9}$$

then

$$\mathbf{P}\{B^r > x\} = \frac{1}{\beta}\int_x^\infty \mathbf{P}\{B > y\}\mathrm{d}y \sim \frac{1}{(\nu-1)\beta} x^{1-\nu} L(x), \quad x \to \infty. \tag{10}$$

A key property of regularly varying probability distributions (and of the larger class of subexponential distributions), specified to the sum of residual service requirements in (8), is that

$$\mathbf{P}\{B_1^r + \ldots + B_n^r > x\} \sim n\mathbf{P}\{B_1^r > x\}, \quad x \to \infty. \tag{11}$$

Put differently: the sum of n independent, identically distributed random variables with regularly varying tail exhibits the same tail behavior as the *maximum* of that sum. This implies that *when such a sum is large, that is most likely due to one of the terms being large.* This observation provides the key intuition to many of the results to be discussed below.

Combining (11) with (8) we obtain Theorem 1. We shall now demonstrate how the following statement, which implies Theorem 1, is easily obtained from the LST expression (7) and Lemma 1. For $\nu > 1$, $x \to \infty$,

$$\mathbf{P}\{B > x\} \sim x^{-\nu} L(x) \Longleftrightarrow \mathbf{P}\{W > x\} \sim \frac{\rho}{1-\rho} \frac{1}{(\nu-1)\beta} x^{1-\nu} L(x). \tag{12}$$

It follows from (9) and Lemma 1 that

$$1 - \beta^r\{s\} = 1 - \frac{1-\beta\{s\}}{\beta s} = -\left(\frac{\Gamma(1-\nu)}{\beta} + \mathrm{o}(1)\right) s^{\nu-1} L(1/s), \quad s \downarrow 0. \tag{13}$$

Combining this result with (7) yields:

$$1 - \mathbf{E}[\mathrm{e}^{-sW}] = \frac{\rho(1-\beta^r\{s\})}{1-\rho\beta^r\{s\}} \sim -\frac{\rho}{1-\rho} \frac{\Gamma(1-\nu)}{\beta} s^{\nu-1} L(1/s), \quad s \downarrow 0.$$

Another application of Lemma 1 gives the $\Longrightarrow$ part of (12). The reverse part is obtained in a similar way.

(ii) The $M/G/1$ PS queue

Theorem 2 indicates that, contrary to the FCFS case, the sojourn time tail in the $M/G/1$ PS queue is just as heavy as the service time tail. We now sketch the proof in [51], which is based on the application of Lemma 1 to an explicit expression of the sojourn time LST.

There are several expressions known for the LST of the sojourn time, cf. [35, 42,45], but they contain contour integrals which are inversion formulas of Laplace transforms. Starting-point in [51] is an expression in [35] for the *conditional* LST of a customer's sojourn time $S_{PS}(\tau)$, given that his service requirement is τ: For $\mathrm{Re}\ s \geq 0$, $\tau \geq 0$,

$$\mathbf{E}[\mathrm{e}^{-sS_{PS}(\tau)}] = \frac{1-\rho}{(1-\rho)H_1(s,\tau) + sH_2(s,\tau)},$$

where the functions $H_1(s,\tau)$ and $H_2(s,\tau)$ are given by their LST w.r.t. τ:

$$\int_0^\infty \mathrm{e}^{-x\tau} \mathrm{d}H_1(s,\tau) = \frac{x - \lambda(1-\beta\{x\})}{x - s - \lambda(1-\beta\{x\})}, \quad \mathrm{Re}\ x > 0,$$

$$\int_0^\infty \mathrm{e}^{-x\tau} \mathrm{d}H_2(s,\tau) = \frac{\rho x - \lambda(1-\beta\{x\})}{x(x - s - \lambda(1-\beta\{x\}))}, \quad \mathrm{Re}\ x > 0.$$

It follows from these relations that, for $\mathrm{Re}\ s \geq 0$ and $\mathrm{Re}\ x > 0$:

$$\int_0^\infty \mathrm{e}^{-x\tau} \mathrm{d}[\mathbf{E}[\mathrm{e}^{-sS_{PS}(\tau)}]]^{-1} = 1 + \frac{1}{1-\rho} \frac{s}{x} \frac{1}{1 - s\mathbf{E}[\mathrm{e}^{-xW}]/(x(1-\rho))}, \tag{14}$$

where W denotes the steady-state waiting time in the $M/G/1$ FCFS queue (we shall denote its distribution by $W(\cdot)$). Formula (14) implies (see [51]) that

$$\mathbf{E}[e^{-sS_{PS}(\tau)}] = \left[\sum_{k=0}^{\infty} \frac{s^k}{k!}\alpha_k(\tau)\right]^{-1}, \tag{15}$$

with $\alpha_0(\tau) := 1$, $\alpha_1(\tau) := \tau/(1-\rho)$, and for $k \geq 2$,

$$\alpha_k(\tau) := \frac{k}{(1-\rho)^k}\int_{x=0}^{\tau}(\tau - x)^{k-1}W^{(k-1)*}(x)\mathrm{d}x.$$

In Corollary 3.2 of [51], Formula (15) is shown to imply that the kth moment of the sojourn time in the $M/G/1$ PS queue is finite iff the kth moment of the service requirement is finite. But Formula (15) is also suitable for applying Lemma 1. With S_{PS} the steady-state sojourn time in the $M/G/1$ PS queue, and using the fact that $\mathbf{E}[e^{-sS_{PS}}] = \int_0^\infty \mathbf{E}[e^{-sS(\tau)}]\mathrm{d}B(\tau)$, it can be shown [51] that, for $1 < \nu < 2$,

$$\mathbf{E}[e^{-sS_{PS}}] - \beta\{\frac{s}{1-\rho}\} = o(s^\nu L(1/s)), \quad s \downarrow 0, \ s \text{ real}.$$

One can now apply Lemma 1. Using the well-known fact that $\mathbf{E}S_{PS} = \beta/(1-\rho)$, it is seen that Theorem 2 holds for $1 < \nu < 2$ (and via a similar approach it is shown in [51] that this holds for all non-integer $\nu > 1$; we ignore the subtleties required in applying Lemma 1 for integer ν). In fact, a two-way application of Lemma 1 yields (cf. [51]): For $\nu > 1$, $x \to \infty$,

$$\mathbf{P}\{B > x\} \sim x^{-\nu}L(x) \Longleftrightarrow \mathbf{P}\{S_{PS} > x\} \sim \frac{1}{(1-\rho)^\nu}x^{-\nu}L(x). \tag{16}$$

(iii) The $M/G/1$ LCFS-PR queue

As observed in Section 2, the sojourn time in the $M/G/1$ LCFS-PR queue has the same distribution as the busy period in the $M/G/1$ queue. De Meyer and Teugels [30] have studied the tail of the latter distribution in the case of a regularly varying service requirement distribution. Their starting-point is the fact that the LST $\mu(s)$ of the steady-state busy period length P is the unique solution of the equation

$$\mu\{s\} = \beta\{s + \lambda(1 - \mu\{s\})\}, \tag{17}$$

with $|\mu\{s\}| \leq 1$ for Re $s \geq 0$. They apply Lemma 1 to show the following equivalence: for $\nu > 1$, $x \to \infty$,

$$\mathbf{P}\{B > x\} \sim x^{-\nu}L(x) \Longleftrightarrow \mathbf{P}\{P > x\} \sim \frac{1}{(1-\rho)^{\nu+1}}x^{-\nu}L(x). \tag{18}$$

Hence the tail of the busy period distribution is just as heavy as that of the service requirement distribution. Theorem 3 immediately follows from (18).

(iv) The $M/G/1$ LCFS-NP queue
Let W_{LNP} denote the steady-state waiting time in the $M/G/1$ LCFS-NP queue. The following is observed in [18], p. 431. If an arriving customer in the $M/G/1$ LCFS-NP queue meets a customer in service with a residual service requirement w, then his waiting-time distribution is that of a busy period with a special first service requirement w. That residual service requirement has distribution $B^r(\cdot)$ with LST $\beta^r\{s\}$ as introduced in the beginning of this section ([18], p. 432). It is now readily seen (cf., e.g., p. 299 of [19]) that

$$\mathbf{E}[\mathrm{e}^{-sW_{LNP}}] = 1 - \rho + \rho\beta^r\{\delta\{s\}\}, \quad \mathrm{Re}\ s \geq 0, \tag{19}$$

with $\delta\{s\}$ the unique zero in Re $s \geq 0$ of $\lambda(1 - \beta\{w\}) - w + s$, Re $w \geq 0$. In fact, cf. (17), $\delta\{s\} = s + \lambda(1 - \mu\{s\})$. In combination with (19), this gives another derivation of Formula (III.3.10) of [18]:

$$\mathbf{E}[\mathrm{e}^{-sW_{LNP}}] = 1 - \rho + \frac{\rho}{\beta}\frac{1 - \mu\{s\}}{s + \lambda(1 - \mu\{s\})}, \quad \mathrm{Re}\ s \geq 0. \tag{20}$$

Using Lemma 1, we can now easily verify that the tail of W_{LNP} is regularly varying of degree one heavier than the tail of the service requirement (as may be expected in view of the possibility of having to wait at least a residual service requirement). If (9) and hence also (13) hold, then it follows from (18) and Lemma 1 that

$$1 - \mu\{s\} - \frac{\beta}{1-\rho}s \sim -\frac{\Gamma(1-\nu)}{(1-\rho)^{\nu+1}}s^{\nu}L(1/s), \quad s \downarrow 0, \tag{21}$$

and therefore

$$1 - \mathbf{E}[\mathrm{e}^{-sW_{LNP}}] \sim -\frac{\lambda\Gamma(1-\nu)}{(1-\rho)^{\nu-1}}s^{\nu-1}L(1/s), \quad s \downarrow 0. \tag{22}$$

On the other hand, starting from (22) and using (20), one gets (21). Application of Lemma 1 and (18) now yields: For $\nu > 1$, $x \to \infty$,

$$\mathbf{P}\{B > x\} \sim x^{-\nu}L(x) \Longleftrightarrow \mathbf{P}\{W_{LNP} > x\} \sim \frac{\lambda}{(\nu-1)(1-\rho)^{\nu-1}}x^{1-\nu}L(x). \tag{23}$$

Both relations imply Theorem 4.

3.2 The Multi-class Case

In this subsection we consider the $M/G/1$ queue with K classes of customers. We study several of the most important service scheduling disciplines, rules that specify at any time which class of customers is being served. We are interested in the question under what conditions, or to what extent, the tail behavior of the service requirements of one class affects the performance of other classes.

The notation is as introduced in Section 2, but quantities relating to class-i customers receive an index i. Hence, class-i customers arrive according to a

Poisson process with rate λ_i, and their service requirements have distribution $B_i(\cdot)$ with mean β_i; $\rho_i := \lambda_i \beta_i$ and $\rho := \sum_{i=1}^{K} \rho_i$.

(i) Fixed priorities: Non-Preemptive priority
Assume that there are only two priority classes, class 1 having Non-Preemptive priority over class 2. Cohen [18], Section III.3.8, gives the following expressions for the LST of the distribution of the steady-state waiting time W_1 of class-1 customers:

$$\mathbf{E}[\mathrm{e}^{-sW_1}] = \frac{1 - \rho + \rho_2 \beta_2^r\{s\}}{1 - \rho_1 \beta_1^r\{s\}}, \quad \mathrm{Re}\, s \geq 0, \quad \rho < 1, \tag{24}$$

$$\mathbf{E}[\mathrm{e}^{-sW_1}] = \frac{(1 - \rho_1)\beta_2^r\{s\}}{1 - \rho_1 \beta_1^r\{s\}}, \quad \mathrm{Re}\, s \geq 0, \quad \rho_1 < 1, \quad \rho \geq 1. \tag{25}$$

In both cases, Lemma 1 can readily be applied to determine the tail behavior of the waiting-time distribution. Actually, this is one of the rare cases in which the LST can be easily inverted. For $\rho < 1$ this gives ($B_{1,i}^r$ has the residual service requirement distribution $B_1^r(\cdot)$, and B_2^r has the residual service requirement distribution $B_2^r(\cdot)$), with $\stackrel{d}{=}$ denoting equality in distribution,

$$W_1 \stackrel{d}{=} B_{1,1}^r + \ldots + B_{1,N}^r + Z,$$

where N is geometrically distributed with parameter ρ_1 while Z is zero with probability $(1-\rho)/(1-\rho_1)$ and $Z = B_2^r$ with probability $\rho_2/(1-\rho_1)$. For $\rho_1 < 1$ but $\rho \geq 1$, inversion of the LST in (25) yields:

$$W_1 \stackrel{d}{=} B_{1,1}^r + \ldots + B_{1,N}^r + B_2^r.$$

These results imply the following. If the service requirement distribution with the heaviest tail is regularly varying at infinity of index $-\nu$, then the waiting-time distribution of the high-priority customers is regularly varying at infinity of index $1 - \nu$. More specifically: If the heaviest tail belongs to class 1, then the waiting-time tail of class-1 customers is as if no class 2 exists. If the heaviest tail belongs to class 2, then the waiting-time tail of class-1 customers behaves like the tail of a residual service requirement of class 2 if $\rho_1 < 1$ and $\rho \geq 1$, and like that tail multiplied by the factor $\rho_2/(1 - \rho_1)$ if $\rho < 1$.

For class 2 the following result has been proven in [14]. If the service requirement distribution with the heaviest tail is regularly varying at infinity of index $-\nu$, then the waiting-time distribution of the low-priority customers is regularly varying at infinity of index $1 - \nu$. This is proven by exploiting a representation for the LST of that waiting-time distribution, as given by Abate and Whitt [1], and then using Lemma 1. The result is not surprising, when one realizes that a low-priority customer may have to wait for a residual service requirement of either class. For the precise asymptotics we refer to [14].

(ii) Fixed priorities: Preemptive-Resume priority
First assume that there are only two priority classes, class 1 having Preemptive-Resume priority over class 2. As is well-known, class-1 customers are not affected by class-2 customers, so the results of Subsection 3.1 (for FCFS) apply to class 1. The waiting-time distribution of the low-priority customers *until the start of the – possibly interrupted – service* is the same as in the Non-Preemptive case. Those possible interruptions consist of full service requirements of high-priority customers, and in the regularly varying case these are less heavy than *residual* service requirements of those customers. Hence, in the scenario of regular variation, the tail behavior of low-priority customers is the same as in the Non-Preemptive case.

If there are $K > 2$ classes, then in studying class j one may aggregate classes $1, \ldots, j-1$ into one high-priority class w.r.t. class j, while the existence of classes $j+1, \ldots, K$ is irrelevant for class j.

(iii) Polling
Deng [21] has considered the extension of the two-class Non-Preemptive priority model to the case in which the server requires a switchover time to move from one class of customers to the other. She proves: If the service requirement distribution *or the switchover-time distribution* with the heaviest tail is regularly varying at infinity of index $-\nu$, then the waiting-time distributions of both classes are regularly varying at infinity of index $1-\nu$. Again the key of the derivation is an explicit expression for the LST of the waiting-time distributions, in combination with Lemma 1.

The above 2-class model may also be viewed as a *polling* model with 2 queues Q_1, Q_2 and a server who alternatingly visits both queues, serving Q_1 exhaustively (i.e., until it is empty) and applying the 1-limited service discipline at Q_2 (i.e., serving one customer, if there is one, and then moving on to the other queue). In [15] a polling model with K queues has been studied, with the exhaustive or gated service discipline being employed at the various queues. In a similar way, the same conclusions as above have been obtained.

(iv) Processor sharing with several customer classes
In the multi-class disciplines that were discussed above, the worst tail behavior of any class determined the waiting-time tail behavior of all classes (except for high-priority customers in the case of Preemptive-Resume priority). Processor sharing turns out to be better able to protect customer classes from the bad behavior of other classes. Zwart [47] showed that the sojourn time distribution of a class-i customer is regularly varying of index $-\nu_i$ iff the service requirement distribution of that class is regularly varying of index $-\nu_i$, *regardless* of the service requirement distributions of the other classes. His method again relied on Lemma 1.

(v) Generalized processor sharing
The Generalized Processor Sharing (GPS) discipline operates as follows [37].

Customer class i is assigned a weight ϕ_i, $i = 1, \ldots, K$, with $\sum_{i=1}^{K} \phi_i = 1$. If customers of all classes are present, then one customer from each class is served simultaneously (processor sharing), a class-i customer receiving a fraction ϕ_i of the server capacity. If only some of the classes are present, then the service capacity is shared in proportion to the weights ϕ_i among the head-of-the-line customers of those classes.

GPS-based scheduling algorithms, such as Weighted Fair Queueing, play a major role in achieving differentiated quality-of-service in integrated-services networks. Hence, it is important to study the extent to which GPS manages to protect one class of customers from the adverse effects of bad traffic characteristics of other classes. Unfortunately, the queueing analysis of GPS is very difficult. A slightly more general model for $K = 2$ is the model with two parallel $M/G/1$ queues with service speeds depending on whether the other queue is empty or not. For general service requirement distributions, the joint distribution of the amounts of work of both classes has been obtained in [19] by solving a Wiener-Hopf problem (see [22] and [28] for the case of exponential service requirement distributions). The results of [19] have been exploited in [8,10,11]. In those papers, service requirements at Q_1 are either exponential or regularly varying; at Q_2 they are regularly varying. Whether the service requirement tail behavior at Q_2 affects the workload tail at Q_1 is shown to depend crucially on whether or not Q_1 is able to handle all its offered work by working at the low speed that occurs while Q_2 is non-empty (i.e., whether or not $\rho_1 < \phi_1$). The method employed in [8,10,11] starts from a – complicated – expression for the workload LST. In some cases Lemma 1 is applicable, but in other cases an extension of this lemma must be used. For $K \geq 3$ coupled queues, respectively for GPS with $K \geq 3$ classes, no explicit results are known. However, the sample-path techniques discussed in Section 5 have proven useful in obtaining tail asymptotics for an arbitrary number of classes [9].

4 Tail Equivalence via Conditional Moments

With heavy-tailed distributions, it is often the case that large occurrences of the variable of interest (e.g., a customer's waiting time or sojourn time) are essentially caused by a *single* large occurrence of one input variable (e.g., a service requirement). In this section we describe a generic approach that may be used to prove that the tails of the distributions of the *causal variable* and the *resultant* variable are *equally heavy*. Specifically, we say that two non-negative random variables X and Y have equally-heavy tailed distributions if $\mathbf{P}\{Y > \overline{g}x\} \sim \mathbf{P}\{X > x\}$ for some constant $\overline{g} > 0$. In the examples below, a customer's own service requirement (denoted with B) or the *residual* service requirement of some other customer (denoted with B^r) will play the role of the causal variable X and the customer's sojourn time (denoted with S) that of the resultant Y. In order to explicitly express the dependence of the sojourn time on the (residual) service requirement, we shall use $S(\tau)$ to denote a customer's sojourn time *given* that the (residual) service requirement equals τ. Consequently, we may alternatively write $S(B)$ or $S(B^r)$ (depending on the causal variable) for the unconditional sojourn time S.

Theorem 7 below relates the tails of the distributions of S and the causal variable X (later replaced with either B or B^r). We shall make two assumptions: one regarding the distribution of the causal variable and one regarding $S(\tau)$. (The first assumption can be relaxed to distributions of *intermediate regular variation*, without invalidating Theorem 7, see [34].)

Assumption 1. $\mathbf{P}\{X > \cdot\} \in \mathcal{R}_{-\alpha}$ for some $\alpha > 0$.

Assumption 2. The following three conditions are satisfied:

(a) $\mathbf{E}S(\tau) \sim \overline{g}\,\tau$, for some $\overline{g} > 0$;

(b) With α as in Assumption 1, there exists $\kappa > \alpha$ such that

$$\mathbf{P}\{S(\tau) - \mathbf{E}S(\tau) > t\} \leq \frac{h(\tau)}{t^{\kappa}},$$

with $h(\tau) = \mathrm{o}(\tau^{\kappa-\delta})$, $\tau \to \infty$, for some $\delta > 0$;

(c) $S(\tau)$ is stochastically increasing in $\tau \geq 0$, i.e., for all $t \geq 0$, the probability $\mathbf{P}\{S(\tau) > t\}$ is non-decreasing in $\tau \geq 0$.

Theorem 7. *Suppose Assumptions 1 and 2 are satisfied. Then the tails of the distributions of the random variables X and $S(X)$ are equally heavy in the sense that:*

$$\mathbf{P}\{S(X) > \overline{g}\,x\} \sim \mathbf{P}\{X > x\}.$$

In particular, the distribution of $S(X)$ is also regularly varying with the same index $-\alpha$ as that of X.

Proof. We only give a sketch of the proof and refer to [34] for details. The proof consists of two parts. For the first part we write, with $\varepsilon > 0$,

$$\mathbf{P}\{S(X) > \overline{g}\,x\} \leq \mathbf{P}\{S(X) > \overline{g}\,x; X \leq x(1-\varepsilon)\} + \mathbf{P}\{X > x(1-\varepsilon)\}. \quad (26)$$

By conditioning on X and integrating over the distribution of X it can be shown (using Assumptions 1 and 2) that

$$\mathbf{P}\{S(X) > \overline{g}\,x; X \leq x(1-\varepsilon)\} = \mathrm{o}(\mathbf{P}\{X > x(1-\varepsilon)\}), \quad x \to \infty.$$

Hence, we may neglect the first term on the right-hand side of (26) and write

$$\limsup_{x\to\infty} \frac{\mathbf{P}\{S(X) > \overline{g}\,x\}}{\mathbf{P}\{X > x\}} \leq \limsup_{x\to\infty} \frac{\mathbf{P}\{X > x(1-\varepsilon)\}}{\mathbf{P}\{X > x\}} = (1-\varepsilon)^{-\alpha}.$$

Letting $\varepsilon \downarrow 0$, the right-hand side tends to 1.
For the second part of the proof we write, for $\varepsilon > 0$,

$$\mathbf{P}\{S(X) > \overline{g}\,x\} \geq \mathbf{P}\{S(X) > \overline{g}\,x; X > x(1+\varepsilon)\}.$$

By conditioning again on X it can be shown that

$$\lim_{x\to\infty} \frac{\mathbf{P}\{S(X) > \overline{g}\, x; X > x(1+\varepsilon)\}}{\mathbf{P}\{X > x(1+\varepsilon)\}} = 1.$$

Hence,

$$\liminf_{x\to\infty} \frac{\mathbf{P}\{S(X) > \overline{g}\, x\}}{\mathbf{P}\{X > x\}} \geq \liminf_{x\to\infty} \frac{\mathbf{P}\{X > x(1+\varepsilon)\}}{\mathbf{P}\{X > x\}} = (1+\varepsilon)^{-\alpha}.$$

Again, the right-hand side tends to 1 as $\varepsilon \downarrow 0$. □

We shall employ Theorem 7 to show for several queueing models that the tail of the sojourn time distribution is as heavy as that of the (residual) service requirement distribution. Assuming that the service requirement distribution is regularly varying, it suffices to verify that $S(\tau)$, the sojourn time conditioned on the (residual) service requirement, satisfies Assumption 2. Parts *(a)* and *(c)* of Assumption 2 are often not hard to verify. We shall use the following variant of Markov's inequality to verify part *(b)*:

$$\mathbf{P}\{S(\tau) > t\} \leq \frac{\mathbf{E}S(\tau)^{\kappa} - (\mathbf{E}S(\tau))^{\kappa}}{(t - \mathbf{E}S(\tau))^{\kappa}}, \qquad \tau \geq 0,\, t > \mathbf{E}S(\tau), \tag{27}$$

where $\kappa \geq 2$. In [34] Markov's inequality itself was used, but for the analysis of the $M/G/1$ LCFS-NP below, the form of (27) is more convenient. To see that this inequality holds, let $c(y)$, $y \geq 0$ be a convex function with a convex derivative $c'(y)$ and $c(0) = c'(0) = 0$. If Y is a non-negative random variable and $t \geq \mathbf{E}Y$,

$$c(Y) - c(\mathbf{E}Y) - c'(\mathbf{E}Y)\,(Y - \mathbf{E}Y) \geq \mathbf{1}_{\{Y>t\}} c(t - \mathbf{E}Y),$$

where $\mathbf{1}_{\{\cdot\}}$ denotes the indicator function. Taking expectations with respect to the distribution of Y, we obtain

$$\mathbf{E}c(Y) - c(\mathbf{E}Y) \geq \mathbf{P}\{Y > t\} c(t - \mathbf{E}Y).$$

Choosing $c(y) = y^{\kappa}$, with $\kappa \geq 2$, leads to the desired result.

The strength of the method described here is that it does not rely on the availability of the LST for the sojourn time distribution. In particular, the method's flexibility was demonstrated in [32] where it was employed in the analysis of an $M/G/1$ PS queue with random service interruptions (for that model even basic performance measures such as mean queue length are not available). A limitation of the method is that it relies on the fact that an extremal occurrence of the performance measure of interest (e.g., the sojourn time) is essentially caused by the occurrence of *a single* extremal input variable.

(i) The $M/G/1$ PS queue

Consider again the $M/G/1$ PS queue described in Section 2. In this section

$S_{PS}(\tau)$ will stand for the sojourn time of a customer with service requirement $\tau \geq 0$, arriving when the system has reached stationarity. As before, the unconditional sojourn time will be denoted with S_{PS}, i.e., $S_{PS} = S_{PS}(B)$, where the random variable B stands for the customer's service requirement. We first list some known results for the moments of $S_{PS}(\tau)$. Then we shall use these to verify Assumption 2 and subsequently apply Theorem 7.

It is well known [26,40] that the mean of the conditional sojourn time is proportional to the service requirement:

$$\mathbf{E}S_{PS}(\tau) = \frac{\tau}{1-\rho}. \tag{28}$$

The variance of $S_{PS}(\tau)$ is given by

$$\mathbf{Var}S_{PS}(\tau) = \frac{2}{(1-\rho)^2} \int_{u=0}^{\tau} (\tau - u)\mathbf{P}\{W > u\}\mathrm{d}u, \tag{29}$$

cf. Yashkov [45]. As before, W is distributed as the stationary waiting time in the $M/G/1$ queue. When the second moment of the service requirement distribution is finite we have for $k = 2, 3, \ldots$, cf. [51],

$$\mathbf{E}S_{PS}(\tau)^k = \left(\frac{\tau}{1-\rho}\right)^k + \frac{\lambda k(k-1)\mathbf{E}B^2}{2(1-\rho)^{k+1}}\tau^{k-1} + \mathrm{o}(\tau^{k-1}), \qquad \tau \to \infty. \tag{30}$$

In the literature these results have mostly been obtained from expressions for the LST of $S_{PS}(\tau)$. However, (28)–(30) can be obtained directly from a set of differential equations instead of deriving the LST of $S_{PS}(\tau)$, see Yashkov [45, Rem. 3] for an outline of how this can be done for the variance of $S_{PS}(\tau)$, and [32,33] for higher moments. Later in this section we use similar ideas to derive differential equations for the moments of the conditional sojourn time in the $M/G/1$ LCFS-NP.

We shall now provide a new proof of Theorem 2. As before, we assume that $B(\cdot) \in \mathcal{R}_{-\nu}$. We further require that $\nu \neq 2$; in [34] it is indicated how this technical assumption can be overcome. Focusing on the sojourn time of a particular customer, its own service requirement B will act as the causal variable X, i.e., in the light of Assumption 1 we choose $\alpha = \nu$. We now verify that Assumption 2 is automatically satisfied. First we note that the monotonicity of $\mathbf{P}\{S_{PS}(\tau) > t\}$ in τ, the last condition in Assumption 2, is easily seen using a sample-path argument: Comparing the sojourn times of two customers, for the same sequences of inter-arrival times and service requirements of other customers, it follows immediately that the one requiring the smaller amount of service leaves before the one with the larger service requirement. As a consequence of (28), we also have that Condition *(a)* of Assumption 2 holds with $\overline{g} = 1/(1-\rho)$.

We now focus on Condition *(b)* and first consider the case that $\nu > 2$, ensuring that $\mathbf{E}B^2 < \infty$. Choose any integer $\kappa > \nu$ and use (30) to conclude that Condition *(b)* is satisfied for any $\delta \in (0, 1)$. Hence, Theorem 7 can be applied.

In the case that $1 < \nu < 2$, it follows from (29) that $\mathbf{Var} S_{PS}(\tau) = \mathrm{o}(\tau^{3-\nu+\varepsilon})$ for all $\varepsilon > 0$. Thus, Assumption 2 is satisfied (with $\kappa = 2$ and $0 < \delta < \nu - 1$) and, hence, Theorem 7 can again be applied. In both cases we conclude that, cf. Theorem 2,

$$\mathbf{P}\{S_{PS} > \frac{x}{1-\rho}\} \sim \mathbf{P}\{B > x\},$$

(ii) The M/G/1 LCFS-NP queue

In the LCFS-NP case we focus on the sojourn time, $S_{LNP}(\tau)$, of a tagged customer that enters the system when the *remaining* service requirement of the customer in service equals τ. Because of the service discipline, if there are any customers in the queue, these are overtaken by the new customer and they will have no influence on $S_{LNP}(\tau)$, which we may write as

$$S_{LNP}(\tau) = \tau + \sum_{n=1}^{N(\tau)} P_n + B,$$

where, by convention, we set the empty sum equal to 0. $N(\tau)$ denotes the number of customers that enter the system during the remaining service requirement τ of the customer in service. P_n, $n = 1, 2, \ldots$, is an i.i.d. sequence having the distribution of the busy period in the $M/G/1$. Indeed, all customers that enter during the time τ overtake the tagged customer, and the same holds for the customers that arrive during their service time, and so on. Finally, B denotes the tagged customer's own service requirement. If there is no customer in service upon arrival, the sojourn time is just equal to the customer's own service requirement B. Note that the probability of arriving to a non-empty system is ρ. We thus have for S_{LNP}, the unconditional sojourn time of the tagged customer,

$$\mathbf{P}\{S_{LNP} \le t\} = (1-\rho)\,\mathbf{P}\{B \le t\} + \rho\,\mathbf{P}\{S_{LNP}(B^r) \le t\}, \qquad t \ge 0. \tag{31}$$

Here B^r denotes the (unconditional) residual service requirement of the customer in service, i.e., B^r has distribution $B^r(x)$, $x \ge 0$, and, hence,

$$\mathbf{P}\{S_{LNP}(B^r) \le t\} = \int_{\tau=0}^{\infty} \mathbf{P}\{S_{LNP}(\tau) \le t\} \mathrm{d}B^r(\tau), \qquad t \ge 0.$$

We now prove Theorem 4 for *non-integer* $\nu > 2$ (see Remark 3 below), by showing that if $B(\cdot) \in \mathcal{R}_{-\nu}$ and, hence, $B^r(\cdot) \in \mathcal{R}_{-\alpha}$ with $\alpha := \nu - 1$, then $S_{LNP}(\tau)$ satisfies Assumption 2 and, by Theorem 7,

$$\mathbf{P}\{S_{LNP}(B^r) > \frac{x}{1-\rho}\} \sim \mathbf{P}\{B^r > x\}.$$

Since $1 - B(x) = \mathrm{o}(1 - B^r(x))$, $x \to \infty$, we have, from (31),

$$\mathbf{P}\{S_{LNP} > \frac{x}{1-\rho}\} \sim \rho\,\mathbf{P}\{B^r > x\}, \tag{32}$$

in accordance with Theorem 4.

Remark 3. The case $1 < \nu < 2$ needs special treatment. As we will see below, the approach aims at verification of Condition *(b)* of Assumption 2, taking κ equal to the nearest integer larger than $\nu - 1$, which in this case would be $\kappa = 1$. However, for $\kappa < 2$ we can not use (27). It is possible to verify Condition *(b)* using different probabilistic arguments which, however, we shall not pursue here.

A different problem occurs when ν is integer-valued. The approach would aim at choosing $\kappa = \nu$. This requires that $\mathbf{E}B^{\nu} < \infty$, which may not be the case. (Recall that in the analysis of the $M/G/1$ PS system we could choose κ equal to any integer larger than ν.)

In order to verify the conditions in Assumption 2 we first derive differential equations for the moments of $S_{LNP}(\tau)$. The random variable P shall have the distribution of the busy period in the $M/G/1$ queue. We assume that $m < \nu < m + 1$, for some integer $m \geq 2$, and therefore $\mathbf{E}B^m < \infty$ and $\mathbf{E}P^m < \infty$.

Remark 4. The fact that $\mathbf{E}P^m < \infty$ if and only if $\mathbf{E}B^m < \infty$ is a consequence of Theorem 3 (since $S_{LPR} \stackrel{d}{=} P$). Note that this result was proven in [30] using Laplace-Transform techniques (cf. (18)). The same can be achieved using (probabilistic) sample-path arguments [49].

Conditioning on whether or not an arrival occurs during a time interval of length $\Delta > 0$ we obtain, for $k = 1, 2, \ldots, m$,

$$\begin{aligned} \mathbf{E}\big[S_{LNP}(\tau + \Delta)^k\big] &= (1 - \lambda\Delta)\mathbf{E}\Big[(\Delta + S_{LNP}(\tau))^k\Big] \\ &\quad + \lambda\Delta\mathbf{E}\Big[(\Delta + S_{LNP}(\tau) + P)^k\Big] + \mathrm{o}(\Delta), \qquad \Delta \to 0. \end{aligned}$$

Re-arranging terms, dividing by Δ, passing $\Delta \to 0$ and using $\mathbf{E}P = \beta/(1 - \rho)$, we obtain

$$\frac{\mathrm{d}}{\mathrm{d}\tau}\mathbf{E}S_{LNP}(\tau)^k = \frac{k}{1 - \rho}\mathbf{E}S_{LNP}(\tau)^{k-1} + \lambda \sum_{j=0}^{k-2} \binom{k}{j} \mathbf{E}S_{LNP}(\tau)^j \mathbf{E}P^{k-j}, \quad (33)$$

with initial condition $\mathbf{E}S(0)^k = \mathbf{E}B^k$. By solving (33) for $k = 1$ (setting the empty sum equal to 0), it can straightforwardly be verified that

$$\mathbf{E}S_{LNP}(\tau) = \beta + \frac{\tau}{1 - \rho},$$

which verifies Condition *(a)* of Assumption 2. Recursively solving (33) for $k = 2, 3, \ldots, m$, leads to the general form

$$\mathbf{E}S_{LNP}(\tau)^k = \left(\frac{\tau}{1 - \rho}\right)^k + p_{k-1}(\tau), \quad (34)$$

where $p_{k-1}(\tau)$ denotes a polynomial in τ of degree $k - 1$. The coefficients of this polynomial can be obtained recursively by substitution into (33); in particular, $p_{k-1}(0) = \mathbf{E}B^k$. Taking $\kappa = m$ we may use (27) and (34) to show that Condition *(b)* of Assumption 2 is satisfied (for any $0 < \delta < 1$). Finally, Condition *(c)* can again be verified by a sample-path argument similar to that in the analysis of the $M/G/1$ PS system.

(iii) The $M/G/1$ FBPS queue
With the FBPS discipline, the customers which so far have received the least amount of service share equally in the total capacity. Using Theorem 7, we shall prove that the sojourn time tail is just as heavy as the service requirement tail if $B(\cdot) \in \mathcal{R}_{-\nu}$ with $1 < \nu < 2$. (For $\nu \geq 2$ we need to study higher moments of the conditional sojourn time.) $S_{FB}(\tau)$ denotes the sojourn time of a customer with service requirement τ. With a straightforward sample-path argument it can be shown that $S_{FB}(\tau)$ is stochastically non-decreasing.

Assuming $B(x)$ is absolutely continuous, the mean and variance of the sojourn time are given by:

$$\mathbf{E}S_{FB}(\tau) = \frac{\tau}{1-\lambda h_1(\tau)} + \frac{\lambda h_2(\tau)}{2(1-\lambda h_1(\tau))^2}, \tag{35}$$

$$\mathbf{Var}S_{FB}(\tau) = \frac{\lambda h_3(\tau)}{3(1-\lambda h_1(\tau))^3} + \frac{\lambda \tau h_2(\tau)}{(1-\lambda h_1(\tau))^3} + \frac{3(\lambda h_2(\tau))^2}{4(1-\lambda h_1(\tau))^4}, \tag{36}$$

cf. Yashkov [46, Form. (6.2) and (6.3)]. The functions $h_j(\tau)$, $j = 1, 2, 3$, are given by

$$h_j(\tau) = j \int_{x=0}^{\tau} x^{j-1} (1 - B(x))\, \mathrm{d}x. \tag{37}$$

These expressions can again be used [34] to prove that, for all $\varepsilon > 0$,

$$\mathbf{E}S_{FB}(\tau) \sim \frac{\tau}{1-\rho}, \qquad \mathbf{Var}S_{FB}(\tau) = \mathrm{o}(\tau^{3-\nu+\varepsilon}), \quad \tau \to \infty.$$

Consequently, Assumption 2 is implied by Assumption 1 (choosing $\kappa = 2$ and $0 < \delta < \nu - 1$) and we may again apply Theorem 7 to show that $\mathbf{P}\{S_{FB} > \frac{x}{1-\rho}\} \sim \mathbf{P}\{B > x\}$, cf. Theorem 5.

(iv) The $M/G/1$ SRPTF queue
Now we consider an $M/G/1$ queue in which the total service capacity is always allocated to the customer with the shortest remaining processing time (Shortest Remaining Processing Time First). The service of a customer is pre-empted when a new customer arrives with a service requirement smaller than the remaining service requirement of the customer being served. The service of the customer that is pre-empted is resumed as soon as there are no other customers with a smaller amount of work in the system.

As in the $M/G/1$ FBPS queue, we restrict ourselves to the case $B(\cdot) \in \mathcal{R}_{-\nu}$ with $1 < \nu < 2$. We further assume that $B(x)$ is a continuous function, hence, with probability 1, no two customers in the system have the same remaining service requirement, see [41].

The sojourn time can be decomposed into two different periods: The waiting time (the time until the customer is first taken into service) and the residence time (the remainder of the sojourn time). The residence time may contain service pre-emption periods caused by customers with a smaller service requirement. For a customer with service requirement τ, we denote the waiting time by $W(\tau)$ and the residence time by $R(\tau)$. Thus, the sojourn time is given by $S_{SR}(\tau) = W(\tau) + R(\tau)$. We define $\rho(\tau)$ as the traffic load of customers with an amount of work less than or equal to τ,

$$\rho(\tau) := \lambda \int_{t=0}^{\tau} t\mathrm{d}B(t). \tag{38}$$

The first two moments of $W(\tau)$ are given by:

$$\mathbf{E}W(\tau) = \lambda \frac{\int_{t=0}^{\tau} t^2 \mathrm{d}B(t) + \tau^2 (1 - B(\tau))}{2\,(1-\rho(\tau))^2}, \tag{39}$$

$$\begin{aligned}\mathbf{E}W(\tau)^2 = {} & \lambda \frac{\int_{t=0}^{\tau} t^3 \mathrm{d}B(t) + \tau^3 (1 - B(\tau))}{3\,(1-\rho(\tau))^3} \\ & + \lambda^2 \int_{t=0}^{\tau} t^2 \mathrm{d}B(t) \frac{\int_{t=0}^{\tau} t^2 \mathrm{d}B(t) + \tau^2 (1 - B(\tau))}{(1-\rho(\tau))^4},\end{aligned} \tag{40}$$

and the mean and variance of $R(\tau)$ by

$$\mathbf{E}R(\tau) = \int_{t=0}^{\tau} \frac{1}{1-\rho(t)} \mathrm{d}t, \tag{41}$$

$$\mathbf{Var}R(\tau) = \lambda \int_{t=0}^{\tau} \frac{\int_{u=0}^{t} u^2 \mathrm{d}B(u)}{(1-\rho(t))^3} \mathrm{d}t, \tag{42}$$

cf. [41]. These expressions may again be used [34] to verify that, when $1 < \nu < 2$, Assumption 1 implies Assumption 2 and, hence, $\mathbf{P}\{S_{SR} > \frac{x}{1-\rho}\} \sim \mathbf{P}\{B > x\}$, cf. Theorem 6.

5 Sample-Path Techniques

In the present section we describe how sample-path techniques may be used to determine the tail asymptotics of the delay distribution in the $M/G/1$ queue for various disciplines. By definition, the tail distribution of a random variable reflects the occurrence of rare events. Large-deviations theory suggests that, given that a rare event occurs, it happens with overwhelming probability in the most likely way. In case light-tailed processes are involved, the most likely path typically consists of an extremely long sequence of slightly unusual events, which conspire to make the rare event under consideration occur, see for instance Anantharam [2]. In contrast, for heavy-tailed characteristics, the most likely scenario usually involves just a single catastrophic event (or in general, a 'minimal combination' of disastrous events that is required to cause the event under consideration to happen). Typically, the scenario entails the arrival of a customer with an exceedingly large service requirement.

The fact that the most likely scenario usually involves just a single exceptional event, provides a heuristic method for obtaining the tail asymptotics by simply computing the probability of that scenario occurring. By way of illustration, we now sketch a heuristic derivation of the tail asymptotics of the workload V in the $M/G/1$ queue as described in Section 2.

Let us focus on the workload in the system at time $t = 0$. The assumption is that a large workload level is most likely due to the prior arrival of a customer with a large service requirement B, let us say at time $t = -y$. (Of course, this assumption is nothing but an educated guess at this stage. However, it turns out that this supposition leads to the correct result, and can actually be strengthened into a rigorous proof, as will be illustrated below.) Note that from time $t = -y$ onward, the workload decreases in a roughly linear fashion at rate $1 - \rho$. So in order for the workload at time $t = 0$ to exceed the level x, the service requirement B must be larger than $x + y(1 - \rho)$. Observing that customers arrive as a Poisson process of rate λ, integrating w.r.t. y, and making the substitution $z = x + y(1 - \rho)$, we obtain, for large x,

$$\mathbf{P}\{V > x\} \approx \int_{y=0}^{\infty} \mathbf{P}\{B > x + y(1 - \rho)\}\lambda \mathrm{d}y = \frac{\lambda}{1 - \rho} \int_{z=x}^{\infty} \mathbf{P}\{B > z\}\mathrm{d}z = \frac{\rho}{1 - \rho}\mathbf{P}\{B^r > x\}. \tag{43}$$

With some additional effort, the heuristic derivation can often be strengthened into a rigorous proof. The typical approach consists of deriving lower and upper bounds which asymptotically coincide. It is often relatively straightforward to convert the heuristic arguments into a strict lower bound by calculating the probability of the most likely scenario occurring. The construction of a suitable upper bound tends to be more challenging. The upper bound usually consists of a dominant term which corresponds to the probability of the most likely scenario. The main difficulty lies in showing that this scenario is indeed the only plausible one, in the sense that all other possible sample paths do not significantly contribute. This is done by partitioning the 'irrelevant' sample paths into a few sets which must then all be shown to have an asymptotically negligible probability.

Although the above approach is fairly typical, it is hard to describe a universal method that can be mechanically executed. The identification of the most likely scenario is problem-specific and requires some sort of an educated guess. Categorizing the 'irrelevant' sample paths is not an automatic task either. The next lemma however characterizes the structure that typically emerges.

Lemma 2. *Suppose that for any $\delta > 0$, $\epsilon > 0$,*

$$\mathbf{P}\{X > x\} \geq F(-\delta)\mathbf{P}\{Y > G(\epsilon)x\} \prod_{i=1}^{K} \mathbf{P}\{D_i^{-\delta,\epsilon}(x)\}, \tag{44}$$

$$\mathbf{P}\{X > x\} \leq F(\delta)\mathbf{P}\{Y > G(-\epsilon)x\} + \sum_{j=1}^{L} \mathbf{P}\{E_j^{\delta,-\epsilon}(x)\}, \tag{45}$$

$\mathbf{P}\{Y > x\}$ is regularly varying of index $-\nu$, $\lim_{\delta \to 0} F(\delta) = F$, $\lim_{\epsilon \to 0} G(\epsilon) = G$, $\mathbf{P}\{D_i^{-\delta,\epsilon}(x)\} \to 1$ as $x \to \infty$, and $\mathbf{P}\{E_j^{\delta,-\epsilon}(x)\} = \mathrm{o}(x^{-\nu})$ as $x \to \infty$. Then

$$\mathbf{P}\{X > x\} \sim F\mathbf{P}\{Y > Gx\}.$$

Proof. The proof is straightforward. Relying on the lower bound (44) and the fact that $\mathbf{P}\{D_i^{-\delta,\epsilon}(x)\} \to 1$ as $x \to \infty$, we obtain

$$\liminf_{x \to \infty} \frac{\mathbf{P}\{X > x\}}{F\mathbf{P}\{Y > Gx\}} \geq \frac{F(-\delta)}{F} \liminf_{x \to \infty} \frac{\mathbf{P}\{Y > G(\epsilon)x\}}{\mathbf{P}\{Y > Gx\}}.$$

Letting $\delta, \epsilon \downarrow 0$, and recalling that $\mathbf{P}\{Y > x\}$ is regularly varying, we find

$$\liminf_{x \to \infty} \frac{\mathbf{P}\{X > x\}}{F\mathbf{P}\{Y > Gx\}} \geq 1.$$

Similarly, using the upper bound (45), the fact that $\mathbf{P}\{E_j^{\delta,-\epsilon}(x)\} = \mathrm{o}(x^{-\nu})$ as $x \to \infty$, and observing that $\mathbf{P}\{Y > x\}$ is regularly varying of index $-\nu$, we deduce

$$\limsup_{x \to \infty} \frac{\mathbf{P}\{X > x\}}{F\mathbf{P}\{Y > Gx\}} \leq \frac{F(\delta)}{F} \liminf_{x \to \infty} \frac{\mathbf{P}\{Y > G(-\epsilon)x\}}{\mathbf{P}\{Y > Gx\}}.$$

Letting $\delta, \epsilon \downarrow 0$, we conclude

$$\limsup_{x \to \infty} \frac{\mathbf{P}\{X > x\}}{F\mathbf{P}\{Y > Gx\}} \leq 1.$$

□

It is worth observing that the above proof technique in fact extends to the class of *intermediately* regularly varying distributions.

As a 'toy example', we now sketch how the above lemma may be used to strengthen the heuristic derivation of (43) into a rigorous proof. The approach is similar as outlined in Chapter 2 of Zwart [48]. We use the time-reversed sample-path representation

$$V \stackrel{d}{=} \sup_{t \geq 0} \{A(0, t) - t\} \tag{46}$$

with $A(0, t)$ denoting the amount of work arriving in the time interval $(0, t)$.

We first construct a lower bound of the form (44). For any $c < \rho$, define $U^c := \sup_{t \geq 0} \{ct - A(0, t)\}$. For any $\delta > 0$, $\epsilon > 0$,

$$\mathbf{P}\{V > x\} \geq \int_{y=0}^{\infty} \mathbf{P}\{A(0, y) + B - y > x\} \lambda \mathrm{d}y$$

$$\geq \lambda \int_{y=0}^{\infty} \mathbf{P}\{A(0,y) - y(\rho - \delta) \geq -\epsilon x\} \mathbf{P}\{B > x(1+\epsilon) + y(1-\rho+\delta)\} \mathrm{d}y$$

$$\geq \mathbf{P}\{\inf_{u \geq 0} \{A(0,u) - u(\rho - \delta)\} \geq -\epsilon x\} \lambda \int_{y=0}^{\infty} \mathbf{P}\{B > x(1+\epsilon) + y(1-\rho+\delta)\} \mathrm{d}y$$

$$= \frac{\rho}{1-\rho+\delta} \mathbf{P}\{B^r > x(1+\epsilon)\} \mathbf{P}\{U^{\rho-\delta} \leq \epsilon x\}.$$

Note that $\mathbf{P}\{U^{\rho-\delta} \leq \epsilon x\} \to 1$ as $x \to \infty$ because of the law of large numbers.

We now proceed to derive an upper bound of the form (45). For any interval $I \subseteq \mathbb{R}^+$, define $V(I) := \sup_{t \in I}\{A(0,t) - t\}$. For any $y \geq 0$, let $N_y(I)$ be the number of customers arriving during the time interval I whose service requirement exceeds the value y. Then, for all $M \geq 0$,

$$\begin{aligned}
&\mathbf{P}\{V > x\} \leq \mathbf{P}\{V([0,Mx]) > x\} + \mathbf{P}\{V((Mx,\infty)) > x\} \\
&= \mathbf{P}\{V([0,Mx]) > x; N_{\epsilon x}([0,Mx]) = 0\} + \mathbf{P}\{V([0,Mx]) > x; N_{\epsilon x}([0,Mx]) = 1\} \\
&+ \mathbf{P}\{V([0,Mx]) > x; N_{\epsilon x}([0,Mx]) \geq 2\} + \mathbf{P}\{V((Mx,\infty)) > x\}.
\end{aligned}$$

The second term corresponds to the only plausible scenario and is dominant. As in [50], it may be shown that for any $\delta > 0$, $\epsilon > 0$, as $x \to \infty$,

$$\begin{aligned}
&\mathbf{P}\{V([0,Mx]) > x; N_{\epsilon x}([0,Mx]) = 1\} \\
&\leq \int_{y=0}^{\infty} \mathbf{P}\{B > x(1-\epsilon) + y(1-\rho-\delta)\} \lambda \mathrm{d}y + \mathrm{o}(x^{1-\nu}) \\
&= \frac{\rho}{1-\rho-\delta} \mathbf{P}\{B^r > x(1-\epsilon)\} + \mathrm{o}(x^{1-\nu}).
\end{aligned}$$

Applying Lemma 2 completes the proof, once we have shown that each of the other three terms can asymptotically be neglected.

For the first term, one may exploit a powerful lemma of Resnick & Samorodnitsky [39] to show that for any $\mu > 0$ there exists an $\epsilon > 0$ such that

$$\mathbf{P}\{V([0,Mx]) > x; N_{\epsilon x}([0,Mx]) = 0\} = \mathrm{o}(x^{-\mu})$$

as $x \to \infty$. The idea is that when there are no large service requirements, the process $\{A(0,t) - t\}$ cannot significantly deviate from its normal drift over long intervals of the order x, so that the workload cannot reach a large level.

In order to control the third term, it may be checked using elementary arguments that $\mathbf{P}\{N_{\epsilon x}([0,Mx]) \geq 2\} = \mathrm{o}(x^{1-\nu})$ as $x \to \infty$. Note that the probability of two large service requirements occurring in a time interval of order x asymptotically vanishes compared to that of just one large service requirement.

Finally, in order to restrain the fourth term, it may be shown using results from Mikosch [31] that $\lim_{M \to \infty} \limsup_{x \to \infty} \mathbf{P}\{V((Mx,\infty)) > x\} / \mathbf{P}\{V > x\} = 0$. The idea is that a large workload level of order x must build up 'in linear time', since otherwise the process $\{A(0,t) - t\}$ must deviate from its normal drift for a prohibitively long period of time.

The above proof exploits and confirms the large-deviations notion that a large workload level is typically due to a single large service requirement by implicitly characterizing the most likely sample path. We refer to Baccelli and Foss [4] for yet stronger characterizations.

It is worth emphasizing that we used the above proof technique for illustration purposes only. The machinery is unnecessarily heavy for determining the workload asymptotics in the ordinary $M/G/1$ queue, given that a convenient expression for the LST is available, which can be explicitly inverted as shown in Section 3. The true merits of the methodology become manifest in more complicated systems, such as fluid queues or GPS models, where typically no useful expression for the LST is available [9,12,50].

5.1 The Single-Class Case

We now turn the attention to the tail asymptotics of the delay distribution in the $M/G/1$ queue. In contrast to the workload distribution, the delay distribution *does* strongly depend on the service discipline that is used.

(i) The $M/G/1$ FCFS queue
For FCFS, the waiting time is simply equal to the workload at the time of arrival. Because of the PASTA property, it then follows from (43) that

$$\mathbf{P}\{W_{FCFS} > x\} \sim \frac{\rho}{1-\rho}\mathbf{P}\{B^r > x\},$$

which agrees with Theorem 1.

(ii) The $M/G/1$ LCFS-NP queue
For LCFS Non-Preemptive priority, the waiting time is equal to 0 with probability $1 - \rho$, and with probability ρ it is equal to a busy period starting with a residual service requirement, which gives

$$\mathbf{P}\{W_{LNP} > x\} \sim \rho\mathbf{P}\{B^r > x(1-\rho)\}, \tag{47}$$

as asserted in Theorem 4.

A heuristic derivation of the above formula proceeds as follows. Consider a tagged customer arriving at time $t = 0$. The premise is that a long waiting time is most likely due to a large service requirement B of the customer in service, if any. The waiting time W of the tagged customer then consists of the remaining service requirement, $B - y$, plus the amount of work arriving during its own waiting time, which is approximately ρW, so that $W \approx B - y + \rho W$, or equivalently, $W \approx (B - y)/(1 - \rho)$. So in order for the waiting time to exceed the value x, the service requirement B must be larger than $y + x(1 - \rho)$. Thus, observing that arrivals occur as a Poisson process of rate λ, and integrating w.r.t. y, we find, for large x,

$$\mathbf{P}\{W_{LNP} > x\} \approx \int_{y=0}^{\infty} \mathbf{P}\{B > x(1-\rho) + y\}\lambda \mathrm{d}y = \rho \mathbf{P}\{B^r > x(1-\rho)\},$$

which is in agreement with (47). The above heuristic derivation may be translated into a rigorous proof in a similar fashion as indicated for the workload asymptotics.

(iii) The $M/G/1$ LCFS-PR queue
For LCFS Preemptive Resume, the sojourn time is simply equal to the busy period, yielding

$$\mathbf{P}\{S_{LPR} > x\} \sim \frac{1}{1-\rho}\mathbf{P}\{B > x(1-\rho)\},$$

as stated in Theorem 3. A sample-path proof of the tail asymptotics of the busy-period distribution may be found in Zwart [49].

(iv) The $M/G/1$ PS queue
We now turn to the tail asymptotics of the sojourn time for the Processor-Sharing discipline. Consider a tagged customer arriving at time $t = 0$. The sojourn time S of the tagged customer consists of its own service requirement B plus the amount of service provided to other customers during its sojourn time. In case of a long sojourn time, the amount of service received by other customers will be approximately ρS, so that $S \approx B + \rho S$, or equivalently, $S \approx B/(1-\rho)$. The assumption is thus that a long sojourn time is most likely due to a large service requirement of the tagged customer itself, suggesting that, for large x,

$$\mathbf{P}\{S_{PS} > x\} \sim \mathbf{P}\{B > x(1-\rho)\}, \tag{48}$$

which corroborates with Theorem 2.

We now show how the above rough derivation may be used as the basis for a rigorous proof of (48) using lower and upper bounds along the lines of Lemma 2. The proof is similar to that in Jelenković & Momcilović [24]. Let B_0 and S_0 be the service requirement and the sojourn time, respectively, of a tagged customer arriving at time $t = 0$. Let B_i and T_i denote the service requirement and the arrival time of the i-th customer arriving after time $t = 0$. Let $L(0)$ be the number of customers in the system just before time $t = 0$, and let B_l^r denote the remaining service requirement of the l-th customer. We use the sample-path representation

$$S_0 = B_0 + \sum_{l=1}^{L(0)} \min\{B_l^r, B_0\} + \sum_{i=1}^{N((0,S_0))} \min\{B_i, R_0(T_i)\}, \tag{49}$$

with $N((0,t))$ denoting the number of customers arriving during the time interval $(0,t)$ and $R_0(t)$ the remaining service requirement of the tagged customer at time t, see for instance Wolff [44].

The next lemma presents a lower bound for the sojourn time of the tagged customer. Denote $Z(t) := \sum_{i=1}^{N((0,t))} \max\{B_i - R_0(T_i), 0\}$.

Lemma 3. *For any* $\delta > 0$,

$$S_0(1-\rho+\delta) \geq B_0 - U^{\rho-\delta} - Z(S_0).$$

Proof. Using the representation (49), we have

$$\begin{aligned}
S_0(1-\rho+\delta) &= B_0 + \sum_{l=1}^{L(0)} \min\{B_l^r, B_0\} + \sum_{i=1}^{N((0,S_0))} \min\{B_i, R_0(T_i)\} - (\rho-\delta)S_0 \\
&\geq B_0 + \sum_{i=1}^{N((0,S_0))} B_i - (\rho-\delta)S_0 + \sum_{i=1}^{N((0,S_0))} \min\{B_i, R_0(T_i)\} - \sum_{i=1}^{N((0,S_0))} B_i \\
&= B_0 + A(0,S_0) - (\rho-\delta)S_0 + \sum_{i=1}^{N((0,S_0))} \min\{R_0(T_i) - B_i, 0\} \\
&\geq B_0 + \inf_{t\geq 0}\{A(0,t) - (\rho-\delta)t\} - \sum_{i=1}^{N((0,S_0))} \max\{B_i - R_0(T_i), 0\} \\
&= B_0 - U^{\rho-\delta} - Z(S_0).
\end{aligned}$$

□

The next lemma provides an upper bound for the sojourn time of the tagged customer. For any $y > 0$, let $A_y(0,t)$ be a version of the process $A(0,t)$ where all service requirements of arriving customers are truncated at the level y. For any $c > \rho$, define $V_y^c := \sup_{t\geq 0}\{A_y(0,t) - ct\}$.

Lemma 4. *For any* $\delta > 0$,

$$(1-\rho-\delta)S_0 \leq \hat{B}_0 + V_{B_0}^{\rho+\delta},$$

with $\hat{B}_0 := B_0 + \sum_{l=1}^{L(0)} \min\{B_l^r, B_0\}$.

Proof. Using the representation (49),

$$S_0(1-\rho-\delta) = B_0 + \sum_{l=1}^{L(0)} \min\{B_l^r, B_0\} + \sum_{i=1}^{N((0,S_0))} \min\{B_i, R_0(T_i)\} - (\rho+\delta)S_0$$

$$\begin{aligned}
&\leq \hat{B}_0 + \sum_{i=1}^{N((0,S_0))} \min\{B_i, B_0\} - (\rho+\delta)S_0 \\
&= \hat{B}_0 + A_{B_0}(0, S_0) - (\rho+\delta)S_0 \\
&\leq \hat{B}_0 + \sup_{t\geq 0}\{A_{B_0}(0,t) - (\rho+\delta)t\} \\
&= \hat{B}_0 + V_{B_0}^{\rho+\delta}.
\end{aligned}$$

□

The above two lemmas provide the necessary ingredients for the proof of (48) along the lines of Lemma 2.

Proof of Theorem 2 (Lower bound) Using Lemma 3, noting that $S_0 \geq B_0$, we obtain

$$\begin{aligned}
&\mathbf{P}\{S_{PS} > x\} \geq \mathbf{P}\{B_0 - U^{\rho-\delta} - Z(S_0) > (1-\rho+\delta)x\} \\
&\geq \mathbf{P}\{B_0 > (1-\rho+\delta+2\epsilon)x\}\mathbf{P}\{U^{\rho-\delta} \leq \epsilon x\} \inf_{y \geq (1-\rho+\delta+2\epsilon)x} \mathbf{P}\{Z(y) > \epsilon x\}.
\end{aligned}$$

Because of the law of large numbers, $\mathbf{P}\{U^{\rho-\delta} \leq \epsilon x\} \to 1$ as $x \to \infty$. As observed in [24], $\inf_{y \geq (1-\rho+\delta+2\epsilon)x} \mathbf{P}\{Z(y) > \epsilon x\} \to 1$ as $x \to \infty$.
(Upper bound) Using Lemma 4, we find

$$\begin{aligned}
\mathbf{P}\{S_{PS} > x\} &\leq \mathbf{P}\{\hat{B}_0 + V_{B_0}^{\rho+\delta} > (1-\rho-\delta)x\} \\
&\leq \mathbf{P}\{\hat{B}_0 > (1-\rho-\delta-\epsilon)x\} + \mathbf{P}\{V_{B_0}^{\rho+\delta} > \epsilon x\}.
\end{aligned}$$

As demonstrated in [24], $\mathbf{P}\{B_0 > x\} \sim \mathbf{P}\{\hat{B}_0 > x\}$ and $\mathbf{P}\{V_{B_0}^{\rho+\delta} > \epsilon x\} = o(x^{1-\nu})$ as $x \to \infty$.
Invoking Lemma 2 then completes the proof. □

5.2 The Multi-class Case

We finally consider the tail asymptotics of the waiting time in the multi-class $M/G/1$ queue with priorities as described in Subsection 3.2. We focus on the case of a Non-Preemptive priority discipline. As mentioned in Subsection 3.2, the tail asymptotics in the case of a Preemptive-Resume policy immediately follow from the results for a high-priority class in isolation and a low-priority class in the Non-Preemptive priority scenario. We assume that the service requirement distribution of at least one of the classes has a regularly varying tail. Let $\mathcal{M}$ be the index set of the classes with the 'heaviest' tail.

Consider a tagged class-k customer arriving at time $t = 0$. The premise is that a long waiting time is most likely due to the prior arrival of a customer with a large service requirement B, let us say at time $t = -y$, which may belong to any of the classes $m \in \mathcal{M}$. Of course, how likely it is for the culprit customer to belong to a given class $m \in \mathcal{M}$ depends on the arrival rates and mean service requirements of the various classes. Due to the Non-Preemptive priority policy, the identity of the culprit customer is not of any relevance for the impact on the tagged customer. However, the effect does strongly depend on the identity of the tagged customer itself. For compactness, denote $\sigma_k = \sum_{l=1}^{k} \rho_l$. Note that from time $t = -y$ onward, the amount of work in the system that has precedence over the service of the tagged customer decreases in a roughly linear fashion at rate $1 - \sigma_k$. In addition, the tagged customer must wait for the amount of work arriving during its waiting time W_k from higher-priority classes at rate σ_{k-1}. Thus, $W_k \approx B - y(1 - \sigma_k) + W_k\sigma_{k-1}$, or equivalently, $W_k \approx (B - y(1 - \sigma_k))/(1 - \sigma_{k-1})$. So in order for the waiting time of the tagged customer to exceed the value x, the service requirement B must be larger than $x(1 - \sigma_{k-1}) + y(1 - \sigma_k)$. Observing that class-$m$ customers arrive as a Poisson process of rate λ_m, integrating w.r.t. y, we obtain, for large x,

$$\begin{aligned}\mathbf{P}\{W_k > x\} &\approx \sum_{m \in \mathcal{M}} \int_{y=0}^{\infty} \mathbf{P}\{B_m > x(1 - \sigma_{k-1}) + y(1 - \sigma_k)\}\lambda_m \mathrm{d}y \\ &= \sum_{m \in \mathcal{M}} \frac{\rho_m}{1 - \sigma_k} \mathbf{P}\{B_m^r > x(1 - \sigma_{k-1})\}.\end{aligned}$$

References

1. Abate, J., Whitt, W. (1997). Asymptotics for $M/G/1$ low-priority waiting-time tail probabilities. *Queueing Systems* **25**, 173–233.
2. Anantharam, V. (1988). How large delays build up in a $GI/G/1$ queue. *Queueing Systems* **5**, 345–368.
3. Anantharam, V. (1999). Scheduling strategies and long-range dependence. *Queueing Systems* **33**, 73–89.
4. Baccelli, F., Foss, S. (2001). Moments and tails in monotone-separable stochastic networks. Research Report RR 4197, INRIA Rocquencourt.
5. Beran, J., Sherman, R., Taqqu, M.S., Willinger, W. (1995). Long-range dependence in variable-bit-rate video traffic. IEEE *Trans. Commun.* **43**, 1566–1579.
6. Bingham, N.H., Doney, R.A. (1974). Asymptotic properties of super-critical branching processes. I: The Galton-Watson process. *Adv. Appl. Prob.* **6**, 711–731.
7. Bingham, N.H., Goldie, C.M., Teugels, J.L. (1987). *Regular Variation* (Cambridge University Press, Cambridge, UK).
8. Borst, S.C., Boxma, O.J., Jelenković, P.R. (2000). Coupled processors with regularly varying service times. In: *Proc. Infocom 2000 Conference*, Tel-Aviv, Israel, 157–164.
9. Borst, S.C., Boxma, O.J., Jelenković, P.R. (2000). Reduced-load equivalence and induced burstiness in GPS queues. *Queueing Systems*, to appear.
10. Borst, S.C., Boxma, O.J., Van Uitert, M.G.J. (2001). Two coupled queues with heterogeneous traffic. In: *Teletraffic Engineering in the Internet Era, Proc. ITC-17*, Salvador da Bahia, Brazil, eds. J. Moreira de Souza, N.L.S. da Fonseca, E.A. de Souza e Silva (North-Holland, Amsterdam), 1003–1014.

11. Borst, S.C., Boxma, O.J., Van Uitert, M.G.J. (2002). The asymptotic workload behavior of two coupled queues. CWI Report PNA-R0202. Submitted for publication.
12. Borst, S.C., Zwart, A.P. (2001). Fluid queues with heavy-tailed $M/G/\infty$ input. SPOR-Report 2001-02, Department of Mathematics and Computer Science, Eindhoven University of Technology. Submitted for publication.
13. Boxma, O.J., Cohen, J.W. (2000). The single server queue: Heavy tails and heavy traffic. In: *Self-similar Network Traffic and Performance Evaluation*, eds. K. Park, W. Willinger (Wiley, New York), 143–169.
14. Boxma, O.J., Cohen, J.W., Deng, Q. (1999). Heavy-traffic analysis of the M/G/1 queue with priority classes. In: *Teletraffic Engineering in a Competitive World, Proc. ITC-16*, Edinburgh, UK, eds. P. Key, D. Smith (North-Holland, Amsterdam), 1157–1167.
15. Boxma, O.J., Deng, Q., Resing, J.A.C. (2000). Polling systems with regularly varying service and/or switchover times. *Adv. Perf. Anal.* **3**, 71–107.
16. Boxma, O.J. Dumas, V. (1998). The busy period in the fluid queue. *Perf. Eval. Review* **26**, 100–110.
17. Cohen, J.W. (1973). Some results on regular variation for distributions in queueing and fluctuation theory. *J. Appl. Prob.* **10**, 343–353.
18. Cohen, J.W. (1982). *The Single Server Queue* (North-Holland Publ. Cy., Amsterdam; revised edition).
19. Cohen, J.W., Boxma, O.J. (1983). *Boundary Value Problems in Queueing System Analysis* (North-Holland Publ. Cy., Amsterdam).
20. Crovella, M., Bestavros, A. (1996). Self-similarity in World Wide Web Traffic: evidence and possible causes. In: *Proc. ACM Sigmetrics '96*, 160–169.
21. Deng, Q. (2001). The two-queue $E/1-L$ polling model with regularly varying service and/or switchover times. SPOR-Report 2001-09, Department of Mathematics and Computer Science, Eindhoven University of Technology.
22. Fayolle, G., Iasnogorodski, R. (1979). Two coupled processors: the reduction to a Riemann-Hilbert problem. *Z. Wahrsch. Verw. Gebiete* **47**, 325–351.
23. Feller, W. (1971). *An Introduction to Probability Theory and its Applications, Vol. II* (Wiley, New York).
24. Jelenković, P.R., Momcilović, P. (2002). Resource sharing with subexponential distributions. In: *Proc. IEEE Infocom 2002*, New York NY, USA, to appear.
25. Karamata, J. (1930). Sur un mode de croissance régulière des fonctions. *Mathematica (Cluj)* **4**, 38–53.
26. Kleinrock, L. (1976). *Queueing Systems, Vol. II: Computer Applications* (Wiley, New York).
27. Klüppelberg, C. (1988). Subexponential distributions and integrated tails. *J. Appl. Prob.* **25**, 132–141.
28. Konheim, A.G., Meilijson, I., Melkman, A. (1981). Processor sharing of two parallel lines. *J. Appl. Prob.* **18**, 952–956.
29. Leland, W.E., Taqqu, M.S., Willinger, W., Wilson, D.V. (1994). On the self-similar nature of Ethernet traffic (extended version). IEEE/ACM *Trans. Netw.* **2**, 1–15.
30. De Meyer, A., Teugels, J.L. (1980). On the asymptotic behaviour of the distribution and the service time in $M/G/1$. *J. Appl. Prob.* **17**, 802–813.
31. Mikosch, T. (1999). Regular variation, subexponentiality and their applications in probability theory. EURANDOM Report 99-013.
32. Núñez-Queija, R. (2000). *Processor-Sharing Models for Integrated-Services Networks.* Ph.D. thesis, Eindhoven University of Technology, ISBN 90-646-4667-8 (also available from the author upon request).

33. Núñez-Queija, R. (2000). Sojourn times in a processor-sharing queue with service interruptions. *Queueing Systems* **34**, 351–386.
34. Núñez-Queija, R. (2002). Queues with equally heavy sojourn time and service requirement distributions. CWI Report PNA-R0201. Submitted for publication.
35. Ott, T.J. (1984). The sojourn-time distribution in the $M/G/1$ queue with processor sharing. *J. Appl. Prob.* **21**, 360–378.
36. Pakes, A.G. (1975). On the tails of waiting-time distributions. *J. Appl. Prob.* **12**, 555–564.
37. Parekh, A.K., Gallager, R.G. (1993). A generalized processor sharing approach to flow control in integrated services networks: the single-node case. IEEE/ACM *Trans. Netw.* **1**, 344–357.
38. Paxson, A., Floyd, S. (1995). Wide area traffic: the failure of Poisson modeling. IEEE/ACM *Trans. Netw.* **3**, 226–244.
39. Resnick, S., Samorodnitsky, G. (1999). Activity periods of an infinite server queue and performance of certain heavy-tailed fluid queues. *Queueing Systems* **33**, 43–71.
40. Sakata, M., Noguchi, S., Oizumi, J. (1971). An analysis of the $M/G/1$ queue under round-robin scheduling. *Oper. Res.* **19**, 371–385.
41. Schrage, L.E., Miller, L.W. (1966). The queue $M/G/1$ with the shortest remaining processing time discipline. *Oper. Res.* **14**, 670–684.
42. Schassberger, R. (1984). A new approach to the $M/G/1$ processor sharing queue. *Adv. Appl. Prob.* **16**, 802–813.
43. Willinger, W., Taqqu, M.S., Sherman, R., Wilson, D.V. (1997). Self-similarity through high-variability: statistical analysis of Ethernet LAN traffic at the source level. IEEE/ACM *Trans. Netw.* **5**, 71–86.
44. Wolff, R.W. (1989). *Stochastic Modeling and the Theory of Queues* (Prentice Hall, Englewood Cliffs).
45. Yashkov, S.F. (1983). A derivation of response time distribution for a $M/G/1$ processor-sharing queue. *Prob. Control Inf. Theory* **12**, 133–148.
46. Yashkov, S.F. (1987). Processor-sharing queues: Some progress in analysis. *Queueing Systems* **2**, 1–17.
47. Zwart, A.P. (1999). Sojourn times in a multiclass processor sharing queue. In: *Teletraffic Engineering in a Competitive World, Proc. ITC-16*, Edinburgh, UK, eds. P. Key, D. Smith (North-Holland, Amsterdam), 335–344.
48. Zwart, A.P. (2001). *Queueing Systems with Heavy Tails.* Ph.D. thesis, Eindhoven University of Technology.
49. Zwart, A.P. (2001). Tail asymptotics for the busy period in the $GI/G/1$ queue. *Math. Oper. Res.* **26**, 485–493.
50. Zwart, A.P., Borst, S.C., Mandjes, M. (2001). Exact asymptotics for fluid queues fed by multiple heavy-tailed On-Off flows. *Ann. Appl. Prob.*, to appear. Shortened version in: *Proc. Infocom 2001*, Anchorage AK, USA, 279–288.
51. Zwart, A.P., Boxma, O.J. (2000). Sojourn time asymptotics in the $M/G/1$ processor sharing queue. *Queueing Systems* **35**, 141–166.

The Möbius State-Level Abstract Functional Interface*

Salem Derisavi[1], Peter Kemper[2], William H. Sanders[1], and Tod Courtney[1]

[1] Coordinated Science Laboratory,
Electrical and Computer Engineering Dept.,
and Computer Science Department
University of Illinois at Urbana-Champaign
1308 W. Main St., Urbana, IL, U.S.A.
{derisavi,whs,tod}@crhc.uiuc.edu
[2] Informatik IV
Universität Dortmund
D-44221 Dortmund, Germany
kemper@ls4.cs.uni-dortmund.de

Abstract. A key advantage of the Möbius modeling environment is the ease with which one can incorporate new modeling formalisms, model composition and connection methods, and model solution methods. In this paper, we describe a new state-level abstract functional interface (AFI) for Möbius that allows numerical solution methods to communicate with Möbius state-level models via the abstraction of a labeled transition system. This abstraction, and its corresponding implementation as a set of containers and iterators, yields an important separation of concerns: It is possible to treat separately the problem of representing large labeled transition systems, like generator matrices of continuous-time Markov chains, and the problem of analyzing these systems. For example, any numerical solver (e.g., Jacobi, SOR, or uniformization) that accesses a model through the Möbius state-level AFI can operate on a variety of state-space representations, including "on-the-fly," disk-based, sparse-matrix, Kronecker, and matrix-diagram representations, without requiring that the implementation be changed to match the state-space representation. This abstraction thus avoids redundant implementations of solvers and state-generation techniques, eases research cooperation, and simplifies comparison of approaches as well as benchmarking. In addition to providing a formal definition of the Möbius state-level AFI, we illustrate its use on two state-space representations (a sparse matrix and a Kronecker representation) and two numerical solvers (Jacobi and SOR). With the help of this implementation and two example models, we demonstrate that the AFI provides the benefits of transparency while introducing only minor slowdowns in solution speed.

* This material is based upon work supported in part by the National Science Foundation under Grant No. 9975019, by the Motorola Center for High-Availability System Validation at the University of Illinois (under the umbrella of the Motorola Communications Center), and by the DFG, Collaborative Research Centre 559.

T. Field et al. (Eds.): TOOLS 2002, LNCS 2324, pp. 31–50, 2002.

1 Introduction

Model-based evaluation tools have been developed for many different modeling formalisms and use many different model solution techniques. Möbius [14, 16, 15, 30] is a recent attempt to build a general multi-formalism multi-solution hierarchical modeling framework that permits the integration of a large number of modeling formalisms and model solution techniques. A key step in achieving this multi-paradigm approach is providing an appropriate separation of concerns between models expressed in different modeling formalisms, model composition and connection methods, and model solvers (e.g., simulators and state-space generators). This is achieved by using the notion of a model-level abstract functional interface (AFI) [19, 14]. The Möbius AFI provides an abstract notion of actions (events), state variables, and properties, and a common set of methods that permits heterogeneous models to interact with one another and solvers without requiring them to understand details of the formalisms in which the constituent models are expressed. There has been a great deal of research in methods for dealing with the state-space explosion problem in state-based models, by either avoiding or tolerating large state spaces. These methods have dramatically increased the size of models that can be analyzed. For example, there have been many attempts to avoid large state spaces by detecting symmetries in models, and exploiting lumping theorems. Approaches with this aim include stochastic well-formed nets [11], stochastic activity networks (SANs) and replicate/join model composition [31], and stochastic process algebras [22, 4, 2, 24], among others. Attempts to tolerate large state spaces include variations of decision diagrams; they appear in the context of stochastic models as multi-terminal binary decision diagrams (MTBDDs) [23, 1, 25], probabilistic decision diagrams [3, 9], and matrix diagrams [12]. These methods are based on the idea of sharing isomorphic substructures to save space and to gain efficiency. Kronecker representations also allow representation of large state transition systems; different variants exist to reflect a modular [7] or hierarchical structure [5,6], or to allow matrix entries to be functions [20,32]. In addition, on-the-fly generation [18] and disk-based methods [17,27] make it possible to avoid the storage of a large state-level model by generating required matrix entries as needed, or by storing them on disk rather than in main memory, respectively.

All of these approaches are interesting candidates for integration into Möbius, even though most of them were developed separately from one another and in the context of single modeling formalisms and/or model solution methods. Interestingly, although there is such a broad spectrum of avoidance and tolerance techniques, the techniques all place very similar requirements on the subsequent numerical model solution methods. In particular, these numerical model solution methods typically involve executing a sequence of matrix-vector multiplications on some variant of the generator matrix of the resulting continuous-time Markov chain (CTMC). Methods that require this include the Power method, the Jacobi method, and the Gauss-Seidel method (for stationary analysis) and uniformization (for transient analysis). Clearly, numerical analysis is much richer in theory (see [32], for example), but the abovementioned rather simple methods are the ones that appear most frequently in combination with the techniques discussed above.

This rich variety of techniques to deal with the state-space explosion problem, and the fact that many numerical solution methods share similar basic operations, have motivated us to develop a state-level, as opposed to the existing model-level, AFI for Möbius. By doing so, we can separate state-space generation and representation issues from issues related to the solution of the resulting state-level models. Creating a state-level AFI also allows us to create and implement numerical solution methods that do not require information about the data structures used to represent a state-level model. The key idea of this approach is to formulate a state-level AFI that allows numerical solution methods to see a model as a set of states and state transitions or, in other words, as a labeled transition system (LTS). The state-level interface we have created supports access to states and transitions in an efficient way via container and iterator classes. Clearly, we are not the first ones to build an interface that allows one to iterate on an LTS; e.g., in the field of protocol verification, the Caesar/Aldebaran tool [21] provides different iterators for this purpose that seem to rely on preprocessor expansion, and in his thesis [28], Knottenbelt gives an abstract C++ representation of states in the form of a non-template class. In contrast, we follow an object-oriented approach that uses templates similar to those used in the C++ standard template library (STL) [29].

By creating a state-level AFI, we achieve a further independence than is possible using the model-level Möbius AFI alone; this has advantages for both tool developers and tool users. In particular, our approach, when used together with the Möbius model-level AFI, avoids redundant reimplementations of the three steps (model specification, state-space generation, and numerical analysis) taken when solving models numerically using state-based methods. That significantly reduces the effort that is necessary to implement, validate, and evaluate new approaches. Furthermore, it allows users to perform direct comparison and benchmarking of alternative approaches, without having to reimplement the work of other researchers; thus, they avoid the risk of being unfair when doing a comparison. Finally, it facilitates cooperation among researchers in developing new solution methods and combining existing ones; e.g., within Möbius, largeness-avoidance techniques based on lumpability can be combined with any state-based analysis method. In short, we achieve a situation in which research results that focus on model reduction, state-space exploration, state-space representation, or analysis can be developed independently but can be used with one another. Obviously, tool users profit from this integrated approach, since more state generation and model solution methods become available to them. Likewise, we make the Möbius framework more useful to researchers who are creating techniques to avoid or tolerate large state spaces.

The remainder of this paper is structured as follows: Section 2 specifies the requirements a state-level AFI must meet in order to be effective. In Section 3 we present the state-level AFI in detail, explaining the motivation behind the choices we made in developing it. In Section 4, we describe the implementation of two new state-level objects that use the AFI: an unstructured sparse-matrix representation as it is used in Möbius and a Kronecker representation that is employed in the APNN toolbox. Section 5 then analyzes two examples that are frequently considered in the literature for the performance of numerical analysis approaches. In describing the examples, we show that the overhead induced by the Möbius state-level AFI is small and is outweighed by the advantages it achieves.

2 Requirements

The transformation of a model from a high-level, user-oriented representation into a state-level model by a state-space exploration is a transformation that may be technically complex, but it does not create additional information in the process. Instead, the goal of the transformation process is to create a representation that is as compact as possible, but can efficiently perform the operations needed during numerical solution. To do that, we must study the type and amount of state-space information that algorithms access and the pattern of the accesses. In the following, we describe the characteristics that a state-level AFI should have and summarize how we have considered each one when designing the Möbius state-level AFI.

Functionality. A state-level AFI must have functionality sufficient to serve a large set of analysis techniques. More specifically, it must be easy to use and must include a sufficiently complete set of functions such that all of the analysis algorithms we are interested in can be written using this common interface. After studying a number of transient and steady-state solvers, we decided to include (among other things) function calls in the interface, so that we could access the elements of the rate matrix in a row-oriented, column-oriented, or arbitrary order. More details are given in Section 3.

Economy. The effort to support and implement the AFI for a particular state-space representation must be minimal, so as not to put an unnecessary burden on an AFI implementor. For state-space representations, it should be possible to support the required functionality in a natural, straightforward manner.

Clearly, economy and functionality are in conflict with one another, and a compromise must be reached. In our case, this means that we refrain from defining operations from linear algebra, such as matrix-vector multiplication, in the interface, since that could lead to an endless demand for further operations. We rather follow an approach in which a state-based analysis method reads information via the AFI, but does not transform it using the interface.

Generality. A state-level AFI should be "solution-method neutral," in the sense that it is not tailored toward any particular state-space representation or solution method. For example, many sophisticated algorithms rely on additional structural information. Decompositional methods such as iterative aggregation/disaggregation require a partition of the state space; Kronecker methods are based on a compositional model description; and most variants of decision diagrams require an order on the variables, and heuristics on the order make use of information present in a model.

Flexibility. A state-level AFI must give implementors the opportunity to find creative optimizations in their implementations. For example, it should allow a developer who implements the interface for a particular state-space representation to exploit the special structure that may be present in the underlying state space, in order to optimize the interface implementation. Ideally, all the optimizations that are possible in a traditional "monolithic" implementation should also be applicable to an implementation that uses the developed AFI. In Section 4, we will give an example of such possible state-space-specific optimizations when we describe the implementation of the interface for the Kronecker-based state spaces.

Performance. The performance of implementations using the interface must be competitive with the monolithic implementation. To achieve this we follow two design goals. First, we provide an AFI that is able to exploit the state-space-specific optimizations in the interface implementation. Second, we attempt to minimize the amount of overhead due to separation of the analysis algorithm and the state-space representation. The overhead is mostly caused by non-fully-optimized C++ compilation, extra function calls and assignments, and construction and deconstruction of temporary objects in the stack.

To summarize, we seek an interface that is straightforward to use and implement, is sufficient in functionality to support a wide variety of state-space representations and numerical solution methods, and provides good performance. A compromise among these goals is obviously necessary in any particular practical implementation of such an interface. We believe we have achieved an appropriate balance in our state-level AFI definition, which is described in the next section.

3 State-Level AFI Definition

In this section, we will first formalize the notion of a labeled transition system by giving a definition that contains the key elements that specify a state-level, discrete-event system. Then, we briefly review several solution methods for continuous-time Markov processes, which are a special case of discrete-event systems, to derive the basic operations that a state-level AFI needs to provide so that a wide range of solution methods can be implemented using the AFI. Finally, we show how containers and iterators help us achieve the separation of concerns discussed earlier, and show how our C++ realization of a state-level AFI satisfies the requirements described in Section 2. In particular, with respect to the requirements described in the previous section, we address flexibility of the Möbius state-level AFI in Section 3.2, and its functionality and economy in Sections 3.3 and 5. We illustrate the generality of the AFI by implementing two conceptually different state-space representations in Section 4.

3.1 Labeled Transition System Definition

To define an appropriate state-level abstract functional interface for Möbius, we start by defining a labeled transition system (LTS). We define an $LTS = (S, s_0, \delta, L, \mathcal{R}, \mathcal{C})$, where:

- S is a set of states and $s_0 \in S$ is the initial state
- $\delta \subseteq S \times \mathbb{R} \times L \times S$ is the state transition relation, which describes possible transitions from a state $s \in S$ to a state $s' \in S$ with a label $l \in L$ and a real value $\lambda \in R$
- $\mathcal{R} : S \times \mathbb{N} \to R$ is the value of the nth rate reward for each state in S
- $\mathcal{C} : \delta \times \mathbb{N} \to R$ is the the value of the nth impulse reward for each transition in δ

The label l gives additional information concerning each transition, typically related to the event (in the higher-level model) that performs it. The real value λ can have several different meanings. In the following, it is taken to be the exponential rate of the associated transition, because we are primarily interested in the numerical solution of the CTMC derived from a stochastic model. However, one can also consider probabilistic models, where $\lambda \in [0, 1]$ gives the probability of a transition, or weighted automata, where $\lambda > 0$ denotes a distance, a reward, or costs of a transition. By integrating both rates and labels in the definition of the LTS, we can use the interface based on it for both numerical solution and non-stochastic model checking. In the latter case, transition time is unimportant and one may wish to consider the language that is generated by the transitions that may occur in the LTS. $\mathcal{R}$ and $\mathcal{C}$ are functions that define a set of rate and impulse rewards, respectively, for the LTS. They define what a modeler would like to know about the system being studied.

Since we focus on Markov reward models in this paper, an LTS defines 1) a real-valued $(S \times S)$ rate matrix $R(i, j) = \sum_{e \in E} \lambda_e$, where $E \subset \delta$ is the set of transitions with $(i, \lambda_e, *, j)$, and 2) a set of n reward structures. The generator matrix Q of the associated CTMC is then defined as $Q = R - diag(rowsum(R))$, where the latter term describes a diagonal matrix with row sums of R as diagonal entries. The reward structures associated with the Markov model are determined by $\mathcal{R}$ and $\mathcal{C}$.

3.2 Use of Containers and Iterators

The philosophy we took when designing the state-level AFI and its implementation was inspired by the concept of "generic programming" [29] and the associated "containers" and "iterators" constructs in the STL (Standard Template Library) and generic class libraries. The idea was to decouple the implementations of a data structure and an algorithm operating on it, since the two are conceptually different. In other words, these concepts facilitate the creation of implementations of algorithms that operate on data structures that are different and have different implementations, but support the same functionality. This decoupling is achieved through identification of a set of general requirements (called *concepts* in generic programming terminology and realized as member functions) met by a large family of abstract data structures. In our case, the "set of requirements" is a state-level AFI that provides the functionality necessary to efficiently implement a large class of solution methods. The requirements allow us to separate the numerical solution method that operates on a state-level model from the particular data structure that implements the model. This separation makes it easy to develop numerical solution methods and makes them applicable to any state-level model that complies with the state-level AFI. Since the implementation of the AFI is separate from, and therefore does not interfere with, the analysis algorithm, we have the flexibility to optimize the internal implementation of the AFI for any particular state-level model (one of the characteristics mentioned in Section 2).

The two notions that help achieve this separation are those of "containers" and "iterators." *Containers* are classes (usually template classes) whose purpose is to contain other *objects*; objects are instantiations of classes. *Template* container classes are parameterized classes that can be instantiated so that they can contain objects of any type. A container is a programming abstraction of the notion of a mathematical set. By hiding the implementation of the algorithm for accessing the set elements inside the container class, we give developers both the ability to use a unified interface to access objects inside a container, and the flexibility to optimize the implementation of the container. In the Möbius state-level AFI, a container is used to represent a subset of transitions of an *LTS*. For example, the elements of a row or a column of a rate matrix constitute a row or column container object.

Iterators are the means by which the objects in a container are accessed. They can be considered "generalized" pointers, which allow a programmer to select particular objects to reference. The following operations are usually defined on iterator objects and implemented in the iterators that we define as part of the Möbius state-level AFI:

- *Dereferencing*, which enables us to access the object.
- *Navigation operators*, such as ++ and −−, which return iterators for (respectively) the next element and the previous element relative to the element pointed to by the iterator.
- *Comparison operators*, which define an order on the objects of the container.

3.3 State-Level AFI Classes

We use containers to represent sets of transitions. Before explaining how we do this, we review several common numerical solution methods to illustrate the access patterns they require from a state-space representation. These patterns will suggest how the transitions of a state-level model should be placed in container objects. We then give a precise programming representation for the transitions contained in containers. This implementation, together with a set of functions returning information about the whole model (e.g., the number of states) along with a number of functions to facilitate computation of reward structures defined on the models, provides a complete state-level AFI.

Required Operations. We now briefly recall iteration schemes of some simple but frequently employed iterative solution methods, namely the Power, Jacobi, and Gauss-Seidel methods for stationary analysis, and uniformization for transient analysis. This review will help us determine both the type of container objects that a state-level object should provide to a solver and also the general information the solver needs concerning a model. Table 1 summarizes the iteration schemes. More details can be found, for example, in [32].

Table 1. Iterative solution methods

Method	Iteration scheme
Power	$\pi^{(k+1)} = \pi^{(k)} P$ where $P = (\frac{1}{\alpha} Q + I)$ and $\alpha \geq 1/(max_{i=1}^{n} \lvert Q_{i,i} \rvert)$
Jacobi	$\pi^{(k+1)} = (1-\omega)\pi^{(k)} + \omega\pi^{(k)}(L+U)D^{-1}$ where $0 < \omega < 2$ is the relaxation factor.
Gauss-Seidel	$\pi^{(k+1)} = (1-\omega)\pi^{(k)} + \omega[(\pi^{(k)} L + \pi^{(k+1)} U) D^{-1}]$ where $0 < \omega < 2$ is the relaxation factor.
uniformization	$\pi(t) = \sum_{k=0}^{\infty} e^{-\alpha t} \frac{(\alpha t)^k}{k!} \pi^{(k)}$ where $\pi(t)$ is the transient solution and $\pi^{(k)}$ is obtained as in the Power method.
Notes: 1. Q is the generator matrix of the underlying Markov process. 2. $\pi^{(0)}$ is an arbitrary initial distribution. 3. $Q = D - (L+U)$, where D is a diagonal matrix and L and U are, respectively, strictly lower and strictly upper triangular matrices.	

Notably, all four iteration schemes are based on successive vector-matrix multiplications, where matrices P or Q are only minor transformations of the rate matrix R given by an *LTS* as mentioned above. Typical access patterns for matrix-vector multiplications are accesses by rows or by columns. However, a closer look reveals that only Gauss-Seidel requires a sequential computation of entries $\pi^{(k+1)}(i)$; Gauss-Seidel completes computation of $\pi^{(k+1)}(i)$ before continuing with $\pi^{(k+1)}(j)$ for a $j > i$. This means that Gauss-Seidel implies a multiplication that accesses a matrix by columns. All other iteration schemes can also be formulated with an access by columns or by rows; in fact, the order in which matrix elements are accessed need not be fixed at all, as long as all nonzero matrix elements are considered. This has been frequently exploited for iterative methods on Kronecker representations, e.g., in [7]. Since access by rows is the same as access by columns on a transposed matrix, we consider it to be part of the interface as well.

AFI Classes. Motivated by these numerical solution methods, we now define the data structure that represents a transition and the set of functions that comprise the state-level AFI. Different access patterns are made possible through

```
template <class _StateType, class _RateType, class _LabelType>
class Transition {
 public:
  typedef _StateType StateType;
  typedef _RateType RateType;
  typedef _LabelType LabelType;
  StateType& row();
  StateType& col();
  RateType& rate();
  LabelType& label();
  RateType& reward(int RewardNumber);
};
```

Fig. 1. `Transition` class interface

a number of functions that return container objects that, for example, contain elements in a row or column. We also define functions that return information on the number of states of the model (for dimensioning vectors) and on the initial state (for defining an initial distribution, as in uniformization). Accessing elements of the rate matrix through containers hides the enumeration of the states (mapping of the state representation to the row/column index of the state) in the state-level class. The freedom to choose this mapping creates an opportunity to optimize the implementation of the state-level class. Kronecker-based models take particularly great advantage of this property, as described in Section 4.2.

Figure 1 shows the interface of the template class used to represent a transition. The template parameters are `_StateType`, `_RateType`, and `_LabelType`, which represent the data types used for states (S), transition rates (R), and transition labels (L), respectively. There are a number of methods that return the characteristics of a transition. They are `row()`, `column()`, `rate()`, and `label()`, which are used to access (i.e., read and write), respectively, the starting state and ending state of a transition and a transition rate and label.

Each pattern of access to transitions of an *LTS* corresponds to one container class. Therefore, in order for us to provide the numerical solution methods discussed in Section 3.3 with the different patterns of access they need, the number of functions that return container objects in the AFI must be the same as the number of patterns.

Three container classes are provided by the state-level AFI. They are accessible by the following methods:

- `LTSClass::getRow(Transition::StateType s, row& r)` assigns to `r` the container consisting of transitions originating from a given state `s`.
- `LTSClass::getColumn(Transition::StateType s, column& c)` assigns to `c` the container consisting of transitions leading to a given state `s`.
- `LTSClass::getAllEdges(allEdges& e)` assigns to `e` the container consisting of all transitions.

Each of the methods mentioned above returns a container object that provides iterator classes that are used to scan through the elements of the container. In Section 3.3 we give more details on `column`, an example container class that `LTSClass::getColumn()` returns. The same ideas apply to the definitions of the container classes that the other methods return.

To facilitate the analysis of the *LTS*, we also need the following functions:

- `Transition::StateType LTSClass::getNumberOfStates`() returns $|S|$.
- `Transition::StateType LTSClass::getInitialState`() returns s_0.

In order to have a state-level interface that enables us to compute reward structures for stochastic models, we should also incorporate rate rewards and impulse rewards into the interface. The following are defined to allow access to the reward structure:

- **int** `LTSClass::getNumberOfRewards`() returns the number of reward structures defined on the *LTS*.
- `Transition::RateType Transition::reward(`**int** n`)` returns the value of the nth impulse reward for a transition.
- `Transition::RateType LTSClass::getRateReward(`**int** n`)` returns the set of values of the nth rate reward for all the states. The set is provided through a container class that can itself be accessed using its corresponding iterator class. The values are given in the order of the indices of the states, i.e., the first value corresponds to state 0, the second value to state 1, and so on.

All of the container classes, their associated iterator classes, the functions returning container objects, and the additional functions mentioned above are encapsulated into an `LTSClass` class that provides the complete state-level AFI. Note that all of the implementation details of `LTSClass` are hidden from the solution methods operating on it, and that the only way they can see `LTSClass` is through its interface, i.e., the state-level AFI.

Example Container Class: `column`. Figure 2 illustrates a container and a particular iterator class interface (`get_column`). A container class definition must implement all the functionality described earlier (dereferencing, navigation operators, and comparison operators) as well as provide a prototype of a particular access method (in this case, access by columns). In order to avoid most of the extra function calls, we have inlined all the member function definitions by defining them inside their own classes.

The `column` object is a container that contains the elements of a column of the rate matrix corresponding to the *LTS*. In particular,

- `column::begin`() initializes an iterator such that it corresponds to the first element of the column.
- `column::iterator::end`() returns true if the iterator is past the last element of the column and false otherwise.

```
class LTSClass {
  ...
  class column {
  public:
    class iterator {
    public:
      iterator();
      ~iterator();
      typedef iterator self;
      Transition& operator*();
      Transition* operator->();
      self& operator++();
      self& operator--();
      bool end();
      bool operator==(self &it);
      bool operator!=(self &it);
      const self& operator=(self const &it);
    };
    void begin(iterator& it);
  };
  void getColumn(Transition::StateType _col_index, column& c);
  ...
};
```

Fig. 2. Container class `column` and its associated iterator

- `column::iterator::operator++` (`column::iterator::operator--`) advances the iterator to point to the next (previous) element in the column and returns an iterator for the next (previous) element in the column. This operator, along with `column::begin()`, `column::iterator::end()`, makes it possible to iterate through all elements of a column of the matrix.
- `LTSClass::getColumn()` initializes the `c` object of class `column` to the specified column of the matrix.
- `column::iterator::operator=`, the assignment operator, is used to assign one iterator to another. Notice that the interface should be implemented in such a way that just after `it1=it2` is executed, `it1` and `it2` are two *independent* iterators to the same element in the column, i.e., each of them can advance regardless of the others. This will enable the analysis algorithm to have multiple iterators on different parts of the matrix simultaneously.
- Equality and inequality operators (`operator==` and `operator!=` functions of `column::iterator` class) should be implemented such that two iterators are equal if and only if they point to the same element of the matrix.

Similar to the way `column` class has been defined to provide column-oriented access to the matrix, `row` and `allEdges`, along with their corresponding iterators, can be defined to provide row-oriented access and access to all transitions (with no specific order).

3.4 Evaluation

The state-level AFI defined in this section clearly supports iterative solution methods that are based on the enumeration of matrix elements quite well. Nevertheless, if we consider the wide range of specific state-level representations and solution methods, we find certain cases that remain unsupported so far, e.g.,

- methods that represent probability distributions by some type of decision diagrams, like MTBDDs [23,1,25] or PDGs [3,9]. These so-called "symbolic" approaches perform an iteration step by multiplying numerical values of subsets of states with subsets of matrix entries instead of single elements. The selection of the considered subsets would make it necessary to reveal the underlying compositional structure of the LTS. However, the "hybrid" approach mentioned in [25] not only has the potential to perform better, but also uses a vector representation. This approach could therefore work with the state-level AFI as it is.
- methods, like the shuffle algorithm by Plateau et al. [20,32], that are based on a compositional state-space representation and that divide transitions into conjunctions of partial transitions. Unlike the Kronecker approaches employed in Section 4.2, the shuffle algorithm iterates through submodels, so either 1) it needs to reside behind the state-level AFI, while the state-level AFI supports a matrix-vector multiplication, or 2) it is implemented by a solver, in which case the state-level AFI needs to reveal the compositional structure of the LTS.
- methods that use decompositions of a matrix. Decompositional methods, e.g., the one described in Chapter 6 of [32], consider block-structured matrices and require iterators for block-access of matrices. This is a minor extension to the set of iterators defined so far. An issue that is even more delicate in theory is that of providing additional information on a useful, effective partition into blocks, e.g., to achieve decomposition that is nearly-completely-decomposable (NCD), a property that is important for the efficiency of decompositional methods.

In summary, the basic functionality provided by the state-level AFI is sufficient to allow us to proceed with several solution methods. For specific algorithms, additional functionality may be needed, especially to reveal more information on the structure of the LTS. However, before such extensions can be considered, it is important to ensure that the fundamental approach is applicable in practice and performs sufficiently well. Once that has been established, more elaborate functionality can be built on top of the state-level AFI we defined.

4 Example State-Space Implementations

To demonstrate the generality of the AFI developed in Section 3, we describe how two conceptually different state-space representations can provide the same state-level AFI. In particular, we have implemented two AFI-compliant state-level objects: "flat" unstructured state spaces based on sparse-matrix representation, and structured state spaces amenable to Kronecker representation. To test these representations, we also implemented two solvers (using the Jacobi and Gauss-Seidel methods) that use the state-level AFI to solve models. Since both solvers comply with the AFI, we can use either of them with either of the state-level objects to solve the models. In this section, we describe the implementation details of two complete state-level classes. To make all AFI-compliant numerical solution methods applicable to an AFI-compliant state-level object, we need to implement the complete set of functions described in Section 3.3 for the object. However, for some state-space representations, there may be some access patterns that cannot be implemented efficiently. For example, if we have a sparse-matrix representation for the state space stored in a row-oriented order, it may be considered inefficient (in terms of space or time) to provide both row- and column-oriented access functions. In such cases, a mechanism must notify the analysis algorithm that a specific access pattern has not been implemented efficiently for that state-level object. We use the C++ exception-handling mechanism to do this. In particular, if a state-space class does not provide efficient implementation for a particular access pattern `X`, calling the corresponding `getX` function raises an exception that is caught by the analysis algorithm. Conceptually, this is a signal to the analysis algorithm that it cannot perform efficiently on this state-space representation.

4.1 Flat State-Space Object

In the Möbius modeling tool, the modeler can generate a CTMC from a high-level stochastic model whose transitions' time distributions are all exponential. The CTMC and the associated reward structures are stored in two files that will be, in a later phase, fed into an appropriate numerical solver that solves the Markov chain and computes the measures of the model we are interested in. In an attempt to show the generality of the state-level AFI, we wrapped this interface around the two files.

In Möbius, the state space is stored in a row-oriented format in the file. When read into memory, it is stored in a compressed sparse row format. In order to support both row- and column-oriented access patterns, we had to sacrifice either speed (by converting back and forth between compressed row and column formats) or space (by storing both formats). In order to achieve separation of concerns, it is essential that we be able to dynamically modify the internal data structure of the state space without changing the interface. In the case of flat state-space representation, we chose to sacrifice speed (and save space) because typical solution methods use only one of the formats during their run-times. Considering this, the conversion from one format to another is not done if the solver requires row-oriented access, and is done only once if the solver requires column-oriented access. Notice that this conversion needs only one scan through all the elements of the matrix; that is roughly the same amount of work needed for a single iteration of a fixed-point numerical solution method.

4.2 Kronecker-Based State-Space Object

Kronecker representations of CTMCs can result from several modeling formalisms, including generalized stochastic Petri nets (GSPNs). GSPNs are supported by the APNN toolbox [10], which implements many state-based analysis methods using Kronecker representations. In order to achieve an implementation of an LTS interface, we modified SupGSPN, a numerical solver of the APNN toolbox that uses a modular Kronecker representation and improved algorithms of [7]; the improvement is its avoidance of binary search, as described in [12]. In the following, we focus on iterators to support Jacobi and Gauss-Seidel iteration schemes for fixed-point iteration. One observation in [7] is that a Jacobi solver need not impose any kind of order on a matrix-vector multiplication in an iteration step, and that that degree of freedom can be extensively used to optimize enumeration of matrix elements stored in a Kronecker representation. Jacobi solvers match the behavior of the `allEdges` iterator in the LTS interface. The SupGSPN implementation of the originally recursive algorithm of [7] performs iteratively with an internal data structure to store local variables used in the corresponding recursive approach. Therefore, iteration through a Kronecker representation is far from trivial if performance is of importance. For instance, directed acyclic graphs (or multi-value decision diagrams) are used to restrict the matrix vector multiplication on the reachable set of states. In addition to making obvious functional changes, we moved all local variables and local data structures into an iterator object, such that an increment operation can continue iterating through the Kronecker representation at the very position the last increment operation left the function and with the same local variable space. We modified algorithms *Act-RwCl* and *Act-RwCl*$^+$ of [7] to support an `allEdges` iterator by replacing the multiplication of matrix and vector elements in the last lines, namely 19 and 13, by statements that 1) return the matrix element to the iterator object and 2) ensure that the algorithms proceed to serve a subsequent increment operation right after that line. Algorithms *Act-ClEl*$_2$ and *Act-ClEl*$_2^+$ of [7] are modified accordingly for a column iterator.

To avoid permanent creation and destruction of iterator objects and other data structures, the implementation has a memory management of its own that recycles memory space. Reusing memory reduces the effort needed to initialize an iterator object. For example, in SOR, a `column` iterator is needed for each column, but columns are typically accessed in sequential, increasing order, so that only a partial update of the internals of the $(i+1)^{\text{th}}$ iterator object is necessary upon creation if we reuse memory space of the ith iterator. For the `allEdges` iterator, we implemented one variant that determines single elements and a second, buffered one that pulls a set of elements from the Kronecker representation in order to reduce the number of function calls. Example results suggest that it would be helpful to employ buffers of around 128 elements to exploit the tradeoff between handling additional data structures and saving function calls. Since CMTCs typically have extremely few elements per row or column, other iterators that give an ordered access by columns or rows write all entries into a buffer, so that access to the Kronecker representation takes place only in the iterator `begin()` function. The current implementation mixes C code for accessing Kronecker data structures and C++ code for the LTS and iterator classes.

5 Performance

In order to be useful, the Möbius state-level AFI must not unacceptably degrade the performance of numerical solvers. Clearly, using the AFI does not increase the time complexity of numerical solution methods that are based on the explicit enumeration of all transitions in a state-level representation, since in principle one can always implement the AFI using the original numerical solution algorithm and interrupt its enumeration of matrix elements whenever a single entry is considered. The enumeration then continues with a call for the next increment or decrement operation. This mechanism implies a constant overhead, which is irrelevant in the computation of the order of a numerical solution algorithm. Nevertheless, in practice, constant factors must be sufficiently small.

In this section, we evaluate the performance implications of the use of the Möbius state-level AFI for two examples taken from the literature. We consider the two AFI implementations discussed in the previous section. The first implementation is based on a flat sparse-matrix state-space representation, and originates from the numerical solver of Möbius and *UltraSAN*. The second AFI implementation uses a Kronecker state-space representation and is derived from the SupGSPN numerical solver in the APNN toolbox. Both implementations are evaluated with respect to the existing non-AFI versions of the solvers from which they originate.

We did experiments on different architectures and operating systems, and observed that with the same compiler (gcc version 2.95.2) and optimization parameter settings (-O4), the relative performance of two programs varied significantly across platforms. We considered a Sun Enterprise 400MHz, a Sun Ultra60 450MHz, and a PIII 1GHz PC running Linux. All the machines had enough RAM to hold all the data needed by the programs. The given numbers in the following tables present the running times on the Ultra60 machine. For a Sun Enterprise we observed that APNN was faster than KronLTS by 30 to 60% , and for the PC we observed an inverse relation: the KronLTS was faster by about 20%. We are currently investigating the reasons for the behavior in further detail. Our initial hypothesis is that the variations are due to hardware and/or compiler differences across platforms, such as cache size, register bank size, and instruction re-ordering. So far, we conclude that the overhead is sufficiently limited to retain the same time complexity, and that the constant factors are almost always less than 2.

5.1 Flexible Manufacturing System Example

Ciardo et al. [13] describe a flexible manufacturing system to illustrate the benefits of an approximate analysis technique based on decomposition. This model has been used in many papers as a benchmark model for CTMC analysis (e.g., [34, 8]). For simplicity, we consider a variant in which transitions have marking-independent incidence functions and rates. The model is parameterized by the number of parts that circulate in the FMS. The model distinguishes three types of parts, and we assume that there are the same number of pieces (N) of each type. For the Kronecker methods we partition the model into three components as in [8]. The dimensions of the associated CTMC are shown in Table 3(a); column $|S|$ shows the number of states, and column $NZ(Q)$ gives the number of off-diagonal nonzero matrix entries in Q. For those model configurations, the implementations of a Jacobi and a Gauss-Seidel solver perform as shown in Table 4(a). The first column gives the parameter setting of N. The other columns refer to results obtained with the original Möbius implementation, the sparse-matrix AFI state-space implementation, the APNN toolbox implementation, and the Kronecker AFI state-space implementation. For each tool we present the times using the Jacobi and the Gauss-Seidel solution methods. Each computation time is the average time for a single iteration step, as described in Section 3.3; that is the CPU time in seconds taken to perform one iteration.

Table 2. State spaces of the studied models

N	$\|S\|$	$NZ(Q)$
4	35910	237120
5	152712	1111482
6	537768	4205670
7	1639440	13552968
8	4459455	38533968
9	11058190	99075405

(a) FMS

TWS	$\|S\|$	$NZ(Q)$
1	11700	48330
2	84600	410160
3	419400	2281620
4	1632600	9732330
5	5358600	34424280
6	15410250	105345900

(b) Courier protocol

In the original Möbius and the sparse-matrix AFI implementations, a Gauss-Seidel iteration is about 15% faster than a Jacobi iteration. This happens because 1) computation of $\pi^{(k+1)}$ in each iteration involves only a few accesses to the elements of π and Q, and a few floating-point operations, 2) accessing the memory is much more expensive than a floating-point operation, and 3) in our implementation, the number of accesses to memory (specifically, an element of π) in the Jacobi method is one more than in the Gauss-Seidel method. This is different for Kronecker implementations, which allow the use of more efficient algorithms for enumerating matrix entries in an arbitrary order (the `allEdges` iterator in the interface) than for an order by columns as required for Gauss-Seidel [7]. The "slowdown" columns in Table 4(a) give the percentage of decrease in speed caused by the overhead of the state-level AFI. For the Möbius and sparse-matrix AFI implementations, the slowdown for the Jacobi (SOR) solver is computed by subtracting column two (three) from column four (five) and dividing the result by column two (three). The same formula is used to compute the slowdown column for comparison between the APNN toolbox and Kronecker AFI state-space implementations. As can be seen, the slowdown for the sparse-matrix AFI implementation is almost always less than 10%. In solving the larger models using the Kronecker approach, we use on average 74% more time for the `allEdges`

Table 3. Time per iteration (in seconds) for the studied models

N	Möbius		Flat LTS		slowdown %		APNN		Kron LTS		slowdown %	
	JAC	SOR	JAC	SOR	JAC	SOR	JAC	SOR	JAC	SOR	JAC	SOR
4	0.036	0.030	0.037	0.031	3	3	0.033	0.11	0.065	0.17	97	55
5	0.206	0.181	0.220	0.19	7	5	0.14	0.52	0.30	0.82	114	58
6	0.785	0.693	0.844	0.737	8	6	0.77	1.90	1.24	2.81	61	48
7	2.54	2.23	2.72	2.38	7	7	2.45	6.03	3.88	9.24	58	53
8	–[a]	–	–	–	–	–	6.98	17.5	11.0	25.0	58	43
9	–	–	–	–	–	–	17.9	42.1	28.0	65.9	56	57

[a] The state space is too large to be explicitly constructed.

(a) FMS

TWS	Möbius		Flat LTS		slowdown %		APNN		Kron LTS		slowdown %	
	JAC	SOR	JAC	SOR	JAC	SOR	JAC	SOR	JAC	SOR	JAC	SOR
1	0.0075	0.0059	0.0073	0.0070	-3	19	0.0126	0.0418	0.019	0.060	51	43
2	0.088	0.079	0.088	0.079	0	0	0.0858	0.327	0.143	0.46	67	41
3	0.487	0.423	0.496	0.442	2	4	0.634	1.65	0.831	2.42	31	47
4	2.01	1.76	2.05	1.85	2	5	2.71	7.41	3.56	9.98	31	35
5	–[a]	–	–	–	–	–	9.32	24.5	12.3	34.6	32	41
6	–	–	–	–	–	–	28.6	83.3	36.8	117.0	29	40

[a] The state space is too large to be explicitly constructed.

(b) Courier protocol

iterator (in the Jacobi AFI implementation) and on average 52% more for the `column` iterator. Nevertheless, the `allEdges` iterator remains significantly faster than the `column` iterator (in the SOR implementation). The results use an implementation of an `allEdges` iterator that uses an internal buffer of 128 matrix entries in order to reduce the number of function calls needed to proceed on the Kronecker data structures. For $N \in \{3, 4, \ldots, 7\}$, we run an experiment series with buffer sizes in the range of $2^0, 2^1, \ldots, 2^{14}$. The observed computation times describe a curve that initially decreases sharply, reaches a minimum in an interval that contains 128 matrix entries for all values, and only gradually increases for increasing buffer sizes. Hence, we fixed the buffer size to 128 for the Jacobi `allEdges` iterator reflected in Table 4(a).

5.2 Courier Protocol Software Example

In this subsection, we consider a GSPN model of a parallel communication software system that was originally designed by Woodside and Li [33], and has been considered for benchmarking CTMC analysis techniques (for example, see [26]). The model is parameterized by the transport window size TWS, which limits the number of packets that are simultaneously communicated between the sender and receiver. To obtain a Kronecker representation, we use the same partition into four components that was used in [26]. Table 3(b) shows the number of states in the CTMC and the off-diagonal nonzero entries, much like Table 3(a). Table 4(b) gives the computation times we observed on average for a single iteration step for this model. The selection of columns is the same as in Table 4(a). The results are slightly different from the values we observed for the FMS example. The overhead imposed by the interface is still low in the case of sparse matrices. For the Kronecker approach, the overhead is on average 40% for Jacobi and 41% for SOR. We also exercised different buffer sizes and observed that 128 is always in the range that contains the minimum overhead.

6 Conclusions

In this paper, we have presented a state-level abstract functional interface for models expressed as labeled transition systems, and experimentally evaluated the performance of that interface compared to standard implementations. This interface uses containers and iterators to separate issues related to representing labeled transition systems from issues related to solving such systems. The use of this interface thus yields an important separation of concerns with significant advantages for research related to state-based analysis methods, as well as for applications that use these methods. More specifically, we discussed the requirements that a state-level AFI must fulfill to be useful in practice. The presented AFI was designed accordingly, and we described our experiences and the important design issues involved in implementing this AFI efficiently. In particular, with the help of two examples, we illustrated the usability of our approach and its impact on the performance of different numerical solvers in CTMC analysis. The presented results show that for simple LTS representations, the overhead is negligible, and for complex data structures such as are used for Kronecker representations, computation times increase by a constant factor that is almost always less than 2. We thus conclude that we gain much more from the use of the interface than we lose from the minor performance overhead incurred.

Our ongoing work is on a full integration of different state-space representations in Möbius, based on the AFI and the new state-level AFI. In addition to implementing known state-space representation techniques, we envision the creation of adaptive state-level AFI implementations that internally modify themselves or switch over to other implementations depending on the usage patterns that are dynamically observed. That way, we could dynamically make use of the space-time trade-off that characterizes different labeled transition system representations.

Acknowledgments. We thank Graham Clark for his comments and ideas in our discussions on the design of Möbius interfaces.

References

1. C. Baier, J. P. Katoen, and H. Hermanns. Approximate symbolic model checking of continuous-time Markov chains. In *Proc. Concurrency Theory (CONCUR'99)*, pages 146–162. Springer LNCS 1664, 1999.
2. M. Bernardo and R. Gorrieri. A tutorial on EMPA: A theory of concurrent processes with nondeterminism, priorities, probabilities and time. *Theoretical Computer Science*, 202(1-2):1–54, Jul 1998.
3. M. Bozga and O. Maler. On the representation of probabilities over structured domains. In *Proc. CAV'99*, Springer, LNCS 1633, pages 261–273, 1999.
4. P. Buchholz. Markovian process algebra: Composition and equivalence. In U. Herzog and M. Rettelbach, editors, *Proc. of the 2nd Work. on Process Algebras and Performance Modelling*, pages 11–30. Arbeitsberichte des IMMD, University of Erlangen, no. 27, 1994.
5. P. Buchholz. Hierarchical Markovian models: Symmetries and aggregation. *Performance Evaluation*, 22:93–110, 1995.
6. P. Buchholz. Structured analysis approaches for large Markov chains. *Applied Numerical Mathematics*, 31(4):375–404, 1999.
7. P. Buchholz, G. Ciardo, S. Donatelli, and P. Kemper. Complexity of memory-efficient Kronecker operations with applications to the solution of Markov models. *INFORMS J. on Computing*, 12(3), 2000.
8. P. Buchholz, M. Fischer, and P. Kemper. Distributed steady state analysis using Kronecker algebra. In *Proc. 3rd Int. Workshop on the Numerical Solution of Markov Chains (NSMC'99)*, pages 76–95, Zaragoza, Spain, Sept. 1999.
9. P. Buchholz and P. Kemper. Compact representations of probability distributions in the analysis of superposed GSPNs. In *Proc. of the 9th Int. Workshop on Petri Nets and Perf. Models*, pages 81–90, Aachen, Germany, 2001.
10. P. Buchholz, P. Kemper, and C. Tepper. New features in the APNN toolbox. In P. Kemper, editor, *Tools of Aachen 2001, Int. Multiconference on Measurement, Modelling and Evaluation of Computer-communication Systems*, Tech. report No. 760/2001. Universität Dortmund, FB Informatik, 2001.
11. G. Chiola, C. Dutheillet, G. Franceschinis, and S. Haddad. Stochastic well-formed coloured nets for symmetric modelling applications. *IEEE Transactions on Computers*, 42(11):1343–1360, Nov 1993.
12. G. Ciardo and A. Miner. A data structure for the efficient Kronecker solution of GSPNs. In *Proc. of PNPM'99: 8th Int. Workshop on Petri Nets and Performance Models*, pages 22–31, 1999.
13. G. Ciardo and K. S. Trivedi. A decomposition approach for stochastic reward net models. *Performance Evaluation*, 18(1):37–59, 1993.
14. G. Clark, T. Courtney, D. Daly, D. Deavours, S. Derisavi, J. M. Doyle, W. H. Sanders, and P. Webster. The Möbius modeling tool. In *Proc. of the 9th Int. Workshop on Petri Nets and Performance Models*, pages 241–250, Aachen, Germany, September 2001.
15. D. Deavours and W. H. Sanders. The Möbius execution policy. In *Proc. of PNPM'01: 9th Int. Workshop on Petri Nets and Performance Models*, pages 135–144, Aachen, Germany, 2001.
16. D. Deavours and W. H. Sanders. Möbius: Framework and atomic models. In *Proc. of PNPM'01: 9th Int. Workshop on Petri Nets and Performance Models*, pages 251–260, Aachen, Germany, 2001.

17. D. D. Deavours and W. H. Sanders. An efficient disk-based tool for solving very large Markov models. In *Proceedings of the 9th Int. Conference on Modelling Techniques and Tools for Computer Performance Evaluation (TOOLS '97)*, pages 58–71, June 1997.
18. D. D. Deavours and W. H. Sanders. 'On-the-fly' solution techniques for stochastic Petri nets and extensions. *IEEE Trans. on Software Eng.*, 24(10):889–902, 1998.
19. J. M. Doyle. Abstract model specification using the Möbius modeling tool. Master's thesis, University of Illinois at Urbana-Champaign, January 2000.
20. P. Fernandes, B. Plateau, and W. J. Stewart. Efficient descriptor-vector multiplication in stochastic automata networks. *JACM*, 45(3):381–414, 1998.
21. J. C. Fernandez, H. Garavel, A. Kerbrat, R. Mateescu, L. Mounier, and M. Sighireanu. CADP: A protocol validation and verification toolbox. In *Proc. of the 8th Conference on Computer-Aided Verification*, volume 1102 of *LNCS*, pages 437–440, New Brunswick, USA, August 1996.
22. S. Gilmore, J. Hillston, and M. Ribaudo. An efficient algorithm for aggregating PEPA models. *Software Engineering*, 27(5):449–464, 2001.
23. H. Hermanns, J. Meyer-Kayser, and M. Siegle. Multi terminal binary decision diagrams to represent and analyse continuous time Markov chains. In *Proc. 3rd Int. Workshop on the Numerical Solution of Markov Chains*, pages 188–207, Zaragoza, Spain, 1999.
24. H. Hermanns and M. Ribaudo. Exploiting symmetries in stochastic process algebras. In *Proc. of ESM'98: 12th European Simulation Multiconference*, 1998.
25. J. P. Katoen, M. Kwiatkowska, G. Norman, and D. Parker. Faster and symbolic CTMC model checking. In *Proc. PAPM-PROBMIV'01*, pages 23–38. Springer LNCS 2165, 2001.
26. P. Kemper. Numerical analysis of superposed GSPNs. *IEEE Trans. on Software Eng.*, 22(9):615–628, Sep 1996.
27. W. Knottenbelt and P. G. Harrison. Distributed disk-based solution techniques for large Markov models. In *Proc. of NSMC'99: 3rd International Meeting on the Numerical Solution of Markov Chains, Zaragoza, Spain*, pages 58–75, 1999.
28. W.J. Knottenbelt. Generalised Markovian analysis of timed transition systems. Master's thesis, University of Cape Town, Cape Town, South Africa, July 1996.
29. D. R. Musser, G. J. Derge, and A. Saini. *STL Tutorial and Reference Guide, Second Edition: C++ Programming with the Standard Template Library*. Addison-Wesley, Reading, MA, 2001.
30. W. H. Sanders. Integrated frameworks for multi-level and multi-formalism modeling. In *Proceedings of PNPM'99: 8th Int. Workshop on Petri Nets and Performance Models, Zaragoza, Spain*, pages 2–9, September 1999.
31. W. H. Sanders and J. F. Meyer. Reduced base model construction methods for stochastic activity networks. *IEEE Journal on Selected Areas in Communications*, 9(1):25–36, January 1991.
32. W. J. Stewart. *Introduction to the Numerical Solution of Markov Chains*. Princeton University Press, 1994.
33. C. M. Woodside and Y. Li. Performance Petri net analysis of communications protocol software by delay-equivalent aggregation. In *Proc. of the 4th Int. Workshop on Petri Nets and Performance Models*, pages 64–73, 1991.
34. P. Ziegler and H. Szczerbicka. A structure based decomposition approach for GSPN. In *Proc. of PNPM'95: 6th Int. Workshop on Petri Nets and Performance Models*, pages 261–270, 1995.

The *ProC/B* Toolset for the Modelling and Analysis of Process Chains*

F. Bause, H. Beilner, M. Fischer, P. Kemper, and M. Völker

Fachbereich Informatik
Universität Dortmund
D-44221 Dortmund, Germany
{bause,beilner,fischer,kemper,voelker}@ls4.cs.uni-dortmund.de

Abstract. This paper presents a toolset for modelling and analysing logistic networks. The toolset includes a graphical user interface accommodating a "Process Chains" view. It supports model analysis by a variety of methods including simulative, algebraic and numerical techniques. An object-based, hierarchical structure helps to keep track of large models. The hierarchy employs the notion of function units which may include subordinate function units, where function units provide services to their environments that are internally accomplished by calling services of subordinate function units. This point of view is very much along the structures found in real world organisations. We describe and analyse a model of a supply chain to demonstrate the capabilities of the toolset.

Keywords: Process Chains, E-Business, E-Commerce, Simulation, Queueing Networks, Generalised Stochastic Petri Nets

1 Introduction

Many frameworks for model based analysis of IT systems have been developed, many of them emphasising quantitative system properties. The frameworks generally incorporate both certain means for describing models, and certain solvers for analysing the described models. Analysis techniques share a common view of the dynamics of models/systems, regarding them as Discrete Event Dynamic Systems (DEDSs) [10]; they draw on the reservoir of corresponding basic techniques: Queueing Network techniques, numerical techniques for stochastic chains, Discrete Event Simulation. Modelling means are more manifold. A typical modelling framework provides a specific world view, a modelling paradigm, and supports it by corresponding textual/graphical front ends. Employed modelling paradigms are either related to envisaged analysis techniques (Queueing Networks, time-enhanced Petri Nets, constituents of particular simulation tools), or to specific application areas (protocols, networking, mobile communications), or aim at direct support of IT systems construction (SDL-based, UML-based).

* This research was supported by the Deutsche Forschungsgemeinschaft as part of the Collaborative Research Centre "Modelling of large logistic networks"(559).

T. Field et al. (Eds.): TOOLS 2002, LNCS 2324, pp. 51–70, 2002.

Considerable interest is presently being placed on systems supportive of business activities, in general. Business processes, logistic networks, supply chains, Just-In-Time production/delivery, outsourcing, B2B/B2C, virtual factories/companies are familiar terms denoting particular facets of this development. Mostly large-scale, increasingly automated, IT-supported and -driven ("e-business", "e-commerce"), these systems have attained a considerable complexity, and economic pressures towards their effective tuning/optimisation have noticeably increased. This is obviously another natural domain for model-based analysis, and attempts at developing suitable modelling paradigms, appropriate model analysis techniques and corresponding modelling frameworks are well underway (cf. [19,20]), in spirit very much like the above IT performance and reliability frameworks.

Can the two modelling lines support each other? Focussing on logistics, figures of merit include residence times, populations, throughputs, utilisations, availability, fault-tolerance; all familiar measures that require an analysis of the systems' behaviours. As for a suitable view of these dynamics, DEDSs appear again appropriate. Certainly, not everything is identical or similar: System structures and control disciplines are different, the relative importance of figures of merit differs, etc. On the whole, however, the idea is not far-fetched of connecting the two modelling areas.

This paper describes main ideas and status of a toolset that supports the model based analysis of logistics networks. The toolset has been developed in the context of an organised cooperation of research projects residing in the Mechanical Engineering, Business Science, Statistics and Computer Science departments of the University of Dortmund, and in Dortmund's Fraunhofer Institute for Material Flow and Logistics.

Given an application area, and corresponding, "interesting" application system properties, the development of tool support for model based analysis requires decisions both on suitable model analysis techniques, and on a suitable modelling paradigm. While suitability of analysis techniques is directly related to the system properties to be derived, suitability of a modelling paradigm is basically determined by its "bridging" power, its capability of capturing all information needed, of the application area, for the analysis techniques. We firmly believe that suitability of a paradigm also depends on its understandability for the envisaged community: Users need to "see" their very system in the corresponding model. This purpose seems best served by adopting, for the paradigm, the "usual" views, notions and terms of the application area.

As for the model analysis techniques: In the logistics area, simulation is almost exclusively employed for analysing model behaviour. In the IT performance area, alternative techniques for DEDS analysis are additionally applied. They exhibit, in cases, considerable advantages in terms of efficiency/precision. Attempts at carrying these advantages to the new application area appear but natural. Following this idea, analysis techniques from the Queueing Network domain and from the numerical, Markov Chain based field have been incorporated in the new toolset, additional to simulation. Due to the different characteristics of logistics and IT systems, all ported analysis techniques had to be checked for their applicability, and for any necessary adaptations.

As for the modelling paradigm: In logistics (as in related areas) so-called Process Chains are customary for describing system dynamics: Processes proceed along their prescribed activities, the latter competing for system resources. Various Process Chain versions exist, supported by similar graphical notations. Kuhn et al [17], [18] introduce one particular Process Chain paradigm on which our work builds. This paradigm serving, in essence, but descriptional purposes, variations and extensions had to be devised to yield a modelling paradigm (termed *ProC/B* paradigm) that was sufficiently complete and unambiguous to allow for an automatic mapping to the employed analysis techniques.

The paper is structured as follows: Sect. 2 introduces the *ProC/B* modelling paradigm. Sect. 3 describes the corresponding *ProC/B* toolset and incorporated analysis techniques. Sect. 4 considers the evaluation of costs. Sect. 5 deals with an application example taken from the Supply Chain Management domain. We conclude in Sect. 6.

2 Process Chains

Logistic networks are characterised by a variety of companies which form a network of orderers and suppliers. An order for a product typically induces various activities of production and transportation, step by step refined into sub-activities and delegated to particular companies or their departments. The *ProC/B* paradigm has to account for the specifics of this application area: On the one hand, the structural hierarchy ("includes hierarchy") of the total system needs to be captured: Networks are composed of companies, companies of departments which include sub-departments etc. On the other hand, the behavioural hierarchy ("calls hierarchy") of the involved activities (processes) has to be heeded: Activities are refined into sub-activities which may be further refined etc. These hierarchies are interwoven in practice since order handling processes, in their behavioural refinements, may almost arbitrarily spread across the system structure.

The *ProC/B* paradigm combines the two hierarchies. System structure is captured by Functional Units (FUs) which may include sub-FUs. Behaviour is expressed in Process Chains (PCs), i.e. process patterns made up of activities. FUs provide Services which may be called from their environments, and which are internally, within the FUs, defined by PCs. PCs may use the Services of other FUs to have their activities performed. The hierarchies of "FUs include FUs ..." and "PCs use Services defined by PCs ..." are to some extent independent. They close with predefined "standard" Functional Units providing "standard" Services as modelling time and space consumptions.

The *ProC/B* paradigm employs a variety of modelling constructs. Characteristic properties of a construct are captured by specific attributes. (The term attribute denotes a specification time parameter to be value-assigned before model analysis; the assignment is, in certain cases, achievable via the *ProC/B* experimentation environment.) The description of *ProC/B* models is largely graphical, by canvasses of an appearance like Fig. 1. References to such figures will be indicated by square brackets, [Fig#: ...]. On the description canvasses, *ProC/B* constructs are typically depicted by specific graphical symbols, their attributes given as textual annotations. Relying on the programming language expertise of the reader, the syntax of these annotations is not presented here.

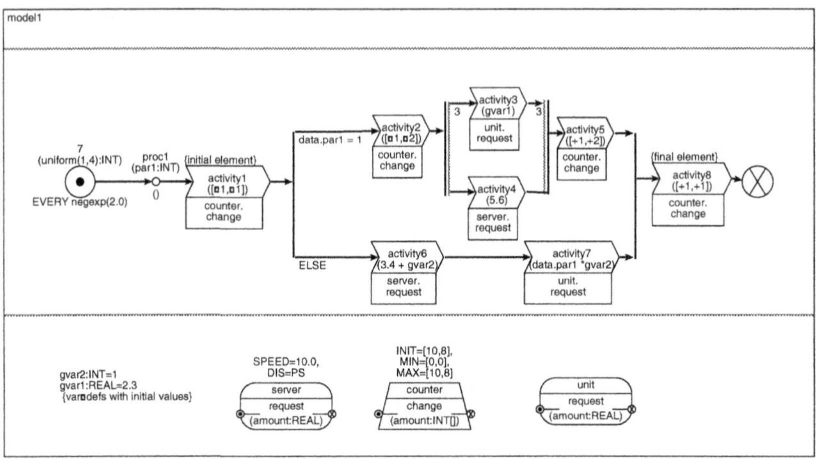

Fig. 1. Example of a flat *ProC/B* model

A *ProC/B* model, short `Model`, is composed of

- a behaviour portion including `Process Chains`, `Sources` and `Sinks`,
- a structure portion including `Function Units` and `Variables`,
- additional information interrelating the behaviour and structure portions.

A `Model` is named and may carry additional attributes. [Fig1: Describes a non-hierarchical, "flat" `Model`, *model1*.]

Every `Process Chain (PC)` captures the behaviour pattern for a particular type of processes, with the understanding that individual processes can be initiated which will subsequently progress, following that behaviour pattern. `PCs` are named and may carry parameters and variables. [Fig1: A single `PC`, *proc1*, is introduced with 1 formal parameter, *par1*. Access notations to parameters and variables of processes are prefixed with keyword *data.* for technical reasons.] A `PC` is composed of a set of `Process Chain Elements (PCEs)`, one for each (sub-)activity of the process type, together with a (partial) order over these `PCEs`. `PCEs` are graphically represented by special arrow symbols. [Fig1: 8 `PCEs`, *activity"n"*, each with its attributes: comment; name and actual parameters; execution notice (to be discussed later).] The ordering information over `PCEs` is specified by `Interconnections` (graphically: arrowhead lines) and `Connector Elements` or `Connectors`, for short (graphically: various vertical bars). An individual process "visits" (a subset of) the specified `PCEs` and `Connectors`, and time may (but need not) be spent traversing any of them; after traversal, a (unique) `Interconnection` determines the next element to be visited, and progress to this element is timeless. [Fig1: A process having completed *activity6* will immediately engage itself in *activity7*.] `Connectors` introduce options for traversing alternate `PC` branches (`Opening` and `Closing OR-Connectors`), and for concurrent branch traversals (`Opening` and `Closing AND-Connectors`). [Fig1: A pair of `OR-Connectors` allows for alternate branches, between *activity1* and *activity8*, the (immediate) decision taken dependent on the parameter, *par1*, of the individual process. A pair of `AND-Connectors` splits the upper branch into 4 concurrently progressing "lightweight" threads, 3 of them engaging themselves in an *activity3*, 1 in *activity4*; the single continuation will only commence after completion of all threads.]

As a peculiarity of the application domain, explicit "loops" are not tolerated in behaviour patterns. (This apparent limitation can be overcome by *ProC/B* constructs not discussed here.) Accordingly, `PCs` exhibit initial elements (`PCEs` or `Connectors`), without predecessors, and final elements, without successors. A `PC` with unique initial and final elements is termed a `Simple PC`. [Fig1: *proc1* is a `Simple PC`; see also `PCE` comments.] The present discussion is restricted to `Simple PCs`; `Composed PCs` will be discussed later.

`Sources` and `Sinks` specify the initiation and termination, respectively, of individual processes. Amongst a variety of *ProC/B* constructs with source/sink character, so-called `Unconditional Sources` and `Sinks` are of prime importance for flat models. An `Unconditional Source` specifies the points in time and the number of individual processes to be initiated, together with any actual parameters for these processes. An `Unconditional Sink` indicates the termination of individual processes. `Sources` (`Sinks`) are graphically depicted by special circle symbols, to be interconnected with an initial (final) element of some particular `PC`. These `Interconnections` determine the type of process to be initiated (terminated) and, for `Sources`, the number and types of parameters to be provided. [Fig1: The leftmost symbol in the behaviour strip specifies an `Unconditional Source`. (Bulks of) 7 individual processes will be initiated (on average) EVERY 1/2 time units (exponential distribution with rate 2). The `Source` is interconnected to `PC`, *proc1*, and sets the parameters *par1* to uniformly, between 1 and 4, distributed values.]

A `Function Unit (FU)` represents a structural entity that is capable of performing (certain) activities; in *ProC/B* terminology: that provides (certain) `Services`. The understanding is that progressing processes have any of their potentially time-consuming activities performed by some `FU`, via calling a particular `Service`. The external view of a `FU` includes its name, a list of provided `Services` together with any formal parameters, and a list of additional attributes. `FUs` are depicted by boxes of various sorts. [Fig1: The structure strip shows 3 `FUs`, *server*, *counter* and *unit*, of 2 different sorts; *server* provides 1 `Service`, *request*, with a parameter, *amount* and with its attributes, SPEED and DIS, set to 10 and PS.] Two options exist for specifying the behaviour of a `FU`: Certain "standard" kinds of behaviour are predefined, as `Standard FU Types`, and may be assigned to in-

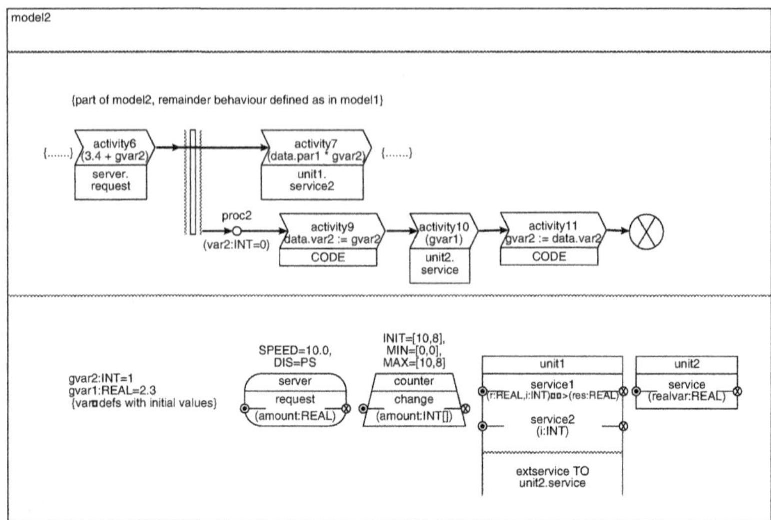

Fig. 2. Part of modified *ProC/B* model

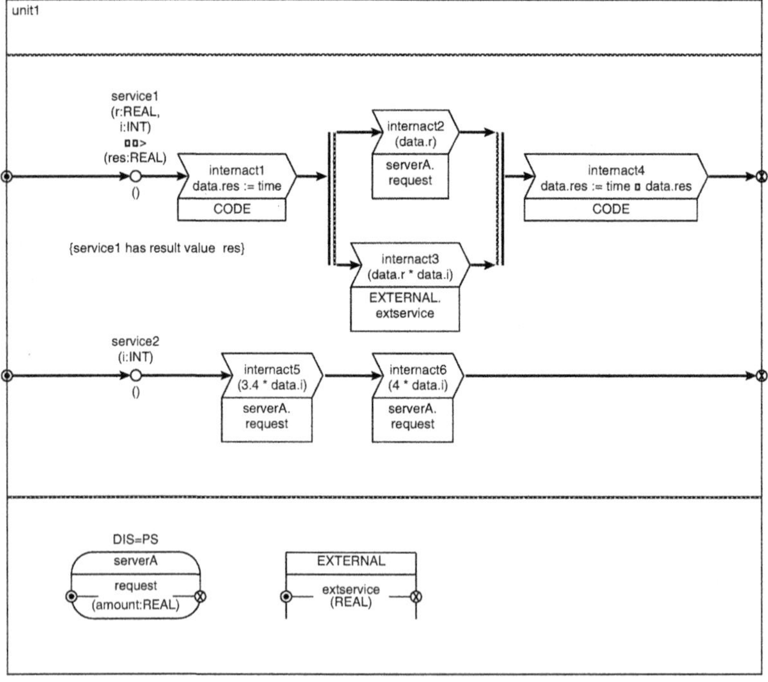

Fig. 3. Example of an internal functional unit importing an external service

dividual FUs; non-standard behaviours can be flexibly defined as `Constructed FUs`, the details to be discussed later. `Servers` capture the familiar behaviours of traditional queues, and `Counters` support the manipulation of passive resources. A change to a `Counter` is immediately granted iff its result respects specified upper and lower bound vectors; otherwise the requesting process gets blocked until the change becomes possible. [Fig1: *server* and *unit* are `Servers` as depicted through their "sort of box"; *server* has its SPEED and DIScipline attributes set to 10 and ProcessorSharing; non-assigned attributes keep default values. *counter* is a `Counter` and governs a 2-dimensional vector, with values between [0,0] and [10,8] and initialised to [10,8].] While process-specific variables have already been introduced as `PC` attributes, additional global `Variables` may be declared for a `FU` and referenced in its `PCs`. [Fig1: leftmost in the structure strip.]

Behaviour and structure portions are interrelated by expressing, for each potentially time-consuming activity, by which `Service` of which `FU` the activity is to be performed; in *ProC/B* terminology: which `FU.Service` pair the activity is referred to (for execution). This information is represented in the execution notice attribute of the corresponding `PCE`. [Fig1: *activity6* is referred to *request* of *server*, with an actual value, *3.4+gvar2*, assigned to *request's* parameter, *amount*. Note the reference to the global *gvar2*.] Execution notices are also exploited for characterising special time-consuming activities (such as pure delay by a notice, DELAY), and for introducing timeless data manipulation activities (by the notice, CODE). [Fig2: *activity9* and *activity11* are CODE `PCEs`.]

We return to the behaviour portion. `Simple PCs` can be connected with `PC Connectors`. The resulting `PC` structures are termed `Composed` PCs, capable of capturing process synchronisations. General `PC Connectors` exhibit a "closing face" and an "opening face", the closing face interconnected with final elements of `Simple PCs`, the opening face with initial elements. `PC Connectors` are depicted by particular vertical bars. [Fig2: Presents *model2*, a variation of *model1*. In the behaviour portion, the variation relates to (1) introducing a general `PC Connector`, between *activity6* and *activity7*, its closing (opening) face to the left (right); (2) further interconnecting it with a `Simple PC`, *proc2*; and (3) slightly changing the execution notice of *activity7*. The remainder of *model2's* behaviour portion is as in *model1* (not copied for space reasons).] A general `PC Connector` collects terminations of processes of interconnected `Simple PCs` (at its closing side), before initiating processes of interconnected `Simple PCs` (at its opening side). The number(s) of terminations/initiations can be individually specified. As an exception to the general `Simple PCs-Simple PCs` connection rule, a continuation of individual processes, across `PC Connectors`, can be expressed. [Fig2: Processes following the *activity6-activity7* line are individually continued (note the crossing line), whereas new (single) process instances, of type *proc2*, are initiated whenever an *activity6* is completed in the upper process (branch).]

We return to the structure portion. `FUs` with non-standard behaviours can be captured by `Constructed FUs`. Their external view (name, provided `Services` with formal parameters, attributes) is depicted in the structure strip - like for `Standard FUs`, but with a different type of box. [Fig2: Compared to *model1*, the variation relates to (1) deleting the `Standard FU`, *unit*, and (2) introducing the `Constructed FUs`, *unit1* and *unit2*. The before-mentioned change to *activity7's* execution notice is in fact a consequence of this structure variation: Where *activity7* of *model1* was referred to a *unit*-`Service`, it is now referred to one of the *unit1*-`Services`.] The definition of `Constructed FUs` is by separate canvasses, describing the `FU` internals with the same constructs that `Models` were described with ("self-similarity"), i.e. mainly with behaviour and structure portions and their interrelations. [Fig2: Defines the `Constructed FU`, *unit1*, of *model2*. The definition of *unit2* will not be detailed here.] Behaviour portions are again composed of `PCs`, `Sources` and `Sinks`. Whereas `Unconditional Sources` and `Sinks` may but need not be employed in `Constructed FUs`, so-called `Virtual Sources` and `Sinks` are mandatory: By interconnecting a `Virtual Source` to a `PC`, and this `PC` to a `Virtual Sink`, the very `PC` is declared a provided `Service` of the `Constructed FU` and defines the behaviour pattern followed whenever this `Service` is called upon. `Virtual Sources` and `Sinks` are depicted on the `FU` borders (both in the external and internal views). [Fig3: *unit1* provides 2 services, *service1* and *service2*, with their formal parameters; please compare with the external view of *unit1* in Fig2; also note that *service1* carries both input and result parameters.] Structure portions are again composed of `FUs`, be they `Standard` or `Constructed` ones (the latter, in repetition, separately defined), and `Variables`. And, again, behaviour and structure portions are interrelated by referring `PCEs` to `FU.Service` pairs. In the latter context, the *ProC/B* paradigm permits that referring `PCE` and referred-to `FU` do not reside in the same `FU`. This objective is accomplished by an option of enhancing a structure portion by a fictitious unit named (fixed keyword:) EXTERNAL. To the interiour of a `FU`, EXTERNAL provides `Services` which may be referred to as usual. In the external view of this FU the ("unsaturated") `Services` of the fictitious EXTERNAL will be visible, and referable to some non-fictitious `FU.Service` pair (or, in turn, to a further EXTERNAL). [Fig3: *internact3* of *service1* is referred to *extservice* of EXTERNAL. Fig2: *extservice* is visible, and referred to *service* of *unit2*.] Please note that the original demand of "letting the behavioural processes almost arbitrarily spread across the system structure" would not be satisfied without the EXTERNAL option since otherwise but tree-like behaviour refinements, along the includes hierarchy, could be attained. Note besides that this option must not be employed creating recursive activations.

3 Analysis of Process Chain Models

Fig. 4 presents the general structure of the toolset. A graphical user interface provides facilities to describe structure and behaviour of the system to be analysed, employing the *ProC/B* notation presented in Sect. 2. Access to various model analysis techniques is by particular transformer modules which map *ProC/B* models to the modelling paradigms and input languages of existing modelling frameworks, with their specific analysis options. At present, mappings to the HIT modelling environment [5,6] and to the APNN Toolbox [8] are available,

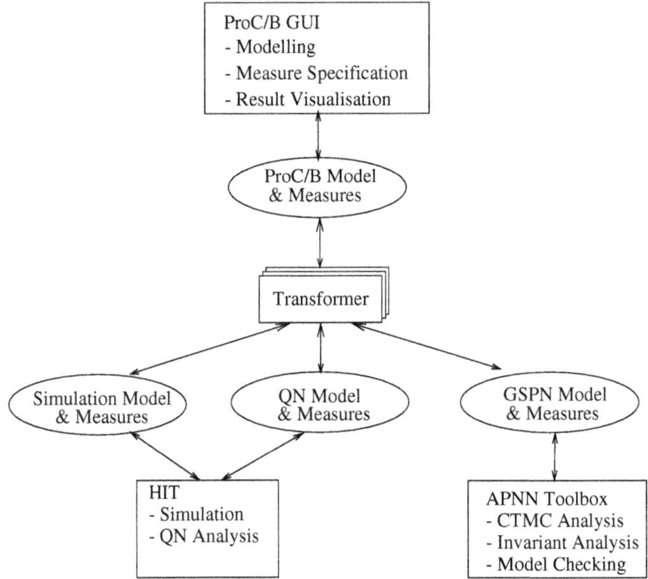

Fig. 4. General structure of the toolset

rendering access to Discrete Event Simulation, to Queueing Networks (QNs) with the familiar exact and approximate techniques, and to Generalised Stochastic Petri Nets (GSPNs) with the related quantitative and functional techniques. The non-simulative techniques are obviously only applicable to restricted *ProC/B* models. The corresponding applicability conditions can however be checked syntactically, at the modelling level. Results from model analysis can optionally be back-transformed and presented within the graphical model representation.

The following subsections describe the basic ideas of the model transformations in more detail.

3.1 Simulation

ProC/B models fall into the DEDS category of models. Hence, Discrete Event Simulation is an obvious analysis option. The question of which particular simulation engine to employ was decided rather pragmatically: So-far unmentioned, many ideas for the *ProC/B* paradigm have been lent and adapted from an existing performance evaluation environment, HIT [5,6]. To name but a few of the important similarities: The HIT modelling paradigm is process-oriented, models are hierarchically structured employing both the "includes" and "calls" hierarchical relations, servers and counters serve as standard types of elements governing time and space, respectively. HIT does include simulation and corresponding statistical evaluations amongst its solution techniques. It was an almost natural choice (for us) to use this simulation engine as our target.

HIT's user interfaces include a particular modelling and programming language, Hi-Slang. Although labour-intensive, the implementation of transformer modules, from the graphical *ProC/B* level, to Hi-Slang, did not encounter any fundamental difficulties (details omitted). All *ProC/B* models are consequently open for simulative analysis via mapping them to Hi-Slang.

HIT is basically tailored to steady-state analysis, based on a single replication approach. Time Series Analysis techniques are applied to individual streams of data produced by simulation, each stream related to one particular (requested) result variable. Data streams (and corresponding statistical techniques) are classified into a set of stream types, between them including the special, performance-related streams for calculating residence times, populations, utilisations and throughputs. For all streams, the usual characteristics can be demanded to be estimated: Means, standard deviations, confidence intervals, histograms, and others. Possibly somewhat particular is, that every data stream may be stratified in detailed (possibly multiple) ways as based on the model structure. Using plain words rather than formulae, and the *ProC/B* terminology: Activities of some lower level `FU` are caused by activities in some higher level `FU`. It may be important to discriminate measurements at the lower level `FU` (say, of service completion times) according to specific, higher level originators. HIT (and thereby *ProC/B*) is in fact capable of furnishing such stratified measurements, streams, results: For any `FU`, and for any of its provided services, results can be obtained as stratified by the causing activities of any other service, of some other `FU`.

3.2 Queueing Network Analysis

QNs are well-established in the area of IT systems performance modelling [7]. They provide very efficient analysis techniques, both for the classic product-form QNs (PF-QNs) [3] and for certain non PF-QNs. In comparison with the expressiveness of general *ProC/B* models, the familiar restrictions of QN techniques appear fairly strong. Their advantages for modelling logistic systems is in the early design phases where gross initial models, with a large number of parameter variations, can be efficiently assessed.

The general scheme of mapping *ProC/B* models onto QNs is fairly natural. A standard QN is characterised by a set of queues and a set of routing chains as capturing system structure and behaviour, respectively. System dynamics is explained by customers moving along chain descriptions, for open chains initiated via particular arrival processes. `FUs` of the `Server` type map naturally onto queues, `PCs` onto routing chains. Customers mirror the progressing *ProC/B* processes. `Unconditional Sources` determine (stochastic) arrival processes. `PCs` with process parameters (with discrete and finite domains) are covered by multiple "copies" of corresponding routing chains where a specific copy is created for each permitted parameter value and the corresponding chain behaviour. Within routing chains, the concept of QN customer classes is exploited for capturing the flexible *ProC/B* interrelations between `PCEs` and `Services`, which often results in multiple queue visits. By way of example we refer to figure 5, where two `PCEs` are referred to `Server` *A* such that the depicted `PC` visits this `Server` twice. In the QN equivalent, customers switch to a different class, indicated by a dashed line, before they enter queue *A* for the second time.

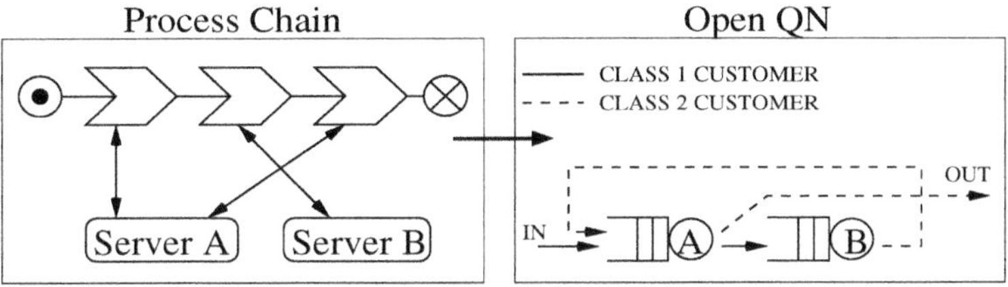

Fig. 5. Mapping *ProC/B* models to QNs

We make extensive use of customer classes when representing the *ProC/B* hierarchical relations: The identity of `Constructed FUs` is preserved to allow for their "offline" evaluation and with it for the construction of corresponding aggregates. During composition of the total model, this decision entails the necessity that `FU Services` have to "remember from which `PCE`, of which `PC`, they have been called". The mapping delegates these distinctions to different customer classes.

Technically, the *ProC/B* - QN mapping is realised in two steps. A first step is onto a general, intermediate QN notation, the second step intended to map onto the input language of some particular QN solver tool. This separation aims at easing the incorporation of different QN solvers, with potentially different solution techniques implemented. Presently operational is a mapping onto HIT comprising the usual MVA/Convolution techniques for PF-QNs and a set of approximate non PF-QN techniques (for class-specific FCFS service times and for priority scheduling disciplines). Further intended is a mapping onto QNA [14].

3.3 Numerical Markov Chain Analysis

Continuous time Markov chains (CTMCs) are able to handle any kind of state-dependent behaviour provided the timing is Markovian. For numerical analysis, CTMCs need to be finite and in case of stationary analysis also ergodic. In case of large state spaces, Kronecker methods have been applied with great success. Since the derivation of a CTMC with a Kronecker structure is known for GSPNs that are composed of components, so called superposed GSPNs (SGSPNs) [12, 15], we can focus on a mapping of *ProC/B* to SGSPNs. Once a SGSPN is attained, it is straightforward to employ existing software tools like SMART [11] or the APNN toolbox [8]. A more direct mapping to a CTMC (with or without Kronecker representation) would avoid limitations of GSPNs but also the ability to use Petri net analysis techniques like invariant analysis.

SGSPNs can describe finite state processes that communicate in a rendezvous manner by synchronized transitions. This goes well with `Process Chains`,

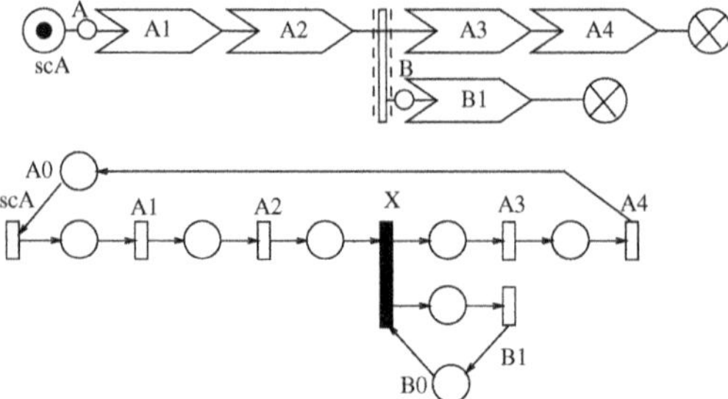

Fig. 6. Mapping Process Chains to Structured Markov Chains via GSPNs

if each chain is mapped to a component. It is a design decision whether to map each instantiation of a chain into a single component – a variant that allows to distinguish each process but dramatically increases the state space – or to map all instantiations of a chain into one component. The latter counts only the number of processes that are in a specific state. It allows us to consider larger models but at a reduced level of detail, it implies the min-match problem in case of fork-join structures as observed in [13]. Clearly, all individual elements of the *ProC/B* paradigm need to be expressed by GSPN places and transitions, e.g., a counter is a natural variable that allows for changes by addition and subtraction, so its representation by a single place for the variable and transitions for each manipulation is fairly natural.

Fig. 6 sketches the mapping of a *ProC/B* model that includes a `PC-connector` to a SGSPN. It shows a `PC` A that at one point starts a second `PC` B. Note that transitions with prefix A (B) refer to chain A (B) and the immediate transition X matches the `PC-conncector`. The SGSPN components achieve finite populations by a short-circuit via transitions scA (X) and places *A0* (*B0*). The initial marking of these places gives the maximum number of simultaneously active instantiations of process chains. Considering the model in short-circuit accomodates a typical construction to build aggregates as a flow-equivalent server (FES), so numerical analysis is employed to build an FES for a rather complex subsystem for a finite range of process instantiations. A FES can be used in a bottom up approach in the design of large systems like logistic networks if prefabricated submodels are taken from a library. In these cases, an approximate, environment-independent aggregate is useful and its multiple usage amortizes its costs of analysis.

A transformer has been implemented that generates a SGSPN in the APNN format of the APNN toolbox from a *ProC/B* model. The full functionality of the APNN toolbox is applicable on the resulting SGSPN. This means, that we can perform the numerous numerical methods for stationary and transient CTMC analysis with modular and hierarchical Kronecker representations. We can also use CSL model-checking of CTMCs to detect more specific measurements than normally expressed by rate and impulse rewards [9]. We frequently apply a functional analysis to detect defects in complex models by checking invariants, liveness, and ergodicity ahead of any CTMC analysis. Clearly, our transformer does only map a suitable subset of the *ProC/B* paradigm to GSPNs, since GSPNs are not able to handle data-dependent decisions and timing, arbitrary time distributions, processes (tokens) that carry a set of local variables and parameters, and alike. These restrictions can be statically checked for a *ProC/B* model ahead of a transformation.

The results that are achieved by numerical analysis, QN analysis or simulation all refer to technical measures related to performance.

4 Economic Measures

In the given application area, results are requested not only with respect to technical properties such as utilisations or throughputs, but also with respect to incurred cost. It is not the proper place, here, to argue about the relative virtues of a variety of existing costing and accounting models. Suffice it to mention that contemporary organisational experience shows a considerable increase of overheads and indirect costs compared to direct costs (costs directly related to labour and material) up to the point where traditional costing schemes have difficulties in determining the costs involved in producing particular goods. Newer approaches at costing therefore emphasise a "correct" assignment of costs, inclusive of indirect costs, to specific (groups of) products and tasks. The activity-based costing model, ABC [2], is a well-known approach along these lines. In the *ProC/B* framework, and referring to the above costing aims, main interest will normally be in assigning/distributing all costs incurred during system operations to/over the `PCs` in the top level `FU`: These `PCs` represent the tasks requested by the system's environment, the latter represented by the `Sources` stimulating the top level `PCs`. A costing scheme has been developed for the *ProC/B* framework which satisfies this interest. The scheme follows an "ex-post" approach, exploiting performance results as available after model (performance) analysis. It is based on the following preconditions:

- Cost figures do not influence the dynamic behaviour of the model/system; otherwise, costing notions would have to be incorporated in the model itself.
- The analysed models reach stationarity, and utilised performance results refer to the stationary phase; thereby, measures such as costs per unit operational time obtain an unambiguous meaning; all cost figures in the following are to be understood as expected values.
- Any cost item considered arises from the existence and/or operations of some particular `FU`; this is a pragmatic, yet realistic, assumption as every `FU` represents a structural system part

The costing scheme introduces a distinction between three kinds of cost, for every `FU`, r:

- FCosts(r) [per unit time], representing "F"ixed costs arising from the sheer existence of r (think of depreciation costs or costs for operations-independent maintenance, etc.);

- PCosts(s, r) [per service call], representing costs that are naturally attributable to the act of "P"erforming a particular activity, i.e. to the execution of an individual instance of some service s provided by r (think of piece-work wages, of energy costs for producing a single item, etc.);
- OCosts(r) [per unit time], representing costs that originate from and only during system "O"perations, generally in a load-dependent manner, but which are not naturally attributable to individual service executions (costs of overall sorting in a storage unit, of management costs in general).

Costing implementations in the *ProC/B* toolset [16] so far cover a basic costing model in which no attempt is undertaken to assign (indirect) FCosts and OCosts to activities (`PCs` or `PCEs`).

Cost figures are constructed in a bottom-up fashion. Given the FCosts contributions of all `FUs` (in the form of corresponding cost parameters), it is obvious how total model FCosts can be calculated along the includes hierarchy. FCosts arise independently of the system dynamics and, hence, of any model analysis. OCosts, on the other hand, are in general load-dependent and therefore depend on the analysis results. Given corresponding dependency functions for all `FUs` (as additional costing parameterisation), total model OCosts can be calculated from the OCosts determined for the `FUs`, along the includes hierarchy, analogously to the above FCosts.

Not so for the PCosts, even for this basic case: Starting at the model bottom, PCosts for standard `FUs` (`Servers` and `Counters`) must first be derived. By way of example: For a server `FU` r, a cost parameter must be given, for the cost of r work per unit time. Next, in order to identify the PCosts contribution, of employing r, to the PCosts of top level `PCs`, the total use of r must be discriminated with respect to these originator `PCs`. The result is again load-dependent. Omitting all formulae: If stratified performance results (cf. Sect. 3) are available, then the calls hierarchy can be followed upwards, repeatedly from called `Service/FU` pair to calling `Service/FU` pair, until eventually the top level `PCs` are reached; in the process, stratified performance results can be exploited for calculating the very PCosts for individual top level chains. Please note besides, that this approach produces precisely the type of PCosts advocated in the mentioned ABC model.

For more general cost models, the objective of also assigning F/OCosts to causing activities needs more support. Corresponding work is in progress along the idea of parameterising all `FUs` with costing functions. These functions will have to capture (exchangeable) prescriptions for calculating FCosts, OCosts and PCosts from the stratified performance results, prescriptions as specific for particular costing models.

5 Application Example: Supply Chains

Supply chain management (SCM) may be considered as a management approach for designing, implementing, and evaluating the flow of materials, products, and information among multiple participants. These act as suppliers, manufacturers, wholesalers, and retailers that are all involved in procuring, producing, and delivering products. In the SCM field the purpose of modelling often concerns the design, implementation and maintenance of supply chains aiming at best-practice implementations as, e.g., predefined in the Supply Chain Operational Reference (SCOR) model [21]. Performance analysis, in particular based on models containing dynamic behaviour, is beyond the scope of tools for supply chain design.

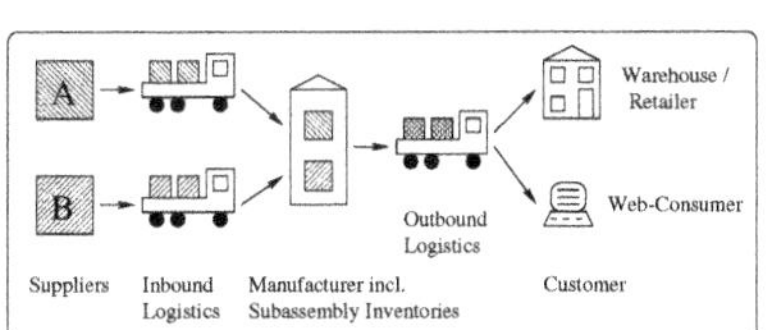

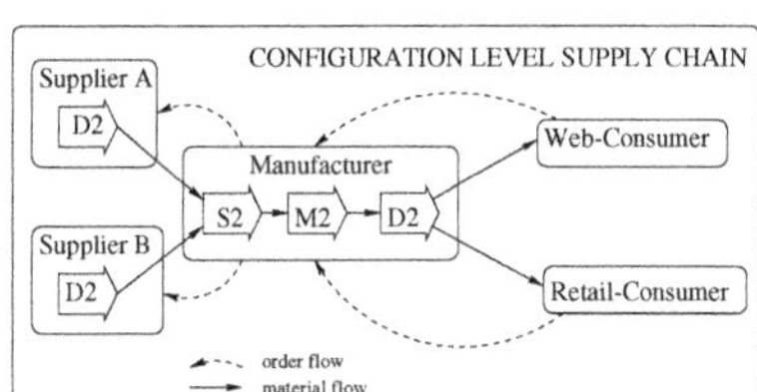

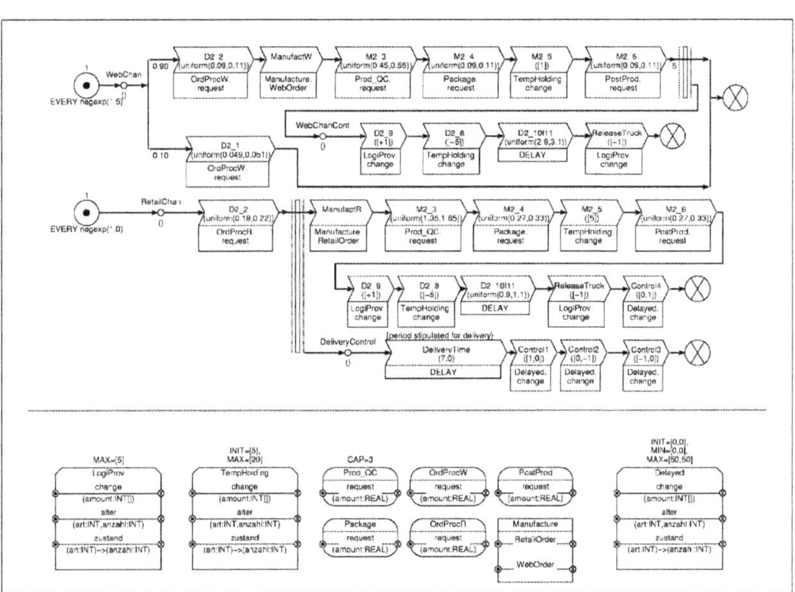

Fig. 7. Supply chain scenario and its stages of modelling: informal, SCOR, and *ProC/B*.

We consider a typical supply chain scenario, see top left of Fig. 7, and investigate the impact of a newly introduced supply chain channel between a manufacture and web-consumers on the overall costs and performance of an already existing channel. Such models arise from trends like E-business and E-commerce. We consider two consumer types: *Retail-Consumer* and *Web-Consumer*. The latter produces typically a larger number of smaller orders, therefore we assume that *Retail-Orders* and *Web-Orders* differ by a factor of five. We further assume, that the manufacture offers exactly one product 'AB' which is assembled from two sub-assemblies of type 'A' and 'B' procured by two suppliers. Both consumer types order product 'AB' with a consumer-specific order quantity. The arrival of customers is governed by Poisson arrival streams. We incorporate in the model a simple warehousing policy for sub-assemblies. The manufacturer procures sub-assemblies from the suppliers with a certain quantity M, if and only if the stock of inventory has been decreased by M. The value of M exceeds the mean consumer order quantity and therefore procurement is not required upon each receipt of consumer orders. Procurement times of in-bound logistic providers are stipulated, whereas delivery times of out-bound logistic are assumed to be uncertain depending on traffic conditions.

In the next step we set up a more formalised model using the SCOR notation, see top right of Fig. 7. SCOR provides a standardised way of supply chain modelling by the use of predefined sets of basic business processes/activities associated with all phases of supply chain processes, for details we refer to [21]. In Fig. 7 arrows indicate such basic processes which are labelled with their short names, e.g., *D2*.

Table 1. Encodings of activities and resources

ACTIV.	DESCRIPTION	RESOURCE	DESCRIPTION
S2_1|2|3	Receive+verify sub-assemblies	*OrdProcW*	Web-order processing system
S2_4	Store sub-assemblies (invent.)	*OrdProcR*	Retail-order processing system
D2_1	Respond to customer inquiries	*InventA*	Store sub-assemblies A
D2_2	Process order	*InventB*	Store sub-assemblies B
D2_8	Pick product from stage	*Prod_QC*	Manufact. + quality control
D2_9	Shipping product (outb. log.)	*Package*	Packaging operation
D2_10|11	Receive, test + install product	*TempHold*	Store + stage finished product
M2_1	Preprocessing steps	*PostProd*	Release product to deliver
M2_2	Issue sub-assemblies from store	*LogiProv*	Out-bound logistic provider
M2_3	Produce and test		
M2_4	Package product		
M2_5	Stage product		
M2_6	Release product to deliver		

In the final stage of modelling we set up the *ProC/B* model, see bottom side of Fig. 7. The model contains two `Sources` generating orders from *Web-Consumers* (top) and from *Retail-Consumers.* The corresponding `PCs` are similar. We first pay attention to the upper `PC` labelled *WebChan.* At first, *WebChan* branches into two sub-chains with a probabilistic selection to decide whether or not the consumer inquiry yields an order. If it is does not, the sub-chain requires no further consideration and ends with a `Sink` immediately. However, inquiries that result in an order are more interesting and contain the actual activities performed by the supply chain. The underlying activities are named according to the SCOR-terminology. For example, the first `PCE` in the `PC` *WebChan* is labelled *D2_2* and encodes all activities concerning the receipt of orders. The remaining activity (`PCE`) and resource (`FU`) encodings are listed in Table 1.

Due to space limitations, we do not go to details and highlight only important characteristics of the model: 1) Both `PCs` interact due to shared resources, except for *OrdProcW* and *OrdProcR*, 2) the *WebChan* `PC` comprises an order combination connector, modelled by a `PC Connector`. We assume, that individual shipping of (small) orders is too costly and therefore always five orders are merged (picking) for one shipment operated by the out-bound logistic provider, 3) the `PCEs` *ManufactW* and *ManufactR* invoke `Services` *WebOrder* and *RetailOrder*, that are defined hierarchically below in the subordinated `Constructed FU` *Manufacture* and 4) in the *RetailChan* `PC` we model a control process *DeliveryControl* in order to measure the mean number of delayed deliveries. We assume that due to contractual penalties additional expenses will be incurred by delayed deliveries.

So far we have identified all activities that consume resources and incur costs. The resulting model does not fulfil restrictions imposed by QN analysis as suggested in Sect. 3.2 and therefore we employ the model translation into a simulative HIT model as proposed in Sect. 3.1. The following results are based on simulation runs that terminate once 95% confidence bands are attained of a width of at most 5% of the estimated means, for all result variables. The model-based performance analysis investigates the impact of a newly introduced supply chain for *Web-Consumer* (`PC` *WebChan*). The chain is assumed to gain importance in terms of increased order rates λ_W, whereas the *Retail-Consumer* order rate λ_R remains fixed ($= 1$). We consider several settings of the model input parameter $\lambda_W = 1.0, \ldots, 3.0$ and address in particular the following questions: 1) How are lead times of retail-orders be affected (due to shared resources) by introducing additional *Web-Consumer* demands and what is the corresponding utilisation? 2) What *Web-Consumer* demand maximises the profit, in particular, does increasing turnover (demand) lead to increasing profit and who are the prime cost drivers?

Tables 2 and 3 give results of simulative performance analysis. Each column contains results for a particular setting of λ_W. The calculation of the turnover requires to specify the income for product 'AB' and order quantities. We assume that *Web-Consumers* [*Retail-Consumers*] order 1 [5] product(s) and pay 82 money units per product, and hence the turnover subject to λ_W is given by $82 \times \lambda_W + 5 \times 82$.

Figures 8–11 visualise computed measures and help to respond to the questions imposed above: 1) As expected, lead times increase, because retail-orders compete with additional load imposed by web-orders, see also Fig. 8. Surprisingly, we observe optimal lead times of web-orders for $\lambda_W \approx 2.5$. As mentioned above, web-orders are merged for shipping and therefore long waiting times for filling up freights occur, if order-rates are too low. Utilisation of resources differ from each other, see Table 2. The bottleneck is determined by *Prod_QC*. 2) The profit is maximised for $\lambda_W \approx 2.0$ and almost all profit is lost for $\lambda_W \approx 2.75$ caused by a cost explosion due to operational costs OC. We observe that performance costs PC increase linearly in accordance with the turnover and for small values of λ_W operational costs can be neglected, but they become more dominant for $\lambda_W \geq 2.5$. For what reason, i.e., who is the prime cost driver? An increased number of delayed deliveries (DD) that extend predefined times lead to increased operational costs OC(DD) $= 100 \times \#(\mathit{Delayed})$, i.e., we assume costs of 100 money units per time unit and delayed delivery. Therefore we state, that an increasing turnover as it is being caused by the Web-consumer demand does not lead to increasing profit, because the current revenue of retail-consumers decreases due to expenses incurred by delayed deliveries.

Table 2. Selected Performance Measures:
T_W,T_R = Lead Times Web/Retail
$\rho(\cdot)$ = Resource Utilisation

$\lambda_W =$	1.0	1.5	2.0	2.5	2.7	3.0
T_W	10.4	8.95	8.40	8.37	8.75	9.9
T_R	5.46	5.67	5.98	6.5	7.17	8.7
ρ(OrdProcW)	9.5	14.2	19.0	23.7	26.1	28.5
ρ(OrdProcR)	20.0	20.0	20.0	20.0	20.0	20.0
ρ(TempHold)	35.2	36.6	38.0	39.5	40.3	41.1
ρ(LogiProv)	30.8	36.2	41.6	47.0	49.7	52.3
ρ(Package)	39.0	43.5	48.0	52.5	54.8	56.9
ρ(PostProd)	39.0	43.5	48.0	52.5	54.8	56.9
ρ(Prod_QC)	65.0	72.5	79.9	87.5	91.2	94.8
#(Delayed)	0.04	0.06	0.13	0.35	0.76	2.0

Table 3. Cost Measures:
PC, OC, FC = perf./operations/ fixed costs
OC(DD) = operational costs due to delayed orders
TO, PF = total turnover/profit

$\lambda_W =$	1.0	1.5	2.0	2.5	2.7	3.0
PC	344.9	374.2	402.7	432.2	446.9	460.6
OC	33.2	38.6	48.5	74.3	116.5	238.2
FC	70.0	70.0	70.0	70.0	70.0	70.0
OC(DD)	3.7	5.9	12.5	35.0	75.5	195.6
TO	492.0	533.0	574.0	615.0	635.5	656.0
PF	44.1	50.0	53.0	38.0	2.5	-112.0

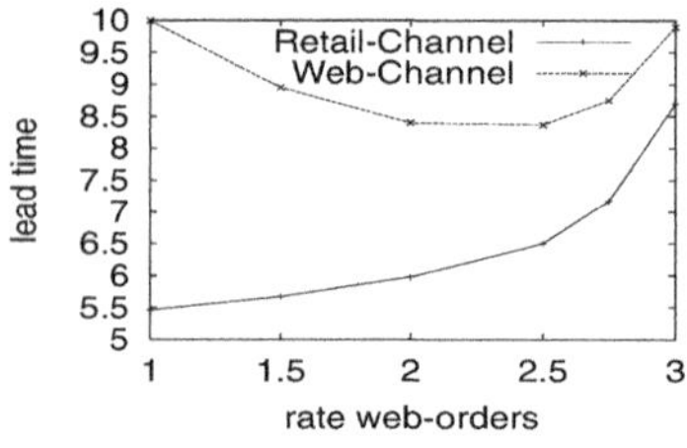

Fig. 8. Order Lead Times

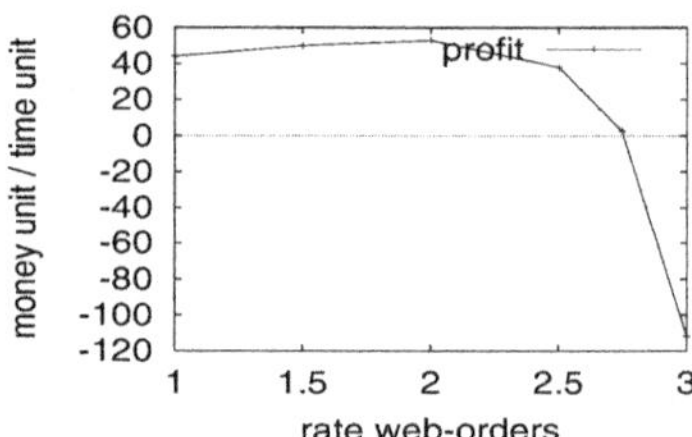

Fig. 10. Profit

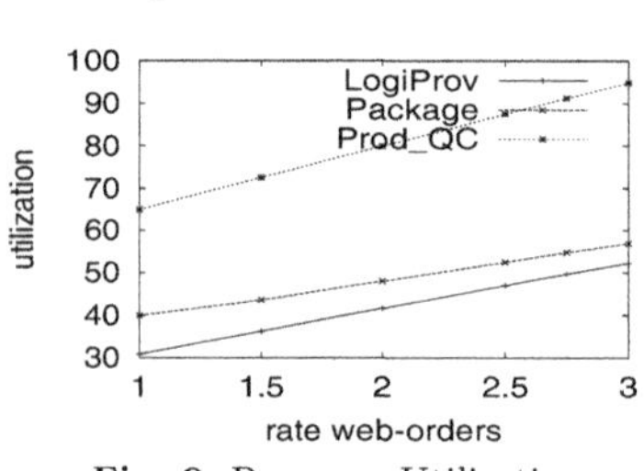

Fig. 9. Resource Utilisation

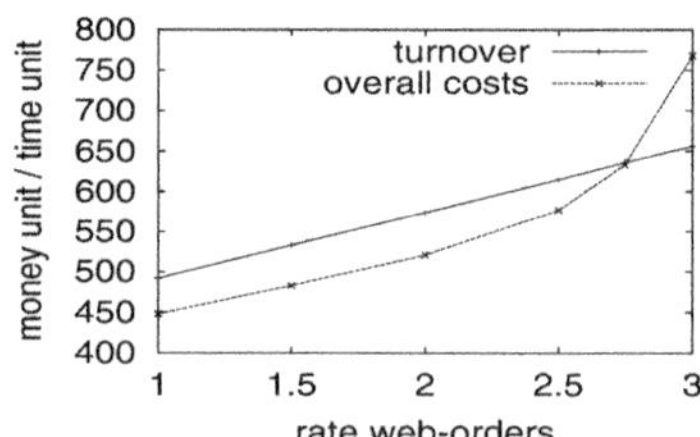

Fig. 11. Turnover and Costs

We conclude with some suggestions for system improvement. Performance analysis has shown, that either negotiations to cut costs incurred by delayed deliveries (cost driver) or investments in the production (elimination of performance bottle-neck) should be started, if the rate of Web-order exceeds the value of 2.5.

6 Conclusions

We presented a toolset that integrates established analysis techniques from the field of computer and communication systems for the analysis of process chains, a modelling notation that is specifically designed for the application field of logistic systems. We employ simulation as a general fall-back technique and wherever applicable highly efficient product-form solution methods for Queueing Networks and numerical analysis techniques for Markov chains. Techniques may be used for complete models or to build aggregates that are subsequently used in simulation.

The toolset makes use of existing tools that implement the above techniques, namely HIT and the APNN toolbox. The contribution is in a notation and graphical user interface to support modelling with discrete event systems in a way that conforms with the real world structures present in logistic systems, namely enterprises (functional units) that own resources, offer services, and rely on services provided by other enterprises. In addition to this support for modelling, we provide mappings to simulation languages, stochastic Petri Nets and Queueing Networks. An important feature of these mappings is to exploit structural information that is present in a model in order to derive structured descriptions that can be analysed efficiently. E.g., the mappings achieve a hierarchical description in Hi-Slang for simulation, the existence of chains in Queueing Networks, and a decomposition into components for GSPNs, so Kronecker methods can be applied. Finally, we present how cost analysis is performed for process chains in a way that is related to the well known activity based costing approach.

The toolset is developed and used within a large, interdisciplinary research project, SFB 559 [22]. From this context, we took supply chain management as an application field of high current interest and presented results of a case study based on the presented notation and toolset.

Ongoing work is dedicated to the integration of further analysis engines, to provide further support for aggregation, functional analysis and to extend the costing approach. The demand for analysis of large and complex models also drives us to work on parallel and distributed algorithms.

References

1. M. Ajmone Marsan G. Balbo G. Conte, S. Donatelli, and G. Franceschinis. Modelling with generalized stochastic Petri nets. Wiley, 1995.
2. A. Arantes, C. Fernandes, A.P. Guedes, and I. Themido. Logistic costs case study-an ABC approach. *J. of the Operational Research Society*, Vol. 51, pp. 1148-1157, 2000
3. F. Baskett, K. Chandy, R. Muntz, and F. Palacios. Open, closed and mixed networks of queues with different classes of customers. *J. of the ACM*, 22(2):248-260, 1975.
4. F. Bause, H. Beilner. Intrinsic Problems in Simulation of Logistic Networks. *11th European Simulation Symposium and Exhibition* (ESS'99), Simulation in Industry, Erlangen, October 26-28, pp. 193-198, 1999.
5. H. Beilner, J. Mäter, N. Weißenberg. Towards a performance modelling environment: News on HIT In: *Modeling techniques and tools for computer performance evaluation* Editors: R. Puigjaner, D. Potier, pp. 57-75, 1989.

6. H. Beilner, J. Mäter, C. Wysocki. The Hierarchical Evaluation Tool HIT In: *Short Papers and Tool Descriptions of the 7th InternationalConference on Modelling Techniques and Tools for Computer Performance Evaluation*, 1994.
7. G. Bolch, S. Greiner, H. de Meer, K.S. Trivedi. Queueing Networks and Markov Chains. *J. Wiley & Sons*, 1998.
8. P. Buchholz, M. Fischer, P. Kemper, and C. Tepper. New features in the APNN toolbox. In P. Kemper (ed), *Tools of Aachen 2001 Int. Multiconference on Measurement, Modeling and Evaluation of Computer-Communication Systems*, pp. 62–68. Universität Dortmund, Fachbereich Informatik, Forschungsbericht Nr. 760, 2001.
9. P. Buchholz, J.P. Katoen, P. Kemper, and C. Tepper. Model-checking large structured Markov-chains. submitted for publication, 2001.
10. C. Cassandras. Discrete Event Systems: modelling and performance analysis. *Irwin, Aksen*, 1993.
11. G. Ciardo and A. Miner. SMART: Simulation and Markovian analyzer for reliability and timing. In: *Proc. of IEEE Int. Computer Performance and Dependability Symposium.* IEEE CS-Press, 1996.
12. S. Donatelli. Superposed Generalized Stochastic Petri nets: definition and efficient solution. In *Proc. 15th int. Conf. Application and Theory of Petri nets*, Springer, 1994.
13. S. Donatelli and G. Franceschinis The PSR methodology: integrating hardware and software models. In Billington,J. and Reisig,W. (eds.), *Application and Theory of Petri Nets 1996*, Springer, LNCS 1091, pp. 133-152, 1996.
14. B.R. Haverkort. Approximate Analysis of Networks of PH/PH/1/K Queues: Theory & Tool Support. In: *Quantitative Evaluation of Computing and Communication Systems*, Editors: H. Beilner, F. Bause, LNCS 977, Springer, pp. 239–253, 1995.
15. P. Kemper. Numerical analysis of superposed GSPNs. *IEEE Transactions on Software Engineering*, 22(9):615–628, 1996.
16. T. Köpp. Visualization of performance and cost measures for logistic systems derived from process chain paradigms. *Master's thesis*, Dept. of Computer Science, University of Dortmund, 2001.
17. A. Kuhn. *Prozessketten in der Logistik - Entwicklungstrends und Umsetzungsstrategien.* Verlag Praxiswissen, Dortmund 1995.
18. A. Kuhn. *Prozesskettenmanagement - Erfolgsbeispiele aus der Praxis.* Verlag Praxiswissen, Dortmund 1999.
19. D.M. Lambert, M.C. Cooper, and J.D. Pagh. Supply Chain Management: Implementation Issues and Research Opportunities. *Int. J. of Logistic Management*, 9(2), pp. 1-19, 1998.
20. A.W. Scheer. *ARIS-Modellierungsmethoden.* Springer, 1998.
21. Supply-Chain Operations Reference Model, SCOR version 4.0, 2000.
22. *Collaborative Research Center 559 "Modelling of Large Logistics Networks".* http://www.sfb559.uni-dortmund.de/eng/index.htm
23. W. J. Stewart. *Introduction to the numerical solution of Markov chains.* Princeton University Press, 1994.

MRMSolve: Distribution Estimation of Large Markov Reward Models*

Sándor Rácz, Árpád Tari, and Miklós Telek

Technical University of Budapest, Hungary,
{raczs,arpi,telek}@webspn.hit.bme.hu

Abstract. MRMSolve is an analysis tool developed for the evaluation of large Markov Reward Models (MRM). The previous version of MRM-Solve [8] provided only the moments of MRMs at arbitrary transient instant of time. This paper presents a new version of MRMSolve with new analysis features and software environment. The most important new functionality of MRMSolve is that it also makes distribution estimation of MRMs. MRMSolve can estimate the distribution of reward measures up to models with $\sim 10^6$ states, and to the best of our knowledge no other algorithm can handle MRMs with more than $\sim 10^4$ states.

Keywords: Markov Reward Models, accumulated reward, completion time, moments based distribution estimation.

1 Introduction

Stochastic reward processes are commonly applied for computer and communication systems' performance analysis. These processes are characterized by a discrete state stochastic process describing the system behaviour and the associated reward structure describing the system performance in different states. When a Continuous time Markov chain (CTMC) describes the system behaviour and there are non-negative *reward rates* associated with the system states the stochastic reward process is referred to as Markov reward model (MRM).

There are two main subclass of measures associated with MRM. The random amount of reward accumulated during a given time interval is referred to as *accumulated reward*, and the random time to accumulate a given amount of reward is referred to as *completion time*. It is easy to compute the mean of these reward measures based on the transient analysis of the underlying CTMC, instead, this paper is about the distribution of the reward measures. Closed form expressions are known for the distribution of accumulated reward [4] and completion time [5] of MRMs in double Laplace transform domain. Unfortunately, the numerical evaluation of these transform domain expressions are infeasible when the

* This work was partially supported by Hungarian Scientific Research Fund (OTKA) under Grant No. T-34972.

T. Field et al. (Eds.): TOOLS 2002, LNCS 2324, pp. 71–81, 2002.

state space of the CTMC is larger than ~20 states[1]. A number of numerical techniques were proposed for the evaluation of MRMs with larger state spaces. Some of them directly calculate the distribution of reward measures [11,2,6,10], while some other of them provides only the moments of the measures [4,14]. Table 1 summarizes their complexity and memory requirement, where m denotes the number of moments, t the time, K (K') the number of different (important) reward rates, T the number of transitions, and N the number of states. Based on Table 1 and our experiences we conclude that the numerical methods that directly provide the distribution of reward measures are applicable for MRMs with less than ~10^4 states while it is possible to evaluate the moments of reward measures up to ~10^6 states [14]. The MRMSolve tool is aimed for the analysis of large MRMs, hence it applies the numerical method presented in [14] to evaluate the moments of reward measures and it estimates the distribution based on the evaluated moments. Especially, the distribution estimation provides upper and lower bounds of the distribution function.

Table 1. *Complexity of numerical analysis methods of MRMs*

Method	CPU time	memory	output
Iyer, Donatiello and Heidelberger [4]	$\mathcal{O}(N^4 \cdot m^2)$	n.a.	moments
Smith, Trivedi and Ramesh [11]	$\mathcal{O}(N^3)$	n.a.	distribution
Donatiello and Grassi [2]	$\mathcal{O}(T \cdot K \cdot t^2)$	$\mathcal{O}(K \cdot N \cdot t)$	distribution
Nabli and Sericola [6]	$\mathcal{O}(T \cdot K \cdot t^2)$	$\mathcal{O}(K \cdot N \cdot t)$	distribution
Silva and Gail [10]	$\mathcal{O}(T \cdot K' \cdot t^2)$	$\mathcal{O}(N \cdot t^2)$	distribution
Telek and Racz [14]	$\mathcal{O}(T \cdot m \cdot t)$	$\mathcal{O}(N \cdot m)$	moments
CTMC transient analysis	$\mathcal{O}(T \cdot t)$	$\mathcal{O}(N)$	

This paper introduces the new features of MRMSolve and its wide range of applicability. To this end several application examples of the literature of system performance analysis are evaluated. Algorithmic details of the applied computation methods are omitted due to space constraint. The rest of the paper is organized as follows. Section 2 introduces the general structure of MRMSolve. Section 3 summarizes the applied distribution estimation method. Section 4 demonstrates the easy use and usefulness of MRMSolve via a number of application examples. The compact MRMSolve descriptions of models, taken from research papers, are presented together with numerical results. Section 5 discusses the computational and memory complexity of MRMSolve and Section 6 provides concluding remarks.

[1] The "~" sign indicates our general the rules of thumb. The complexity of particular procedures depend on several parameters which are not reflected by these general rules.

2 The General Structure of MRMSolve

From the users' point of view the analysis of a MRM using MRMsolve is composed by two main steps: i) description of the MRM and the measures of interest, ii) automatic model analysis. To support the model description MRMSolve applies a MRM description language, which is developed particularly for the effective description of large MRMs. Generally, the large MRMs of practical interest exhibit structural regularity. The description language of MRMSolve describes the structural regularity of the models. The simpler is the structure of the model the easier is to describe it with MRMSolve, and the complexity of the model description is independent of the size of the model. The model description contains the system states identification (state space description), the definition of the possible state transitions, the definition of the system performance in each state and the description of the initial distribution. The input of automatic model analysis is the constructed model and the analysis parameters, which are the time points at which the distribution of the accumulated reward is evaluated, the accuracy of the calculation, and the number of evaluated moments (m). The analysis provides the following information about the investigated performance measures: the first m moments of the accumulated reward, the lower and upper bounds of the distribution function, and the estimation of the quantiles.

The major steps of the analysis procedure of MRMSolve are: the interpretation of the model description and generation of the generator matrix, the initial probability vector and the reward vector of the MRMs; calculation of moments of reward measures; distribution estimation of reward measures.

3 Distribution Estimation

The problem of inversely characterizing distribution from their moments has been studied for over 100 years. Stieltjes, [12], established necessary and sufficient conditions for the existence of a *real valued*, *bounded* and *non-decreasing* function, for example a distribution function, on the interval $[0, \infty)$ such that its moments match given values. An excellent overview of the moment problem and some variations can be found in [1]. Numerous attempts have been made to obtain continuous or discrete distributions from their moments [1,13] or to derive upper and lower bounds on the distribution function. In the case of distribution estimation at a given point x we need to find the distribution with the given moments whose cdf function is the less (the most) at point x. Indeed, we need to find the *domain of feasible distribution functions*. It practically means that this method gives upper and lower bounds on the feasible distribution functions (e.g., if the only information from a non-negative random variable is its mean value (μ_1) then the ideal estimator gives the domain $1 \geq F(x) \geq 1 - \frac{\mu_1}{x}$ based on the Markov-inequality). One can realize that this type of estimation methods give the best and the worst cases for the examined measure.

In several practically interesting cases of performance analysis the probability of extreme cases has to be bounded [10]. E.g., the probability that the stress accumulated by the system is larger than a dangerous threshold should be less than 10^{-3}. The analysis of the domain of feasible distributions can provide this kind of limits. Hence, the method applied in MRMSolve is of the second type and is taken from [7]. The method is based on the following main ideas. The Hankel determinant, $\text{Hankel}(a_0, \ldots, a_{2n}) := \mathbf{Det} \begin{pmatrix} a_0 & \ldots & a_n \\ \vdots & \ddots & \vdots \\ a_n & \ldots & a_{2n} \end{pmatrix}$, of the moments of any distribution is non-negative. The extreme case when the Hankel determinant is 0 is provided by a discrete distribution. The applied algorithm calculates the extreme discrete distribution which has the maximal mass at the evaluated point and its Hankel determinant is 0.

4 Numerical Examples

4.1 Carnegie-Mellon Multiprocessor System

Model construction. The system is similar to the one presented in [11]. The system consists of P processors, M memories and an interconnecting network composed by switches which allows any processor to access any memory. The failure rates per hour for the system are set to be μ_P, μ_M and μ_S for the processors, memories and switches respectively.

Viewing the interconnecting network as S switches and modeling the system at the processor-memory-switch level, the system performance depends on the minimum of the number of operating processors, memories and switches. Each state is thus specified by a triple $(a; b; c)$ indicating the number of operating processors, memories and switches, respectively. We augment the preventive maintenance with state F. Events that decrease the number of operational units are the failures and events that increase the number of operational elements are the repairs. When a component fails, a recovery action must be taken (e.g., shutting down the failed processor, etc.).

Two kinds of repair actions are possible, preventive maintenance is initiated with rate μ_G per hour which restores the system to state $(N; M; S)$ with rate λ_G per hour from state F and local repair which can be thought of as a repair person beginning to fix a component of the system as soon as a component failure occurs. We assume that there is only one repair person for each component type. Let the local repair rates be λ_P, λ_M and λ_S for processors, memories and switches, respectively.

The system starts from the perfect state $(P; M; S)$. The performance of the system is proportional to the number of cooperating processors and memories, whose cooperation is provided by one switch. The system performance (processing power) in a given state is defined as the minimum number of the operational processors, memories and switches. The minimal operational configuration is supposed to have one processor, one memory and one interconnecting switch. We consider the *processing power* of the system averaged over a given time interval, i.e., the reward accumulated in $(0, t)$ is divided by t. Hence the processing power of the system is always between 0 and $min(N, M, S)$ unit.

Model description and automatic analysis. For describing system states the tool allows us to use state variables. Extra states can be represented by state variables with associated logical conditions. A state can be identified by the values of its state variables, e.g., in our example a system state is identified by a triple $(a; b; c)$ or we can use some extra states as state F which cannot match to the state variables description. In general, the modeler makes some restrictions for the feasible values of state variables. There are two ways to do this, to limit the value of state variables and to add complex logical constraints to the state space description. In our example the state space is:

$$\begin{aligned} \mathcal{S} &= \{(a; b; c) \ : \ 0 \leq a \leq P, \ 0 \leq b \leq M, \ 0 \leq c \leq S \ \} \ \bigcup \ \{F\} \\ &= \{(0;0;0), (0;0;1), (0;0;2), \ldots, (P; M; S-1), (P; M; S), F\} \end{aligned}$$

whose cardinality is $(P + 1)\ (M + 1)\ (S + 1) + 1$. Table 2 contains the model description of the examined Carnegie-Mellon multiprocessor system, where the model parameters are as follows: number of processors, memories and switches: $P = 128$, $M = 128$, $S = 32$, failure rate of a processor, a memory and a switch: $\mu_P = 0.5$, $\mu_M = 0.05$, $\mu_S = 0.02$, preventive maintenance rate: $\mu_G = 0.1$, repair rate of processors, memories and switches: $\lambda_P = 2$, $\lambda_M = 1$, $\lambda_S = 0.5$, preventive repair rate: $\lambda_G = 1$, enable/disable flag of preventive maintenance: $GR =$ **True**. This system has 549154 states.

The example was evaluated with the following set of analysis parameters: time points: $t = 0.5 \ldots 10$, calculated moments: $m = 6$, and the distribution of the accumulated reward were calculated in $k = 20$ points from the lower limit $F_l = 0.01$ to the upper limit $F_u = 0.99$ of the estimated distribution and a threshold curve is calculated at $Th = 0.01$ quantile of the estimated distribution.

In Figure 1, we compare the system with allowing preventive maintenance (setting GR to **True**) and the system without preventive maintenance (setting GR to **False**). Allowing preventive maintenance results in higher processing power for larger t but causes very high variance.

4.2 Busy Periods in a M/M/1/K System

[3] studies the transient behavior of an $M/M/1/K$ queue where the arrival rate to the queue is $\lambda = 1$, the service rate is $\mu = 1$ and $K = 1000$. The queue is empty at time 0. The objective is to find the moments of the busy time of the system during the $[0, t]$ interval relative to the length of the interval and also to provide estimation of the 1% quantile. Table 3 shows the specification of this model for MRMSolve and Figure 2 provides the obtained results. MRMSolve provided the same results as [3].

4.3 Serving Rigid, Elastic, and Adaptive Traffic

[9] presents the MRM of a transmission link serving peak bandwidth assured rigid, adaptive and elastic traffic with the Partial Overlap policy. There are two

Table 2. *MRMSolve description of the Carnegie-Mellon multiprocessor system*

State space	
a : 0 **To** P	number of active processors
b : 0 **To** M	number of active memories
c : 0 **To** S	number of active switches
Extra state = { F }	extra state
State-transition rates	
$(a;b;c) \to (a+1;b;c) = \lambda_P$	processor repair
$(a;b;c) \to (a;b+1;c) = \lambda_M$	memory repair
$(a;b;c) \to (a;b;c+1) = \lambda_S$	switch repair
GR : $(F) \to (P;M;S) = \lambda_G$	global repair
$(a;b;c) \to (a-1;b;c) = a \cdot \mu_P$	processor failure
$(a;b;c) \to (a;b-1;c) = b \cdot \mu_M$	memory failure
$(a;b;c) \to (a;b;c-1) = c \cdot \mu_S$	switch failure
GR : $(a;b;c) \to (F) = \mu_G$	global failure
Reward rates	
$(a;b;c) = \mathbf{Min}(a,b,c)$	processing power in state (a;b;c)
Initial distribution	
$(P;M;S) = 1$	starting form the perfect state

Table 3. *MRMSolve description of the M/M/1/K system from [3]*

State space	
a : 0 **To** 1000	actual number of requests
State-transition rates	
$(a) \to (a+1) = 1$	arrival rate
$(a) \to (a-1) = 1$	departure rate
Reward rates	
a!=0 : $(a) = 1$	busy or idle
Initial distribution	
a==0 : $(a) = 1$	starting form empty state
Parameters of the analysis	
$t = 0.1 \ldots 30$	time points of the analysis
$m = 10$	number of calculated moments
$k = 20$	number of points in distribution estimation
$F_l = 0.01$	lower limit of distribution estimation
$F_u = 0.99$	upper limit of distribution estimation
$Th = 0.01$	threshold value

kinds of performance criteria considered, which are criteria for average throughput and criteria for throughput threshold. The first one requires only the steady-state analysis of the mean accumulated reward (which is easy to obtain from the

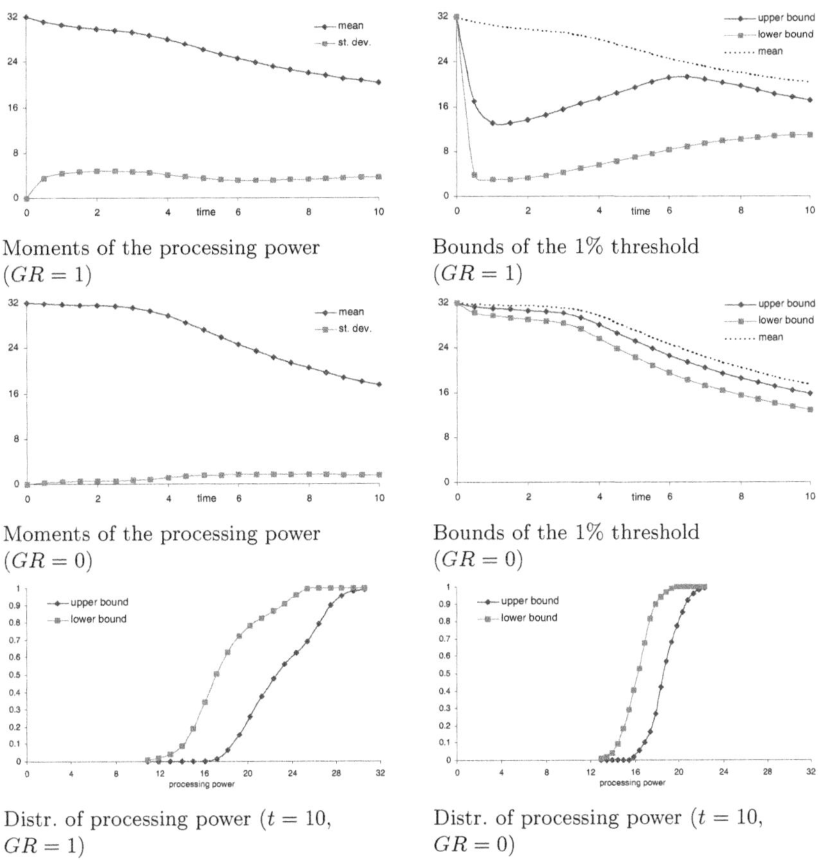

Moments of the processing power ($GR = 1$)

Bounds of the 1% threshold ($GR = 1$)

Moments of the processing power ($GR = 0$)

Bounds of the 1% threshold ($GR = 0$)

Distr. of processing power ($t = 10$, $GR = 1$)

Distr. of processing power ($t = 10$, $GR = 0$)

Fig. 1. Results for Carnegie-Mellon multiprocessor system

steady state distribution of the underlying Markov chain), but the analysis of the throughput threshold is based on the transient analysis of a MRM. Table 4 shows the MRMSolve description of the model, with the following parameters: link capacity and its common part: C, C_{Com}, maximum number of adaptive and elastic flows: N_2, N_3, bandwidth demand of rigid, adaptive and elastic flows: b_1, b_3, b_3, minimum allowed bandwidth of adaptive and elastic flows: b_2^{min}, b_3^{min}, arrival intensity of rigid, adaptive and elastic flows: λ_1, λ_2, λ_3 (ideal) service rate of rigid, adaptive and elastic flows: μ_1, μ_2, μ_3. The bandwidth of adaptive and elastic flows in different states ($r_2(a,b,c)$, $r_2(a,b,c)$) are calculated by an external "awk" functions.

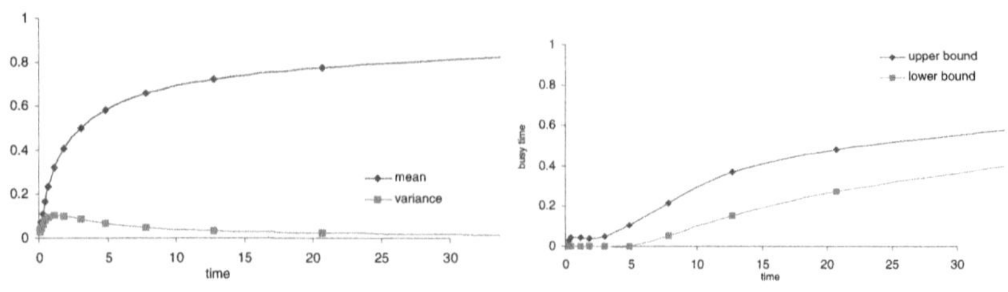

Mean and variance of the busy time in $(0, t)$

Upper and lower limits for the 1% threshold

Fig. 2. Analysis results of the M/M/1/K system

Table 4. *MRM of the transmission link from [9]*

State space	
a : 0 **To** C_{Com}/b_1	number of rigid flows
b : 0 **To** N_2	number of elastic flows
c : 0 **To** N_3	number of adaptive flows
$N_2\ b_2^{min} + N_3\ b_3^{min} \leq C - C_{Com}$	guarantee minimal bandwidths
$b \geq 1$	tagging an adaptive flow
State-transition rates	
$(a; b; c) \to (a + 1; b; c) = \lambda_1$	rigid flows arrival
$(a; b; c) \to (a; b + 1; c) = \lambda_2$	adaptive flows arrival
$(a; b; c) \to (a; b; c + 1) = \lambda_3$	elastic flows arrival
$(a; b; c) \to (a - 1; b; c) = a\ \mu_1$	rigid flows departure
$(a; b; c) \to (a; b - 1; c) = (b - 1)\ \mu_2$	adaptive flows departure (w/o tagged one)
$(a; b; c) \to (a; b; c - 1) = c\ r_3(a, b, c)\ \mu_3$	elastic flows departure
Reward rates	
$(a; b; c) = b_2\ r_2(a, b, c)$	bandwidth of tagged adaptive flow
Initial distribution	
<file name>	result of steady-state analysis

4.4 Buffered Multiprocessor System

In [2,4] authors consider an optimization problem of a "buffered multiprocessor system". The system is an N processor fault-tolerant system with a finite buffer of capacity BS. Table 5 presents the MRMSolve description of the model. The numerical results obtained by MRMSolve based on this description are equivalent with the ones presented in [2,4].

5 Notes on Computational Complexity

The analysis has three main steps, the generation of the reward rate vector, the initial probability vector and the generator matrix of the CTMC; the calculation

Table 5. *MRMSolve description of the buffered multiprocessor system of [2,4]*

State space	
a : 0 **To** N	actual number of processors
b : 0 **To** 1	operation condition
State-transition rates	
$b == 1$: $(a;b) \to (a-1;b) = a\ \mu_P$	
$b == 1$: $(a;b) \to (a;0) = BS\ \mu_b$	
$b == 0$: $(a;b) \to (N;1) = \mu_r/(N+1-a)$	
Reward rates	
$(a;b) = TH(a)$	throughput of a $M/M/p/p+B$ system (external 'awk' function)
Initial distribution	
$a == 0\ \&\&\ b == 1$: $(a;b) = 1$	starting form perfect state

of the moments of accumulated reward; and the distribution estimation based on the moments. The complexity of the second step is provided in Table 1. The computational complexity of the third step is dominated by the numerical evaluation of the roots of an $\sim m/2$ order polynome, where m is the number of known moments. This step is practically immediate using a currently common computer.

The running time complexity of the MRMSolve tool is demonstrated via the running time data of an example introduced above. E.g., the analysis of the fairly large model of Section 4.1 with $N = 549154$ states and $T = 3244608$ transitions required: 7 min. – to generate the generator matrix and the initial probability and reward vectors; 524 min. – to evaluate the moments of accumulated reward at the required time points; ~1 min. – to complete the distribution estimation based on the moments; on a normal PC with Celeron 600MHz processor and 256MB memory.

This example coincides with our general experience that for really large models the calculation of moments dominates the running time. The time of the first step (the generation of the generator matrix and the associated vectors) increases faster than linearly with the size of the model, but it is still acceptable for larger models as well. E.g., the first step took only 25 minutes for the same example with twice that many processors which result in twice that many states and transitions.

The nice feature of the second step is that, in contrast with the first and third steps, its complexity is easy to identify. Since the numerical procedure [14] is based on the randomization technique the dominant element of the generator matrix (the one with the largest absolute value), q, and the largest time instant t characterize the number of required iterations. The precision parameter has minor effect on the number of iterations if qt is large ($qt > 100$). In these cases the number of required iterations is between qt and $2qt$.

In the introduced example we calculate 6 moments at 20 time points form 0.5 to 10 and the dominant element of the generator matrix is $q = 64$, hence $qt = 640$ and the number of iterations is ~1000. In one iteration cycle 6 vector-matrix multiplications, $6 \times 20 \times 2$ vector-vector multiplications and the same number of vector summations are performed. During this computation we had a sparse generator matrix with $(N + T)$ non-zero elements and dense vectors with N non-zero elements. One vector-matrix multiplication of a dense vector and a sparse matrix of $(N + T)$ non-zero elements means $(N + T)$ floating point multiplications and one vector-vector multiplications of dense vectors (N non-zero elements) means N floating point multiplications. The complexity of summation is less than the complexity of multiplication, hence we do not consider it independently, only as an additional factor of the complexity of multiplication.

Based on these data we can relate the obtained calculation time with the performance of the applied computer. We had ~1000 iteration cycles in 524 min., which means ~2 cycle/min. One cycle requires $\sim 1000 \times 6 \times (N + T) + \sim 1000 \times 6 \times 20 \times 2 \times N \approx 140.000.000$ multiplications, hence our computer performed approximately 5.000.000 multiplications with associated data access, data storage and summations in a second.

The memory requirement of the analysis of this model was $(6 + 2) \times 20$ memory blocks for vectors of N floating point numbers and one memory block for the sparse generator matrix of $N + T$ floating point numbers. It is $8 \times 20 \times \sim 500.000 + \sim 3.500.000$ floating point numbers 8 bytes each, hence ~100 MByte. Our computer has 256 MByte memory, hence this example fit to the memory. If it is not the case the number of multiplications drops to 1/10 of the value above.

6 Conclusion

The paper presents a software tool to analyze the distribution of reward measures of large MRMs. To the best of the authors knowledge the applied analysis approach is the only one that can cope with the distribution of MRMs of more than 10^4 states and this tool is the first one which implements this approach.

A model description language is developed for the effective definition of large MRMs. The distribution of reward measures are estimated based on their moments. The accuracy of this estimation method is poorer at around the mean of the distributions, but it is quite tight at around the extreme values. There are several practical examples, among others from the analysis of safety critical systems, when the goal of the analysis is to evaluate the occurrence of extreme cases.

The present implementation of the tool allows to define MRMs, to run the computation and to post-process the results with a widely applied work sheet managing program named Excel.

References

1. N. I. Akhiezer and M. G. Krein, "Some questions in the theory of moments", *Translations of mathematical monographs*, 2, AMS., Providence, R.I., 1962.
2. L. Donatiello and V. Grassi, "On evaluating the cumulative performance distribution of fault-tolerant computer systems", *IEEE Tr. on Computers*, 1991.
3. W.K. Grassmann, "Means and variances of time averages in markovian environment", *European Journal of Operational Research*, Vol. 31, pp 132 – 139, 1987.
4. R. Iyer, L. Donatiello and P. Heidelberger, "Analysis of performability for stochastic models of fault-tolerant systems", *IEEE Tr. on Comp.*, pp 902 – 907, 1986.
5. V. Kulkarni, V. Nicola and K. Trivedi, "On modeling the performance and reliability of multi-mode computer systems", *J. of Syst. and Sw.*, pp 175 – 183, 1986.
6. H. Nabli and B. Sericola, "Performability analysis: A new algorithm", *IEEE Tr. on Computers*, C-45(4), pp 491 – 494, 1996.
7. S. Rácz, "Numerical analysis of communication systems through Markov reward models", *Ph. D. thesis*, Technical University of Budapest, 2000.
8. S. Rácz, B. P. Tóth and M. Telek, "MRMSolve: A Tool for Transient Analysis of Large Markov Reward Models", In *Tools 2000*, pp 337 – 340, LNCS 1786, 2000.
9. S. Rácz, M. Telek and G. Fodor, "Link Capacity Sharing Between Guaranteed- and Best Effort Service on an ATM Transmission Link under GoS Constraints", *Telecommunication Systems*, Vol. 17:1,2, 2001.
10. E. De Souza e Silva and H.R. Gail, "An algorithm to calculate transient distribution of cumulative rate and impulse based reward", *Stoch. Models*, pp 509 – 536, 1998.
11. R. Smith, K. Trivedi and A.V. Ramesh, "Performability analysis: Measures, an algorithm and a case study", *IEEE Tr. on Computers*, C-37, pp 406 – 417, 1988.
12. T. Stieltjes, "Reserches sur les fractions continues", *Ann. Fac. Sci. Univ. Toulouse*, Vol. 2, pp J 1 – 122 , 1894.
13. Aldo Tagliani, "Existence and stability of a discrete probability distribution by maximum entropy approach", *Applied Math. and Computation*, pp 105 – 114, 2000.
14. Miklós Telek and Sándor Rácz, "Numerical analysis of large Markov reward models", *Performance Evaluation*, Vol. 36&37, pp 95 – 114, August 1999.

PhFit: A General Phase-Type Fitting Tool*

András Horváth and Miklós Telek

Dept. of Telecommunications, Technical University of Budapest, 1521 Budapest, Hungary, {horvath,telek}@webspn.hit.bme.hu

Abstract. PhFit, a new Phase-type fitting tool is presented in this paper. The presented tool is novel from several aspects. It allows for approximating distributions or set of samples not only by continuous but by discrete Phase-type distributions as well. The implemented algorithms separate the fitting of the *body* and the *tail* part of the distribution which results in satisfactory fitting also for heavy-tail distributions. Moreover, PhFit allows the user to choose the distance measure according to which the fitting is performed.

1 Introduction

In the recent decades, a lot of research was carried out to handle stochastic models in which durations are Phase-type (PH) distributed. Queuing models with PH distributed interarrival times and/or PH distributed service times are considered in numerous papers. In addition, PH distributions are introduced into different modeling formalisms, e.g. Petri Nets (PN).

In order to exploit advances in handling models with PH distributed activity durations, one needs algorithms to determine the parameters of the applied PH distribution. The two main classes of fitting methods differ in the kind of information they utilize. The methods that use *incomplete* information to perform the fitting results in a PH distribution whose selected parameters match those parameters of the original distribution. These methods typically use the moments of the original distribution. Nevertheless, it is possible to use other parameters as well like, for example, the procedure proposed in [3] that uses the value of the complementary cumulative distribution function (ccdf) at a given set of points. The methods that use the *complete* distribution to perform fitting, i.e. the fitting is aimed at minimizing the *distance* between the original and the approximating distribution according to a given way of measuring the distance between the two distributions. MLAPH and EMPHT implement the maximum-likelihood principle which results in minimizing the cross entropy. The procedure presented in [4] gives the possibility to apply an arbitrary distance measure (a measure of the difference between the original and the approximating PH distribution).

Naturally, it is possible to combine the above concepts in a single fitting procedure. Given a set of samples, MEDA provides a PH distribution whose

* This work was partially supported by Hungarian Scientific Research Fund (OTKA) under Grant No. T-34972.

T. Field et al. (Eds.): TOOLS 2002, LNCS 2324, pp. 82–91, 2002.

first three moments are identical to the empirical moments given by the samples, and, moreover, it minimizes the area difference between the empirical and the approximating cumulative distribution function. A detailed comparison of all the above mentioned fitting procedures can be found in [5].

PhFit performs the fitting using the combined algorithm described in [4]. The body of the distribution is fitted according to a distance measure chosen by the user, while the tail is fitted applying the heuristic method of [3]. In this paper, in addition to the description of the tool, the method described in [4] is reformulated for fitting discrete PH distributions as well.

The paper is organized as follows. Section 2 gives a short overview of both continuous and discrete PH distributions and their properties. Section 3 describes the algorithm implemented in the tool to approximate distributions. Application of the tool is illustrated in Section 4 and the paper is concluded in Section 5.

2 Phase-Type Distributions

A DPH distribution is the distribution of the time to absorption in a DTMC with n transient states and one absorbing state. The one-step transition probability matrix of the corresponding DTMC can be partitioned as

$$\widehat{\boldsymbol{B}} = \begin{bmatrix} \boldsymbol{B} & \boldsymbol{b} \\ \boldsymbol{0} & 1 \end{bmatrix} \tag{1}$$

where $\boldsymbol{B} = [b_{ij}]$ is the $(n \times n)$ matrix collecting the transition probabilities among the transient states, $\boldsymbol{b} = [b_{i,n+1}]^T, 1 \leq i \leq n$ is a vector of length n that groups the probabilities from any state to the absorbing one, and $\boldsymbol{0}$ is the zero vector. The initial probability vector $\widehat{\boldsymbol{\alpha}} = [\boldsymbol{\alpha}, \alpha_{n+1}]$ is of length $(n+1)$ with $\sum_{j=1}^{n} \alpha_j = 1 - \alpha_{n+1}$. In the tool described hereinafter, we consider only the class of DPH distributions for which $\alpha_{n+1} = 0$.

Similarly, a CPH distribution is the distribution of the time to absorption in a CTMC with n transient states and one absorbing state. The infinitesimal generator of the CTMC $\widehat{\mathbf{Q}}$ can be partitioned in the following way:

$$\widehat{\boldsymbol{Q}} = \begin{bmatrix} \boldsymbol{Q} & \boldsymbol{q} \\ \boldsymbol{0} & 0 \end{bmatrix} \tag{2}$$

where $\boldsymbol{Q}$ is a $(n \times n)$ matrix that describes the transient behavior of the *CTMC* and $\boldsymbol{q}$ is a column vector of length n that groups the transition rates to the absorbing state. Let $\hat{\boldsymbol{\alpha}} = [\boldsymbol{\alpha},\ \alpha_{n+1}]$ be the $(n+1)$ initial probability (row) vector with $\sum_{i=1}^{n} \alpha_i = 1 - \alpha_{n+1}$. The tuple $(\boldsymbol{\alpha}, \boldsymbol{Q})$ is called the representation of the CPH, and n the order.

Some properties of continuous and discrete PH distributions are summarized in Table 1, where $\boldsymbol{e}$ denotes the vector with all entries equal 1.

Table 1. Properties of PH distributions

Property	Discrete PH	Continuous PH
probability density (mass) function	$f_i = \boldsymbol{\alpha}\boldsymbol{B}^{i-1}\boldsymbol{b}$	$f(x) = \boldsymbol{\alpha}\exp(\boldsymbol{Q}x)\boldsymbol{q}$
	$f_i \geq 0$	$f(x) > 0,\ x > 0$
cumulative distribution function	$F_i = 1 - \boldsymbol{\alpha}\boldsymbol{B}^i\boldsymbol{e}$	$F(x) = 1 - \boldsymbol{\alpha}\exp(\boldsymbol{Q}x)\boldsymbol{e}$
min. coefficient of variation ($n > 0$)	≥ 0	$\geq 1/n$
max. coefficient of variation ($n > 1$)	∞	∞
support	finite or infinite	infinite
tail decay	geometric	exponential

3 Fitting According to Distribution Functions

3.1 Fitting Method for Arbitrary Distance Measure

The aim of PH fitting is to find a PH distribution with such parameters that according to a given measure the PH distribution is close to the distribution that we aim at approximating. The parameters to be found are the initial probability vector and the transition matrix. In case of an n-phase PH distribution, the number of free parameters in the initial probability vector is $n-1$ when $F(0) = 0$ and n when $F(0) \geq 0$, while it is n^2 in the transition matrix. In order to decrease the number of free parameters, only cyclic Phase-type (APH) distributions are considered[1].

Since any ACPH or ADPH distribution of order n can be transformed into the canonical form (CF1) in Figure 1 [2,1], the approximating PH distribution is looked for in this form, described by the vectors $\boldsymbol{a}$ and $\boldsymbol{q}$. This way the number of free parameters is decreased to $2n - 1$.

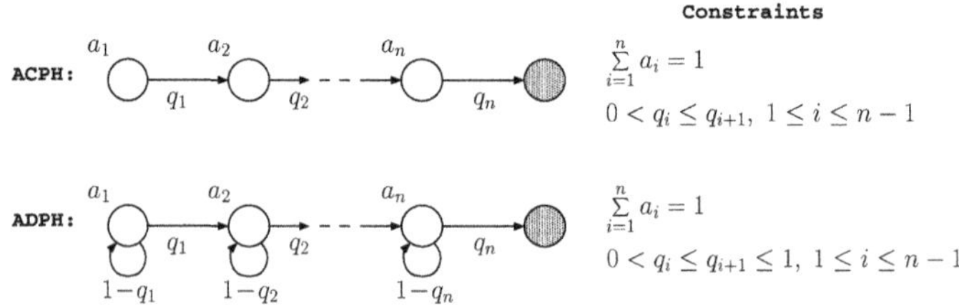

Fig. 1. Canonical form for ACPH and ADPH

The fitting is performed according to a predefined distance measure. Table 2 recites common measures that are implemented in PhFit, where $f(\cdot)$ ($f_.$) denotes the probability density function, pdf, (probability mass function, pmf) of the original and $\hat{f}(\cdot)$ ($\hat{f}_.$) of the approximating CPH (DPH) distribution.

[1] The procedure described in this section would be able to fit any Phase type structure by relaxing some constraints.

Table 2. Distance measures

Distance Measure	Continuous case	Discrete case
Relative entropy	$\int_0^\infty f(t)\, log\left(\frac{f(t)}{\hat{f}(t)}\right) dt$	$\sum_{i=1}^\infty f_i\, log\left(\frac{f_i}{\hat{f}_i}\right)$
pdf area difference	$\int_0^\infty \mid \hat{f}(t) - f(t) \mid dt$	$\sum_{i=1}^\infty \mid \hat{f}_i - f_i \mid$
cdf area difference	$\int_0^\infty (\hat{F}(t) - F(t))^2\, dt$	

The PH fitting algorithm is designed to find the vectors $\boldsymbol{a}$ and $\boldsymbol{q}$ with which the distance between the approximating PH distribution and the original distribution -denoted by $\mathcal{D}(f_{PH}(\boldsymbol{a}, \boldsymbol{q}), f)$- is minimal. The algorithm implemented in the PhFit is the following. The initial point $(\boldsymbol{a}^{(0)}, \boldsymbol{q}^{(0)})$ is the *best* of 1000 random generated pairs of vectors (satisfying the constraints of the applied canonical form) with proper mean. The *best* means the one that gives the least distance according to the applied distance measure. The distance measure $\mathcal{D}(f_{PH}(\boldsymbol{a}^{(0)}, \boldsymbol{q}^{(0)}), f)$ is evaluated numerically.

Starting from the initial guess, the non-linear optimization problem is solved by an iterative linearization method. In each step the partial derivatives with respect to the parameters $(\boldsymbol{a}^{(i)}, \boldsymbol{q}^{(i)})$ are numerically computed:

$$\frac{\partial \mathcal{D}(f_{PH}(\boldsymbol{a}^{(i)}, \boldsymbol{q}^{(i)}), f)}{\partial a_j^{(i)}}, \qquad \frac{\partial \mathcal{D}(f_{PH}(\boldsymbol{a}^{(i)}, \boldsymbol{q}^{(i)}), f)}{\partial q_j^{(i)}}, \qquad j = 1, ..., n.$$

Then, the simplex method is applied to determine the direction in which the distance measure decreases optimally. The constraints of the linear programming is given by probabilistic constraints (the initial probabilities have to sum up to one and, in the discrete case, $0 \leq q_j^{(i+1)} \leq 1, 1 \leq q \leq n$), by the restriction on the structure of the PH distribution (entries of $\boldsymbol{q}^{(i+1)}$ are increasing) and by confining the change of parameters (since the derivatives are valid only in a small area around $(\boldsymbol{a}^{(i)}, \boldsymbol{q}^{(i)})$). A search is performed in the direction indicated by the linear programming. The next point of the iteration $(\boldsymbol{a}^{(i+1)}, \boldsymbol{q}^{(i+1)})$ is chosen to be the border of the linearized area (defined by the allowed maximum change in the parameters) in the optimal direction if the goal function is decreasing in that direction all the way to the border of the area. The next point is set to the (first) minimum if the goal function has a minimum in the optimal direction inside the linearized area. The iteration is stopped if the relative difference of the parameters in consecutive iteration steps are less than a predefined limit (10^{-5}), or if the number of iterations reaches the predefined limit (1000). The allowed relative change of the parameters greater than 10^{-3} is less than Δ, where Δ starts from 0.1 and is multiplied by 0.995 in each step.

3.2 Fitting Heavy-Tailed Distributions

Recent experiences have shown that the method described in Section 3.1 does not provide satisfactory goodness of fitting for distributions with heavy tail [4]. In [3], Feldman and Whitt suggest a simple, heuristic method to fit heavy-tail behavior with mixture of exponential distributions. Their method is computationally cheap, provides good fitting of the tail behavior but it has the disadvantage of being restricted to decreasing probability density functions. In [4] the method described in Section 3.1 and the heuristic method of [3] are combined into a powerful general PH fitting algorithm that is capable of capturing both heavy-tails and not only decreasing probability functions.

Hereinafter we reformulate the method of Feldman and Whitt for discrete distributions, and then, in Section 3.3 describe in short the combined method introduced in [4].

The resulting fitting distribution is a mixture of geometric distributions, and, as a consequence, belongs to the family of DPH distributions. Figure 2 depicts the mixture of m geometric distributions as a DPH distribution and gives the related constraints. The probability mass function and the cumulative distribution function are given by

$$f_n = \sum_{i=1}^{m} b_i (1 - r_i)^{n-1} r_i, \text{ and } F_n = 1 - \sum_{i=1}^{m} b_i (1 - r_i)^n .$$

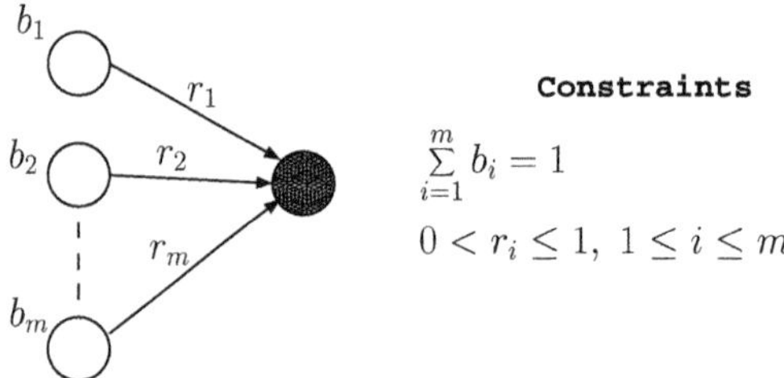

Fig. 2. Mixture of geometric distributions

The proposed heuristic method determines the parameters of the mixture of m geometric distributions ($\boldsymbol{b}$ and $\boldsymbol{r}$) in a recursive manner such that the ccdf of the resulting distribution is "very close" to that of the original distribution at $2m - 1$ points. The $2m - 1$ points are the following:

$$0 < t_c = t_m < t_{m-1} < bt_{m-1} < \ldots < t_1 = t_d < bt_1,$$

with

$$t_i = t_d \delta^{-i+1}, \quad i \in \{1, 2, \ldots, m\}, \quad \text{where } \delta = \sqrt[m-1]{\frac{t_d}{t_c}} \ , \text{ and } b < \delta.$$

In order to avoid cumbersome notation, we assume that the introduced $2m - 1$ points are integers. If this is not the case, instead of a point t its integer part $\lfloor t \rfloor$ has to be used.

The above $2m-1$ points are defined by m, t_c, t_d and b. The points t_c and t_d define the lower and the upper bound of the range in which the distribution is considered. In the present section t_c will be set always to 1. The upper bound t_d can be defined by deciding how far the tail should be considered. The constant b, which defines the distance of adjacent points, is defined by z as $b = \delta^z$ with $0 < z < 1$. Further considerations for the choice of the values m, t_c, t_d and b can be found in [3] for the continuous version of the algorithm. These considerations are valid for the discrete case as well.

First, the algorithm provides such b_1 and r_1 that the ccdf of the approximating distribution matches the ccdf of the original distribution F_t^c at t_1 and bt_1. This is done by assuming that the other components of the mixture will not impact the ccdf significantly at t_1 and bt_1, i.e. we assume that $r_i, i = 2, \ldots, m$ will be significantly larger than r_1, and so that

$$\sum_{i=1}^{m} b_i(1-r_i)^t \sim b_1(1-r_1)^t \quad \text{for } t \geq t_1. \tag{3}$$

The parameters b_1 and r_1 are obtained by arranging the two equations

$$b_1(1-r_1)^{t_1} = F_{t_1}^c, \quad \text{and} \quad b_1(1-r_1)^{bt_1} = F_{bt_1}^c,$$

as

$$r_1 = 1 - \sqrt[t_1(1-b)]{\frac{F_{t_1}^c}{F_{bt_1}^c}}, \quad \text{and} \quad b_1 = F_{t_1}^c(1-r_1)^{-t_1}.$$

In the ith step, $2 \leq i \leq m-1$, the algorithm determines b_i and r_i such way that the ccdf of the mixture of geometric distributions matches F_t^c at t_i and bt_i. As when determining b_i and r_i, this is done by assuming that $r_j, j = i+1, \ldots, m$ will be significantly smaller than r_i, so that

$$\sum_{j=1}^{m} b_j(1-r_j)^t \sim \sum_{j=1}^{i} b_j(1-r_j)^t, \qquad \text{for } t \geq t_i. \tag{4}$$

The parameters b_i and r_i are obtained by the equalities

$$b_i(1-r_i)^{t_i} = F_{t_i}^c - \sum_{j=1}^{i-1} b_j(1-r_j)^{t_i}, \tag{5}$$

$$b_i(1-r_i)^{bt_i} = F_{bt_i}^c - \sum_{j=1}^{i-1} b_j(1-r_j)^{bt_i}, \tag{6}$$

where the contribution of the components with index lower than i is considered by the extraction on the right hand side of the equations. Using the notation

$$F_{i,t}^c = F_t^c - \sum_{j=1}^{i-1} b_j(1-r_j)^t,$$

rearranging (5) and (6), b_i and r_i are obtained as

$$r_i = 1 - \sqrt[t_i(1-b)]{\frac{F^c_{i,t_i}}{F^c_{i,bt_i}}}, \qquad b_i = F^c_{i,t_i}\,(1 - r_i)^{-t_i}. \tag{7}$$

In the mth step, since b_m is already determined by the constraint

$$\sum_{i=1}^{m} b_i = 1, \text{ as } b_m = 1 - \sum_{i=1}^{m-1} b_i,$$

we cannot have both (5) and (6) for $i = m$. So that, instead of using both the points t_m and bt_m, we determine r_m using

$$b_i(1 - r_i)^{t_i} = F^c_{m,t_i}, \text{ as } r_i = 1 - \sqrt[t_i]{\frac{F^c_{m,t_i}}{b_i}}.$$

We have guarantee neither that properties (3) and (4), which are assumed throughout the procedure, hold, nor that the sum of the initial probabilities associated with the hyper-geometric part of the Phase type structure ($\sum_{i=1}^{m} b_i$) is lower than 1. However, these can be easily checked after the procedure is completed, and in general it is not a problem to define the set of points in such way that these properties hold. For example, if the sum is greater than 1 it may help to increase t_d or m. It is discussed in details in [3] how the $2m - 1$ points may be chosen efficiently.

In order to illustrate the application of the procedure, let us define the following heavy-tail discrete distribution function with Pareto-like tail:

$$f_n = \frac{1}{\mathcal{Z}(a+1)} n^{-(1+a)}, \tag{8}$$

where $\mathcal{Z}(\cdot)$ denotes the Riemann zeta-function and a determines the decay of the tail.

Figure 3 and 4 depicts the probability mass function (pmf) of approximations of the above defined distribution for different values of a with either 6 or 8 phases.

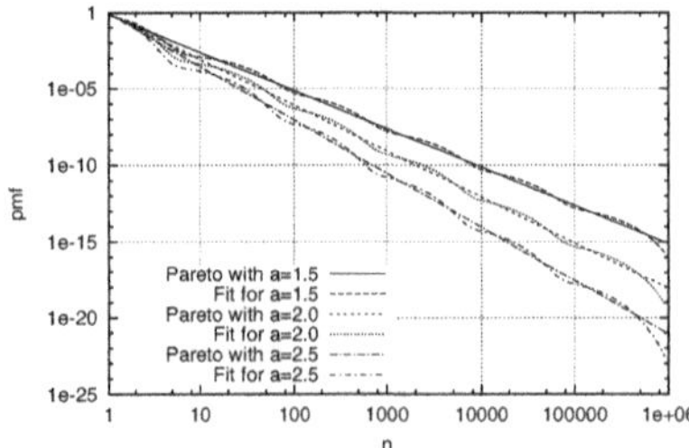

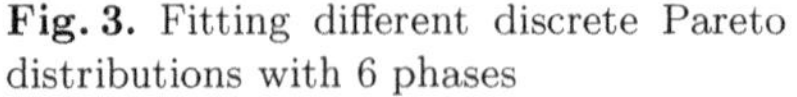

Fig. 3. Fitting different discrete Pareto distributions with 6 phases

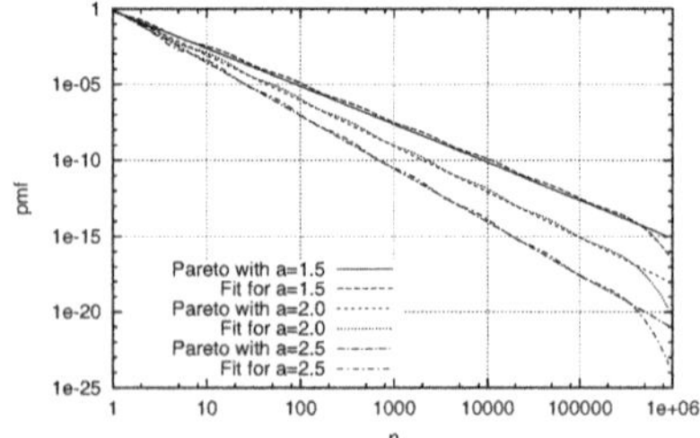

Fig. 4. Fitting different discrete Pareto distributions with 8 phases

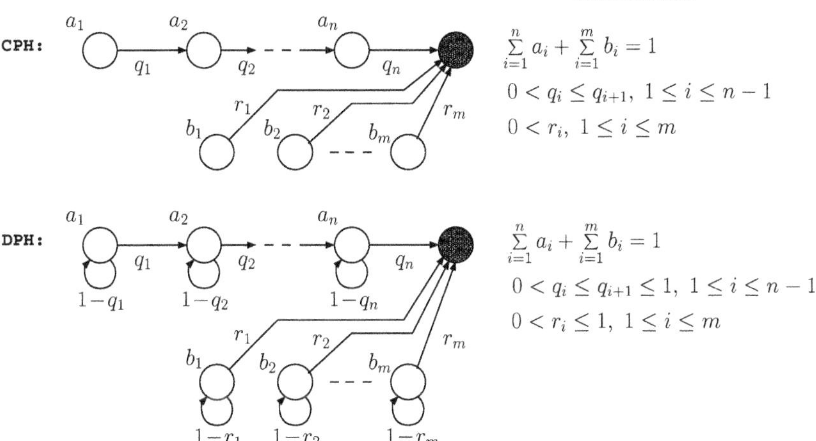

Fig. 5. Structured by CF1 and mixtures

3.3 Combined Fitting Method

As we mentioned before, the heuristic method presented in Section 3.2 provides distributions with decreasing probability mass function. In order to relax this limitation, the heuristic method is combined with the one described in Section 3.1. Figure 5 depicts the structure and constraints of the resulting PH distribution both for continuous and discrete case.

To this end, we modify the step of the algorithm in which b_m and r_m are defined. As the parameters $b_i, r_i, 2 \leq i \leq m-1$, also the parameters b_m and r_m are defined based on (7). Now the requirement for $\sum_{i=1}^{m} b_i$ is to be less than 1.

In case of fitting with continuous PH distributions the continuous counterpart of the algorithm presented in Section 3.2 is used to determine $\boldsymbol{b}$ and $\boldsymbol{r}$ (see [4]).

Having $\boldsymbol{b}$ and $\boldsymbol{r}$ we use the algorithm described in Section 3.1 to fit the body of the distribution with two differences:

1. Having the hyper-geometric (or hyper-exponential) part the constraint on the initial probabilities modifies to $\sum_{i=1}^{n} a_i = 1 - \sum_{i=1}^{m} b_i$.
2. The structure of the approximate PH distribution differs from the one used before (Figure 1). The parameters associated with the additional m phases ($\boldsymbol{b}$ and $\boldsymbol{r}$) are fixed during this stage of the fitting process.

4 Application of the Tool

In this section, we illustrate how the tool can be applied to fit a set of data, in particular, we describe an example with heavy-tail behavior. The fittings are performed with discrete PH distributions.

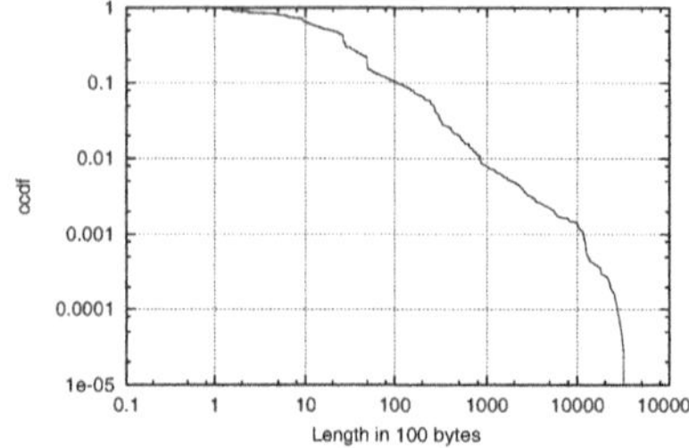

Fig. 6. Experimental ccdf of the length of requests arriving to the server

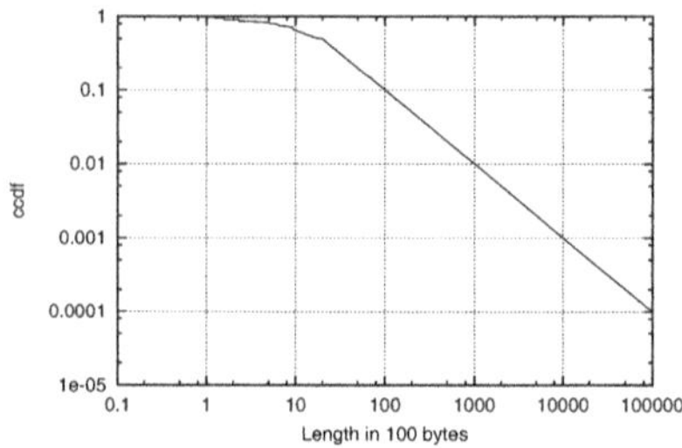

Fig. 7. The ccdf applied during the fitting

Table 3. Parameters used to perform fitting

Parameter	Fitting I	Fitting II
Number of phases to fit the body	4	
Measure to fit the body	cdf area difference	
Upper bound of fitting the body	100	
Number of phases to fit the tail	3	
Lower limit of fitting the tail (t_3)	100	
Upper limit of fitting the tail (t_1)	10^4	6×10^3
Distance of adjacent points (z)	0.4	

The chosen data set, which is called EPA_HTTP and can be downloaded from [6], contains a day of HTTP logs with about 40000 entries. The experimental ccdf of the length of the requests is depicted in Figure 6.

The linearity of the ccdf in the interval [20:10000] (Figure 6) suggests that the tail behavior can be approximated accurately by polynomial (Pareto-like) tail. In order to determine the parameter of the tail, regression is applied to the log-log curve of the ccdf in the interval [20:10000]. Having the parameter, the tail of the experimental ccdf is replaced with a polynomial tail in the interval $[20 : \infty]$ as depicted in Figure 7. The value of the ccdf at 20 is 0.503, so that the tail has this value at 20, and then it has the decay given by the regression.

Having defined the shape and parameter of the tail, the parameters of the fitting itself have to be chosen. Hereinafter two fittings are presented. Table 3 collects the parameters of these two fittings. For both cases, the stepsize of the DPH distribution corresponds to 100 bytes.

Figure 8 and 9 depicts the body and the tail of the ccdf of the two approximations of the data set. As it can be observed, the only difference between the two fittings is the upper limit of the tail fitting. This difference is clearly reflected by the tails of the two PH distributions. One could easily find such upper limit for the fitting of the tail that the tail of the ccdf of the approximating distribution breaks down where the tail of the experimental ccdf breaks down. However, in general, it is not easy to justify that the end of the tail of the random variable

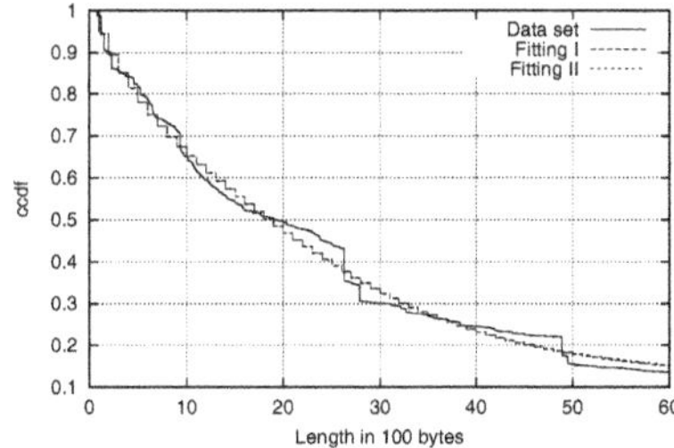

Fig. 8. Body of the approximating distributions

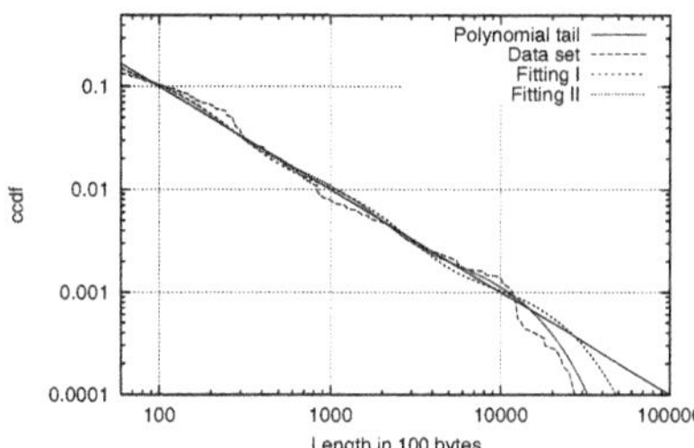

Fig. 9. Tail of the approximating distributions

under observation is really there where it is suggested to be by its samples. The break we see in the experimental ccdf can easily be caused by the low number of observations as well. This is why -apart from the difficulty of identifying it automatically- we allow the user to choose the upper limit of the tail fitting.

5 Conclusion

This paper presented a new Phase-type fitting tool, PhFit. PhFit offers advanced functionality compared to existing tools from several points of view: i) PhFit allows fitting with both discrete and continuous PH distributions; ii) PhFit offers special treatment to fit slowly decaying tail behavior; iii) PhFit allows to set the measure according to which the fitting is performed.

References

1. A. Bobbio, A. Horváth, M. Scarpa, and M. Telek. Acyclic discrete phase type distributions: Properties and a parameter estimation algorithm. Technical Report of Budapest University of Technology and Economics, 2000.
2. A. Cumani. On the canonical representation of homogeneous Markov processes modelling failure-time distributions. *Microelectronics and Reliability*, 22:583–602, 1982.
3. A. Feldman and W. Whitt. Fitting mixtures of exponentials to long-tail distributions to analyze network performance models. *Performance Evaluation*, 31:245–279, 1998.
4. A. Horváth and M. Telek. Approximating heavy tailed behavior with phase type distributions. In *3rd International Conference on Matrix-Analytic Methods in Stochastic models*, Leuven, Belgium, 2000.
5. A. Lang and J. L. Arthur. Parameter approximation for phase-type distributions. In S. R. Chakravarty and A. S. Alfa, editors, *Matrix-analytic methods in stochastic models*, pages 151–206. Marcel Dekker, Inc., 1996.
6. EPA-HTTP Trace, The Internet Traffic Archive. At `http://ita.ee.lbl.gov`. Collected by Laura Bottomley (`laurab@ee.duke.edu`) of Duke University.

Traffic Modeling of IP Networks Using the Batch Markovian Arrival Process

Alexander Klemm, Christoph Lindemann, and Marco Lohmann

University of Dortmund
Department of Computer Science
August-Schmidt-Str. 12
44227 Dortmund, Germany
{ak, cl, ml}@ls4.cs.uni-dortmund.de
http://www4.cs.uni-dortmund.de/~Lindemann/

Abstract. In this paper, we identify the batch Markovian arrival process (BMAP) as an analytically tractable model of choice for aggregated traffic modeling of IP networks. The key idea of this aggregated traffic model lies in customizing the batch Markovian arrival process such that the different lengths of IP packets are represented by rewards (i.e., batch sizes of arrivals) of the BMAP. The utilization of the BMAP is encouraged by the observation that IP packet lengths follow to a large extent a discrete distribution. A comparative study with the MMPP and the Poisson process illustrates the effectiveness of the customized BMAP for IP traffic modeling by visual inspection of sample paths over four different time-scales, by presenting important statistical properties, and by analysis of traffic burstiness using R/S statistics. Additionally, we show that the BMAP model outperforms MMPP and Poisson traffic models by comparison of queuing performance.

1 Introduction

Traffic characterization and modeling constitute important steps towards understanding and solving performance-related problems in future IP networks. In order to perform reliable traffic characterization and traffic modeling accurate and detailed IP network measurements have to be conducted. Various detailed measurements have been performed in local area networks (LAN), e.g. [6], [11], as well as in wide area networks (WAN), e.g. [7], [10]. The central idea of traffic modeling lies in constructing models that capture important statistical properties of the underlying measured trace data [2]. For IP traffic, important statistical properties are *burstiness* and *self-similarity*. Intuitively, this means that measured IP traffic shows noticeable sustained periods with arrivals above the mean (i.e., bursts) over a wide range of different time-scales [15]. Aggregated traffic models capture the entire traffic stream without explicitly considering individual traffic sources, e.g. the traffic originated by individual users. The problem of accurately capturing these properties in aggregated traffic models has been solved for non-analytically tractable models but is still subject of current research interest for analytically tractable models. Non-analytically tractable models, e.g.

T. Field et al. (Eds.): TOOLS 2002, LNCS 2324, pp. 92–110, 2002.

fractional Gaussian noise (fGN) and fractional autoregressive integrated moving average (fARIMA), naturally capture burstiness as well as self-similarity. Various research papers have subjected these models, e.g., Ledesma and Liu reported the effective construction of fGN in [8].

For analytically tractable models, e.g. the Markov-modulated Poisson process (MMPP, [4]), recent work has been proposed that utilizes the MMPP in order to mimic self-similar behavior [1], [16]. Skelly, Schwartz, and Dixit [13] utilized the MMPP for video traffic modeling. They described a simple and efficient method for parameter estimation of a general MMPP based on the match of the marginal distribution of the arrival rate. The class of batch Markovian arrival process (BMAP, [9]) includes the well known Poisson-process, MMPP, and Markovian arrival process (MAP, [9]) as special cases and additionally associates rewards (i.e., batch sizes of arrivals) to arrival-times. However, due to the addition of rewards the BMAP provides a more comprehensive model for representing IP traffic than the MMPP or the MAP, while still being analytically tractable.

The challenge for employing BMAPs to model IP traffic constitutes the proper parameter estimation for this arrival process from the given trace data. In fact, measured trace data does not contain all statistical properties required for the unique specification of a corresponding BMAP. Due to this incomplete data, the parameters for a BMAP cannot be properly estimated by standard statistical techniques, e.g. moment matching. Dempster, Laird, and Rubin introduced the expectation-maximization (EM) algorithm [3] for computing maximum likelihood estimates from incomplete data. Ryden tailored the EM algorithm for the MMPP and developed an implementation [12]. To the best of our knowledge, tailoring the EM algorithm for BMAPs, developing a numerical stable implementation and utilizing the BMAP for traffic modeling is an open research problem.

In this paper, we present a detailed analysis of IP traffic measurements recently conducted at an Internet service provider (ISP) dial-up link. We derive parameterized general distributions for session-level, connection-level, and packet-level characteristics according to different application-types. Because of the nature of generally distributed sources, this detailed synthetic traffic model constitutes a non-analytically tractable traffic model. According to [14], our analysis confirms that 80% of the mass of the packet-length distribution is concentrated on the three packet length 40 bytes, 576 bytes, and 1500 bytes. Based on these observations, we introduce an aggregated traffic model for IP networks that is both analytically tractable and closely captures the statistics of the measured traffic data. The key idea of this aggregated traffic model lies in customizing the batch Markovian arrival process such that these different lengths of IP packets are represented by rewards of the BMAP. We introduce an efficient method for estimating the parameters of a BMAP with the EM algorithm. Furthermore, we present computational formulas for the E-step of the EM algorithm and show how to utilize the EM algorithm for the effective parameter estimation of BMAPs. In order to show the advantage of the BMAP modeling approach over other widely used analytically tractable models, we compare the customized

BMAP with the MMPP and the Poisson process by means of visual inspection of sample paths over four different time-scales, by presenting important statistical properties, by formal analysis of traffic burstiness using R/S statistics, and by queuing system analysis.

The paper is organized as follows. Section 2 presents the analysis and characterization of the measured IP traffic. To make the paper self-contained, Sect. 3 recalls the definition and properties of the BMAP and provides a primer to the EM algorithm. Moreover, we introduce effective computational formulas for the expectation step (E-step) and the maximization step (M-step) tailored to the BMAP, and present a framework for traffic modeling of aggregated IP traffic that utilizes the BMAP. In Sect. 4, a comparative study illustrates the effectiveness and accuracy of the proposed traffic model. Finally, concluding remarks are given.

2 IP Traffic Measurement and Characterization

2.1 Dial-Up Modem/ISDN Traffic Measurements

We conducted detailed traffic measurements at the ISP dial-up modem/ISDN link of the University of Dortmund. At the time of performing these measurements in January 2001 the university offered free Internet access for students and employees, so the users' costs depend on the telecommunication-tariffs and session duration only. Therefore, measurements in an ISP environment can be regarded as characteristic for session-oriented Internet traffic. In the four-week measurement period approximately 110,000 user sessions with a total data volume of 120 GB have been logged.

The measurements were performed by the software package *TCPdump* running on a Linux host that sniffs all IP packets in the Ethernet segment between the MaxTNT dial-up routers and the Internet router (see Fig. 1). For all IP datagrams sourced or targeted by dial-up modems the TCP/IP header information in conjunction with a timestamp of the arrival-time have been recorded and stored for offline processing. The header information includes source and target IP addresses, the port numbers, the packet length, and the TCP header flags. In addition to the header trace we use the log-files generated by the MaxTNT dial-up routers. For each dial-up session they provide information about session start- and end-time, the assigned IP address, and the link bandwidth. By aligning the measured trace data with the MaxTNT log-files, the header trace can be split into separate trace files for each dial-up session. Furthermore, the session interarrival-time and session volume distributions are determined.

In order to derive the connection interarrival-time and connection volume distributions, for each application-type all TCP connections within each session are reconstructed by means of IP address and port number pairs. We observed that many HTTP connections persist a relatively long period related to the transmitted data volume. Further investigations of this phenomenon showed, that many HTTP connections are closed with a *reset* packet, which is transmitted a very large time after the other packets of this connection. This is caused by

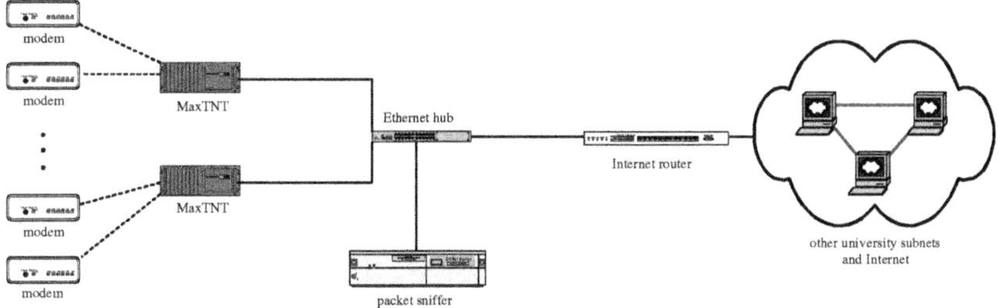

Fig. 1. Measurement environment at the dial-up modem/ISDN links

the HTTP implementations of most Internet browsers, which keep connections open in order to transmit several documents within the same connection and thus avoid overhead for connection establishment. The reset packets abortively release the connections when the user terminates the HTTP application. For our traffic analysis we ignore these "late reset" packets for the following reasons: (1) they do not contribute to the transmission of documents and (2) they affect the packet interarrival-time distribution in a way that the measured data cannot be well represented by fittings to general distributions.

2.2 Traffic Analysis and Traffic Characterization

This section presents fundamental characteristics of the IP traffic measured at our university. First, we analyzed the trace data in order to obtain the application usage pattern of the modem/ISDN users. The data volume fractions are broken down to HTTP, FTP, e-mail, Napster, UDP, and other TCP applications. As Fig. 2 shows, HTTP applications, e.g. Web browsing, dominate with a fraction of 73%, followed by the popular music download application Napster with 9% and e-mail with 6% of the overall transmitted data volume. Note, that the court decision against Napster was not effective when conducting the measurements. The relatively small fraction of 2% for FTP applications and the observation, that there is a significant number of HTTP connections comprising very large data volume, show that file downloads are increasingly performed via HTTP. With 4% of the total data volume UDP applications form a relatively small part of the overall application usage. Taking into account that DNS lookups are performed via UDP the fraction of real-time UDP applications is so small, that realistic statistical measures about real-time traffic cannot be derived from this data. Therefore, we focus our investigations on non real-time traffic.

The analysis is performed at three different traffic-levels: session-level, connection-level, and packet-level.

1. The session-level describes the dial-up behavior of the individual users, characterized by the session interarrival-time distribution and the session data-volume distribution.

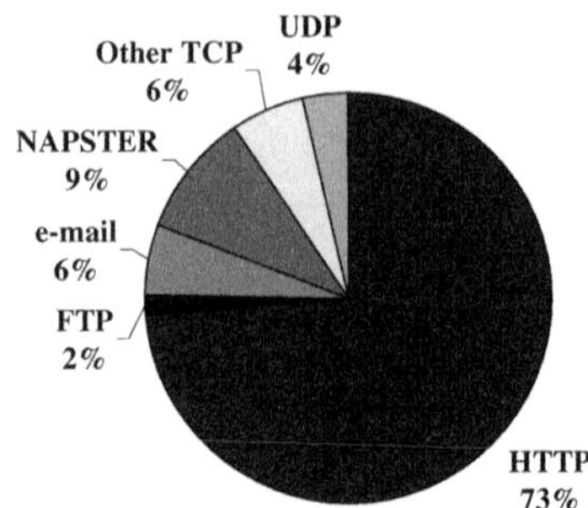

Fig. 2. Application usage distribution with respect to data volume

2. The connection-level describes for each individual application the corresponding distribution of connection interarrival-times within a user-session as well as the distribution of connection data volume.
3. The packet-level characterizes the packet interarrival-time distribution and the packet length distribution within the application specific connections.

According to the users' different application-types parameterized distributions have been derived for the statistical measures at each traffic-level. We observe that each statistical measure comprises a *characteristic distribution*, e.g. the HTTP connection interarrival-times are distributed according to a lognormal distribution. In order to find such a characteristic distribution for a specific statistical measure we use a least-squares regression, utilizing the following set of probability density functions (pdf): Lognormal, Pareto, Weibull, Gamma, and Exponential. The detailed statistics of this analysis are omitted because of space limitations.

The analysis of the packet length distributions revealed that the packet lengths of all relevant TCP applications follow to a large extent a discrete distribution. In Fig. 3 the probability density of packet lengths is depicted and shows, that the packet lengths 40 bytes, 576 bytes and 1500 bytes dominate with an overall percentage of 80% of all TCP packets. This observation can be explained with the maximum transfer units (MTU) of the used network protocols. Most application protocols like FTP, HTTP, POP3, and SMTP are used to transfer relatively large data blocks (as opposed to many small packets in real-time applications). Therefore, in order to reduce overhead, as many packets as possible are filled up to the MTU of the underlying protocol, which typically comprises 1500 bytes in the Ethernet protocol and 576 bytes in the serial line Internet protocol (SLIP). The choice between a MTU of 576 bytes or 1500 bytes depends on the network configuration of the dial-up client. The huge amount of 40 bytes packets is to a large extent caused by TCP acknowledgments with an empty data field. Recall, that the TCP and IP headers without any options consist of 40 bytes. Furthermore, we observe that the remaining packet lengths are distributed uniformly between 40 bytes and 1500 bytes. Table 1 presents the fractions of these

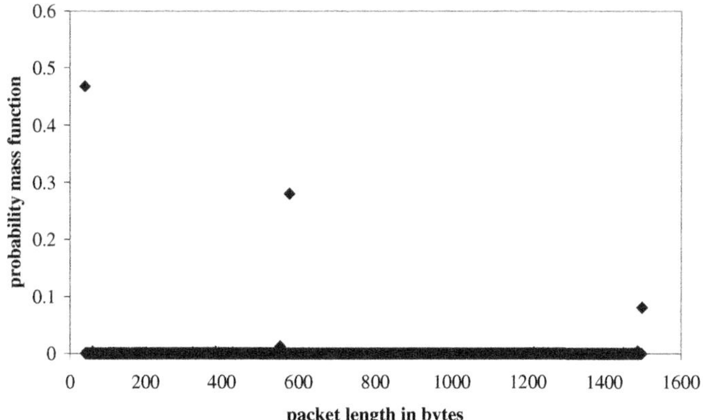

Fig. 3. Probability mass function of TCP packets lengths

discrete packet lengths for HTTP, e-mail, Napster, and FTP. In contrast to TCP packets, UDP packet lengths follow lognormal distribution. Note, that similar characteristics concerning discrete packet size distributions have been observed for local area networks (LAN) and wide area networks (WAN), [14]. Thus, the basic ideas outlined in the next section can also be applied for traffic modeling in LAN and WAN.

The statistical properties on the three different traffic-levels can be employed for synthetic traffic generation that an individual user generates: A single user can run different applications that may be concurrently active, e.g. WWW browsing while downloading Napster music files. Each application is completely described by its statistical properties. These statistical properties comprise an alternating process of ON- and OFF-periods with some application specific length or data volume distribution, respectively. During an ON-period, i.e. an application specific connection, the user applies the appropriate application in an active fashion. The interarrival-time between two successive connection starting points of the same application-type and the data volume of each connection are drawn from the parameterized general distributions. Within each ON-period the packet

Table 1. Fractions of different packet lengths in overall traffic

	40 bytes	576 bytes	1500 bytes	other
HTTP	46.77%	27.96%	8.10%	17.17%
e-mail	38.25%	25.98%	9.51%	26.26%
Napster	34.98%	45.54%	4.18%	15.30%
FTP	40.43%	18.08%	9.33%	32.16%

arrival process is completely captured by the packet interarrival-times, drawn according to an application dependent distribution, and the corresponding packet lengths. The overall traffic stream of one user constitutes of the superposition of the packet arrival processes of all application connections within the user's session. Moreover, new users enter the considered system environment according to a session interarrival-time distribution and leave the system after transferring a specific data-volume drawn according to a session volume distribution.

Because of the nature of generally distributed sources, this detailed synthetic traffic model constitutes a non-analytically tractable traffic model. Thus, this traffic model can be utilized as traffic generation component in simulation studies on a per-user basis. Based on this model, performance studies for changing traffic characteristics can easily be conducted by new parameterization of the characteristic distribution for the considered statistical measure. This is easily accomplished by changing the values of expectation and standard deviation of the characteristic distribution of the considered statistical measure. For example, experiments for increasing file sizes can be easily performed by changing the parameters of the connection data volume distribution. In order to get an analytically tractable traffic model that can be integrated as a traffic generation component within analytical models, we identified the batch Markovian arrival process. The utilization of the BMAP is encouraged by the observation that IP packet lengths follow to a large extent a discrete distribution. The key idea of this aggregated traffic model lies in customizing the batch Markovian arrival process such that the different lengths of IP packets are represented by rewards of the BMAP. Recall, that aggregated traffic models capture the entire traffic stream without explicitly considering individual traffic sources. Thus, the aggregated traffic stream comprises a sequence of interarrival-times of packet arrivals and packet lengths.

3 Traffic Modeling Using the Batch Markovian Arrival Process

3.1 The Batch Markovian Arrival Process

The batch Markovian arrival process (BMAP) belongs to the class of Markov renewal processes. Consider a continuous-time Markov chain (CTMC, [9]) with $(N+1)$ states $\{0, 1, \ldots, N\}$, where the states $\{1, 2, \ldots, N\}$ are transient states and 0 is the absorbing state. Moreover, $\boldsymbol{\pi}$ denotes the initial state probability vector of the CTMC. Based on this governing CTMC, the BMAP can be constructed as follows: The CTMC evolves until an absorption in state 0 occurs. The chain is then instantaneously restarted in one of the transient states $\{1, 2, \ldots, N\}$. When restarting the BMAP after absorption in a transient state j, the probability for selecting state j is allowed to depend on state i from which absorption has occurred. Thus, the distribution of the next arrival may depend on the previous history. Furthermore, there may exist multiple paths between two states i and j corresponding to different rewards, i.e., batch sizes of arrivals. Due to the addition of rewards the BMAP provides a more comprehensive model for representing IP traffic than the MMPP and the MAP, while still being analytically tractable.

Formally, assume the BMAP is in a transient state i for an exponentially distributed time with rate λ_i. When the sojourn time has elapsed, there are $(M+1)$ possible cases for state transitions: With probability $\boldsymbol{P}(m)_{i,j}$ the BMAP enters the absorbing state 0 and an arrival of batch size m occurs. Then, the process is instantaneously restarted in state j. Note that the selection of state j $(1 \leq j \leq N)$ and batch size m $(1 \leq m \leq M)$ is uniquely determined by $\boldsymbol{P}(m)_{i,j}$. On the other hand, with probability $\boldsymbol{P}(0)_{i,j}$ the BMAP enters another transient state j, $j \neq i$, without arrivals. We can define $\boldsymbol{D}(0)_{i,j} = \lambda_i \cdot \boldsymbol{P}(0)_{i,j}$ for $i \neq j$, $\boldsymbol{D}(0)_{i,i} = -\lambda_i$, and $\boldsymbol{D}(m)_{i,j} = \lambda_i \cdot \boldsymbol{P}(m)_{i,j}$. Here, $\boldsymbol{D}(0)$ defines the rate matrix of transitions without arrivals, whereas the matrices $\boldsymbol{D}(m)$ define rate matrices of transitions with arrivals of batch size m $(1 \leq m \leq M)$. Summing up $\boldsymbol{D}(0)$ and $\boldsymbol{D}(m)$ $(1 \leq m \leq M)$ leads to $\boldsymbol{D} = \boldsymbol{D}(0) + \sum_{m=1}^{M} \boldsymbol{D}(m)$, where $\boldsymbol{D}$ is the infinitesimal generator matrix of the CTMC underlying the BMAP. Furthermore, the matrix $\boldsymbol{f}_m(t)$ of probability density functions (pdf) defines probability laws for state changes in the CTMC from i to j with an arrival of batch size m at time t. The matrices $\boldsymbol{f}_m(t)$ are given by $\boldsymbol{f}_m(t) = e^{\boldsymbol{D}(0)\,t} \cdot \boldsymbol{D}(m)$.

3.2 Parameter Estimation Procedure

We derived a computational efficient and numerical robust EM (expectation-maximization) algorithm [3] for the parameter estimation process of BMAPs, i.e., estimation of the parameter set $\boldsymbol{\Phi}$(comprising the probability vector $\boldsymbol{\pi}$ and the transition rate matrices $\boldsymbol{D}(0), \ldots, \boldsymbol{D}(M)$. The EM algorithm implements maximum likelihood estimation in case of incomplete data. Such incomplete data can be thought of as partial observations of a larger experiment. In fact, for a BMAP only arrival-times and batch sizes of arrivals, e.g. arrival-times of IP packets and their packet lengths, are observable. All state changes in the governing CTMC not hitting the absorbing state are not observable and, thus, *cannot* be derived from measured trace data.

Formally, suppose that $\boldsymbol{y}$ is the observable part of a considered experiment. This experiment can be described completely by $\boldsymbol{y}$ and the non-observable data $\boldsymbol{x}$ denoted as the *missing data*. Let $\mathcal{L}(\boldsymbol{\Phi}, \boldsymbol{y})$ be the *likelihood* of a parameter set $\boldsymbol{\Phi}$ given the observation $\boldsymbol{y}$ and let $\mathcal{L}^c(\boldsymbol{\Phi}, \boldsymbol{x}, \boldsymbol{y})$ be the so-called *complete likelihood* of the parameter set $\boldsymbol{\Phi}$ including the missing data $\boldsymbol{x}$. Assume $\boldsymbol{y} = \{(t_1, b_1), (t_2, b_2), \ldots, (t_n, b_n)\}$ is the observed sequence of interarrival-times t_k and the corresponding batch sizes b_k. Define $\Delta t_k = t_k - t_{k-1}$ for $1 \leq k \leq n$. Then, the likelihood of a BMAP with parameter set $\boldsymbol{\Phi}$ is given by:

$$\mathcal{L}(\boldsymbol{\Phi}, \boldsymbol{y}) = \boldsymbol{\pi} \cdot \prod_{k=1}^{n} \boldsymbol{f}_{b_k}(\Delta t_k) \cdot \mathbf{1} \ . \tag{1}$$

Recall, that in (1), $\boldsymbol{\pi}$ denotes the initial state probability vector of the CTMC, $\boldsymbol{f}_{b_k}(t)$ defines the matrix of probability density functions, and $\boldsymbol{\Phi}$ is a specific parameter set for the BMAP comprising $\boldsymbol{\pi}$ and the transition rate matrices

$\boldsymbol{D}(0), \ldots, \boldsymbol{D}(M)$. The vector $\mathbf{1}$ represents a vector of appropriate dimension comprising 1s in each entry. Note, that the (logarithm of the) likelihood measures the quality of the estimated parameter set.

The EM algorithm iteratively determines estimates of the missing parameter set $\boldsymbol{\Phi}$ of the BMAP. Denote by $\boldsymbol{\Phi}(r)$ the parameter set calculated in the r-th iteration of the EM algorithm. We denote further by $\mathbb{P}_{\boldsymbol{\Phi}}$ and $\mathbb{E}_{\boldsymbol{\Phi}}$ the conditional probability and the conditional expectation given the estimate $\boldsymbol{\Phi}$, respectively. As shown in [3], the estimate

$$\hat{\boldsymbol{\Phi}} = \arg\max_{\Phi} \left\{ \mathbb{E}_{\boldsymbol{\Phi}(r)} \left(\log \mathcal{L}^c \left(\boldsymbol{\Phi}, \boldsymbol{x}, \boldsymbol{y} \right) | \boldsymbol{y} \right) \right\} \quad , \text{for } r = 0,\ 1,\ 2,\ \ldots, \tag{2}$$

satisfies $\mathcal{L}(\hat{\boldsymbol{\Phi}}, \boldsymbol{y}) \geq \mathcal{L}(\boldsymbol{\Phi}(r), \boldsymbol{y})$ and $\boldsymbol{\Phi}(r+1) = \hat{\boldsymbol{\Phi}}$ is the estimate for the parameter set determined in the $(r+1)$-th step of the algorithm. This iterative procedure is repeated until a predefined maximum number of iterations is reached or until convergence criteria holds. That is, each component of $\boldsymbol{\Phi}(r)$ and $\boldsymbol{\Phi}(r+1)$ differs only up to a predefined ϵ, respectively. The computation of the conditional expectation in (2) is called the E-step whereas the derivation of the maximum in (2) constitutes the M-step of the EM algorithm. As described in [3], the likelihood $\mathcal{L}(\boldsymbol{\Phi}, \boldsymbol{y})$ is highly non-linear in $\boldsymbol{\Phi}$ and is difficult to maximize, while the complete likelihood $\mathcal{L}^c(\boldsymbol{\Phi}, \boldsymbol{x}, \boldsymbol{y})$ employed in the M-step can often be computed in closed form. This is the main reason for the widespread use of the EM algorithm. A further advantage of the EM algorithm over other maximum likelihood methods lies in the good convergence behavior of the iterative scheme.

3.3 Effective Computational Formulas for the BMAP

Recall, the observed data in a BMAP is $\{(t_1, b_1), (t_2, b_2), \ldots, (t_n, b_n)\}$. The generator of the CTMC $\{X(t) : t \geq 0\}$ underlying the BMAP constitutes the missing data. We assume that $N(t)$ is the counting process of the batch sizes for arrivals. Let $\{t_k : 1 \leq k \leq n\}$ be the sequence of arrival-times. Without loss of generality, we assume $t_0 = 0$ and $t_n = T$. Considering the likelihood estimates of the EM algorithm introduced above, we show in the following how to maximize the likelihood for the parameter set of a BMAP.

First of all, we have to define the complete likelihood of the BMAP using the observed data $\boldsymbol{y}$ and the non-observable data $\boldsymbol{x}$. Let $m(k)$ be the number of transient states entered during the k-th interarrival-time. Moreover, let $i_l(k)$ and $s_l(k)$ denote the l-th transient state and the sojourn time of the l-th transient state during the k-th interarrival-time, respectively. Then the complete likelihood of the BMAP is given by

$$\begin{aligned} \mathcal{L}^c(\boldsymbol{\Phi}, \boldsymbol{x}, \boldsymbol{y}) = \boldsymbol{\pi}_{i_0(1)} \times \prod_{k=1}^{n} \prod_{l=0}^{m(k)-1} & \lambda_{i_l(k)} \cdot e^{-\lambda_{i_l(k)} \cdot s_l(k)} \cdot \boldsymbol{P}(0)_{i_l(k), i_{l+1}(k)} \\ & \times \lambda_{i_{m(k)}(k)} \cdot e^{-\lambda_{i_{m(k)}(k)} \cdot s_{m(k)}(k)} \cdot \boldsymbol{P}(b_k)_{i_{m(k)}(k), i_0(k+1)} \end{aligned} \quad , \tag{3}$$

where $\boldsymbol{P}(m)$ and λ_i are defined as above, $\sum_{j=0}^{m(k)} s_j(k) = \Delta t_k$, and b_k is the batch size of the k-th arrival. The first term of the right hand side of (3) specifies the probability of starting the CTMC in state $i_0(1)$. For each arrival epoch of the BMAP, the second term describes the transient trajectory up to a state $i_{m(k)}(k)$ from which absorption occurs. The last portion of (3) represents the transition from the transient state $i_{m(k)}(k)$ to the absorbing state 0 and the restarting of the process in state $i_0(k+1)$ with an arrival of batch size b_k.

In order to simplify the notation in the estimation step, we define the *sufficient statistics* $\boldsymbol{T}$, $\boldsymbol{A}(1), \ldots, \boldsymbol{A}(M)$ and $\boldsymbol{s}$ as follows. For $1 \leq i, j \leq N$ and $i \neq j$ we define $\boldsymbol{T}_{i,j}$ as:

$$\boldsymbol{T}_{i,j} = \#\{t \,|\, 0 \leq t \leq T, X(t-) = i, X(t) = j, N(t) = N(t-)\} \; . \tag{4}$$

$\boldsymbol{T}_{i,j}$ is the number of *transient state transitions* from state i to state j without an arrival. For $1 \leq m \leq M$ and $1 \leq i, j \leq N$ we define $\boldsymbol{A}(m)_{i,j}$ as:

$$\begin{aligned} \boldsymbol{A}(m)_{i,j} = \; \#\{t_k \,|\, 1 \leq k \leq n, X(t_k-) = i, X(t_k) = j,& \\ N(t_k) = N(t_k-) + m\}& \; . \end{aligned} \tag{5}$$

$\boldsymbol{A}(m)_{i,j}$ is the number of *absorbing state transitions* from state i to state j with an arrival of batch size m at arrival-times t_k. Finally, for $1 \leq i \leq N$ we define $\boldsymbol{s}_i$ as:

$$\boldsymbol{s}_i = \int_0^T \mathcal{I}(X(t) = i)\, dt \;\; , \text{ where } \mathcal{I}(\cdot) \text{ is the indicator function.} \tag{6}$$

$\boldsymbol{s}_i$ captures the total time the CTMC resides in state i.

The key idea of these sufficient statistics is to capture the complete likelihood expression in a more intuitive fashion. Typically, the sufficient statistics can be determined by numerically tractable characteristics of the CTMC. Applying some calculus, these sufficient statistics can easily be used to rewrite and simplify the expression of the complete likelihood in (3). That is:

$$\begin{aligned} \mathcal{L}^c(\boldsymbol{\Phi}, \boldsymbol{x}, \boldsymbol{y}) = \prod_{i=1}^{N} \pi_i^{\mathcal{I}(X(0)=i)} \cdot \prod_{i=1}^{N} e^{\boldsymbol{D}(0)_{i,i} \cdot \boldsymbol{s}_i} \cdot \prod_{i=1}^{N} \prod_{j=1, j \neq i}^{N} \boldsymbol{D}(0)_{i,j}^{\boldsymbol{T}_{i,j}}& \\ \cdot \prod_{m=1}^{M} \prod_{i=1}^{N} \prod_{j=1}^{N} \boldsymbol{D}(m)_{i,j}^{\boldsymbol{A}(m)_{i,j}}& \; . \end{aligned} \tag{7}$$

Intuitively, the second product of (7) symbolizes the sojourn time of the CTMC for each state i. The third product of (7) captures the behavior for all transient state transitions between states i and j. Similarly, the last product of (7) represents the absorbing state transitions between states i and j with arrivals of batch size m.

When adopting (2) to the considered case of a BMAP, we have to recognize that $\boldsymbol{y} = \{(t_1, b_1), (t_2, b_2), \ldots, (t_n, b_n)\}$ is completely characterized by the counting process $N(t)$ introduced above. This leads directly to (8) with the following abbreviations (9) to (12) for ease of notation. In (8), the maximization $\hat{\boldsymbol{\pi}}_i$ of $\boldsymbol{\pi}_i$ is already given in a natural way. Furthermore, it can be shown that using the definition of a BMAP and appropriate partial differentiation, (8) is maximized by (13). Additionally to the maximization by partial differentiation, each of the expressions in (13) utilizes the *maximized sufficient statistics* (9) to (12) in a very intuitive manner. For example, $\hat{\boldsymbol{D}}(0)_{i,j}$ is the ratio of the total number of transient state transitions between states i and j and the total time spent in state i.

The expressions (8) to (12) in Fig. 4 represent the E-step of the EM algorithm, while the expressions in Fig. 5 represent the M-Step of the EM algorithm. For ease of notation, we define $\boldsymbol{R}(k)$ for $k = n+1, \ldots, 1$ as $\boldsymbol{R}(n+1) = \mathbf{1}$ and $\boldsymbol{R}(k) = \boldsymbol{f}_{b_k}(\Delta t_k) \cdot \boldsymbol{R}(k+1)$. Let $\mathbf{1}_i$ denote the i-th unity column vector. Equations (10) and (11) can be transformed to integrals over matrix exponentials by means of probability laws. We omit these transformations as well as the detailed evaluation of (9) and (12) because of space limitations. Already for an MMPP, the problem with the practical applicability of the EM algorithm for parameter estimation lies in the stable numerical computation of integrals over matrix exponentials as specified in such equations. Ryden [12] proposed a diagonalization method to compute $e^{\boldsymbol{Q}t}$, but this approach relies on the diagonalization property of the matrix $\boldsymbol{Q}$. It is known that decomposition techniques like diagonalization are in general not stable numerical methods for computing matrix exponentials.

For efficient and reliable calculation of (integrals over) matrix exponentials of the transformed equations of (9) to (12), we have derived effective computational formulas based on the randomization technique [5] enhanced by a stable calculation of Poisson probabilities. Again, we omit these formulas because of space limitations. Furthermore, we adopted the scaling procedure proposed in [12] for calculating the sufficient statistics $\hat{\boldsymbol{T}}_{i,j}$, $\hat{\boldsymbol{A}}(1)_{i,j}, \ldots, \hat{\boldsymbol{A}}(M)_{i,j}$, $\hat{\boldsymbol{s}}_i$, $\hat{\boldsymbol{\pi}}_i$, and the likelihood estimate $\mathcal{L}(\boldsymbol{\Phi}(r), \boldsymbol{y})$. This scaling procedure is necessary because these quantities can take extremely small or extremely large values.

3.4 BMAP Traffic Modeling Framework

As stated above, we customize the batch Markovian arrival process such that different lengths of IP packets are represented by rewards of the BMAP. In order to represent an aggregated traffic stream utilizing the BMAP, we apply the parameter estimation procedure introduced above for a BMAP with N transient states and M distinct batch sizes. The choice of N and M is crucial for an accurate capturing of the interarrival process and the reward process of the aggregated traffic, respectively. Note, that the run-time of the EM algorithm scales linearly with respect to the number of samples n of the considered trace, but is independent of the choice of M. Thus, this modeling approach can be effectively applied for arbitrary packet length (i.e., reward) distributions by an increasing value of M.

The underlying trace file, which constitutes the aggregated traffic, comprises packet interarrival-times as well as the corresponding packet lengths. Recalling the BMAP definition, the mapping process of packet lengths to BMAP rewards results in a BMAP parameter set, i.e., $\boldsymbol{\pi}$ and $\boldsymbol{D}(0), \ldots, \boldsymbol{D}(M)$, of reasonable size $(M+1)N^2+N$. We map the packet lengths onto the discrete packet lengths s_m, for $1 \leq m \leq M$, where s_m is the average packet length of all packets of the considered trace comprising packet lengths between $L \cdot (m-1)/M$ bytes and

E-step:

$$\mathbb{E}_{\boldsymbol{\Phi}(r)}\left\{\log \mathcal{L}^c\left(\boldsymbol{\Phi},\boldsymbol{x},\boldsymbol{y}\right)|N\left(u\right),0\le u\le T\right\} = \sum_{i=1}^{N}\hat{\boldsymbol{\pi}}_i\cdot\log\boldsymbol{\pi}_i + \sum_{i=1}^{N}\boldsymbol{D}\left(0\right)_{i,i}\cdot\hat{\boldsymbol{s}}_i$$
$$+\sum_{i=1}^{N}\sum_{j=1,j\ne i}^{N}\hat{\boldsymbol{T}}_{i,j}\cdot\log\boldsymbol{D}\left(0\right)_{i,j} + \sum_{m=1}^{M}\sum_{i=1}^{N}\sum_{j=1}^{N}\hat{\boldsymbol{A}}\left(m\right)_{i,j}\cdot\log\boldsymbol{D}\left(m\right)_{i,j} \ , \tag{8}$$

where

$$\hat{\boldsymbol{\pi}}_i = \mathbb{P}_{\boldsymbol{\Phi}(r)}\left\{X\left(0\right)=i\,|N\left(u\right),0\le u\le T\right\} \ , \tag{9}$$

$$\hat{\boldsymbol{s}}_i = \mathbb{E}_{\boldsymbol{\Phi}(r)}\left\{s_i\,|N\left(u\right),0\le u\le T\right\} = \int_0^T \mathbb{P}_{\boldsymbol{\Phi}(r)}\left(X\left(t\right)=i\,|N\left(u\right),0\le u\le T\right)dt \ , \tag{10}$$

$$\hat{\boldsymbol{T}}_{i,j} = \int_0^T \mathbb{P}_{\boldsymbol{\Phi}(r)}\left\{X\left(t-\right)=i,X\left(t\right)=j,N\left(t\right)=N\left(t-\right)|N\left(u\right),0\le u\le T\right\}dt \ , \tag{11}$$

$$\hat{\boldsymbol{A}}\left(m\right)_{i,j} = \sum_{k=1}^{n}\mathbb{P}_{\boldsymbol{\Phi}(r)}\left\{X\left(t_k-\right)=i,X\left(t_k\right)=j,N\left(t_k\right)=N\left(t_k-\right)+m \;|N\left(u\right),0\le u\le T\right\} \ . \tag{12}$$

Fig. 4. E-step for parameter estimation of BMAPs

M-step:

$$\hat{\boldsymbol{\pi}}_i = \boldsymbol{\pi}_i\left(r\right)\cdot\mathbf{1}_i\cdot\boldsymbol{R}(1)/\mathcal{L}\left(\boldsymbol{\Phi}\left(r\right),\boldsymbol{y}\right) \ , \text{ for } i=1,\ldots,N \ .$$
$$\hat{\boldsymbol{D}}\left(0\right)_{i,j} = \hat{\boldsymbol{T}}_{i,j}/\hat{\boldsymbol{s}}_i \text{ and } \hat{\boldsymbol{D}}\left(m\right)_{i,j} = \hat{\boldsymbol{A}}\left(m\right)_{i,j}/\hat{\boldsymbol{s}}_i \ , \text{ for } i,j=1,\ldots,N \ . \tag{13}$$
$$\hat{\boldsymbol{D}}\left(0\right)_{i,i} = -\sum_{j=1,j\ne i}^{N}\hat{\boldsymbol{D}}\left(0\right)_{i,j} - \sum_{m=1}^{M}\sum_{j=1}^{N}\hat{\boldsymbol{D}}\left(m\right)_{i,j} \ , \text{ for } i=1,\ldots,N \ .$$

Fig. 5. M-step for parameter estimation of BMAPs

$L\cdot m/M$ bytes, where L denotes the maximum packet length of the considered IP network. In the case of Ethernet LAN the maximum transfer unit (MTU) of 1500 bytes determines this maximum packet length. Therefore, arrivals with batch size m, $1\le m\le M$, represent packet arrivals with a packet length of s_m bytes. Note, that this mapping process is applied for ease of notation only. Without this mapping, the proposed estimation procedure can be applied for estimating the rate matrices $\boldsymbol{D}\left(0\right),\boldsymbol{D}\left(s_1\right),\ldots,\boldsymbol{D}\left(s_M\right)$, where rate matrices $\boldsymbol{D}\left(m\right)$, $m\notin\{0,s_1,\ldots,s_M\}$, are empty. The estimation of these matrices obviously requires the same computational effort. Moreover, the estimated matrices are identical to the matrices $\boldsymbol{D}\left(0\right),\ldots,\boldsymbol{D}\left(M\right)$, which are computed when the mapping process is applied.

4 Comparative Study of Aggregated IP Traffic Modeling

As stated above, the synthetic traffic model comprising generally distributed sources is not analytically tractable. Thus, it can be employed for simulation studies only. To overcome this restriction, we utilize the traffic modeling framework introduced in the previous section with a trace file comprising 1,500,000 samples (measured 10.00 a.m. 13 December 2000 at the dial-up modem/ISDN link). This trace file comprises packet interarrival-times and the corresponding packet lengths. Based on this trace file the BMAP parameter estimation procedure is applied for a 3-state BMAP ($N = 3$) with $M = 3$ distinct batch sizes. Recall, the choice of M is crucial for the mapping process of packet lengths to BMAP rewards and corresponds to, but is not restricted by the fact that a large amount of packets comprise three different packet lengths (see Table 1 and Fig. 3). Recalling the mapping process of packet lengths to BMAP rewards, arrivals with batch size m, $1 \leq m \leq M$, represent packet arrivals with a packet length of s_m bytes. The average packet lengths s_m ($M = 3$) of our measurements are as follows: $s_1 = 94$ bytes, $s_2 = 575$ bytes, and $s_3 = 1469$ bytes. The considered estimation procedure is quite effective and requires less than 20 minutes of CPU time on a Pentium III PC with 128 MB of main memory.

The following shows the effectiveness of our BMAP modeling approach, compared with a 3-state MMPP ($N = 3$) and Poisson process, by means of visual inspection of sample paths over multiple time-scales, by presenting important statistical properties, by formal analysis of traffic burstiness as well as by investigations of queuing behavior. Figures 6 and 7 plot sample paths of the measured traffic (Fig. 6, left) compared with the sample paths of the aggregated traffic streams of the customized BMAP (Fig. 6, right), the MMPP (Fig. 7, left), and the Poisson process (Fig. 7, right), respectively. For sample-path construction of the MMPP and the Poisson process, we associate the average packet length of all IP packets comprising 315 bytes to the arrival-times of the MMPP and the Poisson process. The aggregated traffic streams of the MMPP and the Poisson utilized for sample-path construction comprise the same number of samples as the measured trace file. Note, that the parameter matrices $\boldsymbol{D}(0)$ and $\boldsymbol{D}(1)$ of the MMPP have also been estimated by application of the EM algorithm for BMAP. This is accomplished by restriction of $\boldsymbol{D}(1)$ to diagonal entries that are associated with the state-dependent Poisson arrival-rates of the MMPP. The arrival-rate of the Poisson process is naturally given by the mean arrival-rate of the measured trace file. In order to show the effectiveness of our approach these sample paths are plotted on four different time-scales, i.e. 0.001 sec, 0.01 sec, 0.1 sec, and 1.0 sec. Figures 6 and 7 evidently show that the customized BMAP authentically captures the average transferred data volume per time unit and exhibits traffic burstiness over multiple time-scales in the considered scenario. Moreover, these sample paths show the clear advantage of the customized BMAP over the MMPP and the Poisson process, which fail to capture the original sample path over almost all time-scales.

Table 2 presents additionally statistical properties for the data rates of the measured traffic, the BMAP, the MMPP, and the Poisson process, on different time-scales in terms of mean, standard deviation, skewness, and kurtosis. Recall,

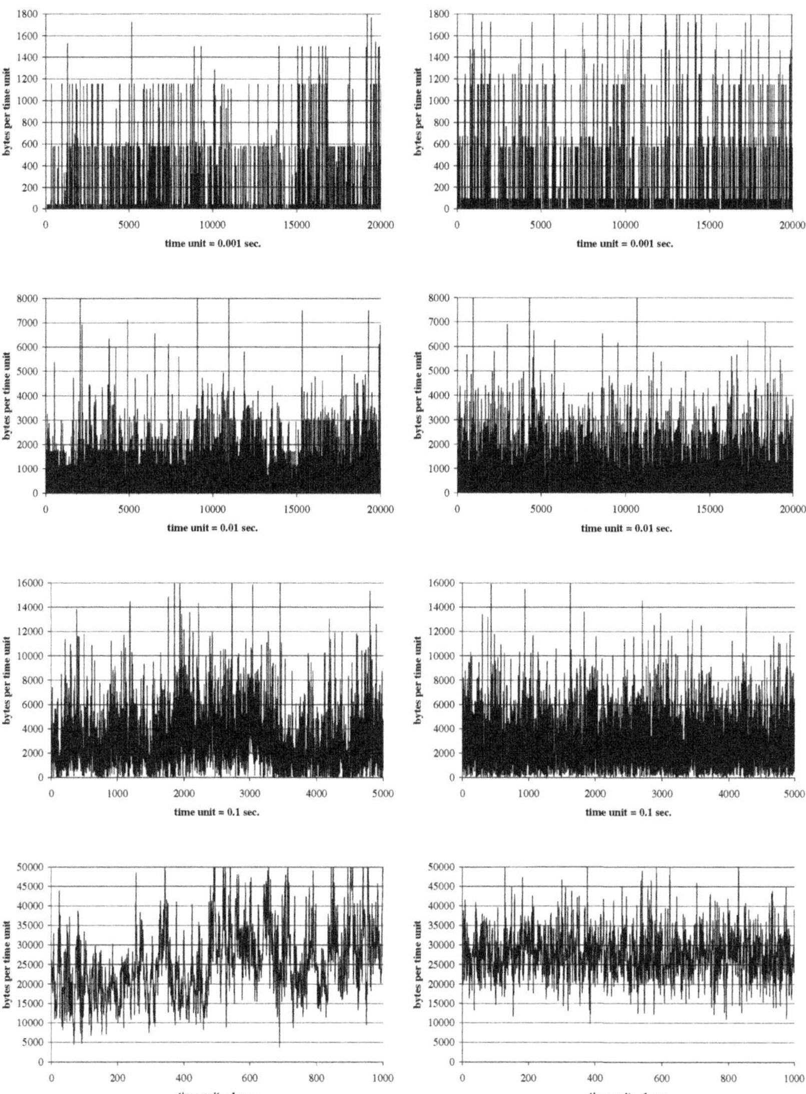

Fig. 6. Sample paths of the measured traffic (left) and the customized BMAP (right) at different time-scales

that the mean gives the center of the distribution and the standard deviation measures the dispersion about the mean. The third moment about the mean measures skewness, the lack of symmetry, while the forth moment measures

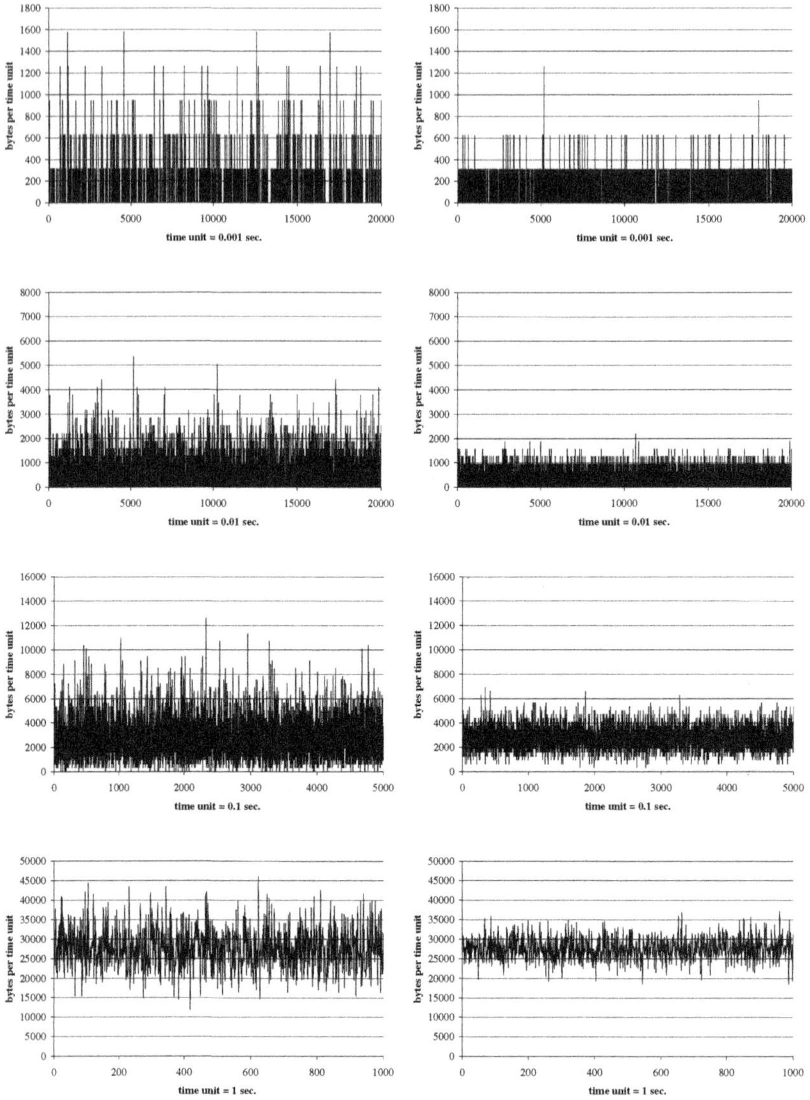

Fig. 7. Sample paths of the MMPP (left) and the Poisson process (right) at different time-scales

kurtosis, the degree to which the distribution is peaked. In Table 2, skewness and kurtosis are standardized by an appropriate power of the standard deviation. We observe, that mean and standard deviation of the measured traffic and

Table 2. Statistical properties of data rates on different time-scales

time unit in sec.	traffic model	mean	std. dev.	skewness	kurtosis
	measured traffic	27.63	153.02	6.72	52.77
0.001	customized BMAP	27.70	157.90	8.12	84.34
	MMPP	27.65	118.39	5.58	42.73
	Poisson process	27.65	93.37	3.38	14.46
	measured traffic	276.27	697.46	4.21	29.03
0.01	customized BMAP	277.01	662.32	3.82	23.14
	MMPP	276.47	491.13	2.81	13.84
	Poisson process	276.49	295.82	1.07	4.14
	measured traffic	2762.64	2240.81	1.44	6.15
0.1	customized BMAP	2770.10	2191.71	1.27	5.15
	MMPP	2764.61	1672.45	0.90	4.21
	Poisson process	2764.86	933.00	0.33	3.11
	measured traffic	27621.50	10954.80	0.60	3.21
1.0	customized BMAP	27697.30	6929.95	0.41	3.19
	MMPP	27643.70	5413.94	0.28	3.05
	Poisson process	27643.70	2972.29	0.03	2.94

the customized BMAP perform quite similar over the considered time-scales, with exception of the BMAPs standard deviation on the largest time-scale. The skewness of the measured traffic is quite similar on medium time-scales, i.e., 0.01 sec and 0.1 sec, while the customized BMAP overestimates the skewness on the smallest time-scale and underestimates it on the largest time-scale. Furthermore, the last column of Table 2 indicates, that kurtosis, i.e., peakedness, is well captured on the three largest time-scales, whereas the BMAP significantly exceeds the measured traffic on the smallest time-scale. This is, because on the smallest time-scale the various packet lengths of the measured traffic cannot be represented exactly by only three ($M = 3$) different reward values, i.e., packet lengths. This effect diminishes with increasing value of M. Moreover, Table 2 evidently shows, that the MMPP as well as the Poisson process are clearly inferior compared with the customized BMAP and loosely capture standard deviation, skewness and kurtosis, over all considered time-scales.

These observations are emphasized by the analysis of traffic burstiness, which can be expressed in terms of the Hurst parameter H. Figure 8 plots the R/S statistics [15] of the measured traffic, the customized BMAP, the MMPP as well as the Poisson process. The degree of traffic burstiness H, can easily derived by the slopes of linear regression plots of the R/S statistics. As expected, the Poisson process ($H = 0.5558$) fails to capture the traffic burstiness, while the MMPP ($H = 0.6408$) and the customized BMAP ($H = 0.6418$) both indicate a significant amount of traffic burstiness compared with the Hurst parameter of the measured traffic ($H = 0.6785$).

The practical applicability of our BMAP modeling approach can be emphasized by the analysis of the queuing performance. As proposed in [1], we utilize

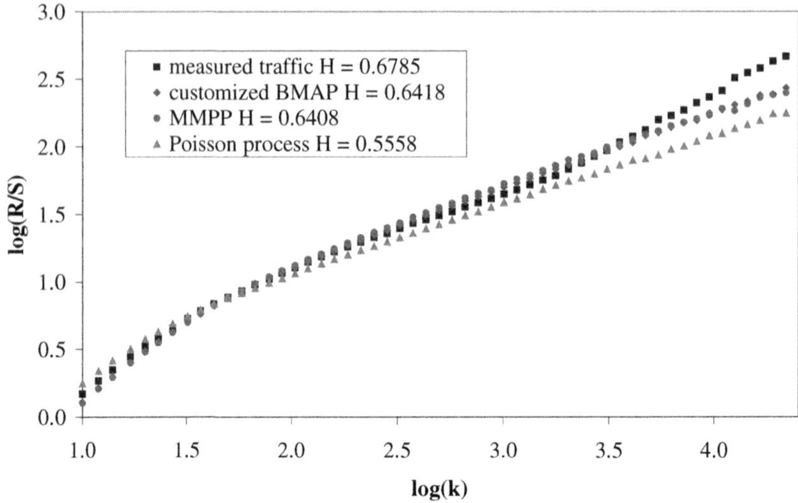

Fig. 8. R/S statistic plot of the trace and the analytically tractable models

a simple queuing model with deterministic service time and unlimited capacity for investigations of the complement distribution of the queue length. Figure 9 depicts the complement distribution of the queue length Q of the BMAP/D/1 queuing system, the MMPP/D/1 queuing system and the M/D/1 queuing system (using the Poisson process), compared with the simulations performed with the measured traffic for different traffic intensities ρ. It is obvious that the BMAP model shows a similar behavior in terms of queuing performance for low traffic intensities, i.e., $\rho = 0.3$ and $\rho = 0.4$. For traffic intensities of $\rho = 0.5$ and $\rho = 0.6$ the customized BMAP matches the distribution of the measured traffic up to medium queue length. As expected, the Poisson process performs badly for all considered traffic intensities. Obviously, the MMPP outperforms the Poisson process, but is significantly inferior in capturing the complement distribution of the queuing length, compared with the customized BMAP for all considered traffic intensities.

Conclusions

We present a detailed analysis of IP traffic measurements recently conducted at an Internet service provider (ISP) dial-up link and derive parameterized general distributions for session-level, connection-level, and packet-level characteristics. Moreover, we observe that almost all IP packets comprise three dominating packet lengths. Based on these observations, we introduce an aggregated traffic model for IP networks that is both analytically tractable and closely captures the statistics of the measured traffic data. The key idea of this aggregated traffic

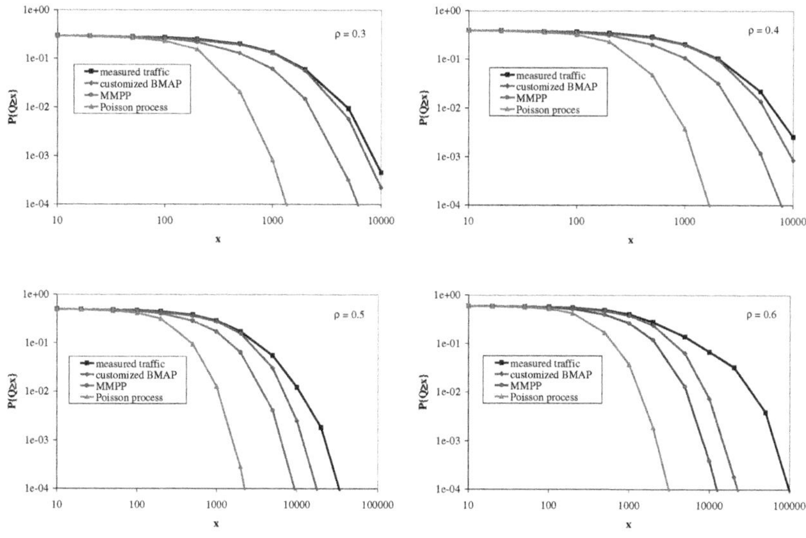

Fig. 9. Complement distribution of queue length Q of single server queue with deterministic service time for different traffic intensities ρ

model lies in customizing the batch Markovian arrival process such that these different lengths of IP packets are represented by rewards (i.e., batch sizes of arrivals) of the BMAP. We introduce an efficient method for estimating the parameters of a BMAP with the EM algorithm. In fact, we present efficient computational formulas for the E-step of the EM algorithm and show how to utilize the EM algorithm for the effective parameter estimation of BMAPs. In order to demonstrate the advantages of the BMAP modeling approach over other widely used analytically tractable models, we compare the customized BMAP with the MMPP and the Poisson process by means of visual inspection of sample paths over four different time-scales, by presenting important statistical properties, by formal analysis of traffic burstiness, and by queuing system analysis.

References

1. Andersson, S., Ryden, T.: Maximum Likelihood Estimation of a Structured MMPP with Applications to Traffic Modeling. Proc. 13th ITC Specialist Seminar on Measurement and Modeling of IP Traffic, Monterey CA (2000) 20.1–20.10
2. Ash, G.R.: Traffic Engineering & QoS Methods for IP-, ATM-, & TDM-Based Multiservice Networks. Internet Draft draft-ietf-tewg-qos-routing-01.txt (2001)
3. Dempster, A.P., Laird, N.M., Rubin, D.B.: Maximum Likelihood from Incomplete Data via the EM Algorithm. Journal of the Royal Statistical Society **39** (1976) 1–38

4. Fischer, W., Meier-Hellstern, K.: The Markov-modulated Poisson Process (MMPP) Cookbook. Performance Evaluation **18** (1993) 149–171
5. Gross, D., Miller, D.R.: The Randomization Technique as a Modeling Tool and Solution Procedure for Transient Markov Processes. Operations Research **32** (1984) 345–361
6. Kilpi, J., Norros, I.: Call Level Traffic Analysis of a Large ISP. Proc. 13th ITC Specialist Seminar on Measurement and Modeling of IP Traffic, Monterey CA (2000) 6.1–6.9
7. Kruse, H., Allman, M., Griner, J., Ostermann, S., Helvey, E.: Satellite Network Performance Measurements Using Simulated Multi-User Internet Traffic. Proc. 7th Int. Conf. on Telecommunication Systems (1999)
8. Ledesma, S., Liu, D.: Synthesis of Fractional Gaussian Noise using Linear Approximation for Generating Self-similar Network Traffic. Computer Communication Review **30** (2000) 4–17
9. Lucantoni, D. M.: New Results on the Single Server Queue with a Batch Markovian Arrival Process. Comm. in Statistics: Stochastic Models **7** (1991) 1–46
10. McCreary, S., Claffy K.C.: Trends in Wide Area IP Traffic Patterns: A View from Ames Internet Exchange. Proc. 13th ITC Specialist Seminar on Measurement and Modeling of IP Traffic, Monterey CA (2000) 1.1–1.12
11. Nuzman, C. J., Saniee, I., Sweldens, W., Weiss, A.: A Compound Model for TCP Connection Arrivals. Proc. 13th ITC Specialist Seminar on Measurement and Modeling of IP Traffic, Monterey CA (2000) 1–9
12. Ryden, T.: An EM Algorithm for Parameter Estimation in Markov Modulated Poisson Processes. Computational Statistics and Data Analysis **21** (1996) 431–447
13. Skelly, P., Schwartz, M., Dixit, S.: A Histogram-Based Model for Video Traffic Behavior in an ATM Multiplexer. IEEE Trans. on Networking **1** (1993) 446–459
14. Thompson, K., Miller, G.J., Wilder, R.: Wide-Area Internet Traffic Patterns and Characteristics. IEEE Network Magazine **11** (1997) 10–23
15. Willinger, W., Paxson, V., Taqqu, M.S.: Self-similarity and Heavy Tails: Structural Modeling of Network Traffic. In: A Practical Guide to Heavy Tails. Chapman & Hall (1998) 27–53
16. Yoshihara, T., Kasahara, S., Takahashi, Y.: Practical Time-Scale Fitting of Self-Similar Traffic with Markov-Modulated Poisson Process. Telecommunication Systems **17** (2001) 185–211

PEPA Nets: A Structured Performance Modelling Formalism

Stephen Gilmore[1], Jane Hillston[1], and Marina Ribaudo[2]

[1] Laboratory for Foundations of Computer Science, The University of Edinburgh, Edinburgh EH9 3JZ, Scotland. {stg,jeh}@dcs.ed.ac.uk

[2] Dipartimento di Informatica e Scienze dell'Informazione, Università di Genova, Via Dodecaneso 35, 16146 Genova, Italia. ribaudo@disi.unige.it

Abstract. In this paper we describe a formalism which uses the stochastic process algebra PEPA as the inscription language for labelled stochastic Petri nets. Viewed in another way, the net is used to provide a structure for combining related PEPA systems. The combined modelling language naturally represents such applications as mobile code systems where the PEPA terms are used to model the program code which moves between network hosts (the places in the net). We describe the implementation of a tool to support this modelling formalism and apply this to model a peer-to-peer filestore.

1 Introduction

Variants of Petri nets have been widely used in the description and performance analysis of computer, telecommunications and manufacturing systems [1]. The appeal of Petri nets as a modelling formalism is easy to see. They provide a graphical presentation of a model which has an easily accessible interpretation and they also have the advantage of being supported by an unambiguous formal interpretation.

In their use as performance modelling languages stochastic Petri nets have recently been joined by stochastic process algebras such as PEPA [2], EMPA [3] and IMC [4]. Stochastic process algebras lack the attractive graphical presentation of Petri nets and properties such as the depiction of causality and conflict in a model. In contrast though, in stochastic process algebras an explicit compositional structure is imposed on the model. This structure makes the model easy to understand, may alleviate problems of model construction and can be exploited for both qualitative and quantitative analysis. A comparison of these two modelling formalisms [5] concludes that "there is scope for future work incorporating the attractive characteristics of the formalisms, such as structural analysis or functional abstraction, from one paradigm into the other". Some work has been done in this area in beginning to develop a structural theory for process algebras [6] on the one hand and in importing composition operations from stochastic process algebras into Well-formed nets on the other [7]. The present work considers using both Petri nets and process algebras together as

T. Field et al. (Eds.): TOOLS 2002, LNCS 2324, pp. 111–130, 2002.

a single, structured performance modelling formalism. There is some reason to believe that these two formalisms would complement each other. A recent paper [8] gives an example of a system which can be modelled more easily in one formalism than the other.

Petri nets have previously been combined with other modelling formalisms such as the lazy functional programming language Haskell (used with non-stochastic Petri nets in [9]) and queueing models (used with generalised stochastic Petri nets in [10]). The combination of stochastic Petri nets with queueing networks in particular has been a source of inspiration to several authors. Earlier work in this area includes Bause's *Queueing Petri nets* [11] and Haverkort's *Dynamic Queueing Networks* [12]. An extension of (non-stochastic) Petri nets which provides modelling concepts similar to ours is Valk's *Elementary Object systems* [13]. The tokens in an elementary object system are themselves Petri nets having individual dynamic behaviour.

Coloured Petri nets are a high-level form of classical Petri nets. The plain (indistinguishable) tokens of a classical Petri net are replaced by arbitrary terms which are distinguishable. In stochastic Petri nets the transitions from one marking to another are associated with a random variable drawn from an exponential distribution. Here we consider coloured stochastic Petri nets where the colours used as the tokens of the net are PEPA components. We refer to these as *PEPA nets* from here on.

Section 2 introduces the notation and terminology of PEPA nets, to give the reader an informal explanation of the ideas. However, PEPA is a formal language with a precise semantic definition and so in Section 3 we present the operational semantics of PEPA nets. In Section 4 we present a case study of a simple mobile agent system modelled as a PEPA net. Having presented the reader an example of modelling with PEPA nets we then compare them to the related modelling formalisms of Petri nets and the PEPA stochastic process algebra in Section 5. In each case we seek to show that PEPA nets offer some expressivity which is not directly offered by the other formalisms. In Section 6 we discuss tool support for this formalism. Section 7 is a more detailed case study. Further work is listed in Section 8. Concluding remarks are presented in Section 9.

2 PEPA Nets

In this section we present the concepts and definitions used in PEPA nets. We assume that the reader is familiar with the basic concepts of process algebras and Petri nets. Readers who are unfamiliar with the PEPA process algebra are referred to Appendix A for an introduction.

There are two types of change of state in a PEPA net. We refer to these as *firings* of the net and as *transitions* of PEPA components. The intention behind having two types of change of state is that we can use these to model changes which take place on different scales. Transitions of PEPA components will typically be used to model small-scale (or *local*) changes of state as components undertake activities. Firings of the net will typically be used to model macro-step (or *global*) changes of state such as context switches, breakdowns and repairs, one thread yielding to another, or a mobile software agent moving from one network host to another. We will return to a mobile agent example later but here we wish just to point out that our motivation is primarily to model systems which have two levels of change of state and not to develop a stochastic process algebra for specifically modelling mobile code applications. A suitable formalism already exists for the latter purpose, Priami's *stochastic* π*-calculus* [14].

A firing in a PEPA net causes the transfer of one token from one place to another. The token which is moved is a PEPA component, which causes a change in the remainder of the evaluation both in the source (where existing co-operations with other components now can no longer take place) and in the target (where previously disabled co-operations are now enabled by the arrival of an incoming component which can participate in these interactions). Firings have global effect because they involve components at more than one place in the net.

A transition in a PEPA net takes place whenever a transition of a PEPA component can occur (either individually, or in co-operation with another component). Transitions can only take place between components which are resident in the same place in the net. The PEPA net formalism does not allow components at different places in the net to co-operate on a shared activity. An analogy is with message-passing distributed systems without shared-memory where software components on the same host can exchange information without incurring a communication overhead but software components on different hosts cannot. Transitions in a PEPA net have local effect because they involve only components at one place in the net.

A PEPA net is made up of PEPA *contexts*, one at each place in the net. The notion of context might seem an unusual one to have to employ here but contexts have previously proved useful in definitions of classical process algebras [15], and in the PEPA stochastic process algebra [16]. Contexts contain *cells*. Like a memory location in an imperative program, a cell is a storage area to be filled by a datum of a particular type. In particular in a PEPA net, a cell is a storage area dedicated to storing a PEPA component. The components which fill cells can circulate as the tokens of the net. Components which are not in a designated cell are static and cannot move. Static components which cannot move are not included in most versions of Petri nets; the closest commonly-known idea is that of "self loops" where a token is deleted from a place and then immediately added again. They prove useful here because our concept of token is more complex than most. Static components act as cooperation partners in synchronisation activities with tokens.

We use the notation $P[\_]$ to denote a context which could be filled by the PEPA component P or one with the same alphabet. If P has derivatives P' and P'' only and no other component has the same alphabet as P then there are four possible values for such a context: $P[\_]$, $P[P]$, $P[P']$ and $P[P'']$. $P[\_]$ enables no transitions. $P[P]$ enables the same transitions as P. $P[P']$ enables the same transitions as P'. $P[P'']$ enables the same transitions as P''.

2.1 Markings in a PEPA Net

The *marking* of a classical Petri net records the number of tokens which are resident at each place in the net. Since the tokens of a classical Petri net are indistinguishable it is sufficient only to record their number and one could present the marking of a Petri net with places P_1, P_2 and P_3 as shown below.

$$\begin{array}{l} P_1 : 2 \\ P_2 : 1 \\ P_3 : 0 \end{array}$$

If an ordering is imposed on the places of the net a more compact representation of the marking can be used. Place names are omitted and the marking can be written using vector notation thus, $(2, 1, 0)$.

Consider now a PEPA net with places P_1, P_2 and P_3 as shown below.

$$P_1[p] \stackrel{\mathit{def}}{=} P[p] \underset{L}{\bowtie} Q$$

$$P_2[p] \stackrel{\mathit{def}}{=} P[p] \underset{K}{\bowtie} R$$

$$P_3[p] \stackrel{\mathit{def}}{=} P[p] \underset{K \cup L}{\bowtie} (Q \parallel R)$$

From their uses in the contexts at each place we see that P is a component which can move as a token around the net whereas Q and R are static components which cannot move. There is a copy of Q at place P_1 and another at P_3. There is a copy of R at place P_2 and another at P_3.

Given the above definitions for the places in this PEPA net, we can denote a marking of this net by $(P_1[P], P_2[\_], P_3[\_])$. In general, a context may have more than one parameter, to be filled by PEPA components of different types, so the vector of lists notation which we have used here is needed in general. Where an ordering is imposed on places and each context has only a single cell to be filled we can abbreviate such a marking by $(P, \_, \_)$.

2.2 Net-Level Transitions in a PEPA Net

Transitions at the net-level of a PEPA net are labelled in a similar way to the labelled multi-transition system which records the unfolding of the state space of a PEPA model. A labelling function ℓ maps transition names into pairs of names such as (α, r) where it is possible that $\ell(t_i) = \ell(t_j)$ but $t_i \neq t_j$. The first element of a pair (α, r) specifies an *activity* which must be performed in order for a component to move from the input place of the transition to the output place. The activity type records formally the activity which must be performed if the transition is to fire. The second element is an exponentially-distributed random variable which quantifies the *rate* at which the activity can progress in conjuction with the component which is performing it.

As an example, suppose that Q is a component which is currently at place P_1 and that it can perform an activity α with rate r_1 to produce the derivative Q'.

Further, say that the net has a transition between P_1 and P_2 labelled by (α, r_2). If Q performs activity α in this setting it will be removed from P_1 (leaving behind an empty cell) and deposited into P_2 (filling an empty cell there).

3 Semantics

The PEPA language is formally defined by a small-step operational semantics as used in the definition of Milner's CCS and other process algebras. In order to describe the firing rule for PEPA nets formally we need a relational operator which is to be used to express the fact that there exists a particular transition in the net superstructure. This operator must have the properties that it identifies the source and target of the transition and that it records the activity which is to be performed in order for a component to cross this transition, moving from the source to the target. We use the notation

$$P_1 \overset{(\alpha, r)}{\rightarrow\!\!\square\!\!\rightarrow} P_2$$

to capture the information that there is a transition connecting place P_1 to place P_2 labelled by (α, r). This relation captures static information about the structure of the net, not dynamic information about its behaviour. We could describe the net structure in a PEPA net using a list of such assertions but the more familiar graphical presentation of a net presents the same information in a more accessible way.

When we wish to express the fact that no such labelled transition exists connecting place P_1 to place P_2, we draw a stroke through the box in the middle of the arrow symbol. This relation can be defined in terms of the relation above.

$$P_1 \overset{(\alpha, r)}{\rightarrow\!\!\not\square\!\!\rightarrow} P_2 \;=\; \nexists P_2 \cdot P_1 \overset{(\alpha, r)}{\rightarrow\!\!\square\!\!\rightarrow} P_2$$

The introduction of contexts requires an extension to the syntax of PEPA. This extension is presented in Figure 1.

The semantic rules for PEPA nets are provided in Figure 2. The Cell rule conservatively extends the PEPA semantics to define that a cell which is filled by a component P has the same transitions as P itself. A healthiness condition on the rule (also called a *typing judgement*) requires a context such as $P[\_]$ to be filled with a component which has the same alphabet as P. We write $P =_a P'$ to state that P and P' have the same alphabet. There are no rules to infer transitions for an empty cell because an empty cell enables no transitions.

The Transition rule states that the net has local transitions which change only a single component in the marking vector. This rule also states that these transitions agree with the transitions which are generated by the PEPA semantics (including the extension for contexts). The second premise of the Transition rule mandates that a local transition α can only occur in a place in the net which does not have an outgoing arc labelled by α. Note that this negative requirement is a static requirement related to the structure of the net, not the negation of

$N ::= D^+M$ (net)	$M ::= (P, \ldots)$ (marking)	$D ::= I \stackrel{def}{=} S$ (defn)
(definitions and marking)	(a vector of components)	(identifier declaration)
$S ::= (\alpha, r).S$ (prefix)	$P ::= P \underset{L}{\bowtie} P$ (cooperation)	$C ::=$ '_' (empty)
$\mid S + S$ (choice)	$\mid P/L$ (hiding)	$\mid P$ (full)
$\mid I$ (identifier)	$\mid P[C]$ (cell)	
	$\mid I$ (identifier)	
(sequential components)	(concurrent components)	(cell term expressionss)

Fig. 1. The syntax of PEPA extended with contexts

the transition relation which is being defined. Thus, the rule cannot fail to be *stratifiable* [17].

The Firing rule takes one marking of the net to another marking by performing a PEPA activity and moving a PEPA component from the input place to the output place. This has the effect that two entries in the marking vector change simultaneously. The rate at which the activity is performed is calculated as in the PEPA semantics of co-operation. That is, the rate is adjusted to reflect the inability of the slower co-operand to function at the rate of the faster co-operand, using the well-known notion of *apparent rate*. The definition of apparent rate can be found in [2].

Cell:

$$\frac{P' \xrightarrow{(\alpha,r)} P''}{P[P'] \xrightarrow{(\alpha,r)} P[P'']} \quad (P =_a P')$$

Transition:

$$\frac{P \xrightarrow{(\alpha,r)} P' \qquad P \not\xrightarrow{(\alpha,r')} Q}{(\ldots, P, \ldots) \xrightarrow{(\alpha,r)} (\ldots, P', \ldots)}$$

Firing:

$$\frac{Q \xrightarrow{(\alpha,r_1)} Q' \qquad P_i \xrightarrow{(\alpha,r_2)}\!\!\!\!\!\!\!\!\Vert\;\;\;\; P_j}{(\ldots, P_i[Q], \ldots, P_j[\_], \ldots) \xrightarrow{(\alpha,R)} (\ldots, P_i[\_], \ldots, P_j[Q'], \ldots)}$$

Fig. 2. Semantics of PEPA net firings

4 Example: A Mobile Agent System

We present a small example to reinforce the reader's understanding of PEPA nets. In this example a roving agent visits three sites. It interacts with static software components at these sites and has two kinds of interactions. When visiting a site where a network probe is present it interrogates the probe for the data which it has gathered on recent patterns of network traffic. When it returns to the central co-ordinating site it dumps the data which it has harvested to the master probe. The master probe performs a computationally expensive statistical analysis of the data. The structure of the system allows this computation to be overlapped with the agent's communication and data gathering. The marshalling and unmarshalling costs for mobile code applications are a significant expense so overlapping this with data processing allows some of this expense to be offset.

The structure of the application is as represented by the PEPA net in Figure 3. This marking of the net shows the mobile agent resident at the central co-ordinating site. As a mnemonic, in both the net and the PEPA description, we print in bold the names of those activities which can cause a firing of the net. In this example, those activities are ***go*** and ***return***.

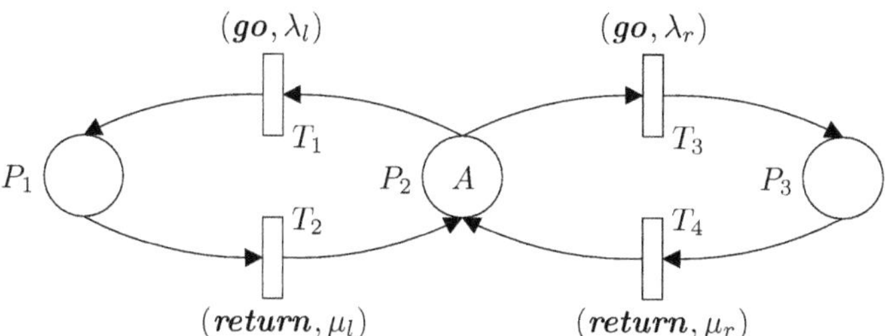

Fig. 3. A simple mobile agent system

Formally, we define the places of the net as shown in the PEPA context definitions below. P_2 has a local state denoted by P_2'.

$$P_1[A] \stackrel{def}{=} Agent[A] \underset{\{interrogate\}}{\bowtie} Probe \qquad P_3[A] \stackrel{def}{=} Agent[A] \underset{\{interrogate\}}{\bowtie} Probe$$

$$P_2[A] \stackrel{def}{=} Agent[A] \underset{\{dump\}}{\bowtie} Master \qquad P_2'[A] \stackrel{def}{=} Agent[A] \underset{\{dump\}}{\bowtie} Master'$$

The initial marking of the net is $(\_, Agent, \_)$. The behaviour of the components is given by the following PEPA definitions.

$$\begin{aligned} Agent &\stackrel{def}{=} (\boldsymbol{go}, \lambda).Agent' & Master &\stackrel{def}{=} (dump, \top).Master' \\ Agent' &\stackrel{def}{=} (interrogate, r_i).Agent'' & Master' &\stackrel{def}{=} (analyse, r_a).Master \\ Agent'' &\stackrel{def}{=} (\mathbf{return}, \mu).Agent''' & Probe &\stackrel{def}{=} (monitor, r_m).Probe + \\ Agent''' &\stackrel{def}{=} (dump, r_d).Agent & & \quad (interrogate, \top).Probe \end{aligned}$$

The transition system underlying this model is shown in Figure 4. The derivation of such a transition system is the first step in the performance analysis of such a system. The transition system contains the specification of a Continuous-Time Markov Chain model of the system. This CTMC is solved for its stationary distribution and performance measures are calculated from that. For a model as simple as this one we can solve it simply with Gaussian elimination. We also have available solvers such as an efficient implementation of the preconditioned biconjugate gradient method.

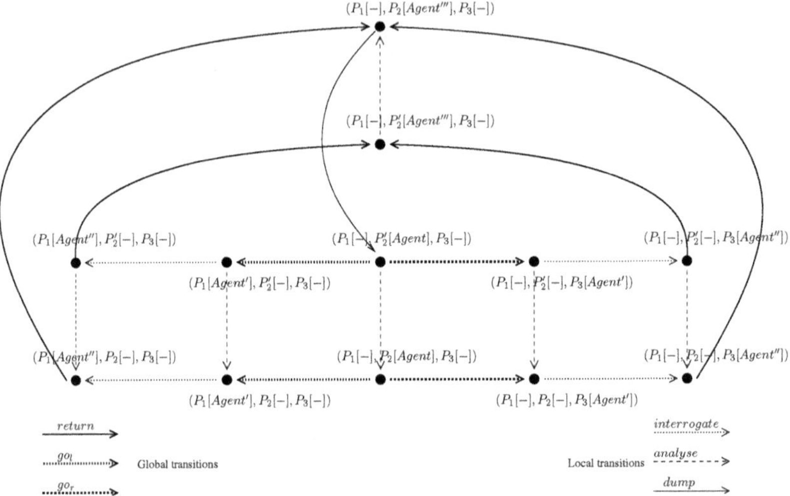

Fig. 4. The transition system of the mobile agent example

5 Relating PEPA Nets to Other Modelling Formalisms

If they were to be viewed purely formally as high-level description languages for specifying continuous-time Markov chains, then PEPA nets, stochastic Petri nets and the PEPA stochastic process algebra would be considered to be equally expressive. That is to say, for a given CTMC C, it is possible to construct a high-level model in each of these three formalisms such that the underlying CTMC derived from the model is isomporphic to C.

In practice, the three languages present different sets of conceptual tools to the modeller. From the pragmatic perspective of a performance modeller who wishes to reliably encode a high-level model of a particular system then there might be reasons to select one of the languages instead of the others for this particular modelling study. In the remainder of this section we compare modelling with PEPA nets with modelling with Petri nets and the PEPA stochastic process algebra.

5.1 Relating PEPA Nets to Petri Nets

To illustrate the difference between PEPA nets and Petri nets we first show how to represent an ordinary k-safe stochastic Petri net as a PEPA net. In a classical stochastic Petri net tokens are indistinguishable. We can replicate this in a PEPA net by having only a single class of tokens which have only one (PEPA) state. The definition of such a token would also need to always permit firings of the net to take place. We define these tokens by summing over all of the transition activity names, for all of the transitions of the net ($tn_i \in T$).

$$Token \stackrel{def}{=} \sum_{tn_i \in T} (tn_i, \top).Token$$

To define a k-safe stochastic Petri net with a PEPA net we then need simply to specify the places of the net as being capable of storing up to k of these tokens, and making no use of static components.

$$P_i[tk_1, \ldots, tk_k] \stackrel{def}{=} Token[tk_1] \parallel \cdots \parallel Token[tk_k]$$

This reconstruction of ordinary k-safe stochastic Petri nets from PEPA nets points to the difference between the two formalisms. A PEPA net can be viewed as a Petri net where the tokens are *programmable*. The tokens of a PEPA net have state, can count, can observe activities, and can even refuse to be fired from the place where they reside. We believe that this gives the PEPA net modeller a novel conceptual modelling tool which can be used to express natural descriptions of systems with active, stateful mobile agents.

5.2 Relating PEPA Nets to PEPA

The relationship between PEPA nets and PEPA is straightforward. A PEPA net with only one place and no transitions is simply a PEPA stochastic process algebra model. To explain how a PEPA net can offer added expressive power we consider a PEPA net with more than one place, such as that shown in Figure 5.

In this model a token of type P moves between place P_1 and place P_2. In doing so it decouples itself from a static component Q, located at P_1. The token thereby moves out of the scope of the cooperation set L. Cooperation sets are used to configure copies of components, coupling them to communication partners. In this way they restrict the behaviour of a component, requiring it to perform some activities (those in the cooperation set) only if they have a partner who is able to cooperate in performing them. In the example in Figure 5 if Q is unwilling to perform some of these activities then the behaviour of P will be restricted. Even if Q is willing to perform all of the activities in the cooperation

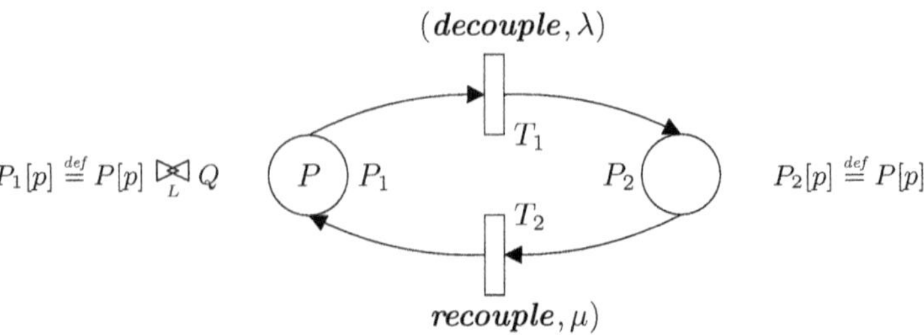

Fig. 5. Tokens in a PEPA net can decouple from a static component

set L then it can still influence the rate at which they are performed. In contrast when the token P is resident in P_2 then it is subject to no such restriction and can perform all of its activities at the rates which it itself specifies.

This concept cannot be expressed in a PEPA stochastic process algebra model. The cooperation sets used in a PEPA model impose a static communication topology on the model. In contrast a PEPA net has dynamically varying communication structure and, in consequence, a given action in a component might sometimes be performed in isolation and sometimes be performed in cooperation. The ability to express the concept of dynamically varying communication structure offers an additional conceptual tool to the performance modeller which is not available when modelling in PEPA. In this way PEPA nets strictly extend the expressiveness of the PEPA stochastic process algebra.

6 Implementation

The PEPA stochastic process algebra is supported by a range of tools including the PEPA Workbench [18] and the Möbius Modelling Framework [19]. In this section we explain the use of PEPA nets with these tools. In the first case we have extended the tool to directly support the extended formalism. In the second case we explain how to translate PEPA nets into the extension of PEPA supported by Möbius, PEPA$_k$.

6.1 The PEPA Workbench for PEPA Nets

We have implemented the PEPA nets formalism as an extension of the PEPA Workbench, an existing modelling tool for PEPA. The PEPA Workbench exists in two distinct versions. The first version is an experimental research tool which is coded in the functional programming language Standard ML [20]. The second is a re-implementation of this in the Java programming language. These are known as "the ML edition" and "the Java edition" respectively.

Standard ML and Java have very different strengths. For a visual language such as the notation of Petri nets the Java language's visualisation capabilities

```
PEPA Workbench for PEPA nets Version 0.72.2 "Cramond" [14-08-2001]
Filename: agent.pepa
Compiling the model
Generating the derivation graph
The model has 12 states
The model has 35 transitions
The model has 8 firings
Writing the hash table file to agent.hash
Exiting PEPA Workbench.
```

Fig. 6. The PEPA Workbench for PEPA nets processing the mobile agent model

would suit the task much better than Standard ML. Further, there are existing Java tools for Petri nets which could be extended to provide an implementation of PEPA nets. After initial experimentation with the Standard ML version of the PEPA Workbench for PEPA nets, a graphical presentation of PEPA nets could be incorporated into the Java version of the Workbench. This implementation plan is ongoing, but at an early stage.

The Standard ML language is well suited to implementing symbolic processing applications and provides built-in support for describing datatypes such as those needed to present the abstract syntax of a formal language such as PEPA. These features made it possible to rapidly adapt the routines for generating PEPA derivation graphs to generate derivation graphs for PEPA nets. The compact transition rules presented in Figure 2 look simple on the page but they proved to be a challege to implement efficiently. Here again, the higher-order features of the Standard ML programming language proved to be useful in allowing us to form function closures from higher-order functions which fixed some of their formal parameters. This allowed us to unroll the derivation graph for the PEPA nets model without suffering a performance penalty due to accumulated parameter information.

The use of the PEPA Workbench for PEPA nets is illustrated in Figure 6. Comparing the results with the picture of the labelled transition system in Figure 4 we see that the number of states and firings agree. Two self-loops are omitted from every state in the diagram in order to avoid clutter. This accounts for the additional twenty-four transitions reported by the PEPA Workbench for PEPA nets.

The input language to the tool is an extension of the concrete syntax used for storing PEPA language models. The topology of the net is specified by providing a textual description of the places and the arcs connecting them. Providing a visual editor for PEPA nets remains as future work.

6.2 Using PEPA Nets in the Möbius Modelling Framework

Möbius is a multi-formalism performance and dependability modelling tool. The modeller can specify atomic models in a number of component-based modelling formalisms, including stochastic activity networks (SANs), stochastic Petri nets (SPNs), Markov processes specified in "bucket and ball" style, queueing networks and the PEPA stochastic process algebra [21]. These atomic models are configured and composed using a graphical notation to make a structured high-level model which is composed from atomic submodels. The ability to interconnect models expressed in different formalisms is achieved through the use of an *abstract functional interface* to the models. Models can be solved either by discrete event simulation or by state-based, analytical and numerical techniques. The Möbius solvers use efficient implementations of classical sparse matrix solution methods.

Möbius implements an extension of PEPA called PEPA$_k$. It is shown in [21] that PEPA$_k$ models can be mapped to PEPA models. Here we explain how to map PEPA nets to PEPA$_k$ models.

PEPA$_k$ extends PEPA with formal parameters, guards and value passing. It might at first seem that we can use parameter passing to describe the firing of a PEPA net and the communication of a token from one place to another. However, the parameters of a PEPA$_k$ component must have integer values. That is, the component definitions cannot describe *higher-order components*, which are themselves parameterised by another component. In PEPA$_k$, guards are used to restrict the evaluation of process expressions to those cases where the guard evaluates to *true* under the current assignment of (integer) values to parameters. In PEPA nets, cells are storage locations for components where the behaviour of the component is either fully enabled (because the cell contains a token) or fully disabled (because the cell is empty). Accordingly, we can use guarded components to model cells if we can write guards which evaluate to *true* exactly when the token is present and *false* otherwise.

Each PEPA net has a finite number of places and each token has a finite number of colours (local states). Because of this, we can encode the information that a token of a particular colour is at a particular place by a pair of integer variables. Call these variables `place` and `colour` respectively. We can now encode a PEPA net cell in place j as a sum of PEPA$_k$ guarded components as shown below.

$$\underbrace{P[\cdot]}_{\substack{\text{PEPA net cell at place } j, \\ \text{tokens } = \{\, P_0, \ldots, P_n \,\}}} \quad \rightsquigarrow \quad \underbrace{\sum_{i=0}^{n} [(\texttt{place} = j) \wedge (\texttt{colour} = i)] \Rightarrow P_i}_{\text{PEPA}_k \text{ expression in atomic submodel } j}$$

The Möbius implementation of a PEPA net is built up as a composition of atomic submodels, each implemented in PEPA$_k$, one for each place in the PEPA net.

To model the firing of a PEPA net where the place of a token and its colour are simultaneously updated we update the variables to store the new place and the new colour, e.g. (`place` = k, `colour` = c). The definition of the variables is placed at a higher level of the Möbius Replicate/Join tree to allow the variables to be shared between the atomic submodels.

To implement dynamically varying communication structure in PEPA$_k$ it would be necessary to replicate some components or rename some activities.

7 Case Study: A Peer-to-Peer File System

We have used the PEPA Workbench for PEPA nets to analyse performance aspects of a modern networked application, Freenet [22], modelled as a PEPA net. The Freenet project began in the Division of Informatics of The University of Edinburgh. Its purpose is to develop a de-centralised networked application which allows users to publish information for retrieval over the network. Publications are replicated at a subset of the nodes in the network and requests to retrieve them cause them to be further replicated at other nodes nearer to the requestor. Little-accessed publications can be dropped from nodes. In this way, in time, a little-used publication could eventually disappear from the network entirely (it would "go out of print").

Up to this point one could simply think of Freenet as a probabilistic filestore but one striking novelty of the Freenet platform is that it attempts to ensure the anonymity of both authors and readers and the ability of node maintainers to deny knowledge of the contents stored at their node. Additional layers of indirection mean that it is not feasible to determine the origin of a file passing through the network. No centralised server is used to maintain a registry of publications on the network (this is a peer-to-peer architecture) so there is no central control to be held accountable for the contents of the network as a whole.

Clients built on Freenet include *Frost.* Frost is a file-sharing tool similar to Napster and Morpheus. It additionally provides a message board system that allows anonymous Usenet-style communication. Applications of this include enabling free speech in countries without freedom of speech laws.

Because the system architecture contains no centralised index, retrieving a file in Freenet consists of making a request to a Freenet host. This becomes a series of requests as one host interrogates another to satisfy the request. Files on Freenet are stored under descriptions which are hashed to provide search keys and searching for a file proceeds by steepest-ascent hill-climbing. To prevent infinite chains of requests, each request has a "hops-to-live" count which is decreased each time that it hops from one Freenet node to another. When the hops-to-live count reaches zero the search is abandoned and it is reported that the file could not be found.

The behaviour of a Freenet node is modelled as a static PEPA net component. The node first receives a request which comes from either the user or from another node. It checks its own store to see if the data is found. It returns the data if found, allowing another request to be initiated. If not found a further request, found/notfound iteration is initiated.

$$
\begin{aligned}
\mathit{Node} &\stackrel{\mathit{def}}{=} (\mathit{request}, r).\mathit{Node}_2 \\
\mathit{Node}_2 &\stackrel{\mathit{def}}{=} (\mathit{found}, p \times f).\mathit{Node}_3 + (\mathit{notfound}, (1-p) \times f).\mathit{Node} \\
\mathit{Node}_3 &\stackrel{\mathit{def}}{=} (\mathit{return}, rt).\mathit{Node}
\end{aligned}
$$

The request is a PEPA net token, moving around the network via the ***hop*** activity. We model failure due to exceeding the hops-to-live count (*die*). The subscript on a request counts down the number of hops left to live. The request dies if it has not found the file and has no more hops left. When it dies, the component becomes "recycled" as a new request (for a different file).

$$\begin{array}{lll}
Request_h \stackrel{\text{def}}{=} (request, \top).Request'_h & & (h_{max} \geq h \geq 0) \\
Request'_h \stackrel{\text{def}}{=} (found, \top).Request'_{h_{max}} & & \\
\qquad\qquad + (notfound, \top).Request''_h & & (h_{max} \geq h \geq 0) \\
Request''_h \stackrel{\text{def}}{=} (\mathbf{hop}, \kappa).Request_{h-1} & & (h_{max} \geq h > 0) \\
Request''_0 \stackrel{\text{def}}{=} (die, d).Request_{h_{max}} & &
\end{array}$$

Each place in the net combines a slot for a request with a node as shown below.

$$P_i[R] \stackrel{\text{def}}{=} Request[R] \underset{\{\, request,\ found,\ notfound \,\}}{\bowtie} Node$$

We have processed a modest-sized model of this system with the PEPA Workbench for PEPA nets and solved it with the Maple computer algebra system to find performance measures of the system. One such performance measure was the dependency of the number of requests on the probability of finding the file at a given node, subject to two simplifying assumptions of uniform request origins and uniform file distribution. We found the PEPA nets formalism to give a relatively natural means of expressing the structure of a system such as this one, where mobile components have local state which evolves at places in the net.

8 Further Work

We have defined a language which provides an extension to the PEPA stochastic process algebra by allowing a number of distinct PEPA models to be arranged into a net. These models communicate via the transfer of tokens from one place to another. We have implemented this new language and applied it to some case studies. In the light of additional experience gained from further case studies it could be possible that we would discover that other language constructs would be helpful to the modeller.

One possibility would be an independent evolution of the net system, akin to the *transport transitions* of elementary object systems, where tokens are forcibly moved from one place to another without the option to refuse this or change state in transit. We have omitted this feature at present because it seems at odds with the process algebra notion of every component having behaviour. Additional language design decisions and extensions remain as future work.

Other future work includes the continued development of our implementation of the PEPA Workbench for PEPA nets. The additional of a graphical editor for PEPA nets is a likely next step with this tool.

Together with Norman and Parker at Birmingham we have recently extended the PRISM probabilistic symbolic model checker [23] to support the PEPA stochastic process algebra as an additional modelling language. An extension of that work to support PEPA nets would greatly enhance our ability to experiment with models on a large scale.

9 Conclusions

The PEPA nets formalism is new and, as yet, relatively unproven. It is our belief that it can provide a suitable framework for the description of performance models of systems which have distinct notions of changes of state. Our experience with the PEPA formalism has been that the combination of a well-defined formal semantics for the language and the availability of a range of tools to implement the language has enabled us and others to use it effectively in the performance modelling and analysis of systems. By following a similar development path we would hope that the PEPA nets formalism could also prove to be useful.

The combination of a process algebra with a Petri net presents many opportunities to import developments from the Petri net community into the practices in the process algebra community. Further, it is to be hoped that these developments can be imported more directly through the use of a Petri net with algebraic terms as tokens than if one was to rework them and to re-apply them in the process algebra context.

Acknowledgements. Stephen Gilmore and Jane Hillston are supported by the DEGAS (Design Environments for Global ApplicationS) project funded by the FET Proactive Initiative on Global Computing. Our thanks go to Salem Derisavi of the Möbius project for providing insights into the operation of PEPA$_k$ in Möbius. Thanks also to Giuliana Franceschinis for her advice on coloured Petri nets. The authors are grateful to the anonymous referees of the Tools conference for their comments on the paper. An earlier version of this paper appeared as [24].

References

1. M. Ajmone Marsan, A. Bobbio, and S. Donatelli. Petri nets in performance analysis: An introduction. In Reisig, W. and Rozenberg, G., editors, *Lectures on Petri Nets I: Basic Models*, volume 1491 of *LNCS*, pages 211–256. Springer-Verlag, 1998.
2. J. Hillston. *A Compositional Approach to Performance Modelling*. Cambridge University Press, 1996.
3. M. Bernardo and R. Gorrieri. A tutorial on EMPA: a theory of concurrent processes with nondeterminism, priorities, probabilities and time. *Theoretical Computer Science*, 202:1–54, 1998.
4. H. Hermanns. *Interactive Markov Chains*. PhD thesis, Universität Erlangen-Nürnberg, 1999.
5. S. Donatelli, J. Hillston, and M. Ribaudo. A comparison of Performance Evaluation Process Algebra and Generalized Stochastic Petri Nets. In *Proc. 6th International Workshop on Petri Nets and Performance Models*, Durham, North Carolina, 1995.
6. S. Gilmore, J. Hillston, and L. Recalde. Elementary structural analysis for PEPA. Technical Report ECS-LFCS-97-377, Laboratory for Foundations of Computer Science, Department of Computer Science, The University of Edinburgh, 1997.
7. I. C. Rojas M. *Compositional construction and analysis of Petri net systems*. PhD thesis, The University of Edinburgh, 1997.

8. J. Hillston, L. Recalde, M. Ribaudo, and M. Silva. A comparison of the expressiveness of SPA and bounded SPN models. In B. Haverkort and R. German, editors, *Proceedings of the 9th International Workshop on Petri Nets and Performance Models*, Aachen, Germany, September 2001. IEEE Computer Science Press.
9. C. Reinke. Haskell-Coloured Petri Nets. In *Implementation of Functional Languages, 11th International Workshop*, volume 1868 of *LNCS*, pages 165–180, Lochem, The Netherlands, September 1999. Springer-Verlag.
10. M. Becker and H. Szczerbicka. PNiQ: Integration of queuing networks in generalized stochastic petri nets. *IEE Proceedings—Software*, 146(1):27–33, February 1999. Special issue of the proceedings of the Fourteenth UK Performance Engineering Workshop.
11. F. Bause. Queueing Petri nets—a formalism for the combined qualitative and quantitative analysis of systems. In *5th International Workshop on Petri Nets and Performance Models*, pages 14–23, Toulouse, France, October 1993.
12. B.R. Haverkort, I.G. Niemegeers, and P Veldhuyzen van Zanten. DyQNtool—a performability modelling tool based on the dynamic queueing network concept. In G. Balbo and G. Serazzi, editors, *Modelling Techniques and Tools for Computer Performance Evaluation*, pages 181–195. North-Holland, 1992.
13. R. Valk. Petri nets as token objects—an introduction to Elementary Object Nets. In J. Desel and M. Silva, editors, *Proceedings of the 19th International Conference on Application and Theory of Petri Nets*, volume 1420 of *Lecture Notes in Computer Science*, pages 1–25, Lisbon, Portugal, 1998. Springer-Verlag.
14. C. Priami. Stochastic π-calculus. In S. Gilmore and J. Hillston, editors, *Proceedings of the Third International Workshop on Process Algebras and Performance Modelling*, pages 578–589. Special Issue of *The Computer Journal*, 38(7), December 1995.
15. K.G. Larsen. Compositional theories based on an operational semantics of contexts. In *REX Workshop on Stepwise Refinement of Parallel Systems*, volume 430 of *LNCS*, pages 487–518. Springer-Verlag, May 1989.
16. G. Clark. *Techniques for the Construction and Analysis of Algebraic Performance Models*. PhD thesis, The University of Edinburgh, 2000.
17. J.F. Groote. Transition system specifications with negative premises. *Theoretical Computer Science*, 118(2):263–299, 1993.
18. S. Gilmore and J. Hillston. The PEPA Workbench: A Tool to Support a Process Algebra-based Approach to Performance Modelling. In *Proceedings of the Seventh International Conference on Modelling Techniques and Tools for Computer Performance Evaluation*, number 794 in Lecture Notes in Computer Science, pages 353–368, Vienna, May 1994. Springer-Verlag.
19. G. Clark, T. Courtney, D. Daly, D. Deavours, S. Derisavi, J. M. Doyle, W. H. Sanders, and P. Webster. The Möbius modeling tool. In *Proceedings of the 9th International Workshop on Petri Nets and Performance Models*, pages 241–250, Aachen, Germany, September 2001.
20. R. Milner, M. Tofte, R. Harper, and D. MacQueen. *The Definition of Standard ML: Revised 1996*. The MIT Press, 1996.
21. G. Clark and W.H. Sanders. Implementing a stochastic process algebra within the Möbius modeling framework. In L. de Alfaro and S. Gilmore, editors, *Proceedings of the first joint PAPM-PROBMIV Workshop*, volume 2165 of *Lecture Notes in Computer Science*, pages 200–215, Aachen, Germany, September 2001. Springer-Verlag.

22. I. Clarke, O. Sandberg, B. Wiley, and T.W. Hong. Freenet: A distributed anonymous information storage and retrieval system. In H. Federrath, editor, *Designing Privacy Enhancing Technologies: International Workshop on Design Issues in Anonymity and Unobservability*, volume 2009 of *Lecture Notes in Computer Science*, pages 46–66, Berkeley, California, 2001. Springer-Verlag.
23. M. Kwiatkowska, G. Norman, and D. Parker. PRISM: Probabilistic symbolic model checker. This volume, 2002.
24. S. Gilmore, J. Hillston, and M. Ribaudo. PEPA-coloured stochastic Petri nets. In K. Djemame and M. Kara, editors, *Proceedings of the Seventeenth UK Performance Engineering Workshop*, pages 155–166, University of Leeds, July 2001.

A Summary of the PEPA Language

The PEPA language provides a small set of combinators. These allow language terms to be constructed defining the behaviour of components, via the activities they undertake and the interactions between them. The syntax may be formally introduced by means of the grammar which was shown in Figure 1. In that grammar S denotes a *sequential component* and P denotes a *model component* which executes in parallel. C stands for a constant which denotes either a sequential or a model component, as defined by a defining equation. C when subscripted with an S stands for constants which denote sequential components. The component combinators, together with their names and interpretations, are presented informally below.

Prefix: The basic mechanism for describing the behaviour of a system is to give a component a designated first action using the prefix combinator, denoted by a full stop. For example, the component $(\alpha, r).S$ carries out activity (α, r), which has action type α and an exponentially distributed duration with parameter r, and it subsequently behaves as S. Sequences of actions can be combined to build up a life cycle for a component.

Choice: The life cycle of a sequential component may be more complex than any behaviour which can be expressed using the prefix combinator alone. The choice combinator captures the possibility of competition between different possible activities. The component $P + Q$ represents a system which may behave either as P or as Q. The activities of both P and Q are enabled. The first activity to complete distinguishes one of them: the other is discarded. The system will behave as the derivative resulting from the evolution of the chosen component.

Constant: It is convenient to be able to assign names to patterns of behaviour associated with components. Constants are components whose meaning is given by a defining equation.

Hiding: The possibility to abstract away some aspects of a component's behaviour is provided by the hiding operator, denoted by the division sign in P/L. Here, the set L of visible action types identifies those activities which are to be considered internal or private to the component. These activities are not visible to an external observer, nor are they accessible to other components for cooperation. Once an activity is hidden it only appears as the unknown type τ; the rate of the activity, however, remains unaffected.

Cooperation: Most systems are comprised of several components which interact. In PEPA direct interaction, or *cooperation*, between components is represented by the butterfly combinator. The set which is used as the subscript to the cooperation symbol determines those activities on which the *cooperands* are forced to synchronise. Thus the cooperation combinator is in fact an indexed family of combinators, one for each possible *cooperation set* L (we write $P \parallel Q$ as an abbreviation for $P \underset{L}{\bowtie} Q$ when L is empty). When cooperation is not imposed, namely for action types not in L, the components proceed independently and concurrently with their enabled activities. However if a component enables an activity whose action type is in the cooperation set it will not be able to proceed with that activity until the other component also enables an activity of that type. The two components then proceed together to complete the *shared activity*. The rate of the shared activity may be altered to reflect the work carried out by both components to complete the activity.

In some cases, when an activity is known to be carried out in cooperation with another component, a component may be *passive* with respect to that activity. This means that the rate of the activity is left unspecified and is determined upon cooperation, by the rate of the activity in the other component. All passive actions must be synchronised in the final model.

Model components capture the structure of the system in terms of its *static* components. The dynamic behaviour of the system is represented by the evolution of these components, either individually or in cooperation. The form of this evolution is governed by a set of formal rules which give an operational semantics of PEPA terms. The semantic rules, in the structured operational style, are presented in Figure 7 without further comment; the interested reader is referred to [2] for more details. The rules are read as follows: if the transition(s) above the inference line can be inferred, then we can infer the transition below the line. The notation $r_\alpha(E)$ which is used in the third cooperation rule denotes the apparent rate of α in E.

Thus, as in classical process algebra, the semantics of each term in PEPA is given via a labelled *multi-transition* system—the multiplicities of arcs are significant. In the transition system a state corresponds to each syntactic term of the language, or *derivative*, and an arc represents the activity which causes one derivative to evolve into another. The complete set of reachable states is termed the *derivative set* of a model and these form the nodes of the *derivation graph* formed by applying the semantic rules exhaustively.

The timing aspects of components' behaviour are not represented in the states of the derivation graph, but on each arc as the parameter of the negative exponential distribution governing the duration of the corresponding activity. The interpretation is as follows: when enabled an activity $a = (\alpha, r)$ will delay for a period sampled from the negative exponential distribution which has pa-

Prefix

$$\frac{}{(\alpha, r).E \xrightarrow{(\alpha,r)} E}$$

Cooperation

$$\frac{E \xrightarrow{(\alpha,r)} E'}{E \underset{L}{\bowtie} F \xrightarrow{(\alpha,r)} E' \underset{L}{\bowtie} F} (\alpha \notin L) \qquad \frac{F \xrightarrow{(\alpha,r)} F'}{E \underset{L}{\bowtie} F \xrightarrow{(\alpha,r)} E \underset{L}{\bowtie} F'} (\alpha \notin L)$$

$$\frac{E \xrightarrow{(\alpha,r_1)} E' \quad F \xrightarrow{(\alpha,r_2)} F'}{E \underset{L}{\bowtie} F \xrightarrow{(\alpha,R)} E' \underset{L}{\bowtie} F'} (\alpha \in L) \qquad \text{where } R = \frac{r_1}{r_\alpha^E}\frac{r_2}{r_\alpha^F}\min(r_\alpha(E), r_\alpha(F))$$

Choice

$$\frac{E \xrightarrow{(\alpha,r)} E'}{E + F \xrightarrow{(\alpha,r)} E'} \qquad \frac{F \xrightarrow{(\alpha,r)} F'}{E + F \xrightarrow{(\alpha,r)} F'}$$

Hiding

$$\frac{E \xrightarrow{(\alpha,r)} E'}{E/L \xrightarrow{(\alpha,r)} E'/L} (\alpha \notin L) \qquad \frac{E \xrightarrow{(\alpha,r)} E'}{E/L \xrightarrow{(\tau,r)} E'/L} (\alpha \in L)$$

Constant

$$\frac{E \xrightarrow{(\alpha,r)} E'}{A \xrightarrow{(\alpha,r)} E'} (A \stackrel{\mathit{def}}{=} E)$$

Fig. 7. The operational semantics of PEPA

rameter r. If several activities are enabled concurrently, either in competition or independently, we assume that a *race condition* exists between them. Thus the activity whose delay before completion is the least will be the one to succeed. The evolution of the model will determine whether the other activities have been *aborted* or simply *interrupted* by the state change. In either case the memoryless property of the negative exponential distribution eliminates the need to record the previous execution time.

When two components carry out an activity in cooperation the rate of the shared activity will reflect the working capacity of the slower component. We assume that each component has a capacity for performing an activity type α, which cannot be enhanced by working in cooperation (it still must carry out its own work), unless the component is passive with respect to that activity type. For a component P and an action type α, this capacity is termed the *apparent rate* of α in P. It is the sum of the rates of the α type activities enabled in P. The apparent rate of α in a cooperation between P and Q over α will be the minimum of the apparent rate of α in P and the apparent rate of α in Q.

The derivation graph is the basis of the underlying Continuous Time Markov Chain (CTMC) which is used to derive performance measures from a PEPA model. The graph is systematically reduced to a form where it can be treated as the state transition diagram of the underlying CTMC. Each derivative is then a state in the CTMC. The *transition rate* between two derivatives P and Q in the derivation graph is the rate at which the system changes from behaving as component P to behaving as Q. It is denoted by $q(P, Q)$ and is the sum of the activity rates labelling arcs connecting node P to node Q. In order for the CTMC to be *ergodic* its derivation graph must be strongly connected. Some necessary conditions for ergodicity, at the syntactic level of a PEPA model, have been defined [2]. These syntactic conditions are imposed by the grammar introduced earlier.

A.1 Definition of PEPA Nets Equality on Alphabets

The relation $=_a$ is used in the PEPA nets semantics. Its definition is straightforward but is included here for completeness.

$$P =_a Q \quad \text{if} \quad \text{alph}\, P = \text{alph}\, Q$$

The alphabet of a PEPA nets component is the least set satisfying the following equations.

$$\begin{aligned}
\text{alph}\,(P \underset{L}{\bowtie} Q) &= ((\text{alph}\, P) \setminus L) \cup ((\text{alph}\, Q) \setminus L) \cup ((\text{alph}\, P) \cap L \cap (\text{alph}\, Q)) \\
\text{alph}\,(P/L) &= (\text{alph}\, P) \setminus L \\
\text{alph}\,(P[C]) &= \text{alph}\, P \\
\text{alph}\, I &= \text{alph}\, S \text{ where } I \stackrel{def}{=} S \\
\text{alph}((\alpha, r).S) &= \{\, \alpha \,\} \cup \text{alph}\, S \\
\text{alph}(R + S) &= \text{alph}\, R \cup \text{alph}\, S
\end{aligned}$$

A.2 Availability of the Modelling Tools

The PEPA modelling tools, together with user documentation and papers and example PEPA models are available from the PEPA Web page which is located at `http://www.dcs.ed.ac.uk/pepa`. The PEPA Workbench for PEPA nets is available for download from this page in versions for Linux, Solaris and Windows.

Validation of GSPN and SWN Models through the PROD Tool

Susanna Donatelli and Liliana Ferro

Dip. di Informatica, Università di Torino, Corso Svizzera 185, 10149 Torino, Italy
susi@di.unito.it

Abstract. This paper presents an extension of the GreatSPN tool for Generalized stochastic Petri nets (GSPN) and Stochastic well-formed nets (SWN) solution that allows a check of state space properties: the extension is based on a translation of GSPN and SWN nets in GreatSPN format into high level Petri nets that are a valid input to the validation tool PROD and on a definition of a number of "analysis" macros that can be used by non-PROD experts to validate the model.

1 Introduction

Generalized stochastic Petri nets[1] (GSPN) and their colored extension Stochastic well-formed nets [5] (SWN) have gained wide acceptance in the performance evaluation community. A number of tools allows (often among other features) the definition and solution of GSPN models: GreatSPN [4], TimeNET [16], UltraSAN [14], SMART [6] and APNNtoolbox [11], while the solution of SWN is allowed only by the tool GreatSPN and by CPN-AMI [8] (although through an export to GreatSPN).

Both an accurate description of a small system and a rather abstract description of a very large one may easily lead to quite complex models that need to be validated from a functional point of view before being used to estimate performance analytically or via simulation. Validation in GSPN is usually supported by the computation of a number of structural properties, like P- and T-semiflows, conflict sets, structural deadlocks and traps, while a much smaller number of properties are available, and implemented, for SWN. For example, to the best of our knowledge, the only available computation of SWN semiflows is the one in CPN- AMI, but for P-semiflows [7] only and with a number of restrictions on the class of accepted models. Moreover there is in most tools a limited possibility of examining the state space, for GSPN but especially for SWN: the GreatSPN tool provides a textual description of the reachability graph (possibly symbolic for SWN) together with the list of deadlock states, livelocks, and number of strongly connected components.

The approach followed to add validation facilities to the stochastic solution of GSPN and SWN has been that of building a bridge between two tools: GreatSPN [4] and PROD [15]. GreatSPN is a graphical tool for the definition and solution of GSPN and SWN models. With respect to the classical Stochastic

T. Field et al. (Eds.): TOOLS 2002, LNCS 2324, pp. 131–140, 2002.

Petri nets (SPN), GSPNs allow the use of immediate transitions of different levels of priorities (that fire with priority over exponential ones), and the use of inhibitor arcs. SWN is a colored extension of GSPN.

PROD is a tool for the definition and validation of place/transition nets and of the high level Petri net class known as Predicate/Transition (Pr/T) nets. It is possible to define precedence among transitions, while inhibitor arcs are not allowed. It has no graphical interface, but a rather large set of efficient solution methods to build the reachability graph and check properties. The positive characteristics of PROD from the point of view of GSPN and SWN verification is that SWN and Pr/T nets are not "too distant" (as we shall see in the rest of the paper), it has a large set of properties that can be checked (including a CTL model-checker) and it has a number of optimized method for the construction and analysis of the reachability graph. Less positive characteristics are instead the absence of a graphical interface and of an user-friendly analysis environment that makes its use difficult for non-experts, and a number of limitations on the application of the optimization tools, in particular if priorities are associated to transitions none of the optimization methods can be applied.

The bridge is one way, from GreatSPN to PROD, and it is made out of two basic ingredients: a translator from GSPN and SWN (in GreatSPN format) to Pr/T nets (in PROD format), and a generator of PROD macro that allows to query PROD in a easy manner. As we shall see in this paper the translation is not only a syntactic matter, since there are some discrepancies among the basic net models of the two tools.

Before concentrating our attention on PROD we have considered a number of possible alternatives : actually just two, CPN-AMI [8] and Maria [12], since these are the only tools we found that could do reachability analysis and CTL model checking for colored nets (other tools do, but they are actually based on the Model-Checking Kit [13] that allows only safe nets). Maria does not allow precedence among transitions, and therefore it becomes very difficult to work with immediate transitions, a non acceptable limitation for GSPN and SWN users. CPN-AMI instead allows to check SWN nets, actually through an export to PROD, but only for SWN without priorities and inhibitor arcs.

The paper is organized as follows: Section 2 briefly introduces some of the PROD functionalities and the properties that can be checked on SWN using PROD, Section 3 presents the translation from GreatSPN to PROD and Section 4 shows an example of a GreatSPN-to-PROD interactive analysis session. The conclusive remarks are in Section 5.

2 GreatSPN-to-PROD: The User Perspective

The component of PROD we are mostly interested in is `probe`, that allows to build a reachability graph of a Pr/T net and to analyze it interactively using a set of queries. The answer to a query is always a (set of) path(s), since even markings are considered as zero-length path.

The GreatSPN-to-PROD module translates a GSPN/SWN model defined in GreatSPN format into the corresponding model described in PROD format.

The GreatSPN-to-PROD translator also produces a file containing a list of useful macros to be used during a `probe` session.

The translation procedure produces the PROD description of the net in the *netname.net* and *.def* files, the list of the properties macros n the *netname.macro* file and color-related definitions in C-like syntax in the *netname_funz.c* and *.h* files. The script file `ExploreRG` is also created to avoid the use of a list of PROD commands: `ExploreRG netname` generates the reachability graph (RG) of `netname`, it allows the inspection of the RG using `probe` queries, both in the original PROD syntax and through the GreatSPN-to-PROD created macros, and it finally deletes all files created during the RG generation.

The translation procedure is totally transparent to the user, but for the case of nets with inhibitor arcs. Since PROD does not allow the definition of inhibitor arcs, they are translated as test arcs over complementary places, using a technique that for GSPN is rather standard [3], and that it has here been adapted to SWN. To compute the initial marking of a complementary place it is necessary to know a bound on the number of tokens in the inhibiting place. This cannot be automated for the cases in which the net is not covered by P-semiflows or their computation is not allowed by the tool (as it is the case for SWN in GreatSPN), and therefore this information is asked to the user.

GreatSPN-to-PROD defines a number of macros to query PROD using `probe` that we list in the following.

Computing sets of Markings: `TangMark VanMark Deadlock Livelock` detects the set of tangible markings of the net (vanishing, deadlocks and livelocks components respectively); `MarkBelongSet`(mark,markSet) verifies if the marking mark belongs to the set of markings markSet; `LogicCond`(formula) detects and displays the set of markings that satisfy condition expressed by formula, where formula is a propositional logic expression in which the basic predicates are C-like marking expressions (pretty much as in GreatSPN).

Compute sets of markings based on transition enabling: `AllMarkEnabOnly`(transSet) detects and displays the set of markings in which only transitions in transSet are enabled; `MarkingSetEnab`(trans) detects and displays the set of markings that enable transition trans; `MarkSetEnabOR`(setT1,setT2) detects and displays the set of markings that enable at least either a transition of the set setT1 or a transition of the set setT2; `MarkSetEnabAND`(setT1,setT2) (same as before but with AND condition) `Successor`(mark, trans) detects and displays the marking M_1 reached from mark after the firing of trans.

Marking display: `Mark`(node) displays the marking identified by the number node;

Transition enabling: `TransEnab`(mark) detects and displays the set of transitions enabled in marking mark; `Enable`(mark,trans) verifies if the marking mark enables transition trans;

Path computations: `MOpathTO`(markSet) detects and displays the set of shortest paths from the initial marking to each marking in markSet; `PathTO`(markSet) (same as before, but for the "current" marking); `MOpathTOdeadlock` detects and displays the set of the shortest paths from M_0 to each deadlock marking; `PathTOdeadlock` (same as before, but from the "current marking"); `MOpathTOlivelock`(livelockSet); detects and displays the set of the shortest paths from M_0 to each marking belonging to the livelock; `PathTOlivelock`(livelockSet) (same as before, but from the "current marking"); `ExistPathM1toM2`(mark1,mark2) detects and displays the shortest path from marking mark1 to the mark2, if any; `AllPathM1toM2`(mark1,mark2) detects and displays all the paths, without loops, from mark1 to mark2, if any.

Some of these macros have a simple definition in PROD syntax, but other do not, for example the definition of `AllMarkEnabOnly`(lastset,transSet) is:

```
#define AllMarkEnabOnly(lastset,transSet) qmn not not
fire((transSet)) true # qmn not not fire(! (transSet)) true
# build verbose %(lastset +1) - %(lastset +2)
```

Obviously during a `probe` session the user can check the properties above and any property defined in the PROD syntax, among them also the classical CTL operators.

3 A Closer Look to the Translation

To take a closer look to the translation we consider the SWN model (Figure 1) of a multicomputer programmable logic controller (MPLC), but we use it in a rather syntactic manner, only to discuss color domains and arc functions.

In SWN each place is assigned a color domain that is a cartesian product of basic color classes, where a basic color class is a set of elements called colors, and the basic color classes are disjoint. Each basic color class can be split into disjoint sets (static subclasses) and, for a GreatSPN idiosyncrasy, at least one per class should be defined. PROD has instead no concept of color classes (there is a single color type in Pr/T nets, the set of integer).

The SWN model has two basic color classes CB, of static subclass Buf, and C, of static subclass El, defined as: CB = u Buf, with Buf= { b1, b2, b3} and CE = El, with EL={ e1, e2}. Places *p1, p2, p6* and *p7* have color domain CE, while "CE,CE" means the Cartesian product of CE and CE, so that tokens in *p3* are pairs in the Cartesian product $\{e1, e2\} \times \{e1, e2\}$.

The PROD net file generated by the GreatSPN-to-PROD translator is shown in Figure 2, while the macros and functions defined to implement colors are shown in the right portion of Figure 1. We now consider the most salient features of the translation.

Translating colors classes, place's domains and markings. Each SWN basic color class is defined as a set or as an ordered list of static subclasses, and each static subclass is a set (or an ordered list) of colored tokens that are named in a symbolic manner. The Pr/T formalism of PROD has no explicit definition of color class and subclass, since each token is a tuple of integers.

To translate the SWN net in such a way as to be able to still distinguish the colors we have decided to define a PROD macro for each basic color: the macro associates to each color a different integer (therefore distinct classes have disjoint numerical values) in such a way as to respect ordering of colors, so for

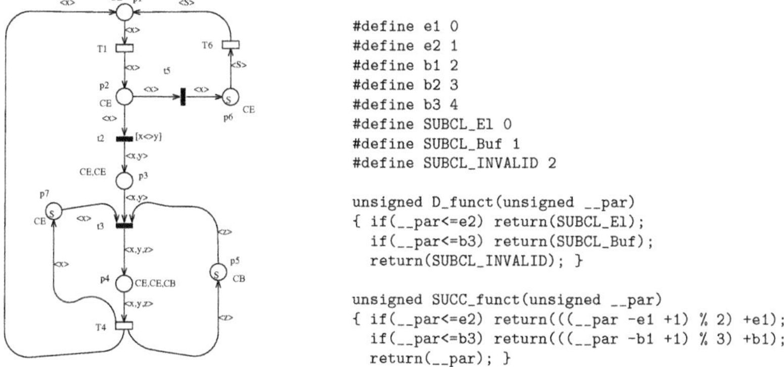

```
#define e1 0
#define e2 1
#define b1 2
#define b2 3
#define b3 4
#define SUBCL_El 0
#define SUBCL_Buf 1
#define SUBCL_INVALID 2

unsigned D_funct(unsigned __par)
{ if(__par<=e2) return(SUBCL_El);
  if(__par<=b3) return(SUBCL_Buf);
  return(SUBCL_INVALID); }

unsigned SUCC_funct(unsigned __par)
{ if(__par<=e2) return(((__par -e1 +1) % 2) +e1);
  if(__par<=b3) return(((__par -b1 +1) % 3) +b1);
  return(__par); }
```

Fig. 1. SWN example model and color translation in PROD

the class $El = \{e1, e2\}$, the GreatSPN-to-PROD translator defines two macros: `#define e1 0` and `#define e2 1`.

PROD has no explicit definition of color domain of a place, although it is possible to state what is the range of values of "legal" tokens for a place through the **lo** and **hi** keyword. We therefore associate to each place in PROD a range derived from the color domain of the place in SWN. Again with reference to Figure 1, the domain of place *p4* is CE,CE,CB and it is translated into the PROD place definition: `#place p4 lo(<.e1,e1,b1.>) hi(<.e2,e2,b3.>)`, where *e1* and *e2* correspond to the first and last color in CE, and *b1* e *b3* to the first and last token in CB.

The initial marking of a place is defined in SWN as a sum of tuples, where each element of a tuple may indicate a single token or a set of tokens: for example a single tuple containing function S indicates the sum of all tokens over the color domain of the place. Using again our PLC model of Figure 1 let us consider two examples of SWN initial markings and their PROD translations:

1. $M_0(\text{p5}) = < b1 > + < b2 >$ $\longrightarrow$ `#place p5 ... mk(<.b1.>+<.b2.>)`
2. $M_0(\text{p4}) = < S, S, S >$ $\longrightarrow$ `#place p4 ... mk(<.e1..e2,e1..e2,b1..b3.>)`

In the first case in M_0 place *p5* contains tokens *b1* and *b2*, while in the second case the color domain of place *p4* is the composition of three basic color classes(CE,CE,CB), and the marking is $< S, S, S >$, therefore the translation assigns to *p4* the initial marking mk(<.e1..e2,e1..e2,b1..b3.>), that is to say the Cartesian product of {e1,e2} × {e1,e2} × {b1,b2,b3}. The translation of the initial marking of the MPLC net as in Figure 1 is shown in the translation of the places given in Figure 2.

Transitions, guards and priorities. Translation of transitions is rather straightforward (apart from arc functions) and some examples are shown in Figure 2. Priority is called precedence in PROD, but is essentially a global priority like in GSPN and SWN, that is to say each transition belongs to an unique priority

```
#prec TEMP_PRI << IMM_PRI_G1
#place p3_y_t2 lo(<.e1.>)  hi(<.e2.>) mk(1<.e1..e2.>)
#place p4 lo(<.e1,e1,b1.>)\
     hi(<.e2,e2,b3.>)
#place p5 lo(<.b1.>)\
     hi(<.b3.>)\
    mk(1<.b1..b3.>)
#place p7 lo(<.e1.>)\
     hi(<.e2.>)\
    mk(1<.e1..e2.>)
#place p3 lo(<.e1,e1.>)\
     hi(<.e2,e2.>)
#place p6 lo(<.e1.>)\
     hi(<.e2.>)\
    mk(1<.e1..e2.>)
#trans T6
 in { p6 : 1<.e1.>+1<.e2.>;}
 out    { p1 : 1<.e1.>+1<.e2.>;}
 comp   { Precedence(TEMP_PRI); Accept(); }
#endtr
#trans T4
 in { p4 : 1<.x,y,z.>;}
 out    { p1 : 1<.x.>;
     p7 : 1<.x.>;
     p5 : 1<.z.>;}
 comp   { Precedence(TEMP_PRI); Accept(); }
#endtr
#trans t5
 in { p2 : 1<.x.>;}
 out    { p6 : 1<.x.>;}
 comp   { Precedence(IMM_PRI_G1); Accept(); }
#endtr
#trans t2
 in { p3_y_t2 : <.y.>;
     p2 : 1<.x.>;}
 out    { p3_y_t2 : <.y.>;
     p3 : 1<.x,y.>;}
 gate    x!=y ;
 comp   { Precedence(IMM_PRI_G1); Accept(); }
#endtr
```

Fig. 2. The PROD translation

level. In the case of the example there are two levels called TEMP_PRI and IMM_PRI_G1, for timed and immediate transitions of priority 1, respectively.

In SWN guards are boolean expressions that can be associated to transitions. Since PROD has a `gate` construct that is a boolean expression associated to transitions, the translation is, in the simplest cases, quite straightforward. For

example the MPLC model has a guard ($x <> y$) associated to transition *t2* that is translated as `gate x != y;`. But guards may also make use of the subclass function $d(x)$: the guard $[d(x) <> d(y)]$ means that x and y have to belong to two different static subclasses. Checking if an element belongs to a class is realized in PROD through a function automatically produced by the translation called D_funct, that is shown in Figure 1, so:
[x<>y and d(x)<>El] $\longrightarrow$ `gate (x!=y) && (D_funct(x) == SUB_CL_Elab);`

Variable instantiation. In PROD it is not possible to use "free variables", that is to say variables that appear in output arcs of a transition, but that do not appear in any of the input arcs to the transition, while this is quite common with SWN models. The reason is that in PROD there is no explicit definition of color domain for places, and it is therefore necessary to modify the net by adding a place and a self loop, and to associate the free variable to the arc of the self loop. More precisely: given a transition *t1* with a free variable x on an arc from *t1* to place *p1* the net is modified as follows: 1) a new place of name *p1_x_t1* is added to the net, its color domain is the color class of x; 2) an arc from *p1_x_t1* to *t1* and one from *t1* to *p1_x_t1* are added to the net, with associated function x.
An example of free variable is variable y out of transition *t2* in the SWN of Figure 1, whose translation is shown in Figure 2.

Arc functions. Arc functions can be rather complex expressions, built as sums of tuples, each with a multiplicative coefficient; each element of the tuple can be a sum of variables and of predefined functions: the constant function S, the successor function !x, and the predecessor function ^x , the last two can be applied only to ordered color classes. If place *p1* has color domain D, examples of functions that can be on an arc out of *p1* are: $< x >$ that denotes a color in the domain D, $< S > + < x >$ that denotes all the colors in D, with an element repeated twice, $< S - x >$ that denotes all the colors of D, but one.

In PROD functions on arcs are sum of tuples, each with its own coefficient, and each element of the tuple is a C-like expression that must evaluate to an integer value. SWN and PROD therefore mainly differ in the use of the S, !x, and ^x functions, and in the absence of the difference operator -.

For !x, and ^x the choice has been that of defining two functions SUCC_funct and PRED_funct that work for any color class, thanks to the fact that in PROD each color is an integer. These functions are shown in Figure 2. Observe that in PROD the SUCC and PRED functions can be applied to any color classes, while in SWN the application is allowed only to ordered color classes, but this is not a problem, since we assume that the SWN has been syntactically checked by GreatSPN before proceeding to the translation.

Function S represents the set of all colors of a color class or of a color domain, and it is translated as a sum of tuples, for example in the MPLC model there is an arc labelled with S from p_6 to T_6 and from $T6$ to p_6. The translation of the arcs is shown in Figure 2 associated to transition $T6$: function S becomes a sum of unary tuples, one per each color in class El. More complicated cases exists, for example assume that the arc from t_2 to p_3 is changed to $< S, S >$, then the translation is:

arc $< S, S >$ from *t2* to *p3* $\longrightarrow$ `#trans t2 .....`
cdom(p3)= CE×CE

```
out {p3:<.e1,e1.>+<.e1,e2.>+
    <.e2,e1.>+<.e2,e2.>;}
```

Additional difficulties arise when the arc function is a difference of terms, like $< S - x >$, since differences among tuples are not allowed in PROD, and therefore the translation requires a transformation at the net level. Given a place *p1* of domain D={d1,d2,...,dn} connected to transition *t1* through an arc of associated function $< S - x >$, the following transformation takes place:

- $< S - x >$ is replaced by $\sum_{i=1}^{n-1} < x_i >$, where x_i are free variables (they do not appear in any other arc connected to *t1*);
- a place p_{new} is added, with color domain equal to that of S.
- a self-loop is created between p_{new} and *t1* with function $x + \sum_{i=1}^{n-1} < x_i >$

4 Example of a Probe Session

The analysis in GreatSPN of the model in Figure 1 for the case of class Buf= { b1} and EL={ e1, e2, e3, e4} reveals 1516 tangible states, 1298 vanishing states, no deadlocks and the initial marking is a home state.

By launching the ExploreRG command the net is translated in PROD and the `probe` interactive environment is entered. We can start the analysis by asking the default statistics about the RG construction using the "statistics" command, while we can list the tangible markings using "TangMark" and the vanishing marking using "VanMark" (the use of .... means that omission of a part).

```
0#statistics
Number of nodes: 2814
Number of arrows: 6905
Number of terminal nodes: 0
Number of nodes that have been completely processed: 2814
Number of strongly connected components: 1
Number of nontrivial terminal strongly connected components: 0
0#TangMark
0,        1,        6,  .........
..............  2594,     2595,     2596,     2597
1516 paths;   Built set %3
0#VanMark
   2,        3,        4,        ...................
................. 2810,     2811, 2812,     2813
1298 paths;    Built set %4
```

A state can be visualized in terms of distribution of tokens over places by the following query:

```
0#Mark(2807)
Node 2807, belongs to strongly connected component %%0
  p3_y_t2: <.0.> + <.1.> + <.2.> + <.3.>
  p5: <.4.>
  p7: <.0.> + <.1.> + <.2.> + <.3.>
```

```
  p3: <.0,3.> + <.1,0.> + <.2,3.>
  p1: <.3.>
-------------------------------------------------
```

Due to space limitations we do not show a complete validation session, but the interested reader can find in [2] a full case study.

5 Conclusions

This paper describes a translator from GSPN and SWN nets, expressed through the GreatSPN tool, into a valid input format for the PROD tool. The translator also provides a number of predefined macros that allow performance modellers, presumably not very deeply acquainted with state space verification tools to validate their performance model through reachability analysis.

The need for reachability based validation is particularly relevant for SWN models, due to the fact that very few structural properties can be computed in the available tools, and due to the fact that some of the complexity is hidden in the colored functions associated to arcs, so that some subtle errors may go undetected, but even when an uncorrect behaviour, like a deadlock, or transitions with zero throughput are detected, it may be very difficult to trace the problem back to its causes.

The GreatSPN-to-PROD tool has been implemented in C using Lex and Yacc, as GreatSPN, and up to now it is able to deal with all GSPN models and with most SWN models. Functionalities that are not translated for SWN are: the use of a name of a function over an arc (the translator assume that the full expression is given), variable names and color names should be distinct, functions of the form $< S-!x >$, $< S-$ ^x $>$, and $< S,S > - < x,y >$ are not translated (this restriction is not very significant since it is possible to rewrite them in terms of functions that are translated). The translator is available to interested users, by sending an email to the papers's authors, and it will be included in the next distribution of GreatSPN-to-PROD.

Future work is to gain more confidence with the method, to extend the set of macros and to consider the possibility of model checking GSPN and SWN using the ETMCC [10] tool against CSL logic (CTL extended with stochastic aspects), along the way of the example presented in [9]

References

1. M. Ajmone Marsan, G. Balbo, G. Conte, S. Donatelli, and G. Franceschinis. Modelling with Generalized Stochastic Petri Nets. J. Wiley, 1995.
2. P. Ballarini, S. Bernardi, and S. Donatelli. Validation and evaluation of a software solution for fault tolerant distributed synchronization. *Submitted for publication – available on request to susi@di.unito.it.*
3. G. Chiola, S. Donatelli, and G. Franceschinis. GSPN versus SPN: what is the actual role of immediate transitions? In *Proc. 4th Intern. Workshop on Petri Nets and Performance Models*, pages 20–31, Melbourne, Australia, December 1991. IEEE-CS Press.

4. G. Chiola, G. Franceschinis, R. Gaeta, and M. Ribaudo. GreatSPN 1.7: GRaphical Editor and Analyzer for Timed and Stochastic Petri Nets. *Performance Evaluation*, special issue on Performance Modelling Tools, (1), 24, 1996.
5. G. Chiola, C. Dutheillet, G. Franceschinis, and S. Haddad. A Symbolic Reachability Graph for Colored Petri Nets. *Theoretical Computer Science B (Logic, semantics and theory of programming)*, 176(1&2):39–65, April 1997.
6. G. Ciardo and A. S. Miner. SMART: Simulation and Markovian Analyzer for Reliability and Timing. In *Proc. IEEE International Computer Performance and Dependability Symposium (IPDS'96)*, Urbana-Champaign, IL, USA. Sept. 1996. IEEE Comp. Soc. Press.
7. J.M. Couvreur and J. Martinez. Linear invariants in commutative high-level nets. In *Proc.* 10th *Intern. Conference on Application and Theory of Petri Nets*, Bonn, Germany, June 1989.
8. *The CPN-AMI environment.* `http://www-src.lip6.fr/logiciels/framekit/cpn-ami.html`.
9. B. Haverkort, H. Hermanns, J.P. Katoen. The Use of Model Checking Techniques for Quantitative Dependability Evaluation In *IEEE Symposium on Reliable Distributed Systems* (SRDS), IEEE CS Press, October 2000
10. H. Hermanns, J. P. Katoen, J. Meyer-Kayser, and M. Siegle. A Markov Chain Model Checker In *Tools and Algorithms for the Construction and Analysis of Systems*, LNCS 1785: pp. 347-362, 2000
11. P. Kemper F. Bause, P. Buchholz. A toolbox for functional and quantitative analysis of DEDS. Short paper at TOOLS'98, LNCS 1469, Springer-Verlag.
12. Maria: a Reachability Analyser for Algebraic System Nets, `http://www.tcs.hut.fi/Software/maria`
13. The Model-Checking Kit, `http://wwwbrauer.informatik.tu-muenchen.de/gruppen/theorie/KIT`.
14. W. D. Obal II, M. A. Qureshi, D. D. Deavours, and W. H. Sanders. Overview of UltraSAN. *Proc. IEEE Int. Performance and Dependability Symposium*, Urbana, IL, USA, Sept. 4-6, 1996. `http://www.crhc.uiuc.edu/UltraSAN`.
15. K. Varpaaniemi, J. Halme, K. Hiekkanen, and T. Pyssysalo. PROD reference manual. Technical Report Series B, number 13, Helsinki University of Technology, August 1995. `http://www.tcs.hut.fi/prod`
16. A. Zimmermann, J. Freiheit, R. German, and G. Hommel. Petri Net Modelling and Performability Evaluation with TimeNET 3.0. *Proc. of TOOLS2000*, LNCS 1786, pp. 188-202, Springer-Verlag.

Software Performance Models from System Scenarios in Use Case Maps

Dorin C. Petriu and Murray Woodside

Dept. of Systems and Computer Engineering
Carleton University, Ottawa K1S 5B6, Canada.
{dorin,cmw}@sce.carleton.ca

Abstract. Software performance concerns begin at the very outset of a new project. The first definition of a software system may be in the form of Use Cases, which may be elaborated as scenarios: this work creates performance models from scenarios. The Use Case Maps notation captures the causal flow of intended execution in terms of responsibilities, which may be allocated to components, and which are annotated with expected resource demands. The SPT algorithm was developed to transform scenario models into performance models. The UCM2LQN tool implements SPT and converts UCM scenario models to layered queueing performance models, allowing rapid evaluation of an evolving scenario definition. The same reasoning can be applied to other scenario models such as Message Sequence Charts, UML Activity Graphs (or Collaboration Diagrams, or Sequence Diagrams), but UCMs are particularly powerful, in that they can combine interacting scenarios and show scenario interactions. Thus a solution for UCMs can be applied to multiple scenarios defined with other notations.

1 Introduction

Software performance analysis often begins from scenario definitions, which describe the system behaviour during a response. For example Smith's Execution Graphs [28][29] can be used to capture a performance analyst's version of system scenarios, and can be used in the earliest stages of planning. Kahkipuro [16] used scenarios expressed as UML collaborations, and this approach has been extended in a proposed UML performance profile [26]. Other authors have used Petri nets to capture the scenarios.

Because software designers are (usually) not also performance analysts, the performance-specific scenario models (such as Execution Graphs) create a conceptual gap between the design and the performance analysis. To avoid this gap, it would be better to use a *software engineering* scenario notation. This work is based on a well-developed scenario language called Use Case Maps (UCMs) [7], but it is extensible to other notations such as UML. UCMs expand Use Cases into scenarios described as causal sequences of responsibilities, either unbound or associated with components. UCMs can be used to reason about architecture and to develop an architecture within a structural notation, possibly based on the UML, such as is described by Hofmeister, Nord and Soni [15].

T. Field et al. (Eds.): TOOLS 2002, LNCS 2324, pp. 141-158, 2002.

To provide continuous re-evaluation during the evolution of an architecture there must be automation. This paper describes the UCM2LQN converter, a tool which automates the conversion of UCM scenario models into Layered Queueing Network (LQN) performance models. It is integrated into the UCM Navigator, which is an editor and repository tool for UCMs, so that the UCMNav can be used as a front-end editor for design models which are also performance models. The concepts of the converter can in principle be extended to other scenario modeling tools such as Stories [8] or UML [5] which provides Activity Diagrams, Collaboration Diagrams and Sequence Diagrams. Conversion of Collaboration models into layered queues has previously been described by Kahkipuro [16]. Eventually the ideas of UCM2LQN may be applied to annotated UML models using a standard profile for performance annotations [26].

The performance model notation used here is Layered Queueing, because this form of model captures logical resource effects and provides good traceability between the performance measures and the emerging software architecture. It incorporates the software components as servers, and logical resources (such as buffers, locks and threads), as well as the hardware resources. Essentially, layered queueing is a canonical form for simultaneous resource queues, that are common in software resources. Simpler queueing models could be used instead, but they would model fewer features of the resource architecture, as described in [32]. Petri net models capture these features very well, as described by Pooley [23], but sometimes have problems with larger system scales.

The difficult problem solved by UCM2LQN applies to any scenario notation which binds actions to software components, and not just to Use Case Maps. The problem is in interpreting paths as interactions between software objects which may have resource attributes. Interactions which imply waiting for logical resources (blocking) have performance effects and are captured by analyzing the entire path. A second kind of difficulty comes from interactions between scenarios, either in competition or in collaboration.

There has been considerable effort expended on methods for Software Performance Engineering (SPE), and an overview can be obtained from the proceedings of the two international Workshops on Software and Performance (WOSP'98 [33] and WOSP2000 [34]). Despite this effort, SPE has proven to be more appealing in concept than in practice. The effort needed to cross into the realm of performance analysis, in the course of any design project, is too high, and the concepts are alien to the developer. Using automated model-building reduces the need for special performance expertise. There is still a requirement to specify the appropriate performance data - such as service demands by responsibilities, arrival rates at start points, branching probabilities, loop repetitions, and device speed factors - as annotations in the UCM in order to get meaningful results. These values can be obtained from known workloads or they can be approximated by using a budgeting approach and supplying values based on an estimate of much time operations have to complete [27][30]. The results may validate the performance aspects of the design by confirming the budgets, or may identify problems such as bottlenecks, and this work can be a partnership between the designer and the performance expert.

This research pins its hopes on embedding most of the description into the software definition as it emerges, and on tracking this definition through its stages into code. It is important to begin early, and the automatic converter described here captures the first step in design.

2 Models for Scenarios and Performance

2.1 Use Case Maps

UCM notation was invented by Buhr and his co-workers [6][7] to capture designer intentions while reasoning about concurrency and partitioning of a system, in the earliest stages of design. It was derived by watching designers discussing and massaging ideas into architectures, and is intended to be intuitive, and high-level. Details can be represented, but are not the purpose. Compared to the Unified Modeling Language (UML), UCMs fit in between Use Cases and UML behavioural diagrams. In UML Class Diagrams are used to describe how a system is constructed, but do not describe how it works; this task is taken up by UCM's. Collaboration Diagrams do provide a high-level description of how the system works, but only one scenario at a time [3].

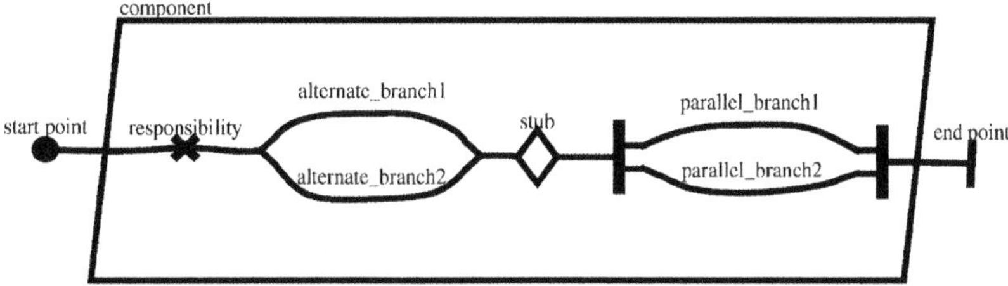

Fig. 1. Example of the UCM notation.

A Use Case Map is a collection of elements that describe one or more scenarios unfolding throughout a system [7] [6]. The basic elements of the notation are shown in Figure 1. A scenario is represented by a path, shown as a line from a start point (a filled circle) to an end point (a bar), and traversed by a token from start to end. Paths can be overlaid on components which represent functional or logical entities, which may represent hardware or software resources. Responsibilities, denoted with an X-shaped mark on the path, represent functions to be accomplished. The performance modeling assumes that the computational workload is associated with responsibilities, or is overhead implied by crossings between components. Responsibilities are annotated by service demands (number of CPU or disk operations, or calls to other services) and data store operations.

A path can be traversed by many tokens, and several tokens may occupy a single path at once. The workload of a path is indicated by annotations to its start point (closed or open arrivals, arrival rates and external delays). A path can be refined hierarchically by adding stubs, which represent separately specified maps called plug-ins. There may also be several alternative plug-ins for any stub.

Paths have the usual behaviour constructs of OR fork/joins (representing alternative paths), AND fork/joins (representing parallel paths) and loops. OR forks and loops are annotated by choice probabilities and mean loop counts. AND and OR forks do not have to be nested, that is they do not have to join later. This is realistic for software design, but creates problems for model creation, as the structured workload graph reduction used by Smith ([28], chapter 4) does not always apply.

The UCM Navigator (UCMNav) [17] was developed by Miga as an editor and repository manager, and has been used by our industrial associates to create large, industry-scale scenario specifications. It supports

- drawing and editing UCMs, including multiple scenarios, and storing in an XML format.
- annotations for deployment on system devices and for performance, as well as comments and pseudo code,
- specifying delay requirements along a path,
- generating Message Sequence Charts (MSC) as well as performance models.

The UCM2LQN converter (to be described below) is implemented as an add-on to UCMNav, and generates a file in the LQN language which can then be used (outside the UCMNav) to compute performance measures using either a simulator called LQSim, or an analytic solver LQNS.

2.2 Layered Queueing Networks

Layered Queueing Networks (LQN) model contention for both software and hardware resources, based on requests for services. Entities in the role of clients make service requests and queue at the server. In ordinary queueing networks there is one layer of servers; in LQN, servers may make requests to other servers, with any number of layers [24][48]. An LQN can thus model the performance impact of the software structure and interactions, and be used to detect software bottlenecks as well as hardware performance bottlenecks [19]. There have been many applications [22][31][51].

In an LQN the software resources are called tasks, (representing a software process with its own thread of execution, or some other resource such as a buffer) and the hardware resources are called devices (typical devices are CPUs and disks). Tasks can have priority on their CPU. The workload of a LQN is driven by arrival streams of external requests, and by tasks which cycle and make requests, called *reference tasks*.

An LQN can be represented by a graph with nodes for tasks and devices, and arrows for service requests (labelled by the mean number of messages sent). There are two types of arc to represent asynchronous messages, with no reply, and synchronous messages which block the sender until there is a reply (synchronous messages are also called task calls; the model was created originally for Ada software). Tasks receive either kind of request message at designated interface points called *entries*. A task has a different entry for every kind of service it provides; an entry also represents a class of service. Internally an entry has service demands defined by sequences of smaller computational blocks called *activities*, which are related in sequence, loop, parallel

(AND fork/joins) and alternative (OR fork/joins) configurations. Activities have processor service demands and generate calls to entries in other tasks.

A third type of interaction called forwarding is a combination of synchronous and asynchronous behaviour. The sending client task makes a synchronous call and blocks until it receives a reply. The receiving task partially processes the call and then forwards it to another server which becomes responsible for sending a reply to the blocked client task; it can be forwarded with a probability, and any number of times. The intermediate server task can begin a new operation after forwarding the call.

Models are created in a textual language which can be edited as text or with a simple graphical editor, and can be solved either by simulation, or by analytic approximations by the solver LQNS. LQNS is based on [31] and the Method of Layers [24], with a number of additional approximations [10][11][12]. The approximations have limitations in dealing with priorities (poor accuracy) and with AND-joins that do not have an AND-fork in the same task, so simulation is often useful.

The interactions in LQN's can be understood more clearly using UCMs to show the sequences of events. Figure 2 has a series of UCMs describing the interactions which must be detected when building an LQN model:

(a) a basic synchronous interaction between two tasks taskA and taskB has a path launched by an activity (which is an inferred overhead activity for communications); the reply returns the path to the same activity. The interpretation of this message is the same if the path goes on from taskB to other tasks, returning to taskB before returning to taskA.

(b) two activities in taskA send messages, one to taskB and a later one to taskC.

(c) taskA sends an asynchronous message to taskB. The interpretation of the message is the same if the path goes on from there, but never returns to taskA. The LQN notation is an open arrowhead, here shown with one side only.

(d) taskA sends a message to taskB which is forwarded to taskC, before returning directly to taskA. The forwarding path can include any number of intermediate tasks; the assumption is that taskA (or a thread of the task) waits blocked for the return, unless there is a fork in taskA before sending the request. The LQN notation for the forwarding steps is a solid arrow for the original blocking call, and dashed arrows for the other, non-blocking messages.

Figure 2 also shows the LQN notations for forks and joins and for loops.

3 Extracting a Layered Performance Model

The novel contribution in this work is finding disguised synchronous and forwarding interactions. These identify potential software blocking which may have significant performance implications. Compared to many scenario analyses (such as used in [28]), which only determine device demands by class, the layered model also retains the component context of each demand. Other models which retain the software context of demand, e.g. Kahkipuro's AQN [16], require that blocking interactions be explicitly identified.

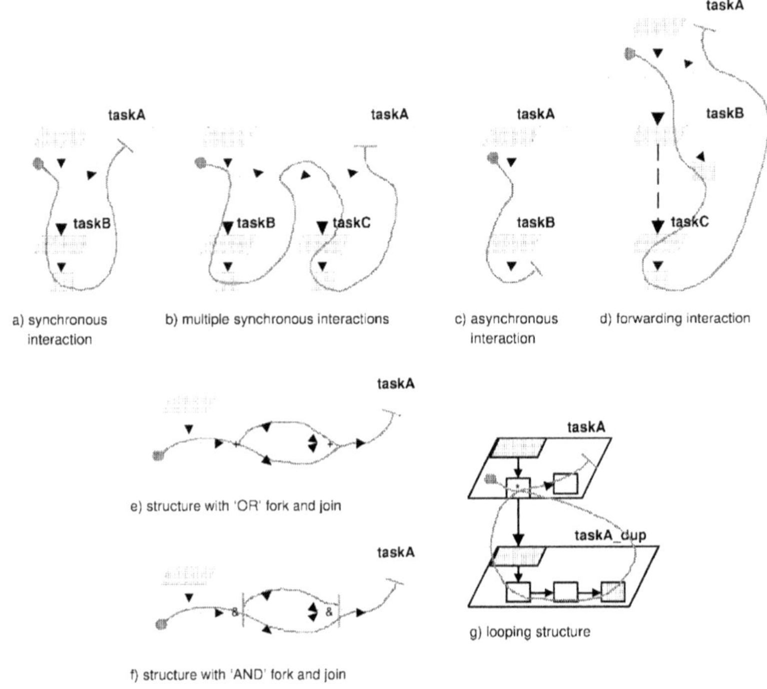

Fig. 2. Corresponding interactions and structures in UCM and LQN.

3.1 Correspondences between UCMs and LQN's

There are some quite close correspondences between some of the scenario entities, and LQN model entities that can represent them.

Table 1. Corresponding UCM and LQN constructs.

UCM Construct	LQN Construct
start point	reference task
responsibility	activity
AND/OR forks and joins	LQN AND/OR forks and joins
component	task
device	device
service	entry in a task (with a dedicated processor)

Considering these in order,

- A reference task can serve either as an open workload generator inserting asynchronous requests, or a closed workload generator, in which case it has a multiplicity equal to the population, and each task makes synchronous requests (and waits for the response).
- A UCM responsibility can represent an arbitrarily complex set of operations, however here we are restricting its significance to a sequential operation, which can make calls to services. A complex operation can be captured in many cases by these calls, which are mapped to servers and service requests in the LQN.
- A component may represent an operating system process, or an object or module of some kind. An LQN task has a primary meaning as a separate operating system process, but it also represent an object or module executing in the context of some task. A synchronous call to the module is effectively sequential, because of the blocking of the main task, so it is equivalent to including the module inside the main task... modeling a module in this way exposes its contributions to performance.
- A "service" in UCM is an annotation representing a service used by the software but outside the scope of the UCM, such as a file service or a database service. Ultimately a submodel for this subsystem will be added to the model, but as a placeholder, a task with a dedicated processor is inserted to take the calls for the service.

3.2 Correspondences of Path Structure in LQN

Within a component the scenario expression of path structure translates directly to the LQN activity sequence notation, with the usual constructs of alternate and parallel branching (and joining), as well as looping. The LQN notation supports the same constructs. Figure 2(e) shows a UCM interpretation of an LQN task with an OR fork and join (in the LQN model the OR is indicated by a '+' connector). Figure 2(f) shows an AND fork and join (the LQN model uses '&' in the connector). A UCM loop point is indicated by an OR join followed immediately by an OR fork; the LQN notation has a loop traversal count. A complex loop body can be represented in the LQN by a pseudo-task which is "called" by the loop controller and executes the activities of the body, as indicated in Figure 2(g).

3.2.1 Fork and Join in Separate Components

In a scenario, paths may fork in one component and join in another. Both UCMs and LQN's support this feature; the path is conveyed from the first component to the second by asynchronous or forwarding interactions. Simulation evaluation in our tools assumes that any token on the joining paths is a candidate, but applications may require that only tokens that are siblings from the fork should be allowed to join. If the scenario is such that tokens cannot pass each other this is no problem, otherwise it is a headache both to model and (indeed) to implement.

3.3 Performance Annotations in UCMs

The performance annotations on UCM elements were mentioned in the description of the UCM notation above, but it is worth summarizing them more formally since they provide the parameters and some of the elements of the performance model. Table 2 shows the annotations and their default values.

Table 2. UCM constructs, the necessary performance data needed to create meaningful LQNs, UCMNav support for entering the data, and default values used if the data is not specified.

UCM Element	Performance Annotation	Default
responsibility	number of calls	1.0 calls
component	associated devices	one infinite processor
device	speed-up factor	1.0
OR fork	probability of each branch (as a weight)	equal probability for each branch
loop	number of loop iterations	1.0 iterations
start point	open system arrival rate and distribution	1 arrival/sec, with deterministic delay
	OR closed system popula tion and delay	10 jobs with deterministic delay of 1 sec.

4 Scenario to Performance Model Transformation Algorithm

The algorithm for scenario to performance transformation (SPT) must do the following:

- identify when the path crosses component boundaries
- determine the type of messages sent or received when crossing component boundaries
- capture the path structure and the correct sequence of path elements
    - create the LQN objects that correspond directly to UCM elements
    - handle forks, joins, and loops

The UCM is transformed into an LQN on a path by path basis. Each start point is assumed to begin an independent path, and as such is assigned to its own reference task. Reference tasks act as the work generators for the LQN model. Each reference tasks is assigned arrival rates and distributions as specified by the start points in the UCM. Similarly, LQN activities are assigned workload demands as specified in the corresponding UCM responsibility and OR branches are assigned probabilities set in the UCM. If any performance data is missing from the UCM, default values are assigned as noted in Table 2.

The SPT algorithm follows a UCM path from its start point. Each element along the path is checked for its enclosing component, and if the enclosing component has changed then a boundary has been crossed. Each boundary crossing corresponds to a message between components. The message may be a synchronous call, a reply, an asynchronous call, or a forwarding; to resolve its role in an interaction requires examining a portion of the history of the path. This is called *resolving* the interaction. Therefore there is a need to keep track of all messages that have been discovered, but not yet resolved.

4.1 Call and Reply Stack (CRS)

The Call and Reply Stack (CRS) is the mechanism that stores the unresolved message history as the path is traversed. Whenever a component boundary is crossed, the message event is pushed onto the stack and then the pattern of messages in the stack is analyzed to see if they satisfy one of the interaction patterns illustrated in Figure 2. For example, if the most recent message can be interpreted as a reply to a previous message on the CRS, the interpretation is performed and a synchronous interaction is generated and attached to the LQN elements. The priority in resolving interactions is to interpret them first as synchronous, and then as forwarding; interactions are interpreted as asynchronous only as a last resort. The operations of the CRS can be summarized as follows:

- unresolved messages, with the LQN entries and activities involved in sending and receiving, are pushed on the CRS
- when messages are resolved as LQN interactions, the associated LQN entries and activities are popped off the CRS
- any messages remaining on the CRS when the end of the path is reached are resolved as being involved in asynchronous calls.

A result of this approach is that no message (with its associated workload) is ever lost.

Figure 3 shows a UCM with multiple boundary crossings and the state of the CRS after each of those crossings.

The path traversal is made more complicated by the presence of forks and joins. If a fork is encountered along the path, then the outgoing branches are followed one by one, until either a join or an end point is reached. Figure 4 shows the order in which a set of path segments with forks and joins are traversed, starting from the start point on the left. When a join is encountered the traversal proceeds past it only after all the incoming branches that can be reached from the current start point have been traversed.

Branching can also affect the structure of the CRS. When a fork is encountered the CRS is also forked, so that there is a separate CRS sub-stack for each branch of the fork. Branches are explored in an arbitrary order. When exploring a branch, interactions are resolved as they are found. If, after an OR fork, the resolution of messages on a branch involves messages sent before the fork (and therefore in a previous CRS sub-stack), then the fork is moved back to just before them. The CRS elements back to the new fork are duplicated for all branches.

CRS contents after boundary crossing a:
[1] - message sent by taskA

CRS contents after boundary crossing b:
[1] - call made from taskA to taskB

CRS contents after boundary crossing c:
[2] - message sent by taskB
[1] - call made from taskA to taskB

CRS contents after boundary crossing d:
[2] - call made from taskB to taskC
[1] - call made from taskA to taskB

CRS contents after boundary crossing e:
[3] - message sent by taskC
[2] - call made from taskB to taskC
[1] - call made from taskA to taskB

CRS contents after boundary crossing f:
(empty)

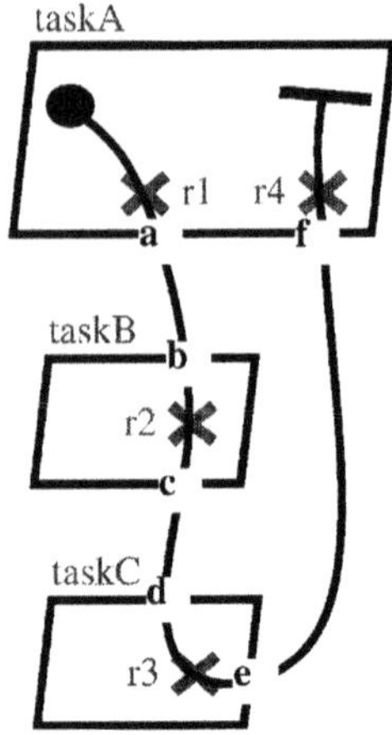

Final resolution of messages after boundary crossing f:
....taskA makes a synchronous call to taskB
....taskB makes a forwarding call to taskC
...taskC sends a reply to taskA

Fig. 3. UCM showing the contents of the CRS after each of a series of component boundary crossings.

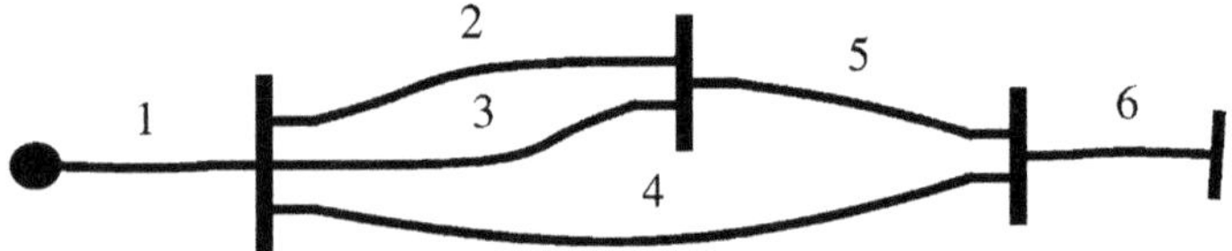

Fig. 4. UCM path showing the order in which branches are traversed.

4.2 SPT Algorithm

The following high-level description of the algorithm describes the operations carried out at each point along the path:

(a) create appropriate LQN objects for the current path point

1.1. *if* the current point is a start point *then*

1.1.1. create a reference task for the start point

1.2. *if* the current point is an end point *then* go to step 4

1.3. *if* the current point is a responsibility or a stub with no plugin *then*

1.3.1. create an LQN activity and update it with the service requests of the responsibility or stub

1.4. *if* the current point is a fork *then*

1.4.1. create an LQN fork of an appropriate type

1.4.2. create a branch CRS for the next branch path to be traversed

1.5. *if* the current point is a join *then*

1.5.1. *if* all the incoming branches have been traversed *then* proceed past the join and merge the CRS for the last branch to be traversed with the main path CRS before the branch

1.5.2. *else* go back and traverse the next incoming branch

1.5.2.1. create a branch CRS for the next branch path to be traversed

1.6. *if* the current point is a loop head *then*

1.6.1. create a repeated LQN activity to be the loop control activity

1.6.2. create an LQN task to handle the loop body

1.6.3. add a synchronous call from the loop control activity to the loop body

(b) look ahead to the next point on the path

(c) analyze inter-component interactions (identify any component boundary crossings and resolve the nature of the inter-component messages)

3.1. *if* the current point resides in a component *then*

3.1.1. *if* the next point does not reside in a component *then* create an unresolved message, with an activity to send it, and push them on the CRS

3.1.2. *else if* the next point resides in a different component that has a message pending on the CRS *then* identify a synchronous or forwarding interaction and resolve it

3.1.3. `else if the next point resides in a different component that does not have any message pending on the CRS then identify a call of unknown type (synchronous, forwarding, or asynchronous).`

3.2. `else the current point does not reside in a component`

3.2.1. `if the next point resides in a component that does not have any message pending on the CRS then identify the reception of a call`

3.2.2. `else if the next point resides in a component that has a message pending on the CRS then identify a synchronous or forwarding interaction and resolve it`

(d) *if* the current point is an end point *then* any unresolved interactions are asynchronous

(e) *else* set the next point as the current path point and go to step 1

The algorithm ensures that every responsibility in the scenario is traversed and that a corresponding LQN activity is generated with the specified service demands. A more detailed description of the algorithm can be found in [20].

5 Example - Ticket Reservation System

The Ticket Reservation System (TRS) allows users to browse through a catalogue of events and seat availability, and to buy tickets using a credit card. The UCM design for the TRS is shown in Figure 5, with the components being as follows:

- *User*: TRS customer
- *WebServer*: web interface to the TRS, executes CGI scripts
- *Netware*: the underlying network software and the network itself
- *CCReq*: credit card verification and authorization server
- *Database*: database server

A *User* can access the TRS can be used either to browse events by displaying an event schedule and seating availability, or to buy tickets using a credit card. A typical scenario involves the *User* logging on to the system by requesting a connection. The *WebServer* then logs the user on and opens a session, then confirms that the connection was made. Once she is connected to the system, the *User* enters a loop where she has two options. She can either choose to browse and check information about an event, or she can buy a ticket. If the browsing option is chosen, the *WebServer* sends an event information request to the *Database*, through the *Netware*. The *Database* is responsible for retrieving the data requested and send it to the *WebServer*. The information can then be displayed back to the *User*, who can now choose whether to continue browsing, purchase tickets or disconnect. If the ticket purchasing option is chosen, the *User* must supply a credit card number to which the purchase price can be billed. The *WebServer* then begins to confirm the transaction by contacting the *CCReq* through the *Netware* and requesting that the credit card be verified. Once the credit card is checks out, *CCReq* forwards the purchase request to the *Database* so it may update its records. The transaction is now completed and a confirmation is sent to the *WebServer*, which in turn relays it back to the *User*. The *User* may continue to browse or purchase more tickets as she wishes. Once the *User* is done, she can make a disconnection request and the *WebServer* closes the session and confirms that the she has been logged out.

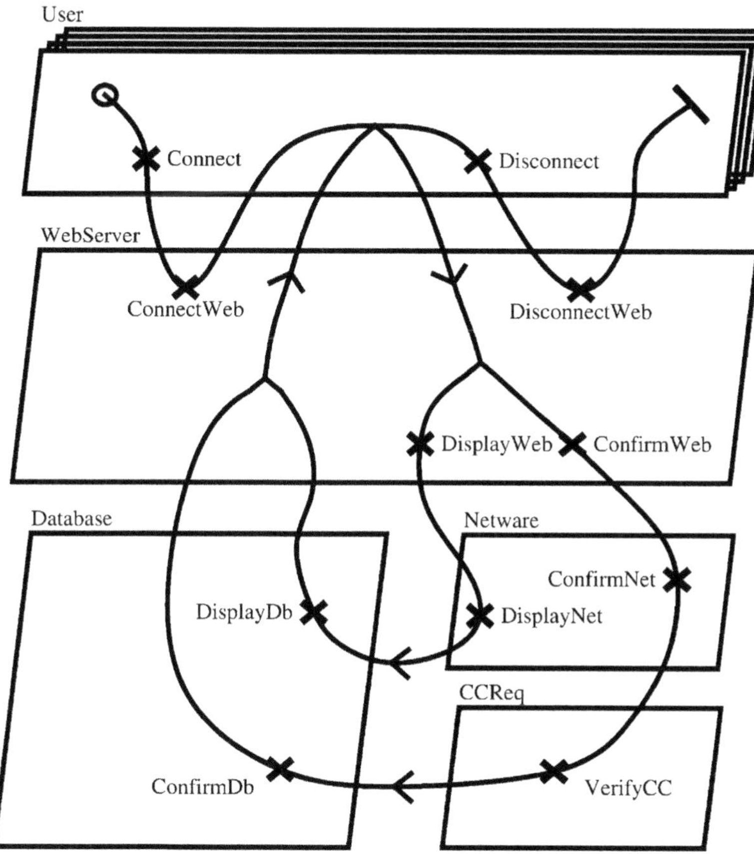

Fig. 5. Ticket Reservation System Use Case Map model.

The TRS LQN is shown in Figure 6. The LQN shows an initial asynchronous call from the reference task to the *User*, due to the open nature of the model's arrivals. This example requires the conversion of a complex loop, the body of which features forking and joining and makes service requests of other tasks.

Examining the flow of activities and messages in the LQN, the UCM path is readily identifiable. The loop control activity is shown as the diagonally shaded activity marked with an asterisk in the *User* task. The loop body was abstracted away from the loop head and is represented by the *User_dup1* task. The rest of the loop body is taken care of by the activities in *User_dup1*. The activities for the *WebServer* task incorporate the OR fork and join necessary to separate the sequence of actions for browsing or buying. Calls from the *WebServer* are forwarded by the *Netware*, and by the *CCReq* if a reservation was made, before being replied to by the *Database*.

The resulting LQN file has been solved by the solver LQNS, to demonstrate that it is a correctly formed model definition. However the model results are not critical to the present discussion and will not be presented here. With the model, one could address such issues as

- the CPU load imposed by the servers
- the levels of concurrency needed in the servers,
- the impact on capacity, if there are longer sessions or longer internet delays for each interaction.

6 Transforming Other Scenario Models (e.g. UML Sequence Diagrams)

The SPT algorithm can work with any scenario notation which is based on the sequence connectors described here (sequence, alternative paths, AND forks and joins, and loops), and which binds elements to components. Thus any of the three UML diagrams which show scenarios (Sequence Diagrams, Collaboration Diagrams, and Activity Diagrams) can be transformed by the SPT algorithm. Other scenario notations that can be handled include the ITU standards, Message Sequence charts and High-Level Message Sequence Charts.

For example, in Sequence Diagrams, each participating instance will be treated as a component and transformed to a LQN task. If necessary these can be aggregated later on the basis of concurrent processes. Messages are clearly identified and do not need to be inferred. Looping may be represented by an enclosed set of interactions, which is identifiable as a loop body for the transformation. AND forks (and joins) have to be recognized implictly by multiple message send events (or receive events). OR forks may occur in two ways; by multiple messages leaving the same point, or by a split in the instance lifeline (the vertical timeline associated witht he instance). An OR join may be shown by a merging of the split lifelines, or by messages arriving at the same point. Operations can be inferred for handling the receipt of messages (which activate methods) and for the purposes of the transformation can be treated similarly to UCM responsibilities. This covers all the key elements of the scenario, so the interaction types can be determined by the SPT algorithm. The problem of parameter annotations may be resolved by a proposed standard profile for this purpose [26].

7 Conclusions

The tool described here addresses the problem of capturing performance issues in the earliest software design efforts. The UCM2LQN converter connects high level design in the form of Use Case Maps with performance analysis using Layered Queueing

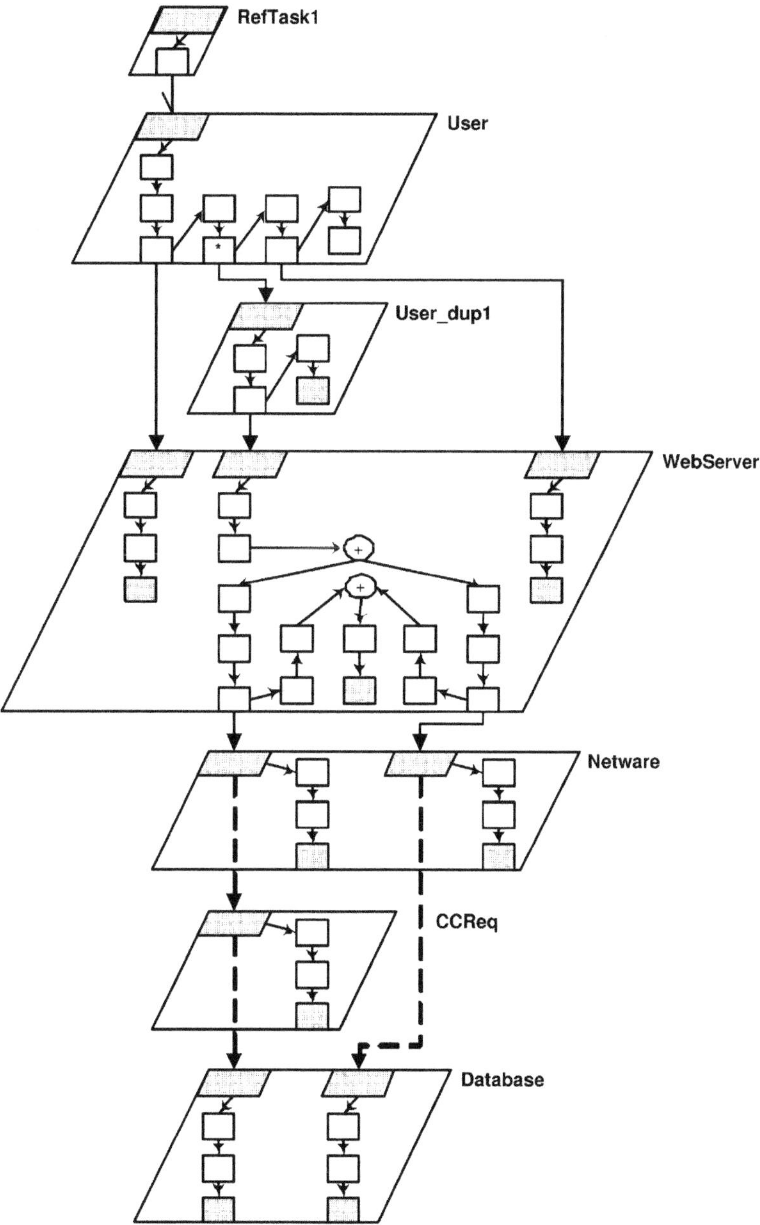

Fig. 6. TRS LQN showing activity connections based on the output generated by the UCM2LQN converter from the UCM shown in Figure 5.

Networks. It demonstrates close integration between the software specification tool (the UCMNav editor) and the performance analysis programs (the LQNS analytic solver and the LQSim simulator).

The SPT algorithm used in UCM2LQN can be applied equally to scenario specifications in other languages, such as sequence diagrams in UML. Some interpretation of the sequence diagram is needed to establish the corresponding constructs for the purposes of the algorithm. Only a sketch of the interpretation of sequence is given here, but it does not appear to be difficult to fill in the details. Since one UCM may present many paths, the equivalent conversion may involve many sequence diagrams.

The key difficulty in the conversion is in identifying blocking interactions between software entities, and potential contention for servers and other logical resources. This involves matching patterns for two kinds of synchronous interactions (synchronous and forwarding), delaying the matching to obtain sufficient information from the path traversal, and careful handling of forks in the path that occur during one of these interactions.

The model-building tool is integrated into the UCM Navigator, which is freely distributed and has over a hundred users (see the web site `www.usecasemaps.org` for the UCM User Group).

Some improvements to the model building are still needed in the use of data conditions to define which paths are part of a given scenario, and the handling of paths which are parts of larger paths.

Acknowledgements. This research was funded by the Natural Sciences and Engineering Research Council of Canada (NSERC), through its program of Research Grants, and by Communications and Information Technology Ontario (CITO).

References

1. D. Amyot, L. Charfi, N. Gorse, T. Gray, L. Logrippo, J. Sincennes, B. Stepien, and T. Ware, "Feature Description and Feature Interaction Analysis with Use Case Maps and LOTOS", Sixth International Workshop on Feature Interactions in Telecommunications and Software Systems (FIW'00), Glasgow, Scotland, May 2000
2. D. Amyot, L. Logrippo, R.J.A. Buhr, and T. Gray, "Use Case Maps for the Capture and Validation of Distributed Systems Requirements", Fourth International Symposium on Requirements Engineering (RE'99), Limerick, Ireland, June 1999
3. D. Amyot and G. Mussbacher, "On the Extension of UML with Use Case Maps Concepts", The 3rd International Conference on the Unified Modeling Language (UML2000), York, UK, October 2000.
4. S. Balsamo and M. Simeoni, "Deriving Performance Models from Software Architecture Specifications", European Simulation Multiconference 2001 (ESM 2001), Prague, June 2001
5. G. Booch, J. Rumbaugh, and I. Jacobson, The Unified Modeling Language User Guide. Addison-Wesley, 1998.
6. R. J. A. Buhr, "Use Case Maps as Architectural Entities for Complex Systems," IEEE Transactions on Software Engineering, vol. 24, no. 12 pp. 1131 - 1155, 1998.
7. R.J.A. Buhr and R.S. Casselman, "Use Case Maps for Object-Oriented Systems", Prentice Hall, 1996

8. L. Constantine, L. Lockwood , "Software for Use", Addison Wesley 1999
9. V. Cortellessa and R. Mirandola, "Deriving a Queueing Network-based Performance Model from UML Diagrams", ACM Proceedings of the Workshop on Software and Performance (WOSP2000), Ottawa, Canada, 2000, pp. 58-70
10. G. Franks and M. Woodside, "Effectiveness of early replies in client-server systems," Performance Evaluation, vol. 36--37, pp. 165-183, August 1999.
11. G. Franks and M. Woodside, "Performance of Multi-level Client-Server Systems with Parallel Service Operations," in Proc. of Workshop on Software Performance (WOSP98), October 1998, pp. 120-130.
12. Greg Franks, "Performance Analysis of Distributed Server Systems", Report OCIEE-00-01, Ph.D. thesis, Carleton University, Ottawa, Jan. 2000
13. H. Gomaa and D. A. Menasce, "Design and Performance Modeling of Component Interconnection Patterns for Distributed Software Architectures", ACM Proceedings of the Workshop on Software and Performance (WOSP2000), Ottawa, Canada, 2000, pp. 117-126
14. J. Hodges and J. Visser, "Accelerating Wireless Intelligent Network Standards Through Formal Techniques", IEEE 1999 Vehicular Technology Conference (VTC'99), Houston, 1999
15. C. Hofmeister, R. Nord, and D. Soni, Applied Software Architecture. Addison-Wesley, 1999.
16. P. Kahkipuro, "UML Based Performance Modeling Framework for Object Oriented Systems," in UML99, The Unified Modeling Language, Beyond the Standard, LNCS 1723, Springer-Verlag, Berlin, 1999, pp. 356-371.
17. A. Miga, "Application of Use Case Maps to System Design With Tool Support", M.Eng. Thesis, Department of Systems and Computer Engineering, Carleton University, Ottawa, Canada, 1998
18. O. Monkewich, "NEW QUESTION 12: URN: User Requirements Notation", ITU-T Study Group 10, Temporary Document 99, November 1999
19. J.E. Neilson, C.M. Woodside, D.C. Petriu and S. Majumdar, "Software Bottlenecking in Client-Server Systems and Rendez-vous Networks", IEEE Trans. On Software Engineering, Vol. 21, No. 9, pp. 776-782, September 1995
20. Dorin Petriu, "Layered Software Performance Models Constructed from Use Case Map Specifications", M.A.Sc thesis, Carleton University, May 2001.
21. Dorin Petriu and C. M. Woodside, "Evaluating the Performance of Software Architectures", The 5th Mitel Workshop (MICON2000), Mitel Networks, Ottawa, August 2000
22. D. C. Petriu, C. Shousha, and A. Jalnapurkar, "Architecture-Based Performance Analysis Applied to a Telecommunication System", IEEE Transactions on Software Engineering, Vol. 26, No. 11, Nov 2000, pp. 1049-1065
23. R. Pooley, "Software Engineering and Performance: a Roadmap," in The Future of Software Engineering, part of the 22nd Int. Conf. on Software Engineering (ICSE2000), Limerick, Ireland, June 2000, pp. 189-200.
24. J. A. Rolia, K. C. Sevcik, "The Method of Layers", IEEE Transactions on Software Engineering, Vol. 21, No. 8, 1995, pp. 682-688
25. C. Scratchley, C. M. Woodside, "Evaluating Concurrency Options in Software Specifications", Proceedings of the 7th International Symposium on Modeling, Analysis and Simulation of Computer and Telecomm Systems (MASCOTS99), College Park, Md., October 1999, pp 330 - 338
26. B. Selic, A. Moore, M. Bjorkander, M. Gerhardt, B. Watson, and M. Woodside, "Response to the OMG RFP for Schedulability, Performance and Time," Obect Management Group, OMG document ad/01-06-14, June 12,2001.

27. K. H. Siddiqui, C. M. Woodside, "A description of Time/Performance Budgeting for UCM Designs", The 5th Mitel Workshop (MICON2000), Mitel Networks, Ottawa, August 2000
28. C. U. Smith, "Performance Engineering of Software Systems", Addison-Wesley, 1990
29. C. U. Smith, L.G. Williams, "Performance Engineering Evaluation of Object Oriented Systems with SPE-ED", Computer Performance Evaluation: Modeling Techniques and Tools (LNCS 1245), Springer-Verlag, 1997
30. C. U. Smith, Murray Woodside, "Performance Validation at Early Stages of Development", Position paper, Performance 99, Istanbul, Turkey, October 99
31. C. M. Woodside, J. E. Neilson, D. C. Petriu and S. Majumdar, "The Stochastic Rendezvous Network Model for Performance of Synchronous Client-Server-Like Distributed Software", IEEE Transactions on Computers, Vol. 44, No. 1, Jan 1995, pp. 20-34
32. Murray Woodside, "Software Resource Architecture", to appear in Int. Journal on Software Engineering and Knowledge Engineering (IJSEKE), 2001
33. ACM Proceedings of the Workshop on Software and Performance (WOSP'98), Santa Fe, USA, 1998
34. ACM Proceedings of the Workshop on Software and Performance (WOSP2000), Ottawa, Canada, 2000

Applying the UML Performance Profile: Graph Grammar-Based Derivation of LQN Models from UML Specifications

Dorina C. Petriu and Hui Shen

Carleton University,
Systems and Computer Engineering
Ottawa ON Canada, K1S 5B6
petriu@sce.carleton.ca

Abstract. The Object Management Group (OMG) is in the process of defining a UML Profile for Schedulability, Performance and Time that will enable the construction of models for making quantitative predictions regarding these characteristics. The paper proposes a graph-grammar based method for transforming automatically a UML model annotated with performance information into a Layered Queueing Network (LQN) performance model. The input to our transformation algorithm is an XML file that contains the UML model in XML format according to the standard XMI interface. The output is the corresponding LQN model description file, which can be read directly by existing LQN solvers. The LQN model structure is generated from the high-level software architecture and from deployment diagrams indicating the allocation of software components to hardware devices. The LQN model parameters are obtained from detailed models of key performance scenarios, represented as UML interaction or activity diagrams.

1 Introduction

The Object Management Group (OMG) is in the process of defining a UML Profile for Schedulability, Performance and Time [10] that would enable the construction of models that can be used for making quantitative predictions regarding these characteristics. The original RFP issued in March 1999 was followed by the first "Response to RFP" submission in August 2000, and by a revised submission in June 2001 [10]. The later includes some additional aspects not covered in the former, among which is a section dealing with performance analysis. The proposed performance profile extends the UML metamodel with stereotypes, tagged values and constraints, which make it possible to attach performance annotations (such as resource demands and visit ratios) to a UML model. In order to conduct quantitative performance analysis of an annotated UML model, one must first translate it into a performance model, use an existing performance analysis tool for solving the performance model and then import the performance analysis results back in the UML model. The focus of this paper is the first step of the process. The paper proposes a graph-grammar based method

T. Field et al. (Eds.): TOOLS 2002, LNCS 2324, pp. 159–177, 2002.

for transforming a UML model annotated with performance information into a Layered Queueing Network (LQN) performance model [20], [21]. The input to our transformation algorithm is an XML file that contains an annotated UML model in XML format according to the standard XMI interface [9], and the output is the corresponding LQN model description file, which can be read directly by existing LQN solvers [5]. The transformation algorithm described in the paper was completely implemented in Java on top of a rather large open source Java library that implements and manipulates the UML metamodel [23]. More work is necessary for the present implementation to become a tool prototype, especially the addition of a suitable GUI.

The transformation approach is as follows: the LQN model structure is generated from the high-level software architecture, more exactly from the architectural patterns showing high-level software components and their relationships, and from deployment diagrams indicating the allocation of software components to hardware devices. The LQN model parameters are obtained from detailed models of key performance scenarios, represented as UML interaction or activity diagrams, annotated with performance information.

The paper continues previous work of the authors from [12], [11], [13], [1]. In [12] the system's architectural patterns were used to build LQN performance models, but the model derivation was not automated. In [11] an automated graph transformation was proposed to derive the LQN model structure from the high-level architecture and the architectural patterns. The transformation was implemented by using an existing graph rewriting tool named PROGRES [17]. The PROGRES-based transformation was extended in [1] to obtain the whole LQN model (including its parameters) from a UML model represented as a PROGRES input graph. The merit of the PROGRES-based approach is that it represents a proof of concept that graph-transformation techniques can be applied successfully to the derivation of performance models from UML models. Although PROGRES had the advantage of freeing us from low-level operations of graph matching and manipulation, it also brought the disadvantage of introducing additional steps in the process. For example, we had to express the UML metamodel as a PROGRES schema, and to convert each UML model into a PROGRES input-graph format. The solution presented in this paper eliminates the general-purpose graph rewriting tool from the loop by performing the manipulation and transformation of the UML model directly at the metamodel level. This solution is more efficient than the PROGRES-based one, as it has fewer steps; also, the ad-hoc transformation is faster, as it is tailored to the problem at hand. Another advantage of working directly at the UML metamodel level is that it becomes possible to merge the performance model builder with a UML tool.

Since the introduction of the Software Performance Engineering technique in [18], there has been a significant effort to integrate performance analysis into the software development process throughout all lifecycle phases. This requires the ability to derive performance models from software design specifications. A survey of the techniques developed in the recent years for deriving performance models from UML models is given in [2]. Among the techniques surveyed, the one from [3] follows the SPE methodology very closely. Information from UML use case, deployment, and sequence diagrams is used to generate SPE scenario descriptions in the form of flow diagrams similar to those used in [18], [19]. The work presented in [8] introduces an UML-based notation and framework for describing performance models, and a set of special techniques for modelling component-based distributed systems. In [4] the idea of patterns is used to investigate the design and performance modelling of interconnection patterns for client/server systems.

Compared to the existing research, our paper is a unique combination of the following characteristics: a) it accepts as input XML files produced by UML tools, b) it generates LQN performance models by applying graph transformation techniques to graphs of metaobjects that represent different UML diagrams of the input model, and c) it uses the UML performance profile for adding performance annotations to the input model.

2 Background

2.1 UML Performance Profile

According to [10], the UML Performance Profile provides facilities for:

- capturing performance requirements within the design context,
- associating performance-related Q0S characteristics with selected elements of the UML model,
- specifying execution parameters which can be used by modelling tools to compute predicted performance characteristics,
- presenting performance results computed by modelling tools or found by measurement.

The Profile describes a domain model, shown in Fig. 1, which identifies basic abstractions used in performance analysis. Scenarios define response paths through the system, and can have QoS requirements such as response times

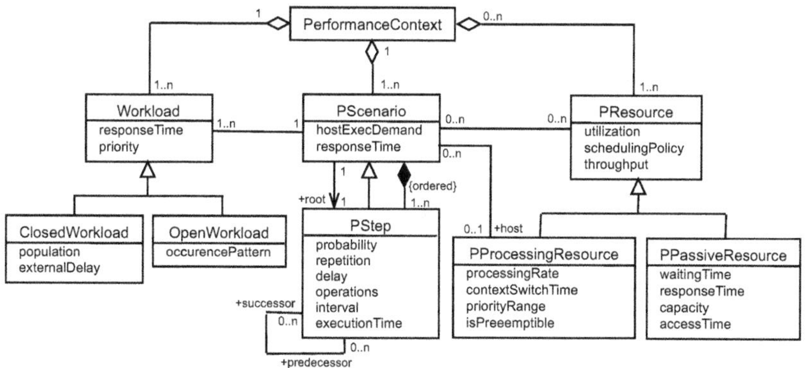

Fig. 1. Domain model in the UML Performance Profile

or throughputs. Each scenario is executed by a job class, called here a workload, which can be closed or open and has the usual characteristics (number of clients or arrival rate, etc.) Scenarios are composed of scenario steps that can be joined in sequence, loops, branches, fork/joins, etc. A scenario step may be an elementary operation at the lowest level of granularity, or may be a complex sub-scenario composed of many basic steps. Each step has a mean number of repetitions, a host execution demand, other demand to resources and its own QoS characteristics. Resources are another basic abstraction, and can be active or passive, each with their own attributes. The Performance profile maps the classes from Fig. 1 to a stereotype that can be applied to a number of UML model elements, and each class attribute to a tagged value. For example, the basic abstraction PStep is mapped to the stereotype <<PAstep>> that can be applied to the following UML model elements:Message and Stimulus (when the scenario is represented by an interaction diagram) or ActionState and SubactivityState (when the scenario is represented by an activity diagram).

In our implementation, we process XML files produced by current UML tools, which obviously do not support the Performance Profile yet. Therefore, we have attached the tagged values associated with the stereotypes "by hand" to different model elements.

Fig. 2 illustrates the inter-operability of the different tools involved: a UML tool (such as Rational Rose or ArgoUML [22]), a performance model solver (LQN analytical solver or simulator) and our UML to LQN transformation implementation. So far we have made progress on the forward path (represented with black arrows) but have not attempted the backward path yet (represented with gray arrows).

2.2 The LQN Model

LQN was developed as an extension of the well-known QN model, at first independently in [20], [21] and [15], then as a joint effort [5]. The LQN toolset presented in [5] includes both simulation and analytical solvers. The main difference with respect to QN is that LQN can easily represent nested services: a server which receives and serves client requests, may become in turn a client to other servers from which it requires nested services while serving its own clients.

A LQN model is represented as an acyclic graph, whose nodes represent software entities and hardware devices, and arcs denote service requests. The

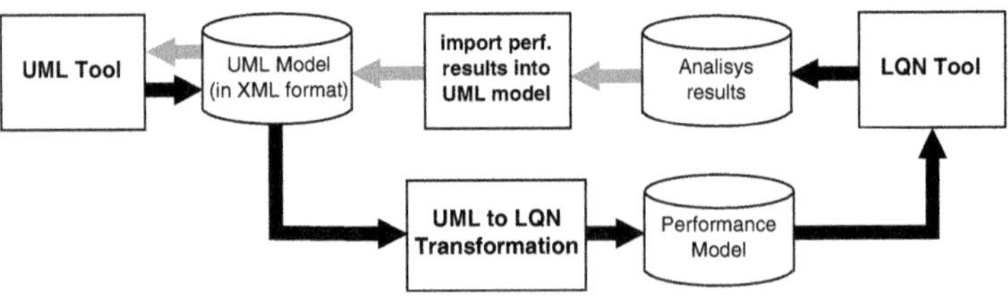

Fig. 2. Tool inter-operability

software entities (also known as tasks) are drawn as parallelograms, and the hardware devices as circles. The nodes with outgoing but no incoming arcs play the role of clients, the intermediate nodes with both incoming and outgoing arcs are usually software servers and the leaf nodes are hardware servers (such as processors, I/O devices, communication network, etc.) A software or hardware server node can be either a single-server or a multi-server. Fig. 3 shows a simple example of a LQN model of a web server: at the top there is a customer class with a given number of stochastical identical clients. Each client sends demands for different services of the WebServer. Each kind of service offered by a LQN task is modelled as a so-called entry, drawn as a parallelogram "slice" in the figure. Every entry has its own execution times and demands for other services, given as model parameters. In this case, the WebServer entries require services from different entries of the Database task. Each software task is running on a processor shown as a circle. Also as circles are shown the communication network delays and the disk device used by the Database.

It is worth mentioning that the word layered in the LQN name does not imply a strict layering of tasks (for example, tasks in a layer may call each other or skip over layers). All the arcs used in this example represent synchronous requests, where the sender of a request message is blocked until it receives a reply from the provider of service. It is possible to have also asynchronous request messages, where the sender does not block after sending a request and the server does not send any reply back. Another communication style in LQN allows for a client request to be processed by a chain of servers instead of a single server, as shown in section 4. The first server in the chain will forward the request to the second, etc., and the last server will reply to the client. Although not explicitly illustrated in the LQN notation, every server, be it software or hardware, has an implicit message queue where incoming requests are waiting their turn to be served. Servers with more then one entry have a single input queue, where requests for different entries wait together.

A server entry may be decomposed in two or more sequential phases of service. Phase 1 is the portion of service during which the client is blocked, waiting for a reply from the server (it is assumed that the client has made a synchronous request). At the end of phase 1, the server will reply to the client, which will unblock and continue its execution. The remaining phases, if any, will be executed in parallel with the client. A recent extension to LQN [6] allows for an entry to be further decomposed into activities if more details are required to describe its execution. The activities are connected together to form a directed graph, which may branch into parallel threads of control, or may choose randomly between different branches. Just like phases, activities have execution time demands, and can make service requests to other tasks. Examples of LQN with activities are given in Fig. 8 and Fig. 10.

The parameters of a LQN model are as follows:

- customer (client) classes and their associated populations or arrival rates,
- for each phase (activity) of a software task entry: average execution time,
- for each phase (activity) making a request to a device: average service time at the device, and average number of visits,

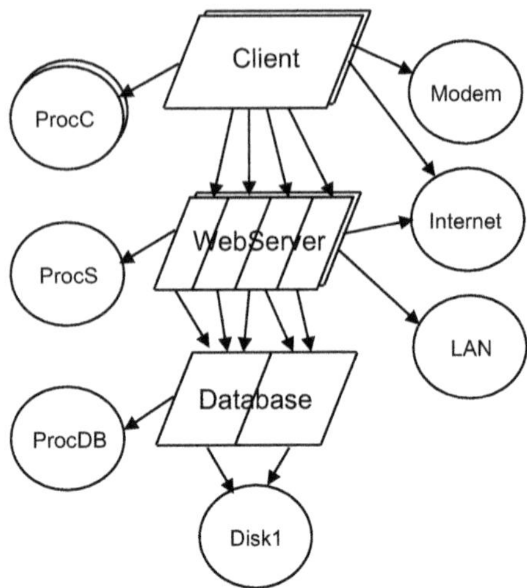

Fig. 3. LQN model example

- for each phase (activity) making a request to another task entry: average number of visits,
- for each request arc: average communication delay,
- for each software and hardware server: scheduling discipline.

2.3 Architectural Patterns

In our approach, the structure of the LQN model is generated from the high-level architecture, and more exactly from the architectural patterns used in the system. Frequently used architectural solutions are identified in literature as architectural patterns (such as pipeline and filters, client/server, broker, layers, master-slave, blackboard, etc.) A pattern introduces a higher-level of abstraction design artifact by describing a specific type of collaboration between a set of prototypical components playing well-defined roles, and helps our understanding of complex systems. Each architectural pattern describes two inter-related aspects: its structure (what are the components) and behaviour (how they interact). In the case of high-level architectural patterns, the components are usually concurrent entities that are executed in different threads of control, compete for resources, and their interaction may require some synchronization. The patterns are represented as UML collaborations [9]. The symbol for a collaboration is an ellipse with dashed lines that may have an "embedded" square showing the roles played by different pattern participants.

In Fig. 4 and Fig. 5 are shown the structure and behaviour of two patterns used in our case study: Client Server and Forwarding Server Chain. The Client Server pattern has two alternatives: the one shown in Fig. 4.b is using a synchronous communication style (where the client sends the request then remains

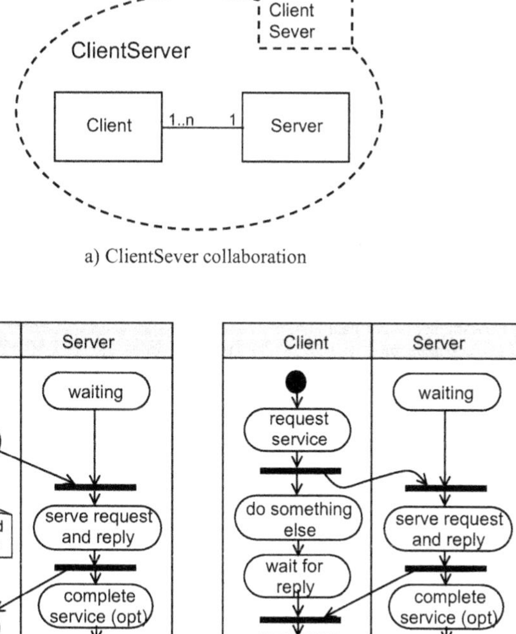

a) ClientSever collaboration

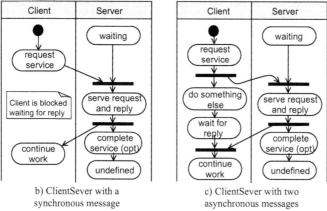

b) ClientSever with a synchronous message

c) ClientSever with two asynchronous messages

Fig. 4. Client Server architectural pattern

blocked until the sender replies), whereas the one from Fig. 4.c is using an asynchronous communication style (where the client continues its work after sending the request, and will accept the server's replay later). The Forwarding Server Chain, shown in Fig. 5, is an extension of the Client Server pattern, where the client's request is served by a series of servers instead of a single one. There may be more than two servers in the chain (only two are shown in Fig. 5) . The servers in the middle play the role of ForwardingServer, as each one forwards the request to the next server in the chain after doing their part of service. The last server in the chain plays the role of ReplyingServer, as it sends the reply back to the client. In this paper we show how these two patterns are converted into LQN models. More architectural patterns and the corresponding rules for translating them into LQN are described by the authors of the present paper in [10, 11].

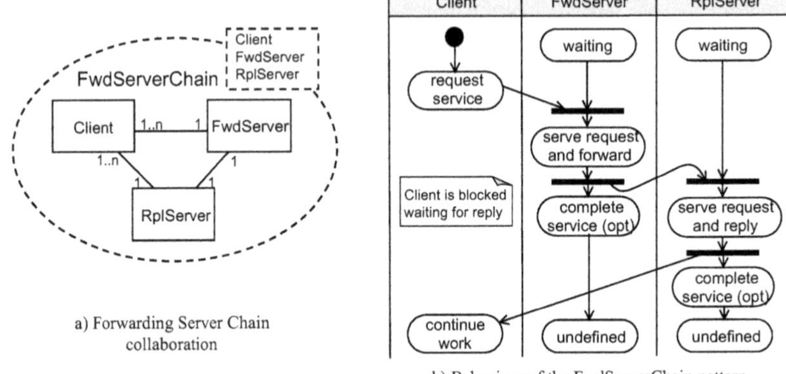

a) Forwarding Server Chain collaboration

b) Behaviour of the FwdServerChain pattern

Fig. 5. Forwarding Server Chain architectural pattern

3 Transformation from UML to LQN

Similar to the SPE methodology from [16, 17], the starting point for our algo rithm is a set of key performance scenarios annotated with performance inform ation. For each scenario we derive a LQN submodel, then merge the submodels together. The approach for merging is similar with the one used in [6], where LQN submodels were derived from execution traces. The derivation of each LQN submodel is done in two big steps:

a) The submodel structure (i.e., the software and hardware tasks and their connecting arcs) is obtained from the high-level architecture of the UML model and from the deployment of software components to hardware devices. Two kinds of UML diagrams are taken into account in this step: a high-level collaboration diagram that shows the concurrent/distributed high-level component instances and the patterns in which they participate, and the deployment diagram. Fig. 6 shows these two diagrams for the web server model that was used to derive the LQN model from Fig. 3 (devices and tasks without entries.) Each high-level software component is mapped to a LQN software task, and each hardware device (processor, disk, communication network, etc.) is mapped to a LQN hardware task. The arcs between LQN nodes correspond to the links from the UML diagrams. It is important to mention that in the first transformation step from UML to LQN we take into account only the structural aspect of the architectural patterns; their behavioural aspect will be considered in the next step.
b) LQN task details are obtained from UML scenario models represented as activity diagrams, over which we overlay the behavioural aspect of the architectural pattern, making sure that the scenario is consistent with the patterns. By "LQN details" we understand the following elements of each task: entries, phases, activities (if any) and their execution time demands and

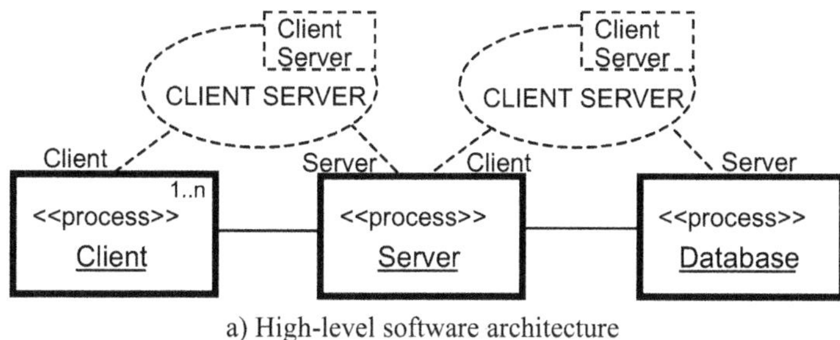

a) High-level software architecture

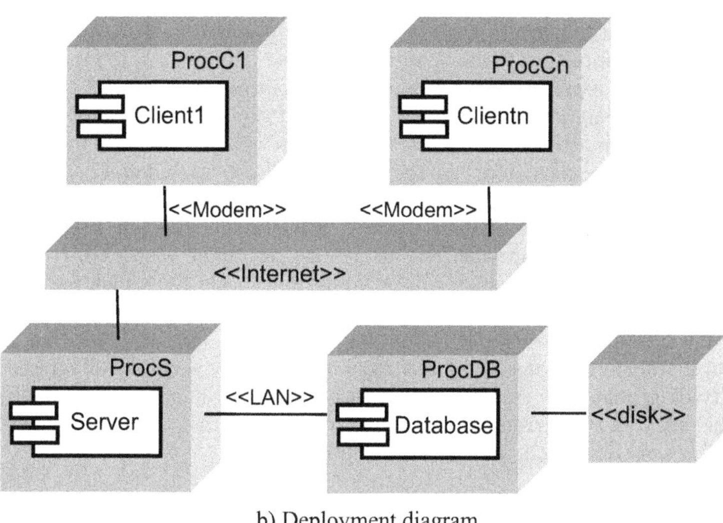

b) Deployment diagram

Fig. 6. UML diagrams used to generate the structure of the LQN model from Fig.3

visit ratio parameters, as described in section 2.2. A task entry is generated for each kind of service offered by the corresponding software component instance. The services offered by each instance are identified by looking at the messages received by it in every scenario taken into account for performance analysis.

Scenarios can be represented in UML by sequence, collaboration or activity diagrams. (The first two are very close as descriptive power and have similar metamodel representation). UML statecharts are another kind of diagrams for behaviour description, but are not appropriate for describing scenarios. A statechart describes the behaviour of an object, not the cooperation between several objects, as needed in a scenario.

In the proposed approach, we decided to use activity diagrams for translation to LQN. The main reason is that sequence (collaboration) diagrams are not well defined in UML yet, as they are lacking convenient features for representing loops, branches and fork/join structures. Other authors who are building performance models from UML designs have pointed out this deficiency of the present UML standard, and are using instead extended sequence diagrams that look like the Message Sequence Chart standard (see [19] for a well known example). We did not take the approach of extending the sequence diagrams with the missing features because our algorithm takes in XML files generated by UML tools, and parses graphs of UML metaobjects. Our implementation is consistent with the present UML metamodel and XMI interface; moreover, it uses an open-source library, named Novosoft Metadata Framework and UML Library [23], which implements the standard UML metamodel as defined in [9]. Therefore, our choice was to use activity diagrams that are able to represent branch/merge, fork/join and activity composition without any extensions.

However, the activity diagrams have a disadvantage with respect to sequence (collaboration) diagrams: they do not show what objects are responsible for different actions. An attempt to counterbalance this weakness was the introduction of "swimlanes" (or partitions) in the UML standard. A swimlane contains actions that are performed by a certain instance or set of instances (for example, a swimlane can be associated to a whole department when modeling a work flow problem). In our approach, we associate a swimlane with each concurrent (distributed) component, which will be translated into a LQN task (see Figures 4, 5 and 9.c). Since many UML modellers prefer sequence diagrams for expressing the cooperation between objects, we proposed in [13] an algorithm based on graph transformations for converting automatically sequence diagrams into activity diagrams. The transformation associates a swimlane to all the objects that belong to a concurrent (distributed) component, and therefore adjusts the level of abstraction of the model to our needs.

4 From Activity Diagrams to LQN Entries, Phases, and Activities

This section presents the graph grammar-based transformation of activity diagrams into LQN detailed features (i.e., the realization of step (b) from the previous section). The graph-grammar formalism is appropriate in this case because both UML and LQN models are described by graphs. The essential idea of all graph grammars or graph rewriting systems is that they are generalization of the string grammars that are used in compilers. The terms "graph grammars" and "graph rewriting systems" are often considered synonymous. However, a graph grammar is a set of production rules that generates a language of terminal graphs and produces nonterminal graphs as intermediate results, whereas a graph rewriting system is a set of rules that transforms one instance of a given class of graphs into another instance of the same class of graphs, without distinguishing between terminals and nonterminals graphs. The main component of a graph grammar is a finite set of production rules. A production is a triple

(L, R, E), where L and R are graphs (the left-hand side and right-hand side, respectively) and E is some embedding mechanism. Such a production rule can be applied to a host graph H as follows: when an occurrence of L is found in H, it is removed end replaced with a copy of R; finally, the embedding mechanism E is applied to attach R to the remainder of H [14].

In our case, the initial host graph is the set of metaobjects that represents a given activity diagram (the metaobjects are the nodes and the links between them are the edges of the graph). According to the UML metamodel, the nodes (i.e., metaobjects) are of type `StateVertex` and `Transition`. A `StateVertex` type has a number of subtypes, among which `State` and `Pseudostate` are the most important. `State` is associated eventually with the actions represented in the diagram, whereas the special diagram blocks such as "fork", "join", "choice", etc., are `Pseudostates` (see [9] for more details).

Our purpose is to parse the activity diagram graph to check first whether it is correct, then to divide it into subgraphs that correspond to various LQN elements (entries, phases, etc.). In general, it is quite difficult to parse graph grammars, and in some cases even impossible [14]. In the case discussed in this paper we have found a shortcut by decomposing the original host graph into a set of subgraphs, each corresponding to a swimlane from the activity diagram. Each subgraph is described by a simpler graph-grammar, very similar to the string grammars used in compilers. This is not so surprising, since a swimlane describes the behaviour of a single component, dealing with sequences of scenario steps and nested structures such as loops, alternative branches and fork/joins. After disconecting the swimlanes as shown below, each swimlane subgraph has a structure known as an AND/OR graph. We defined a context-free grammar describing these subgraphs and implemented a top-down parser with recursive functions for parsing them. Our algorithm for the step (b) from the previous section contains two substeps:

b.1) Overlay the behaviour of the architectural patterns extracted in step (a) from the high-level collaboration diagram over the activity diagram, and verify whether the communication between concurrent components is consistent with the pattern. This is done by traversing the graph, by identifying the cross-transitions between swimlanes, and by checking if they follow the protocol defined by the pattern. Then, apply a graph transformation rule corresponding to the respective pattern, and attach appropriate nonterminal symbols to the subgraphs identified (see Fig. 7 and Fig. 8). This disconnects practically the subgraphs corresponding to each swimlane from its neighbors. Repeat this step for all inter-component communication (we assume that all are covered by some architectural pattern).

b.2) Parse separately the subgraph within each swimlane. This will deal with sequences, loops, alternative branches and fork/join structures. When parsing a subgraph corresponding to a certain LQN element (phase or activity) identified in the previous step, compute its execution time S from the execution times of the contained scenario steps as follows: $S = \sum_{i=1}^{n} r_i s_i$, where r_i is the number of repetitions and s_i the host execution time of scenario step i.

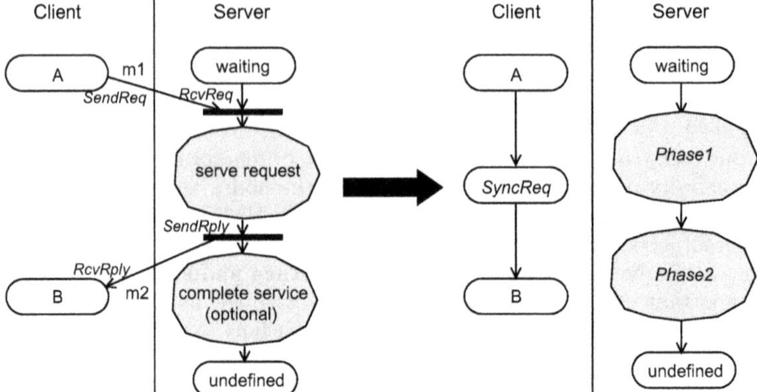

a) Graph transformation rule for the Client Server pattern with synchronous communication

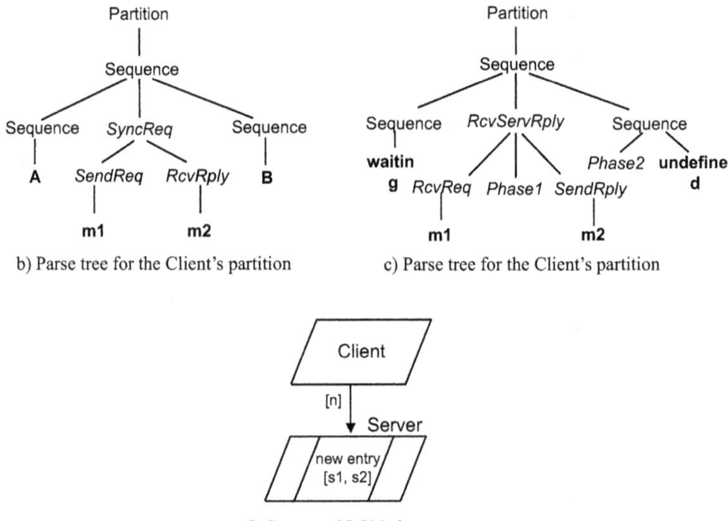

b) Parse tree for the Client's partition

c) Parse tree for the Client's partition

d) Generated LQN elements

Fig. 7. Transformation rule and parsing trees for the ClientServer pattern with synchronous communication

The graph transformation rule and parsing tree for the ClientServer pattern with synchronous communication are illustrated in Fig. 7, whereas those for the variant with asynchronous communication are illustrated in Fig. 8. The right-hand side R of the rule from Fig. 7.a contains some nodes and edges carried over from the left-hand side L (which will be kept in the graph), and some new ones (which will be added). Also, some nodes and edges from L do not appear in R, meaning that they will be deleted from the graph. The embedding mechanism assumes that (i) all the nodes that are kept in R from L will keep also their links with the remaining of the graph, (ii) the links of the deleted nodes with the remaining of the graph will be deleted as well, and (iii) the new nodes are explicitly connected only to nodes from R as shown in R.

According to Fig. 7.a, two subgraphs are identified on the server side. One corresponds to the phase 1 of service and is found between the "join" Pseudostate marking the receiving of the client request and the "fork" Pseudostate marking the sending of the reply. The other subgraph corresponds to the second phase of service, is optional, and can found between the "fork" marking the sending of the reply and either a "waiting" state for a new request or the "undefined" state used by default to mark the end of the respective component behaviour on behalf of the current scenario. The subgraphs will be labeled with the nonterminal symbols *Phase1* and *Phase2*, respectively, and will be parsed after step (b.1). On the client side a new node `SyncRec`, which symbolizes the making of the request, will replace the transitions `m1` and `m2`, which represent the sending of the request and the receiving of the reply, respectively. The partial parsing trees for the client and server side are shown in Fig. 7.b and 7.c. It is important to emphasize that the semantic of the nonterminals in italic is related to the abstraction level represented by the high-level pattern. These nonteminals are used to identify and label the subgraphs that correspond to smaller LQN elements, such as phases and activities.

Fig. 7.d illustrates the LQN elements generated in this case. A new entry of the Server task is generated for each new type of request accepted by the server. In the case shown in the figure, the entry has two phases, and their service times are computed as explained in step (b.2). A LQN request arc is generated between the Clients phase (or activity) containing the new `SyncRec` node inserted by the rule from Fig. 7.a and the new server entry. Its visit ratio n is identical with the number of repetitions of state `A` that originates the synchronous request.

Fig. 8.a shows a similar transformation rule for the ClientServer pattern with asynchronous communication. The difference here is that the client does not block immediately after sending the reply to the server. A fork/join structure is inserted in the client side, as seen in Fig. 8.a and 8.b. The LQN elements generated are shown in Fig. 8.c. The new entry contains LQN activities and a similar fork/join structure. The transformation rules for other patterns are not given here due to space limitations.

5 Case Study: Group Communication Server

In this section is presented the application of the proposed UML to LQN transformation algorithm to a case study [16]. A group communication server accepts two classes of documents from its subscribers, private and public, each with its own access rights. The documents are kept in two different files: the private documents on disk1 and the public ones on disk2. Five use cases were analyzed for the system: subscribe, unsubscribe, submit document, retrieve document and update document. However, only one scenario, namely Retrieve, is presented here.

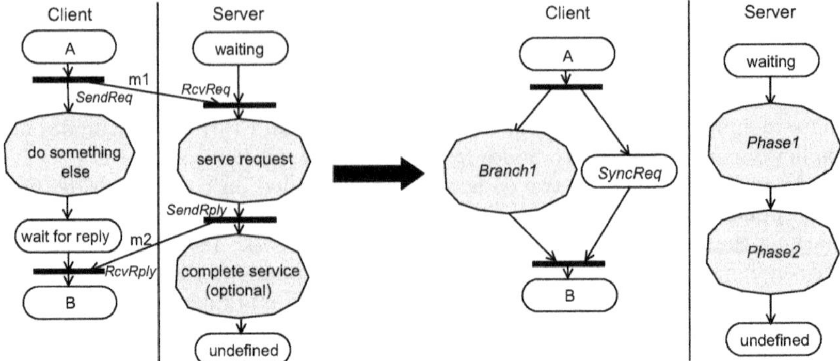

a) Graph transformation rule for the Client Server pattern with asynchronous communication

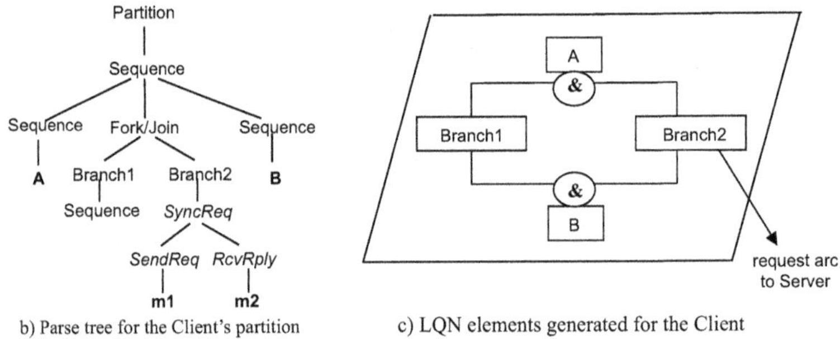

b) Parse tree for the Client's partition

c) LQN elements generated for the Client

Fig. 8. Transformation rule and parsing trees for the ClientServer pattern with asynchronous communication

Fig. 9.a shows the architectural patterns in which are participating the components involved in this scenario, and Fig. 9.b gives the deployment diagram. The activity diagram with performance annotations describing the scenario is given in Fig. 9.c. A User process sends a request for a specific document to the Main process of the server, which determines the request type and forwards it to another process named RetrieveProc. This process is rctually esponsible for retrieving the documents. Half of all the requests will refer to documents found in the buffer, so no disk access is necessary. The other half is split as follows: 20% of the requests will refer to private documents, and 30% to public documents. In each case, RetrievProc delegates the responsibility of reading the document to the corresponding disk process.

Disk1Proc reads private documents from a sequential file, so it makes a number of F accesses to an external operation named "readDisk1" in order to find the desired document. On the other hand, Disk2Proc reads public documents from an indexed file, so it will make only one access to the external operation

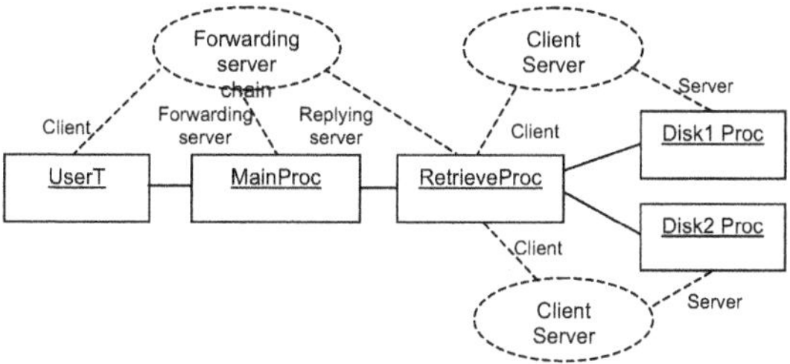

a) High-level architecture for "retrieve" scenario

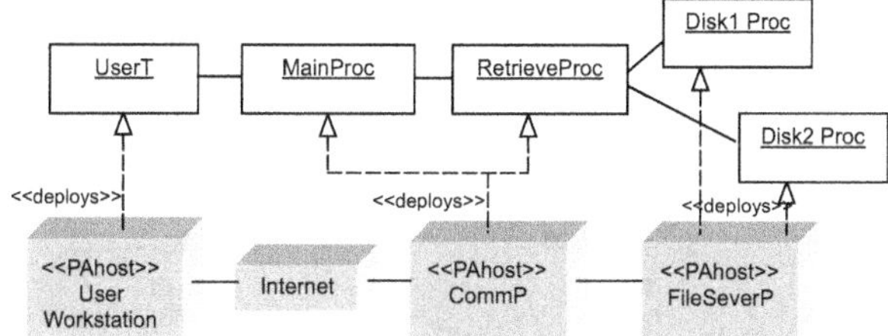

b) Deployment diagram for the components involved in "Retrieve" scenario

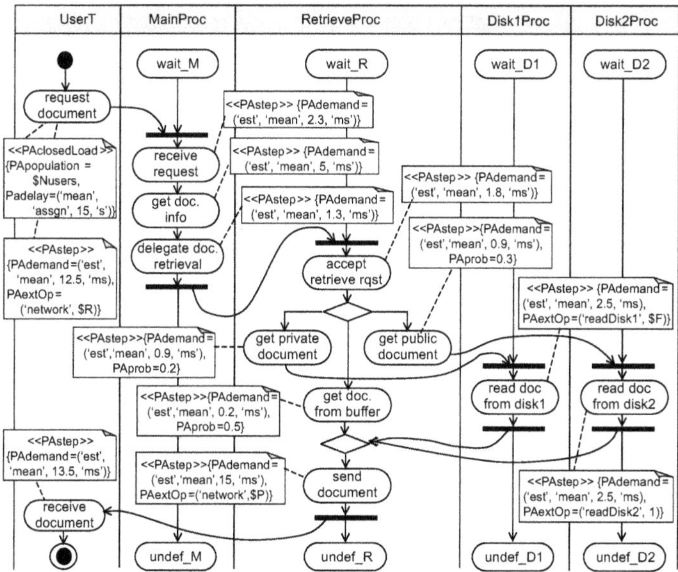

c) Activity Diagram with performance annotations for "Retrieve" scenario

Fig. 9. Group communication server: high-level architecture, deployment and activity diagram for "Retrieve" scenario

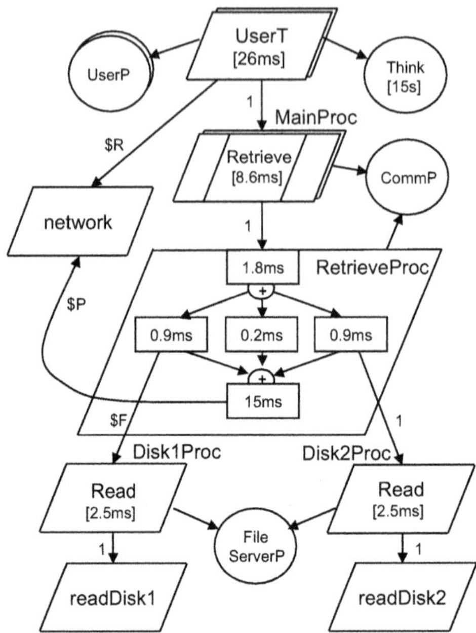

Fig. 10. LQN submodel generated for the scenario "Retrieve"

"readDisk2". The performance characteristics and the resources required for the external operations are described elsewhere. The external operations were specially provided in the UML performance profile to allow the UML modeler to describe the system at the right level of abstraction.

After getting the desired document either from file or from memory, RetrieveProc sends it back to the user. The scenario steps that send messages over the Internet invoke an external operation "network" once for every packet transmitted . This will allow to introduce in the performance model communication network delays that are not fully represented in the UML model.

Every scenario step in Fig. 9.c has a `PAdemand` tagged value indicating its estimated mean execution time on the host processor. The workload for the Retrieve scenario is closed, with a number of $Nusers clients. A user "thinks" for a mean delay of 15s. (The identifiers starting with '$' indicate variables that must be assigned concrete values before doing the actual performance analysis).

The LQN model obtained by applying our method is shown in Fig. 10. A LQN task was generated for each of the five software components from Fig. 9. Additional tasks were generated for the external operations `readDisk1`, `readDisk2` and `network`. The task `MainProc` has many entries, one for each type of requests it accepts. However, only one of its entries is determined from this scenario. This entry forwards the client request to `RetrieveProc` (forwarding is represented by a dotted request arc). `RetrieveProc` has one entry with internal branching, represented as a LQN activity graph that mirrors the scenario steps from the activity diagram from fig.9.c.

The purpose of this paper is to present the proposed UML to LQN transformation, so no performance analysis results are presented here. Our experience with the UML Performance Profile shows that it is relatively easy to understand, and that it provides enough performance annotations for generating working LQN models. However, we would like to add a few items on the "wish list" for the Performance Profile. Firstly, an additional tagged value is needed for expressing the size of messages, which is necessary for calculating the network delays. Secondly, it would be very useful to use parameterized expressions instead of concrete numbers for the tagged values. Thirdly, sometime it's useful to be able to define a workload over a set of scenarios that are composed in a certain way (sequentially, random choice, etc.)

6 Conclusions

Our experience with the graph-grammar formalism shows that it is very powerful and modularized by nature. The rule-based transformation approach lends itself rather easily to extensions. We are working right now on adding new transformation rules for other architectural patterns, such as pipeline and filters, critical section, blackboard, master-slave, etc. Another kind of extension we are planning on doing is the addition of a suitable GUI. An area that is completely uncovered is the backward path to bring back into the UML model the results from the performance analysis solver (represented with gray arrows in Fig. 2).

Regarding the inter-operability with UML tools, we have met with some problems due to the fact that the present UML tools do not support entirely the current UML standard. For example, Rational Rose does not support yet the following features: collaborations (i.e., the dashed ellipse symbol), object flow in activity diagrams and tagged values. Another tool we have been using, ArgoUML[22], does not support swimlanes and object flow in activity diagrams, etc. In order to test our algorithm, we have obtained XML files from the existing UML tools, but had to change them by hand in order to add the missing features. We hope that this problem will disappear with time, so that tool inter-operability will become a true reality.

Acknowledgements. This work was partially supported by grants from the Natural Sciences and Engineering Research Council of Canada (NSERC) and Communications and Information Technology Ontario (CITO).

References

1. Amer, H., Petriu, D.C.: Software Performance Evaluation: Graph Grammar-based Transformation of UML Design Models into Performance Models. submitted for publication, 33 pages (2002)
2. Balsamo, S., Simeoni, M.: On transforming UML models into performance models. In: Proc. of Workshop on Transformations in the Unified Modeling Language, Genova, Italy (2001)

3. Cortellessa, V., Mirandola, R.: Deriving a Queueing Network based Performance Model from UML Diagrams. In: Proc. of 2nd ACM Workshop on Software and Performance, Ottawa, Canada (2000) 58–70
4. Gomaa, H., Menasce, D.A.: Design and Performance Modeling of Component Interconnections Patterns for Distributed Software Architectures. In: Proc. of 2nd ACM Workshop on Software and Performance, Ottawa, Canada (2000) 117–126
5. Franks, G., Hubbard, A., Majumdar, S., Petriu, D.C., Rolia, J., Woodside, C.M: A toolset for Performance Engineering and Software Design of Client-Server Systems. Performance Evaluation, Vol. 24, Nb. 1-2 (1995) 117–135
6. Franks, G.: Performance Analysis of Distributed Server Systems. Report OCIEE-00-01, Ph.D. Thesis, Carleton University, Ottawa, Canada (2000)
7. Hrischuk, C.E., Woodside, C.M., Rolia, J.A.: Trace-Based Load Characterization for Generating Software Performance Models. IEEE Trans. on Software Eng., V.25, No.1 (1999) 122–135
8. Kähkipuro, P.: UML-Based Performance Modeling Framework for Component-Based Distributed Systems. In: R.Dumke et al.(eds): Performance Engineering, Lecture Notes in Computer Science, Vol. 2047. Springer-Verlag, Berlin Heidelberg New York (2001) 167–184
9. Object Management Group: UML Specification Version 1.3. OMG Doc. ad/99-06-08 (1999)
10. Object Management Group: UML Profile for Schedulability, Performance and Time. OMG Document ad/2001-06-14, `http://www.omg.org/cgi-bin/doc?ad/2001-06-14` (2001)
11. Petriu, D.C., Wang, X.: From UML Description of High-Level Software Architecture to LQN performance models. In: Nagl, M., et al.(eds): Applications of Graph Transformations with Industrial Relevance AGTIVE'99. Lecture Notes in Computer Science, Vol. 1779. Springer-Verlag, Berlin Heidelberg New York (2000) 47–62
12. Petriu, D.C., Shousha, C., Jalnapurkar, A.: Architecture-Based Performance Analysis Applied to a Telecommunication System. In: IEEE Transactions on Software Eng., Vol.26, No.11 (2000) 1049–1065
13. Petriu, D.C., Sun, Y.: Consistent Behaviour Representation in Activity and Sequence Diagrams. In: Evans, A., et al.(eds): UML'2000 The Unified Modeling Language - Advancing the Standard. Lecture Notes in Computer Science, Vol. 1939 (2000) 369–382
14. G.Rozenberg (ed): Hanbook of Graph Grammars and Computing by Graph Transformation, Vol.1. World Scientific (1997)
15. Rolia, J.A., Sevcik, K.C.: The Method of Layers. EEE Trans. on Software Engineering, Vol. 21, Nb. 8 (1995) 689–700
16. Scratchley, W.C.: Evaluation and Diagnosis of Concurrency Architectures. Ph.D Thesis, Carleton University, Dept. of Systems and Computer Eng. (2000)
17. Schürr, A.: Programmed Graph Replacement Systems. In G.Rozenberg (ed): Handbook of Graph Grammars and Computing by Graph Transformation. (1997) 479–546
18. Smith, C.U.: Performance Engineering of Software Systems. Addison Wesley (1990)
19. Smith, C.U., Williams, L.G.: Performance Solutions: A Practical Guide to Creating Responsive, Scalable Software. Addison Wesley (2001)
20. Woodside, C.M.: Throughput Calculation for Basic Stochastic Rendezvous Networks. In: Performance Evaluation, Vol.9, No.2 (1998) 143–160

21. Woodside, C.M., Neilson, J.E., Petriu, D.C., Majumdar, S.: The Stochastic Rendezvous Network Model for Performance of Synchronous Client-Server-like Distributed Software. In: IEEE Transactions on Computers, Vol.44, Nb.1 (1995) 20-34
22. ArgoUML tool. to be found at `http://argouml.tigris.org/`
23. Novosoft Metadata Framework and UML Library, open source library to be found at `http://nsuml.sourceforge.net/`

A Passage-Time Preserving Equivalence for Semi-Markov Processes

J.T. Bradley

Department of Computing,
Imperial College of Science, Technology and Medicine,
Huxley Building, 180 Queen's Gate, London SW7 2BZ.
jb@doc.ic.ac.uk

Abstract. An equivalence for semi-Markov processes is presented which preserves passage-time distributions between pairs of states in a given set. The equivalence is based upon a state-based aggregation procedure which is $O(n^2)$ per state in the worst case.

1 Introduction

An equivalence compares two systems and defines whether they are in some way *equal in behaviour* for a given property. The concept of an equivalence for a stochastic model which preserves stochastic behaviour is not new (i.e. Markovian lumping [1] and within Markovian process algebras [2,3,4,5]). As far as we are aware, the existence of similar useful equivalences for more distribution-rich stochastic models, such as semi-Markov processes is new.

In this paper, the property we are seeking to preserve is that of having identical passage-time distributions between pairs of states. This, in stochastic terms, is a very strong constraint compared to say having similar steady-state behaviour or reward behaviour.

The equivalence is based on an aggregation technique for SMPs which is fully defined here and this provides us with opportunities for model reduction. Controlling SMP state space size so that transient [6], steady-state and passage-time techniques [7] can be undertaken tractably is an important goal. We make heavy use of Laplace transforms in manipulating the semi-Markov state space; this is justified by the fairly recent developments in Laplace inversion algorithms [8] that can provide numerically stable inversions for even discontinuous functions.

The paper is structured as follows: the equivalence is defined in the next section and related to the aggregation function. An example aggregation is given for a 4-complete transition graph. The individual aggregation steps are discussed and justified stochastically. Finally, the whole algorithm is formally presented and the complexity is discussed.

T. Field et al. (Eds.): TOOLS 2002, LNCS 2324, pp. 178–187, 2002.

2 Definition of Equivalence

2.1 Introduction

We specify a semi-Markov process, $M \in SMP$, as made up of the tuple (S, P, L) where S is the finite set of states, P is the underlying DTMC and L is the distribution matrix. M_X is used to access the X element of the tuple.

We define the equivalence operator, $(\overset{m,n}{\sim})$, for two semi-Markov processes, M, N:

$$M \overset{m,n}{\sim} N \tag{1}$$

where $m \subseteq M_S$ and $n \subseteq N_S$. This says that two systems M and N are passage-time equivalent over the state subsets m and n. This means that all passage-time distributions between states in m over M are identical to a specific reordering of passage-time distributions between states in n over N.

2.2 Formal Definition

In formal terms, $M \overset{m,n}{\sim} N$ iff M^* and N^* are isomorphic upto state relabelling.

M^* and N^* are defined by using the aggregation function, *aggregate_smp* and the subsidiary function *fold* (defined in section 3.3).

$$\begin{aligned} M^* &= \mathit{fold}(\mathit{aggregate\_smp}, M, M_S \setminus m) \\ N^* &= \mathit{fold}(\mathit{aggregate\_smp}, N, N_S \setminus n) \end{aligned} \tag{2}$$

where *aggregate_smp* satisfies the following property. Given a first passage-time distribution function between two states:

$$\mathit{passage\_time} : SMP \times (S \times S) \to ([0,1] \to \mathbb{R}^+) \tag{3}$$

For $M_2 = \mathit{aggregate\_smp}(M_1, i)$ such that $M_{1_S} = \{i\} \cup M_{2_S}$:

$$\forall r, s \in M_{2_S}, \mathit{passage\_time}(M_2, (r, s)) = \mathit{passage\_time}(M_1, (r, s)) \tag{4}$$

3 SMP State Lumping

3.1 An Example of SMP State Lumping

We illustrate the state-aggregation of SMPs with an example of a 4-complete graph, representing the transitions of an SMP. This situation is shown in figure 1.

In the first instance, a state is selected for aggregation. For a state with m in-transitions and n out-transitions, there are mn two-transition paths that pass

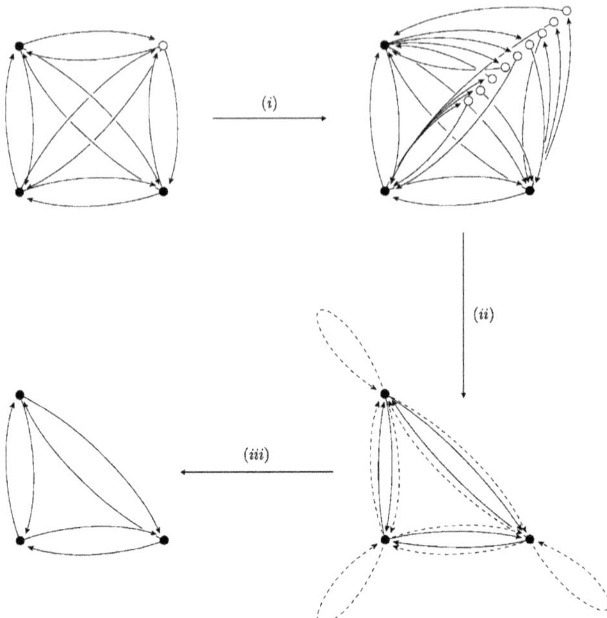

Fig. 1. Reducing a complete 4 state graph to a complete 3 state graph.

through the state. In the worst case (for a k-complete graph) there are $(k-1)^2$ such transitions.

After stage (i) of the process in figure 1, these transitions are represented explicitly by replicating the chosen node (shown in white) and transitions.

In step (ii), the 9 two-transition paths are aggregated to give 9 single transitions consist of cycles and non-cycles (shown as dashed edges). The non-cyclic transitions shadow transitions from the original SMP graph.

In the final step, the non-cyclic transitions are combined with their shadow transitions and the cyclic transitions are absorbed into the non-cycle distributions. This leaves us with a 3-complete graph.

The process for a single aggregation is worst case $O(k^2)$, and for aggregating the state space of most of an SMP, $O(k^3)$.

In the next sections, we will show how the aggregation process preserves the stochastic effect of the aggregated state in such a way that passage-time distributions between unaggregated states are kept in tact.

3.2 Basic Reduction Steps

Sequential Reduction. From figure 2: $Y = X_1 + X_2$ is a convolution and therefore in Laplace form, $L_Y(z) = L_{X_1}(z)L_{X_2}(z)$. If there are probabilistic weightings p_1 and p_2 on respectively of the transitions, then the overall weighting for the path is $p_1 p_2$. This is used in the *agg_seq* function, equation (13).

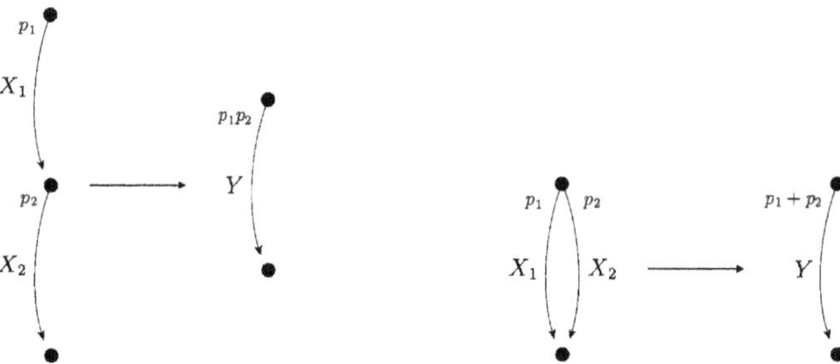

Fig. 2. Aggregating sequential transitions in an SMP.

Fig. 3. Aggregating branching transitions in an SMP.

Branch reduction. To aggregate the type of branch structure shown in figure 3, we can sum the respective probabilities and distributions. Thus the aggregate probability for the branch is $p_1 + p_2$ and the overall distribution Y for the sojourn is given by $L_{X_1}(z) + L_{X_2}(z)$. This is used in the *agg_branch* function, equation (14).

Cycle Reduction. In a semi-Markov process, cycle reduction may be necessary (and indeed is in the next section) if we create a state with at least one out-transition and a transition to itself (or cycle). We can remove the cycle by making its stochastic effect part of the out-going transitions.

Therefore we need to modify those out-transitions, and this section describes that modification. We picture our state system as being in the first stage of figure 4: with $(n-1)$ out-transitions with probability p_i of departure along edge i; each out-transition carries a sojourn of X_i; the cycle probability is p_n and carries a delay of X_n.

The first step, (i), is to isolate the cycle and treat is separately from the branching out-transitions. We do this by introducing an instantaneous delay and extra state after the cycle, $Z \sim \delta(0)$; the introduction of an extra state is only to aid our visualisation of the problem and is not necessary or indeed performed in the actual aggregation algorithm. Clearly the probability of doing this instantaneous transition is $(1 - p_n)$ (this is just the probability of performing any of the out-transitions from our original state). We now have to renormalise the p_i probabilities on the branching state to become $q_i = p_i/(1 - p_n)$.

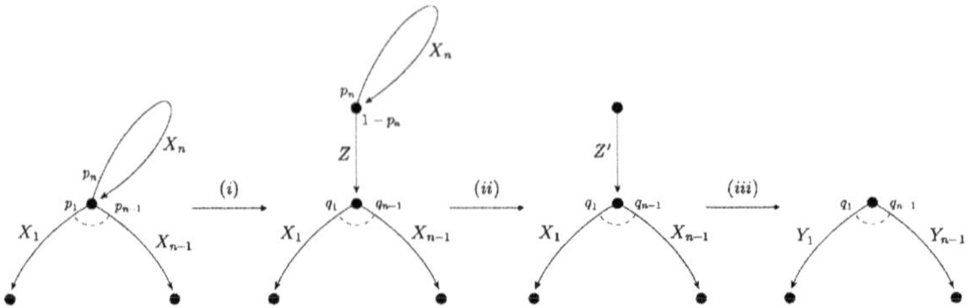

Fig. 4. The three-step removal of a cycle from an SMP.

In step (ii) of figure 4, we aggregate the delay of the cycle into the instantaneous transition creating a new transition with distribution Z'. This can be done in one of two ways: either by treating the system as a random sum of the random variable, X_n, or by considering a linear system of Laplace transforms. In the latter case:

$$L_{Z'}(z) = p_n L_{X_n}(z) L_{Z'}(z) + (1 - p_n) \underbrace{L_Z(z)}_{1} \tag{5}$$

This gives us:

$$L_{Z'}(z) = \frac{1 - p_n}{1 - p_n L_{X_n}(z)} \tag{6}$$

In stage (iii) of the process, the Z' delay is simply sequentially convolved onto the X_i events to give us our final system.

In summary then: we have reduced an n-out-transition state where one of the transitions was a cycle to an $(n-1)$-out-transition state with no cycle such that:

$$q_i = \frac{p_i}{1 - p_n} \tag{7}$$

and:

$$L_{Y_i}(z) = \frac{1 - p_n}{1 - p_n L_{X_n}(z)} L_{X_i}(z) \tag{8}$$

This form is used explicitly in equation (15), the *agg_cycle* function of the next section.

3.3 State Lumping Definition

Notation. In the description below, the following notation is used:

A semi-Markov process, $M \in SMP$, is made up of the tuple (S, P, L) where S is the finite set of states, P is the underlying DTMC and L is the distribution matrix in Laplace form.

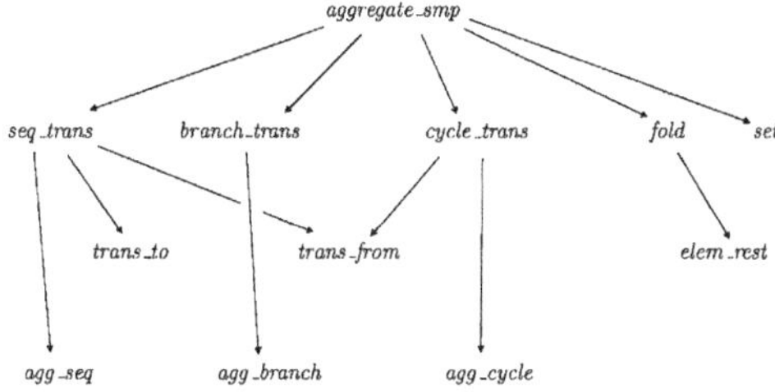

Fig. 5. The functional dependency diagram for the algebraic description of *aggregate_smp*.

Also: $Prob = [0,1]$, $LaplaceT = \mathbb{C} \to \mathbb{C}$, $PD = (Prob, LaplaceT)$ and finally $T = (S \times S) \times PD$.

So more specifically, $P : S \times S \to [0,1]$ such that $\sum_{j \in S} P(i,j) = 1$ and $L : S \times S \to LaplaceT$.

As before, for $M \in SMP$, $M_S = S$, $M_P = P$ and $M_L = L$ so that we can define $i \stackrel{M}{\to} j$ to mean that, there exists a transition from state i to state j in M, or formally $M_P(i,j) > 0$.

Finally, figure 5 shows the functional dependencies in the definition of *aggregate_smp*.

Main aggregation algorithm. In this section, we define the overarching aggregation function, *aggregate_smp*, which is defined on an SMP and a state. The lumping procedure can be applied to any state of an irreducible semi-Markov process or to any except absorbing or initial states of a transient SMP.

The general algorithm for aggregating a single state into an SMP such that the passage-times are preserved follows the pattern seen in the example aggregation of section 3.1.

Reading from the bottom up in equation (9), the general method works as follows, for a state i to be aggregated in an SMP, M:

1. Find all valid paths of length two that have i as the middle state and combine into a set of single transitions using the techniques of section 3.2. Call this set ts.
2. Separate ts transitions into a set of cycles, ts_c, and a set of branching transitions to other states, ts_b.
3. Apply the branching reduction of section 3.2 to the set of branching transitions, ts_b. Where a new transition from ts_b that does not already exist in M, then the transition from ts_b is to be placed unchanged into the new SMP. Call the new set of transitions, us.

4. Overwrite all the transition mentioned in us in M and call the new SMP, M'.
5. Aggregate all the cyclic transitions in ts_c, using the method shown in section 3.2. Place rewritten transitions of M' in vs.
6. Finally, integrate all the vs transitions into M' and return the final SMP.
7. The result will have a disconnected state, i, which can be removed.

$$\begin{aligned}
&\mathit{aggregate_smp} : SMP \times S \rightarrow SMP \\
&\mathit{aggregate_smp} \quad (M, i) = \mathit{fold}(set, M', vs) \;.\; vs = \mathit{cycle_trans}(M', ts_c), \\
&\qquad\qquad\qquad M' = \mathit{fold}(set, M, us), \\
&\qquad\qquad\qquad us = \mathit{branch_trans}(M, ts_b), \\
&\qquad\qquad\qquad ts_b = ts \setminus ts_c, \\
&\qquad\qquad\qquad ts_c = \{((i,j),t) \;.\; ((i,j),t) \in ts, i = j\}, \\
&\qquad\qquad\qquad ts = \mathit{seq_trans}(M, i)
\end{aligned} \tag{9}$$

Higher-level aggregation functions. From figure 5, we define the key functions used by *aggregate_smp*: *seq_trans*, *branch_trans* and *cycle_trans*.

seq_trans takes a state, i, to be aggregated and the SMP and returns a set of transitions which represent all the paths (from one state preceding to one state after i) which pass through i. The paths have been aggregated into single transitions using *agg_seq*. The number of transitions generated by *seq_trans* is equal to the product the number transitions leading into i and the number leaving the state.

$$\begin{aligned}
&\mathit{seq_trans} : SMP \times S \rightarrow \mathcal{P}(T) \\
&\mathit{seq_trans} \quad (M, i) = \{((i,j), \mathit{agg_seq}(t, t')) \\
&\qquad\qquad\qquad .\; (i,t) \in \mathit{trans_to}(i, M), (j, t') \in \mathit{trans_from}(i, M)\}
\end{aligned} \tag{10}$$

branch_trans processes an SMP, M, and a set of transitions, R, which must not contain any cycles. The transitions are to be integrated into the SMP, M. If there is a pre-existing transition in M for a given member of R, then the two are combined using *agg_branch*, otherwise the transition in R is just returned unchanged.

$$\begin{aligned}
&\mathit{branch_trans} : SMP \times \mathcal{P}(T) \rightarrow \mathcal{P}(T) \\
&\mathit{branch_trans} \quad (M, R) = \{((i,j), \mathit{agg_branch}(t, t')) \;.\; ((i,j),t)) \in R, \\
&\qquad\qquad\qquad t' = \;\mathsf{if}\; i \overset{M}{\rightarrow} j \;\mathsf{then}\; (M_P(i,j), M_L(i,j)) \;\mathsf{else}\; (0,0)\}
\end{aligned} \tag{11}$$

cycle_trans processes an SMP, M, and a set of transitions, R, which must only contain cyclic transitions. For each cycle defined in R from i to i, the set of leaving transitions is selected from the SMP, M. For each member of that set, the aggregation function *agg_cycle* is applied. All the modified transitions are unified into a single set and returned.

$$
\begin{aligned}
&\mathit{cycle\_trans} : \mathit{SMP} \times \mathcal{P}(T) \to \mathcal{P}(T) \\
&\mathit{cycle\_trans} \quad (M, R) = \bigcup_{i:((i,i),t') \in R} X \\
&\qquad . \; X = \{((i,j), \mathit{agg\_cycle}(t,t')) \; . \; (j,t) \in \mathit{trans\_from}(i, M)\}
\end{aligned}
\tag{12}
$$

Basic aggregation functions. This section describes the three basic structure aggregation operations, displayed in section 3.2. These are:

Sequential Aggregation. Used to represent two transitions in sequence as a single transition.

$$
\begin{aligned}
&\mathit{agg\_seq} : PD \times PD \to PD \\
&\mathit{agg\_seq} \quad ((p, d(z)), (p', d'(z))) = (pp', d(z)d'(z))
\end{aligned}
\tag{13}
$$

Branching Aggregation. Used to represent two branching transitions which terminate in the same state as a single transition.

$$
\begin{aligned}
&\mathit{agg\_branch} : PD \times PD \to PD \\
&\mathit{agg\_branch} \quad ((p, d(z)), (p', d'(z))) = (p + p', d(z) + d'(z))
\end{aligned}
\tag{14}
$$

Cycle Aggregation. Used to represent a cycle to the same state and a leaving transition as a single transition. The first argument is the leaving transition and the second is the cyclic transition. As described in section 3.2, if there is more than one out-transition then the transformation will need to be applied to each in turn.

$$
\begin{aligned}
&\mathit{agg\_cycle} : PD \times PD \to PD \\
&\mathit{agg\_cycle} \quad ((p, d(z)), (p_c, d_c(z))) = \left(\frac{p}{1 - p_c}, \frac{(1 - p_c)d(z)}{1 - p_c d_c(z)} \right)
\end{aligned}
\tag{15}
$$

Subsidiary Functions. The function *trans_from* takes a state, i, and returns the set of states, probabilities and distributions which succeed i.

$$\begin{aligned} &\mathit{trans\_from} : S \times SMP \to \mathcal{P}(S \times PD) \\ &\mathit{trans\_from} \quad (i, M) = \{(j, (M_P(i,j), M_L(i,j))) \,.\, j \in M_S, i \overset{M}{\to} j\} \end{aligned} \tag{16}$$

The function *trans_to* takes a state, i, and returns the set of states, probabilities and distributions which connect to i.

$$\begin{aligned} &\mathit{trans\_to} : S \times SMP \to \mathcal{P}(S \times PD) \\ &\mathit{trans\_to} \quad (i, M) = \{(j, (M_P(j,i), M_L(j,i))) \,.\, j \in M_S, j \overset{M}{\to} i\} \end{aligned} \tag{17}$$

The *set* function is used to set a given transition in the DTMC and distribution matrix of an SMP. If necessary the current transition is overwritten.

$$\begin{aligned} &\mathit{set} : T \times SMP \to SMP \\ &\mathit{set} \quad (((i,j),(p,d(z))), M) = (M_S, P', L') \\ &\qquad .\ P'(k,l) = \begin{cases} p & \text{if } (k,l) = (i,j) \\ M_P(k,l) & \text{otherwise} \end{cases} \\ &\qquad\ \ L'(k,l) = \begin{cases} d(z) & \text{if } (k,l) = (i,j) \\ M_L(k,l) & \text{otherwise} \end{cases} \end{aligned} \tag{18}$$

fold is used in this context to take one transition at a time, from a set of probability-distribution transitions, and apply each of the new transitions to a given SMP. This occurs across the entire supplied transition set until there are none left to apply.

$$\begin{aligned} &\mathit{fold} : (A \times B \to B) \times B \times \mathcal{P}(A) \to B \\ &\mathit{fold} \quad (f, r, \Gamma) = \begin{cases} r & \text{if } \Gamma = \emptyset \\ f(x, r, \mathit{fold}(f, r, \Gamma')) & \\ \quad .\ (x, \Gamma') = \mathit{elem\_rest}(\Gamma) & \text{otherwise} \end{cases} \end{aligned} \tag{19}$$

The function, *elem_rest*, is used by *fold* to select an arbitrary element from a set and return a tuple containing that element and the set minus that element.

$$\begin{aligned} &\mathit{elem\_rest} : \mathcal{P}(A) \to (A, \mathcal{P}(A)) \\ &\mathit{elem\_rest} \quad (T) = \begin{cases} \bot & \text{if } T = \emptyset \\ (x \,.\, x \in T, \{t \,.\, t \in T, t \neq x\}) & \text{otherwise} \end{cases} \end{aligned} \tag{20}$$

4 Conclusion

We have specified and defined an indexed equivalence over semi-Markov processes which is based on a state aggregation of the SMP. The aggregation is $O(n^3)$ for all states in the worst case and $O(n^2)$ for a single state if heavily interconnected.

By preserving passage-times within an SMP we also preserve transient and steady-state results as well, so if a modeller is seeking to perform multiple analysis on an SMP then expending some initial computational effort to reduce the size of the model to concentrate on the key states would be a useful exercise. It is appreciated that if a system is only being analysed once for say steady-state or transient-state results (for which the complexity is $O(n^3)$) then there is not much to be gained from using this technique unless $< O(n)$ states are to be aggregated.

It is envisaged that in much the same way that lumpability [1] has been embodied in various Markovian equivalences, we would like to embed this passage-time equivalence in a process algebraic context. In doing so, of course, we will either need to perform analysis solely at the component level or construct some technique for approximating interleaved concurrent state space as a sequential state space.

References

1. J. G. Kemeny and J. L. Snell, *Finite Markov Chains.* Van Nostrand, 1960.
2. H. Hermanns and M. Rettelbach, "Syntax, semantics, equivalences, and axioms for MTIPP," in *Process Algebra and Performance Modelling Workshop* (U. Herzog and M. Rettelbach, eds.), pp. 69–88, Arbeitsberichte des IMMD, Universtät Erlangen-Nürnberg, Regensberg, July 1994.
3. J. Hillston, *A Compositional Approach to Performance Modelling*, vol. 12 of *Distinguished Dissertations in Computer Science.* Cambridge University Press, 1996. ISBN 0 521 57189 8.
4. H. Hermanns, *Interactive Markov Chains.* PhD thesis, Universität Erlangen-Nürnberg, July 1998.
5. M. Bernardo and R. Gorrieri, "Extended Markovian Process Algebra," in *CONCUR'96, Proceedings of the 7th International Conference on Concurrency Theory* (U. Montanari and V. Sassone, eds.), vol. 1119 of *Lecture Notes in Computer Science*, pp. 315–330, Springer-Verlag, Pisa, August 1996.
6. R. Pyke, "Markov renewal processes with finitely many states," *Annals of Mathematical Statistics*, vol. 32, pp. 1243–1259, December 1961.
7. J. T. Bradley and N. J. Davies, "A matrix-based method for analysing stochastic process algebras," in *ICALP Workshops 2000, Process Algebra and Performance Modelling Workshop* (J. D. P. Rolim, ed.), pp. 579–590, University of Waterloo, Ontario, Canada, Carleton Scientific, Geneva, July 2000.
8. J. Abate and W. Whitt, "The Fourier-series method for inverting transforms of probability distributions," *Queueing Systems*, vol. 10, no. 1, pp. 5–88, 1992.

Symbolic Methods for the State Space Exploration of GSPN Models

Ian Davies[1], William J. Knottenbelt[2], and Pieter S. Kritzinger[1]

[1] Department of Computer Science, University of Cape Town, Rondebosch 7700, South Africa; {idavies,psk}@cs.uct.ac.za
[2] Department of Computing, Imperial College of Science, Technology and Medicine, 180 Queen's Gate, London SW7 2BZ, United Kingdom; wjk@doc.ic.ac.uk

Abstract. Generalised Stochastic Petri Nets (GSPNs) suffer from the same problem as any other state-transition modelling technique: it is difficult to represent sufficient states so that *general*, real life systems can be analysed. In this paper we use symbolic techniques to perform state space exploration for *unstructured* GSPNs. We present an algorithm for finding an encoding function which attempts to minimize the height of BDDs used to encode GSPN state spaces. This technique brings together and extends a spectrum of ad-hoc heuristics in a formal algorithm. We also develop a BDD state exploration algorithm which incorporates an adjustable memory threshold. Our results show the ability to encode over 10^8 states using just 13.7MB of memory.

1 Introduction

As communication systems evolve and become more complex, the need for software tools to analyse these systems grows. A popular way of analysing such systems is to model their behaviour using a high-level abstraction such as Generalised Stochastic Petri Nets (GSPNs) [1]. Qualitative and quantitative properties of the system can then be assessed by analysing the low-level state space and state graph underlying the model. However, even relatively simple models can suffer from the *state space explosion problem*, where the number of states reachable from the initial state becomes too large to store.

In order to cope with increasingly complex models we therefore require advanced techniques for constructing and storing state spaces and state graphs. Based upon earlier work in electronic circuit theory (e.g. [6,12,15]), this paper describes our technique to explore and store the state space and state graph of GSPN models, using Binary Decision Diagrams (BDDs) [5] and Multi-terminal BDDs (MTBDDs) [9] as data storage structures. The application of BDDs to modelling formalisms is an active research area and has been investigated by, amongst others, Pastor *et al* [7,8] and Hermanns *et al* [11]. More recently Ciardo *et al* have successfully applied another BDD variant, Multi-valued Decision Diagrams (MDDs), to construct structured Petri net model state spaces [2,10].

T. Field et al. (Eds.): TOOLS 2002, LNCS 2324, pp. 188–199, 2002.

The focus of the present study is twofold. Firstly, in Section 3, we bring together and extend a spectrum of known ad-hoc heuristics in a formal algorithm for finding an encoding function for BDDs used to encode GSPN state spaces. Secondly, in Section 4, we present a BDD state exploration algorithm for unstructured GSPNs which has an adjustable memory threshold. Experimental results are presented in Section 5.

2 Background Theory

A BDD is a rooted, directed, acyclic graph which contains a set of vertices. Each vertex is associated with an *index* that describes its height in the BDD and a unique *identifier* that distinguishes it from the other vertices. There are two types of vertices in a BDD: *non-terminal* vertices, each of which has two child vertices; and *terminal* vertices that have a Boolean value but no children. Each BDD vertex can have any number of parent vertices. The two children of a non-terminal vertex associated with the Boolean values true and false are called the *high* and *low* child respectively.

A BDD is *ordered* if and only if each non-terminal vertex has a lower index than its child vertices. Further, an ordered BDD is *reduced* if it contains no vertex v such that $low(v) = high(v)$, nor does it contain distinct vertices v and v' such that the subgraphs rooted at v and v' are isomorphic [6]. Reduced, ordered BDDs are therefore *canonical* representations of Boolean functions. This means that two functions are equivalent if and only if the reduced, ordered BDDs for the two functions are isomorphic.

Boolean operators may be applied to BDD data-structure operands. In 1990, Brace *et al.* [14] devised the efficient *ite*-algorithm for manipulating Boolean functions based on the Boolean ternary operator *if-then-else*. We refer the interested reader to [14] for further details.

MTBDDs are an extension of BDDs proposed by Fujita *et al* [9]. They contend that MTBDDs are a superior data structure, in terms of memory utilisation, particularly for the representation of sparse matrices. In fact, the matrix need not be sparse. If several of the matrix elements have the same value then the isomorphism of MTBDD subgraphs may be exploited to gain further advantage over standard sparse matrix packages. MTBDDs represent functions of the form $f : \tilde{D} \rightarrow \mathbb{R}$ where $\tilde{D}$ is a arbitrary finite set. One can encode the members of $\tilde{D}$ using $\lceil \log_2 |\tilde{D}| \rceil$ Boolean variables. In the case where $\tilde{D}$ is the set of integers $\{0, ..., n-1\}$, then the MTBDD represents a vector of length n. In the case where $\tilde{D}$ is the finite set $\{0, ..., n-1\} \times \{0, ..., m-1\}$, then the MTBDD represents a matrix of dimension $n \times m$.

The individual positions of elements in a vector or matrix can be encoded by a unique combination of Boolean variables. MTBDDs are both *reduced* and *ordered* and form a canonical representation of the vector or matrix they encode.

Information about the length of the vector or dimension of the matrix is lost in the MTBDD representation, and this must be stored separately from the data structure. Readers interested in more background regarding MTBDDs are referred to [9], [18] and [11].

3 Encoding Functions

Central to using BDDs for GSPN state space exploration is the *encoding function*, which symbolically represents a state by its *characteristic function* encoded as a BDD. The encoding function determines the height of the BDD and thereby directly influences the time taken for BDD-based operations. In the context of state-space exploration, the encoding function must provide a *one-to-one* mapping from each marking (or state of the GSPN) onto $\{true, false\}^n$. Thus we need to determine how many bits to allocate for each place in the net in order that it can be identified uniquely in each possible marking.

This section presents a technique for encoding GSPN states in BDDs that combines and extends the heuristics found by Haverkort [4] *et al*, Pastor and Cortadella [8] and Hermanns *et al* [11] in a formal algorithm. For brevity we have a assumed a basic knowledge of Petri net invariant theory in the explanations that follow; interested readers should consult [17].

3.1 Using P-Invariants

A P-invariant describes a weighted sum of place markings which remains the same for any reachable marking of the Petri net. A P-invariant is characterised by an equation of the following form:

$$C_{p_1} p_1 + \ldots + C_{p_n} p_n = U \tag{1}$$

where p_i represents the marking on place i, C_{p_i} represents the coefficient (weight) of p_i in the invariant equation, and U is the upper bound imposed by the equation. An upper bound on p_k is thus given by (for non-zero C_{p_k}):

$$p_k \leq U/(C_{p_k}) \tag{2}$$

Rearranging Equation 1 we find (again for non-zero C_{p_k}):

$$p_k = (U - (C_{p_1} p_1 + ... + C_{p_{k-1}} p_{k-1} + C_{p_{k+1}} p_{k+1} + ... + C_{p_n} p_n))/C_{p_k} \tag{3}$$

Since, we can compute p_k given $\{p_1, \ldots, p_{k-1}, p_{k+1}, \ldots, p_n\}$, it is only necessary to store $n-1$ of the places in that equation. We can apply this procedure for each P-invariant equation.

The places of the GSPN can therefore be divided into two categories: those which must be stored, and those which can be computed. The challenge is to attempt to minimise the number of bits used for the stored places that are actually encoded in the BDD. Our heuristic algorithm for this is shown in Figure 1. The P-invariant equations are sorted in order of increasing right-hand-side. This way the equation with the smallest RHS will be used first and require the smallest number of bits for each of its stored places. This is only effective in cases where the place concerned appears in more than one invariant equation. In this case we use the minimum of the upper bounds. We also sort each equation's left-hand-side terms in order of decreasing coefficient so that the place added to the computed set would have required the highest number of bits to store.

```
program Invariant Encoding
begin
    initialise set S of stored places = φ
    initialise set C of computed places = φ
    Sort invariant equations on RHS
    for each equation do
     Sort equation in order of decreasing coefficient
    for each equation e in order do
    begin
     for each place p in order do
     begin
      if (p ∉ S) ∧ (p ∉ C) ∧ (¬(p is the last place in e))
       add p to S
      if p is the last place in e
       insert p at end of C
     end
    end
end.
```

Fig. 1. Algorithm for selecting places to be encoded.

This is a *greedy* algorithm which may not result in the optimal encoding, but it improves on the technique of simply using P-invariants to remove one place per equation by greedily selecting the places required to be stored with the smallest number of bits first. Results using this technique are reported in Section 5.

3.2 Partitions and BDD Ordering

Variable ordering can have a dramatic effect on the amount of memory and time needed to construct a BDD-based representation of the model's state space. In our experiments, we have observed state space searches completing in *less than half* the time when a good variable ordering is chosen. It is known to be an

NP-complete problem to *a priori* decide on the optimal ordering of variables [3]. However, good orderings can often be constructed using heuristics.

In our technique, each component place of a marking is binary encoded with the separate encodings being concatenated making a bit-vector describing the marking. The variables for the individual markings are stored with least significant bit first. We noted no difference between least significant bit versus most significant bit first. Therefore, in order to improve the encoding we look to the ordering of the places themselves. We have experimented with two different GSPN partitioning techniques.

First, we tried to cluster the places into logical partitions, based on the transitions of the GSPN. For each transition we construct a partition consisting of all places connected to it via incoming arcs. If any of those places are already elements of other partitions, then the partitions are combined. Once this operation is completed we are left with distinct sets of places which enable certain transition sets.

Breaking the net into partitions in this way turns out to be the close to the worst thing one can do. The aggregation of places enabling the same transitions does not lead to a suitable place ordering. One needs to *interleave* similarly affected places in the Petri net. This is true for the interleaving of row and column matrices in MTBDDs [11], and the same theory applies here. That is, finding two similar sub-nets and interleaving the corresponding places bit-vectors. To try to automate this process for Petri nets with no obvious structure, we grouped together those places whose number of incoming and outgoing arcs are equal. Our experience was that this resulted in a great improvement upon the previous technique, as discussed in Section 5.

4 State Space Exploration

Having found an efficient encoding method and having chosen a good variable ordering, we are in a position to conduct an efficient state space exploration. Typically symbolic state space exploration methods use breadth-first searches. The algorithm in Figure 2 shows how the set N of *new* states, initialised to the starting state, is used as a *frontier set*. That is, all those states whose successors have not been found. The states reachable in one-step from the states in N are determined by the function *findSuccessorStatesFrom* and stored in U, the *unexplored* state set. E accumulates all the *explored* states and, at each iteration, the frontier set is found by performing a set minus of U from E.

The most flexible part of this algorithm is the function *findSuccessorStatesFrom*. We can find all the states stored in N by a simple BDD traversal during which we maintain an array of values indicating whether the low child path or the high child path was taken, or whether we skipped a node, or number of nodes. If we do skip a number of nodes, then for each index, we need to set the corresponding

```
program Breadth-First Exploration
var
    Set E, U, N = φ
begin
    insert the initial state into N
    while N ≠ φ do
    begin
        let U = findSuccessorStatesFrom(N)
        E = E ∪ N {add the newly explored states to the explored BDD}
        N = U − E {find the frontier set}
    end
end.
```

Fig. 2. Breadth-First State Space Exploration Algorithm

path array value to a "don't care" value. Whenever we reach the true terminal, we use the path array to set the marking of the GSPN under analysis, which we store separately in memory. If the path array contains "don't care" values then all the permutations of the array are set one at a time.

For each permutation in N, we find and fire the enabled transitions. This process, encapsulated by the function *findAllSuccessorsOf*, changes the marking of the Petri net via transition firing. The new marking can then be inserted into the BDD denoted U (see Fig. 3) representing the set of states found at this depth of the state graph. These are the unexplored states, which will contribute to the frontier set in the next iteration of the state search algorithm.

The most time-consuming part of this algorithm is the collection of the successor states by the function *findSuccessorStatesFrom* from the algorithm in Figure 2. We could make use of the BDD *ite* (if-then-else) algorithm in [14] to insert each newly found successor state into the set of found successor states, but, in practice, this is very time consuming and impractical. A much more efficient way to add the new states is to realise that a new state simply means a new path in the BDD. This new path would simply be a worst-case $O(D)$ insertion, where D is the depth of the BDD. Unfortunately, since the BDDs are reduced we cannot simply add a new path to the existing BDD because arbitrarily adding new paths would violate this property.

We developed a new technique to avoid this problem. If the BDD is *un*reduced, we *can* simply add the nodes to build the new path from root to *true* terminal. This reduces the time complexity of adding a new state to $O(D)$. Unfortunately, unreduced BDDs lose their compactness. Parent nodes are still re-used in the unreduced BDDs, but isomorphic child sub-graphs are not re-used, thus leading to a blow-up in memory usage. We therefore cannot leave BDDs in their unreduced form indefinitely.

Our technique makes use of two BDDs for the successor state computation. The first is an ordinary reduced BDD, U, which simply stores the states found

```
procedure findSuccessorStatesFrom(BDD : U, BDD : T, Vertex : v, array of integers : path)
begin
1       if (value(v) == 0) return
2       elseif (value(v) == 1)
        begin
3               foreach (combination of path) do
4               findAllSuccessorsOf(path, T)
5               if (|T| >maxSize)
6               U = U ∪ T
7               T = false
        end
8       else
        begin
9               path[index(v)] = false
10              fillInDontCares(index(v), index(low(v)), path)
11              findSuccessorStatesFrom(U, T, low(v), path)
12              path[index(v)] = true
13              fillInDontCares(index(v), index(high(v)), path)
14              findSuccessorStatesFrom(U, T, high(v), path)
        end
end.
```

Fig. 3. Our algorithm for incremental reduction during state space exploration.

to that point. The second is an *unreduced* temporary BDD denoted T. The temporary BDD has states added to it by simply inserting the new paths to the *true* terminal. This is done until the temporary BDD reaches a user-defined upper-bound for the number of nodes used.

Once this upper-bound is reached, the *ite* algorithm is used to *union* T, the unreduced graph, with U, the reduced graph. Since the *ite* algorithm always returns a reduced BDD, this process has the effect of reducing the size of the BDD needed to store the newly explored states. Since the reduced BDD is normally several orders of magnitude smaller than its unreduced counterpart, this algorithm effectively allows the user to place an upper-bound on the amount of memory used for the exploration. In this way the maximum amount of memory required during the exploration is limited and the user can ensure that the problem will fit in the available memory. Naturally, the lower this limit the less time efficient the algorithm becomes.

The algorithm just described and shown in Figure 3 finds all the successors of all the states in N, some of which may have been already explored. In order to ensure that we do not re-explore them, they are removed at the next step in the algorithm in the *set-minus* operation on line 8. We implemented an enhancement to this. For each state found, we first check whether it is in the BDD for the explored states, which involves a worst-case $O(D)$ comparison. This is more efficient than re-inserting and then removing the states; in our experiments, this generally lead to a time improvement of approximately 25%.

A final enhancement we made was in the detection of enabled transitions. As described in Section 3, some place values are stored in the BDD, while others are computed. Transitions have places from either category in their input set. As the BDD is traversed, place values are determined in the order in which they are stored from root to terminal node. Some transitions may rely only on places stored near the root of the BDD, and other transitions may rely on computed place values derived from places stored near the BDD root. Our algorithm for detecting enabled transitions is applied at every recursive step of the function *findSuccessorStatesFrom*. When the recursion reaches the base case, a much smaller subset of the transitions only need be tested to see if they are enabled. This enhancement typically led to an average 70% reduction in the state space exploration time compared with our previous results.

During the exploration, all state-to-state rates are recorded in an MTBDD matrix. States are added in exactly the same way as above, also incrementally reducing the MTBDD used to store the states when it becomes too large.

Note that it is more common in symbolic state space search algorithms to find all the successor states of the frontier set in one computation using the transition relation BDD in the predicate transformation. For highly structured models this is an extremely efficient approach, but for more non-structured examples the state space sizes that can be explored are dramatically reduced. This is because the BDD depth for the transition relation is double that of BDD needed to store the state space. The transition relation BDD is thus normally a very large BDD and each predicate transformation takes an impractically long time.

We conclude this section with a short discussion of how vanishing state elimination is incorporated into our algorithm. So-called "vanishing" states occur in GSPN state spaces because enabled immediate transitions lead to states with a sojourn time of zero. We eliminate these states on-the-fly using a standard technique that makes use of a vanishing state depth-first stack [13]. The alternative approach of removing vanishing states at the end of a traversal involves a matrix inversion operation which, except in some specialised cases, is inefficient in MTBDD data structures [9]. This can be attributed to the fact that inversions typically involve a large amount of *fill-in*.

5 Experimental Results

The results below are based on our own implementation of a BDD package, using hashing to improve the time taken for each run of the *ite* algorithm.

Invariant-Based Encoding Function: The height of the BDD directly impacts on the time taken of any BDD-based manipulation and the encoding function determines the height of the BDD. We compared our invariant-based GSPN encoding function with a naive binary encoding, where the number of tokens on every place is converted to its unsigned binary form. The smallest improvement upon this technique was a 70% reduction in the height of the corresponding BDD. The greatest improvement we found reduced the BDD height to just 20% of its original size.

Table 1. Comparative performance of classical and BDD storage methods. Dashed entries indicate that the process ran out out memory on a SPARC Station 5 with 256MB total memory.

No. of Phil.	No. of states	Classical	Binary		Invariant	
			Peak	Final	Peak	Final
5	81	256 KB	27 KB	12 KB	5 KB	1 KB
7	477	296 KB	198 KB	33 KB	29 KB	2.4 KB
10	6725	800 KB	-	-	398 KB	3.7 KB
12	39201	3.3 MB	-		2.2 MB	4.6 KB
15	551,613	44.9 MB	-	-	13.2 MB	3.3 KB
17	3,215,041	-	-	-	13.7 MB	9.1 KB
21	110 Million	-	-	-	13.7 MB	11.7 KB

State Space Exploration: Using BDDs for this purpose lead to a remarkable saving in space, allowing us to represent systems with as many as 10^8 states on a single workstation using 13.7MB of memory. While our BDD-based approach is slower for smaller state spaces, the speed of our implementation became comparable to a published classical technique (Knottenbelt *et al* [20]) at about the million-state mark on a single workstation. We are able to explore approximately 11 million states, and save the state to state rates for performance analysis in an MTBDD, in 6 hours on a single workstation using 4.5MB of memory. This is compared with a tool (DNAmaca [13]) using a probabilistic hashing-based technique which fails after 20 hours having explored only 5 million states in nearly 800MB of memory.

Table 1 shows results from the scalable Petri net model of the Dining Philosophers problem. It demonstrates how the use of BDDs in state space explorations, in combination with our computational invariant encoding technique, improves on the memory usage of both classical storage techniques as well as a naive binary encoding technique.

Partitions and Variable Ordering: We found that memory and time efficiency can be improved by ensuring that the Boolean variables encoding the state vectors are ordered felicitously by exploiting the structure of the GSPN. We found that the most efficient variable ordering technique *interleaved* the places of similar sub-areas in the GSPN.

The graph in Figure 4 shows some interesting general trends we have found in the course of our experimentation. Each bar corresponds to the number of states per second the technique allowed, given a particular model. For example, the leftmost bar shows that approximately 2 800 states per second were found using a random ordering on the Kanban [16] model with 3 kanbans. For each technique,

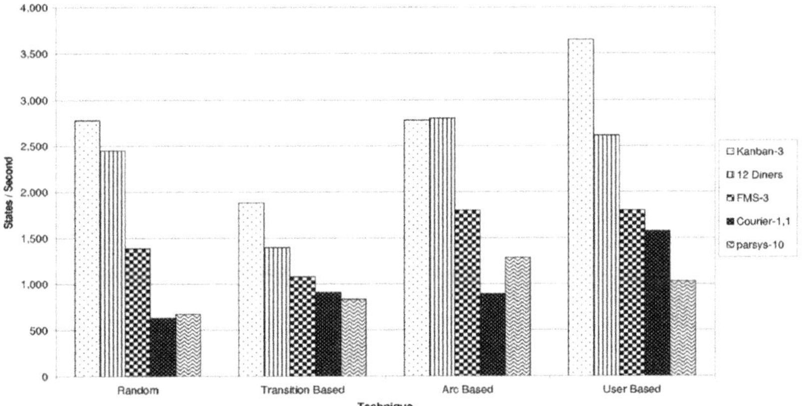

Fig. 4. A graph showing the relative performance of different variable ordering techniques in states per second.

the bars corresponding to each model are in order of decreasing regular structure. The most structured model is the Kanban model and the least structured is the parsys [19] GSPN. In general, there is a decrease in states per second as the regularity of the model structure decreases. This confirms the intuition that, generally, symbolic methods are less efficient on less regular GSPNs. The graphs also show that a user-chosen ordering method was better than the others in almost every case. However, our automated technique comes close to achieve similar throughputs as the user-chosen ordering. This shows that interleaving the places of individual subnets yields a better ordering than clustering places into partitions based on the transitions to which they are connected.

6 Conclusion

We have reported on our experience with symbolic methods for GSPN state space exploration. In this work we are not constrained to solving only regularly structured models, any model structure is suitable. We presented our GSPN encoding technique which brings together in a formal algorithm several heuristics found in existing work. We found that memory and time efficiency can be improved drastically by a well-chosen variable ordering, which, in our experience, involves *interleaving* the places of similar, but not necessarily the same, subnets in the GSPN. We presented results showing how our techniques improve over the memory and time efficiency of probabilistic hashing-based methods for large models on a single workstation.

BDD-based techniques move the focus from the search for space efficient methods, to a search for time efficient ones. In the future we plan to develop more efficient MTBDD-based matrix manipulation algorithms so that the good memory efficiency of MTBDDs can be complemented with good time-savings. Furthermore, we intend to investigate the possibility of distributing our techniques over a network of workstations.

References

1. M. Ajmone-Marsan, G. Conte, and G. Balbo. A class of Generalised Stochastic Petri Nets for the performance evaluation of multiprocessor systems. *ACM Transactions on Computer Systems*, 2:93–122, 1984.
2. A.S. Miner and G. Ciardo. Efficient reachability set generation and storage using decision diagrams. *LNCS 1639, Proc. 20th Intl. Conf. of the Application and Theory of Petri Nets*, pages 6–25, 1999.
3. B. Bollig and I. Wegener. Improving the variable ordering of OBBDs is NP-complete. *IEEE Transactions on Computers*, 45(9):993–1006, 1996.
4. B.R. Haverkort, A. Bell, H.C. Bohnenkamp. On the efficient sequential and distributed generation of very large Markov chains from stochastic Petri nets. *Proc. 8th Intl Conf. Petri Nets and Perf. Models (PNPM'99)*, pages 12–21, 1999.
5. R.E. Bryant. Graph-Based Algorithms for Boolean Function Manipulation. *IEEE Transactions on Computer Science*, C-35(8):677–691, August 1986.
6. R.E. Bryant. Symbolic boolean manipulation with ordered binary decision diagrams. *ACM Computing Surveys*, 24(3):293–318, September 1992.
7. E. Pastor and J. Cortadella. Petri net analysis using boolean function manipulation. *Technical Report, University of Zaragoza*, 1993.
8. E. Pastor and J. Cortadella. Efficient Encoding Schemes for Symbolic Analysis of Petri nets. *Proc. Design, Automation and Test in Europe*, pages 790–795, 1998.
9. M. Fujita, P. McGeer, and J.-Y. Yang. Multi-terminal binary decision diagrams: an efficient data structure for matrix representations. *Formal Methods in System Design*, 10(2/3):149–169, 1997.
10. G. Ciardo, G. Luettgen, R. Siminiceanu. Efficient symbolic state-space construction for asynchronous systems. *ICASE Report No. 99-50*, December 1999.
11. H. Hermanns, J. Meyer-Kayser, and M. Siegle. Multi Terminal Binary Decision Diagrams to Represent and Analyse Continuous Time Markov Chains. *In Proc. 3rd Int. Workshop on the Num. Solution of Markov Chains*, pages 188–207, 1999.
12. J.R. Burch, E.M. Clarke, K.L. McMillan, D.L. Dill, L.J. Hwang. Symbolic Model Checking: 10^{20} States and Beyond. *Proc. 5th IEEE Symp. on Logic in Computer Science*, pages 428–439, 1990.
13. W. Knottenbelt. Generalised Markovian Analysis of Timed Transition Systems. Master's thesis, University of Cape Town, June 1996.
14. K.S. Brace, R.L. Rudell, R.E. Bryant. Efficient implementation of a BDD package. *27th ACM/IEEE Design Automation Conference*, pages 40–45, 1990.
15. O. Coudert, C. Berthet, J-C. Madre. Verification of Sequential Machines Using Boolean Functional Vectors. *Applied Formal Methods For Correct VLSI Design*, 1:111–128, 1990.
16. P. Buchholz, G. Ciardo, S. Donatelli and P. Kemper. Kronecker operations and sparse matrices with applications to the solution of Markov models. *ICASE Report No. 97-66*, December 1997.
17. P.S. Kritzinger and F. Bause. *Stochastic Petri Nets: An Introduction to the Theory.* Verlag Vieweg, Wiesbaden, Germany, 1995.

18. R.I. Bahar, E.A. Frohm, C.M. Gaona, G.D. Hactel, E. Macii, A. Pardo, F. Somenzi. Algebraic Decision Diagrams and their Applications. *In Proc. International Conf. Computer-Aided Design (ICCAD)*, pages 188–191, 1993.
19. S. Caselli, G. Conte, P. Marenzoni. Parallel State Space Exploration for GSPN Models. *LNCS 935, Proc. 16th Intl Conference on the Application and Theory of Petri Nets*, pages 181–200, June 1995.
20. W.J. Knottenbelt, P.G. Harrison, M.A. Mestern, P.S. Kritzinger. A probabilistic dynamic technique for the distributed generation of very large state spaces. *Performance Evaluation*, pages 127–148, February 2000.

PRISM: Probabilistic Symbolic Model Checker*

Marta Kwiatkowska, Gethin Norman, and David Parker

School of Computer Science, University of Birmingham,
Birmingham B15 2TT, United Kingdom
{mzk,gxn,dxp}@cs.bham.ac.uk

Abstract. In this paper we describe PRISM, a tool being developed at the University of Birmingham for the analysis of probabilistic systems. PRISM supports three probabilistic models: discrete-time Markov chains, Markov decision processes and continuous-time Markov chains. Analysis is performed through model checking such systems against specifications written in the probabilistic temporal logics PCTL and CSL. The tool features three model checking engines: one symbolic, using BDDs (binary decision diagrams) and MTBDDs (multi-terminal BDDs); one based on sparse matrices; and one which combines both symbolic and sparse matrix methods. PRISM has been successfully used to analyse probabilistic termination, performance, and quality of service properties for a range of systems, including randomized distributed algorithms, manufacturing systems and workstation clusters.

1 Introduction

Probability is widely used in the design and analysis of software and hardware systems: as a means to derive efficient algorithms (e.g. the use of electronic coin flipping in decision making); as a model for unreliable or unpredictable behaviour (e.g. fault-tolerant systems, computer networks); and as a tool to analyse system performance (e.g. the use of steady-state probabilities in the calculation of throughput and mean waiting time). *Probabilistic model checking* refers to a range of techniques for calculating the likelihood of the occurrence of certain events during the execution of the system, and can be useful to establish properties such as "shutdown occurs with probability at most 0.01" and "the video frame will be delivered within 5ms with probability at least 0.97".

In this paper we introduce PRISM, a probabilistic model checking tool being developed at the University of Birmingham. Conventional model checkers input a description of a model, represented as a state transition system, and a specification, typically a formula in some temporal logic, and return "yes" or "no", indicating whether or not the model satisfies the specification. In the case of probabilistic model checking, the models are probabilistic, in the sense that they encode the *probability* of making a transition between states instead of simply the existence of such a transition, and analysis normally entails calculation of the actual likelihoods through appropriate numerical or analytical methods.

* Supported in part by EPSRC grant GR/M04617 and MathFIT studentship for David Parker.

T. Field et al. (Eds.): TOOLS 2002, LNCS 2324, pp. 200–204, 2002.

2 Probabilistic Model Checking

A number of probabilistic models exist. The simplest are *discrete-time Markov chains* (DTMCs), which specify the probability $\mathbf{P}(s, s')$ of making a transition from state s to some target state s'. *Markov decision processes* (MDPs) extend DTMCs by allowing both probabilistic and non-deterministic behaviour. Non-determinism enables the modelling of asynchronous parallel composition, and permits the under-specification of certain aspects of a system. *Continuous-time Markov chains* (CTMCs), on the other hand, specify the rate $\mathbf{R}(s, s')$ of making a transition from state s to s', with the interpretation that the probability of moving from s to s' within t ($\in \mathbb{R}^{>0}$) time units is $1 - e^{-\mathbf{R}(s,s')t}$.

To analyse these models, we use probabilistic extensions of the temporal logic CTL: PCTL [12] for specifying properties of DTMCs and MDPs; and CSL [4] for CTMCs. PCTL allows us to express properties of the form "under any fair scheduling, the probability that event A occurs is at least p (at most p)". By way of illustration, consider an asynchronous randomized leader election protocol. In PCTL we can specify the properties:

- $\mathcal{P}_{\geq 1}[\ \Diamond\ \mathit{leader}\ ]$ - "a leader is eventually elected with probability 1"
- $\mathcal{P}_{\leq 0.5}[\ \Diamond^{\leq k}\ \mathit{leader}\ ]$ - "the probability of electing a leader within k discrete time steps is at most 0.5"

In CSL, we can describe steady-state and transient behaviour of CTMCs:

- $\mathcal{P}_{\leq 0.01}[\ \Diamond^{\leq t}\ \mathit{full}\ ]$ - "the probability that the queue becomes full within t time units is less than or equal to 0.01"
- $\mathcal{S}_{\geq 0.98}[\ \neg \mathit{full}\ ]$ - "in the long run, the chance that the queue is not full is greater than or equal to 0.98".

Algorithms for model checking PCTL and CSL formulas can be found in [12,6, 5,3] and [4,15] respectively. These reduce to a combination of reachability-based computation and numerical calculation, the latter of which can be performed using iterative methods.

3 The Tool

PRISM takes as input a description of a system written in a probabilistic variant of Reactive Modules [1], and a set of PCTL or CSL specifications. It constructs the model – either a DTMC, an MDP or a CTMC – from the system description, computes the set of reachable states, and then performs model checking to determine which states of the system satisfy each specification. Fig. 1 shows the structure of the tool and Fig. 2 shows a screen-shot of the tool running.

PRISM is a *symbolic* model checker: the underlying data structures are BDDs (binary decision diagrams) and MTBDDs (multi-terminal BDDs) [10]. Model construction is always performed using MTBDDs and BDDs. As mentioned above, probabilistic model checking reduces to reachability-based computation and numerical calculation. The former is performed using BDDs, which has been

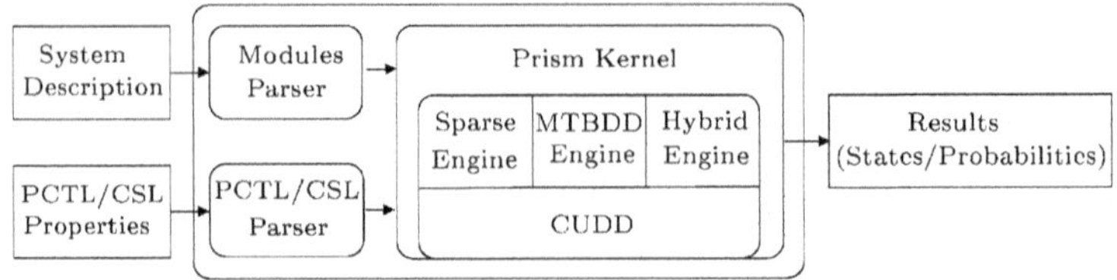

Fig. 1. PRISM System Architecture

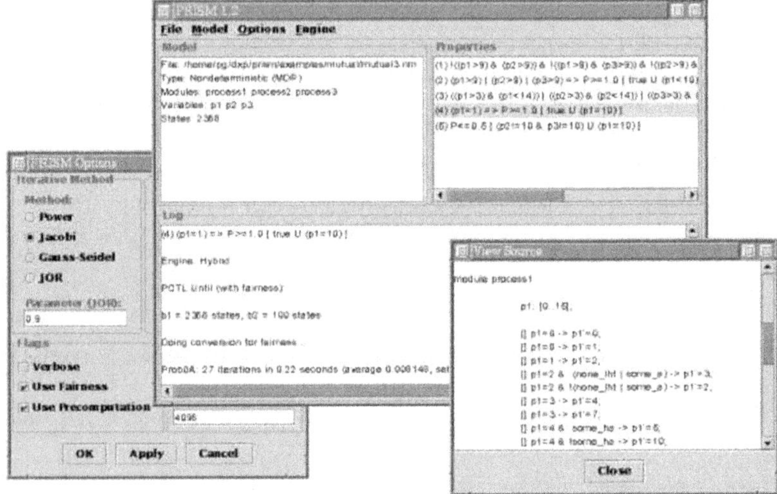

Fig. 2. The PRISM User Interface

shown to be extremely efficient for dealing with large, structured models [7,11]. For the latter, MTBDDs have also been successful in analysing large, structured models [17], but often, their performance is inefficient.

For this reason, PRISM supports three separate *engines* for numerical computation. The first uses MTBDDs to store the model and iteration vector. The second uses conventional data structures for numerical analysis: sparse matrices and full vectors. This engine nearly always provides faster numerical computation than its MTBDD counterpart, but sacrifices the ability to exploit structure. The third, *hybrid* engine provides a compromise. It stores models in a MTBDD-like structure which is adapted so that numerical computation can be carried out in combination with a full vector. This hybrid approach [16] is generally faster than MTBDDs, while handling larger systems than sparse matrices.

A number of other tools exist for analysing probabilistic models. We mention E⊢MC[2] [13], a CSL model checker for CTMCs. PRISM is the only fully-fledged model checking tool which allows the quantitative model checking of MDPs. There are also numerous tools available which support steady-state and transient analysis of CTMCs, without the use of model checking, e.g. MARCA [20].

4 Case Studies

We have used PRISM to build and analyse probabilistic models for a number of case studies. For MDP models, we have considered several randomised distributed algorithms, including randomised mutual exclusion protocols, a randomized Byzantine agreement protocol [8] and a randomised consensus protocol [2]. In the latter case, we were able to verify quantitative PCTL properties for MDPs with up to 10^9 states using the MTBDD engine [17]. We have also considered a number of CTMC models, including queueing systems, workstation clusters and manufacturing systems. For example, in [16], we use the hybrid engine to analyse a Kanban manufacturing system [9] with 40 million states. Fig. 3 below shows statistics for these two examples and a third from [14]. More information about these and many additional case studies can be found on the PRISM web site [18].

Model	States	Construction time (sec.)	Iterations	Time per iteration (sec.)		
				MTBDD	Sparse	Hybrid
Randomized	9.1×10^6	5.5	140,887	2.9	-	11.7
consensus	4.4×10^8	13.2	227,665	6.9	-	-
protocol	7.6×10^9	12.6	63,241	9.8	-	-
Kanban	58,400	0.3	300	41.7	0.04	0.05
manufacturing	2,546,432	3.9	663	-	2.76	3.15
system	41,644,800	10.7	1,148	-	-	58.9
Cyclic	15,360	0.3	406	13.09	0.01	0.01
polling	344,064	0.5	606	-	0.30	0.30
server	7,077,888	0.7	814	-	-	7.84

Fig. 3. Statistics for model checking with PRISM

5 Conclusions and Future Work

We have introduced PRISM, a tool to build and analyse probabilistic systems which supports DTMCs, MDPs and CTMCs and the logics PCTL and CSL. The tool and its source code are freely available from the PRISM web page [18]. It is written in Java and C++, using the CUDD package [19] for BDDs and MTBDDs. Development of PRISM is an ongoing activity. Future plans include extending the input language to allow process algebra terms, expanding the supported logics to include expected time and long run average specifications, and developing parallel and distributed engines.

References

1. R. Alur and T. Henzinger. Reactive modules. In *Proc. LICS'96*, 1996.
2. J. Aspnes and M. Herlihy. Fast Randomized Consensus using Shared Memory. *Journal of Algorithms*, 15(1), 1990.
3. C. Baier. On algorithmic verification methods for probabilistic systems. Universität Mannheim, 1998.
4. C. Baier, B. Haverkort, H. Hermanns, and J.-P. Katoen. Model checking continuous-time Markov chains by transient analysis. In *CAV 2000*, volume 1855 of *LNCS*, 2000.
5. C. Baier and M. Kwiatkowska. Model checking for a probabilistic branching time logic with fairness. *Distributed Computing*, 11(3), 1998.
6. A. Bianco and L. de Alfaro. Model checking of probabilistic and nondeterministic systems. In *Proc. FST & TCS*, 1995.
7. J. R. Burch, E. M. Clarke, K. L. McMillan, D. L. Dill, and J. Hwang. Symbolic model checking: 10^{20} states and beyond. In *Proc. LICS'90*, 1990.
8. C. Cachin, K. Kursawe, and V. Shoup. Random oracles in Constantinople: Practical asynchronous Byzantine agreement using cryptography (extended abstract). In *Proc. PODC'00*, 2000.
9. G. Ciardo and M. Tilgner. On the use of Kronecker operators for the solution of generalized stocastic Petri nets. ICASE Report 96-35, Institute for Computer Applications in Science and Engineering, 1996.
10. E. Clarke, M. Fujita, P. McGeer, J. Yang, and X. Zhao. Multi-terminal binary decision diagrams: An efficient data structure for matrix representation. In *Proc. IWLS'93*, 1993.
11. L. de Alfaro, M. Kwiatkowska, G. Norman, D. Parker, and R. Segala. Symbolic model checking of concurrent probabilistic processes using MTBDDs and the Kronecker representation. In *Proc. TACAS 2000*, volume 1785 of *LNCS*, 2000.
12. H. Hansson and B. Jonsson. A logic for reasoning about time and probability. *Formal Aspects of Computing*, 6, 1994.
13. H. Hermanns, J.-P. Katoen, J. Meyer-Kayser, and M. Siegle. A Markov Chain Model Checker. In *Proc. TACAS 2000*, volume 1785 of *LNCS*, 2000.
14. O. Ibe and K. Trivedi. Stochastic Petri net models of polling systems. *IEEE Journal on Selected Areas in Communications*, 8(9), 1990.
15. J.-P. Katoen, M. Kwiatkowska, G. Norman, and D. Parker. Faster and symbolic ctmc model checking. In *PAPM/PROBMIV'01*, volume 2165 of *LNCS*, 2001.
16. M. Kwiatkowska, G. Norman, and D. Parker. Probabilistic symbolic model checking with PRISM: A hybrid approach. In *Proc. TACAS 2002*, 2002. To appear.
17. M. Kwiatkowska, G. Norman, and R. Segala. Automated verification of a randomized distributed consensus protocol using Cadence SMV and PRISM. In *Proc. CAV'01*, volume 2102 of *LNCS*, 2001.
18. PRISM web page. `http://www.cs.bham.ac.uk/~dxp/prism/`.
19. F. Somenzi. CUDD: CU Decision Diagram package. Public software, Colorado University, Boulder, 1997.
20. W. Stewart. MARCA: Marcov chain analyzer. a software package for Markov modelling. In *Proc. NSMC'91*, 1991.

MAMSolver: A Matrix Analytic Methods Tool*

Alma Riska and Evgenia Smirni

Department of Computer Science
College of William and Mary
Williamsburg, VA 23187-8795, USA
{riska,esmirni}@cs.wm.edu

Abstract. MAMsolver is a software tool for the solution of M/G/1-type, GI/M/1-type, and QBD processes. The collection of solution algorithms implemented by MAMsolver are known as *matrix-analytic methods* and are used to compute stationary measures of interest such as the probability vector, the queue length distribution, the waiting time, the system queue length, and any higher moments of the queue length. The tool also provides probabilistic measures that describe the stability of the queueing system such as the caudal characteristic.

1 Introduction

Matrix analytic techniques, pioneered by Marcel Neuts [7,8], provide a framework that is widely used for the exact analysis of a general and frequently encountered class of queueing models. In these models, the embedded Markov chains are two-dimensional generalizations of elementary GI/M/1 and M/G/1 queues and their intersection, i.e., quasi-birth-death (QBD) processes. Such processes are often referred to as "processes with repetitive structure", because their state space $\mathcal{S}$ can be partitioned into subsets $\mathcal{S}^{(i)}$ for $i \geq 0$, whose states have identical interactions, except maybe the states in $\mathcal{S}^{(0)}$ known as the "boundary portion of the process" (see Section 2 for more details). Matrix analytic techniques have been successfully used for modeling and analysis of complex computer systems. Representative classes of Markov chains that can be solved using matrix analytic techniques are BMAP/PH/1 and MAP/PH/1 queues which can be used for modeling queueing systems that experience both correlation and high variability, salient characteristics of Internet traffic. MAMSolver is a collection of the most efficient solution methodologies for M/G/1-type, GI/M/1-type, and QBD processes. In contrast to existing tools such as MAGIC [12] and MGMTool [4], which provide solutions only for QBD processes, MAMSolver provides implementations for the classical and the most efficient algorithms that solve M/G/1-type, GI/M/1-type, and QBD processes. The solution provided by MAMSolver consists of the stationary probability vector for the processes under study, the computation of simple measures of interest, like queue length or response time of the queueing system, as well as probabilistic indicators for the processes such as the caudal characteristic [5].

* This work was partially supported by National Science Foundation under grants EIA-9974992, EIA-77030, CCR-0098278, and ACI-0090221.

T. Field et al. (Eds.): TOOLS 2002, LNCS 2324, pp. 205–211, 2002.

2 MAMSolver Framework

MAMSolver deals with the solution of processes with repetitive structure, namely M/G/1-type, GI/M/1-type, and QBD processes. MAMSolver provides solution for both continuous and discrete time Markov processes but for the sake of brevity we refer only to continuous time Markov processes throughout this exposition. The formal representation of processes under study is given by a block partitioned infinitesimal generator as follows:

$$\mathbf{Q}_{M/G/1} = \begin{bmatrix} \widehat{\mathbf{L}} & \widehat{\mathbf{F}}^{(1)} & \widehat{\mathbf{F}}^{(2)} & \widehat{\mathbf{F}}^{(3)} & \cdots \\ \widehat{\mathbf{B}} & \mathbf{L} & \mathbf{F}^{(1)} & \mathbf{F}^{(2)} & \cdots \\ \mathbf{0} & \mathbf{B} & \mathbf{L} & \mathbf{F}^{(1)} & \cdots \\ \mathbf{0} & \mathbf{0} & \mathbf{B} & \mathbf{L} & \cdots \\ \vdots & \vdots & \vdots & \vdots & \ddots \end{bmatrix}, \quad \mathbf{Q}_{GI/M/1} = \begin{bmatrix} \widehat{\mathbf{L}} & \widehat{\mathbf{F}} & \mathbf{0} & \mathbf{0} & \cdots \\ \widehat{\mathbf{B}}^{(1)} & \mathbf{L} & \mathbf{F} & \mathbf{0} & \cdots \\ \widehat{\mathbf{B}}^{(2)} & \mathbf{B}^{(1)} & \mathbf{L} & \mathbf{F} & \cdots \\ \widehat{\mathbf{B}}^{(3)} & \mathbf{B}^{(2)} & \mathbf{B}^{(1)} & \mathbf{L} & \cdots \\ \vdots & \vdots & \vdots & \vdots & \ddots \end{bmatrix}, \quad \mathbf{Q}_{QBD} = \begin{bmatrix} \widehat{\mathbf{L}} & \widehat{\mathbf{F}} & \mathbf{0} & \mathbf{0} & \cdots \\ \widehat{\mathbf{B}} & \mathbf{L} & \mathbf{F} & \mathbf{0} & \cdots \\ \mathbf{0} & \mathbf{B} & \mathbf{L} & \mathbf{F} & \cdots \\ \mathbf{0} & \mathbf{0} & \mathbf{B} & \mathbf{L} & \cdots \\ \vdots & \vdots & \vdots & \vdots & \ddots \end{bmatrix}.$$

We use the letters "L", "B", and "F" to describe submatrices corresponding to "local", "backward", and "forward" transitions respectively, in relation to states in $\mathcal{S}^{(i)}$ for $i \geq 1$, and we use "$\widehat{\ }$" to describe those matrices related to states in $\mathcal{S}^{(0)}$, i.e., the boundary portion of the process. This block partitioning of the infinitesimal generator defines a partition of the corresponding stationary probability vector in sub-vectors $\boldsymbol{\pi}^{(i)}$ for $i \geq 0$.

2.1 M/G/1-Type Processes

For the class of M/G/1-type continuous Markov chains, the infinitesimal generator is of the $\mathbf{Q}_{M/G/1}$ form. Key to all algorithms that solve M/G/1-type processes is the computation of the matrix $\mathbf{G}$, which is given by the solution of the following matrix equation:

$$\mathbf{B} + \mathbf{L}\mathbf{G} + \sum_{j=1}^{\infty} \mathbf{F}^{(j)}\mathbf{G}^{j+1} = \mathbf{0}. \tag{1}$$

Matrix $\mathbf{G}$ has an important probabilistic interpretation: an entry (k, l) in $\mathbf{G}$ expresses the conditional probability of the process first entering $\mathcal{S}^{(j-1)}$ through state l, given that it starts from state k of $\mathcal{S}^{(j)}$[8, page 81]. Recent advances show that the computation of $\mathbf{G}$ is more efficient when displacement structures are used based on the representation of M/G/1-type processes by means of QBD processes [1,5]. The most efficient algorithm for the computation of $\mathbf{G}$ is cyclic-reduction [1]. The calculation of the stationary probability vector is based on the stable recursive Ramaswami's formula [9], which defines the following recursive relation among stationary probability vectors $\boldsymbol{\pi}^{(i)}$ for $i \geq 0$:

$$\boldsymbol{\pi}^{(j)} = -\left(\boldsymbol{\pi}^{(0)}\widehat{\mathbf{S}}^{(j)} + \sum_{k=1}^{j-1} \boldsymbol{\pi}^{(k)}\mathbf{S}^{(j-k)}\right) \mathbf{S}^{(0)^{-1}} \quad \forall j \geq 1. \tag{2}$$

Matrices $\widehat{\mathbf{S}}^{(j)}$ and $\mathbf{S}^{(j)}$ are defined as follows:

$$\widehat{\mathbf{S}}^{(j)} = \sum_{l=j}^{\infty} \widehat{\mathbf{F}}^{(l)}\mathbf{G}^{l-j}, \; j \geq 1, \qquad \mathbf{S}^{(j)} = \sum_{l=j}^{\infty} \mathbf{F}^{(l)}\mathbf{G}^{l-j}, \; j \geq 0 \text{ (letting } \mathbf{F}^{(0)} \equiv \mathbf{L}),$$

Given the above definition of $\boldsymbol{\pi}^{(j)}$ and the normalization condition, a unique vector $\boldsymbol{\pi}^{(0)}$ can be obtained by solving the following system of linear equations:

$$\boldsymbol{\pi}^{(0)} \left[\left(\widehat{\mathbf{L}} - \widehat{\mathbf{S}}^{(1)} \mathbf{S}^{(0)^{-1}} \widehat{\mathbf{B}} \right)^{\diamond} \;\middle|\; \mathbf{1}^T - \left(\sum_{j=1}^{\infty} \widehat{\mathbf{S}}^{(j)} \right) \left(\sum_{j=0}^{\infty} \mathbf{S}^{(j)} \right)^{-1} \mathbf{1}^T \right] = [\mathbf{0} \mid 1].$$

where the symbol "$\diamond$" indicates that we discard one (any) column of the corresponding matrix, since we added a column representing the normalization condition[1]. Once $\boldsymbol{\pi}^{(0)}$ is known, one can then iteratively compute $\boldsymbol{\pi}^{(i)}$ for $i \geq 1$, stopping when the accumulated probability mass is close to one. After this point, measures of interest can be computed. [6] gives an improved version of Ramaswami's formula, where the stationary probability vector is computed using matrix-generating functions associated with triangular Toeplitz matrices. These matrix-generating functions are computed efficiently by using fast Fourier transforms (FFT).

2.2 GI/M/1-Type Processes

The continuous GI/M/1-type Markov processes, with infinitesimal generator of the $\mathbf{Q}_{GI/M/1}$ form, admit the very-elegant matrix-geometric solutions proposed by Neuts [7]. In matrix-geometric solutions the relation between the stationary probability vectors $\boldsymbol{\pi}^{(i)}$ is:

$$\boldsymbol{\pi}^{(i)} = \boldsymbol{\pi}^{(1)} \cdot \mathbf{R}^{i-1}, \qquad \forall i \geq 1 \tag{3}$$

where $\mathbf{R}$ is the solution of the matrix equation

$$\mathbf{F} + \mathbf{R} \cdot \mathbf{L} + \sum_{k=1}^{\infty} \mathbf{R}^{k+1} \cdot \mathbf{B}^{(k)} = \mathbf{0}. \tag{4}$$

Matrix $\mathbf{R}$ has an important probabilistic interpretation: $\mathbf{R}$ records the expected number of visits to each state in $\mathcal{S}^{(i)}$, starting from each state in $\mathcal{S}^{(i-1)}$, before reentering $\mathcal{S}^{(i-1)}$ [5]. $\mathbf{R}$ can be obtained using iterative methods. Eq.(4) together with the normalization condition are then used to obtain $\boldsymbol{\pi}^{(0)}$ and $\boldsymbol{\pi}^{(1)}$ by solving the following system of linear equations:

$$[\boldsymbol{\pi}^{(0)}, \boldsymbol{\pi}^{(1)}] \cdot \left[\begin{array}{c|c|c} \widehat{\mathbf{L}}^{\diamond} & \widehat{\mathbf{F}}^{(1)} & \mathbf{1}^T \\ (\sum_{k=1}^{\infty} \mathbf{R}^{k-1} \cdot \widehat{\mathbf{B}}^{(k)})^{\diamond} & \mathbf{L} + \sum_{k=1}^{\infty} \mathbf{R}^{k} \cdot \mathbf{B}^{(k)} & (\mathbf{I} - \mathbf{R})^{-1} \cdot \mathbf{1}^T \end{array} \right] = [\mathbf{0} \mid 1].$$

For $i > 1$, $\boldsymbol{\pi}^{(i)}$ can be obtained numerically from Eq.(3). More importantly, many useful performance metrics, such as the expected number of jobs in the service node, can be computed exactly in explicit form using $\boldsymbol{\pi}^{(0)}$, $\boldsymbol{\pi}^{(1)}$, and $\mathbf{R}$ alone based on the formula $\boldsymbol{\pi}^{(1)}(\mathbf{I} - \mathbf{R})^{-2}$.

[1] $\mathbf{1}^T$ denotes a column vector of ones with the appropriate dimension, while $[\mathbf{0} \mid 1]$ denotes a row vector of zeros except its last element which is one.

2.3 QBD Processes

The intersection of GI/M/1 and M/G/1 type processes results on quasi birth-death processes, whose infinitesimal generator is of the $\mathbf{Q}_{QBD}$ form. QBD processes are most commonly associated with GI/M/1-type processes because they can be solved using the very elegant matrix-geometric approach [7]. In the case of QBD processes, Eq.(4) reduces to the matrix quadratic equation

$$\mathbf{F} + \mathbf{R} \cdot \mathbf{L} + \mathbf{R}^2 \cdot \mathbf{B} = \mathbf{0}. \tag{5}$$

Since QBD is a special case of an M/G/1 process, matrix $\mathbf{G}$ of Eq.(1) is defined and widely used on generating efficient solutions for QBDs, The most efficient solution of Eq.(5) is provided by the logarithmic reduction algorithm [5], which first computes $\mathbf{G}$, and then derives $\mathbf{R}$ based on the relation $\mathbf{R} = -\mathbf{F}(\mathbf{L}+\mathbf{F}\dot{\mathbf{G}})^{-1}$. Vectors $\boldsymbol{\pi}^{(0)}$ and $\boldsymbol{\pi}^{(1)}$ are obtained by solving the following system of linear equations:

$$[\boldsymbol{\pi}^{(0)}, \ \boldsymbol{\pi}^{(1)}] \cdot \left[\begin{array}{c|c|c} \widehat{\mathbf{L}}^{\diamond} & \widehat{\mathbf{F}} & \mathbf{1}^T \\ \widehat{\mathbf{B}}^{\diamond} & \mathbf{L} + \mathbf{R} \cdot \mathbf{B} & (\mathbf{I} - \mathbf{R})^{-1} \cdot \mathbf{1}^T \end{array} \right] = [\mathbf{0} \mid 1].$$

Similarly to GI/M/1-type processes, several measures of interest have closed form formulas depending only on $\boldsymbol{\pi}^{(0)}$, $\boldsymbol{\pi}^{(1)}$, and $\mathbf{R}$.

2.4 ETAQA Methodology

[11,2,3] propose a methodology to compute only *aggregate* probabilities instead of the whole stationary probability vector for M/G/1 and QBD processes. This aggregate methodology, known as ETAQA is exact, numerically stable and most importantly very efficient with respect to both its time and space complexity. For an ergodic CTMC, it requires only the knowledge of matrix $\mathbf{G}$. The aggregate solution of an M/G/1 process is obtained as the solution of the following system of linear equations:

$$[\boldsymbol{\pi}^{(0)}, \ \boldsymbol{\pi}^{(1)}, \ \boldsymbol{\pi}^{(*)}] \cdot \left[\begin{array}{c|c|c|c} \mathbf{1}^T & \widehat{\mathbf{L}} & \widehat{\mathbf{F}}^{(1)} - \sum_{i=3}^{\infty} \widehat{\mathbf{S}}^{(i)} \cdot \mathbf{G} & (\sum_{i=2}^{\infty} \widehat{\mathbf{F}}^{(i)} + \sum_{i=3}^{\infty} \widehat{\mathbf{S}}^{(i)} \cdot \mathbf{G})^{\diamond} \\ \mathbf{1}^T & \widehat{\mathbf{B}} & \mathbf{L} - \sum_{i=2}^{\infty} \mathbf{S}^{(i)} \cdot \mathbf{G} & (\sum_{i=1}^{\infty} \mathbf{F}^{(i)} + \sum_{i=2}^{\infty} \mathbf{S}^{(i)} \cdot \mathbf{G})^{\diamond} \\ \mathbf{1}^T & \mathbf{0} & \mathbf{B} - \sum_{i=1}^{\infty} \mathbf{S}^{(i)} \cdot \mathbf{G} & (\sum_{i=1}^{\infty} \mathbf{F}^{(i)} + \mathbf{L} + \sum_{i=1}^{\infty} \mathbf{S}^{(i)} \cdot \mathbf{G})^{\diamond} \end{array} \right] = [1, \mathbf{0}],$$

where $\boldsymbol{\pi}^{(*)}$ is the aggregate probability vector defined as $\boldsymbol{\pi}^{(*)} = \sum_{i=2}^{\infty} \boldsymbol{\pi}^{(i)}$.

Since QBDs are a special case of M/G/1-type processes, they can be solved using this aggregate approach with the following system of linear equations:

$$[\boldsymbol{\pi}^{(0)}, \ \boldsymbol{\pi}^{(1)}, \ \boldsymbol{\pi}^{(*)}] \cdot \left[\begin{array}{c|c|c|c} \mathbf{1}^T & \widehat{\mathbf{L}} & \widehat{\mathbf{F}} & \mathbf{0}^{\diamond} \\ \mathbf{1}^T & \widehat{\mathbf{B}} & \mathbf{L} & \mathbf{F}^{\diamond} \\ \mathbf{1}^T & \mathbf{0} & \mathbf{B} - \mathbf{F} \cdot \mathbf{G} & (\mathbf{L} + \mathbf{F} + \mathbf{F} \cdot \mathbf{G})^{\diamond} \end{array} \right] = [1, \mathbf{0}],$$

[11,2,3] provide algorithms for the computation of measures of interest based on the computed aggregate probability $[\boldsymbol{\pi}^{(0)}, \ \boldsymbol{\pi}^{(1)}, \ \boldsymbol{\pi}^{(*)}]$.

3 MAMSolver

MAMSolver is a tool that provides implementation of the algorithms highlighted in Section 2. The tool provides solutions for both DTMCs and CTMCs. The matrix-analytic algorithms that we take into consideration are defined in terms of matrices, making matrix manipulations and operations the basic elements of the tool. The input to MAMSolver, in the form of a structured text file, is the finite set of matrices that accurately describe the process to be solved. Since there are different algorithms that provide solution for the same process, the user specifies the method to be used. However several tests are performed within the tool to insure that special cases are treated separately and therefore more efficiently. MAMSolver is implemented in C++, and classes define the basic components of the type of processes under consideration.

Matrix is the module that implements all the basic matrix operations such as matrix assignments, additions, subtractions, multiplications, and inversions. To address possible numerical problems that may arise during matrix operations, we use well known and heavily tested routines provided by the Lapack and BLAS packages[2]. Since solution of system of linear equations is very common for matrix-analytic algorithms, MAMSolver provides several methods depending on the size of the problem, i.e., the size of the coefficient matrices. For small-size problems exact methods such as LU-decomposition are used, otherwise the Lapack implementation of numerical methods like GMRES and BiCGSTAB, are chosen.

Matrix-analytic modules handle both CTMC and DTMC processes. First these modules serve as storage for the input matrices. In addition, these modules provide all the routines necessary for the implementation of the algorithms outlined in Section 2. Both data structures and routines of the matrix-analytic modules are based on the data-structures and routines provided by the matrix module.

The solution of **QBD** processes, requires computation of $\mathbf{R}$ (and sometimes of $\mathbf{G}$ depending on the solution algorithm). Matrix $\mathbf{R}$ is computed using the logarithmic reduction algorithm [5], however for completeness we provide also the classical numerical algorithm. There are cases when $\mathbf{G}$ (and $\mathbf{R}$) can be computed explicitly [10]. We check if the conditions for the explicit computation hold in order to simplify and speedup the solution. The available solution methods for QBD processes are matrix-geometric and ETAQA.

GI/M/1 processes require the computation of matrix $\mathbf{R}$. The classic matrix geometric solution is implemented to solve this type of processes. The algorithm goes first through a classic iterative procedure to compute $\mathbf{R}$ (to our knowledge, there is no alternative more efficient one). Then, it computes the boundary part of the stationary probability vector. Since there exists a geometric relations between vectors $\boldsymbol{\pi}^{(i)}$ for $i \geq 1$, there is no need to compute the whole stationary probability vector.

---

[2] Available from http://www.netlib.org.

M/G/1 processes require the computation of matrix **G**. More effort has been placed on efficient solution of M/G/1 processes. MAMSolver provides the classic iterative algorithm, the cyclic-reduction algorithm, and the explicit one for special cases. The stationary probability vector is computed recursively using either Ramaswami's formula or its fast FFT version. ETAQA is the other alternative for the solution of M/G/1 processes.

MAMsolver computes and stores the stationary probability vector, allowing the user to compute any measures of interest. MAMSolver computes a customized first moment of the form:

$$r = \boldsymbol{\pi}^{(0)} \cdot \boldsymbol{\rho}^{(0)} + \boldsymbol{\pi}^{(1)} \cdot \boldsymbol{\rho}^{(1)} + \sum_{i=2}^{infty} \boldsymbol{\pi}^{(i)}(\mathbf{a}^{[0]} + \mathbf{a}^{[1]} \cdot i).$$

All the coefficient vectors $\boldsymbol{\rho}^{(0)}$, $\boldsymbol{\rho}^{(1)}$, $\mathbf{a}^{[0]}$, $\mathbf{a}^{[1]}$ are to be read from a text file with default values: $\boldsymbol{\rho}^{(0)} = \mathbf{0}$, $\boldsymbol{\rho}^{(1)} = \mathbf{1}$, $\mathbf{a}^{[0]} = \mathbf{0}$, $\mathbf{a}^{[1]} = \mathbf{1}$. Computation of higher moments can be achieved by introducing additional coefficient vectors $\mathbf{a}^{[j]}$, in the above formula.

For lack of space we do not present here any MAMSolver input or output examples. Although at the moment there is no graphical interface for the tool, the input can be constructed easily in text format. The output files are stored in text format as well. For a set of input and output examples and the source code of MAMSolver, we point the interested reader to the tool's website `http://www.cs.wm.edu/MAMSolver/`.

Acknowledgments. We thank Beatrice Meini for providing us with her Fortran implementation of the cyclic reduction algorithm for computation of matrix **G** and the fast FFT Ramaswami's formula. We also thank Daniela Puiu for her contribution in earlier versions of the tool.

References

1. D.A. Bini and B. Meini. Using displacement structure for solving non-skip-free M/G/1 type Markov chains. In A. Alfa and S. Chakravarthy Eds. *Advances in Matrix Analytic Methods for Stochastic Models*, pages 17-37, Notable Publications Inc, NJ, 1998.
2. G. Ciardo, A. Riska, and E. Smirni. An aggregation-based solution method for M/G/1-type processes. In B. Plateau, W. J. Stewart, and M. Silva, editors, *Numerical Solution of Markov Chains*, pages 21–40. Prensas Universitarias de Zaragoza, Zaragoza, Spain, Sept. 1999.
3. G. Ciardo and E. Smirni. ETAQA: an efficient technique for the analysis of QBD-processes by aggregation. *Performance Evaluation*, Vol.(36-37), pages 71–93, 1999.
4. B.R. Haverkort, A.P.A. Van Moorsel and A. Dijkstra. MGMtool: A Performance Analysis Tool Based on Matrix Geometric Methods. In R. Pooley, and J. Hillston, editors *Modelling Techniques and Tools*, pages 312–316, Edinburgh University Press, 1993.

5. G. Latouche and V. Ramaswami. *Introduction to Matrix Geometric Methods in Stochastic Modeling.* ASA-SIAM Series on Statistics and Applied Probability, SIAM Press, Philadelphia, PA, 1999.
6. B. Meini. An improved FFT-based version of Ramaswami's formula. *Comm. Statist. Stochastic Models*, Vol. 13 pages 223-238, 1997.
7. M. F. Neuts. *Matrix-geometric solutions in stochastic models.* Johns Hopkins University Press, Baltimore, MD, 1981.
8. M. F. Neuts. *Structured stochastic matrices of M/G/1 type and their applications.* Marcel Dekker, New York, NY, 1989.
9. V. Ramaswami. A stable recursion for the steady state vector in Markov chains of M/G/1 type. *Commun. Statist.- Stochastic Models*, Vol. 4 pages 183-263, 1988.
10. V. Ramaswami and G. Latouche. A general class of Markov processes with explicit matrix-geometric solutions. *OR Spektrum*, 8:209–218, Aug. 1986.
11. A. Riska, and E. Smirni. An exact aggregation approach for M/G/1-type Markov chains. to appear at ACM SIGMETRICS'02 Conference, Marina Del Rey, CA, June 2002.
12. Mark.S.Squillante. MAGIC: A computer performance modeling tool based on matrix-geometric techniques. In Proc. *Fifth International Conference on Modelling Techniques and Tools for Computer Performance Evaluation*, 1991.

The MOMBASA Software Environment – A Toolkit for Performance Evaluation of Multicast-Based Mobility Support*

Andreas Festag, Lars Westerhoff, and Adam Wolisz

Technical University of Berlin, Telecommunication Networks Group (TKN)
Sekr. FT5-2, Einsteinufer 25, 10587 Berlin, Germany
{festag|westerhoff|wolisz}@ee.tu-berlin.de

Abstract. The *MOMBASA Software Environment* is a toolkit that implements mobility-related functionalities complementing multicast protocols for multicast-based mobility support. The functionalities provided by the *MOMBASA Software Environment* include detection of link availability, registration, location update, paging, address translation, handoff initiation, handoff control, rerouting, prevention of handoff oscillation and inactive handoff suppression.
The *MOMBASA Software Environment* is targeted for researchers investigating the support of host mobility in IP-based cellular networks. It aims at performance evaluation of mobility support by means of measurements. The software is easy to maintain, to configure and to extend: a) It has a clear design, b) it provides well-defined configuration and management interfaces, c) policies can be used to control and tune the system behavior and d) it has a generic interface to the multicast which facilitates to investigate multicast protocols of different types.
This paper describes the functionalities, features and structure of the *MOMBASA Software Environment* and presents a framework for evaluating the performance of mobility support using the *MOMBASA Software Environment*. The *MOMBASA Software Environment* is open software under GNU Public License. It is freely available, extensively tested and well documented.

1 Introduction

Performance is one of the key criteria in communication software. Measurement represents an accepted evaluation technique which gives accurate results for certain scenarios. However, measurement-based performance evaluation requires an implementation, at least a prototype. The *MOMBASA Software Environment* provides a prototype implementation for multicast-based mobility support in all-IP cellular networks. As will be explained later, the *MOMBASA Software Environment* is well designed for performance evaluation by means of measurements.

* This work was partly supported by a grant of SIEMENS.

T. Field et al. (Eds.): TOOLS 2002, LNCS 2324, pp. 212–219, 2002.

The growing importance of mobile communication deserves support for host mobility in IP-based cellular networks. A general problem of IP networks needs to be solved, which arises from the double meaning of the IP address as a host identifier and as identification of the host's current point of attachment. There exist several solutions for the general mobility problem, the most important approaches are *Address translation and indirect routing* (e.g. Mobile IP [7, 5], RAT [9]) and *Host-based routing* (e.g. Cellular IP [1], HAWAII [8]).

MOMBASA (**MObility support – a Multicast-BASed Approach**) pursues a different approach. The general mobility problem (separation of identity and location) is solved by multicast. The main idea of *MOMBASA* is to utilize location-independent addressing and routing to support host mobility which is already provided by multicast. In *MOMBASA*, each mobile is assigned a multicast group address (which is independent of the current network point of attachment). The mobile host subscribes to the multicast group using its current access point to the network. Handoff between access points is performed by multicast operations, namely subscribe/un-subscribe to/from a multicast group. Data packets are distributed via a dynamic multicast tree with branches reaching the current locations of the mobile host while the mobile host roams through the coverage of the cells. The branches of the multicast tree grow and shrink and, hence, follow the mobile's location. In comparison to other mobility approaches, e.g. IETF Mobile IP, MOMBASA has some advantages: *First*, re-routing for handoff is done in the network node where the path to the old and from the new access point diverge (and not in a software agent in the mobile's home network as in the Mobile IP approach which might be distant to the current mobile's location.). *Second*, a *handoff-specific* signaling and infrastructure is in principle not necessary. Instead a multicast infrastructure and protocols – which are expected to exist in future networks – are reused for mobility purposes And *third*, multicast offers inherently mechanisms to minimize the service interruption caused by a handoff between access points.

The *MOMBASA Software Environment* is a toolkit that implements mobility-related functionalities complementing multicast protocols. These functionalities include detection of link availability, registration, location update, paging, address translation, handoff initiation, handoff control, rerouting, prevention of handoff oscillation and suppression of handoff for inactive mobile hosts.

This paper presents the *MOMBASA Software Environment*[1] as a toolkit for measurement-based performance evaluation of mobility mechanisms with different types of multicast. The next section details the implemented functionalities and features. Then the implementation design, configuration and extensibility are described. In the last section, metrics for a performance evaluation are listed.

[1] In the following abbreviated as *MOMBASA SE*

2 Functionalities and Features of MOMBASA SE

The *MOMBASA SE* implements the following functionalities:

- **Detection of link availability:** Access points advertise their availability on the links they provide service for. Mobile hosts may solicit advertisements from access points.
- **Registration:** A mobile registers with the access point which relays the registration to a gateway. A mobile can be registered indirectly by another access point.
- **Location update:** A mobile host updates its current location with the network.
- **Address translation:** The gateway and the access point perform address translation from unicast to multicast addresses and vice versa. The address translation works either by NAT[2] or tunneling.
- **Handoff initiation:** A handoff can be triggered by the expiration of an advertisement lifetime or a link layer trigger. Alternatively, a handoff can be forced by the network.
- **Handoff control:** Handoff is controlled by the mobile host based on a *handoff request/reply*-scheme. Handoff can be hard, soft or predictive.
- **Rerouting:** Rerouting is based on multicast operations. It can be executed in a *break-make* and *make-break* order.[3] Additionally, access points can be added to the multicast tree in advance.
- **Prevention of handoff oscillation:** This prevents a mobile host from being constantly handed over when it is simultaneously reachable by multiple access points.
- **Suppression of handoff for inactive mobile hosts:** Mobile hosts which do not send or receive for a certain duration go into an inactive state and re-register less often. For inactive mobile hosts, the handoff initiation is suppressed.
- **Paging:** Inactive mobile hosts provide the network with uncertain location information. The gateway uses paging to locate these mobile hosts.

Moreover, the *MOMBASA SE* can be characterized by the following features:

- Network components and protocols are based on IP version 4.
- Multicast is used in the wire-line part of the access network. The access point acts as a multicast proxy for the mobile host.
- Minimal modifications to the multicast protocols.
- No modifications to correspondent (fixed) hosts.
- Mobility is supported in the access network.
- Support of heterogeneous access networks, support of handoff between access points providing different wireless technologies (vertical or inter-technology handoff).
- Differentiation between inactive and active mobile hosts.

[2] Network address translation

[3] This refers to the sequence of multicast un-subscribe and subscribe operation.

- Buffering and forwarding of packets for predictive handoff and paging.
- Certain functionalities can be controlled and tuned by policies (handoff type, algorithms for access point selection, paging, buffering and forwarding).
- The system uses soft state, i.e. every state needs to be refreshed or times out.

3 Implementation Design

The main software components of *MOMBASA SE* are: **Mobile Agent (MA)**, **Mobility Enabling Proxy (MEP)** and **Gateway Proxy (GW-P)** which are executed in the mobile host, access point and gateway proxy, respectively. These components complement the multicast routing daemons in the multicast routers. The components are implemented as daemons running in user space. *MOMBASA SE* employs certain design concepts: *First*, it is object-oriented which reduces the complexity of the software. *Second*, all components are based on the same main implementation design. Each implementation has the same basic structure of classes. *Third*, all agents employ an event-driven concept with external and internal events (protocol messages and timer events, respectively).

The *MOMBASA SE* is implemented for Linux systems running on an x86 architecture. Modifications of the Linux standard kernel were necessary for address translation between unicast and multicast addresses and for paging. The software is developed in C++ and uses only standard C and C++ libraries (including the Standard Template Library).

The default configuration of *MOMBASA SE* works with the multicast provided by the standard Linux kernel (IGMPv2 and kernel support for a PIM-SM Version 2 daemon) and a publically available multicast routing daemon for PIM-SM[4] (see [6]). However, the implementation of the MOMBASA SE does not depend on a specific multicast routing daemon (see also the discussion in the next section).

The implementation of *MOMBASA SE* utilizes certain technologies, among others *link-layer (packet) sockets* to intercept packets for buffering, *Linux socket filters* for idle detection, *network address translation* between unicast and multicast addresses and vice versa, and *multi-threading* for buffering.

4 Extensibility

The *MOMBASA Software Environment* is targeted for researchers investigating multicast-based mobility support. While the basic network architecture is assumed to be fixed, the software was designed to become extended in a flexible and easy manner. This includes features for utilization of other multicast types, implementation of enhanced features for mobility support, portability, configuration and testing:

[4] pimd-2.1.0-alpha28

- **Support of multiple multicast types:** The actual version of the *MOMBASA SE* works with IP multicast as it is defined by the standard IP multicast service model in RFC 1112 [2]. The interface to the multicast is provided by IGMPv2 and hence, *MOMBASA SE* supports all multicast routing protocols according RFC 1112[5]. But *MOMBASA SE* is not limited to these multicast types: Multicast has been the subject of research efforts for the next generation Internet and new schemes have been proposed. Some of them break the standard IP multicast service model. An example is single source multicast, such as PIM-SSM [4]. *MOMBASA SE* is prepared for *Single-source multicast*, its usage requires *IGMPv3* and only minor modifications of the implementation. Moreover, in the next development stage, the *MOMBASA SE* implementation will be extended to support *generic multicast*, where the multicast is regarded as an abstract service for multicast group creation and release, multicast group subscribe and un-subscribe operations and packet delivery. This facilitates the examination of multicast types, which offers interesting features for mobility support (such as third party signaling, sub-casting, etc.) without being limited to IGMPv2/v3 as a multicast group management protocol.
- **Implementation of enhanced features for mobility support:** *MOMBASA SE* has a clear design, detailed documentation about specification and implementation design [2, 4] exists, and it has been extensively tested [5]. Therefore enhanced features can be easily implemented. Moreover, certain system behavior can be controlled and fine-tuned by policies. The software provides hooks for policy handlers to control time and destination of handoff, control buffering and flushing of packets and to retrieve signal quality for handoff trigger. Hence, *MOMBASA SE* ensures that enhanced algorithms can be easily implemented without redesigning major parts. Typical examples for extensions are buffering and flushing strategies and paging algorithms.
- **Portability:** In *MOMBASA SE* only standard libraries are used. This facilitates porting *MOMBASA SE* to other architectures. For example, the mobile agent of the *MOMBASA SE* has been ported to a hand-held PC architecture running with a Linux operating system. This was tested with a *iPAQ* by COMPAQ.
- **Configuration and Testing:** The software is instrumented with capabilities for easy configuration. Management interfaces offer debugging facilities at configurable levels. Moreover, the implementation has been instrumented with testing facilities (such as accessing the actual state, access to databases, etc.)

[5] However, there are multicast routing protocols which are less suitable for mobility support (such as broadcast- and prune protocols, like DVMRP [10]) and some which better meet the requirements of host mobility (such as PIM-SM [3] which is based on a concept of rendezvous points and shared trees).

5 Framework for Performance Evaluation

MOMBASA SE can be used to estimate the performance of multicast-based mobility support. This includes a quantitative evaluation of mobility-related performance metrics and a comparison of selected policies. Moreover, the impact of mobility on transport and application layer can be estimated. Suppose a typical testbed setup as shown in Fig. 1, which basically consists of an access network and an emulated WAN representing the Internet. The gateway executing the *gateway proxy GW-P* and a multicast routing daemon, interconnects the access network with the Internet. Additional components of the access network are multicast routers and access points executing *Mobility Enabling Proxies (MEPs)* and providing service in a wireless cells. A mobile can move freely within the coverage of the cells. This setup represents a typical topology and can be used in various scenarios for different mobility patterns, wireless technologies, workloads, buffer sizes and multicast approaches.

Two types of metrics can be identified: *mobility-related metrics* are general to all multicast approaches. *Multicast-related metrics* refer to a certain multicast approach. Typical mobility-related metrics for performance evaluation are:

- Handoff and rerouting latency,
- Throughput and packet loss caused by handoff,
- Sequence of packet delivery,
- Signaling overhead for handoff,
- TCP-specific parameters (window size, sequence numbers, retransmissions).

The metrics can be used for comparison with other mobility approaches, such as Mobile IP and its variations since the metrics do not include multicast-specific features. Clearly, the particular multicast type has an impact on the mobility-related metrics. Hence, the multicast-related metrics give quantitative measures for the suitability of a multicast type for mobility support. Typical metrics are:

- Costs of the multicast distribution tree (e.g. distance between source and each receiver, and probably including other metrics, such as delay),
- Signaling overhead and latencies for multicast operations, such as subscribing and un-subscribing to/from multicast channels,
- Number of states in multicast routers per multicast group.

These multicast-related metrics can be used to compare different multicast approaches with respect to their support of host mobility. However, they are dependent on the particular multicast type.

6 Conclusions

The *MOMBASA Software Environment* is a collection of mobility-related functionalities. Together with multicast protocols these functionalities are assembled to a software environment for multicast-based mobility support in all-IP cellular networks. The *MOMBASA Software Environment* offers already a rich set of functionalities. Nevertheless it is designed to be extended. Since IP and IP-style

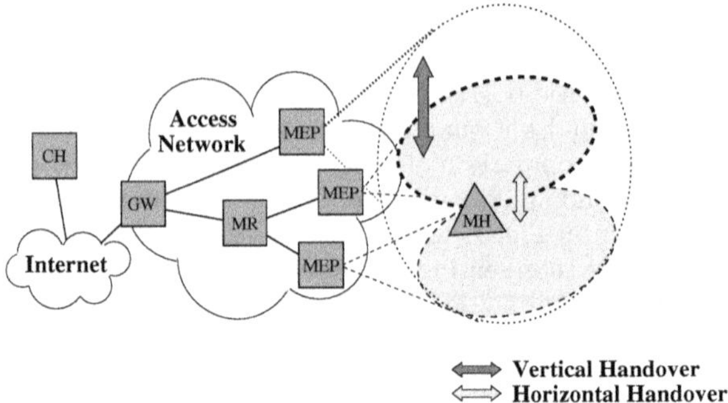

Fig. 1. Setup for performance evaluation

multicast are the subject of growing research efforts, this software environment facilitates the investigation of multicast-based mobility support using available and future multicast approaches and enhanced mobility mechanisms. Therefore the toolkit offers at least a valuable base for experimentation and measurements.

General References

[1] A. Campell, J. Gomez, S. Kim, A. Valko, C.-Y. Wan, and Z. Turanyi. Design, Implementation, and Evaluation of Cellular IP. *IEEE Personal Communication*, pages 42–49, August 2000.

[2] S. Deering. Host Extensions for IP Multicasting. RFC 1112, August 1989.

[3] D. Estrin, D. Farinacci, A. Helmy, D. Thaler, S. Deering, M. Handley, V. Jacobson, C. Liu, P. Sharma, and L. Wei. Protocol Independent Multicast-Sparse Mode (PIM-SM): Protocol Specification. RFC 2362, June 1998.

[4] B. Fenner, M. Handley, H. Holbrook, and I. Kouvelas. Protocol Independent Multicast - Sparse Mode (PIM-SM): Protocol Specification (Revised). Internet Draft, work in progress, March 2001.

[5] D. Johnson and C. Perkins. Mobility Support in IPv6. Internet Draft, work in progress, November 2000.

[6] University of Southern California. USC pimd. `http://catarina.usc.edu/pim/`, 2000. PIM-SM Version 2 Multicast routing daemon.

[7] C. Perkins. IPv4 Mobility Support. Request for Comments 2002, October 1996.

[8] R. Ramjee, T. LaPorta, S. Thuel, K. Varadhan, and S. Wang. HAWAII: A Domain-based Approach for Supporting Mobility in Wide-area Wireless Networks. In *Proceedings of ICNP'99*, Toronto,Canada, October/November 1999.

[9] R. Singh and Y. Tay. IP Relocation Through Twice-NAT (RAT) Motivation, Protocol and Extensions. Technical Report Work in progress rev 1.44, National University of Singapore, 1999.

[10] D. Waitzmann, C. Patridge, and S. Deering. Distance Vector Multicast Routing Protocol (DVMRP). RFC 1075, November 1988.

More Documents about MOMBASA SE (see also http://www-tkn.ee.tu-berlin.de/research/mombasa/)

[1] A. Festag and L. Westerhoff. Design, Implementation and Performance of Multicast-Based Paging for IP Mobility (Extended Version). Technical Report TKN-01-015, TKN, TU Berlin, Berlin, Germany, October 2001.

[2] A. Festag and L. Westerhoff. Protocol Specification of the MOMBASA Software Environment. Technical Report TKN-01-014, TKN, TU Berlin, Berlin, Germany, May 2001.

[3] A. Festag and A. Wolisz. MOMBASA: Mobility Support - A Multicast-based Approach. In *Proceedings of European Wireless 2000 together with ECRR'2000*, Dresden, Germany, September 2000.

[4] L. Westerhoff and A. Festag. Implementation Design of the MOMBASA Software Environment. Technical Report TKN-01-017, TKN, TU Berlin, Berlin, Germany, November 2001.

[5] L. Westerhoff and A. Festag. Testing the Implementation of the MOMBASA Software Environment. Technical Report TKN-01-018, TKN, TU Berlin, Berlin, Germany, October 2001.

GILK: A Dynamic Instrumentation Tool for the Linux Kernel

David J. Pearce, Paul H.J. Kelly, Tony Field, and Uli Harder

Imperial College of Science, Technology and Medicine
180 Queen's Gate, London, Exhibition Road, UK

Abstract. *This paper describes a dynamic instrumentation tool for the Linux Kernel which allows a stock Linux kernel to be modified while in execution, with instruments implemented as kernel modules. The Intel x86 architecture poses a particular problem, due to variable length instructions, which this paper addresses for the first time. Finally we present a short case study illustrating its use in understanding i/o behaviour in the kernel. The source code is freely available for download.*

1 Introduction

In this paper we describe an instrumentation tool called GILK that has been developed specifically for the Linux Kernel. It permits sensitive instrumentation code to be added to an unmodified kernel in execution with low instrumentation overhead. This is achieved through an implementation of *runtime code splicing*, which allows arbitrary code to be inserted in the kernel without affecting its behaviour. Currently the tool works only for kernels running on the Intel x86 architecture, although in principle there is no reason why it could not work on others. Through a graphical interface, the user may choose how and where to instrument, when to begin and end individual instruments and what to do with the information produced. We make the following contributions:

- An implementation of runtime code splicing for the Intel x86 architecture is outlined.
- A new technique for code splicing, called *local bounce allocation*, is described.

2 Related Work

Much of the foundation for this project has been laid by Tamches, *et al.* [1,2, 3] with the *KernInst* dynamic instrumentation tool. This works on the Solaris kernel and UltraSparc architecture and its techniques are applicable to a fixed length instruction set and multi-threaded kernel.

Binary rewriters such as QP/QPT [4], EEL [5], BIT [6] and ATOM [7] introduce instrumentation code by modifying the executable statically.

T. Field et al. (Eds.): TOOLS 2002, LNCS 2324, pp. 220–226, 2002.

This is, arguably, a safer approach than runtime modification, but is more cumbersome. It is our belief that GILK provides a more practical solution, as its *dynamic* approach is more suited to the exploratory nature of performance monitoring and debugging.

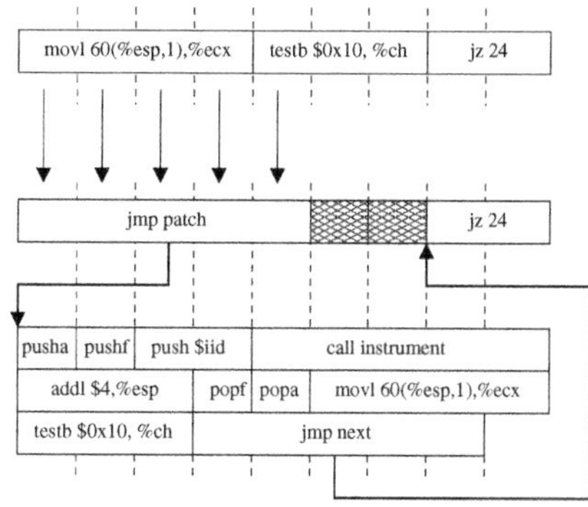

Fig. 1. *Illustrating the process of placing a code splice. In the new sequence two bytes are now redundant, as they are no longer in the flow of control. The two overwritten instructions are relocated to the patch.*

3 GILK Overview

The GILK tool consists of two components: a device driver (called ILK) and a client. The client does the bulk of the work, with the device driver providing access to kernel space. The client begins with a scanning phase to establish the set of valid instrumentation points. The user then specifies what instrumentation should take place, which amounts to selecting instruments, choosing points and specifying start and finish times. The tool supports staggered launching and termination of instruments, which provides greater flexibility.

There are two instrument points associated with each basic block of a kernel function: the pre- and post-hook. A pre-hook instrument gets executed before the first instruction of the block, while a post-hook instrument is executed after the last *non-branching* statement.

Each of the instruments is assigned a unique identifier (iid) which is logged, along with any additional data, to a buffer in the kernel, which the client periodically flushes. Eventually, they are written to disk. The client keeps a record of the active instruments so that the kernel can be safely restored to its original form.

3.1 Code Splicing

The idea behind code splicing is to write a branch instruction or *splice* at the instrument point. Clearly, this will overwrite instructions at that point and, therefore, those affected are first relocated into a *code patch*. The splice targets this code patch, which must also save and restore the machine state and call the instrument function. This is illustrated in Figure 1.

Under the Intel x86 architecture, the splice used is 5 bytes long. However, an instruction may be a single byte in length, making it possible for the splice to overwrite more than one instruction. If an overwritten instruction (other than the first) is the target of a branch, control could be passed into the middle of the splice!

It is for this reason that GILK must generate the Control Flow Graph for each kernel symbol. With this knowledge the above problem can be reduced to saying that it is unsafe to straddle the splice across a basic block boundary.

There is a second problem with variable length architectures that is similar to the first. This time, consider what happens if a thread is suspended at an overwritten instruction. Again, when the thread awakens, control could be passed into the middle of the splice. At this point, the methodology of the Linux Kernel comes to the rescue. There are three main points:

- *A process executing in kernel space must run to completion unless it voluntarily relinquishes control.*
- *Processes running in kernel space may be interrupted by hardware interrupts.*
- *An interrupt handler cannot be interrupted by a process running in kernel space.*

These three points, taken together, allow us to overcome this second problem. Firstly, the ability to block interrupts means the device driver can write the splice without fear of interruption. Secondly, although a process may relinquish control it can only do so through indirectly calling the `schedule()` function. This means that, so long as we don't instrument this function, the sleeping thread problem can be ignored. Further discussions on these topics can be found in [8].

3.2 Local Bouncing

It is sometimes the case that a basic block is less than five bytes in length. This means we cannot always place a splice without straddling a block boundary. However, the Intel x86 architecture also supports a two byte branch instruction with limited range. In general, this is not enough to reach the code patch directly.

Therefore, GILK attempts to place a normal splice within this range. This is termed *bouncing*. The problem, then, is where to position these bounces. Luckily, it is often the case that space is made available by splices for other instruments. To understand this better, consider again Figure 1. If the second overwritten instruction was three or more bytes longer then there would be (at least) five redundant bytes available for use as a bounce. If no other instruments are active, or there are simply not enough redundant bytes, then GILK will relocate instructions *solely for the purpose of finding space.*

This strategy is termed *local bounce allocation* because GILK only attempts to allocate bounces within the function being instrumented.

3.3 Instrument Functions

The instruments themselves are implemented as kernel modules, as this simplifies some of the dynamic linking issues. Each instrument module initially registers itself with the ILK device driver, providing a pointer to the *instrument function.* The instrument function accepts, as parameters, at least the unique instrument identifier and possibly other arguments depending upon which code patch template was used. An example function is:

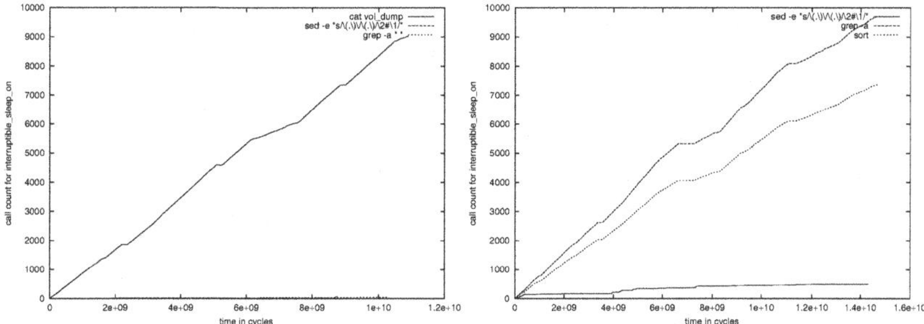

Fig. 2.

```
void simple_instr(unsigned int iid) {
 ilk_log_integer_sample(jiffies,iid);
}
```

This function simply logs the value of the global variable "jiffies" when it is called. Being a kernel module, it has access to all the structures of the kernel which it can report on. Also, as a 'C' function it could easily be more sophisticated.

4 Experimental Results

4.1 Pipe Blocking

This experiment provides a simple case study to show GILK being used to understand kernel and process behaviour. The idea behind it was this: suppose we have a series of UNIX commands concatenated with the "pipe" operator and we wish to determine which of the commands is the bottleneck. One way of using GILK to determine this is by instrumenting the kernel symbol `pipe_write`. Part of the code for this symbol is:

```
while ((PIPE_FREE(*inode) < free) || PIPE_LOCK(*inode)) {
        ...
        interruptible_sleep_on(&PIPE_WAIT(*inode));
```

The function `interruptible_sleep_on()` puts the process to sleep, pending a wake up call from the pipe reader. So, the above can be simplified to saying that the process is put to sleep when there isn't enough space in the buffer *or* the pipe is locked by a reader. Therefore, it is reasonable to assume that a process in a pipeline will make a lot of calls to `interruptible_sleep_on()` if it is producing data faster that it can be consumed.

To measure this, GILK was used to place a pre-hook instrument on the basic block which makes the call to `interruptible_sleep_on()`. The instrument recorded the Process ID and a timestamp. A large file, called "vol_dump" was created with random data and the following pipeline used:

```
% cat vol_dump | sed -e "s/\(.\)\/\(.\)/\2#\1/" | grep -a " " | sort
```

The results can be seen in the left graph of Figure 2. They indicate that the "cat" process is making a large number of calls to `interruptible_sleep_on()` whilst the others are making relatively little. This means that "cat" is producing data faster than it can be consumed and this is causing it to block. The suspicion is, therefore, that "sed" is the bottleneck for this pipeline.

If this was the case then we would expect processes after it to be blocking on their read operations. To confirm this a second experiment was performed in which the pipe read operation was monitored for calls to `interruptible_sleep_on()`. The results from this are shown in right graph of Figure 2 and they show that all processes in the pipeline after "sed" are blocking whilst waiting for data to be produced. Hence, the conclusion that "sed" is the bottleneck seems reasonable.

4.2 Network Traffic Analysis

The experiments outlined in this section form part of ongoing research into self-similarity of network traffic at Imperial College. This particular experiment used GILK to investigate the properties of artificial network traffic. For this a simple multi-threaded JAVA server was constructed that transferred data across the network to a number of clients.

The experiment requires *inter-arrival* times for packets to be measured. The utility `tcpdump` was initially used for this, but it occasionally reported inter-arrival times of zero. Clearly, this is a mistake and it was unclear whether the generated power spectra was being affected.

Thus, GILK was deployed to confirm that inter-arrival times of zero were not real and ascertain if they were affecting the original data. It was used to instrument functions within the Linux TCP/IP stack as well as the Ethernet

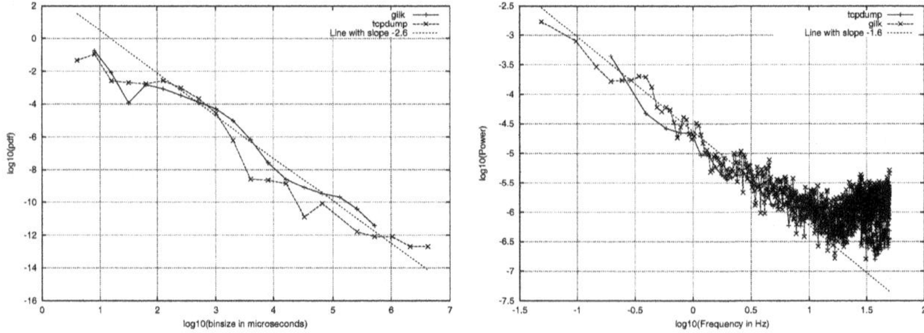

Fig. 3. These plots show a comparison of the histograms (left) and power spectra based on data from `GILK` and `tcpdump`.

driver. The measurements taken confirmed that interarrival times were always positive and it was concluded that there was negligible difference between the power spectra generated with `tcpdump`. Figure 3 illustrates the comparison.

The significance of the power spectra and self-similarity are beyond the scope of this paper and the reader is referred to [9] for more information.

5 Conclusion

GILK provides a useful instrumentation tool and provides an example implementation of runtime code splicing for a variable length architecture, which has not been done before. Experimental evidence shows that it as an accurate and reasonably low overhead way of performing instrumentation.

There remains, however, some scope for improvement. Particularly, the sample logging process appears expensive. Live register analysis could also be used to make machine state saving less expensive. Also, the need to implement instruments as kernel modules adds to the overhead by requiring an extra function call. This could be prevented by employing a more sophisticated dynamic loader. The custom disassembler could be reworked to allow easy updating for new instruction set extensions and, finally, the client interface could be extended to provide more instrumentation strategies and easier navigation through the kernel.

The source code for the tool has been placed under the GNU General Public License and is available for download, along with an extended version of this paper [10].

Acknowledgements. Uli Harder is supported by an EPSRC grant (QUAINT). David Pearce is supported by an EPSRC grant.

References

1. Ariel Tamches and Barton P. Miller. Fine-grained dynamic instrumentation of commodity operating system kernels. In *Operating Systems Design and Implementation*, pages 117–130, 1999.
2. Ariel Tamches and Barton P. Miller. Using dynamic kernel instrumentation for kernel and application tuning. *The International Journal of High Performance Computing Applications*, 13(3):263–276, Fall 1999.
3. Ariel Tamches. *Fine-Grained Dynamic Instrumentation of Commodity Operating System Kernels*. PhD thesis, University of Wisconsin, 2001.
4. James R. Larus and Thomas Ball. Rewriting executable files to measure program behavior. *Software - Practice and Experience*, 24(2):197–218, February 1994.
5. James R. Larus and Eric Schnarr. EEL: machine-independent executable editing. *ACM SIGPLAN Notices*, 30(6):291–300, June 1995.
6. Han Bok Lee and Benjamin G. Zorn. BIT: A tool for instrumenting Java bytecodes. In *Proceedings of the USENIX Symposium on Internet Technologies and Systems (ITS-97)*, pages 73–82, Berkeley, December 8–11 1997. USENIX Association.
7. Amitabh Srivastava and Alan Eustace. Atom: A system for building customized program analysis tools. *ACM SIGPLAN Notices*, 29(6):196–205, June 1994.

8. Michael Beck et al. *Linux kernel internals.* Addison-Wesley, Reading, MA, USA, second edition, 1998.
9. P. Harrison T. Field, U. Harder. Analysis of network traffic in switched ethernet systems. `http://xxx.soton.ac.uk/abs/cs.PF/0107001`, 2001.
10. Gilk: A dynamic instrumentation tool for the linux kernel, `http://www.doc.ic.ac.uk/~djp1/gilk.html`

Geist: A Web Traffic Generation Tool

Krishna Kant, Vijay Tewari, and Ravishankar Iyer

Intel Corporation, Hillsboro, OR
{krishna.kant|vijay.tewari|ravishankar.iyer}@.intel.com

Abstract. This paper briefly describes the design of Geist, a traffic generator for stress testing of web/e-commerce servers. The generator provides a large number of dialable parameters that allow traffic characteristics to range from simple static web-page browsing to the transactional traffic seen by e-commerce front end servers. Unlike other traffic generators, Geist concentrates on the characteristics of the aggregate traffic arriving at the server, which allows for realistic traffic generation without any explicit modeling of users or network components.

1 Introduction

The work reported here was motivated by the need to understand the implications of web traffic characteristics on the architectural aspects of a web/e-commerce server. This requires generation of the aggregate Internet traffic from a server's perspective without having to explicitly emulate users, network components, or network protocols. This *server-centric* focus also means that client-level aspects of the traffic are relevant only to the extent they affect the aggregate traffic. Furthermore, lab testing environment often requires that the servers be driven to their capacity (and in fact beyond the capacity into overload region). This requires the capability to generate heavy traffic (e.g., more than 10K requests per second). It has been amply noted in the literature that the traditional socket interface makes it very difficult to overload web-servers [10]. Finally, the increasing dynamic content of web pages makes generation of realistic transactional characteristics particularly challenging, especially in e-commerce environments. In this paper, we present a tool called Geist (Generator of E-Commerce and Internet Server Traffic), that has been designed to deal with these and other important issues.

The aggregate traffic generation approach used by Geist allows for a more scalable traffic generation since the request-send and response-receive operations on the client side can be completely decoupled. In particular, it is possible to keep generating successive requests at prescribed times irrespective of how long the server takes to send back the responses. Furthermore, the traffic impact of network components and protocols (e.g., queuing delays, flow-control, retransmission, rerouting, etc.) can be captured without having to explicitly represent the network or the protocols. In effect, the approach converts the inherently "closed loop" traffic characterization/handling problem to an "open loop" problem where the traffic properties are modeled directly at the server. The main disadvantage of this approach is the difficulty in directly modeling the user behavior. Geist handles this by carving out a set of "virtual users" from the aggregate traffic as discussed later.

Generation of aggregate traffic with complex characteristics is often computationally intensive, which makes it difficult to ensure that a request is actually generated very

T. Field et al. (Eds.): TOOLS 2002, LNCS 2324, pp. 227–232, 2002.

close to the intended time. Geist addresses this issue by splitting the generation into two steps referred to as *trace generation* and *traffic generation* respectively. Trace generation handles all the complexities of computing the actual time and parameters for the requests, whereas the traffic generation step simply reads the trace and issues the requests. The added advantage of this approach is that the trace could very well have been derived from HTTP logs from a live site. The traffic generator part still has to deal with several O/S related issues to ensure accurate timing of the generated traffic. These issues are discussed in Section 3.

In related work, some other well known tools are Microsoft's Web Application Stress Tool, HTTP-perf [10] from HP Labs, and SURGE [1] from Boston University. These tools mostly take the user emulation approach whereas Geist attempts to generate aggregate traffic directly. The first two tools are very limited in terms of the temporal properties that the traffic is allowed to have. SURGE, on the other hand, supports self-similarity by making each "user equivalent" an on-off process. In contrast, Geist supports asymptotically self-similar, multifractal, and non-stationary arrival process. However, Geist is not locked into producing self-similar traffic; it can also generate traffic with much shorter dependencies, including none. Geist also supports detailed transactional characterization of the traffic. However, SURGE does explicitly support embedded requests, a feature, that is currently not implemented in Geist. Geist's model for temporal locality in accesses is taken from SPECweb96/99 benchmarks, rather than emulated explicitly as in SURGE. Unlike the current version of Geist, the HTTP-perf tool supports multiple requests per connection and cookies; however, it is designed basically for deterministic inter-request time on a single client. Of the above tools, only Geist and WAST can generate a mix of non-secure and secure traffic. Geist also allows for complex temporal characteristics including long-range dependence, traffic irregularities at intermediate time scales, and nonstationarity.

2 Traffic Properties Considered in Geist

In this section, we briefly discuss the major traffic properties considered in Geist and how they are introduced. A more detailed discussion of Geist's design may be found in [8].

Temporal Distribution of the traffic: The temporal properties of the traffic can be examined either in terms of inter-arrival times or the arrival counting process (i.e., number of arrivals in a "slot" of certain duration). The latter is usually more robust, and is used in Geist. An appropriate slot duration is the time-period over which the average number of arrivals are in the range of a few 10s. Geist allows control over the first two moments of the arrival counting process as discussed later in this section. The arrivals belonging to a slot are distributed uniformly so that the inter-arrival time distribution within a slot is negative exponential.

User Behavior Impact on Temporal Properties of the traffic: Apart from the distributional properties, the correlation structure of the arrival process is crucial from a temporal characterization point of view. Over large time scales, these correlational properties are a result of the user behavior, which is often characterized by low and high activity periods, each with a heavy-tailed distribution. The aggregate traffic in such cases exhibits long-range dependence or *self-similarity* [11]. Although self-similarity is now established as a universal property of high-speed networks, most of the studies in the literature take a *network centric view* where the traffic metric of interest is the bytes traveling over a link. In contrast, ours is a *server centric view*, where the interest lies in the requests coming into the server. Our extensive analysis of web and e-commerce request traffic [4, 7] confirms that the self-similarity is observed at the request level as well.

The correlations in the arrivals process (and, in particular, the self-similarity) can substantially affect the queuing behavior of the traffic depending on the time-scales captured by the queue. Since we do not know a priori what time-scales are of interest, it is crucial that the traffic generator be able to generate self-similar traffic, if needed. Geist provides this capability. Geist also supports generation of traffic with medium and short range correlations, including no correlations at all (i.e., generation of a renewal process).

Geist controls the temporal properties of the traffic by using the $M/G/\infty$ paradigm that can generate asymptotically self-similar as well as short and medium range dependent traffic. As such, the marginal distribution of the generated arrival process is Poisson (the occupancy distribution in a $M/G/\infty$ queue), however, it can be easily transformed to a process with the desired distribution as detailed in [9]. Such a transformation is adequate at least as far as second order properties are concerned.

Network Dynamics Effects on the traffic: As the traffic passes through the network elements, its characteristics are affected not only by the usual queuing/processing delays at the nodes but also by network level mechanisms such as TCP flow and congestion control and segmentation/reassembly of packets at intermediate nodes. The time constants of these activities usually fall in 100 ms range which is much less than the time constants involved in user activities. Consequently, self-similarity aspects of the traffic are typically not affected by the network dynamics but network dynamics has a substantial influence on the queuing performance of the traffic.

A direct emulation of network effects on the traffic makes sense only for network-centric studies; with server-centric studies that we are interested in, representation of network effects would require too much additional machinery. Thus an indirect representation of these effects in the aggregate traffic is ideal for our purposes. It has been shown recently that these effects can be captured by using the concept of *multi-fractal* properties which are defined as an extension of self-similarity [2]. As with self-similarity, much of the work to date on this aspect considers byte traffic on a network link, however, it is likely that similar properties apply at the request level also. Geist provides the capability of introducing multifractal-like properties in the traffic in case such effects are deemed important. This is done by accumulating arrivals over some 2^K time-slots and using a *semi-random cascade generator* to distribute the mass down to individual slots. More details on this may be found in [6].

Traffic Nonstationarity: Much of the work on web-traffic analysis assumes that the traffic is approximately stationary, which has been confirmed by our own analysis of web traffic from several sources. However, our recent analysis of traffic logs from several business to business (B2B) and business to consumer (B2C) sites shows that even over short intervals of 10-15 minutes, the traffic is often nonstationary [7]. Geist provides the capability to introduce nonstationarity in the traffic should this be important in studies such as dynamic resource-provisioning.

In order to avoid any perturbation to the M/G/∞ paradigm, the nonstationarity is introduced at the output end by modulating the number of arrivals during the last slot given by the M/G/∞ process. This is done using a level-shift process, the details of which may be found in [7].

Transactional Composition of the traffic: Representation of transactional behavior is another important aspect of e-commerce traffic generation. Basically, this involves a classification of the transactions based on the server-side scripts invoked by a request which in turn invoke middleware (e.g., shopping cart, search server) or backend functions (e.g., product availability, pricing, etc.). The primary motivation for this classification is that different scripts may have very different characteristics in terms of CPU and I/O requirements. Another important aspect of transactional composition is the use of secure HTTP (or HTTPS) for some (possibly all) transactions. As shown in [5], an HTTPS is far more expensive than a corresponding HTTP transaction, thereby making the distinction necessary.

The transactional characteristics can be easily represented using a "state machine" or a Markov chain, where the state represents the transaction type and the transitions represent ordering between them. In Geist, each state could be further classified as "secure" or "nonsecure" and is associated with a server side script.

It is important to note that the transactional classification applies to individual users, whereas Geist generates only the aggregate traffic. Therefore, the generated traffic needs to be split up into requests for an individual "virtual" user. Geist does this as follows: First it computes the number of virtual users K as the product of the aggregate mean arrival rate and the inter-request time for an individual user, both of which are input parameters to Geist. The successive arrivals are then marked equiprobably to belong to one of the K user streams. Each user stream is then assigned a unique-id and the transactions are marked according to the Markov chain model.

Access Characteristics of the traffic: The actual server-side script executed by a transaction embodies the resource requirements in processing the transaction. Geist only indicates which scripts are executed and how often; it does not explicitly specify the properties of these scripts or even their parameters. Such an approach gives maximum flexibility to the experimenter in writing the scripts (or simply using the existing scripts for the e-commerce application of interest). The parameter issue can be resolved by writing a wrapper script that generates the desired parameter values. We plan to provide some sample wrapper scripts along with the tool.

Irrespective of the type of access (dynamic or static), it is important to control the characteristics of the response sent out by the server. This is done in Geist by requiring that every Get request retrieve a "file" from a given "file-set". As in the SPECweb99 benchmark, it is assumed that a dynamic GET simply creates some additional data (assumed to be rather small in size), which is appended or prepended to the static file being requested. The details of file-set and file-access specification are similar to those in SPECweb96 and SPECweb99 benchmarks (`www.specbench.org/osg/`). In fact, Geist's approach is somewhat more general and can easily emulate access characteristics of both of these benchmarks.

3 Geist Capabilities and Traffic Generation Issues

Geist trace generator defines 30 or so control parameters to which values can be assigned in an input file. The generated trace is written to an output file, which can be further split up into multiple files for use by each client in the traffic generator part. The input file can contain 3 types of statements: (1) declaration of auxiliary variables (scalars or arrays), (2) assignments of expressions to scalar or array variables (predefined or declared in the input file), (3) Miscellaneous controls (diagnostic, pause, change values and resume, etc.). Currently, there is no graphics interface for the input, nor is one planned.

In addition to trace generation, the generator also includes the following capabilities: (1) Simulation of a simple single-server queuing system directly driven by the generated traffic, (2) Emulation of a file-cache also directly driven by the generated traffic, (3) Creation of the file-system that will be exercised by the traffic generator, and (4) Automated analysis of the temporal properties of the generated traffic. These capabilities allow study of various properties of the generated traffic in a convenient way. The entire trace generator is written in C and runs on both Unix and Windows environments. It should be relatively straightforward to port it to other environments as well.

The traffic generator part can use multiple (say, N) client boxes, in which case the requests in the trace file are assigned to each client such that (a) all requests issues by a "virtual user" stay on the same client, and (b) load is spread evenly across all clients. This splitting of the original trace file is done offline in order to avoid any timing issues. Each client runs an instance of the Geist traffic generation engine which includes a pool of (request) sender threads, (response) receiver threads and a timer thread (to watch run duration). One of the clients called *prime client* is responsible for sending global information to the other client boxes including IP address of the server, duration of the test, number of sender/receiver threads, etc. Additionally the prime client performs time synchronization amongst all clients by broadcasting a time interval after which all the clients reset their virtual clocks to zero. All time decisions are based on this time zero from here on. After performing these functions the prime client behaves like any other client box. Like the trace generator, the behavior of traffic generator is controlled by assigning values to a set of predefined parameters in an input file.

The current request generation engine has been implemented in the C language on the Win32 platform. In this implementation, the communication between the prime client and the other clients is based on UDP broadcast. This restricts the implementation to having all clients in the same subnet. A more flexible implementation including the integration of *pthreads library* is planned for the future.

In order to avoid timing skew due to I/O delays, the input file created by the trace generated is locked in the memory at the beginning. Secure requests are supported via the OpenSSL library (see `www.openssl.org`). Geist also supports secure and non-secure requests via proxies. Furthermore, it is possible to add custom headers in the configuration file which will be used at the time of making the request. This makes the architecture extensible to support new HTTP request headers.

An important issue for the traffic generator is to ensure that the temporal properties of the generated requests are close to those of the traffic specified by the trace file. A logging utility has been provided for this purpose. A study of the accuracy of the generated traffic may be found in [8].

4 Uses and Availability of Geist

We have used Geist already in generating traffic for a number of projects including a study of overload control strategies for web servers [3] a proxy server study and architectural studies like SSL performance implications [5]. Reference [3] uses GEIST to show the impact of loading a web server beyond its capacity. One of the advantages of using Geist (as opposed other traffic generators like Microsoft's WAS tool) here was that the traffic generated by the clients was not dependent on the implicit feedback of the varying load on the server. Geist was modified to receive the overload feedback (via a UDP channel) and respond by throttling the inter-arrival rate of the outgoing traffic. This further shows the flexibility of Geist's architecture for performing studies that require dynamic source traffic modifications based on the feedback.

Geist is to be regarded as work in progress, and can be enhanced in many ways. In particular, Geist currently does not support the new features of HTTP 1.1 or the detailed specification of scripts executed by the server. Our ongoing work shall address these and related issues. The entire tool along with the documentation can be downloaded from `kkant.ccwebhost.com/download.html`.

References

1. P. Barford, and M. Crovella, "Generating Representative Web Workloads for Network and Server Performance Evaluation", Proc. ACM Sigmetrics, pp. 151-160, July 1998.
2. A. Feldmann, A.C. Gilbert and W. Willinger, "Data Networks as Cascades: Investigating the multifractal nature of Internet WAN traffic", Proc. ACM Sigcomm 98, pp42-55.
3. R. Iyer, V. Tewari and K. Kant, "Overload Control Mechanisms for Web Servers", Performance and QoS of Next Generation Networks, Naogya, Japan, Nov 2000.
4. K. Kant and Y. Won, "Server Capacity Planning for Web Traffic Workload", IEEE transactions on knowledge and data engineering, Oct 1999. pp731-747.
5. K. Kant, R. Iyer and P. Mohapatra, "Architectural Impact of Secure Socket Layer on Internet Servers", Proc. of ICCD, Sept 2000.
6. K. Kant, "On Aggregate Traffic Generation with Multifractal Properties", Proc. of GLOBECOM'99, Rio de Janeiro, Brazil, pp 1179-1183.
7. K. Kant and M. Venkatachelam, "Modeling traffic non-stationarity in e-commerce servers", available at `kkant.ccwebhost.com/download.htm`.
8. K. Kant, V. Tewari and R. Iyer, "Geist: A generator of e-commerce and internet server traffic", Proc. of ISPASS, Tucson, AZ, Nov 2001, pp 49-56.
9. M. Krunz and A. Makowski, "A source model for VBR Video traffic based on $M/G/\infty$ Input", Tech. Report, Univ of Maryland.
10. D. Mosberger and T. Jin, "HTTPPERF: Atool for measuring web server performance", Technical Report, HP Labs, 1998.
11. W. Willinger, M.S. Taqqu, R. Sherman, and D.V. Wilson, "Self-Similarity through High Variability: Statistical Analysis of Ethernet LAN traffic at the source level", Proc. of Sigcomm 95, pp100-113.

DrawNET++: Model Objects to Support Performance Analysis and Simulation of Systems

Giuliana Franceschinis[1], M. Gribaudo[2], M. Iacono[3], N. Mazzocca[3], and V. Vittorini[4]

[1] Di.S.T.A., Univ. del Piemonte Orientale, AL, Italy. giuliana@mfn.unipmn.it
[2] Dip. di Informatica, Univ. di Torino, Italy. marcog@di.unito.it
[3] Dip. di Ingegneria dell'Informazione, Seconda Univ. di Napoli, Italy {mauro.iacono,nicola.mazzocca}@unina2.it
[4] D.I.S., Univ. degli Studi di Napoli Federico II, Italy. vittorin@unina.it

Abstract. This paper describes DrawNET++, a prototype version of a model design framework based on the definition of model objects. DrawNET++ provides a graphical front-end to existing performance tools and a practical mean to study compositionality issues in multi-formalism environments. The object oriented features of DrawNET++ provide a flexible architecture for structuring complex models.

Keywords: Model Objects, Model composition, Performance Analysis Framework.

1 Introduction

The complexity of nowadays computer and communication systems calls for suitable software tools to support design decisions. As pointed out in [8] there is a need for *open* frameworks and software environments able to embed and integrate different modeling formalisms and solution/simulation techniques.

The philosophy behind the tool we are proposing in this paper goes in the direction of providing a framework where different formalisms can be easily defined, extended, and composed, and models descriptions can be exported in XML form. The type of formalisms supported by the tool are those for which it is natural to define a representation in terms of a graph. The elements of the graph can be (sub)models. The tool supports compositional approaches to model construction, facilitating model structuring and (sub)model reuse in a style inspired by the Object Oriented (OO) paradigm.

Since new formalisms can be invented and easily integrated in the tool without any programming effort, domain specific formalisms can be defined: in this case the nodes may represent domain specific submodels expressed in some underlying formalism by an expert model designer, and presented to the final user as black boxes with proper interface and connectors.

The framework can exploit existing or newly created analysis/simulation engines by providing the model description as well as the description of performance indices to be computed in XML. Filters (e.g. XSL styles) need to be developed to

T. Field et al. (Eds.): TOOLS 2002, LNCS 2324, pp. 233–238, 2002.

transform the XML model and performance indices representation in a format suitable for the specific analysis/simulation engine. Following this approach we believe that different solvers might be plugged-in as they become available at the (hopefully reasonable) price of writing proper filters.

This approach differs substantially from that advocated in the Möbius project [8] where new formalisms, composition operators and solvers are actually implemented within a unique comprehensive tool. In Möbius all formalisms are required to be compatible with a predefined general framework [5].

The experiments done so far with DrawNET++ have allowed us to experiment with a Fault Tree formalism (Parametric Fault Trees), to study compositionality of Stochastic Well Formed Net (SWN) models through the *algebra* tool [2] included in *GreatSPN* [3], and to mix the two things.

In Sec. 2 the features of DrawNET++ are presented. In Sec. 3 we discuss a possible approach for connecting DrawNET++ with existing model analyzers.

2 DrawNET++ Features

Defining formalisms and models. *DrawNET* is a tool that can be used to rapidly develop user interfaces for performance evaluation engines: it provides a GUI to any graph-based formalism defined by the user such as queueing networks, Petri Nets, Fault trees, Bayesian networks and many more.

A formalism defines the kinds of nodes and edges models may include. Nodes, edges, and formalisms themselves are all *elements*, each with an associated name and set of *properties*. A property is a pair $(name, value)$ used to specify a characteristic of a particular element. Since also formalisms are elements, they can have some properties used to define attributes of the whole model. Edges can connect elements, and have an associated set of *constraints* that tell which kind of elements may be connected by that edge, and how many edges of a given type can be connected to a given element. An edge can connect not only two basic nodes, but also other edges, or (sub)models.

Formalisms and models are described in DrawNET by means of two different *data definition languages*[7]. Formalisms are specified by using a custom XML dialect called **FDL**. This dialect specifies which types of nodes and edges a formalism may have. Properties may be included into the tags that specify nodes and edges. Models are specified by using another custom XML dialect called **GDL**: models are collections of nodes, edges and sub-models satisfying a given FDL specification.

All elements of a model have a *visibility* attribute, which allows to hide internal details of sub-models. Edges can connect any element of the model, and any *visible* element of its sub-models.

Sub-models specified by means of distinct formalisms can coexist to build a more complex model. The only restriction is imposed on connections: visible elements of a sub-model (or the sub-model itself) may be connected to elements of the container model, only if suitable edges exist.

Specifying model objects. The DrawNET++ tool can be used as a support to an OO approach to performance model construction, as explained hereafter. Some extensions that have been implemented to this purpose are described at the end of this section. Three levels can be defined in designing compositional models:

• **model class**: can be defined as a formalism, expressed though an FDL specification (e.g. BlackBox.xml, Machine.xml and FaultyMachine.xml in Fig.1);

• **model object**: it belongs to a given model class, is defined by the designer creating a model in DrawNET++, and is exported by the tool as an XML document following the GDL specification (e.g. the XML description of FaultyMachine indicated as a Template Model Object in Fig.1);

• **instance object**: it is an instance of a model object and it is expressed by means of the resulting XML specification exported by DrawNET. An instance object is created by the end user when building a complex system model (e.g. Robot1 or Cell1 in Fig.1). Several instances of a given model object can be included as *submodels* within a more complex model at a higher level.

A model object represents an abstraction of a system component: it comprises an **interface** and an **inner set of data**. The interface includes the relevant characteristics for the interaction of the modeled component with other components, that is the information that needs to be exchanged between the model and the environment in which it is integrated (*ExpInterface,ImpInterface*) or the parameters that need to be specified to complete the component description when it has some parametric part (*InstInterface*). It also includes the information about the interface points visible to the external world and usable for actually composing a model instance with other model instances (*InputInterface,OutputInterface*). The visibility property of both the *InputInterface* and *OutputInterface* elements should be set to true, so that they may be used to compose the model instance with other elements. This however does not imply that the properties of input/output interfaces will also be visible, only the interface elements will be visible so that they can be connected with external world elements through appropriate edges.

The inner set of data (the *Internal* node) consists of the internal details of the component behavior: it might include a graph directly drawn with DrawNET, or it may be a pointer to a model defined within another tool (e.g., a Stochastic Petri Net model defined in GreatSPN): in this paper we shall consider only the second option. In any case the inner set of data will not be visible when the model is included as a submodel in a more complex structure.

Up to now we have seen how model classes can be defined, and how model objects can be defined and instantiated: these features are present also in other existing tools (for example Tangram-II[4]). Our proposal goes one step further and implements some additional OO features described hereafter.

Inheritance of model specifications: inheritance between model classes can be defined at the formalism level since DrawNET++ allows to define model class hierarchies. A new FDL specification may derive from an existing FDL (e.g. see BlackBox.xml, Machine.xml and FaultyMachine.xml in Fig.1). In this context,

inheritance is a form of model reusability, in which new model classes are created from existing ones by absorbing their elements (nodes and/or edges) and overriding some of them or extending their properties.
Templates: Once a model object is defined, the property values of its nodes become hidden, however it is possible to define *template model objects* by declaring some properties as *parametric* so that they can be modified after instantiation (e.g. parameter *Fault Rate* in the FaultyMachine template model object).
Weak Aggregation: An object may be *aggregated* to other objects by means of proper composition operators. By now we have just explored a simple synchronization operator that is implemented as an edge that connects an *InputInterface* node with an *OutputInterface* node and vice-versa. More complex operators might be needed, that connect more than two elements, requiring the definition of "connection nodes" (for example to compose several output interfaces to several input interfaces, through a Cartesian product operator). The complete model of a system is obtained by instantiating and aggregating model objects as shown in Fig.1 for a simple FMS model.
Strong Aggregation: new model objects may be created that embed other model objects. When a new model is created by composing submodels, it is possible to exploit an information hiding feature of DrawNET++ to obtain strong aggregation. For example, in Fig.1 a model object *Cell* is created by aggregating a machine and a buffer, and hiding the *OutputInterface* of the machine and the *InputInterface* of the buffer so that they are no longer accessible when a *Cell* instance is included in a higher level model.

3 Performance Analysis of DrawNET++ Models

The work presented in this paper stemmed from the need of defining a framework for the compositional construction of SWN models using a library of (domain specific) models and an intuitive composition method based on black boxes and connectors [6,1]. Although the framework can be used in a more general setting, for space reasons this section will be focused on this specific use of DrawNET++, and in particular on how it can be interfaced with GreatSPN.

The steps that allow to obtain performance results out of a DrawNET++ model similar to that shown in Fig. 1 are: (1) generate the (sub)model description files accepted by GreatSPN, (2) invoke the GreatSPN composition tool *algebra*, (3) invoke GreatSPN analysis/simulation facilities, (4) retrieve the performance results from the files generated by GreatSPN and save them in a form that can be read and displayed by DrawNET++.
Generation of SWN models for GreatSPN: In the model class descriptions of Fig 1 two properties allow to declare the formalism and associated analysis tool for the model objects in that class: in our case they are set to SWN and GreatSPN respectively. In this case a GreatSPN description of each *basic* model object behavior already exists: the part that must be implemented in a post-processor integrated into DrawNET++ is (1) the automatic generation of the connection structure, in the form of a GreatSPN labeled SWN model, (2) the

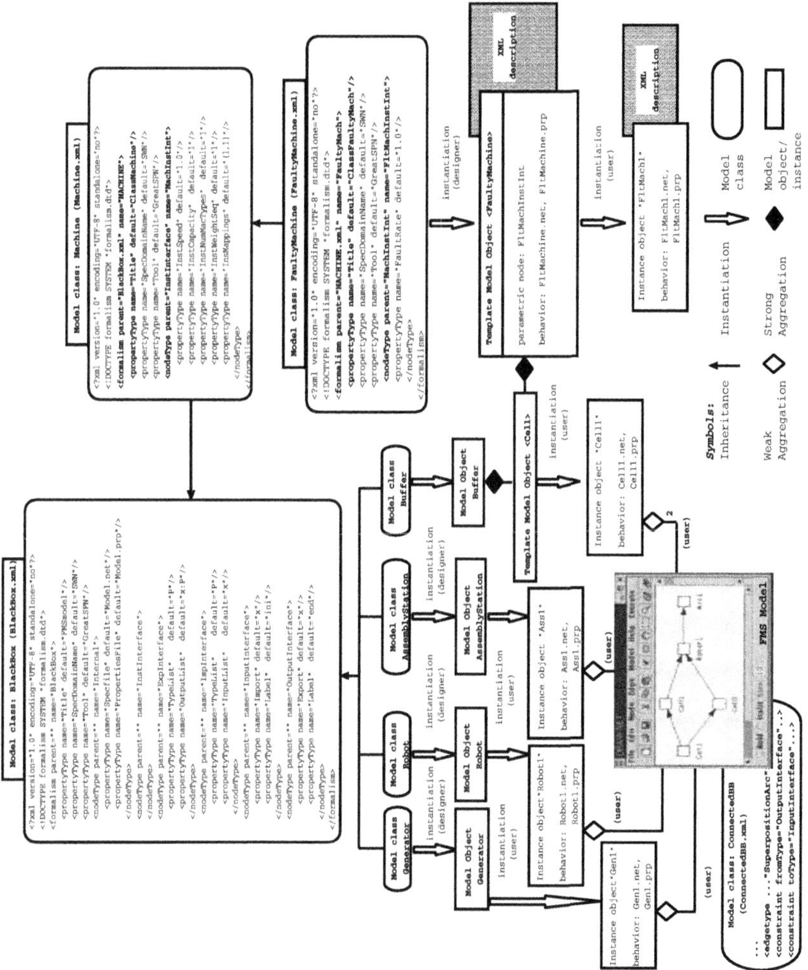

Fig. 1. Construction of a complete model

instantiation of the subnets represented by the DrawNET++ submodels, (3) the automatic generation of a script for calling *algebra* on the proper submodels, finally getting the complete composed model, ready for being solved/simulated.

Retrieving results: the results that can be obtained by analysis and/or simulation are dependent on the specific tool used. A simple language as been defined to implement the communication of results , called Result Description Language (RDL). Based on the RDL, an XML Result Data Specification (RDS) defines the performance results by pairs (name, value). The RDS is used to back-propagate the information from a simulation/solution engine to the GUI: at the end of a simulation/solution process the post-processor retrieves the results and makes them available to DrawNET++ by filling a proper RDS definition.

4 Conclusions

In this paper we presented DrawNET++, a prototype system that has been developed to support an OO design process of system models and to provide a graphical front-end to existing performance tools. The current version of the tool together with a complete demonstration example can be downloaded from:
http://www.di.unito.it/~greatspn/DrawNET/

References

1. F.Basile, P. Chiacchio, N. Mazzocca, and V. Vittorini Specification and Modeling of Flexible Manufacturing Systems Using Behaviours and Petri Nets Building Blocks In *Proc. of the International Symposium on Software Engineering for Parallel and Distributed Systems (PDSE99)*, Los Angeles, USA, 17-18 May 1999.
2. S. Bernardi, S. Donatelli, and A. Horváth. Compositionality in the GreatSPN tool and its use to the modelling of industrial applications. Accepted for publication on *Software Tools for Technology Transfer.*
3. G. Chiola, G. Franceschinis, R. Gaeta, and M. Ribaudo. GreatSPN 1.7: GRaphical Editor and Analyzer for Timed and Stochastic Petri Nets. *in Performance Evaluation, vol. 24, no.1-2, Nov. 1995*, 1995. 47-68. http://www.di.unito.it/ greatspn/
4. R.M.L.R. Carmo, L.R. de Carvalho, E. de Souza e Silva, M.C. Diniz and R.R. Muntz. Performance/availability modeling with the Tangram-II modeling environment. Performance Evaluation 33 (1998), 45–46.
5. D. Deavours and W. Sanders, Möbius: Framework and Atomic Models. In Proc. 9th International Workshop on Petri Nets and Performance Models, Aachen, Germany, September 2001
6. G. Franceschinis, C. Bertoncello, G. Bruno, G. Lungo Vaschetti and A. Pigozzi SWN models of a contact center: a case study In Proc. 9th International Workshop on Petri Nets and Performance Models, Aachen, Germany, September 2001
7. M. Gribaudo, A. Valente. Framework for Graph-based Formalisms. In *Proceeding of the first International Conference on Software Engineering Applied to Networking and Parallel Distributed Computing 2000, SNPD'00*, pages 233-236 Reims, France, May 2000, ACIS.
8. W.H. Sanders. Integrated frameworks for multi-level and multi-formalism modeling. *Proceedings of the 8th International Workshop on Petri Nets and Performance Models, 1999*, 1999. 2-9.

A Visual Formalism for the Composition of Stochastic Petri Nets

Richard Hopkins and Peter King

Dept. Computing and Electrical Engineering, Heriot Watt University
{rph,pjbk}@cee.hw.ac.uk

Abstract. We introduce a graphically based formalism for parallel system designs, covering both functional and stochastic behaviour. This paper focuses on the combination in one formalism of characteristics of two major approaches to formalisms for concurrent systems, namely Process Algebras and Petri Nets. We define a general form of composition on nets with stochastic delays for transitions. This incorporates place and transition fusion. Then, following the general method of CCS, we define inference rules for deriving the behaviour of a composed net from the behaviour of its components. We give a number of examples to illustrate this synthesis of Petri Nets and Process Algebras.

1 Introduction

This paper introduces an initial version of STOCON — Stochastic Composable Nets — which provides a graphically based formalism for parallel system designs, covering both functional and stochastic behaviour. The goal of this version is to provide a synthesis of two major approaches to the representation and analysis of concurrent systems, namely Process Algebras and Petri Nets.

1.1 Process Algebras

A Process Algebra (PA) (e.g. CCS), provides: A small number of general composition operators by which a larger system can be built up from its components; A representation of behaviour that abstracts from details of internal operation; A form of compositional reasoning, behavioural inference, whereby the abstract behaviour of a composed system is derived from that of its components, and thus properties of the overall system can be derived from, or verified via, independently-established properties of individual components. Originally PAs dealt with only functional properties of systems, that is, a system either can or cannot exhibit a particular behaviour, whereas more recently stochastic PAs, such as PEPA[9], TIPP[8] or sPBC[12], have been developed to deal also with the probabilistic and timing aspects of the behaviours that a system exhibits.

T. Field et al. (Eds.): TOOLS 2002, LNCS 2324, pp. 239–258, 2002.

1.2 Petri Nets

A Petri Net (PN) is a graph consisting of places representing local state and transitions representing local change. The behaviour model is tokens residing on places and being moved by the firing of transitions. Compared with PAs, the benefits of PNs include the following.

Expressivity. There is a graphical, rather than textual, representation of the system design which makes it more intuitive and easier to work with (assuming tool support), allows great freedom in the expression of system structure, and is arguably more appropriate as a semantic model for graphical system design notations. The basic framework of places, transitions, arcs and tokens supports a variety of expressivity elaborations in which various kinds of information can be associated with these elements. Of particular relevance here are various forms of stochastic PNs[1,14] in which a net is annotated with timing and possibly probability information, and high-level nets [7,11] in which tokens carry values.

Structural Analysis. There is an explicit representation of local state and a separation between static system structure of places and transitions vs. dynamic system behaviour of token flow (whereas in a PA the changing state of the system is the evolution into different structures of the expression representing it). For PAs, analysis is generally over all possible system behaviours, with the inherent danger of exponential explosion as system size increases. In contrast, for PNs the static structure and explicit local state allows analysis techniques (particularly state invariants) based on system structure, and thus greater system size before intractability sets in.

There are two broad approaches to compositionality of PNs —

The "native" approach, exemplified by Hierarchic Coloured Petri Nets [11], where the composition structures are developed from the PN perspective and comprise some combination of element (place or transition) refinement where an element in an outer net is itself a sub-net, and element fusion where elements appearing in a number of nets are declared to be actually the same element. In these approaches the behavioural inference of PAs is absent. The compositional reasoning is based on native PN structural analysis techniques.

The PA approach, e.g. [16], involving the definition of PA-like composition operators on nets, often in the form of giving a net semantics for a pre-existing PA. The net composition structures provide transition refinement and place and transition fusion, but only as required to support specific PA compositions rather than with the generality of the native PN approaches. The PA approach to PN composition has the compositionality benefits of PAs, but misses out on many of the benefits of PNs themselves.

1.3 STOCON Contributions and Structure of the Paper

Our aim is to obtain a synthesis of the PA and PN approaches which is more thorough than has previously been achieved. Currently this synthesis is:

(i) (Section 2) Providing a form of composition which incorporates transition/place refinement/fusion with the generality of a native PN approach, whilst also supporting PA-like composition operators;

(ii) (Section 3) Applying to PN composition the CCS approach of abstract behavioural model (LTS) and behavioural inference rules.

We thus have the basis for the compositional reasoning of PAs, although we have not yet determined how well that works in practice, and we have not yet addressed compositionality of net structural analysis in this framework. Also we have so far restricted ourselves to fundamentals of PN structure, without features such as priorities, marking-dependent weights or inhibitor arcs. We have incorporated stochastic characteristics of system behaviour through delays on transitions (currently restricted to exponential, immediate and passive), but not yet probabilistic choice. In this paper our concern is composition structure rather than e.g. stochastic analysis.

Most of the remainder of the paper is devoted to further examples, to:

(i) (section 4) Exhibit structures which are natural to express using PNs but are not convenient to express using PA compositions.

(ii) (Section 5) Show how standard PA compositions are expressible in the STOCON framework.

(iii) (Section 6) Show an example which cannot be achieved in any existing PN or PA approach known to the authors, as a basis for discussion of the relationship between STOCON and other approaches.

Finally in Section 7 we discuss future development of STOCON, including its potential as a basis for combining different formalisms within one tool framework and in this regard the difference of approach here from that in Möbius[4].

2 Multi-level Nets

The basis for STOCON nets is Place-Transition nets [15], that is: a net structure comprises places, transitions, weighted arcs from places to transitions and vice-versa, a capacity for each place (ignored in this presentation); a net marking comprises zero or more tokens on each place. There are enhancements to this basis to incorporate: (i) compositionality; (ii) stochastic delays. We will illustrate the main ideas using Fig. 1 and 2, and then give the formal definitions.

2.1 Compositionality Elements

In Fig. 1, (c) shows a multi-level net, an m-net — an outer net with two boxes, called "holons" (meaning elements of a hierarchy) each of which contains an inner m-net. This is derived by refinement of M in (a) by M' in (b). The result (c) can be "flattened" to give the holon-free m-net of (d). Flattening is of theoretic importance in relating m-nets back to standard PNs.

Overall the example is the composition (in sequence) of two copies of the same basic queue represented by M'. Place p holds one token for each queued item. Transition t receives new items into the queue. It can fire, in synchronisation with some external transition, to place a token on p (with a concurrent firing rule, there could be multiple concurrent firings of this transition). Transition u removes items from the queue. Provided there is a token on both places, it can

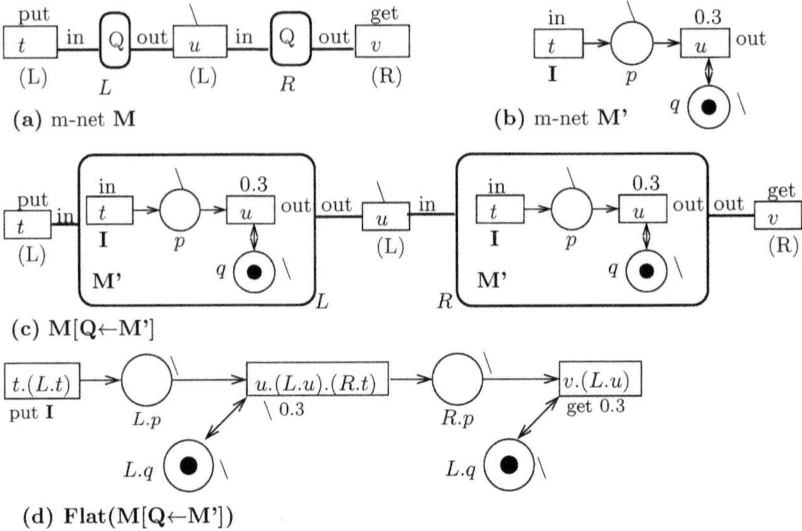

Fig. 1. A Composition using Transition Fusion

fire, in synchronisation with some external transition, to remove a token from p. Place q enforces sequentiality of firings of u; it represents a resource (e.g. a processor) which is required for u to fire but is not consumed by the firing. The m-net of (d) is the flattened composition in which there are now two places to hold queued items, with the middle transition transferring elements from one to the other.

The compositionality enhancements are: holons as well as places and transitions; labels on transitions and places; labelled associations between a place and some holons which define fusions of that place with places from the associated holons; similarly, labelled transition-holon associations for transition fusions. In figures italics are used for the (arbitrary, unique) names of elements, e.g. L, t, p, to distinguish them from other information, such as (non-unique) labels.

A holon, e.g. L in (a) and (c), is a sub-structuring element which can be bound either to a net variable, L bound to Q in (a), or to an inner m-net, L bound to M' in (c). The refinement operation, $M[Q \leftarrow M']$, has the effect that every holon that was bound to variable Q is now bound to a copy of m-net M'.

A transition has a label, e.g. *put*, *get* or $\backslash$ in (a)/(c). Also a transition-holon association has a label, e.g. in (c) u has an *out* association with L and *in* association with R. The meaning is that firing of u must synchronise with firing of an *out*-labelled transition in L and firing of an *in*-labelled transition in R. In this case the only candidates are u from L and t from R. The effect can be seen in (d) where the required synchronisation becomes one fusion transition $u.(L.u).(R.t)$. That name indicates its derivation from: outer m-net u; u from L; t from R. The label is inherited from the outer m-net transition. This label is $\backslash$, for an "private" transition (corresponding to a silent, τ, action of CCS) which fires independently of external transitions, and in further compositions cannot form part of transition fusions.

Generally in the flattening: all \-labelled transitions from inner m-nets are carried forward unchanged to the result m-net; a transition in the outer m-net generates in the result m-net one fusion transition for every combination of the appropriately-labelled transitions of the inner m-nets for the holons with which it has association arcs. The fusion transition inherits the connectivity of all the original transitions. (In the general case this involves an "arc sum", see formal definition and Fig. 3.)

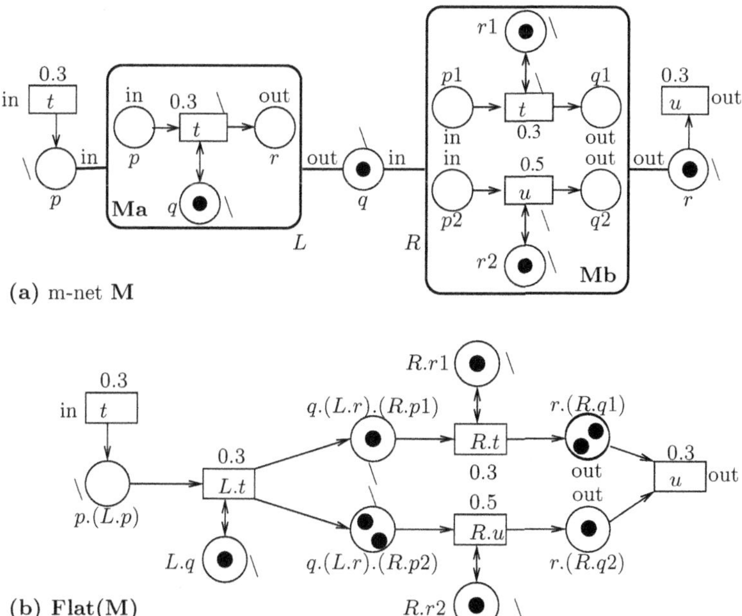

Fig. 2. A Composition using Place Fusion

There is an exactly analogous structure for places, illustrated in Fig. 2 where (b) is the flattening of multi-level m-net (a), with the additional considerations that the marking of a fusion place is the sum of the markings of the places from which it is derived.

This example is again a sequential composition of components. The overall construct, (a) or (b), has the same interface, *in*- and *out*- labelled transitions, as the M' component in Fig. 1, and so could be used in its place. The differences in the internal structure here are: (i) the components are accessed via places —

the outer m-net achieves the composition by identifying *out*-labelled places of the L component with *in*-labelled places of the R component; (ii) the second component has parallel processing — putting a token on outer m-net place q has the effect of putting a token on both places $p1$ and $p2$ of Mb (which in (b) manifest as fusion places $q.(L.r).(R.p1)$ and $q.(L.r).(R.p2)$), so that different aspects of the processing of that item are carried out in parallel.

The example of Fig. 1 corresponds to place refinement — both L and R are structurally place-like in being connected just to transitions, and the composition mechanism is transition fusion. Conversely, the example of Fig. 2 corresponds to transition refinement. Later, e.g. Fig. 3, there are examples where one holon is connected to both places and transitions and therefore is neither pure place refinement nor pure transition refinement. Our nets are unusual in that we require no structural restrictions (note e.g. absence of input places for t of Fig. 1(b)) and allow infinite markings.

2.2 Stochastic Elements

The stochastic information in a m-net consists of an annotation on each transition. This can be a basic stochastic delay, r, which is the rate parameter for an exponential distribution, with $\mathbf{I}$ as infinite rate for an immediate transition, and $\mathbf{0}$ as indefinite rate for a passive transition. Also it can be an expression for deriving a fusion transition's rate from the rates for its constituent. In Fig. 1(a) transition u has annotation (L) denoting the rate from the transition from L. Thus in (d) the resulting transition has annotation 0.3 which is the same as that for u within L in (c). We could also have used say $min(L, R)$, giving the same result since the rate from R is infinite.

2.3 Definition of Structural Aspects of M-Nets

Preliminaries. $\mathbf{I}$ $(= 1/0)$ represents infinity, and $\mathbf{0}$ a null element. $\Re^{\mathbf{0}}_{\mathbf{I}}$ is the positive reals enhanced with $\{\mathbf{I}, \mathbf{0}\}$. $\mathcal{N}$ is the non-negative integers.
$\mathcal{M}^{\mathbf{I}}(D) : D \to \mathcal{N} \cup \{\mathbf{I}\}$ and $\mathcal{M}(D)$:$D \to \mathcal{N}$ are the multi-sets on D with and without the possibility of infinite element occurrences.
$\mathcal{L}$ is the set of labels excluding $\backslash$. $\mathcal{V}$ is the set of net variables.
$\mathcal{S}^H$ is the set of (stochastic) expression involving constants from $\Re^{\mathbf{0}}_{\mathbf{I}}$, variables from H, and operators $. + .$, $min(.,.)$, $max(.,.)$, $. \cdot .$ (product) and $1/.$ (reciprocal), with the restrictions that: an expression cannot evaluate to 0; variable-free expressions are constants, i.e. $\mathcal{S}^{\emptyset} = \Re^{\mathbf{0}}_{\mathbf{I}}$.
For $E \in \mathcal{S}^H$ and $sub : H \to \Re^{\mathbf{0}}_{\mathbf{I}}$, we define $E[sub] \stackrel{def}{=} r \in \Re^{\mathbf{0}}_{\mathbf{I}}$ where r is the evaluation of E under the variable substitution given by sub, with $\mathbf{0}$ acting as a unit of all dyadic operators and with $1/\mathbf{0} = \mathbf{0}$.

Net structure. A net N is a structure $N = (P, T, H, \overline{F}, \underline{F}, L, A, S)$. ($P$, T, $\overline{F}$ and $\underline{F}$ constitute a Place/Transition net structure).

P, T, H are mutually disjoint finite sets of place, transition and holon names.

$\overline{F}$, $\underline{F}$: $T \to \mathcal{M}(P)$. $\overline{F}(t)$ is the input marking for t. E.g. for u in L of Fig. 3, $\overline{F}(u) = \{p1, q, q\}$. We can use this as $\overline{F} : T \times P \to \mathcal{N}$. Likewise $\underline{F}(t)$ for the output marking.

L: $P \cup T \to \mathcal{L} \cup \{\backslash\}$ is the place/transition labelling.

A: $(P \cup T) \times H \to \mathcal{L} \cup \{\mathbf{0}\}$. $A(x, h)$ is the label of the association between place or transition x and holon h, if there is one, and otherwise $\mathbf{0}$.

S: $T \to \mathcal{S}^H$. This gives the stochastic annotations, subject to the restriction that $S(t) \in \mathcal{S}^{\{h|A(t,h)\neq\mathbf{0}\}}$, i.e. the variables in a transition's annotation are restricted to the names of its associated holons.

We define component selectors: $N^P = P$, $N^T = T$ etc.

For a net N and a holon $h \in N^H$ we define the net interface and holon interface as the non-\ labels on the net's places and the holon's associations:

$$NI(N) \stackrel{def}{=} \{l \in \mathcal{L} | \exists p \in N^P : N^L(p) = l\};$$
$$HI(N, h) \stackrel{def}{=} \{l \in \mathcal{L} | \exists p \in N^P : N^A(p, h) = l\}.$$

M-nets. We can inductively define a domain of *MNets*, such that for N being a net structure, $B : N^H \to MNets \cup \mathcal{V}$ being a holon binding, and $\sigma \in \mathcal{M}^{\mathbf{I}}(N^P)$ being a marking for its places, also in *MNets* is $M = N(B; \sigma)$, subject to two restriction:

(i) If $B(h) = M' = (N', \ldots) \in MNets$ then $NI(N') = HI(N, h)$ (Interface matching).

(ii) $NFL_N(\sigma)$ where $NFL_N(\sigma) \stackrel{def}{=} \forall l \in NI(N) : \exists p : \sigma(p) = 0 \wedge N^L(p) = l$, that is the "No Full Label" condition that at least one of the places with a particular interface label has no tokens, e.g. in Fig. 2(a) there cannot be a token on r of L, nor on both *p1* and *p2* - tokens are kept at the outermost possible level (in a notional environment for a top-level m-net).

Refinement. For $M = N(B; \sigma)$ and $R : \mathcal{V}' \to MNets$ with $\mathcal{V}' \subseteq \mathcal{V}$:
$M[R] \stackrel{def}{=} M' = N(B'; \sigma)$ where:
if $B(h) \in \mathcal{V}'$ then $B'(h) = R(B(h))$ provided $NI(R(B(h)) = HI(N, h)$;
if $B(h) \in MNets$ then $B'(h) = B(h)[R]$ provided that is defined
(i.e. that the previous condition is recursively satisfied);
if $B(h) \in \mathcal{V} - \mathcal{V}'$ then $B'(h) = B(h)$.

M-net Flattening. For (relative) simplicity here we will only consider fully-refined 1-level m-nets, i.e. an m-net $M_0 = (N_0, P_0, \ldots)(B_0; \sigma_0)$ such that taking $H_0 = \{h_1, \ldots, h_n\}$ we have for $i \in \{1, \ldots, n\}$:

$$MNets \ni B(h_i) = M_i = (P_i, T_i, \emptyset, \overline{F}_i, \underline{F}_i, L_i, \emptyset, S_i)(\emptyset; \sigma_i).$$

Without loss of generality we can assume disjointness of all the net structures involved, i.e. for $i, j \in \{0, \ldots, n\}$, $i \neq j$, $(P_i \cup T_i) \cap (P_j \cup T_j) = \emptyset$, and so for a place/transition x we define its origin's index $I(x)$ such that $x \in P_{I(x)} \cup T_{I(x)}$.

The flattening of M_0, $Flat(M_0) \stackrel{def}{=} M' = (P', T', \emptyset, \overline{F}', \underline{F}', L', \emptyset, S')(\emptyset, \sigma')$ is constructed as follows, where an element of M' is a, possibly singleton, set of original elements:

$P' \stackrel{def}{=}$ Union of:
(i) promoted internal places, $\{\{p\} \mid p \in P_1 \cup \ldots \cup P_n \ \wedge \ L_{I(p)}(p) = \backslash\}$;
(ii) fusion places: the set of all minimal $\{p, p_1, \ldots, p_m\}$ such that $p \in P_0$ and with $\{h_{k_1}, \ldots, h_{k_m}\} = \{h \in H_0 | A_0(p, h) \neq \mathbf{0}\}$, for $i = 1 \ldots m : p_i \in P_{k_i} \ \wedge \ L_{k_i}(p_i) = A_0(p, h_{k_i})$.

$T' \stackrel{def}{=}$ Exactly analogous to definition of P.
$\overline{F}' \stackrel{def}{=}$ such that $\overline{F}'(tt, pp) = \sum_{t \in tt, p \in pp} w(t, p)$ where if $I(t) = I(p) = i$ then $w(t, p) = \overline{F}_i(t, p)$, otherwise $w(t, p) = 0$. (The arc-sum construction.)
$\underline{F}' \stackrel{def}{=}$ Exactly analogous to definition of $\overline{F}'$.
$L' \stackrel{def}{=}$ such that: $L'(\{x\}) = L_{I(x)}$; for $I(x) = 0$, $L'(\{x, \ldots\}) = L_0(x)$.
$S' \stackrel{def}{=}$ such that: $S'(\{t\}) = S_{I(t)}$; for $I(t) = 0$, $S'(\{t, t_1, \ldots, t_m\}) = S_0(t)[sub]$ where for $i = 1 \ldots m : sub(h_{I(t_i)}) = S_{I(t_i)}(t_i)$.
$\sigma' \stackrel{def}{=}$ such that $\sigma'(pp) = \sum_{p \in pp} \sigma_{I(p)}(p)$.

3 Behavioural Aspects of M-Nets

3.1 Behavioural Model

Our model of behaviour is a structure corresponding to a PN reachability graph, or a PA labelled (state-)transition system (LTS). That is, a set of states, each of which will be an m-net, and Transitions as arcs directed from pre-state to post-state, with the arc being decorated with information about the Transition. We use "Transition" to refer to an LTS global state change, as opposed to "transition" for a net element.

A Transition from state M to M' is $M \stackrel{[\overline{\lambda}_1, \ldots, \overline{\lambda}_n | l, r | \underline{\lambda}_1, \ldots, \underline{\lambda}_m]}{\longrightarrow}_{tag} M'$. Here, in the Transition decoration: $l \in \mathcal{L}$ is the Transition's label; $r \in \Re^0_{\mathbf{I}}$ is the Transition's rate; $\overline{\lambda} = \{\overline{\lambda}_1, \ldots, \overline{\lambda}_n\}$, $\underline{\lambda} = \{\underline{\lambda}_1, \ldots, \underline{\lambda}_m\} \in \mathcal{M}(\mathcal{L})$ are "import" and "export" multi-sets of place labels; *tag* (which will be ignored in examples) identifies the underlying transition, this being necessary for cases such as $M \stackrel{[\overline{\lambda}|l,r|\underline{\lambda}]}{\longrightarrow}_{t1} M'$ and $M \stackrel{[\overline{\lambda}|l,r|\underline{\lambda}]}{\longrightarrow}_{t2} M'$ in order to obtain, for stochastic analysis, the true rate from M to M' being $2 \cdot r$.

The l, r parts of the decoration follow the usual form in defining transition systems for stochastic PAs. The additional elements here are the $\overline{\lambda}$ and $\underline{\lambda}$. These place labels (which we will also refer to as label-tokens) are dual to the transition label l. As in any LTS, the label l associated with a Transition, T, means that (in some environment) T provides l for the synchronisation requirements of the environment, and requires a matching label from the environment, i.e. in PN terms the l specifies the <u>transition</u> interaction with the environment. Analogously

$\overline{\lambda}$ and $\underline{\lambda}$ specify the place interaction with the environment. In order for T to occur the environment must hold tokens corresponding to $\overline{\lambda}$, and these are imported; having occurred T produces tokens corresponding to $\underline{\lambda}$, and these are exported to the environment.

For $M \stackrel{[l|\ldots|l']}{\longrightarrow} M'$ the (single label-token) l means one token for every l-labelled place of M, which, for M bound to holon h of environment net N, corresponds to one token on every place in N which has an l-labelled association with h (and similarly for l'); this extends to multi-sets of label tokens by taking multi-set sum over the places corresponding to the labels.

3.2 Example of Behaviour Inference

We will illustrate this notation by an example of behaviour inference shown in Fig. 3, referring to inference rules defined below. Henceforth we take the default label as \, and the default stochastic annotation as h if the transition has one holon associate, h, and **I** otherwise.

The top layer of Fig. 3 shows m-net *M1* as a composition of *Ma1* and *Mb1*, and its flattening, *Flat*(*M1*). From this we show (by dotted arcs) three Transitions to the second layer: A transition of the composed m-net, $M1 \stackrel{[|\backslash,\mathbf{I}|]}{\longrightarrow} M2$; the Transition of the component, L, from which that is inferred, $Ma1 \stackrel{[in|\backslash,\mathbf{I}|]}{\longrightarrow} Ma2$; the corresponding transition for the flattened m-net, $Flat(M1) \stackrel{[|\backslash,\mathbf{I}|]}{\longrightarrow} Flat(M2)$, which necessarily matches that for $M1 \stackrel{[\ldots]}{\longrightarrow} M2$. In each case we also indicate the transition, for the outer, inner, or flattened m-net, which fires in that Transition, if any. In understanding the Transitions for the structured m-nets it may be help to follow the corresponding Transitions for the flattened m-net, using the normal PN firing rule (a special case of Rule 3).

The leftmost Transition, $Ma1 \stackrel{[in|\backslash,\mathbf{I}|]}{\longrightarrow} Ma2$, corresponds to the firing of transition v (Rule 3). The firing of v requires a token on *p2*. Because *p2* has label *in*, this requires importing an *in* label-token from the environment, which provides a token for both *p1* and *p2* (all the *in*-labelled places). One of these is used in the firing and the other remains in the post-state *Ma2*. In the rest of this Transition decoration, the \ and **I** are taken from the fired transition; no tokens are exported.

This is for a private Transition (label \) which means that there are no transition synchronisation requirements — it can occur as a Transition of the outer m-net provided the outer m-net provides the tokens that it imports (Rule 2). In this case the requirement is for one token on every *in*-labelled place of the inner m-net; that maps into one token on every place of the outer m-net which has an *in*-labelled association with the appropriate holon (here L). The token on place r meets that requirement, and so in the outer Transition, $M1 \stackrel{[|\backslash,\mathbf{I}|]}{\longrightarrow} M2$, it is imported into the inner m-net. Note that in the outer Transition's post-state (*M2*) we use the post-state(s) from the inner Transitions from which it is inferred — the *Ma1* of *M1* has become *Ma2*. The movement of tokens between

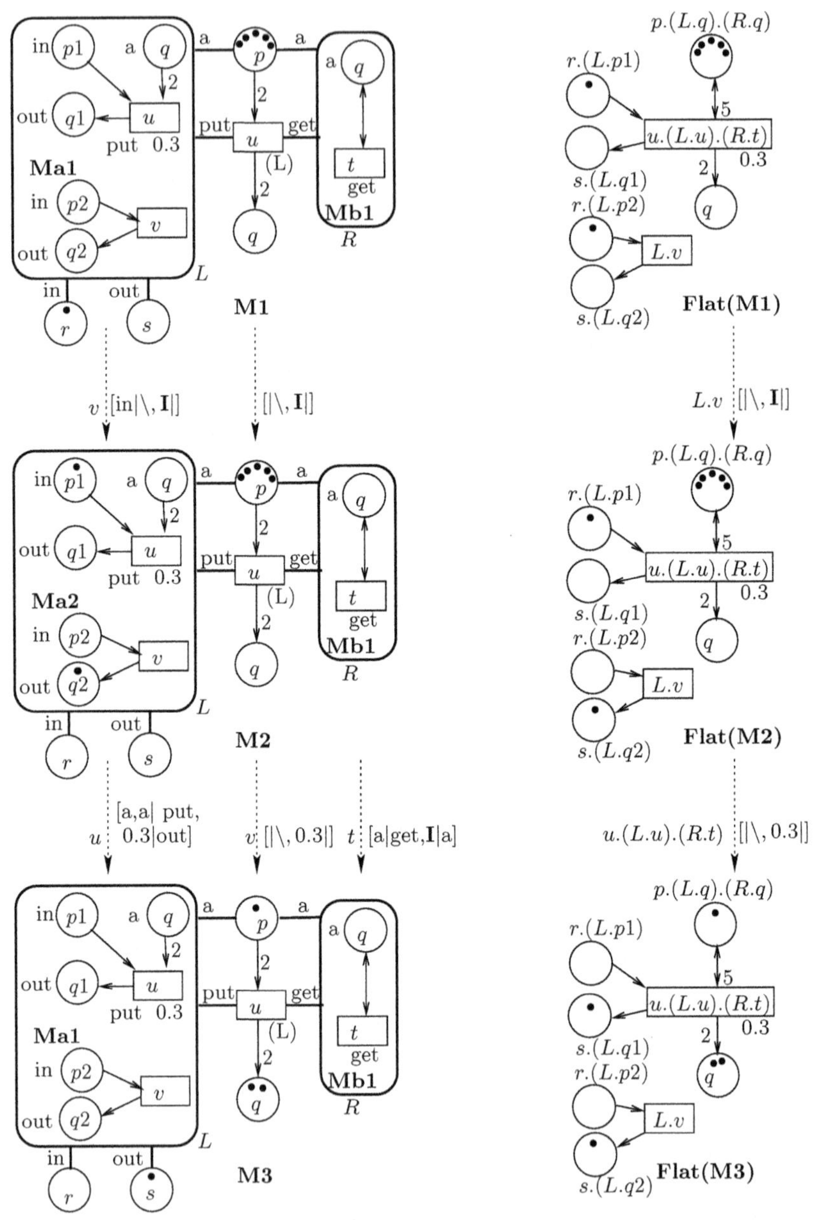

Fig. 3. Examples of Behaviour Inference

inner and outer m-nets is multi-level. If the place r were labelled *input* and was un-marked, then the outer Transition produced for this example would be $M1 \xrightarrow{[input|\backslash,\mathbf{I}|]} M2$ — importing of an *in* label-token by *Mb1* requiring importing of an *input* label-token by *M1*.

The next stage, $M2 \xrightarrow{[\ldots]} M3$ etc., shows the synchronisation of inner m-net transitions which is achieved by transition fusions, and gives a more general example of token movement between levels (all these transitions are examples of Rule 3). The outer Transition $M2 \xrightarrow{[|\backslash,0.3|]} M3$ is the firing of transition u of the outer m-net. Due to the associations of this transition with holons L and R, this requires (is a synchronisation of) a firing of a *put*-labelled Transition from L, provided by the $Ma2 \xrightarrow{[a,a|put,0.3|out]} Ma1$, with a firing of an *get*-labelled Transition from R, provided by the $Mb1 \xrightarrow{[a|get,\mathbf{I}|a]} Mb1$. In the former of these, the firing of u in *Ma2*, the weight 2 on the arc from q to u means that two a label-tokens are imported. Its firing results in nominal marking $\{q1, q2\}$ which is one token on every *out*-labelled place, so the Transition exports these as one *out* label token, leaving no tokens for *Ma3* and a token on s of *M3*.

The firing of the outer Transition requires 5 tokens on place p. The $\{a, a\}$ requirement of the inner Transition for *Ma2* maps onto 2 tokens on p; the $\{a\}$ requirement from *Mb1* maps onto one token on p; the ordinary firing of the outer transition u requires 2 tokens on p. The effect of the Transition is to remove those 5 tokens from p, and produce: 1 on p, provided by the Transition for *Mb1*; 2 on q, by the ordinary firing of outer transition u.

3.3 The Inference Rules

We take $N = (P, T, \ldots)$, with a holon ordering $H = \{h_1, \ldots h_n\}$, and write an an m-net (expression) as $M = N(B(h_1), \ldots B(h_n); \sigma)$. We will consider Transitions from $M = N(M_1, \ldots, M_n; \sigma)$ to $M' = N(M'_1, \ldots, M'_n; \sigma')$, provided $M_i \in MNets$ (i.e. only fully-refined m-nets). We define $I = \{1, \ldots, n\}$ and employ the constructs *IM* (In Map) and *OM* (Out Map) —

$IM : H \times \mathcal{M}(\mathcal{L}) \to \mathcal{M}(P)$. $IM(h, \lambda) \stackrel{def}{=} \sigma$ where: if $A(p, h) = l \neq \mathbf{0}$ then $\sigma(p) = \lambda(l)$; otherwise $\sigma(p) = 0$. This gives the place marking σ corresponding to the label-tokens λ imported/exported by the h component.

$OM : \mathcal{M}(\mathcal{L}) \to \mathcal{M}(P)$. $OM(\lambda) \stackrel{def}{=} \sigma$ where if $L(p) \neq \backslash$ then $\sigma(p) = \lambda(l)$, and otherwise $\sigma(p) = 0$. This gives the place marking σ corresponding to the label-tokens λ imported/exported from/to the environment.

Rule 1 — Universal Null Transition (to simplify rule 3)

$$M \xrightarrow{[|\mathbf{0},\mathbf{I}|]}_{\mathbf{0}} M$$

Rule 2 — Promotion of Private Transitions (for M_l, $l \in I$)

$$\text{From} \qquad M_l \overset{[\overline{\lambda}_l|\backslash,r|\underline{\lambda}_l]}{\longrightarrow}_{t_l} M_l'$$

$$\text{Infer} \quad N(M_1,\ldots,M_l,\ldots,M_n;\,\sigma) \overset{[\overline{\lambda}|\backslash,r|\underline{\lambda}]}{\longrightarrow}_{l.t_l} N(M_1,\ldots,M_l',\ldots,M_n;\,\sigma')$$

where $\sigma' = \sigma + OM(\overline{\lambda}) - IM(h_l,\overline{\lambda}_l) + IM(h_l,\underline{\lambda}_l) - OM(\underline{\lambda})$

provided $\sigma + OM(\overline{\lambda}) \geq IM(h_l,\overline{\lambda}_l)$

and $NFL_N(\sigma')$, $NFL_N(\sigma + OM(\overline{\lambda}) - IM(h_l,\overline{\lambda}_l))$
to ensure $\underline{\lambda}$ is maximal and $\overline{\lambda}$ is minimal.

Rule 3 — (Synchronisation via) Outer m-net transition (for $t \in T$)

$$\text{From} \quad \forall i \in I: \quad M_i \overset{[\overline{\lambda}_i|A(t,h_i),r_i|\underline{\lambda}_i]}{\longrightarrow}_{t_i} M_i'$$

$$\text{Infer} \quad N(M_1,\ldots,M_n;\sigma) \overset{[\overline{\lambda}|L(t),r|\underline{\lambda}]}{\longrightarrow}_{(t,1.t_1,\ldots,n.t_n)} N(M_1',\ldots,M_n';\sigma')$$

where $r = S(t)[sub]$, where $\forall i \in I: sub(h_i) = r_i$

$$\sigma' = \sigma + OM(\overline{\lambda}) - \textstyle\sum_{i\in I} IM(h_i,\overline{\lambda}_i) - \overline{F}(t) + \sum_{i\in I} IM(h_i,\underline{\lambda}_i) + \underline{F}(t) - OM(\underline{\lambda})$$

provided $\sigma + OM(\overline{\lambda}) \geq \sum_{i\in I} IM(h_i,\overline{\lambda}_i) + \overline{F}(t)$

and $NFL_N(\sigma')$, $NFL_N(\sigma + OM(\overline{\lambda}) - \sum_{i\in I} IM(h_i,\overline{\lambda}_i) - \overline{F}(t))$

The LTS produced for an m-net can provide the basis for stochastic analysis, by eliminating everything in the Transition decorations apart from the rates. We can interface with other formalisms. For example if a component is defined via an appropriate stochastic PA it will generate an LTS with decorations of form $[l,r]$. Enhancing those to $[|l,r|]$ allows the behaviour of that component to be used as that for a notional m-net in a higher-level m-net structure.

4 State Dependence in Queue/Server Networks

In this section we give further examples, building on the basic queue structure of Fig. 1, which illustrate ways in which place labelling can be used to achieve the behaviour of a component being dependent on state elsewhere in the system. In all cases the basic component interface is, as for the component m-nets of Fig. 1(a), an *in*-labelled transition by which a task or queue item is provided, and an *out*-labelled transition by which it is removed.

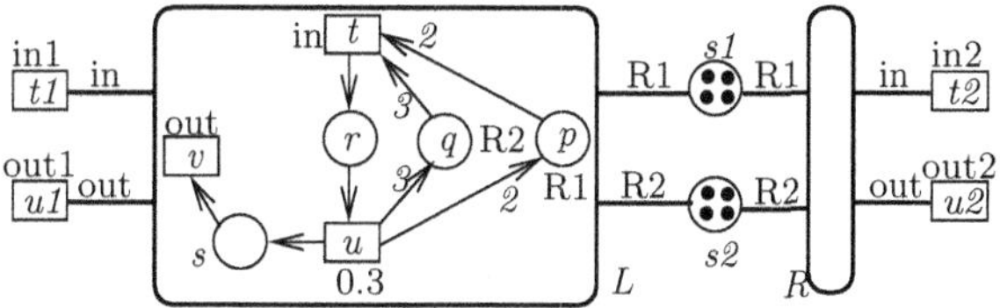

Fig. 4. Multiple Multi-instanced Shared Resource Dependence

4.1 Multiple Shared Resources

Fig. 4 shows a structure of two components, both of which make use of shared multi-instanced resources *R1* and *R2*. In the outer m-net, the number of tokens on place *s1* is the number of instances of resource *R1* available, and likewise *s2* for *R2*. The m-net for holon *L* represents a service that requires two instances of *R1* and three instances of *R2*. Its transition *t* to receive a task cannot fire unless those resources are available and it keeps them unavailable until the completion of the actual processing represented by the timed transition *u*. That task is then represented by a token on place *s* which enables a firing of the *v* transition, for the removal of that task to the environment. The outer m-net provides an interface to two such services (which compete for those resources), with access to the service in *L* being by labels *in1* and *out1*, and to that for *R* being by labels *in2* and *out2*. This is a case where there might be infinite marking for *s1* and/or *s2* to remove resource limitations.

One of the behaviours of component *L* is firing sequence *t*, *u*, *v* giving Transitions . $\stackrel{[2\cdot R1,3\cdot R2|in,\mathbf{I}|]}{\longrightarrow}$. $\stackrel{[|\backslash,0.3|2\cdot R1,3\cdot R2]}{\longrightarrow}$. $\stackrel{[|out,\mathbf{I}|]}{\longrightarrow}$. (with "." for anonymous states). This shows (in terms of abstract labels rather than concrete transitions and places) the dependency on resource availability and the sequencing of resource acquisition and release — the *R1* and *R2* resources are acquired in the same Transition as the *in* action, and so the task is not accepted unless the required resources are available; whereas those resources are released prior to the *out* action and so the resource release is not dependent on the environment being ready to accept the end of the task.

4.2 Switch Setting

Fig. 5 shows a structure in which there are two alternative versions of a service, *L* and *R*, controlled by a switch. If the environment has the switch *on* there will be a token available for place *p*, enabling the firing of *t1* and thus the use of *L*; and conversely for *off*, *t2* and *R*. The outer net provides, in addition to the *in/out* interface, a *flip* interface which changes the setting of the switch. Note that, unlike the *R1* and *R2* of the previous example, the *on* and *of* are not acquired resources because (within the inner net) they are used as side conditions, i.e. they are imported and exported in the same Transition, e.g. $\stackrel{[off|in,\mathbf{I}|off]}{\longrightarrow}$ for a firing of *t2*.

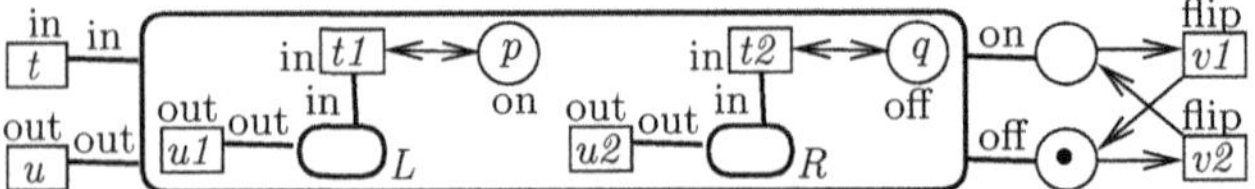

Fig. 5. Switch Setting

4.3 Queue Length Dependence

Fig. 6 shows a way in which the routing of a task to different servers can be made dependent how many tasks are in internal queues for each. Here we have anticipated a high level net version of STOCON similar to Predicate/Transition nets [7]. A token can carry a value (e.g. value 1 for token on place *pl*). An arc between a place and a transition can be annotated with a variable (e.g.: a on arc p to v; b on arc v to p; a on arcs *pl* to *ul* and vice-versa). A transition can be annotated with an expression - in a potential firing of a transition the variable(s) on an arc are bound to the value(s) carried by the token(s) that move on that arc in the firing, and the potential firing can only be an actual firing if with that binding the expression evaluates to *TRUE*. For example, the annotation $b = a + 1$ on transition v has the effect that it adds 1 to some token on p.

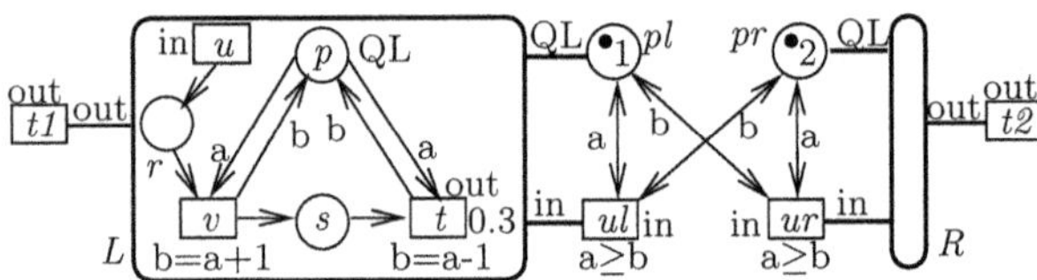

Fig. 6. Queue Length Dependence - High-Level Net Version

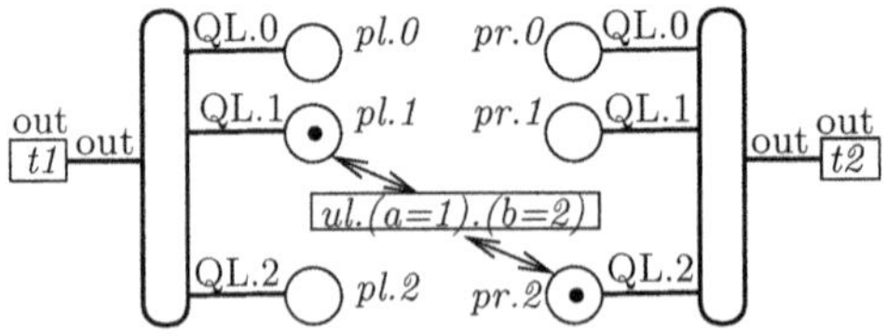

Fig. 7. Queue Length Dependence - Unfolded Version

For our purposes here a high level m-net can be viewed as just an abbreviation for a larger equivalent low level m-net which is obtained by "unfolding" it. Fig. 7 shows part of the unfolding of the outer m-net in Fig. 6. Assuming a token on place *pl* or *pr* can have values in $\{0, 1, 2\}$, the place *pl* unfolds to the family of places $pl.0, \ldots, pl.2$ such that a token with value x on *pl* becomes a plain token on $pl.x$ and label QL for *pl* becomes $QL.x$ for $pl.x$; and similarly for *pr*. The transition *ul* unfolds to a family of transitions, of which only one, $ul.(a = 1).(b = 2)$, is shown. There is one such unfolded transition for every binding of values to variables which makes its expression *TRUE*. For this case the bindings are $a = 1$ and $b = 2$, and the arcs with high-level places in Fig. 6 have now become arcs with the appropriate low-level places in Fig. 7, as determined by that binding of variables.

In Fig. 6 the basic queue structure has been enhanced by a place labelled QL (Queue Length) to carry a token whose value is the number of items which have been received by v but not yet processed by t. This place is made visible in the external environment (and thus subject to abuse!) so that the outer m-net can make decisions based on that information. Here the outer m-net has two *in* interface transitions, namely : *ul* to synchronise with the *in* interface transition of L and thus route tasks to that server, which (by the $a \leq b$ annotation) it can only do if the Queue Length for L is no greater than that for R; and *ur* which conversely routes tasks to the server in R.

5 Process Algebra Compositions

Fig. 8 shows various PA operators translated into m-nets. Here labels are inside transitions/places and place/transition names are usually omitted. For transition labels we use a set of actions $\mathcal{A}$, with conjugation $\overline{a}$ as in CCS. We also introduce quantifications such as in (f) the $i : \mathcal{A}$ which means, $\forall i \in \mathcal{A}$: a copy of that transition and its immediate structure. There are only two place labels, E (entry) and X (exit). The initial marking is all (and only) E-labelled places marked and the final marking (if reached) is all (and only) X-labelled places marked. The behaviours we are interested in are those which start by importing an E label-token, and thereafter neither import nor export label-tokens until termination with the export of an X label-token which produces again the initial state - $M_0 \stackrel{[E|\alpha_0,r_0|]}{\longrightarrow} M_1 \stackrel{[|\alpha_1,r_1|]}{\longrightarrow} \ldots M_m \stackrel{[|\alpha_m,r_m|X]}{\longrightarrow} M_0$. This is seen most clearly in (a), the m-net for a basic action (r, a) where r is a rate and a is an action which becomes the transition's label.

Our use of entry places and exit places is standard in work defining PA-like compositions on nets. (Exit places are only needed if sequential composition or iteration is included). Common compositions are: choice (b) is fusion of entry places and fusion of exit places; sequential (h) is fusion of the first component's exit places with the second component's entry places; parallel, (c) and (d), keep independent entry and exit places for the components.

Non-standard is that the manipulation of transitions is achieved through explicit transitions in the outer m-net and their associations to holons for the components. This means we can express a variety of synchronisation styles, rather than having one style built-in to the net composition formalism. As exemplars

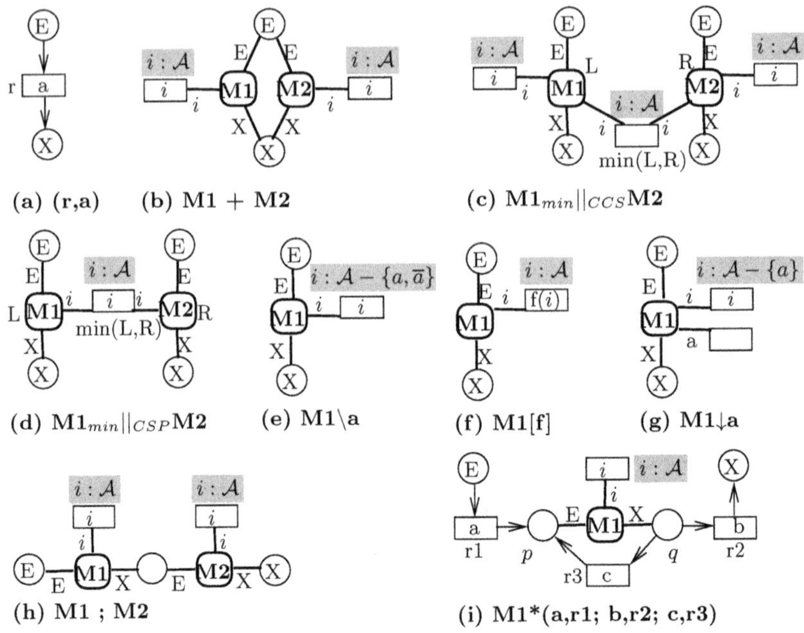

Fig. 8. M-net Semantics for some PA Operators

of this: (c) shows CCS style synchronisation with the rate for the resulting transition being the minimum of the rates for the original transitions; (d) similarly shows CSP style synchronisation. We also show CCS style restriction (e) and re-labelling (f), and CSP style hiding (g).

Recursion presents some difficulty for PN approaches, and we have not yet formulated recursively-defined m-nets. Instead we have included iteration (i). This is iteration of M with: start guard $(a, r1)$; end guard $(b, r2)$; repeat guard $(c, r3)$. In PA terms this is $(a, r1); rec(P = (\ M\ ;\ ((b, r2)\ +\ ((c, r3); P))\ ))$. The start and end guards are needed to obtain the expected behaviour when this construct is immediately within choice. The repeat guard is needed to obtain an expected net property (1-safeness) in some cases of M being a parallel composition.

One mode of reasoning about STOCON m-nets in general is to derive, from the outer m-net and general inference rules, specific inference rules for use with that composition for different sets of components (e.g. one set of components being "specifications" and other sets being different implementations). For example, for choice composition Fig. 8(c), with the above assumption about behaviours of interest, and a suitable definition of a behavioural equivalence $\approx$, we can derive the standard inference rule for choice composition —

$$\begin{array}{ll} \text{from} & M1 \stackrel{[e|l,r|]}{\longrightarrow} M1' \\ \text{infer } (M1 + M2) & \stackrel{[e|l,r|]}{\longrightarrow} (M1' + M2) \approx M1' \end{array}$$

6 Comparison with Other Composition Approaches

The two broad approaches to net composition are the native-style, as in e.g. hierarchic/modular nets [11,3], and the PA-style of PA-like composition operators on nets, as above and in e.g. [16,2,17]. For the latter we will first consider those based on single-action PAs (which includes CCS and CSP), that is where the labels/actions used have no sub-structure utilisable in synchronisation.

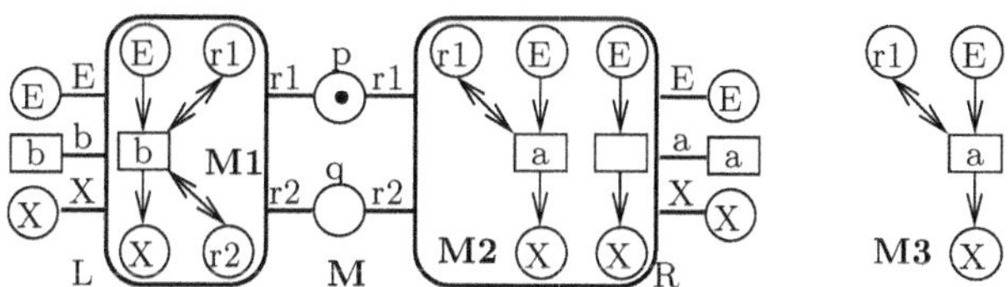

Fig. 9. Combination of PA-like Composition and Multiple Shared Resources

Fig. 9 shows an example which cannot be achieved as a "black-box" composition in either of these approaches. This example combines: the PA approach of Fig. 8, involving parallel composition on components with entry and exit places; the use of shared resources, *r1* and *r2* represented by places p and q, as in Fig. 4. For a true black-box compositionality we could substitute *M3* for *M2* (which has the same interface) without changing the formulation of the composition, as we can here for composition $N(M1, M2; p)$ becoming $N(M1, M3; p)$.

In native-style compositions the place fusions required for this composition are defined by identifying specific places to be fused, and, because the number of interface (to-be-fused) places in *M2* and *M3* is different, black-box substitutivity is not possible. In effect these approaches have an injective place/transition labelling which does not support PA-like compositions. This is particularly problematic for transition fusions to achieve synchronisation where there may be many candidate synchronising transitions within one component, perhaps coming from deep within its structure, and very different numbers thereof in different interchangeable component versions.

PA-style compositions of course have no difficulty with the substitutivity aspect of this example. The problem is with the shared resources represented here by places p and q. The only possible general approach is for each such place to be another component in parallel composition with *M1* and *M2*. Using CCS, p could be expressed as $R1_n = \sum_{l>0,0<m\leq n}(r1_l^+.R1_{n+l} + r1_m^-.R1_{n-m})$, where $R1_n$ is p with n tokens, and $r1_l^+$ and $r1_m^-$ are actions to add/remove l/m tokens. With a similar representation for q, the transition within *M1* would be translated

as say action sequence $\overline{r1_1^-}.\overline{r2_1^-}.b.\overline{r2_1^+}.\overline{r1_1^+}$, and that within *M2* as $\overline{r1_1^-}.a.\overline{r1_1^+}$. The difficulty of course is that this can lead to the classic deadlock situation with *M1* first having removed the token from p and then being unable to proceed, leaving *M2* unable to do its first action. That deadlock does not occur in the m-net behaviour. Any other compositional translation of this example encounters some such difficulty.

To deal effectively with this situation, a PA needs multi-actions. The two main multi-action PAs are CCS[13] and PBC[2]. In both, an action is a multi-set $\{a, b, \ldots\}$ of simultaneous independently-synchronisable sub-actions, accommodating this example by *M1*'s transition being $\{\overline{r1_1^-}, \overline{r2_1^-}, b, \overline{r2_1^+}, \overline{r1_1^+}\}$. There are however some difficulties with this. Firstly, without an a priori finite capacity for a place, its translation into a multi-action PA produces infinite behaviour, which is a problem for tool-supported analysis methods. In fact a proper rendering in PBC requires infinite parallel composition, which exacerbates this problem. There are also problems from a stochastic perspective. SCCS is a synchronous calculus — in parallel composition the components proceed in lock-step, which may present difficulties for adding (continuous time) stochastic delays. PBC is asynchronous, but has its own difficulties here, as seen in [12] which gives a gives a stochastic extension. The difficulty is that the inference rule for synchronisation is complex (making manual reasoning difficult) and depends on internal process structure rather than just on LTS Transitions, thereby compromising the notion of an abstract behaviour model.

7 Conclusions

This paper has presented the starting point for a formalism, STOCON, which enables the composition of stochastic PNs. Its notable features are—

- Generality of composition, subsuming native PN and PA compositionality.
- Visual representation of place/transition fusions, which is important if the formalism is to provide a basis for design tools.
- LTS model and behaviour inference rules through which PA-style compositional reasoning is applicable to native PN compositionality.

The main lines of development envisaged for STOCON's m-nets are —

(i) Developing translations to m-nets of various notations/formalism ranging over e.g. PA-based notations such as LOTOS, queuing networks, graphical notations such as UML (see [10]), programming notations such as CSP, and of course various forms of PAs and PNs. The graphical nature of m-nets may aid the comprehensibility of such semantics, e.g. in Fig. 8, (a)-(c), (e)-(f) and (g) define the complete m-net semantics for a CCS-like stochastic PA with sequential composition and the m-net inference rules are the route to proving consistency with the PA's native semantics.

(ii) Partly driven by (i), increasing the expressiveness of the m-net structure itself by e.g. the inclusion of some form of probabilistic choice, needed for a full treatment of stochastic aspects of systems; a treatment of recursion; the development of a high-level net version, along the lines of Fig. 6, which is necessary for dealing with the detailed behaviour of substantial systems; incorporation of other common PN features such as inhibitor arcs.

(iii) Developing specific theory and (stochastic and functional) analysis techniques, drawing on that for formalism which by (i) become subsumed with STOCON, particularly that for (stochastic) PNs and (stochastic) PAs.

With the above developments, STOCON would have the potential for use within system development tools as a "gateway" model allowing: the combination of components defined in different notations/formalism, provided an m-net semantics for each has been defined; (subject to applicability properties) the combination of analysis tools and techniques from different formalism domains. Such a development would have goals similar to the Möbius project [4,6]. A fundamental difference between STOCON and Möbius is the approach to composition of, and interaction between, components from different formalisms. For example, consider: a component defined as a PA expression, E, which has Fig. 8(i) as its m-net semantics; the combination of E with components defined in other formalisms. In STOCON, the only way those other components could interact with E is via its interface of place labels E and X and transition labels $a, \ldots, !z$. In Möbius however, as shown in [5], another component could make a change to E's state a-kin to moving a token from place p to q. From our perspective that seems to violate the integrity of E's native PA formalism and prohibits an overall compositional semantics. Although tools using STOCON as a gateway formalism would not necessary implement compositions by translating components to m-nets, those translations would provide a semantics of the composition demonstrably consistent with the components' native semantics.

References

1. F. Bause and P. S. Kritzinger. *Stochastic Petri Nets - An Introduction to the Theory.* Advanced Studies in Computer Science. Vieweg, 1996.
2. E. Best, R. Devillers, and J. Hall. The Petri Box Calculus: A new causal algebra with multi-label communication. In G. Rozenberg, editor, *Advances in Petri Nets '92*, volume 609 of *Lecture Notes in Computer Science*, pages 21–69. Springer-Verlag, 1992.
3. S. Christensen and L. Petrucci. Towards a modular analysis of coloured petri nets. In *Proc. 13th Int. Conf. on Applications and Theory of Petri Nets*, volume 616 of *Lecture Notes in Computer Science*, pages 113–133. Springer-Verlag, 1992.
4. G. Clark et al. The Möbius modelling tool. In *Proceedings 10th International Workshop on Petri Nets and Performance Models*, pages 241–250. IEEE Comput. Soc., 2001.
5. G. Clark and W. H. Sanders. Implementing a stochastic process algebra within the Möbius execution modeling framework. In *Proceedings 9th International Workshop on Process Algebras and Performance Models*, 2001.
6. D. D. Deavours and W. H. Sanders. Möbius: Framework and atomic models. In *Proceedings 10th International Workshop on Petri Nets and Performance Models*, pages 251–260. IEEE Comput. Soc., 2001.

7. H. J. Genrich. Predicate/Transition nets. In *Petri Nets: Central Models and their Properties*, number 254 in Lecture Notes in Computer Science, pages 207–247. Springer-Verlag, 1986.
8. H. Hermanns and M. Rerrelbach. Syntax, semantics, equivalences and axioms for MTIPP. Technical report, Univ. Erlangen-Nurnberg, 1995.
9. J. Hilston. *A Compositional Approach to Performance Modelling.* PhD thesis, University of Edinburgh, 1994.
10. R. P. Hopkins and M. Smith. Stochastic UML and its STOCON semantics. Memo, Dept. CEE, Heriot Watt University, Edinburgh, 2002.
11. K. Jensen. *Coloured Petri Nets.* EATCS Monographs on Theoretical Compputer Science. Springer-Verlag, 1992.
12. H. Macia, V. Valero, and D. de Frutos-Escrig. sPBC: a markovian extension of finite Petri Box Calculus. In *Proceedings 9th International Workshop on Petri Nets and Performance Models*, pages 207–216. IEEE Comput. Soc., 2001.
13. R. Milner. *Communication and Concurrency.* Computer Science. Prentice Hall, 1989.
14. A. Pagnoni. Stochastic nets and performance evaluation. In *Petri Nets: Central Models and their Properties*, number 254 in Lecture Notes in Computer Science, pages 460–478. Springer-Verlag, 1986.
15. W. Reisig. Place/Transition systems. In *Petri Nets: Central Models and their Properties*, number 254 in Lecture Notes in Computer Science, pages 117–141. Springer-Verlag, 1986.
16. M. Ribaudo. On the aggregation techniques in stochastic Petri nets and stochastic process algebras. *The Computer Journal (Special Issue - Process Algebra and Performance Modelling)*, 38(7):600–611, 1995.
17. I. Rojas. Compositional construction of SWN models. *The Computer Journal (Special Issue - Process Algebra and Performance Modelling)*, 38(7):613–621, 1995.

Symbolic Performance Prediction of Data-Dependent Parallel Programs

Hasyim Gautama and Arjan J.C. van Gemund

Dept. of Information Technology and Systems
Delft University of Technology
P.O. Box 5031, NL-2600 GA Delft, The Netherlands
{H.Gautama, A.J.C.vanGemund}@ITS.TUDelft.NL

Abstract. Analytically predicting the performance of data-dependent programs is an extremely challenging problem. Even for a fixed problem size the variety of typical input data sets may cause a considerable execution time variance. Especially for time-critical applications, merely predicting the mean execution time does not suffice and knowledge of the execution time distribution is essential. In this paper we present a compositional analytic method to approximate the first four statistical moments of the program execution time in terms of the first four moments of the loop bounds, the branch conditions, and the execution time delays of the constituent tasks. The approach applies to sequential and parallel programs of which the associated DAG has a series-parallel structure. For each binary or N-ary sequential, parallel, or conditional composition the solution complexity is merely $O(1)$. The method is exact for sequential and conditional composition. Furthermore, for N-ary parallel compositions experimental results of synthetic and real workloads show that the actual prediction error of the moments method is in the percent range. The analytic method is implemented in terms of the performance modeling language PAMELA. Apart from the theory, in this paper we also present a symbolic PAMELA compiler. Provided with a PAMELA process model of the (parallel) program, the PAMELA compiler symbolically translates this source to closed-form expressions that express the first four moments of the program execution time.

1 Introduction

Static approaches to program performance prediction aim to provide an analytic, compositional model that predicts program execution time in terms of program parameters such as loop bounds, branching probabilities, and basic instruction workload models in order to maximize diagnostic insight in program performance. For instance, consider the following loop

```
for (i=1; i<=N; i++)
    if (C)
        S;
```

T. Field et al. (Eds.): TOOLS 2002, LNCS 2324, pp. 259–278, 2002.

that contains a branch and a statement (block). Assuming that the truth probability of the branch condition is p, and the average workload of statement S is X, both profiled over a representative set of input data vectors, the program execution time Y is predicted by

$$Y = \sum_{i=1}^{N} pX = NpX \tag{1}$$

While Eq. (1) is correct in terms of its mean value $\mathsf{E}[Y]$, the model is inadequate to predict the execution time *distribution* of Y over the whole spectrum of input data sets. However, for highly data-dependent programs, such as sorting programs and simulation programs, knowledge about the distribution of Y can be crucial, for instance in time-critical (e.g., real-time) applications where only some percentage of runs (or none) is allowed to exceed some execution time threshold. In the above example, the variance of Y, being determined by N, p, and X, can be quite significant. Hence program performance prediction using stochastic parameters is more effective and realistic than using deterministic parameters [23].

There are a number of probabilistic approaches to program execution time analysis, the specific trade-off between analysis cost and prediction accuracy depending on how workload distributions are represented. For instance, consider the sequential composition of two statements with execution time X_1 and X_2, respectively, the total execution time being $Y = X_1 + X_2$. If the probability density function (pdf) of X_1 and X_2 is given, solving Y requires a convolution of pdf(X_1) and pdf(X_2). While the solution is exact, the complexity involved with program-wide convolution of anything but the simplest of distributions prohibits practical application. In addition, the fact that over the whole *spectrum* of input data sets loop bounds and branching behavior also typically exhibit *stochastic* behavior, considerably complicates the analysis [1,22].

Aimed at balancing prediction accuracy and solution complexity, many approaches have been proposed to characterize probability densities, ranging from the use of specific distributions or series approximations to the use of mean and variance. Recently, an analytic approach has been presented where the distributions are represented in terms of the first four moments [4,5,6]. The method permits the first four moments of the execution time $\mathsf{E}[Y^r]$ to be analytically expressed at $O(1)$ solution complexity in terms of the first four moments of the basic block execution times, sequential loop bounds, and branch truth probability values. For parallel compositions the analysis is approximate, though equally low-cost. This low-cost, parametric approach provides rapid, diagnostic insight in execution time distribution of (parallel) applications during the first design stages where low cost still outweighes accuracy.

While previous papers have focused on particular compositions (e.g., sequential [4], parallel [5,6]), in the current paper we give an overall presentation of the moments analysis technique. In particular, we present an implementation of the methodology in terms of a process-algebraic modeling language and compiler. The language is called Pamela (PerformAnce ModEling LAnguage [8]) of which a prototype version based on the use of deterministic variables has been presented at the 1995 instance of this Conference [9]. In contrast however, the current language version fully supports the use of *stochastic* variables. Most notably, the methodology is now also supported by a public-domain research *compiler* that automatically translates a PAMELA process model into an analytic model that predicts the first four moments of the execution time at minimum cost.

The paper is organized as follows. In Section 2 we review related approaches towards predicting the execution time distribution of sequential, conditional, and parallel task compositions. In Section 3 we summarize our moments analysis for sequential, conditional, and parallel compositions, and report on the accuracy and complexity of our analysis. In Section 4 we present a number of case studies involving the execution time prediction of real (parallel) programs in order to show the accuracy of our technique in practice. In Section 5 we present the language and compiler implementation, including two example applications. Finally, in Section 6 we draw our conclusions.

2 Related Work

In this section we review related approaches towards analytically predicting the execution time distribution of sequential, conditional, and parallel task compositions. An approach using the pdf is introduced by Gelenbe [7] to determine the completion times of block-structured parallel programs (SP graphs). However, the high cost numerical integration prohibits practical use. Lester [15] uses the z-transform to approximate the pdf. While the real pdf can be approximated well, the solution complexity of the underlying numeric process is still high.

To decrease solution complexity, there have been a number of approaches based on the use of representations other than the pdf, where generality is traded for cost. Some approaches introduce restrictions to specific distributions which are characterized by a limited number of parameters. Sahner and Trivedi [21] use exponomial distributions. While proven a powerful tool for reliability modeling and analytical performance analysis, exponomial workloads are hardly measured in real programs. Aimed at analyzing parallelism (order statistics) Kruskal and Weiss [14] use increasing failure rate (IFR) distributions while Axelrod [2], Gumbel [11], Madala and Sinclair [17], and Robinson [20] use symmetric distributions. Although the approximation error is quite reasonable, only the first moment can be obtained. As mean and variance are required it is impossible to analyze applications with nested parallelism. Sötz [26] uses an exponential distribution combined with a deterministic offset. While the analysis is straightforward, the approach may introduce significant errors. Sarkar [22] determines the mean and variance for sequential compositions only. Schopf and Berman [24] use normal distributions. While the application to sequential programs is straightforward, binary parallelism is approximated heuristically so that the application to N-ary parallelism would cause severe errors.

Lüthi *et al.* [16] characterize parameter variabilities in terms of histograms. In contrast to program (task graph) analysis they address the problem of solving queuing models with load variabilities. Also Schopf and Berman [24] use histograms with a limited number of intervals. However, the analysis complexity grows rapidly with the number of histogram intervals needed to accurately characterize a distribution.

Another way of characterizing the pdf is based on series approximation, for example the Gram-Charlier series of type A [5]. While the analysis is asymptotically exact, the number of Gram-Charlier terms needed for a sufficiently accurate approximation is prohibitive.

In summary, the above approaches deal with sequential and parallel compositions. Some impose restrictions on the allowable distributions. Some allow a mere characterization in terms of mean and variance. None of the approaches addresses the effect of stochastic loop bounds or branching, which are essential in stochastic program modeling. An exception is the approach taken by Adve and Vernon [1] who allow a sequential loop bound to be stochastic.

Table 1 summarizes the related work in terms of the distribution type used, and whether the approach addresses sequential composition (SC), and stochastic loop bounds (LB), condition probabilities (CP), binary parallel composition (BP) and N-ary parallel composition (NP). Our approach is included for reference.

Table 1. Summary of related work from program analysis perspective.

First author	Distr. type	SC	LB	CP	BP	NP
Adve [1]	Mean & Var	-	+	-	-	-
Axelrod [2]	Normal	-	-	-	-	+
Gautama [5]	Series	-	-	-	+	+
Gautama (this paper)	Moments (4)	+	+	+	+	+
Gelenbe [7]	PDF	+	-	-	+	+
Gumbel [11]	Normal	-	-	-	-	+
Kruskal [14]	IFR	-	-	-	-	+
Lester [15]	Z-transform	+	-	-	-	+
Madala [17]	Normal	-	-	-	-	+
Robinson [20]	Normal	-	-	-	-	+
Sahner [21]	Exponomial	+	-	-	+	+
Sarkar [22]	Mean & Var	+	-	-	-	-
Schopf [24]	Histogram	+	-	-	+	-
Schopf [24]	Normal	+	-	-	+	-
Sötz [26]	Det & Exp	+	-	-	+	+
Lüthi [16]	Histogram	Queuing network				

3 Analysis

In order to provide a proper understanding of our performance prediction approach, in this section we summarize the moments analysis corresponding to sequential, conditional and parallel compositions. Due to space limitations only the main results are presented while the interested reader is referred to [3,4,5,6].

The moments analysis represents a stochastic variable X by a 4-tuple denoting the first four central moments $X = (\mathsf{E}[X], \mathrm{Var}[X], \mathrm{Skw}[X], \mathrm{Kur}[X])$, i.e., the mean, variance, skewness and kurtosis of X, respectively. When X is deterministic ($\mathrm{Var}[X] = 0$), the tuple simply becomes $X = (\mathsf{E}[X], 0, 0, 3)$. A limited number of moments are incorporated in the analysis since higher moments are less important to the accuracy of X. Moreover, evaluation cost is significantly reduced.

The four moment values can distinguish between well-known standard distributions. For example an exponentially distributed random variable X with parameter μ is expressed by $X = (\mu, \mu^2, 2, 9)$, a uniformly distributed X with sample space $[a, b]$ is expressed by $X = ((a+b)/2, (b-a)^2/12, 0, 1.8)$, and a normally distributed X with parameters $[\mu, \sigma]$ is expressed by $X = (\mu, \sigma^2, 0, 3)$. Other distribution types can be distinguished from the skewness and kurtosis values. For any valid empirical workload evaluating the four moment values is straightforward without *a priori* assumption to a certain distribution.

In the following we summarize the analysis of the moments of composition's execution time Y in terms of its constituent parts X_i. For readability the formulae are presented in terms of rth moments ($\mathsf{E}[X^r]$) rather than the central moments and independence assumptions are made wherever required.

3.1 Sequential Composition

Consider an addition of two random variables $Y = X_1 + X_2$. The moments of Y are given by [4]

$$\mathsf{E}[Y^r] = \sum_j^r \binom{r}{j} \mathsf{E}[X_1^{r-j}]\mathsf{E}[X_2^j] \tag{2}$$

For N additions of a random variable X given by $Y = \sum_{i=1}^N X$, it holds [4]

$$\mathsf{E}[Y^r] = \mathsf{E}\left[\frac{\mathrm{d}^r}{\mathrm{d}t^r} \left(\sum_{j=0}^r \frac{t^j \mathsf{E}[X^j]}{j!} \right)^N \Bigg|_{t=0} \right] \tag{3}$$

where N may be stochastic. In particular, the mean and variance of Y in Eq. (3) are given by

$$\mathsf{E}[Y] = \mathsf{E}[N]\mathsf{E}[X] \tag{4}$$

$$\mathrm{Var}[Y] = \mathsf{E}[N]\mathrm{Var}[X] + \mathsf{E}[X]^2\mathrm{Var}[N] \tag{5}$$

while the skewness and kurtosis of Y are according to

$$\begin{aligned}\mathrm{Skw}[Y] &= (\mathsf{E}[N]\mathrm{Skw}[X]\mathrm{Std}[X]^3 + \mathsf{E}[X]^3\mathrm{Skw}[N]\mathrm{Std}[N]^3 + \\ &\quad 3\mathsf{E}[X]\mathrm{Var}[X]\mathrm{Var}[N])/\mathrm{Std}[Y]^3 \qquad (6)\\ \mathrm{Kur}[Y] &= (\mathsf{E}[N]\mathrm{Var}[X]^2(\mathrm{Kur}[X]-3) + \mathsf{E}[X]^4\mathrm{Kur}[N]\mathrm{Var}[N]^2 + \\ &\quad 6\mathsf{E}[X]^2\mathrm{Var}[X](\mathrm{Skw}[N]\mathrm{Std}[N]^3 + \mathsf{E}[N]\mathrm{Var}[N]) + \\ &\quad \mathsf{E}[N]\mathrm{Var}[N]) + 4\mathsf{E}[X]\mathrm{Var}[N]\mathrm{Skw}[X]\mathrm{Std}[X]^3 + \\ &\quad 3\mathrm{Var}[X]^2(\mathsf{E}[N]^2 + \mathrm{Var}[N]))/\mathrm{Std}[Y]^4 \qquad (7)\end{aligned}$$

where $\mathrm{Std}[X]$ denotes the standard deviation of X. Since Eqs. (2) and (3) are exact, we present no experimental results. More details can be found in [4].

3.2 Conditional Composition

Consider a random variable Y which is defined by $Y = X$ if $C =$ true and 0 otherwise, where C has the truth probability P. Then the moments of Y are given by [4]

$$\mathsf{E}[Y^r] = \mathsf{E}\left[\frac{\mathrm{d}^r}{\mathrm{d}t^r}\left(\sum_{j=0}^{r}\frac{t^j\mathsf{E}[X^j]}{j!}\right)^P\Bigg|_{t=0}\right] \qquad (8)$$

Similar to Eq. (3), Eq. (8) can also be expressed in terms of $\mathsf{E}[P^r]$ as given in Eqs. (4) to (7) when N is replaced by P.

Modeling stochastic branch behavior focuses on modeling (measuring) P. Conventional branch modeling implicitly assumes P to be a Bernoulli trial with a *deterministic* parameter p that does not model input data variability. As the memoryless Bernoulli process does not model typical branch behavior, we therefore use an alternative statistical model based on the use of Alternating Renewal Processes (ARP). The ARP model allows branching probability to have a wide range of distributions across the space of input data sets. Instead of measuring P in terms of a deterministic Bernoulli parameter p ("average truth probability"), we measure P in terms of U and D which are random variables denoting the length of consecutive true and false branch invocations, respectively. In our ARP approach we model the branch truth probability P by beta distributions whose moments are given by

$$\mathsf{E}[P^r] = \frac{\Gamma(a+b)\Gamma(a+r)}{\Gamma(a)\Gamma(a+b+r)} \qquad (9)$$

where Γ denotes the gamma function, and

$$a = \frac{(\mathsf{E}[D]^2(\mathsf{E}[U] - \mathrm{Var}[U]) + \mathsf{E}[U]^2(\mathsf{E}[D] - \mathrm{Var}[D]))\mathsf{E}[U]}{(\mathsf{E}[D] + \mathsf{E}[U])(\mathsf{E}[D]^2\mathrm{Var}[U] + \mathsf{E}[U]^2\mathrm{Var}[D])}, \quad b = \frac{\mathsf{E}[D]}{\mathsf{E}[U]}\,a. \qquad (10)$$

This approach is completely compatible with our moment analysis. Experiments reported in [3] show an accuracy improvement by an order of magnitude compared to Bernoulli modeling approach. More details can be found in [3].

3.3 Parallel Composition

Consider the N-ary parallel composition corresponding to $Y = \max_{i=1}^{N} X_i$ where X_i are N identical and independent distributed (iid) variates of X. Due to integration problems, however, there is no exact explicit expression for $\mathsf{E}[Y^r]$ in terms of $\mathsf{E}[X^r]$. To obtain an explicit solution in terms of $\mathsf{E}[X^r]$ we first express X in terms of the lambda distribution defined by the percentile function R as function of the cummulative distribution function (cdf), $0 \leq F \leq 1$, according to [12]

$$X = R_X(F) = \lambda_1 + \frac{F^{\lambda_3} - (1-F)^{\lambda_4}}{\lambda_2} \tag{11}$$

where λ_1 is a location parameter, λ_2 is a scale parameter and λ_3 and λ_4 are shape parameters. The λ values are a simple function of $\mathsf{E}[X^r]$. Without loss of generality let $\lambda_1 = 0$. Due to the inverse formulation of F in terms of Eq. (11), $\mathsf{E}[Y^r]$ can now be explicitly derived in terms of $\mathsf{E}[X^r]$ (through λ_j) according to [5]

$$\mathsf{E}[Y^r] = \frac{N}{\lambda_2^r} \sum_{i=0}^{r} \binom{r}{i} (-1)^i \mathrm{B}(\lambda_3(r-i) + N, \lambda_4 i + 1) \tag{12}$$

where B denotes the beta function. More details can be found in [5].

The binary parallel composition, corresponding to $Y = \max(X_1, X_2)$, can also be analytically treated by first modeling X_1 and X_2 in terms of lambda distributions. In this case the moments of Y are approximated by [6]

$$\mathsf{E}[Y^r] = \int_0^1 (\max(R_{X_1}(F), R_{X_2}(F)) + \Delta x)^r \mathrm{d}F \tag{13}$$

where Δx denotes the difference between $R_Y(F)$ and $\max(R_{X_1}(F), R_{X_2}(F))$. The worst case relative error of $\mathsf{E}[Y]$ in Eq. (13) is 35% which occurs for equal workloads, while sharply decreasing for diverging workloads. Furthermore, measurements using real programs suggest that the worst case error may actually be much less (approximately 5%). Note that Eq. (13) only requires integration on a fixed bound of interval $[0, 1]$. For N-ary parallel composition experimental results on synthetic as well as empirical iid distributions show that the relative error is in the percent range, even for large N (e.g., 4% for $N = 10^4$). More details can be found in [5,6].

4 Experiments

To illustrate the application of our moment analysis approach, in this section we describe the results of the moment analysis approach for three small example codes. The first code features a simple branch condition which is memoryless. The second code features a branch condition that has memory. While the above codes are sequential examples, the third code features two data parallel loops which exhibit various degrees of workload correlation. For all codes, the measured distributions Y_m (moments, measured execution times) are based on running the program for 6,000 input data sets while the execution time is determined through counter-based program instrumentation. The predicted execution time Y_p is directly based on Eq. (2) to Eq. (13). The prediction error for the rth moment is defined by

$$\varepsilon_r = |Y_m^r - Y_p^r| / Y_m^r \tag{14}$$

The results show that ε_r is in the percent range as long as branch and workload correlation effects are small.

4.1 Sparse Vector Scaling

In this section we apply the moment method to the example loop which has been described in Section 1, instantiated to a sparse vector scaling routine where `C` equals to `x[i] != 0` and `S` is equal to `x[i] *= alpha` where `alpha` is a scaling factor. Let the execution time of interest be given by the multiplication time between `x[i]` and `alpha` which is assumed to take unit execution time while ignoring other program contributions.

In the experiment the elements of vector `x` are generated according to a Bernoulli distribution with probability $p = 0.1$ to resemble data sets with average density $p = 0.1$. The moments of N and P are given in Table 2. Applying Eqs. (8) and (3) yields an execution time prediction Y_p which is compared to the measured execution time Y_m in Table 3. The table shows that $\mathsf{E}[Y_p]$ is approximately exact while the relative error of $\mathrm{Var}[Y_p]$ is 1% due to measurement inaccuracies.

Table 2. $\mathsf{E}[N^r]$ and $\mathsf{E}[P^r]$ for vector scaling.

X	$\mathsf{E}[X]$	$\mathrm{Var}[X]$	$\mathrm{Skw}[X]$	$\mathrm{Kur}[X]$
N	10,000	0	0	3
P	0.1	$9\ 10^{-2}$	2.7	8.1

Table 3. $\mathsf{E}[Y^r]$ for vector scaling.

Y	$\mathsf{E}[Y]$	$\mathrm{Var}[Y]$	$\mathrm{Skw}[Y]$	$\mathrm{Kur}[Y]$
Y_m	999	891	0.0	3.0
Y_p	1,000	901	0.0	3.0

4.2 Straight Selection Sort

Straight Selection Sort sorts an N elements vector `x` according to

```
for (i=N; i>=2; i--) {
    k = i;
    for (j=i-1; j>=1; j--)
        if (x[j]>x[k])
            k = j;
    swap(x[i],x[k]);
}
```

where `swap` exchanges the value between two elements. To define program performance we choose the statement `k = j` to take unit execution time while the rest of the constructs are assumed to take zero execution time. Although in practice the statement `k = j` will not represent any significant execution time, this choice provides the most interesting (i.e., stochastic) scenario.

For this experiment we let $N = 1,000$ and the elements of array `x` are generated uniformly with sample space $[0, 1]$. The measured input parameters are shown in Table 4 while the predicted and measured execution times are shown in Table 5. The Y_p value is determined by evaluating Eqs. (8) and (3). While ε_1 is very small, the relative variance error is 28%, which is caused by correlation of the branch condition between different invocations. While traditional branch models such as a Bernoulli trial would yield variance errors of 74%, our ARP model provides much better estimates [3].

Table 4. $\mathsf{E}[N^r]$ and $\mathsf{E}[P^r]$ for selection sort.

X	$\mathsf{E}[X]$	Var$[X]$	Skw$[X]$	Kur$[X]$
N	1000	0	0	3
P	$1.1\ 10^{-2}$	$3.0\ 10^{-2}$	8.3	60

Table 5. $\mathsf{E}[Y^r]$ for selection sort.

Y	$\mathsf{E}[Y]$	Var$[Y]$	Skw$[Y]$	Kur$[Y]$
Y_m	5,492	21,143	-0.1	3.0
Y_p	5,477	15,126	0.0	3.0

4.3 PSRS

PSRS (Parallel Sorting by Regular Sampling [25]) sorts an N elements vector `x` into a vector `y`. A pseudo code of PSRS for P processors is as follows

```
forall (p=0;p<P;p++)
    sort1(x[p*N/P;(p+1)*N/P-1]);
<select pivots>
<disjoin>
forall (p=0;p<N;p++)
    sort2(y[p*N/P;(p+1)*N/P-1]);
```

The algorithm comprises two data parallel sorting loops. The first parallel section (using Quicksort), called `sort1`, divides the array in P equal subarrays, and sorts each partition in parallel, after which a number of global pivots are determined. Based in these pivots, the subarray is redivided in P parts (`disjoin`), after which P new partitions are created based on the pivots index. The second section (using Mergesort), called `sort2`, sorts the new partitions, after which a sorted array is obtained. The working of `sort1` implies that each task has an iid workload, as we generate the input array with a uniform random variable using a sample space $[0, 1]$. In contrast, the task workloads in `sort2` are correlated, since their workload depends on the common global pivot values. As workload X_i we choose the number of floating point operations per task.

In the experiments we assign each processor a constant array length $N/P = 1,000$ while P ranges from 2 to 128. In Figs. 1 and 2 we show ε_r for `sort1` and `sort2`, respectively. The results of the Gumbel method [11] are included for

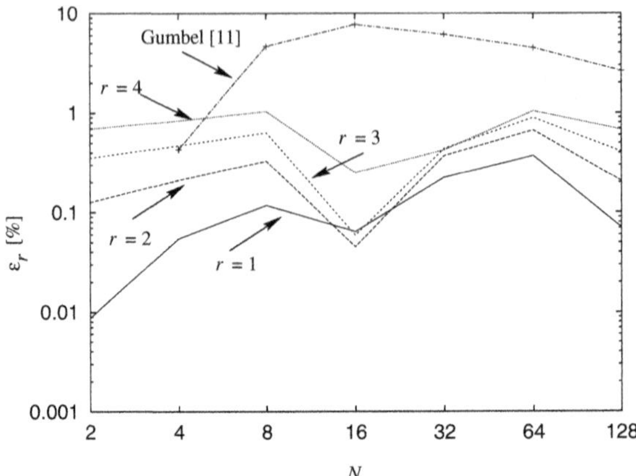

Fig. 1. Error [%] for `sort1`.

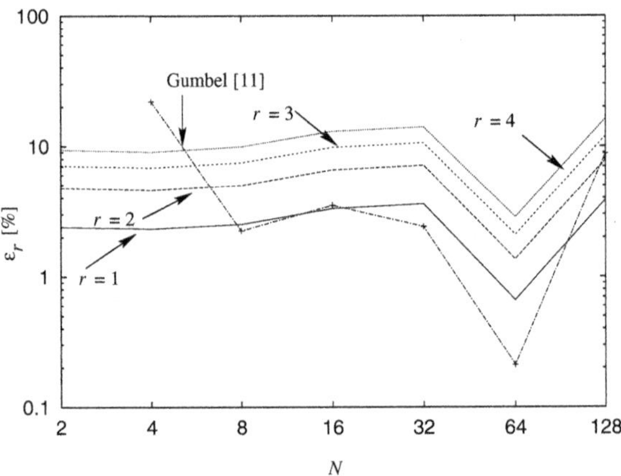

Fig. 2. Error [%] for `sort2`.

comparison. While `sort1` produces excellent accuracy, the correlation effects in `sort2` clearly degrade ε_r.

In summary, the above 3 experiments show that the moments analysis yields quite an acceptable accuracy in view of the $O(1)$ solution complexity of our symbolic analysis technique, while outperforming comparable low-cost analysis methods. More example codes and results can be found in [5,6].

5 Tool Implementation

The moments analysis method has been implemented in terms of a performance modeling language called Pamela (PerformAnce ModEling LAnguage). The language allows an application to be described in terms of a process-algebraic, performance simulation model which is subsequently compiled to an analytic execution time model. An initial version of the language and associated analysis technique has been presented in [9], which was restricted to deterministic variables only. In this section we present the new version that supports the statistical moments analysis technique, featuring a compiler that implements the symbolic analysis technique. The compiler is available in the public domain [18].

5.1 Modeling Language

Pamela is a process-algebraic language that allows a parallel program-machine combination to be modeled in terms of a sequential, conditional, and parallel composition of processes, modeling workload, condition synchronization, and resource contention. Work is described by the use *process*. The construct use(r,t) exclusively acquires service from *resource* r for t units time (excluding possible queuing delay). The scheduling policy that is currently supported is FCFS with non-deterministic conflict arbitration. The service time t may be deterministic or stochastic. In the latter case, its distribution is expressed in terms of the first four moments. A resource r has a multiplicity that may be larger than 1. As in queuing networks, it is convenient to define an infinite-server resource called rho that has infinite multiplicity. Instead of writing use(rho,t) we will simply write delay(t).

Pamela features the following process composition operators:

- ; for binary sequential composition,
- seq (<index> = <lb>, <ub>) for N-ary sequential composition,
- || for binary parallel composition,
- par (<index> = <lb>, <ub>) for N-ary parallel composition,
- if (<cond>) [else] for conditional composition.

Pamela is a strongly typed language. Variables can be of three types: process, resource, or numeric. The latter type is used for time expressions, parameters, indices, and loop bounds. Each lhs variable can have a formal parameter list. The scope of these parameters is limited to the rhs expression.

The following Pamela equations model a Machine Repair Model (MRM) in which P clients either spend a mean time t_l on local processing, or request service from a server s with service time t_s with a total cycle count of N iterations (unlike steady-state analysis, in our approach we require models to terminate; however N may be kept symbolic).

```
%-----------------------------------------------------------------
% mrm.pam -- Machine Repair Model
%-----------------------------------------------------------------
numeric exponential(mu) = moments(mu,mu*mu,2,9)  % appr exp distr

numeric P = 1000                                % # clients
numeric N = 1000000                             % # iterations
numeric t_l = exponential(10)                   % exp distr (mu = 10)
numeric t_s = exponential(0.1)                  % exp distr (mu = 0.1)

resource s = fcfs(0,1)     % fcfs is a predefined FCFS resource array
                           % 1st arg index, 2nd arg its multiplicity

process main =    par (p = 1, P)                % fork P clients
                      seq (i = 1, N) {          % each loops N times
                          delay(t_l) ;
                          use(s,t_s)
                      }
```

The example illustrates the top-down, *material-oriented* modeling approach [13] taken in PAMELA, in which the server is modeled by a *passive* resource. In a *machine-oriented* approach (the dual modeling paradigm), the server would have been modeled by a separate *process* that synchronizes through explicit message-passing. Unlike our approach however, the latter paradigm is not amenable to a mechanic analysis process where a PAMELA model is *automatically compiled* to analytic execution time expressions. This is due to the inherent difference in modeling condition synchronization and mutual exclusion. In message-passing paradigms both forms of synchronizations are implicitly expressed through the *same* constructs, i.e., synchronous communication, combined with a non-deterministic choice operator (selective communications). This makes it impossible to symbolically and mechanically express the separate timing effects of both synchronization types, which is the basis of our analytic approach. In the PAMELA top-down modeling approach, problem parallelism (including condition synchronization) is modeled explicitly in terms of `par` (or `;`) operators, explicitly constrained by mutual exclusion (`use`) as a result of scheduling when the processes need to share resources such as, e.g., software locks, file servers, processors, communication links, memories, and/or I/O disk handlers, The PAMELA modeling paradigm is further discussed in [10].

Due to the ultra-low solution complexity of the performance model high parameter values can be specified as the resulting models typically evaluate within a second. When no numeric value is specified for a variable, this implies that the parameter will also occur in the symbolic performance model. This language feature is described in the next section.

As in ordinary mathematics, the semantics of a PAMELA model is based on expression substitution. Although for readability a model may be coded in terms of many equations, internally each expression is evaluated by recursively substituting every global variable by its corresponding rhs expression. Consequently, the above MRM model is internally rewritten to the equivalent normal-form model below (relevant equations shown only).

```
numeric t_l = moments(10,100,2,9)
numeric t_s = moments(0.1,0.01,2,9)

process main =  par (p = 1, 1000)
                    seq (i = 1, 100000) {
                        delay(moments(10,100,2,9)) ;
                        use(fcfs(0,1),moments(0.1,0.01,2,9))
                    }
```

Apart from the process operators mentioned above, PAMELA includes the usual unary and binary numeric operators such as +, *, /, mod, div, ==, <, max, etc., as well as the reduction operators sum (<index> = <lb>, <ub>) and max (<index> = <lb>, <ub>). Conditional numeric expressions are described using if-then just like conditional process expressions. Furthermore, as parts of the analysis result is expressed in terms of vectors, the numeric abstract data-type includes vectors as well as scalars, implying that all numeric operators are overloaded. A vector is denoted [<scalar>, ..., <scalar>]. Hence, the expression [1,2,3] * 4 is legal and, incidentally, will be compiled to [4,8,12]. In order to generate unbounded, symbolic vectors PAMELA features the unitvec operator which returns a unit vector in the dimension (base 0) given by its argument. For instance, the expression 10 * unitvec(3) will be compiled to [0,0,0,10].

5.2 Symbolic Compilation

A PAMELA model is translated to a time-domain performance model by substituting every process equation by a numeric equation that models the execution time associated with the original process. The lhs is derived from the original lhs by prefixing T_. Thus the cost model of a process expression main is denoted T_main. The result is a PAMELA model that only comprises numeric equations as the original process and resource equations are no longer relevant. The fact that the cost model is again a PAMELA model is for reasons of convenience as explained later on.

The analytic approach underlying the translation process is based on a combination of critical path analysis of the delays due to condition synchronization ("task synchronization"), and a lower bound approximation of the delays due to mutual exclusion synchronization ("queuing delay") as a result of resource contention. Per process equation four numeric equations are generated, whose lhs identifiers are derived from the original process variable by prefixing specific strings. Let L denote the lhs of a process equation. The first equation generated is phi_L which computes the effect of condition synchronization. The second equation generated is delta_L which computes the aggregate workload per resource (index). The combined mutual exclusion delay is computed by the third equation denoted omega_L. The three above equations are combined into the fourth equation T_L which denotes the execution time. A more detailed background can be found in [9].

Returning to the MRM example, the PAMELA model of the MRM is compiled to the following time domain model (`T_main` shown only):

```
numeric T_main = max(max (p = 1, 1000) {
                     sum (i = 1, 1000000) {
                         (moments(10,100,2,9) +
                          moments(0.1,0.01,2,9))
                     }
                 },max(sum (p = 1, 1000) {
                           sum (i = 1, 1000000) {
                               moments(0.1,0.01,2,9) * unitvec(0)
                           }
                 })
```

Since all parameters are numerically bound, this intermediate result is automatically reduced (evaluated) to

```
numeric T_main = moments(1.01+07,4.11+03,4.69-01,3.23+00)
```

During this evaluation process Eqs. (2), (3), and (12) are used.

5.3 Parameterization

By virtue of the symbolic nature of the analysis process, PAMELA process models are typically parameterized, thus preserving parameters into the resulting time domain model. In order to enable parameterization PAMELA supports the `parameter` modifier, which blocks the substitution process from attempting to substitute a rhs expression for the particular variable that is intended to become a parameter. Consider the MRM model presented earlier. As all variables were bound to numeric values the compiler evaluates the model for the given values of `P`, `N`, `t_l`, and `t_c`. In order to investigate the effect of, say, `P` and `N`, we would redefine these variables according to

```
numeric parameter P
numeric parameter N
```

Symbolic compilation now yields the intermediate result (`T_main` shown only)

```
numeric T_main = max(max (p = 1, P) {
                     sum (i = 1, N) {
                         (moments(10,100,2,9) +
                          moments(0.1,0.01,2,9))
                     }
                 },max(sum (p = 1, P) {
                           sum (i = 1, N) {
                               moments(0.1,0.01,2,9) * unitvec(0)
                           }
                 }))
```

Although parameterized, this model is automatically further reduced as a result of simple transformation rules such as

```
sum (i = a, b) scalar = (b-a+1) * scalar
```

yielding the following result symbolic performance model:

```
numeric T_main = max(max (p = 1, P) {
                              N * moments(10.1,100.01,2,9)
                          },(P * N * (moments(0.1,0.01,2,9))))
```

This model can be evaluated for different values of `P` and `N`, possibly using mathematical tools other than the PAMELA compiler. In PAMELA further evaluation is achieved as described earlier, by recompiling the above result after removing one or both **`parameter`** modifiers and providing a numeric rhs expression.

In order to assess the prediction quality of the above result, we derive the mean cycle time of the MRM as function of `P` by dividing `T_main` by `N`. The resulting prediction T_{MOM} = `T_main/N` is compared with the result T_{MVA} of Mean Value Analysis [19] (as `t_l` and `t_s` are approximately exponential) as shown in Table 6.

Table 6. MRM mean cycle time.

P	1	2	5	10	20	50	100	200	500
T_{MVA}	10.10	10.10	10.11	10.12	10.12	10.19	10.82	20	50
T_{MOM}	10.10	10.11	10.12	10.12	10.12	10.12	10.13	20	50

Table 6 illustrates the effects of the low-cost, lower bound approximation in PAMELA of the effects of mutual exclusion (queuing). While the prediction error ε_1 for $P = 0$ and $P \to \infty$ is zero, near to the saturation point ($P = 100$) the error is around 8%. Experiments [10] indicate that for very large systems ($O(1000)$ resources) the worst case average error is limited to 50%. However, these situations seldom occur as typically systems are either dominated by condition synchronization or mutual exclusion, in which case the approximation error is in the percent range.

Note that in this particular example the introduction of variance in `t_l` and `t_s` has a negligible effect on the prediction. For small P the prediction values are slightly higher than the deterministic lower bound $T = t_l + t_s$ which is caused by the order statistics effect computed by Eq. (12).

Given the ultra-low solution complexity, the accuracy provided by the compiler is quite acceptable in scenarios where a user conducts, e.g., application scalability studies as a function of various machine parameters, to obtain an initial assessment of the parameter sensitivities of the application. In particular, note that on a Pentium II 350 MHz the symbolic performance model of the MRM merely requires 0.9 CPU s per point in Table 6 (irrespective of N and P) where most of the CPU time is required to evaluate Eqs. (12) and (13). In contrast, the evaluation of the intermediate model would take approximately 22,500 CPU s where most of the CPU time is required to repeatedly evaluate Eq. (2) for `P*N` times.

5.4 Modeling Example

We end this section with an example of how PSRS can be modeled using PAMELA when run on a shared-memory architecture. In contrast to the exposition in Section 4.3, which merely focused on the prediction error of the two parallel sorting sections (`sort1` and `sort2`), we now model the entire algorithm, including the effect of communication delays.

In the PAMELA model of PSRS, given in Fig. 3, some numeric variables are declared in the first seven lines of the model, i.e., the array length `N`, the processor number `P`. The moments of `c1`, `c2` and `c3` are obtained from profiling. Note that `c` in `sort` must be profiled separately for each function call. The next lines declare the CPU resources and the shared memory resource. Although in the current model the workload of each parallel process is mapped onto a unique CPU (see the `flop` model), the explicit use of CPU resources allows the modeler to also investigate the effects of multithreading. Note that the `shmem` multiplicity is currently set to a value such that no contention will ever occur. The evaluation of the model starts from the `main` process which consists of 3 parallel and 2 sequential sections. In order to simplify the modeling example, we have chosen straight selection sort (described in Section 4.2) instead of quicksort (which requires a much larger sequential model). The `main` process calls the other 3 processes, i.e., the program (sub)model `sort` (straight selection sort), and the machine models `flop` and `move` which model the floating point operation, and the shared memory load/store operation, respectively. The last 2 processes represent workloads with exponential time delay `t_f` and `t_m`. Note, that the `move` interface allows the possibility of modeling, e.g., memory contention (e.g., `use(mem,t_m)` for a single memory bank), without requiring further model modification.

In our experiments we use random input vectors of size $\mathtt{N} = 81,920$. Instead of comparing our predictions with the run times of the actually running parallel program (which would require a much more detailed PAMELA model) we use a counter-based measurement approach, in which we run a multithreaded version of PSRS that is instrumented with counters at the appropriate places in the program. The predicted execution time for $\mathtt{P} \geq 2$ are obtained from profiling and running Fig. 3, respectively, while for $\mathtt{P} = 1$ we choose straight selection sort given in Section 4.2 as the sequential program, instead of simply running PSRS for $\mathtt{P} = 1$.

To observe the effect of memory communication on the execution time speedup we consider both $\mathtt{t\_m} = 0$ and `t_m = moments(10,100,2,9)`. In Fig. 4 the measured and predicted speedup are shown by solid and dashed lines, respectively, for $\mathtt{P} \leq 128$. The speedup increases linearly with the number of processors for $\mathtt{P} \leq 64$ and decreases for large `P` since the working of PSRS becomes inefficient for small array size. We measure a super linear speedup for $\mathtt{t\_m} = 0$ due to the choice of straight selection sort for the sequential version as well. For example the speedup is 10 for $\mathtt{P} = 8$. Furthermore, assigning `t_m = moments(10,100,2,9)` degrades the speedup such that for $\mathtt{P} = 2$ the speedup is less than 1. For both values of `t_m` the speedup prediction is approximately accurate while the error is mainly caused by the inaccuracy in profiling `c`. Note that the moments of `c`

```
%-----------------------------------------------------------------------
% psrs.pam -- Parallel Sorting by Regular Sampling Model
%-----------------------------------------------------------------------
numeric parameter N                              % array length
numeric parameter P                              % # processors
numeric t_f = moments(1,1,2,9)                   % computation time
numeric t_m = moments(10,100,2,9)                % communication time
numeric c1 = moments(5e-3, 2e+0, 4e+0, 2e+1)     % profiled for # runs
numeric c2 = moments(1e-2, 3e-2, 9e+0, 7e+1)     % profiled for # runs
numeric c3 = moments(4e-3, 5e+0, 2e+0, 6e+0)     % profiled for # runs
resource cpu(p) = fcfs(p,1)                      % the P CPUs
resource shmem = fcfs(P,P)                       % shared memory

process main = par (p=0, P-1) {                  % sort1:
                 sort(p*N/P,(p+1)*N/P-1,p,c1) ; % sort subarray
                 seq (i=0, P-1)                  % collect samples
                   move(p)
               } ;
               sort(0,P*P-1,p,c2) ;              % sort samples
               seq (i=0, P-2) {                  % choose pivots
                 move(p)
               } ;
               par (p=0, P-1) {                  % disjoin:
                 seq (i=0, P-1) {
                   seq (j=0, (N-N/P)/(P*P)-1) {
                     flop(p) ;
                     move(p)
                   }
                 }
               } ;
               par (p=0, P-1) {                  % sort2:
                 seq (i=0, P-1) {                % collect subarray
                   seq (j=0, (N-N/P)/(P*P)-1)
                     move(p)
                 } ;
                 sort(p*N/P,(p+1)*N/P-1,p,c3)   % sort subarray
               }

process sort(lb,ub,p,c) = seq (i=lb+1, ub) {     % sort
                            seq (j=lb, i-1) {
                              if (c)
                                flop(p)
                            } ;
                            move(p)              % swap
                          }

process flop(p) = use(cpu(p),t_f)                % computation
process move(p) = use(shmem,t_m)                 % memory communication
```

Fig. 3. PAMELA model of PSRS

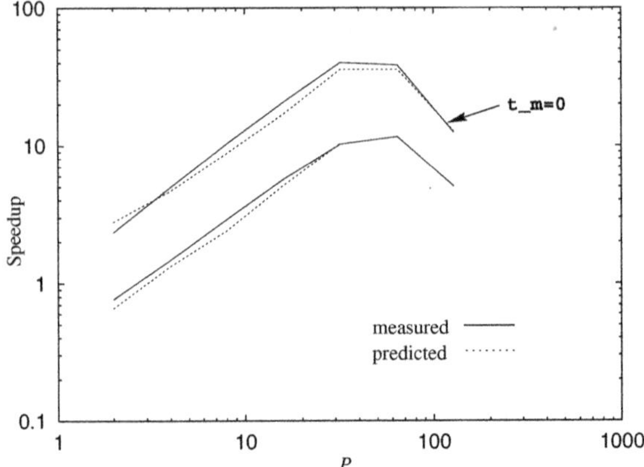

Fig. 4. Measured and predicted speedup.

are very sensitive to the program execution times since `c` is located in a loop nest with high invocation frequency.

The corresponding ε_1 of Fig. 4 is shown in Fig. 5. The highest error is $\varepsilon_1 =$ 18% at $\mathtt{P} = 16$ for $\mathtt{t\_m} = 0$ and $\varepsilon_1 = 15\%$ at $\mathtt{P} = 2$ ε_1 decreases as `P` large since our measurements show that the correlation in **`sort`** is high for large array size. While the error is quite acceptable, the evaluation of the compiled version of above model only requires 1.7 CPU s.

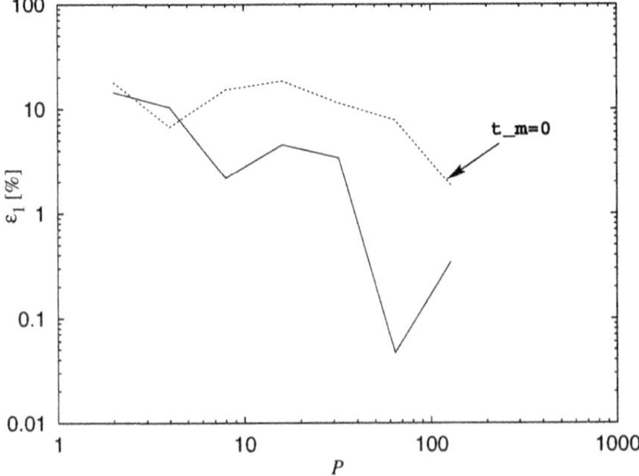

Fig. 5. ε_1 [%] for PSRS.

6 Conclusion

In this paper we have presented a compositional, analytic method to derive symbolic performance models of data-dependent parallel programs. Our approach approximates the first four statistical moments of program execution time in terms of the first four moments of the loop bounds, the branch conditions, and the execution time delays of the constituent tasks. The approach is intended to allow the use of stochastic workloads for modeling accuracy, while at the same time offering execution time expressions of $O(1)$ solution complexity.

Our moments method is implemented in terms of PAMELA, offering modeling support by automatically generating the analytic performance models. Apart from a deterministic version, a first version of the compiler has been developed that completely supports stochastic workloads, automatically producing the first four moments of program execution time. Our experimental results show that the prediction error is in the percent range while the evaluation of the models only takes a few seconds. Future work is mainly directed to analyzing larger parallel programs.

Acknowledgements. The authors gratefully acknowledge the anonymous reviewers for their insightful comments.

References

1. V.S. Adve and M.K. Vernon, "The influence of random delays on parallel execution times," in *Proc. of the 1993 ACM SIGMETRICS Conference on Measurement and Modeling of Computer Systems*, May 1993, pp. 61–73.
2. T.S. Axelrod, "Effects of synchronization barriers on multiprocessor performance," *Parallel Computing*, vol. 3, May 1986, pp. 129–140.
3. H. Gautama, "Static branch performance prediction using alternating renewal processes," Tech. Rep. 1-68340-44(2001)04, Delft University of Technology, Delft, The Netherlands, Mar. 2001.
4. H. Gautama and A.J.C. van Gemund, "Static performance prediction of data-dependent programs," in *ACM Proc. on The Second Int. Workshop on Software and Performance (WOSP 2000)*, Sept. 2000, pp. 216–226. Ottawa, Canada.
5. H. Gautama and A.J.C. van Gemund, "Low-cost performance prediction of data-dependent data parallel programs," in *Proc. of the 9th Int. Symp. on Modeling, Analysis, and Simulation of Computer and Telecommunication Systems (MASCOTS 2001)*, IEEE Computer Society Press, Aug. 2001, pp. 173–182. Cincinnati, Ohio.
6. H. Gautama and A.J.C. van Gemund, "Performance prediction of data-dependent task parallel programs," in *Proc. of the 7th Int. Conference on Parallel Processing (EuroPar 2001)*, Aug. 2001, pp. 106–116. Manchester, United Kingdom.
7. E. Gelenbe, E. Montagne, R. Suros and C.M. Woodside, "Performance of block-structured parallel programs," in *Parallel Algorithms and Architectures* (M. Cosnard *et al.*, eds.), Amsterdam: North-Holland, 1986, pp. 127–138.
8. A.J.C. van Gemund, "Performance prediction of parallel processing systems: The PAMELA methodology," in *Proc. 7th ACM Int. Conf. on Supercomputing*, Tokyo, July 1993, pp. 318–327.

9. A.J.C. van Gemund, "Compile-time performance prediction of parallel systems," in *Proc. Computer Performance Evaluation: Modelling Techniques and Tools (Tools'95), LNCS 977*, Heidelberg, Sept. 1995, pp. 299–313.
10. A.J.C. van Gemund, *Performance Modeling of Parallel Systems.* Delft University Press, 1996.
11. E.J. Gumbel, "Statistical theory of extreme values (main results)," in *Contributions to Order Statistics* (A.E. Sarhan and B.G. Greenberg, eds.), New York: John Wiley & Sons, 1962, pp. 56–93.
12. E.J. Dudewicz J.S. Ramberg, P.R. Tadikamalla and F.M. Mykytka, "A probability distribution and its uses in fitting data," *Technometrics*, vol. 21, May 1979, pp. 201–214.
13. W. Kreutzer, *System simulation, programming styles and languages.* Addison-Wesley, 1986.
14. C.P. Kruskal and A. Weiss, "Allocating independent subtasks on parallel processors," *IEEE Trans. on Software Engineering*, vol. 11, Oct. 1985, pp. 1001–1016.
15. B.P. Lester, "A system for the speedup of parallel programs," in *Proc. of the 1986 Int. Conference on Parallel Processing*, IEEE, Aug. 1986, pp. 145–152. Maharishi Int. U, Fairfield, Iowa.
16. J. Lüthi, S. Majumdar, G. Kotsis and G. Haring, "Performance bounds for distributed systems with workload variabilities and uncertainties," *Parallel Computing*, vol. 22, Feb. 1997, pp. 1789–1806.
17. S. Madala and J.B. Sinclair, "Performance of synchronous parallel algorithms with regular structures," *IEEE Trans. on Parallel and Distributed Systems*, vol. 2, Jan. 1991, pp. 105–116.
18. PAMELA Project Web Site, `http://ce.et.tudelft.nl/~hasyim/Pamela`.
19. M. Reiser and S.S. Lavenberg, "Mean value analysis of closed multichain queueing networks," *Journal of the ACM*, vol. 27, Apr. 1980, pp. 313–322.
20. J.T. Robinson, "Some analysis techniques for asynchronous multiprocessor algorithms," *IEEE Trans. on Software Engineering*, vol. 5, Jan. 1979, pp. 24–31.
21. R.A. Sahner and K.S. Trivedi, "Performance and reliability analysis using directed acyclic graphs," *IEEE Trans. on Software Engineering*, vol. 13, Oct. 1987, pp. 1105–1114.
22. V. Sarkar, "Determining average program execution times and their variance," in *Proc. of the SIGPLAN '89 Conference on Programming Language Design and Implementation*, 1989, pp. 298–312.
23. J.M. Schopf and F. Berman, "Performance prediction in production environments," in *Proc. of the 1st Merged Int. Parallel Processing Symposium and Symposium on Parallel and Distributed Processing (IPPS/SPDP-98)*, Los Alamitos, IEEE Computer Society, Mar. 30–Apr. 3 1998, pp. 647–653.
24. J.M. Schopf and F. Berman, "Using stochastic information to predict application behavior on contended resources," *IJFCS: Int. Journal of Foundations of Computer Science*, vol. 12, 2001.
25. H. Shi and J. Schaeffer, "Parallel sorting by regular sampling," *Journal of Parallel and Distributed Computing*, vol. 14, no. 4, 1992, pp. 361–372.
26. F. Sötz, "A method for performance prediction of parallel programs," in *Proc. CONPAR 90-VAPP IV (LNCS 457)* (H. Burkhart, ed.), Springer-Verlag, 1990, pp. 98–107.

Analysis of a Transaction System with Checkpointing, Failures, and Rollback

L. Kumar[1], M. Misra[1], and I. Mitrani[2]

[1] Indian Institute of Technology, Roorkee
[2] University of Newcastle upon Tyne, UK

Abstract. We consider a system where transactions are processed by a single server subject to faults and recovery. A checkpoint is attempted after a fixed number of transactions have been completed, and takes some time to establish. The occurrence of a fault causes a rollback to the last checkpoint, after which all intervening transactions are reprocessed. The system is modelled by a two-dimensional Markov process with one unbounded variable (the number of transactions in the queue), and one bounded variable (the number of transactions processed since the last checkpoint). The joint steady-state distribution of the process, and hence the performance measures of interest, is found by two different methods: generating functions and spectral expansion. The problem of determining the optimal checkpointing parameter is considered.

1 Introduction

Checkpointing and rollback-recovery are common techniques that allow processes to make progress in the presence of faults. A process takes a checkpoint by saving its current state in the stable storage at intermediate points. When a fault occurs, it rolls back to the last checkpoint and starts executing from there. This reduces the lost execution time.

Many checkpointing strategies have been proposed and analyzed in the literature [2,4,5,6,9,10]. A survey and a classification of results can be found in Nicola and Spanje [10], who distinguish three categories of checkpointing strategies and three recovery models. The interval between consecutive checkpoints may be state-independent and random (exponentially distributed) [4,5], it may be fixed [2], or it may be based on a specified number of transactions [6,9,10] (combinations of these policies are also possible). Similarly, the time taken to recover from a fault may be modelled as a random variable with a given distribution (exponential), whose parameter depends on the work done since the last checkpoint [4,5,6]; it may involve an independent re-sampling of the services since the last checkpoint [9,10]; or it may ba a deterministic repetition of the work done since the last checkpoint.

Exact analytical results are available only under the simplest set of assumptions (exponentially distributed checkpoint and recovery intervals). All other models involve various approximations. In a step towards remedying this situation, we present an exact analysis of the transaction system model introduced

T. Field et al. (Eds.): TOOLS 2002, LNCS 2324, pp. 279–288, 2002.

in [9], where the assumptions are quite general and realistic. A checkpoint is established after a fixed number of transactions have been completed. After a fault (which may occur also during the checkpointing operation), all transactions completed since the last checkpoint are returned to the queue and receive new services. The aim of the analysis is to determine the joint steady-state distribution of the numbers of queued transactions and those completed since the last checkpoint. Various performance measures can be obtained from that distribution.

The detailed assumptions of the model, and the resulting equations, are described in section 2. Section 3 presents a solution which uses generating functions. A different solution, based on spectral expansion, is described in section 4. Section 5 contains the results of numerical experiments, where the efficiency of the two solution methods is compared, and the question of the optimal number of transactions between checkpoints is examined.

2 Model and Analysis

We consider a system where transactions, arriving according to a Poisson process with rate λ, are served in FIFO order by a single server. The service times are i.i.d. random variables distributed exponentially with mean μ^{-1}. After N consecutive transactions have been completed, the system performs a checkpoint operation whose duration is an i.i.d. random variable distributed exponentially with mean β^{-1}. Once a checkpoint is established, the N completed transactions are deemed to have departed. However, both transaction processing and checkpointing may be interrupted by the occurrence of a fault. The latter arrive according to an independent Poisson process with rate ξ. When a fault occurs, the system instantaneously rolls back to the last established checkpoint; all transactions which arrived since that moment either remain in the queue, if they have not been processed, or return to it, in order to be processed again (it is assumed that repeated service times are resampled independently).

The above assumptions imply that the system state at time t can be described by two integer random variables, $I(t)$ and $J(t)$, where

$I(t)$ is the number of transactions that have completed service since the last checkpoint;

$J(t)$ is the number of transactions present that have not completed service (including those requiring re-processing).

The process $X = \{[I(t), J(t)]\ ;\ t \geq 0\}$, is an irreducible Markov process with a state space $\{0, 1, \ldots, N\} \times \{0, 1, \ldots\}$. The possible transitions of X out of state (i, j) are:

- To state $(i, j+1)$, with rate λ (arrival of a new transaction);
- To state $(i+1, j-1)$, with rate μ, for $i = 0, 1, \ldots, N-1$ and $j > 0$ (service completion);
- To state $(0, j)$, with rate β, when $i = N$ (checkpoint completion);
- To state $(0, j+i)$, with rate ξ, for $i = 1, 2, \ldots, N$ (fault occurrence).

Denote by $\pi_{i,j}$ the joint steady state distribution of $I(t)$ and $J(t)$:

$$\pi_{i,j} = \lim_{t\to\infty} P[I(t) = i, J(t) = j] \; ; \; i = 0, 1, \ldots, N \; ; \; j = 0, 1, \ldots . \tag{1}$$

These probabilities should satisfy the following balance equations:

$$\pi_{i,j}[\lambda + \mu\delta(j > 0)\delta(i < N) + \xi\delta(i > 0) + \beta\delta(i = N)] =$$
$$\lambda\pi_{i,j-1} + \mu\pi_{i-1,j+1} + \beta\delta(i = 0)\pi_{N,j} + \xi\delta(i = 0) \sum_{k=1}^{\min(j,N)} \pi_{k,j-k} \; , \tag{2}$$

where $\pi_{-1,j} = \pi_{i,-1} = 0$ by definition, and $\delta(B)$ is the indicator function of the boolean B: $\delta(B) = 1$ if B is true, 0 if false. Also, the standard normalizing equation must be satisfied:

$$\sum_{i=0}^{N}\sum_{j=0}^{\infty} \pi_{i,j} = 1 \; . \tag{3}$$

An explicit ergodicity condition, ensuring the existence of a solution for (2) and (3), can be obtained by considering the queue size at consecutive instants when X enters a state of the form $(0, j)$. Those are the moments when either a new checkpoint is successfully established, or an old one is returned to as a result of a fault; we shall refer to them as 'checkpointing instants'. Let t_n be the n'th checkpointing instant, and let J_n be the number of transactions present immediately after it: $J_n = J(t_n+)$. The Markov process X is ergodic if, and only if, the embedded Markov chain $Y = \{J_n \; ; \; n = 1, 2, \ldots\}$, is ergodic. According to Foster's criterion (e.g., see [1]), Y is ergodic iff its average drift is strictly negative:

$$E(J_{n+1} - J_n \,|\, J_n = j) < -\varepsilon \; , \tag{4}$$

for some $\varepsilon > 0$ and all sufficiently large j.

Let $V = t_{n+1} - t_n$ be the interval between two consecutive checkpointing instants, assuming that at time t_n there are at least N transactions present in the queue. Let K be the number of successfully completed operations during V, where an 'operation' is either a service of a transaction or a setting of a checkpoint. Since the latter is done after N services are completed, we have $K < N$ if a service is interrupted by a fault; $K = N$ if the checkpointing operation is interrupted by a fault; $K = N + 1$ if all N services *and* the checkpointing completed successfully.

For values of K strictly less than N we can write

$$P(K = k) = \left(\frac{\mu}{\mu+\xi}\right)^k \frac{\xi}{\mu+\xi} \; ; \; k = 0, 1, \ldots, N-1 \; , \tag{5}$$

and

$$E(V \,|\, K = k) = \frac{k+1}{\mu+\xi} \; ; \; k = 0, 1, \ldots, N-1 \; . \tag{6}$$

When $K = N$, the operation which is interrupted by a fault is checkpointing. Hence,

$$P(K = N) = \left(\frac{\mu}{\mu + \xi}\right)^N \frac{\xi}{\beta + \xi} , \tag{7}$$

and

$$E(V \mid K = N) = \frac{N}{\mu + \xi} + \frac{1}{\beta + \xi} . \tag{8}$$

Finally, all $N + 1$ operations complete successfully when none of them is interrupted by a fault:

$$P(K = N + 1) = \left(\frac{\mu}{\mu + \xi}\right)^N \frac{\beta}{\beta + \xi} , \tag{9}$$

and

$$E(V \mid K = N + 1) = \frac{N}{\mu + \xi} + \frac{1}{\beta + \xi} . \tag{10}$$

The unconditional average interval between two consecutive checkpointing instants can be shown, after straightforward manipulations, to be equal to

$$E(V) = \frac{1}{\xi}\left[1 - \left(\frac{\mu}{\mu + \xi}\right)^N \frac{\beta}{\beta + \xi}\right] . \tag{11}$$

The average number of arrivals during the interval V is $\lambda E(V)$. On the other hand, the number of departures is equal to 0 if the interval is terminated by a fault (i.e., if $K \leq N$), and to N otherwise (remember that at the start of the interval the queue size is at least N). Hence, the average number of departures during V is equal to $N\,P(K = N+1)$. In other words, for all $j \geq N$, the average drift appearing in (4) is equal to

$$E(J_{n+1} - J_n \mid J_n = j) = \lambda E(V) - N\,P(K = N + 1) . \tag{12}$$

This, together with (11) and (9), establishes the following:

Proposition 1 *The Markov process X and the Markov chain Y are ergodic if, and only if,*

$$\frac{\lambda}{\xi}\left[1 - \left(\frac{\mu}{\mu + \xi}\right)^N \frac{\beta}{\beta + \xi}\right] < N\left(\frac{\mu}{\mu + \xi}\right)^N \frac{\beta}{\beta + \xi} . \tag{13}$$

When the above condition is satisfied, the balance and normalizing equations (2) and (3) can be solved numerically, in order to determine performance measures such as the steady state average number of transactions in the queue, $E(J)$, or in the system, $E(I + J)$, or the steady state average response time of a transaction, given by $E(I + J)/\lambda$. This is the subject of the following two sections.

3 Solution by Generating Functions

The infinite set of equations (2) can be transformed into a finite set of functional recurrences. Let $g_i(z)$ be the generating function of the stationary probabilities for states with i completed transactions:

$$g_i(z) = \sum_{j=0}^{\infty} \pi_{i,j} z^j \; ; \quad i = 0, 1, \ldots, N \; . \tag{14}$$

It is convenient to introduce the following notation:

$$\rho = \frac{\lambda}{\mu} \; ; \quad \sigma = \frac{\beta}{\mu} \; ; \quad \tau = \frac{\xi}{\mu} \; ; \quad a(z) = \rho(1-z) + \tau \; .$$

Then, multiplying both sides of (2) by z^j and summing over all j, we obtain, for $0 < i < N$,

$$z[a(z)+1]g_i(z) = g_{i-1}(z) + z\pi_{i,0} - \pi_{i-1,0} \; ; \quad i = 1, 2, \ldots, N-1 \; . \tag{15}$$

Similarly, for $i = N$, we have

$$z[a(z)+\sigma]g_N(z) = g_{N-1}(z) - \pi_{N-1,0} \; . \tag{16}$$

When $i = 0$, the corresponding equation is

$$[a(z) - \tau + 1]g_0(z) = (\sigma + \tau z^N)g_N(z) + \pi_{0,0} + \tau \sum_{k=1}^{N-1} z^k g_k(z) \; . \tag{17}$$

By consecutive elimination, using equations (16) and (15), we can express $g_N(z)$ in terms of $g_0(z)$:

$$\begin{aligned} &z^N[a(z)+1]^{N-1}[a(z)+\sigma]g_N(z) = \\ &g_0(z) - \pi_{0,0} - za(z)\sum_{k=1}^{N-1} z^{k-1}[a(z)+1]^{k-1}\pi_{k,0} \; . \end{aligned} \tag{18}$$

Next, multiply equation (15) by z^{i-1} and sum for $i = 1, 2, \ldots, N-1$. This yields, after cancellation and grouping similar terms,

$$a(z)\sum_{k=1}^{N-1} z^k g_k(z) = g_0(z) - z^{N-1}g_{N-1}(z) - \pi_{0,0} + z^{N-1}\pi_{N-1,0} \; . \tag{19}$$

This last equation can be rewritten, after replacing $g_{N-1}(z)$ with $g_N(z)$ via (16), as

$$a(z)\sum_{k=1}^{N-1} z^k g_k(z) = g_0(z) - z^N[a(z)+\sigma]g_N(z) - \pi_{0,0} \; . \tag{20}$$

Substituting (20) into (17) and eliminating $g_N(z)$ with the aid of (18), we obtain an expression for $g_0(z)$:

$$g_0(z) = \frac{b(z)}{R(z)} , \tag{21}$$

where

$$b(z) = \{\rho(1-z)z^N[a(z)+\sigma][a(z)+1]^{N-1} - \sigma[a(z)-\tau z^N]\}\pi_{0,0}$$
$$- \sigma z a(z)[a(z)-\tau z^N]\sum_{k=1}^{N-1} z^{k-1}[a(z)+1]^{k-1}\pi_{i,0} ,$$

and

$$R(z) = \rho(1-z)z^N[a(z)+\sigma][a(z)+1]^N - \sigma[a(z)-\tau z^N] .$$

Thus, $g_0(z)$ is given in terms of N unknown constants, $\pi_{0,0}$, $\pi_{1,0}$, ..., $\pi_{N-1,0}$. These are determined by the requirement that $g_0(z)$ should be analytic in the unit disc (since it is a power series which converges at $z = 1$). In particular, if there is a point z such that $z < 1$ and $R(z) = 0$, then the numerator in the right-hand side of (21) must also vanish at that point.

The polynomial $R(z)$ is of degree $2N + 2$. One of its zeros is at $z = 1$, as can be seen directly. When the process is ergodic, the other zeros are positioned according to the following:

Proposition 2 *If the inequality (13) holds, then $R(z)$ has $N-1$ zeros, z_1, z_2, ..., z_{N-1}, such that $|z_l| < 1$ ($l = 1, 2, \ldots, N-1$), and $N+2$ zeros, u_1, u_2, ..., u_{N+2}, such that $|u_l| > 1$ ($l = 1, 2, \ldots, N+2$).*

The justification of this Proposition will be left until the next section. It suffices to mention here that similar results have been established elsewhere in the literature (for a thorough analysis, see Gail, Hantler and Taylor [3]). (It is worth pointing out that the ergodicity condition is equivalent to the requirement that $R(z)$ be strictly increasing at $z = 1$, i.e., $R'(1) > 0$.)

Hence, we have

$$b(z_l) = 0 ; \quad l = 1, 2, \ldots, N-1 . \tag{22}$$

Moreover, by using the fact that $R(z_l) = 0$, (22) can be simplified and reduced to

$$-a(z_l)\pi_{0,0} + \sum_{k=1}^{N-1} z_l^k[a(z_l)+1]^k\pi_{i,0} = 0 ; \quad l = 1, 2, \ldots, N-1 . \tag{23}$$

This is a set of $N-1$ independent linear equations for the unknown probabilities $\pi_{i,0}$. Together with the normalizing equation,

$$\sum_{i=0}^{N} g_i(1) = 1 , \tag{24}$$

they determine the unknowns uniquely.

The average number of transactions in the queue, $E(J)$, and in the system, $E(I+J)$, are obtained from

$$E(J) = \sum_{i=0}^{N} g_i'(1) , \tag{25}$$

and

$$E(I+J) = \sum_{i=0}^{N} [g_i'(1) + i g_i(1)] . \tag{26}$$

4 Spectral Expansion Solution

Define the row vectors of state probabilities where the *total number* of transactions present is j, for $j \geq N$:

$$\mathbf{v}_j = (p_{0,j}, p_{1,j-1}, \ldots, p_{N,j-N}) \; ; \; j = N, N+1, \ldots . \tag{27}$$

Then the balance equations (2) can be rewritten in the form of vector recurrences of the M/G/1 type:

$$\mathbf{v}_j A = \mathbf{v}_{j-1} B + \mathbf{v}_j C + \mathbf{v}_{j+N} D \; ; \; j = N+1, N+2, \ldots , \tag{28}$$

where the $(N+1) \times (N+1)$ matrices A, B, C and D are defined as

$$A = \begin{bmatrix} \lambda+\mu & 0 & & & \\ 0 & \lambda+\mu+\xi & & & \\ & & \ddots & & \\ & & & \lambda+\mu+\xi & 0 \\ & & & 0 & \lambda+\xi+\beta \end{bmatrix} ,$$

$$B = \begin{bmatrix} \lambda & 0 & & & \\ 0 & \lambda & & & \\ & & \ddots & & \\ & & & & 0 \\ & & & 0 & \lambda \end{bmatrix} , \quad C = \begin{bmatrix} 0 & \mu & & & \\ \xi & 0 & \mu & & \\ \vdots & & \ddots & \ddots & \\ \xi & & & 0 & \mu \\ \xi & & & & 0 \end{bmatrix} , \quad D = \begin{bmatrix} 0 & & & \\ \vdots & & & \\ 0 & & & \\ \beta & 0 & \cdots & 0 \end{bmatrix} .$$

The recurrences (28) can be rewritten as a vector difference equation of order $N+1$ with constant coefficients:

$$\mathbf{v}_j Q_0 + \mathbf{v}_{j+1} Q_1 + \mathbf{v}_{j+N+1} Q_{N+1} = 0 \; ; \; j = N, N+1, \ldots , \tag{29}$$

where $Q_0 = B$, $Q_1 = C - A$ and $Q_{N+1} = D$. Associated with that equation is the matrix polynomial

$$Q(z) = Q_0 + Q_1 z + Q_{N+1} z^{N+1} , \tag{30}$$

which is given by

$$Q(z) = \begin{bmatrix} \lambda - (\lambda+\mu)z & \mu z & & \\ \xi z & \lambda - (\lambda+\mu+\xi)z & \mu z & \\ \vdots & & \ddots & \\ \xi z + \beta z^{N+1} & & & \lambda - (\lambda+\beta+\xi)z \end{bmatrix} . \tag{31}$$

Since $det[Q(z)]$ is a polynomial of degree $2N+1$, $Q(z)$ has $2N+1$ generalized eigenvalues, z_l, and left eigenvectors, $\boldsymbol{\psi}_l$ $(l = 1, 2, \ldots, 2N+1)$, which satisfy

$$\boldsymbol{\psi}_l Q(z_l) = 0 \; ; \; l = 1, 2, \ldots, 2N+1 . \tag{32}$$

The general solution of the difference equation (29) is of the form

$$\mathbf{v}_j = \sum_{l=1}^{2N+1} x_l \boldsymbol{\psi}_l z_l^j \; ; \; j = N, N+1, \ldots , \tag{33}$$

where x_l are arbitrary coefficients. However, in order that the solution be normalizeable, one should include only the eigenvalues z_l which satisfy $|z_l| < 1$, together with their corresponding eigenvectors. That is, the coefficients x_l corresponding to eigenvalues on, or outside the unit circle, must be equal to 0.

Suppose that there are M eigenvalues z_l with $|z_l| < 1$. Then there are M coefficients x_l to be determined in the expansion (33). In addition, the probabilities $\pi_{i,j}$, for $i + j < N$, are not covered by (33). That makes a total of $M + N(N+1)/2$ unknown constants. On the other hand, the balance equations (2), for $i+j \le N$, are still to be used. One of those is dependent on the others and should be replaced by the normalizing equation. Thus we have $(N+1)(N+2)/2$ independent linear equations for $M + N(N+1)/2$ unknowns. That set has a unique solution if, and only if, $M = N+1$. We know, however, that a unique solution exists when the process is ergodic. Hence, when the condition (13) is satisfied, the matrix polynomial $Q(z)$ has $N+1$ generalized eigenvalues in the interior of the unit disc.

The polynomials involved in the spectral expansion and generating function solutions, $det[Q(z)]$ and $R(z)$, are closely related. Specifically, by expanding the determinant in (31) along its first column and performing appropriate manipulations, we see that

$$det[Q(z)] = \frac{(-\mu)^{N+1} z^{2N+1}}{a(1/z)} R(1/z) . \tag{34}$$

Hence, the zeros of $det[Q(z)]$ *inside* the unit disc are precisely the reciprocals of the zeros of $R(z)$ *outside* the unit disc, with the exception of the one which is also a zero of $a(z)$. This observation, together with the fact that $det[Q(z)]$ has $N+1$ such zeros, shows that $R(z)$ has $N+2$ zeros outside the unit disc (one of which is the zero of $a(z)$). This leaves the zero of $R(z)$ at $z = 1$ and $N-1$ zeros inside the unit disc, which establishes Proposition 2.

Having determined the coefficients x_l and the probabilities $\pi_{i,j}$ for $i+j < N$, the performance measures can be obtained without difficulty. For example, the average total number of transactions in the system is given by

$$E(I+J) = \sum_{k=1}^{N-1} k \sum_{j=0}^{k} \pi_{k-j,j} + \sum_{l=1}^{N+1} x_l \psi_l z_l^N \frac{1}{1-z_l} \left[N + \frac{z_l}{1-z_l} \right] . \quad (35)$$

5 Numerical Results

Either of the above solution methods can be used to evaluate the performance of the system. The choice is influenced by considerations of efficiency, and also by the nature of the required performance measures. If the only quantities of interest are the averages $E(I)$ and $E(J)$, then the generating functions approach is faster (it requires only the determination of $N-1$ roots and the solution of an $N \times N$ set of linear equations). If, on the other hand, one is also interested in marginal distributions (e.g., the probability that there are more than 100 transactions in the queue), then the generating functions are not very useful, whereas spectral expansion provides the answer readily. The spectral expansion solution tends to be slower because, in addition to the $N+1$ eigenvalues, eigenvectors and expansion coefficients, one has to determine $N(N+1)/2$ boundary probabilities. There are ways of improving the efficiency of this solution, but we have not explored these fully.

Of major practical interest is the effect of the parameter N, the number of transactions between two checkpoints, on the performance of the system. Clearly, it is inefficient to set N too small, because that causes service capacity to be wasted on establishing checkpoints. On the other hand, setting it too large is also inefficient, because when a fault occurs, many transactions will have to be reprocessed. Indeed, even a lightly loaded system (low arrival rate, high service rate) becomes saturated when N increases beyond a certain threshold. Table 1 shows the minimum, maximum and optimum values of the number of transactions between checkpoints, N_{min}, N_{max} and N_{opt}, for different values of the arrival rate, λ. The first two numbers are given by the ergodicity condition, they do not require the model to be solved. The third number was obtained using the spectral expansion solution. The performance measure to be optimized was the total number of transactions in the system, $E(I+J)$.

It can be observed that, for these parameter values, N_{opt} is much closer to N_{min} than to N_{max}. In fact, one may be tempted to dispense with the tedium of model solution, and use a simple heuristic as an approximation of N_{opt}. The quality of that approximation would depend, of course, on how steep, or shallow, is the change in performance when N varies. In the present example, an approximation replacing N_{opt} by $\min(2N_{min}, (N_{min}+N_{max})/2$ would work very well. To find out whether this can be recommended as a general 'rule of thumb' would require more experimentation.

Table 1. $\mu = 1$, $\beta = 0.06$, $\xi = 0.01$

λ	N_{min}	N_{max}	N_{opt}
0.1	2	343	5
0.2	5	244	10
0.3	8	181	15
0.4	14	130	23
0.5	25	83	38

6 Conclusion

In this paper we have considered a system that provides fault tolerance by taking a checkpoint after completing a fixed number of transactions. Two exact methods for evaluating the performance of that system are presented: one using generating functions and the other based on spectral expansion. The first method is numerically faster, but is suitable mainly for computing averages. The second method tends to be slower, but yields directly the joint and marginal distributions of the numbers of transactions in the queue and in the system.

References

1. S. Asmussen, Applied Probability and Queues, Wiley, 1987.
2. K.M. Chandy, J.C. Browne, C.W. Dissly and W.R. Uhrig, "Analytic models for rollback and recovery strategies in database systems", IEEE Trans. Soft. Engin., 1, 100-110, 1975.
3. H.R. Gail, S.L. Hantler and B.A. Taylor, "Spectral analysis of $M/G/1$ and $G/M/1$ type Markov chains", Adv. Appl. Prob., 28, 114-165, 1996.
4. E. Gelenbe, "On the optimum checkpoint interval", JACM, 26, 259-270, 1979.
5. E. Gelenbe and D. Derochette, "Performance of rollback recovery systems under intermittent failures", CACM, 21, 493-499, 1979.
6. N. Mikou and S. Tucci, "Analyse et optimisation d'une procédure de reprise dans un système de gestion de données centralisées", Acta informatica, 12, 321-338, 1979.
7. I. Mitrani and R. Chakka, "Spectral expansion solution for a class of Markov models: application and comparision with the matrix-gemometric method", Performance Evaluation, 23, 241-260, 1995.
8. I. Mitrani and P.J.B. King, "Multiprocessor systems with preemptive priorities", Performance Evaluation 1, 118-125, 1981.
9. V.F. Nicola and F.J. Kylstra, "A model of checkpointing and recovery with a specified number of transactions between checkpoints", Procs., Performance'83, North-Holland, 83-100, 1983.
10. V.F. Nicola and J.M. van Spanje, "Comparative analysis of different models of checkpointing and recovery", IEEE Transactions on Software Engineering, 16, 8, 807-821, 1990.
11. K.S. Trivedi, Probability and statistics with reliability, queueing and computer science applications, Prentice-Hall, 1982.

Analyzing Voice-over-IP Subjective Quality as a Function of Network QoS: A Simulation-Based Methodology and Tool

Adrian E. Conway[1] and Yali Zhu[2]

[1]Verizon Laboratories, 40 Sylvan Road, Waltham, MA 02451, USA
adrian.conway@verizon.com
[2]Computer Science Department, Worcester Polytechnic Institute, 100 Institute Road, Worcester, MA 01609, USA
yaliz@wpi.edu

Abstract. A simulation-based methodology is developed for analyzing the subjective quality of voice-over-IP calls as a function of network QoS parameters and choices in implementation and configuration. The proposed method combines the use of existing objective voice-quality measurement algorithms, such as the ITU-T P.861 PSQM, and artificial voice reference signals, such as the ITU-T P.50, with the discrete-event simulation of a network QoS model. A significant advantage of the method is that it does not involve the use of human subjects in evaluating subjective voice quality levels. This enables one to entirely automate the process of quantifying call quality as a function of network QoS and implementation choices such as packet size and codec type. Such automation enables one to realize significant time and cost savings in obtaining experimental results. A tool implementation is described that includes basic network packet loss and delay jitter models. Example numerical results are presented for the G.711 codec. The extension of the method to the subjective quality evaluation of audio, video, and multimedia signals is also described. The paper also introduces the concepts of 'subjective teletraffic engineering' and 'subjective equivalent bandwidths.'

1 Introduction

A recent phenomenon in telephony is the increasing use of IP networks and IP-based technologies for the transport of voice calls [20]. In a typical voice-over-IP (VoIP) call, the voice signal is digitally encoded with a codec such as G.711, G.723, or G.729, and packetized into RTP/UDP/IP packets for streaming over the Internet. At the receiving end, the arriving packet stream is buffered, depacketized, and decoded into the received voice signal. In traversing the Internet, the VoIP packet stream may be perturbed by a number of network impairments such as packet loss, packet reordering, and packet delay jitter. These perturbations all combine to degrade the perceived quality of the received voice signal.

T. Field et al. (Eds.): TOOLS 2002, LNCS 2324, pp. 289-308, 2002.

To ensure that the voice quality, as perceived by the end-users, will be at an acceptable level or at a level required by a service level agreement (SLA) [25], the VoIP network should be engineered to meet the target quality requirements [18]. A natural approach towards engineering a VoIP network is to first establish the end-to-end network quality-of-service (QoS) that is required to support the target voice quality level, assign portions of the overall QoS 'budget' to the various sub-networks that are traversed by the VoIP call, and engineer or design each sub-network to meet its QoS budget allotment. Each QoS allotment will typically be specified in terms of a combination of loss, delay, and delay jitter metrics.

A fundamental problem at the foundation of VoIP network traffic engineering methodology is, therefore, to be able to quantify how the subjective quality, as perceived by human end-users, depends on the network QoS parameters and choices in implementation and configuration. A subjective quality metric that is now widely adopted in telephony is the mean opinion score (MOS) [14]. The grades of MOS are found in the Absolute Category Rating (ACR) method of ITU-T P.800 [14]. As shown in Table 1, they provide a quality score in the range of 1 to 5. Hence, the relationship between MOS and network QoS parameter values needs to be analyzed for different codec types, packetization methods, buffering mechanisms, play-out algorithms, and the combinations thereof.

Table 1. Mean Opinion Score Scale

5	Excellent
4	Good
3	Fair
2	Poor
1	Bad

There are several approaches that may be adopted to determine how the MOS depends on network QoS. A direct approach to this problem is to build a test VoIP network in a lab environment and use human subjects to evaluate signal quality for different network QoS conditions and VoIP equipment configurations. This is the most comprehensive and realistic approach towards testing. However, a difficulty with this solution is that it is very expensive and time consuming to use real human subjects, especially when there are many different subjective experiments to be conducted. The construction and operation of a test network in a lab environment is also expensive. It is also time-consuming and expensive to modify a test network for many different experimental configurations. Another problem with the approach is that the experimental results are not, in general, reproducible since subjective evaluation is carried out using real human subjects whose opinions are variable.

An alternate method of evaluating VoIP quality in a network lab environment is to use commercially available test equipment that uses objective methods for the subjective quality measurement of voice signals. In contrast to using human subjects, an objective method applies a machine-executable algorithm to determine the quality of a received voice signal as compared to an original transmitted signal [29]. An example of an objective method is the standardized ITU-T P.861 objective quality measurement method based on the Perceptual Speech Quality Measure (PSQM) [15]. This method was developed originally for comparing the subjective quality of different speech codecs. It is now also being applied to objectively measure subjective voice quality in packet-switched networks. Examples of commercially available test equipment that use PSQM include the Abacus system from Zarak Systems Corporation [1], the VoIP Test System from Hammer Technologies, the 935AT Telecom Test Set from Sage Instruments, and the OPERA™ tool from Opticom GmbH [19].

Although objective signal quality measurement equipment can be used to replace the use of human subjects in evaluating voice signal quality in a laboratory network, using such equipment in a lab environment can still be time consuming and expensive especially when there are many different experiments to be carried out. To reduce the time and costs of measuring voice quality in a lab environment, one could automate the control of the objective measurement equipment. One could also replace the test VoIP network by a network emulator such as NIST Net [22].

In this paper, we develop an automated software-based simulation method for analyzing VoIP subjective quality as a function of network QoS and choices in implementation and configuration. Compared to the approaches described above, the proposed method is a significant further step forward in reducing the time and costs involved in subjective testing. The method combines the use of existing objective voice quality measurement algorithms, such as the ITU-T P.861 PSQM, and artificial voice reference signals, such as the ITU-T P.50, with the discrete-event simulation of a network QoS model. As a simulation-based method that can be implemented entirely in software, it provides a number of significant advantages. It replaces live human voices by artificial voice signals. It replaces subjective human evaluation by a machine-executable algorithm. It allows one to entirely automate the process of quantifying voice quality as a function of a plethora of network QoS conditions and choices in implementation and configuration. The simulation methodology enables significant time and cost savings, especially when there are a large number of experiments to be carried out. The methodology can also be extended to audio, video, and multimedia signals.

In the following section, we first survey related work in order to properly situate the proposed simulation-based method. The general proposed methodology is then described in Section 3. Our implementation of the method in a tool is described in Section 4. This tool includes basic network models for packet loss and delay jitter. In Section 5, we present some example numerical results for the G.711 codec to illustrate the operation of the present tool. In Section 6, we indicate directions in which the present work is being extended and explain how the proposed simulation-based methodology may be extended to the automated objective quality evaluation of packetized audio, video, and multimedia signals. We also explain how the tool may be applied in the development of 'subjective teletraffic engineering' rules and methods for VoIP. The concept of 'subjective equivalent bandwidth' is also introduced.

2 Related Work

We first survey related work to situate the present contribution. The subjective human evaluation of the quality of traditional circuit-switched voice calls as a function of circuit QoS (i.e. propagation delay, group delay, SNR, and echo) has, of course, already been studied extensively since the early days of telephony [8]. In the more recent timeframe, the subjective human evaluation of packet-switched voice calls as a function of virtual circuit QoS (i.e. packet loss, delay, and delay jitter) has also been studied [4, 21, 23]. An introduction to the use of test equipment, that implements computer-based objective methods (e.g. PSQM) for the subjective evaluation of voice call quality, is provided in [7]. Recent work in the area of the objective quality analysis of voice in packet networks as a function of network QoS includes [2], [5], [10], and [28].

In [2], a method called *VQmon* is developed for estimating the transmission quality of VoIP calls. The method is intended for the non-intrusive real-time passive monitoring of VoIP calls. It uses an extended version of the ITU G.107 E-model. The method is much simpler computationally than the existing objective methods such as PSQM. Hence, it is suitable for embedding in VoIP gateways and IP phones as a real-time passive monitoring method. A different approach towards non-intrusive passive monitoring is presented in [5].

In [10], an automatic speech recognition (ASR) system is used to evaluate VoIP speech quality for the G.723 and G.729 codecs. Results are presented for the 'recognition accuracy' as a function of various packet loss rates and packet sizes, but the recognition accuracy measure is not related to a subjective score such as MOS.

In [28], the effect of the *location* of packet loss on perceived speech quality is studied. A simulation system is implemented to obtain the experimental results. This system uses reference speech files and objective methods of speech quality analysis, including PSQM+ [17]. The simulation approach adopted in [28] is along the same lines as the method developed here. The simulation-based methodology presented here, however, is made in the more general context of the development of a general purpose VoIP engineering tool that is able to handle the analysis of a network QoS model in conjunction with various implementation and configuration choices such as codec type, packetization method, buffering method, and play-out algorithm. To our knowledge, such a general purpose simulation-based methodology and VoIP engineering tool is a new development.

3 Automated Objective Methodology

The methodology proposed here can be used to simplify and automate the process of evaluating the subjective quality of VoIP calls as a function of network QoS parameters, codec type, packetization method, buffering mechanism, play-out algorithm, other implementation choices and parameters, and combinations thereof. The main novel idea in the method is to integrate existing objective voice quality measurement methods, such as PSQM [15], and pre-recorded reference or test signals, such as artificial voice signals [12, 13], in a computer-executable simulation engine that includes the modeling of network-level QoS, codec type, packetization method, buffering mechanism, play-out algorithm, and other related implementation details.

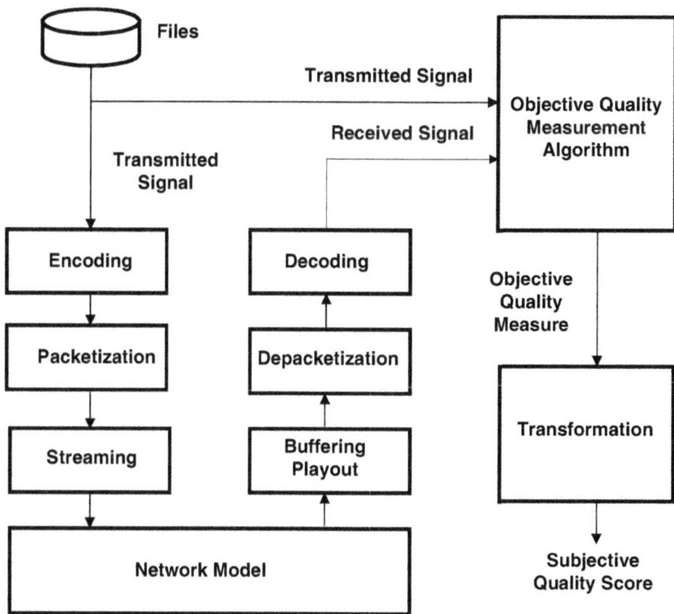

Fig. 1. Block diagram of automated objective methodology for subjective quality evaluation of VoIP

The general methodology is shown in Fig. 1. In the simulation engine, a stored signal such as, for example, an artificial voice signal is encoded into a digital signal following an encoding procedure such as, for example, G.711 or G.729. The encoded digital signal is then packetized into, for example, RTP/UDP/IP packets. The packets are transmitted (or streamed) to the network model shown in Fig. 1. The network model introduces simulated QoS impairments into the transmitted packet stream. Impairments may take the form of, for example, packet loss, packet reordering, and packet delay jitter. The QoS impairments may themselves be generated according to a simulated model. Also, the network model may itself be a simulated network that contains simulated background packet traffic.

The packets that traverse the simulated network model then arrive at a simulated destination where they are buffered and played out according to a specified play-out algorithm. The packet payloads are extracted from the played out packets (depacketization) to form the received encoded digital signal. The received encoded digital signal is then decoded according to the given codec type thus yielding the final received voice signal. The subjective quality of this received signal is then obtained by comparing the final received signal with the original transmitted voice signal using an objective quality measurement algorithm such as PSQM. Finally, the output of the objective quality measurement algorithm may be transformed by a mapping function to provide a subjective quality [15] score such as a MOS score [14].

The proposed simulation methodology has a number of attractive features and advantages compared to other approaches such as the ones mentioned in Section 2. The main advantageous feature is, of course, that it does not require the use of any human subjects to conduct subjective signal quality testing. Another main advantage of the simulation engine approach is that the process of conducting multiple tests with different parameter settings may be automated under software control. This enables one to conduct subjective quality testing for large sets of experiments in a time efficient manner with significant cost savings. The method is also inherently flexible so that it may accommodate different codec types, packetization methods, buffering methods, play-out algorithms, network models, and network QoS impairment models. It may also include new experimental types of codecs that are not yet standardized or implemented in products (e.g. bandwidth-adaptive codecs). As well, the method may incorporate new, improved, or revised, objective quality measurement algorithms, such as the ITU-T P.862 Perceptual Evaluation of Speech Quality (PESQ) method [16], as they become available. Finally, the method provides experimental results that are, of course, reproducible since the method does not rely on the use of any human subjects.

All of these attractive features and advantages do not, of course, make the proposed method a complete replacement for testing in a lab environment using hardware and real subjective human evaluation. However, they do provide the proposed method with a valuable role to be played in the field of VoIP traffic engineering. For example, the method may be applied to the mass testing of different types of configurations and parameter settings in order to obtain the ranges of parameter combinations that map to different quality levels. Such large scale testing may be infeasible in practice using other approaches. Large scale testing may also be used to explore more fully the 'multidimensional' design space so as to gain a better understanding of the critical elements affecting voice quality. As discussed further in Section 6, the method may also be used in the development of 'subjective teletraffic engineering' rules and methods for VoIP. Such developments would be difficult or impractical without the use of a tool that automates the process of conducting subjective evaluation in conjunction with the simulation of a network model that includes QoS.

4 Tool Implementation

The methodology of Section 3 has been implemented in a tool that runs on the Windows NT 4.0 platform. This choice of platform was dictated by the operating system required by the (objective voice quality) measurement software that we integrate into the tool. Fig. 2 illustrates the software architecture of the tool implementation. Reference voice signal input files are stored as standard WAV files. These files are constructed from the raw 16-bit 16-KHz sampled voice signal files that are available in a compact disc from the ITU-T [13]. The voice signals include the reference artificial voice signal P.50, as well as reference voice signals in various different languages for both male and female speakers. The ITU reference voice signals are each of relatively short duration. For example, the P.50 signal is only about 11 seconds long and the English female signal is only about 12 seconds long. In order to run the network QoS simulations for a sufficient length of time to obtain 'equilibrium' results, we construct longer WAV files by simply concatenating copies of the same shorter reference file. Such concatenation produces a periodic voice signal that can lead to non-stationary side effects in the voice quality measurements. However, this method of construction was adopted initially for the sake of immediate simplicity. Other methods of construction can be developed (see Section 6).

The tool takes its inputs from (i) a CONFIG file that specifies all the fixed parameters in running the tool for a set of experiments and (ii) a RUN file that specifies the different individual experiments that are to be run. Each individual experiment is distinguished by a particular set of parameter combinations.

As shown in Fig. 2, the first step in an experimental run is to create and store the input packet list that is to be transmitted or 'streamed' to the network. The construction of the packet list takes into account the voice encoding algorithm to be used, the amount of voice data to be placed in each packet, and the type of packet (e.g. RTP/UDP/IP) to be streamed. Relative timestamps and sequence numbers are assumed to be contained in each packet.

Having constructed the input packet list, the next step is to simulate the arrival of this VoIP packet stream to the network model. This network model consists of a discrete-event network simulation that is driven by the previously constructed VoIP input packet stream. The network simulation model includes the modeling of network QoS effects such as packet loss, delay jitter, packet sequencing, and packet duplication. Both the network modeling and the QoS modeling may be made arbitrarily complex. For the purposes of this paper, however, we limit our attention to three simple models: (i) a simple Bernoulli loss model in which packets are simply discarded at random, (ii) a bursty loss model, and (iii) a delay jitter model that also includes Bernoulli loss. In the bursty loss model, the start of a packet burst is determined according to a Bernoulli trial and the burst length is assumed to be Poisson distributed. The delay jitter model consists of a single FIFO queue with the VoIP traffic stream multiplexed in with other background traffic that is assumed to arrive according to a Poisson process. The background traffic packet lengths are assumed to be Poisson distributed. The effect of the background traffic is to introduce delay jitter into the VoIP packet stream.

The output of the network simulation model is a stream of VoIP packets. These packets are timestamped with their exit time. The effect of the network model is to perturb the original input packet stream. The network perturbations experimented with here are packet loss and delay jitter. Other network perturbations, such as out-of-sequence packets and duplicated packets, may be experimented with using other network simulation models.

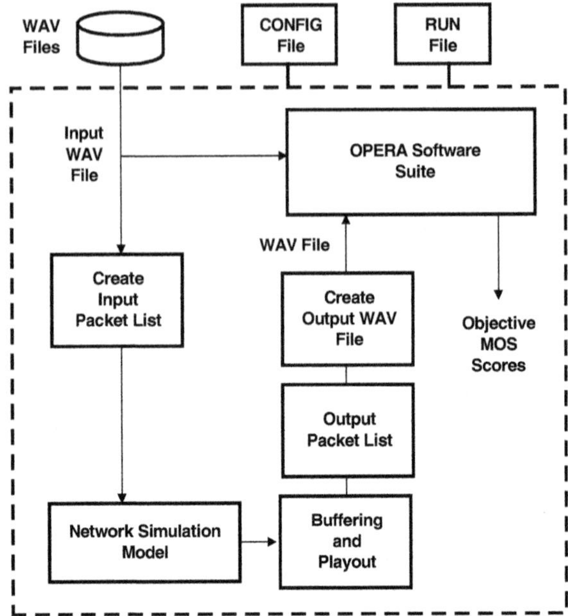

Fig. 2. Software architecture of tool implementation

At the receiving end, the output VoIP stream is fed into a simulated fixed-length packet buffer. The packets are played out from the buffer according to a simulated play-out algorithm. The coded voice data is then extracted from the payloads of the played-out packets and then decoded according to the codec algorithm that is being employed. The voice data associated with a lost packet is simply set to be a silence period (other methods of repairing packet loss [24] may also be adopted). The decoded voice signal data is then arranged together to form an output WAV file. This file contains the final received output voice signal.

Having constructed the output voice signal WAV file, the final step is to determine objectively the subjective quality of this signal as compared to the original input voice signal WAV file. In our tool, this is accomplished using the PSQM and PSQM+ implementations that are included in the OPERA™ Software Suite Version 2.0 that is available from Opticom GmbH. This software is run in a batch file mode with the WAV files as inputs. The PSQM+ algorithm is an improved version of PSQM that is more suitable for VoIP network measurements than the standardized PSQM method. PSQM+ improves the time-alignment of the signals to be compared and also improves how silence periods and packet dropouts are taken into account in evaluating subjective quality. PSQM+ was developed by the original developers of

PSQM (KPN Research of the Netherlands), but PSQM+ is not an ITU-T recommendation [17].

In a single run, the OPERA™ software actually provides three different scores for PSQM and one score for PSQM+. The three PSQM scores correspond to different assumed values of the silent interval weighting factor W_{sil} that enters into the computation of the PSQM score as defined in P.861 (p. 18, in [15]). The three assumed values for W_{sil} are 0.0, 0.2, and 0.4. In P.861 [15], a provisional recommendation of $W_{sil} = 0.2$ is made for speech with about 50% silent intervals. The computation of the PSQM+ score does not involve W_{sil}.

The OPERA™ software also maps the computed PSQM and PSQM+ output values to an objective mean opinion score (OMOS) scale. This scale uses the grades of MOS shown previously in Table 1.

With the scale of Table 1, it has been found [19] using real subjective testing of 'toll-grade' voice calls (64 Kb/s PCM) that the OMOS score never exceeds 4.3. A value of OMOS = 4 is normally considered toll quality [7]. Hence, in analyzing VoIP quality, the OMOS score will usually fall in the range of 1 to 4. The actual functions used in OPERA™ to map the PSQM and PSQM+ values to the OMOS scores are, at present, proprietary, but listening tests have shown high correlations between the PSQM and PSQM+ values and the real subjective results [30]. Note that the problem of having to deal with these proprietary OMOS mapping functions will disappear with the adoption of the improved ITU-T PESQ [16] method (see Section 6) that provides a PESQMOS score defined by an explicit equation [26].

5 Objective MOS Results

We now present the results of a series of experiments which demonstrate the operation of the implementation and provide a set of numerical OMOS results that illustrate how voice quality is affected by network QoS conditions. The experiments assume an 8-bit G.711 μ-law codec with an 8 KHz sampling rate. Each experimental data point corresponds to a single simulation run.

In the following figures, the OPERA™ OMOS output values for PSQM with W_{sil} = 0.0 and 0.2 are denoted by OMOS-W0 and OMOS-W2, respectively. The OPERA™ OMOS output value for PSQM+ is denoted by OMOS+.

5.1 Bernoulli Loss Model

We first consider the case of the Bernoulli loss model described in Section 4. Fig. 3 shows how the OMOS-W0, OMOS-W2, and OMOS+ scores vary as the packet loss rate (lost packets/packet) is changed from 0% to 40%. In this experiment, the voice WAV file is a 22 minute version of the P.50 artificial voice signal (file p50_f.16p in [13]). The packet size is assumed to be 160 samples/packet. This corresponds to a packet rate of 50 packets/s. Fig. 4 shows how the OMOS varies with the loss rate in the case where the voice WAV file is a 22 minute version of the reference female

English voice signal (file A_eng_f2.16p in [13]). The packet size is again assumed to be 160 samples/packet.

Fig. 5 shows how the OMOS varies with the loss rate for the 22 minute P.50 artificial voice signal when the packet size is increased to 320 samples/packet. This corresponds to a packet rate of 25 packets/s. Fig. 6 shows how the OMOS varies with the loss rate for the 22 minute female English voice signal at 25 packets/s.

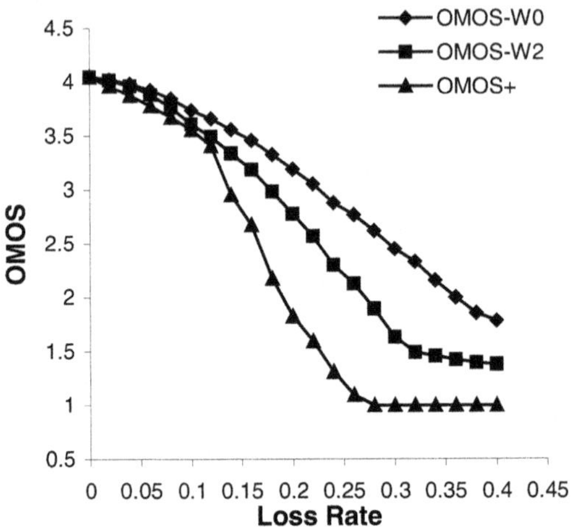

Fig. 3. OMOS vs. packet loss rate for the P.50 artificial voice signal at 50 packets/s

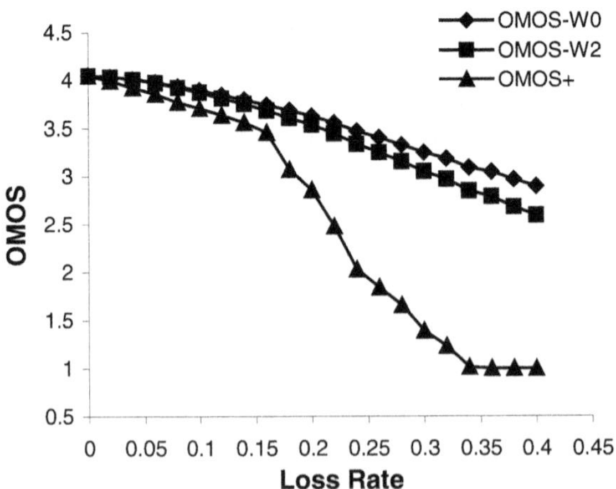

Fig. 4. OMOS vs. packet loss rate for the female English voice signal at 50 packets/s

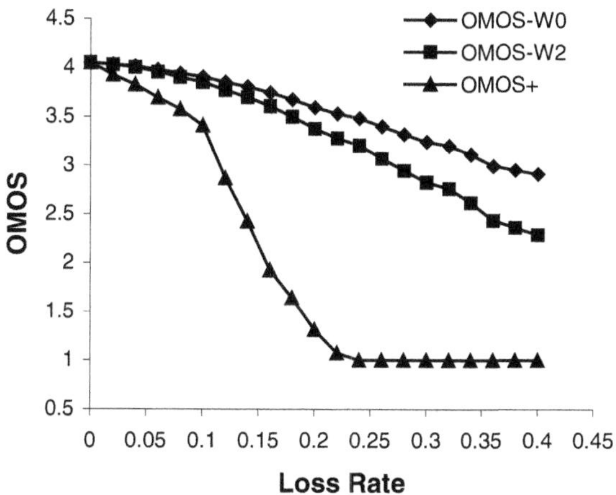

Fig. 5. OMOS vs. packet loss rate for the P.50 artificial voice signal at 25 packets/s

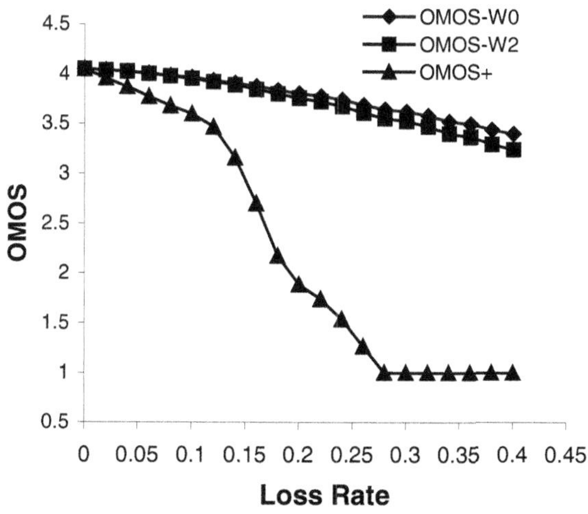

Fig. 6. OMOS vs. packet loss rate for the female English voice signal at 25 packets/s

From the OMOS+ scores in Figs. 3 and 4, we see that good quality voice can be achieved at 50 packets/s with up to about a 13% packet loss rate. From the OMOS+

scores in Figs. 5 and 6, we see good quality voice at 25 packets/s up to about an 11% loss rate.

Fig. 6, in particular, also demonstrates that the OMOS-W0 and OMOS-W2 scores corresponding to the PSQM algorithm do not work very well in estimating voice quality for VoIP since they provide much higher than expected scores when the packet loss rate is above 10%. Published results indicate that, for a G.711 codec with a 20% packet loss rate, the MOS score should be below about 2. See Fig. 5 in [3], where a 20% packet loss rate for a G.711 codec with packet loss concealment gives rise to an I_{ef} value of 40, a R value reduction of 40 (using eq. 3 in [3]), and a corresponding MOS reduction of about 2 (using Fig. 2 in [3]). At a packet loss rate of 20% with *no* packet loss concealment, the MOS score should, therefore, be below about 2 (since the MOS for a G.711 codec with 0% packet loss is equal to about 4). At a 20% packet loss rate, the OMOS+ curve shown in Fig. 6 has a OMOS value of about 1.8 while the OMOS-W0 and OMOS-W2 curves have OMOS values above about 3.3. Hence, the OMOS-W0 and OMOS-W2 curves overestimate the expected MOS. This highlights the need for the PSQM+ method that was designed explicitly as an improvement of PSQM for handling packetized voice such as VoIP. Hence, in the remainder of this section, we limit our attention to OMOS+ results.

The OMOS+ curves in Figs. 3-6 demonstrate how the voice quality of the G.711 codec depends on the packet loss rate through a curve that exhibits a knee. The actual position of the knee depends on the packet transmission rate, or equivalently the packet size. It also depends on the actual test signal. In developing traffic engineering rules and guidelines for VoIP to meet given MOS requirements, it is, therefore, necessary to quantify where the knee occurs for different parameter settings that may arise in practice and different types of voice signals (e.g. male/female, different languages) that may be encountered. The tool presented here provides a cost-effective manner of obtaining the required quantitative results. The OMOS+ curves in Figs. 3-6 also help to validate the tool against the known results mentioned in the previous paragraph (i.e. according to [3], at a packet loss rate of 20% with *no* packet loss concealment, the OMOS+ score should be below about 2, which is the case in Figs. 3, 5, and 6, and approximately the case in Fig. 4).

We can also experiment with how the OMOS+ varies with the packet size (samples per packet) assuming a fixed packet loss rate. Fig. 7 shows how the OMOS+ decreases as we increase the packet size (number of voice samples per packet). Here, we use the 22 minute P.50 artificial voice signal. The random packet loss rate is fixed at 10%. We see that a larger packet size results in lower estimated voice quality. This effect may be explained as follows. With larger packets, the voice signal loss intervals are less frequent but longer. With longer loss intervals, the overall voice signal quality is degraded more compared to the case of shorter packets where the loss intervals are shorter but more frequent. This illustrates again that in developing traffic engineering rules and guidelines for VoIP it is necessary to understand the effects of the different possible implementation settings. Fig. 7 also helps to validate the proper operation of the proposed tool since the results produce a trend that may be expected.

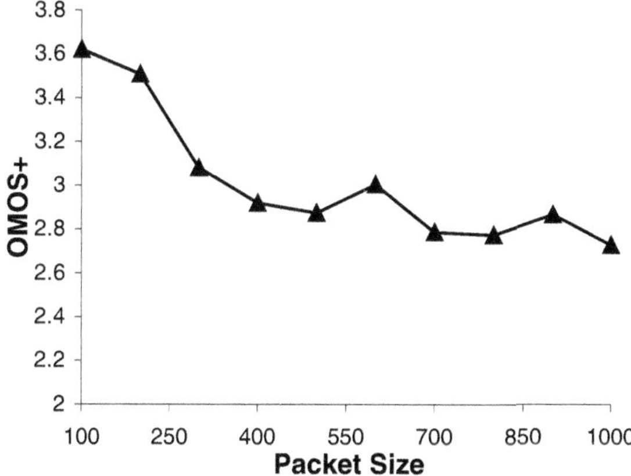

Fig. 7. OMOS+ vs. packet size (samples per packet) for the P.50 artificial voice signal with 10% random packet loss

Note that the curve in Fig. 7 is not monotonically decreasing. This may be attributed to statistical variation in the simulation results. With increasing packet size, there are fewer packets for a given voice signal length. The actual number of lost packets in each simulation run is also a random variable.

5.2 Bursty Loss Model

We now consider the case of the bursty loss model described in Section 4. In this model, we assume that there are bursts of consecutive packet losses in the VoIP packet stream. The number of lost packets in a burst is assumed to be independent and Poisson distributed with mean B. The number of 'non-lost' packets between bursts is assumed to be independent and geometrically distributed with mean G, where $G = P/(1-P)$ and P is the success probability (or the probability that a packet is not the first packet in a burst of packet losses). The overall proportion γ of lost packets is, therefore, $\gamma = B/(B+G)$.

Fig. 8 shows how increasing the mean packet burst length affects the OMOS+ for the 22 minute P.50 artificial voice signal. In this case, P is fixed at 0.99. The packet rate is 50 packets/s. Fig. 9 shows how the burst length affects OMOS+ for the 22 minute female English voice signal, again with P fixed at 0.99 and a packet rate of 50 packets/s. In both cases, the drop off in OMOS+ is expected since increasing the mean burst length B also increases γ, the overall proportion of lost packets.

Figs. 8 and 9 help to further validate the proper operation of the proposed tool since the results continue to produce trends that may be expected.

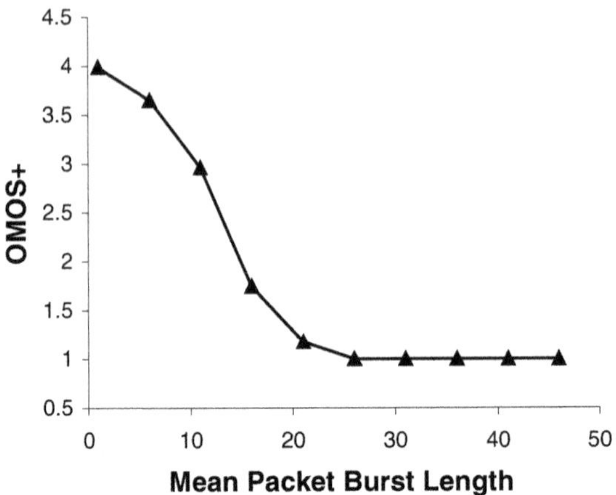

Fig. 8. OMOS+ vs. mean packet burst length for the P.50 artificial voice signal at 50 packets/s with $P = 0.99$

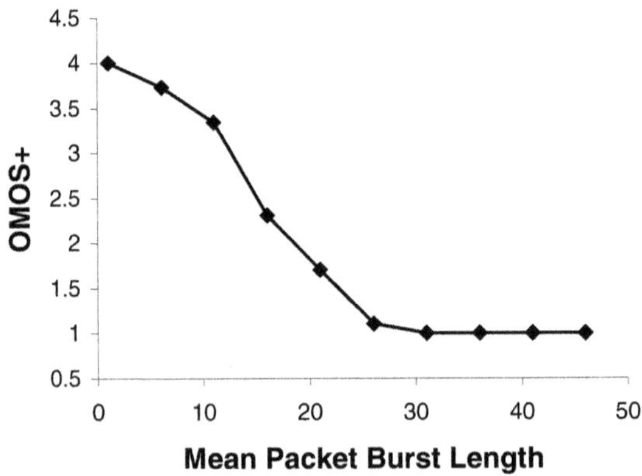

Fig. 9. OMOS+ vs. mean packet burst length for the female English voice signal at 50 packets/s with $P = 0.99$

5.3 Delay Jitter Model

The delay jitter model consists of a single FIFO queue where the VoIP traffic stream is multiplexed in with other background traffic that is assumed to arrive according to a Poisson process. The background traffic packets are assumed to have a length that is independent and Poisson distributed. The delay jitter model also incorporates Bernoulli loss into the VoIP packet stream as it is presented to the input of the FIFO queue. In this way, the delay jitter model can be used to evaluate simultaneously the effects of random loss and delay jitter.

The delay jitter model consisting of a FIFO queue with background traffic can be considered to be a simple model of a VoIP call that traverses an IP router. With the VoIP packet stream competing with the other IP traffic that traverses the router, the effect of this background traffic is to delay certain VoIP packets. The 'delay jitter' may be reduced at the receiving end by a buffer that stores a certain number of packets prior to playing them out at a constant rate. This, however, is at the expense of adding a fixed delay. Packets that are still late in meeting their play-out deadline due to excessive delay jitter are assumed to be discarded.

Fig. 10 shows how the OMOS+ decreases with increasing delay jitter for the 22 minute P.50 artificial voice signal. Here the jitter metric is the '*jitter loss*' proportion, defined to be the proportion of packets discarded due to delay beyond their play-out time deadline. In this case, the VoIP packet rate is set at 50 packets/s and the Bernoulli loss rate is 0%. The mean background traffic rate is 60 packets/s. The depth of the buffer is set at 5 packets. The obtained range in jitter loss was obtained by varying the background traffic mean packet size from 10K to 16K bits. The curve in Fig. 10 exhibits a knee at a jitter loss proportion of about 0.1. This behavior is similar to that observed in Figs. 3-6. This is expected since jitter loss and Bernoulli loss are merely two different types of processes that produce packet loss.

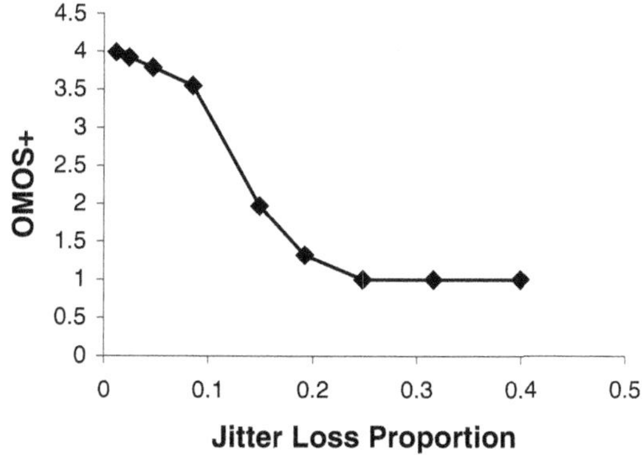

Fig. 10. OMOS+ vs. jitter loss proportion for the P.50 artificial voice signal at 50 packets/s

We now illustrate the combined effects of Bernoulli loss and delay jitter in the delay jitter model. Fig. 11 shows a contour plot of the OMOS+ for the VoIP stream as the random loss rate is varied from 1% to 20% and the mean packet size of the background traffic is varied from 10K to 14K bits. There are three shaded regions for the following ranges of OMOS+ values: 1 to 2, 2 to 3, and 3 to 4. From Fig. 11, we see that to maintain a given OMOS+ score (e.g. OMOS+ = 3), the mean packet size of the background traffic must be decreased as the random loss rate is allowed to increase. By decreasing the mean packet size, the jitter loss is decreased. The 'non-linear' behavior observed in Fig. 11 is expected since the jitter loss and the random loss are additive in an 'average' sense, while the jitter loss is a nonlinear function of the mean packet size.

Fig. 12 shows a contour plot of the OMOS+ of the VoIP stream as a function of the random loss rate and the measured jitter loss proportion (the proportion of packets discarded due to delay beyond their play-out time deadline). The range of jitter loss shown in Fig. 12 was obtained by varying the background mean packet size from 8,950 to 15,050 bits. From Fig. 12, we see that to maintain a given OMOS+ score (e.g. OMOS+ = 3), the jitter loss proportion must be decreased as the random loss rate is increased. The more 'linear' behavior observed in Fig. 12 is expected since the jitter loss and the random loss are additive in an 'average' sense and the OMOS+ is plotted directly in terms of the measured jitter loss proportion.

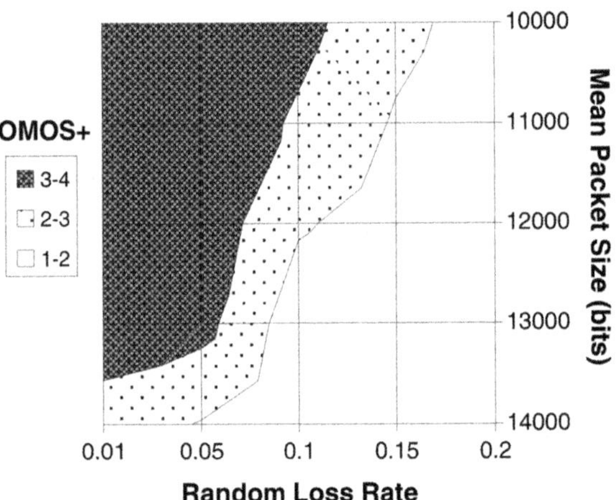

Fig. 11. OMOS+ vs. random loss rate and background traffic mean packet size for the P.50 artificial voice signal at 50 packets/s

The results of Fig. 10-12 help to further validate the implementation and proper operation of the proposed methodology since the experiments provide results that may be expected. The multiplexing model developed in this section also demonstrates how the general methodology developed here provides a general quantitative *perceptual* approach towards analyzing the performance of teletraffic models by incorporating objective methods of perceptual quality evaluation in a system simulation model.

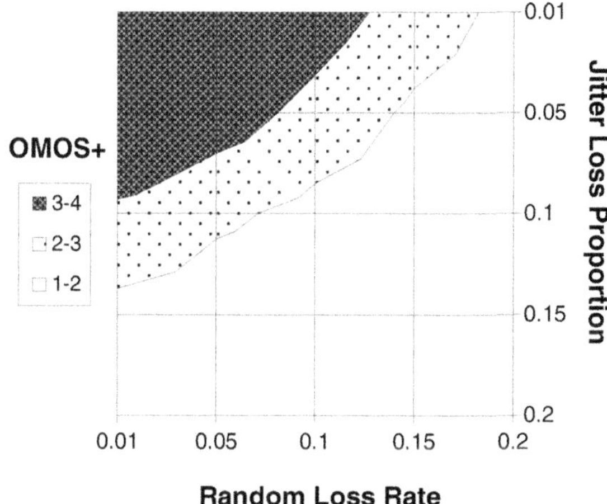

Fig. 12. OMOS+ vs. random loss rate and jitter loss proportion for the P.50 artificial voice signal at 50 packets/s

6 Extensions, Future Directions, and Concluding Remarks

In this paper, we have presented a new methodology and tool for VoIP traffic engineering. It enables the time-efficient and cost-effective evaluation of VoIP subjective quality as a function of network QoS conditions, implementation choices, and configuration settings. As a flexible automated simulation-based tool employing *standardized* reference voice signals and *standardized* methods of objective voice quality measurement, it provides a real practical alternative to the costly and time-consuming process of testing in a lab environment with real human subjects and expensive equipment.

Numerical results have been presented to illustrate and help validate the proper operation of the proposed methodology. The numerical results also demonstrate the dependence of VoIP quality on combinations of network QoS and implementation parameters. Hence, to develop traffic engineering rules and guidelines for VoIP, it is necessary to understand the effects of the different possible combinations, particularly in terms of the location of 'knees.' The analysis of a simple multiplexing model in Section 5.3 has also demonstrated how the methodology and tool provides a general quantitative perceptual approach towards analyzing the performance of teletraffic system models directly in terms of objective perceptual metrics.

A further application area for the methodology and tool is in the development of '*subjective teletraffic engineering*' rules and methods for VoIP or voice-over-packet in general. Traditionally, teletraffic engineering for packet networks is developed in terms of mathematically-oriented performance requirements such as packet loss, packet delay, and packet delay jitter. These requirements, however, do not translate directly into the subjective quality levels that are to be perceived by the end-users. The objective methods that have been standardized for the subjective analysis of voice quality may now provide a vehicle for developing teletraffic enginering methods for VoIP that are based *directly* on objective MOS requirements. As an example in this direction, the simulation tool developed here may be applied to the study of an access link over which multiple VoIP calls are multiplexed. The tool may be used to determine in an automated way how many VoIP calls may be multiplexed subject to specific objective MOS requirements. In this way, we may develop VoIP teletraffic engineering rules and methods based directly on objective MOS requirements. Analogous to the well-known *equivalent bandwidth* concept [9] developed in terms of packet-level QoS requirements, we may also develop the concept of *subjective equivalent bandwidths*. These are directions in which our research is continuing.

There are also several directions in which the tool itself is being extended. It is being extended to include the improved and recently standardized ITU-T P.862 PESQ method [16], the software for which has just recently become available in the OPERA™ Software Suite Version 3.0. With the PESQ method, one can avoid using proprietary methods such as the PSQM+ from Opticom GmbH. The tool is also being extended to include: additional codecs such as G.729, improved methods of constructing long WAV files to reduce or eliminate the possible effects of periodicities mentioned in Section 4, a wider variety of network QoS models, different methods of repairing packet loss, and confidence intervals based on multiple independent simulation runs.

Finally, it is to be noted that the general methodology presented in Section 3 is not restricted in its applicability to only voice signals. It is sufficiently general to also be applied to other telecommunication signal types, such as *audio* and *video*, subject to the condition that a corresponding objective quality measurement method is available now or in the future. For example, the methodology as it stands may be applied to packetized audio signals that are streamed across a packet network since the standardized PEAQ method [11] is currently available for the objective measurement of audio signal quality. In the near future, the proposed methodology may also be applied to packetized video signals since work on developing objective quality measurement methods for video is already well underway [6, 27]. One could also extend the methodology to *multimedia* signals that are combinations of voice, video, and audio, if and when objective methods of subjective quality evaluation for multimedia signals become available.

References

1. "Testing VoIP using PSQM," Abacus Application Note 11, *Zarak Systems Corporation*, Sept. 1999
2. A.D. Clark, "Modeling the effects of burst packet loss and recency on subjective voice quality," 2nd *IP-Telephony Workshop*, Columbia University, New York, April 2001

3. R.G. Cole, and J.H. Rosenbluth, "Voice over IP performance monitoring," *Computer Communication Review*, vol. 31, no. 2, pp. 9-24, 2001
4. A.E. Conway, S.B. Moon, and P. Skelly, "Synchronized two-way voice simulation tool for internet phone performance analysis and evaluation," in *Computer Performance Evaluation Modeling Techniques and Tools*, Lecture Notes in Computer Science, 1245, pp. 108-122, Springer-Verlag, 1997
5. A.E. Conway, "A passive method for monitoring voice-over-IP call quality with ITU-T objective speech quality measurement methods," in *Proc. IEEE International Conference on Communications*, New York, NY, April 2002, in press
6. P. Corriveau, A. Webster, A. Rohaly, J. Libert, "Video Quality Experts Group: the quest for valid objective methods," in Proc. SPIE vol. 3959, *Human Vision and Electronic Imaging V*, B. Rogowitz and T. Pappas, Eds., pp. 129-139, June 2000
7. P. Denisowski, "How does it sound?," *IEEE Spectrum*, vol. 38, no. 2, pp. 60-64, 2001
8. H. Fletcher, and J. Steinberg, "Articulation testing methods," *Bell System Technical Journal*, vol. 8, pp. 806-854, 1929
9. R. Guerin, H. Ahmadi, and M. Naghshineh, "Equivalent capacity and its application to bandwidth allocation in high-speed networks," *IEEE Journal on Selected Areas in Communications*, vol. 9, no.7, pp. 968-981, 1991
10. J.B. Hooper, and M.J. Russell, "Objective quality analysis of a voice over internet protocol system," *IEE Electronics Letters*, vol. 32, no. 22, pp. 1900-1901, Oct. 2000
11. *ITU-R Recommendation BS.1387*, "Method for objective measurements of perceived audio quality (PEAQ)," 1998
12. *ITU-T Recommendation P.50*, "Artificial Voices," 1999
13. *ITU-T Recommendation P.50, Appendix 1*, "Test signals," 1998
14. *ITU-T Recommendation P.800*, "Methods for subjective determination of transmission quality," 1996
15. *ITU-T Recommendation P.861*, "Objective quality measurement of telephone-band (300-3400 Hz) speech codecs," 1998
16. *ITU-T Recommendation P.*862, "Perceptual evaluation of speech quality (PESQ), an objective method for end-to-end speech quality assessment of narrowband telephone networks and speech codecs," 2001
17. *ITU-T Contribution* COM 12-20-E, "Improvement of the P.861 perceptual speech quality measure," KPN Research, Netherlands, Dec. 1997
18. M.J. Karam, and F.A. Tobagi, "Analysis of the delay and jitter of voice traffic over the internet," in *Proc. IEEE INFOCOM 2001*, vol. 2, pp. 824-833, 2001
19. M. Keyhl, C. Schmidmer, and H. Wachter, "A combined measurement tool for the objective, perceptual based evaluation of compressed speech and audio signals," in *Proc. 106th Audio Engineering Society (AES) Convention*, 4931 (M3), Munich, Germany, May 1999
20. T. Kostas, M. Borella, I. Sidhu, G. Schuster, J. Grabiec, and J. Mahler, "Real-time voice over packet-switched networks," *IEEE Network*, pp. 18-27, Jan./Feb. 1998
21. O. Maeshima, Y. Ito, M. Ishikura, and T. Asami, "A method of service quality estimation with a network measurement tool,", in *Proc. IEEE International Performance, Computing and Communications Conference*, pp. 201-209, Feb. 1999
22. NIST Net emulator homepage, www.antd.nist.gov/itg/nistnet/ index.html
23. M. Perkins, K. Evans, D. Pascal, L. Thorpe, "Characterizing the subjective performance of the ITU-T 8 kb/s speech coding algorithm - ITU-T G.729," *IEEE Communications Magazine*, pp. 74-81, vol. 359, Sept. 1997
24. C. Perkins, O. Hodson, and V. Hardman, "A Survey of packet-loss recovery techniques for streaming audio," *IEEE Network Magazine*, vol. 12, no. 5, pp. 40-48, Sept. 1998
25. A. Rayes, and K. Sage, "Integrated management architecture for IP-based networks," *IEEE Communications Magazine*, 2000, vol. 38, no. 4, pp. 48-53, 2000

26. A.W. Rix, J.G. Beerends, M.P. Hollier, and A.P. Hekstra, "Perceptual evaluation of speech quality (PESQ) – A new method for speech quality assessment of telephone networks and codecs," in *Proc. IEEE International Conference on Acoustics, Speech and Signal Processing*, vol. 2, pp. 749-752, 2001
27. A. Rohaly *et al*, "Video Quality Experts Group: current results and future directions," in Proc. SPIE vol. 4067, *Visual Communications and Image Processing 2000*, K. Ngan, T. Sikora, and M. Sun, Eds., pp. 742-753, May 2000
28. L. Sun, G. Wade, B. Lines, and E. Ifeachor, "Impact of packet loss location on perceived speech quality," *2nd IP-Telephony Workshop*, Columbia University, New York, April 2001
29. L. Thorpe, and W. Yang, "Performance of current perceptual objective speech quality measures," in *Proc. IEEE Workshop on Speech Coding*, pp. 144-146, 1999
30. "State of the art voice quality testing," White Paper, Opticom GmbH, Erlangen, Germany, 2000

Hierarchical Workload Characterization for a Busy Web Server

Adeniyi Oke and Rick Bunt

Department of Computer Science
University of Saskatchewan
57 Campus Drive
Saskatoon, Saskatchewan, S7N 5A9
Canada
aao804@cs.usask.ca,bunt@cs.usask.ca

Abstract. This paper introduces the concept of a Web server access hierarchy—a three-tier hierarchy that describes the traffic to a Web server in three levels: as aggregate traffic from multiple clients, as traffic from individual clients, and as traffic within sessions of individual clients. A detailed workload characterization study was undertaken of the Web server access hierarchy of a busy commercial server using an access log of 80 million requests captured over seven days of observation. The behavioural characteristics that emerge from this study show different features at each level and suggest effective stategies for managing resources at busy Internet Web servers.

1 Introduction

The phenomenal growth of the World Wide Web continues to challenge network infrastructure and systems. Web servers are over-loaded with requests, networks become congested, and end-users experience poor response times. This continuing growth has motivated a great deal of research on how to improve the performance and scalability of the Web. Research studies have been conducted at the client-side [7,9,11] and proxy-side [13,15] to achieve these goals, but a common theme is to manage the resources of the Web server effectively [4,5,6, 8,16]. Under proper management, request throughput and data throughput at the server can be increased and network bandwidth can be conserved. The focus of this paper is the different levels through which Web servers can receive requests from prospective clients: as requests from multiple clients, as requests from individual clients, and as requests within sessions from single clients. Our research seeks to shed light on two important questions: how do the characteristics of Web server workload change over the levels of the access hierarchy, and what are the implications of these characteristics for Web server resource management. We believe that the contributions from this study will enable Web server designers to gain insight into the design and provisioning of Web services and suggest ways of improving the effectiveness of Web protocols (HTTP/1.1). Important conclusions of this paper are:

T. Field et al. (Eds.): TOOLS 2002, LNCS 2324, pp. 309–328, 2002.

- The behavioural characteristics of aggregate server workload are generally consistent with other studies [5,6], but there are a few changes. We found that these changes are not due to the effect of upstream caching, but rather to the peculiar nature of the server workload studied where most users requested an extremely small set of documents within the period of observation.
- Both "human" and "non-human" clients were identified at the server, and the behavioural characteristics of their reference patterns are dramatically different. This has implications for performance.
- A client-based resource management policy could be effective at the Web server if the reference pattern of "non-human" clients can be managed separately from the reference pattern of "human" clients.
- A change in the current implementation of HTTP/1.1 persistent connections is suggested. An adaptive or dynamic timeout policy with short timeout values for "human" clients and a fixed timeout policy with short timeout values for "non-human" clients is proposed.

The remainder of the paper is organized as follows. Section 2 presents the background and related work for the study. Section 3 describes the Web server workload characterized. Section 4 summarizes the characteristics of the Web server workload as it relates to the access hierarchy. Section 5 concludes the paper.

2 Background and Related Work

The performance and scalability of the World Wide Web depends on the combined effectiveness of Web resource management strategies at the client, in the network and at the server. Workload characterization is important to the understanding of the behavioural characteristics of Web traffic. Many workload characterization studies have been carried out at both the client side and the server side. These studies focused primarily on aggregate workloads from multiple users, and are therefore useful in designing non-differentiated client policies for the provisioning of document services or to determine the effectiveness of Web protocols. A few of these related studies are briefly discussed.

Catledge and Pitkow [9] first characterized the Web traffic of user sessions at the client side. Three categories of user reference patterns were identified—serendipitous (random), browsing (looking for items of interest) and searching (investigating specific topics). In a much larger study of Web user sessions, Cunha *et al.* [11] identified two types of reference patterns, described as mostly surfing and mostly working. Hine *et al.* [12] observed three user reference patterns referred to as wanderer, resident and sojourner. Barford *et al.* [7] examined whether or not the user reference patterns identified in [11] change over time and the implications of these changes with regards to Web resource management at the client side.

At the server side, Arlitt and Williamson [5] identified ten invariant characteristics of Web server workloads for effective resource management. Arlitt and

Jin [6] analyzed the server workload of 1998 World Cup to explore the extent to which these ten invariant characteristics change over time. Although some of the invariant characteristics were found to have changed over time, the results supported the continued use of the resource management strategies suggested in [5]. Arlitt [4] further characterized an aggregate server workload by grouping it into Web user sessions at the server with a view to understanding the impact of the newly introduced HTTP/1.1 protocol on the resource management of Web servers. A hierarchical approach for characterization of Web server workloads collected at e-business sites and information provider sites has been studied [2,3,16]. Menasce *et al.* [16] used a hierarchical approach to understand whether or not the characteristics and invariants identified in [5] are still valid for e-business workloads. Almeida *et al.* [2,3] applied this approach to identify, characterize and distinguish two major categories of search agents found in Web server workloads, namely *crawlers* and *shopbots*, and further assessed the impact of their reference patterns on caching.

In many respects, our work is similar to these related studies, but differs in that our motivation is to understand how the characteristics of Web server workloads change as users move through three levels of access aggregation. In particular, this paper attempts to investigate how to manage the resources of Web servers effectively by characterizing the aggregate client workloads, individual client workloads and sessions within individual client workloads at the server side. This hierarchical characterization enables Web server designers to gain clearer insight into resource management policies of Web servers in terms of the provisioning of Web services and Web protocol (HTTP/1.1) effectiveness.

3 The Collection, Description, and Analysis of a Web Server Workload

For this study, we obtained Web server access logs from a busy (anonymous) commercial Web site. The Web site has a cluster of Web servers that appear to the users as a single machine. Each server has HP K-class multiprocessor HP-UX boxes running the Open-Market-Secure-Web Server/2.0.5.RCO. Server access logs were collected over a period of seven days from Sunday June 14, 1998 to Saturday June 20, 1998. The logs were preprocessed to preserve the anonymity of users and URLs. Each entry in the access logs is similar to those explained in [5,6,15].

In the workload, there are 644, 187 clients[1] responsible for 328 GB of data transferred over the network within the period of observation. The server daily activity represents two orders of magnitude more workload than the busiest server activity characterized in [5] (tens of million of requests per day, compared to hundreds of thousands of requests per day). However, the original (or raw)

[1] The term client refers to a host with a distinct Internet Protocol (IP) address in the access log. In this case, a client can be seen as a single user host, a timesharing cluster, or a relay host.

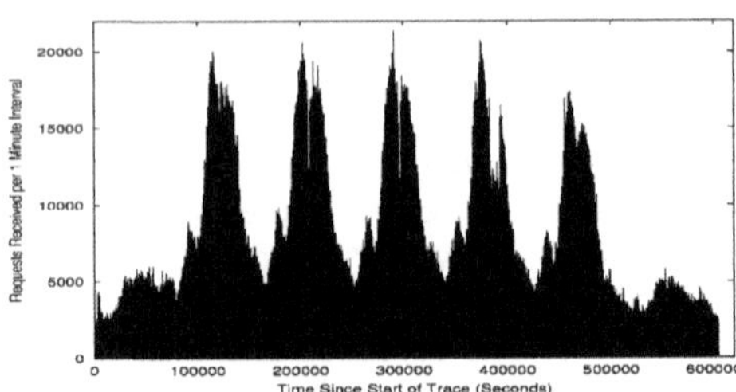

Fig. 1. Seven Days Traffic Profile of Web Server Workload Trace

workload shows a weekend effect because the server received far more requests from clients during the working days than on weekends. Figure 1 illustrates this.

After reducing the raw server access logs by eliminating unsuccessful requests (as was done in [5,6]), there are more than 56 million requests from 620 thousand unique clients over the period of observation. In addition, the server transferred about 101 thousand unique documents. Table 1 gives summary statistics of the reduced access logs. The fact that the median request per day is greater than the mean request per day implies that the observation of weekend effect in the original workload is preserved in the reduced logs. There is evidence that the presence of a few large documents transferred by the server might be responsible for the skewness of the document size distribution since the mean document size (28 kB) is less than the median document size (9 kB). The mean transfer size (5.7 kB) and the median transfer size (1.2 kB) fall within the range reported in [5,8].

One of our goals was to differentiate between documents that are heavily demanded and documents that are rarely or lightly demanded. By grouping the document types as reported in [5,6,15], some important differences are seen in the nature of document types transferred by the Web server. For example, 95.60% of requests were either HTML (9.51%) or Image documents (86.09%). This contrasts with previous studies [5] which found these to be nearly the same. However, the volume of bytes transferred as HTML documents account for 23.66% and Image documents in our study account for 63.28%. This indicates that Image documents have greater impact than HTML documents, whereas the reverse was the case in [5]. The increasing popularity of Image documents over other types of Web documents could be responsible for this difference.

An important phenomenon is "one-timer" referencing with respect to documents and clients. One-timer documents are distinct documents transferred only once by the server during the period of observation. They are important because of their adverse impact on caching strategies. In the reduced server workload, there were 12,357 one-timer documents that represented 12.23% of the overall unique documents and 8.78% of total disk storage. Distinct users that successfully requested a document once from the Web server within the pe-

Table 1. Summary of Workload Statistics (Reduced Data)

Access Log Duration	7 days
Access Log Starting Date	June 14, 1998
Access Log End Date	June 20, 1998
Total Requests	56,458,479
Mean Requests/ Day	8,065,497
Median Requests/ Day	9,517,399
Coefficient of Variation	0.35
Total Bytes Transferred (GB)	323
Mean Transfer Size (Bytes)	5,722
Median Transfer Size (Bytes)	1,227
Coefficient of Variation	5.50
Total Unique Clients	620,041
Total Unique Documents	101,008
Total Storage Size (MB)	2,819
Mean Document Size (Bytes)	27,918
Median Document Size (Bytes)	8,506
Coefficient of Variation	9.74

riod of observation are referred to as one-timer clients. They are also important because of their adverse impact on the effectiveness of HTTP/1.1 persistent connections. There were 33,205 one-timer clients accounting for 5.35% of the number of clients. The large proportion of one-timer documents and one-timer clients in this workload suggests that caching strategies and the HTTP/1.1 protocol might not perform as hoped.

4 Hierarchical Workload Characterization

A number of important characteristics were examined, including document size and transfer size distributions, temporal locality, document concentration, document inter-reference times and phase transition behaviour.

4.1 Characteristics of the Aggregate Workload

The aggregate workload is simply the raw data as seen by the server, with no attempt to isolate its component parts. Requests from the entire user community are presented to the server in an interleaved fashion.

Document and Transfer Size Distributions. The nature of documents either stored or transferred by the Web server is an important consideration for resource management. Figure 2(a) shows the cumulative frequency distribution of document references, document sizes and transfer sizes, and weighted transfer

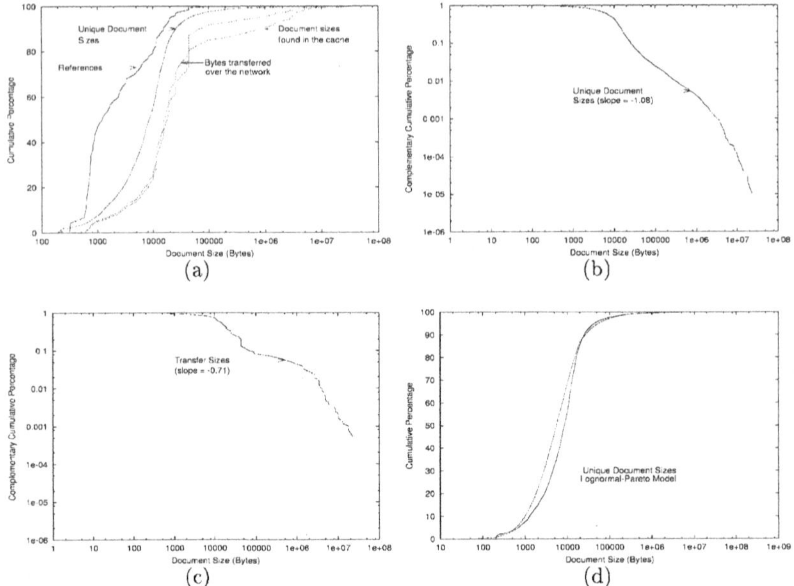

Fig. 2. Document Size Distribution: (a) Cumulative Distribution Frequency by Document Sizes; (b) Log-log Complementary Distribution Plot for Unique Documents; (c) Log-log Complementary Distribution Plot for Transfer Sizes; (d) Comparison of Document Size Distribution and a Hybrid Lognormal-Pareto model

sizes[2]. We observed that documents smaller than 10 kB account for 80.49% of the total requests and 28% of the total bytes transferred, documents between 10-100 kB account for 19.55% of the total requests and 65% of bytes transferred, and documents larger than 100 kB account for only 0.14% of the total requests and 7% of the bytes transferred. This indicates that Web users prefer smaller documents, probably less than 10 kB, while large volume of data traffic on the network is due to a few user requests to fairly large documents at the server. Caching is suggested for resource management of the Web server, even though a tradeoff may exist between caching for improving the server's request throughput and caching for improving the server's data throughput, if cache policies are based on the frequency of user references to documents. The difference in size between the weighted transfer sizes and actual transfer sizes for documents larger than 100 kB suggests that large documents are not fully downloaded before users abort the transfer. Thus, caching may not be applicable to this category of large documents.

[2] This is calculated by multiplying the number of references to a document by the maximum transfer size of the document within the period of observation.

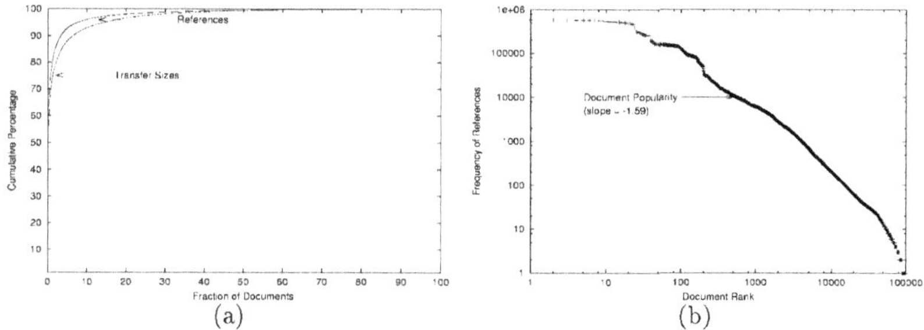

Fig. 3. Concentration of Document References: (a) Cumulative Distribution by References and Bytes Transferred; (b) Zipf Distribution: Reference Count versus Rank

Figures 2(b) and (c) suggest that the distributions of document and transfer sizes are heavy-tailed or Pareto, respectively. This means that, for document sizes, a small set of large documents occupy most of the disk space, while for transfer size, a heavy tail means a small set of documents is responsible for most of the bytes transferred over the network. Applying least-squares estimation (LSE) [5,6,10], the tail index of the document size distribution is $\alpha = -1.08$ (infinite variance) and the tail index of the transfer distribution is $\alpha = -0.71$ (infinite mean). These results differ from earlier results [5,10,11] because of the clustering of medium-sized image and text documents between 10 and 40 kB, which account for most of the bytes transferred over the network. We also found that a hybrid lognormal-Pareto distribution as suggested by Barford *et al.* [7] captures the body and tail of the document distribution at the server. Details are provided in [19].

Concentration of Document References. Several studies [5,6,11,15] have found that Web documents exhibit a non-uniform reference pattern. A small percentage of documents are extremely popular, while a significant number of documents are rarely referenced. Our server workload also exhibits this property as shown in Figure 3. Figure 3(a) illustrates this by arranging distinct documents found in the server workload in decreasing order (from the most popular to the least popular) based on how many times the distinct documents were accessed against the fraction of total documents referenced. The resulting plot shows that 10% of the most frequently accessed documents account for 96% of total requests and 5% of the most frequently referenced documents account for 93% of the overall requests received by the Web server. Similar results are observed for the bytes transferred by the server. The first 10% of distinct documents (representing the most heavy transfer documents at the server) were responsible for 93% of bytes transferred over the network. Our results show the presence of strong document concentration in the aggregate workload and suggest that

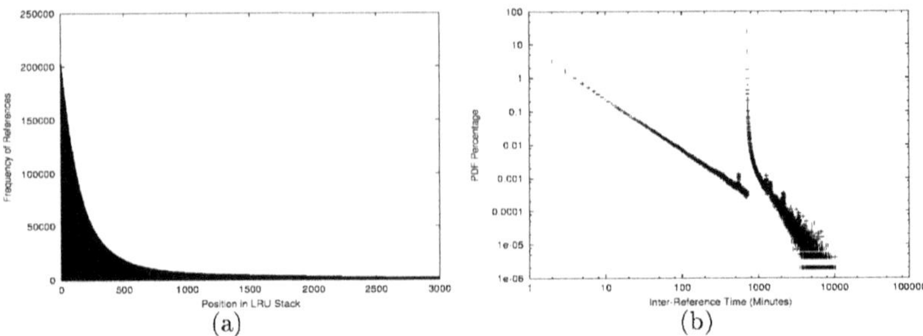

Fig. 4. Document Re-Referencing Behaviour: (a)Temporal Locality using LRU Stack Depth Histogram for 3000 Stack Positions; (b) Inter-Reference Times Probability Density Function Plot

server caching strategies that take into account both the frequency of references and the volume of bytes contributed by documents can be effective.

Figure 3(b) demonstrates the use of Zipf's Law [22] to illustrate the presence of document concentration by plotting a log-log transformation of distinct documents, sorted in decreasing order of popularity, as a function of the document rank. Although the slope of the popularity line is not -1.0, there is evidence of the document concentration property in this workload since the slope of the popularity curve is -1.59. The steeper the slope of the popularity line, the stronger the concentration or frequency of requests to a smaller set of documents. A similar observation was reported in [6]. Therefore, caching is promising for managing the Web server resources over time.

Temporal Locality. This property is essential for the success of caching strategies and a significant factor in the choice of cache management policy. The least recently used (LRU) stack reference model [1,5,20] is used to characterize temporal locality since it reflects the tendency of references to certain documents to persist over time–the probability of users re-referencing documents that have been requested in the past. Figure 4(a) shows the presence of temporal locality in this workload. The x-axis represents the first 3000 stack positions, from the most recently referenced document position to the least recently referenced document position. The y-axis represents the frequency of reference to documents that occupy each of the stack positions. The hyperbolic shape of the LRU stack distance histogram demonstrates that most documents occupy positions closer to the top of the stack, which implies the presence of temporal locality in this aggregate workload.

Re-referencing Behaviour: Document Inter-Reference Times. The degree of document re-referencing by users as exhibited by temporal locality is

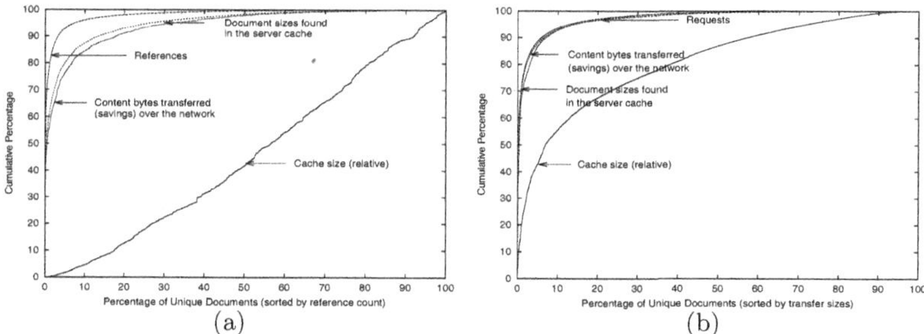

Fig. 5. Caching Implications for Web Server Resource Management

shown by using the probability density function (PDF) to characterize document inter-reference times—the time interval between successive requests to the same documents [13]. The intuition is that stronger (weaker) temporal locality reflects higher (lower) probability to smaller document inter-reference times. After computing and combining the inter-reference times of individual distinct documents in the workload, the PDF of overall document inter-reference time is shown in Figure 4(b). Since the probability of a user re-referencing the same documents decreases rapidly with time, the presence of stronger temporal locality is observed. This result is likely to be due to the presence of popular documents, which tend to be requested frequently, thus exhibiting shorter inter-reference times, while less popular documents exhibit longer inter-reference times. However, the observation of a break in the PDF of document inter-reference times at roughly 24 hour (1440 minute) intervals may reveal the impact of time zone differences in user referencing patterns and the spike may be due to the presence of a non-human referencing pattern in the workload, such as might result from search agents or crawlers [2,3].

Resource Management Implications. There are two approaches to caching at a Web server. One approach is to cache documents that are frequently requested by users in order to improve the request throughput. The other approach is to cache documents that contribute to a large volume of bytes transferred in order to conserve network bandwidth or improve the data throughput. Figure 5 shows the implications of using cache policies based on the number of references to documents or on the volume of bytes contributed by documents on both the request throughput and the data throughput. The y-axis represents the cumulative percentage and the x-axis represents percentage of documents. Arlitt and Williamson [5] first used these graphs in understanding the performance implications of Web servers.

Figure 5(a) depicts the performance results of using caching policies based on the number of references to documents. In this graph, the top line represents the percentage of total requests serviced from the cache. The next two lines report the percentage of total bytes transferred (in terms of transfer sizes and weighted transfer sizes) for servicing requests from the cache. The last line represents the cache size available at the server. The results show that there is a tradeoff in caching performance between the request throughput and the data throughput when the cache size increases. In particular, the cache policies perform better in terms of the request throughput than the data throughput. This implies that caching based on the frequency of requests to documents is effective for managing Web server resources if Web designers identify CPU cycles as the bottleneck.

Figure 5(b) shows the performance results of using caching policies based on the volume of bytes contributed by documents. The labeling of this graph is similar to Figure 5(a). We observed no tradeoff in performance between the request throughput and the data throughput as the cache size increases. This implies that cache policies based on volume of bytes contributed by documents are more effective in managing Web server resources if Web designers identify both CPU cycles and disk I/Os as the bottlenecks.

Frequency-based cache management policies appear to be the most cost effective way of managing the resources at the Web server since the cost of a cache is always proportional to its size. Figures 5(a) and (b) show that in order to achieve comparable performance results, cache policies that use the number of references to documents require about 129 MB to store the top 10% of the most frequently requested documents, while cache policies that use the volume of bytes contributed by documents require about 1,564 MB to store the top 10% of documents that account for most volume of bytes transferred over the network.

4.2 Characteristics of Individual Client Workloads

For this part of our investigation, we decomposed the aggregate workload into separate streams comprising the requests from individual clients, and analyzed each of these client streams separately. In the design of resource management strategies, Web server designers assume (implicitly or explicitly) that client request patterns are similar. We found some dramatic differences that could have profound impact on performance.

The Analysis of Client Workloads. The total requests and total bytes transferred by individual clients are characterized using a log-log complementary distribution [10]. We observed that the distribution of bytes transferred by individual clients is heavier-tailed ($\alpha = -1.24$) than the distribution of total requests generated by individual clients ($\alpha = -1.44$). The fact that both distributions are heavy-tailed indicates that a few clients are responsible for both the disk I/O and the CPU cycle bottlenecks. Therefore, understanding the reference patterns of these few clients may be particularly important to effective Web server resource management.

Table 2 gives statistical information of four selected client workloads that belong to the group of these few clients extracted from the aggregate server

Table 2. Summary of Server Client Access Log Statistics (Reduced Data)

Item Description	Client Number			
	A	B	C	D
Access Log Duration	7 Days			
Total Requests	109,385	97,859	21,122	9,594
Average Requests/Day	15,626	13,980	3,017	1,371
Median Requests/Day	12,139	19,140	4,671	677
Unique Documents	12,235	16,834	10,116	7035
Total Storage Size (MB)	196	333	173	146
Mean Document Size (Bytes)	15,977	19,765	17,061	20,691
Coefficient of Variation	0.71	8.80	6.60	3.27
Total Bytes Transferred (MB)	1,750	919	272	158
Mean Transfer Size (Bytes)	15,997	9,393	12,883	16,499
Median Transfer Size (Bytes)	14,339	1,967	3,089	9,691
Coefficient of Variation	0.73	9.33	7.35	3.55

workload within the period of observation. These are identified as clients A, B, C, and D. Client A has the highest activity per day while clients B, C, and D follow, respectively. As found in the aggregate server workload, a weekend effect is observed in the workloads of clients B and C because their median requests per day are greater than the mean requests per day. More extensive information on these clients including how they were selected is given in [19].

The Reference Patterns of the Selected Clients. The reference pattern of selected client workloads is characterized as shown in Figure 6 by plotting on the y-axis, a sequence of numbers assigned to distinct documents found in each of the client workloads and on the x-axis, the time since the start of the individual client requests. The terms "mostly working" and "mostly surfing" (as coined in [11]) are used in explaining each of the client reference patterns. A mostly working pattern implies that the client keeps re-referencing previously accessed documents most of the time, while a mostly surfing pattern implies that the client rarely keeps re-referencing previously accessed documents. Clients B and C display a mostly working pattern while clients A and D display a mostly surfing pattern. The dense reference pattern of client B indicates a strong working pattern while that of client C is weak. Since the rate of accessing new documents decreases as each day passes, temporal locality can be present in the reference patterns of clients B and C. It is speculated that client B is a firewall or relay, while client C is a time-sharing system. In particular, client B is believed to access the server on behalf of human users with similar document reference patterns, while client C does the same for human users but with dissimilar document reference patterns.

Similarly, the surfing reference pattern of client A reveals a crawling pattern that shows that the client accesses the same number of documents at the server each of the possible nine or ten times it visits the server during the period of

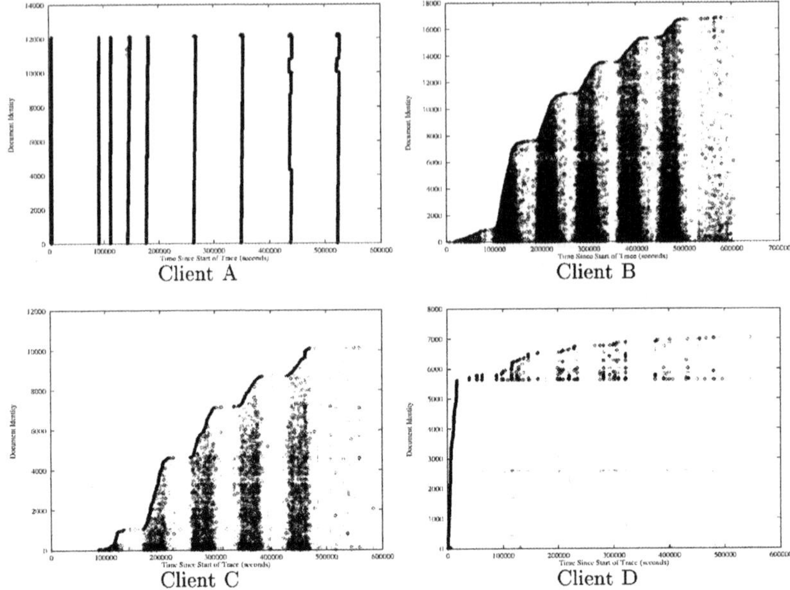

Fig. 6. Reference Patterns of Four Selected Clients

observation. This is quite different from the surfing reference pattern of client D in which the client spends the first day accessing distinct documents alone and uses the subsequent days to make scanty re-referencing to documents previously accessed during the first day. The crawling-surfing reference pattern suggests that client A is a non-human user, perhaps a search agent or crawler [2,3], while the pattern of client D suggests it might be a caching proxy[3].

Concentration of Client Document References. The document referencing patterns of the selected clients are characterized in Figure 7 using Zipf's Law [22] as discussed in Section 2. We observed that client A has a uniform referencing behaviour, which alludes to a cyclic or crawling referencing pattern—the client visits all distinct documents at the server the first time and all subsequent referencing is to traverse this set of previously accessed documents [2,3]. The other clients B, C and D, however, reveal a non-uniform referencing pattern. The result is consistent with the hypothesis that client A is likely to be a non-human

[3] The caching proxy is empty on the setup day and the first document misses of 7,000 requests can be due to cold-start behaviour of an empty cache. The subsequent scanty reference pattern after the first day can be due to capacity misses resulting from a finite-sized cache at the proxy and coherent misses resulting from stale documents in the proxy cache.

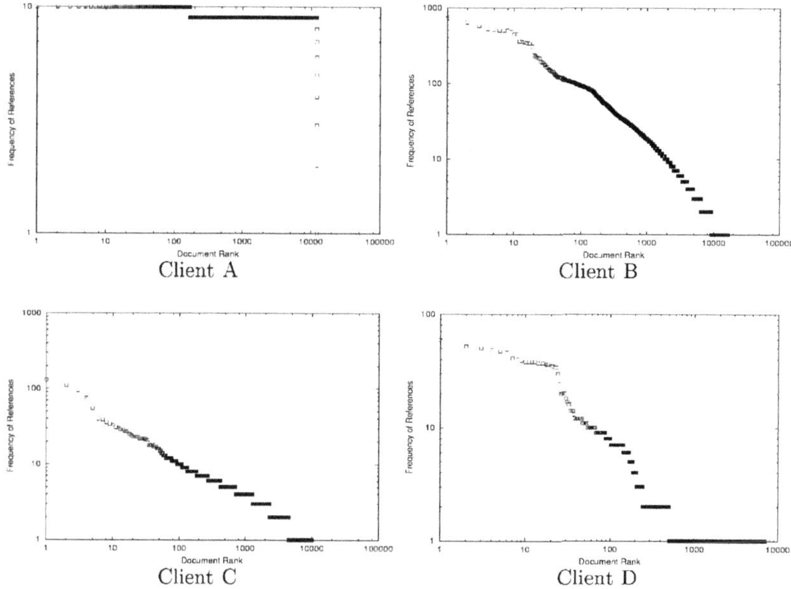

Fig. 7. Test for Zipf Distribution

user such as a search agent or Web crawler, while the other clients are not. It is important to mention that the reference pattern of client A is not amenable to caching, while the reference patterns of client B, C and D are because of the document concentration property reflected by their non-uniform referencing patterns.

Temporal Locality in the Selected Client Workloads. For caching the request streams of clients, temporal locality is an important consideration. By plotting the histogram of stack distances[4] as discussed in Section 2, Figure 8 illustrates that client A has very poor temporal locality and clients B, C and D have weak temporal locality. For client A, most documents referenced occur at the same stack position, which is closer to the bottom of the stack. This further reveals the cyclic or crawling referencing pattern of a fixed set of documents by this client, inferring a non-human referencing pattern [2,3,5,6]. Caching the reference pattern of client A requires the cache to preserve some space ahead of time, or continuously free some space to accommodate the fixed set of documents

[4] A maximum stack length of 1000 yields a satisfactory measure of temporal locality for clients B, C and D. Client A requires an infinite stack due to its crawling document reference pattern.

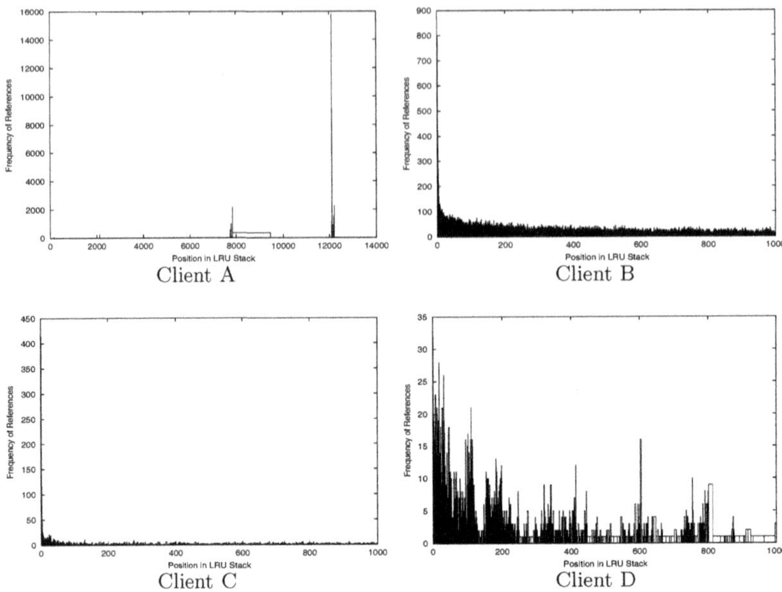

Fig. 8. Distribution of LRU Stack Depths

accessed [2]. The other reference patterns of clients seem amenable to caching, despite the long tail observed in their stack distance distributions.

We applied a relative measure of temporal locality to the document reference pattern of clients using the mean stack distance as reported in [7]. Our results show that client B has the strongest temporal locality, followed by clients D, C, and A, respectively. In addition, we used the assumption of a "perfect cache" discussed in [7,18] to verify the effectiveness of caching the reference patterns of these clients. The results indicate that only the reference patterns of client B and C are likely to be cacheable. The cacheability of client D's reference pattern cannot be ascertained because of the limited number of requests in its workload, but the reference pattern of client A is clearly not amenable to effective caching. Our findings are consistent with the report in [2] that non-human clients such as crawlers have a referencing pattern that completely disrupts locality assumptions while human clients do not.

Inter-Arrival Times of Client-Requested Documents. The cumulative distributions of inter-request arrival times, time intervals between successive requests to documents from single clients, are shown in Figure 9 for the selected client workloads. Client A generates 95% of its requests to documents within one second, while the other clients (B, C and D) generate 80% and almost 100%

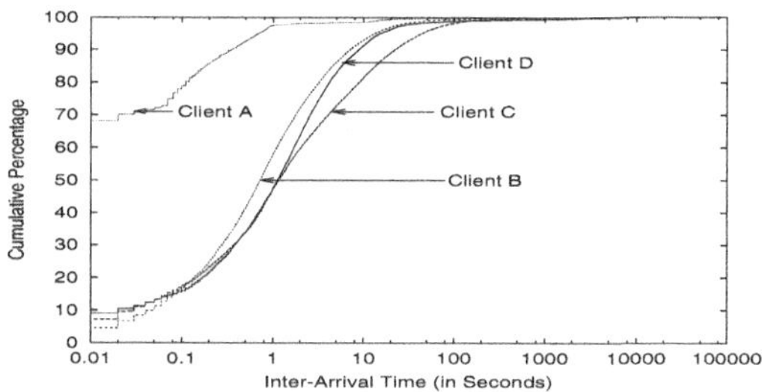

Fig. 9. Cumulative Frequency Distribution of Inter-Arrival Times for the Four Selected Clients

of their requests within 10 and 100 seconds, respectively. This implies that a threshold of inter-request arrival time between 10 and 100 seconds would provide an effective timeout value for HTTP/1.1 persistent connections for these clients. The impossibility that a human user can consistently generate requests within a second for a period of seven days adds weight to the conclusion that client A is a non-human client, while the others are likely to be human clients. In terms of the usage of the HTTP/1.1 protocol, the reference pattern of client A is more closely aligned with the philosophy of persistent connections than other clients because of a smaller inter-request arrival time. This implies that non-human clients are more likely to benefit from HTTP persistent connections than are human clients.

Resource Management Implications. From the characterization results of selected client workloads, two dramatically different reference patterns are identified as human and non-human. The reference pattern of human clients is found to be amenable to caching, while that of non-human clients is not. Since we speculate that these two referencing patterns represent the general referencing patterns of clients at the Web server, there is a need for resource management strategies that treat the request streams of human clients differently from that of non-human clients. Almeida *et al.* [2] suggested Web caching strategies that treat the request streams of non-human clients differently from that of human clients. We believe that caching the request streams of human clients and ignoring the request streams of non-human clients could also be effective for Web server resource management. In implementing such resource management strategies at the Web server, the use of client information will be an important consideration.

4.3 Characteristics of Sessions within Individual Client Workloads

A user's Web request behaviour can differ from one session to another, and this might affect the way these sessions should be managed. For this part of our investigation, we consider the requests comprising individual sessions within client

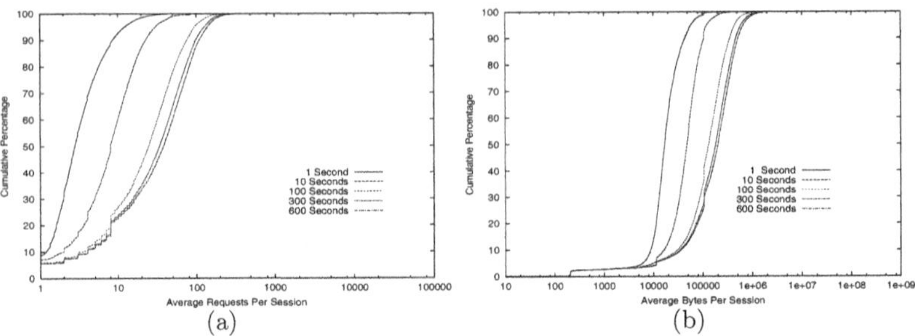

Fig. 10. Analysis of Client Session Activity: (a) Average Requests per Session; (b) Average Bytes Transferred per Session

workloads. We define a session as a stream of requests from a single client with an inter-request time less than a given threshold window time. The threshold window time is referred to as the *timeout value*. If request r_{i+1} from a given client arrives at the server Δt seconds after request r_i from the same client, and $\Delta t \leq T$ (where T is the timeout value), then requests r_i and r_{i+1} are both considered to be part of the same client session. If $\Delta t > T$, then request r_i is the last request in the client session and indicates the end of a client session, while request r_{i+1} initiates the next client session. This method was discussed in [4] to study Web clients. For this study, the sessions within individual client workloads are used to examine the effectiveness of the HTTP/1.1 protocol and to characterize the sequence of document working sets.

Distribution of Requests and Bytes Transferred within Web Sessions. The effectiveness of HTTP/1.1 for the reference patterns of clients is evaluated by characterizing the number of requests and the volume of bytes transferred within sessions of individual client request streams in the aggregate server workload. Fixed timeout values between 1 second and 600 seconds are chosen as a result of the impact of the number of sessions within client workloads reported in [19]. We observed (as shown in Figure 10) that timeout values of 100, 300 and 600 seconds are effective for the persistent connection of HTTP/1.1. The reason is that these timeout values have little impact on both the distribution of requests and the distribution of bytes transferred within sessions of individual client request streams in the aggregate workload. For example, fewer than 10% of clients have an average of one request per session of their individual workloads for all timeout values considered. Additionally, 50% of clients transferred an average of 100-1000 kB per session for a timeout value of 100 seconds.

Since the statistical mean can lead to a spurious measurement if the distribution of data is skewed, the full distributions for total requests and volume of bytes transferred over sequences of sessions within individual clients at the server were analyzed as discussed in [19]. We found a high variation in the total number of requests and the volume of bytes transferred across individual client sessions for timeout values of 1 and 10 seconds. In particular, about 70% of clients that accessed the server are observed to have a coefficient of variation that is close to 1.0 in this regard. This variation decreases as the timeout value reaches 100, 300 and 600 seconds. Since a smaller timeout value is usually preferable owing to memory performance problems [4], a timeout value of 100 seconds offers good utilization of HTTP/1.1 persistent connections[5].

Applying the same approach to client workloads A, B, C and D in Table 2 reveals that client A has the best utilization of HTTP persistent connections for timeout values of 1 second compared to other clients with a higher timeout value of 10-100 seconds. This implies that the reference pattern of supposedly non-human clients like A can more effectively utilize HTTP/1.1 persistent connections at fixed, but smaller timeout values than the human clients like B, C and D.

Phase Transition Behaviour in Web Client Sessions. The sequence of document working sets[6] within sessions of individual client workloads was characterized. The characterization shows the presence of phase transitions if there is a significant change between consecutive document reference patterns of sessions within individual client workloads over the observation period. Adapting Kienzle *et al.*'s [14] method for characterizing memory reference patterns to Web client reference patterns yields the cumulative frequency distributions of the percentage changes in document working sets across consecutive sessions shown in Figure 11. The timeout values that provide the best utilization of HTTP persistent connections for these clients are chosen for identifying a session. The percentage change in document working sets between consecutive sessions can be greater than 100% because the document working set of the current session can be larger than the previous session. The x-axis of the distributions plot represents the percentage change in document working sets of consecutive sessions and the y-axis represents the percentage of consecutive sessions that exceeds the percentage mark on the x-axis. Percentage changes that exceed 500% at the tail of the distributions are cut off for visualization purposes.

We observed that for client A, over 80% of consecutive sessions show a change in document working sets greater than 100%. For clients B, C and D, about 50% of their consecutive sessions have a change in document working sets exceeding 75%, 100% and 100%, respectively, after which a slowly declining pattern evolves. This pattern indicates a clear shift in the activity of clients B, C and D over their sessions. Since most consecutive sessions within the selected client workloads have a change in document working sets greater than 100%, phase transition

[5] This means that the number of TCP connections for the client-server communication on the Web has been reduced substantially by allowing a few clients to maintain the state of their open TCP connections at the server.

[6] The document working set is defined as the number of distinct documents referenced within the session of a client.

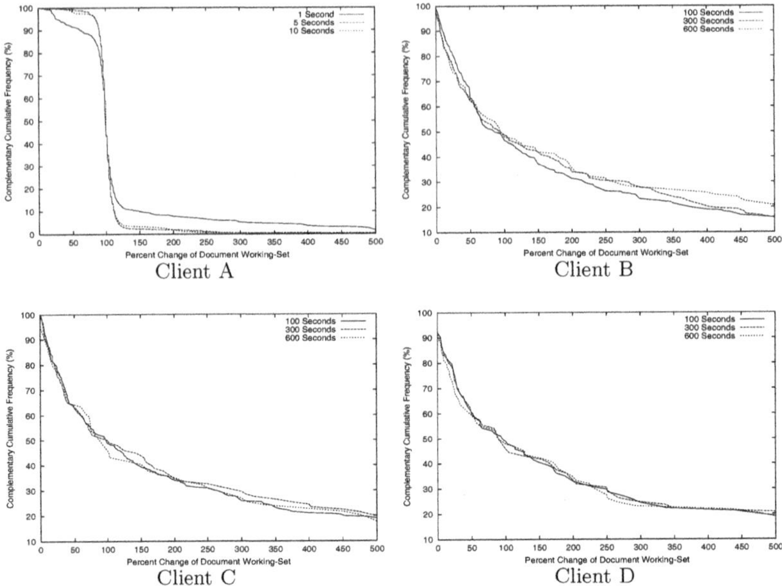

Fig. 11. Distributions of Percentage Changes Between Consecutive Document Working Sets of Client Sessions

behaviour is concluded to be present. This implies that the document reference patterns of sequences of sessions within individual client workloads may present problems for caching at the server.

Resource Management Implications. Arlitt [4] presents an extensive discussion of how the activity of clients using HTTP/1.1 persistent connections [17, 21] can affect the management of Web server resources such as memory. The explanation, however, hinges on how the Web server must reserve the memory resource in order to implement HTTP/1.1 persistent connections effectively. For this workload, the use of fixed but short timeout values less than 100 seconds is found to under-utilize HTTP persistent connections. This in turn wastes the reserved memory resource at the Web server because there is no substantial reduction in the number of TCP connections. On the other hand, a fixed but high timeout value of 100 seconds is found to provide the best utilization of HTTP/1.1 persistent connections. But this fixed and higher timeout value can be effective for resource management only if the memory resource at the Web server is bottleneck-free. Since memory is not bottleneck-free, the implementation of current HTTP/1.1 persistent connections is not likely to be effective at the server.

For effective resource management, our suggestion is that client information be made transparent at the Web server. This would assist in developing policies that use a fixed but short timeout value of 1 second to manage persistent connections of non-human clients, while a dynamic but short timeout value suggested in [4,17] can manage persistent connections of human clients. The presence of phase transition behaviour suggests that the implementation of caching strategies during HTTP/1.1 persistent connections is not likely to be effective at the Web server.

5 Conclusions

A hierarchical workload characterization was undertaken for a busy Web server. This adds to the growing body of knowledge on Web workload characteristics. The results presented can assist Web server designers in the provisioning of Web services as well as improving the effectiveness of the HTTP/1.1 protocol. Differences between clients can significantly impact performance. In particular, the identification of the reference patterns of human and non-human clients further helps in understanding the impact of such patterns on performance. An important observation from this study is that information about clients visiting the Web server (whether human or non-human) can be beneficial to the effective management of server resources. We contend that Web servers can use information based on the reference patterns of isolated clients (such as human and non-human) to provide more effective resource management. Our future research is aimed at the development of such strategies.

Acknowledgements. Funding for this research was provided by the Natural Sciences and Engineering Research Council of Canada, through research grant OGP0003707, and Telecommunications Research Laboratories (TRLabs) in Saskatoon.

References

1. V. Almeida, A. Bestavros, M. Crovella, and A. Oliveira, "Characterizing Reference Locality in the World Wide Web," in *Proceedings of the IEEE Conference on Parallel and Distributed Information Systems*, Miami Beach, Florida, pp. 92-103, December 1996.
2. V. Almeida, D. Menasce, R. Riedi, F. Pelegrinelli, R. Fonseca, and W. Meira, Jr., "Analyzing Web Robots and their Impact on Caching," in *Proceedings of the Sixth Workshop on Web Caching and Content Distribution*, Boston, Massachusetts, June 2001.
3. V. Almeida, D. Menasce, R. Riedi, F. Pelegrinelli, R. Fonseca, and W. Meira, Jr., "Analyzing Robot Behaviour in E-Business Sites," in *Proceedings of the ACM SIGMETRICS Conference*, Cambridge, Massachusetts, pp. 338-339, June 2001.
4. M. F. Arlitt, "Characterizing Web User Sessions," *Performance Evaluation Review*, Vol. 28, No. 2, pp. 50-56, September 2000.

5. M. F. Arlitt and C. L. Williamson, "Internet Web Servers: Workload Characterization and Performance Implications," *IEEE/ACM Transactions on Networking*, Vol. 5, No. 5, pp. 631-645, October 1997.
6. M. Arlitt and T. Jin, "A Workload Characterization Study of the 1998 World Cup Web Site," *IEEE Networks*, Vol. 14, No. 3, pp. 30-37, May/June 2000.
7. P. Barford, A. Bestavros, A. Bradley, and M. Crovella, "Changes in Web Client Access Patterns: Characteristics and Caching Implications," *World Wide Web*, Vol. 2, No. 1, pp. 15-28, January 1999.
8. H. Braun and K. C. Claffy, "Web Traffic Characterization: An Assessment of the Impact of Caching Documents from NCSA's Web Server," *Computer Networks and ISDN Systems*, Vol. 28, pp. 37-51, 1996.
9. L. D. Catledge, and J. E. Pitkow, "Characterizing Browsing Strategies in the World Wide Web," *Computer Networks and ISDN Systems*, Vol. 26, No. 6, pp. 1065-1073, 1995.
10. M. E. Crovella and A. Bestavros, "Self-Similarity in World Wide Web Traffic: Evidence and Possible Causes," in *Proceedings of the ACM SIGMETRICS Conference*, Philadelphia, Pennsylvania, pp. 160-169, May 1996.
11. C. R. Cunha and A. Bestavros, and M. E. Crovella, "Characteristic of World Wide Web Client-Based Traces," Technical Report TR-95-010, Department of Computer Science, Boston University, Boston, Massachussets, April 1995.
12. J. H. Hine, C. E. Wills, A. Martel, and J. Sommers, "Combining Client Knowledge and Resource Dependencies for Improved World Wide Web Performance", in *Proceedings of the INET 1998 Conference*, Geneva, Switzerland, July 1998.
13. S. Jin and A. Bestavros, "Sources and Characteristics of Web Temporal Locality," in *Proceedings of the Eighth International Symposium on Modeling, Analysis and Simulation of Computer and Telecomminucation Systems*, San Francisco, California, August/September 2000.
14. M. G. Kienzle, J. A. Garay, and W. H. Tetzlaff, "Analysis of Page-Reference Strings of an Interactive System," *IBM Journal of Research and Development*, Vol. 32, No. 4, pp. 523-535, July 1988.
15. A. Mahanti, *Web Proxy Workload Characterization and Modeling*, M.Sc. Thesis, Department of Computer Science, University of Saskatchewan, Saskatoon, Saskatchewan, September 1999.
16. D. Menasce, V. Almeida, R. Riedi, F. Peligrinelli, R. Fonseca, W. Meira Jr., "In Search of Invariants for E-Business Workloads," in *Proceedings of the Second ACM Electronic Commerce Conference*, Minneapolis, Minnesota, October 2000.
17. J. C. Mogul, "The Case for Persistent-Connection HTTP," in *Proceedings of the ACM SIGCOMM Conference*, Cambridge, Massachussets, pp. 299-313, August 1995.
18. J. C. Mogul "Network Behavior of a Busy Web Server and Its Clients," WRL Research Report 95/4, Digital Western Research Laboratory, May 1995.
19. A. A. Oke, *Workload Characterization for Resource Management at Web Servers*, M.Sc. Thesis, Department of Computer Science, University of Saskatchewan, Saskatoon, Saskatchewan, October 2000.
20. J. Spirn, "Distance String Models for Program Behaviour," *IEEE Computer*, Vol. 9, No. 11, pp. 14-20, November 1976.
21. K. Yap, "A Technical Overview of the New HTTP/1.1 Specification," in *Proceedings of the Third Australian World Wide Web Conference*, Australia, May 1997.
22. G. K. Zipf, *Human Behaviour and the Principle of Least Effort*, Addison-Wesley, Cambridge, Massachusetts, 1949.

Enabling Network Caching of Dynamic Web Objects

Pankaj K. Garg[1], Kave Eshghi[1], Thomas Gschwind[2], Boudewijn Haverkort[3], and Katinka Wolter[4]

[1] HP Labs, Palo Alto, USA
{garg | keshghi}@hpl.hp.com
[2] Technische Universität Wien, Austria
tom@infosys.tuwien.ac.at
[3] RWTH Aachen, Department of Computer Science, Germany
haverkort@lvs.informatik.rwth-aachen.de
[4] Technische Universität Berlin, Germany
katinka@cs.tu-berlin.de

Abstract. The World Wide Web is an important infrastructure for enabling modern information-rich applications. Businesses can lose value due to lack of timely employee communication, poor employee coordination, or poor brand image with slow or unresponsive web applications. In this paper, we analyze the responsiveness of an Intranet web application, i.e., an application within the corporate firewalls. Using a new Web monitoring tool called WebMon, we found, contrary to our initial expectations, substantial variations in the responsiveness for different users of the Intranet Web application. As in the Internet, traditional caching approaches could improve the responsiveness of the Intranet web-application, as far as static objects are concerned. We provide a solution to enable network caching of *dynamic* web objects, which ordinarily would not be cached by clients and proxies. Overall, our solution significantly improved the performance of the web application and reduced the variance in the response times by three orders of magnitude. Our cache enabling architecture can be used in other web applications.

1 Introduction

Since its inception in the early 1990's, the World Wide Web has evolved into being the most widespread infrastructure for Internet-based information systems. As with traditional information systems, the response time (measured starting from the user's initiation of a request and ending when the complete response is returned to the user) for individual interactions becomes critical in providing the right Quality of Experience (QoE) for a web user. A fast, responsive application gives the impression of a well-designed and well-managed business and web service. A slow, un-responsive application, on the other hand, can suggest poor quality of business and may send users seeking alternative web sites or services [1].

T. Field et al. (Eds.): TOOLS 2002, LNCS 2324, pp. 329–338, 2002.

Unlike traditional information systems, however, not all components required to accomplish a web transaction are necessarily under the control of the organization running the web application. Typically, end-users access a web application with a web browser, through a collection of proxies or caches, which ultimately send the request to a back-end web server farm with application servers and databases. Several networks participate in the intervening layers. Such *organizational heterogeneity*, in addition to the *component heterogeneity*, complicates the designs for responsiveness of web applications.

Caching of web objects has emerged as key enabler for achieving fast, responsive web applications [9]. The main idea is to maintain copies of web objects close to the end-user's browser and serve requests from caches to improve latency and reduce effects of queueing in network elements along the path from the browser to the server. Web browsers maintain cached copies of frequently requested objects. Similarly, large organizations or Internet Service Providers (ISPs) maintain caches of web objects frequently requested and shared by their user community.

To fully utilize the benefits on the Internet or Intranet, effective caching requires web objects available as **static** HTML pages. This means that the HTML page for that web object was not generated when a user requested the object, but was available as a stored HTML file. This is important because the intervening caches, e.g., the browser's cache, will normally not cache **dynamic** content but it will cache static content. Approaches for enabling caching of dynamic content through HTTP headers, e.g., with the `Expires` header, although a step in the right direction, are not universally and uniformly honored by intervening caches.

For performance reasons, web site administrators are well advised to turn dynamic content into static content whenever necessary and possible, to avoid the above problems.

In this paper we provide a framework for: (1) monitoring web applications performance to determine the need for a higher static-to-dynamic web-object ratio, and (2) an architecture to turn dynamic content into static content based on existing file systems and dependency tracking tools, e.g., using the well-known `make` facility [4]. Our approach relies on the fact that some dynamic objects do not change that often, and the data required to construct them is available in files rather than in a database.

We use WebMon [6] to monitor a web application's performance, which determine the requirements for enabling network caching of dynamic content. WebMon monitors the end-user perceived response time for web transactions and reports to a central server. At the same time, WebMon correlates client perceived response times with the server response time for each transaction. Statistical analysis of such client and server response times will help in understanding the requirements with respect to caching. Once a caching solution has been implemented, WebMon can again be used to quantify the benefits of caching.

When we turn dynamic content into static content, the user's request does not usually come all the way to the web server, but may be served by an intermediate cache. Although good for performance reasons, this is a drawback if the web server's administrator would have liked to use that *server hit* to count accesses to the web server. WebMon has a component that monitors every access to a given URL, even though the corresponding request may not come all the way to the web server. With a minor modification, this mechanism also serves for providing an accurate hit count.

In this paper we describe our framework for enabling caching of dynamic objects. We first describe the WebMon tool in Section 2. We describe the analysis of a sample application's response time in Section 3. In Section 4 we describe an architecture for converting most of the dynamic objects of the sample application into static objects. We monitored the altered application and report the results in Section 5. We conclude in Section 6 with a summary and guidelines for future work. An extended version of this paper appears as [5].

2 WebMon: Web Transaction Monitoring

WebMon is a performance monitoring tool for World Wide Web transactions. Typically, a web transaction starts at a Web browser and flows through several *components*: the Internet, a web server, an application server, and finally a database. WebMon monitors and correlates the response times at the browser, web server, and the application server [6].

WebMon relies on a sensor-collector architecture. Sensors are typically shared libraries or script components that intercept the actual processing of a transaction request. Each sensor is logically composed of two parts: the *start* part and the *end* part. The start part of a sensor performs data correlation, whereas the end part forwards monitored data to a collector that gathers and further correlates the data. Since the browser is typically behind a firewall, we use a surrogate sensor web server to forward the browser's data to the collector. This web server can be the same as the original web server that is serving the web pages, or a different one. The collector makes the data available in a file, database, or a measurement server, for further processing.

Browser WebMon sensors are built using JavaScript code sent with each instrumented page. The instrumented page instructs the browser to inject the start and end parts of sensors as the event handlers for the appropriate events for the browser.

The start part of the browser sensor generates a request identifier, and passes the identifier along with its request to the web server. The end part of the browser sensor sends its measurement to the WebMon collector.

The start part of the web server sensor extracts the identifier from the request, and passes the identifier along to the application server. The end part of the web server WebMon sensor sends its measurement along with the request to the collector. Similarly, the application server sensor processes the request and sends its measurement data to the collector. The collector correlates the data received by the individual components on the basis of the unique identifier associated with each transaction. In the prototype we use a single collector, although multiple servers tailored for different deployment architectures are feasible.

3 Response Time Analysis

WebMon enables transactional analysis of web applications from a variety of perspectives. In this paper we are mostly interested in the *response time* perceived by the clients for any **transaction** with the application. A transaction *starts* when the user clicks on a URL, or types a URL in the browser window. The transaction *ends* when the user's browser has finished displaying the complete page associated with that URL.

An application usually offers multiple transactions to its users. In addition to an overall transactional view, WebMon enables transactional segregation that can be used to identify poor performing transactions. Similarly, users of applications come from a variety of network *client nodes*. Accordingly, we analyze WebMon data to cluster and identify user locations that are poorly performing. Such views of the data determine opportunities for improving the web application.

Table 1. Sample mean, median, variance and squared coefficient of variation of the client and server response times.

	mean (ms)	median (ms)	variance (ms^2)	CV^2
clientTime	24 902.9	1993	$1.16413 \cdot 10^{11}$	187.7
serverTime	917.413	721	$3.86337 \cdot 10^{5}$	0.46

In Table 1, we list some statistics for the client and server response times of our sample application, Corporate Source [3]. Corporate Source is an *Intranet* application that enables sharing of source code among HP employees. Corporate Source is a two-tiered web application with a browser accessing web pages using the Apache web server, CGI scripts, and Server Side Include pages.

With respect to the clientTime, we observe that its mean value is very large, in fact, much larger than its median. This indicates that there are measurements that are very large, so large, that the clientTime distribution is skewed to the right. This is also confirmed by the extremely high variance and squared coefficient of variation. We attempted to fit a Pareto distribution to these measurements and found that a reasonable fit could only be obtained when the five largest observations are removed, thus implying that these "outliers" have an extreme impact on the observed mean. In the near future we will consider a fit to a suitably chosen hyperexponential distribution using the EM algorithm, cf. [8].

For the serverTime, we observe a much better behavior in the sense that the mean, which is much lower, is closer to the median, and the variance is very moderate as well. The squared coefficient of variation is only 0.5, indicating that the serverTime is rather deterministic.

By ordering the response times on client IP numbers, we found a dependence of the response times on client IP address. Combining the statistical data from table 1 and the fact that the location of a client is a factor for the perceived performance, we conclude that the network, i.e., the Intranet, is responsible for the large variations and large absolute values of the user-perceived performance. The serverTime is always relatively small, and rather deterministic, so it cannot be the cause of the bad performance perceived at the clients.

Remark. At first instance, we were surprised to see the Intranet performance as bottleneck; we had expected the Intranet to show less variable and lower response times. In the case study at hand, however, it seems that the Intranet is behaving more or less like the ordinary Internet. An explanation for this might be the fact that HP is a global company with offices all over the world, and hence, the Intranet is virtually as widespread as the Internet.

In order to improve the user-perceived performance, we therefore propose to move the objects requested closer to the clients, in order to avoid, as much as possible, the use of the Intranet. This can be achieved by increasing the fraction of web-objects that are cached at the clients. Since many of the objects in the study at hand are dynamic objects, we have to devise a means to enable caching of such dynamic objects. This will be discussed in the next section.

4 Enabling Network Caching of Dynamic Objects

To enable caching of some dynamic web objects from the Corporate Source application, we have to re-engineer the application. We describe this process in Section 4.1. In such re-engineering, determining the appropriate *Cache Update Policies* is quite important. We discuss cache update policies in Section 4.2. Implementation issues are then discussed in Section 4.3, where the issue of counting accesses is given special treatment in Section 4.4.

4.1 Re-engineering "Corporate Source"

The Corporate Source application uses two main file-based data sources: (1) the meta-data source (/usr/local/hpcs), and (2) the source code, with version history (/usr/local/cvsroot).

The application utilizes the two main dynamic page generation capabilities of the Apache web server: (1) server-side includes (.shtml pages), and (2) Common Gateway Interface (CGI) scripts. Out of the nine transactions for the Corporate Source application, four are server-side include pages, and five are CGI scripts. Hence, for the entire application, **none** of the pages are cacheable! This fact explains, at least to a certain extent, the measured response times as shown previously: all requests have to be served over the Intranet, over which many other HP network applications run as well.

To improve the response times for this application, we must transform the service from one that is providing non-cacheable web pages to one that is providing cacheable content. The main change is that instead of directly supplying the pages from the server-side includes or CGI, the web server supplies a set of HTML pages. The HTML pages, in turn, are periodically updated from the CGI and server-side include pages. Hence, for the web browser, *the web server behaves like a cache rather than a server generating dynamic pages.* Periodically, on requests from the `Cache Generator`, it behaves like a web server generating HTML pages from dynamic web objects. This is similar to the idea of a *reverse-proxy*, as used in several web servers, e.g., see `http://developer.netscape.com/docs/manuals/proxy/adminnt/revpxy.htm`. The effect, however, is quite different, since we *enable the caching of the web pages by intervening network entities*, whereas "reverse-proxy'ing" does not achieve this. Note that for our approach to operate correctly, all original HTML links to dynamic objects have to be converted to links to their static counterparts.

4.2 Cache Update Policies

The re-engineering process involves creating a cache of the dynamically generated web pages, and updating these cached pages as needed. For this purpose, it is useful to classify web pages as follows:

- **on-demand** pages are generated on demand; they are dynamic pages;
- **on-change** pages are generated when any underlying content for the page changes;
- **periodic** pages are generated periodically.

In the case of on-demand pages, the information given to the user is always up-to-date, but the disadvantage is possibly poor response time for the end-user. For on-change pages, the users may obtain up-to-date pages, but the machinery required to monitor all possible changes is complex and may be expensive for the web server, e.g., see Challenger et al. [2]. For pages that are updated on a periodic basis, the users may sometimes receive stale information, but the machinery and effort required by the web server are not expensive. Hence, we decided to implement the periodic update policy.

To see how good the periodic update policy is, we consider the following analytical model. Define: the object request rate (λ), the object change rate (τ), and the cached object update rate (γ). We *assume* that both the process of object requests and the process of object changes are Poisson processes. Furthermore, due to the periodic update policy with rate γ, the inter-update time is a constant, denoted $D = 1/\gamma$.

We can now view the time-line as partitioned by updates, all exactly D time units apart. Consider the "arrival" of an object request (as part of a Poisson process). The time that has passed since the last periodic update is a random variable Y, with distribution

$$F_Y(y) = \frac{1 - F_X(y)}{E[X]},$$

with F_X the inter-update time distribution and $E[X] = D$ the mean inter-update time [7, page 102]. $F_X(x)$ is a unit step-function at $x = D$. Accordingly, Y is uniformly distributed on $[0, D]$. This is intuitively appealing; the page change occurs truly randomly in an update interval.

Similarly, we can compute the distribution of Z, the time until the most recent page change. Since the page changes form a Poisson process as well, the time between page changes is a negative exponentially distributed random variable, which is, by definition, memoryless. Hence, Z has a negative exponential distribution with rate τ as well.

The probability that the request for the page will result in an up-to-date copy, then equals the probability $\Pr\{Y < Z\}$, that is, the probability that the last page update took place more recently than the last page change. Conditioning on the time Y until the last update instance, we obtain:

$$\Pr\{\text{"okay"}\} = \Pr\{Y < Z\} = \int_0^D \Pr\{Y < Z | Y = t\} \Pr\{Y = t\}\, dt$$
$$= \int_0^D \frac{e^{-\tau t}}{D} dt = \frac{1}{\tau D}\left(1 - e^{-\tau D}\right). \qquad (1)$$

One can easily show the following properties for this probability, which we for convenience write as $p(x)$, with $x = \tau D \geq 0$. The following limits are obeyed by $p(x)$: $\lim_{x \to 0} p(x) = 1$ and $\lim_{x \to \infty} p(x) = 0$. Furthermore, the derivative $p'(x) < 0$ for $x > 0$, so that $p(x) \in [0, 1]$, and it decreases monotonously from 1 to 0, for $x \geq 0$.

As an example, consider the case where the update rate $\gamma = 10$ per month (every third day an update; $D = 0.1$) and the change rate $\tau = 1$ (per month). The probability that *a* request will result in the right (most recent) copy of the page then equals $p(0.1) = 10(1 - e^{-0.1}) = 0.95$. If we set $\gamma = 30$ (daily updates; $D = \frac{1}{30}$) we obtain success probability 0.984. Notice that the current model does not have λ as one of its parameters. The probability $p(x)$ holds for every request that arrives as part of a Poisson process.

4.3 Implementation Considerations

To implement the periodic updates, we re-engineered the web application to use static HTML pages instead of server-side includes and CGI scripts. We first created a sub-directory "Cache" that contains all the static pages offered by the web server. A Unix "cron" job periodically accesses the CGI and server-side include web pages and generates the static pages for the web server. In the following, we use an example to illustrate the method of converting dynamic pages to static pages.

One of the transactions provided by the Corporate Source application is to describe the details of a given software project, using the meta-data stored about the project. This meta-data is stored as an XML file under the directory:

```
META-DATA/<project-id>/<project-id>.xml
```

To show the meta-data, a CGI PERL script parses the XML file and generates the HTML code for the user's browser to display. The <project-id> is a parameter to the script, through the fat URL method. Hence, the URL to ask information for the project "hpcs" would be:

```
http://src.hpl.hp.com/cgi-bin/sdata.cgi?software=hpcs
```

To develop an effective cache for such web pages, we need a script that converts the XML files into the required HTML files. This script should run only when data in the META-DATA directory has changed. Also, this script should run for all projects submitted to Corporate Source, even projects that may not have been submitted when the script was first written, i.e., we cannot hard-code the projects in the script.

An elegant solution for such a script can be developed using the Unix `make` utility [4]. `make` is a utility that takes a specification (usually called `makefile`) of dependencies among source and derived files, and when executed with the right specification (re-)produces all derived files for which the sources have changed. The user specifies the tools used for transforming the source to the derived files. For our case, we know the source files as the XML files that contain the meta-data. The derived files are the HTML files to be generated. We can use the existing web server and its CGI script as the tools to transform the XML to HTML.

4.4 Counting Accesses

As we will show in the next section, the redesign of the Corporate Source application does significantly improve the user-perceived performance. It does, however, create one problem: in the new architecture, some of the user requests may not make it anymore to the actual web server, so that we do not know anymore how many users have viewed a particular software project, or how many have downloaded it. With the dynamic pages it was easy to obtain this information from the web server logs. This seems to be a general problem when a dynamic page is changed to a static, cacheable page.

To overcome this problem, we again used the WebMon tool [6]. In order to send browser response times back to a measurement data collector, WebMon introduces an extra HTTP request back to a web server that forwards the measured data to the measurement collector. This additional web server can be another web server, on a different network, in case performance of the original web server is an issue. In our case, this additional WebMon request can be used to log accesses to the server, and hence give us the count of dynamic web page access.

To achieve this, we must modify the original WebMon client side instrumentation to include the URL of the previous request in the data collection request.

5 Analysis of the Data with Cached Pages

We adapted the Corporate Source application as described above, and subsequently monitored it for about two weeks.

From the new data set of 521 observations, we computed the sample mean, median, variance and squared coefficient of variation, as given in Table 2. Note that the serverTime could not be monitored for the cached pages, simply because request to these pages do not make it to the server. The serverTime has been observed for only 166 of the 521 entries of the data set.

The serverTime has an extremely small coefficient of variation, which means that there is hardly any variability observed. An Erlang-k distribution with $k \approx 5$ could be used to describe the data. We also observe that the serverTime has decreased (the mean serverTime has decreased to 69% of the former value, the median to 74%), most probably due to the decreased load on the server.

Table 2. New sample mean, median, variance and squared coefficient of variation for serverTime and clientTime

	mean (ms)	median (ms)	variance (ms^2)	CV^2
client	4524.3486	1121	$5.209 \cdot 10^8$	25.4
client-15	1081.2	1549.061	$5.3033 \cdot 10^6$	2.21
server	638.988	539	81219.2	0.2

The mean clientTime is reduced to only 20% of its former value, however, the variance of the clientTime is reduced by three orders of magnitude (which corresponds to a reduction of roughly 99.5%). The coefficient of variation is still large, but considerably smaller than before. The same is true for the variance. Also observe that the mean-to-median ratio (previously equal to 12.5) has reduced to only 4.0; the clientTime distribution is considerably less skewed now.

Interestingly, if we drop the 15 largest observations for the clientTime, the variance is reduced by another two orders of magnitude and end up with a "normal" coefficient of variation. This shows that a few extremely long response times cause these unusual statistics; the majority of the observations is much more moderate. More advanced statistical methods are required to filter these outliers.

6 Conclusions

In this paper, we have proposed and evaluated a performance enhancement of an Intranet web application, resulting, for the case study at hand, in a mean response time reduction of 80% and in a response time variance reduction of three orders of magnitude. The reengineering of the web application was motivated by the insights gained with the novel tool, WebMon, that can monitor end-user perceived response times for web applications and correlate them with server response times. WebMon helped us in determining the performance bottleneck at hand, i.e., the Intranet. In the subsequent reengineering process of the web application studied, we took measures to reduce the load on the Intranet. In particular, we proposed a method which transforms dynamically generated web pages (that cannot be cached) into static web pages. Thus, this transformation enables caching of web objects at the client, and therefore reduced network traffic and load.

Our approach relies only on software tools that are widely available (like the Unix `make` facility), so that it can be used by other web application developers for improving the responsiveness of their web applications.

Although useful for a large number of web applications with dynamic objects, our approach is not directly suitable for web applications with frequently changing objects, such as commonly found in personalized e-commerce shopping web applications and news suppliers. In the future, we will address the performance issues for such web applications as well.

References

1. N. Bhatti, A. Bouch, and A. Kuchinsky. Integrating User-Perceived Quality into Web Server Design. Technical Report HPL-2000-3, Hewlett-Packard Labs, Palo Alto, CA., January 2000.
2. J. Challenger, P. Dantzig, and A. Iyengar. A Scalable System for Consistently Caching Dynamic Web Data. In *Proceedings of the 18th Annual Joint Conference of the IEEE Computer and Communications Societies*, New York, New York, 1999.
3. J. Dinkelacker and P. Garg. Corporate Source: Applying Open Source Concepts to a Corporate Environment: (Position Paper). In *Proceedings of the 1st ICSE International Workshop on Open Source Software Engineering*, Toronto, Canada., May 2001.
4. S. Feldman. Make - A Program to Maintain Programs. *Software Practice and Experience*, 9(3):255–265, March 1979.
5. P. K. Garg, K. Eshghi, T. Gschwind, B. Haverkort, and K. Wolter. Enabling Network Caching of Dynamic Web Objects. Technical report, HP Labs, 1501 Page Mill Road, Palo Alto, Ca 94304, 2002. To Appear.
6. T. Gschwind, K. Eshghi, P. Garg, and K. Wurster. Web Transaction Monitoring. Technical Report HPL-2001-62, Hewlett-Packard Laboratories, Palo Alto, Ca, April 2001.
7. B. R. Haverkort. *Performance of Computer Communication Systems.* John Wiley & Sons, 1998.
8. R. El Abdouni Khayari, R. Sadre, and B.R. Haverkort. Fitting world-wide web request traces with the EM-Algorithm. In R. van der Mei and F. Huebner-Szabo de Bucs, editors, *Proceedings of SPIE: Internet Performance and Control of Network Systems II*, volume 4523, pages 211–220, Denver, USA, August 2001.
9. D. Wessels. *Web Caching.* O'Reilly & Associates, Inc., 101 Morris Street, Sebastopol, CA 95472, June 2001.

A Tool for Controlling Response Time in Real-Time Systems

Pascal Richard

Laboratory of Applied Computer Science
ENSMA - Téléport 2 - BP 40109
86961 Futuroscope Cedex, France
pascal.richard@ensma.fr

Abstract. In hard real-time systems, classical scheduling policies only cope with satisfaction of deadline constraints. In this paper, to every periodic task is associated a weight that models the importance of the task in terms of worst-case response time. These parameters are set off-line by the designers of the real-time software in order to control the quality of the on-line schedule. According to these weights, a set of feasible fixed-priorities are computed so that the mean weighted response time of the tasks is minimized. We propose a branch and bound algorithm to solve this problem. An example is completely detailed and numerical results on randomly generated problems are lastly presented to show the efficiency of the developed tool.

1 Introduction

In hard real-time systems, tasks periodically read data from sensors and respond to the controlled system through actuators. A response to an external event must occur within a fixed interval of time. So, every task occurrence (a job) is subjected to a deadline. These timing constraints are usually inherited from the environment of the controlled system. If one deadline is not met, some dramatic events can occur [1]. Usually, schedulers implemented in commercial real-time operating systems have no knowledge about tasks arriving in the future. From the validation view-point, tasks are a priori known, but the running time of each job is unknown until the job finishes - only worst-case execution times are known.

In some real-time applications, tasks are not only subjected to complete by their deadlines, but more control of the on-line schedule is required. Quality of Service (QoS) is interpreted in many ways (e.g. jitters, response times, etc.). In real-time environments, the objective is then to optimize a performance measure while respecting the release times and the deadlines of the tasks. There are two approaches in order to deal with such optimization problems using schedulers of real-time kernels. On the one hand, we can modify the temporal parameters of the tasks in order to improve the behaviour of the classical priority assignment such as Deadline Monotonic (DM) and Earliest Deadline First (EDF). On the other hand, if we focus on fixed-priority schedulers, we can directly compute a set

T. Field et al. (Eds.): TOOLS 2002, LNCS 2324, pp. 339–348, 2002.

of priorities so that the associated on-line schedule leads to good performances. Such tools are needed at the design step in order to build up a schedule with the expected performances.

In non real-time environments, response time (or flow time) is a widely-used performance metric to optimize continuous job arrivals. When each task has to be responsive in a single processor problem, then the optimized performance measure is the maximum response time of the tasks. For that purpose, the First-In-First-Out rule (FIFO) is an exact algorithm [2]. If the whole system has to be responsive, then the optimized metric is the average response time. It is well-known that the Shortest Remaining Processing Time rule (SRPT) leads to an optimal schedule. Recently, it has been shown that Shortest Processing Time rule is asymptotically optimal for the same problem [3]. But, when deadlines are added to the problem, then it becomes $\mathcal{NP}$-hard [4].

Weighted versions of these problems have also been studied. Their interests are to control the maximum response times of some tasks while keeping the whole system responsive. In particular, the stretch (also called the slowdown) is the weighted sum of response times when weights are the inverse of the processing times. This metric has been used to study the performances of operating systems and parallel systems [5]. The computational complexity of minimizing the average stretch is unknown. But, if arbitrary weights are allowed, then minimizing the weighted total response time is $\mathcal{NP}$-hard in the strong sense [6].

Hereafter, we study periodic tasks that will be on-line scheduled according to fixed priorities. Each task τ_i is defined by four deterministic parameters (C_i, D_i, T_i, w_i), where C_i is the worst-case execution time, D_i is the deadline relative to the arrival of the task in the system, T_i is the period between two successive arrivals and w_i is a real number that models the importance of the task in terms of worst-case response time. The tasks are simultaneously released at time 0 and we also assume that $D_i \leq T_i$, for every task τ_i, $1 \leq i \leq n$. A task τ_i is feasible if its worst-case response time R_i is less than or equal to its relative deadline. Among all feasible priority assignment to the tasks, we aim to find one that minimizes the weighted sum of the worst-case response times. So, the objective function is $\min(\sum_j w_j R_j)$. According to the previous discussion, it is easy to prove that this scheduling problem is $\mathcal{NP}$-hard in the strong sense.

The parameters w_i are set by the designers of the real-time software for defining the importance of task τ_i in terms of worst-case response time. If there are no particular constraints on the response time of a task (but it must be completed by its deadline), then its weight is set to 0. In this way, this task will have no influence on the objective function. We then compute the fixed priorities π_i so that the objective function is minimized and all deadlines are met. Deadline Monotonic policy usually leads to bad performances for minimizing the weighted sum of worst-case response times. The main idea to increase the quality of the schedule is to schedule a task having a small weight as high a priority as possible, even if its deadline is not the lowest one among pending tasks.

The paper is organized as follows. In Section 2 we shall present our branch and bound algorithm. Section 3 presents a detailed example and numerical results on randomly generated problems. Lastly, we conclude and give further perspectives of research.

2 Branch and Bound Algorithm

Branch and Bound algorithms are very used to solve combinatorial problems. When they are applied to scheduling problems, partial schedules are stored in vertices of a search tree. Leaves of the search tree define feasible solutions of the problem. Since the number of feasible solutions is exponential due to the computational complexity of the problem, the only way to find a solution in an acceptable amount of time is to detect as soon as possible vertices that will not lead to an improvement of the best known solution. At each step, the explored vertex is separated, that is to say its children are defined by assigning a priority to one task in the previous partial solution. These vertices are pruned (deleted) if the lower bound of the criterion is greater than or equal to the best known solution or if the constraints of the problem are not satisfied. The implementation of a branch and bound method is based on a set of non-explored vertices, called the Active Set.

2.1 Initial Solution

Before beginning the branch and bound procedure, an initial feasible solution (i.e., a feasible set of priorities) is computed in order to allow comparison of criteria with the first vertices generated in the first level of the search tree. This solution allows the computation of an upper bound of the objective function. Since $D_i \leq T_i$ and tasks are synchronously released at time 0, then:

- Deadline Monotonic policy leads to a feasible schedule if one exists,
- The worst-case response times of the tasks can be computed exactly [7].

Assigning priorities by using the Deadline Monotonic algorithm is performed in polynomial time, but we do not know if there exists a polynomial time algorithm for verifying that every deadline is met in the corresponding schedule (i.e. the complexity status of feasibility of synchronously released and fixed-priority tasks is unknown). But the worst-case response time of a task can be computed in pseudo-polynomial time (i.e., in polynomial time assuming that the input is unary encoded) by using the method presented in [7]. Thus, as far as we know, checking feasibility of given priorities can be performed in pseudo-polynomial time.

We assume hereafter that 1 is the highest priority level. Let $[i]$ denote the index of the task at priority level i. The worst-case response time of a task τ_i depends on the workload of the higher priority tasks. This workload at time t is $W(t)$:

$$W(t) = \sum_{j=1}^{i-1} \left\lceil \frac{t}{T_{[j]}} \right\rceil C_{[j]} \tag{1}$$

The worst-case response time of τ_i is then obtained by solving the recurrent equation $t = C_i + W(t)$, that is to say:

$$\begin{cases} R_i^{(0)} = C_i \\ R_i^{(k)} = W(R_i^{(k-1)}) + C_i \end{cases} \tag{2}$$

$$R_i = R_i^{(k)} = R_i^{(k-1)} \tag{3}$$

According to the Deadline Monotonic priority assignment, we can compute the worst-case response times of the tasks by using (2), and then compute the value of the objective function. The task ordering is performed in polynomial time, as well as computing the objective function. Thus, the computational complexity of this heuristic is due to the feasibility problem of the tasks.

We shall now propose a better heuristic, that always leads to a better solution in comparison to the Deadline Monotonic schedule. We assign the priority in reverse order. Such backward priority ordering is based on an interesting property of fixed-priority schedule.

Lemma 1 *[8] Let the tasks assigned lowest priority levels $i, i+1, \ldots, n$ be feasible under that priority ordering, then there exists a feasible schedule that assigns the same tasks to levels $i, \ldots, n$.*

Our heuristic assigns priorities to the tasks from the lowest priority to the highest one, and at each step it chooses the task that increases as little as possible the objective function among all tasks that are feasible for the current priority level. As a direct consequence of Lemma 1, the heuristic always finds a feasible priority assignment if one exists. In Figure 1, we give the pseudo-code of the heuristic.

```
Heuristic: Backward Priority Rule
   Let X be the set of tasks and n be the number of tasks
   Let z=0 be the objective function
   While X is not empty
      Let X' the tasks feasible at priority level n
       among tasks belonging to X
      Let a be the task with the lowest weighted
       worst-case response time r in X'
      z=z+a.w*r
      Assign priority level n to a
      n=n-1
      X=X\{a}
   End Loop
End
```

Fig. 1. Heuristic pseudo-code

2.2 Vertex Branching Rule

A vertex is simply defined by the index of a task. Levels of the vertices in the tree are interpreted as priority levels of tasks. The first level in the tree defines the tasks assigned to the lowest priority level, and in the same way, the leaves define tasks assigned to the highest priority level. The number of vertices in a search tree is clearly exponential in the size of the problem. Since the number of vertices at level l is the number of permutations of k elements among n, then the number of vertices at level k is: $\frac{n!}{(n-k)!}$. Thus, the total number of vertices in the search tree is: $\sum_{i=0}^{n-1} \prod_{k=0}^{i} (n-k)$.

The vertex branching rule selects the next vertex to be explored. This strategy has an important impact on the largest size of the active set. The most commonly used strategy to solve scheduling problems is the depth-first search one. The main interest of this method is: the size of the active set is polynomially bounded in the size of the problem (it is not the case for other strategies, especially when a breadth-first search is used). In that way, the maximum number of vertices stored simultaneously in the active set is $n(n+1)/2$, generated while reaching the first leaf of the search tree.

When a leaf is reached, the value of its objective function is compared with the best known solution. If it is lower, then the current leaf is used to update the upper bound of the criterion. The search continues while the active set is not empty (i.e., the tree has been completely explored). When the tree has been completely explored, then the best known upper bound, improved during the search, is an optimal solution.

2.3 Lower Bound

For the explored vertex, the value of the criterion associated to the tasks assigned to priority levels can be exactly computed, since their worst-case response times are already known. But for the others, we need a lower bound in order to have an estimation of the quality of the vertex. Note that a task τ_i with a lower priority than another task τ_j cannot increase the response time of τ_j in all feasible schedules.

One way to compute a lower bound of the weighted sum of the worst-case response times is to apply the modified Smith's rule [9]. Tasks without priority are scheduled in non-decreasing order of the ratio C_i/w_i, and we relax three constraints of our problem:

- preemption is allowed
- tasks are periodic.
- tasks are subjected to deadline constraints.

Tasks are then sequenced without preemption using this rule and the relaxed constraints. Their completion times are then computed. Subsequently, the weighted sum of the worst-case response times is computed. We shall prove that this method leads to a lower bound of the objective function for the explored vertex. Figure 2 presents the pseudo-code of the lower bound computation. $t.w$ and $t.C$ denote respectively the weight and the worst-case execution time of a task t ; $v.S$ is the set of tasks with assigned priorities in the vertex v ; $v.R[t]$ is the worst-case response time of t for vertex v ; T is the set of tasks of the system.

```
Algorithm: Lower Bound
Input:   Vertex v
Output: Integer lb
Var : Integer z, Set of Tasks U
Begin
    lb=0
    For every task t in v.S Do
        lb=lb+t.w*v.R[t]
    End For
    U=T\v.S
    z=0
    For every task t in U in non-decreasing order of t.C/t.w Do
        z=z+t.C
        lb=lb+z*t.w
    End For
    Return lb
End
```

Fig. 2. Lower Bound pseudo-code

Theorem 1 *A lower bound of the optimal weighted sum of the worst-case response times is computed by the Lower Bound algorithm.*

Proof: The first loop in the Lower Bound procedure calculates the value of the criterion for the tasks having priorities. Since these tasks are assigned to lower priority levels, then their worst-case response times can exactly be computed using the system of equations (2) and (3). For the other tasks (having no assigned priority levels), their worst-case response times are dependent of the assignment of the higher priority levels. We shall show for these tasks that a lower bound of the criterion is obtained by applying the modified Smith's rule [9]. Since we relax the assumption of the periodic arrival of tasks, higher priority tasks occurs strictly one time. Thus, the worst-case response times cannot increase. Subsequently, consider two priority assignments of the tasks: σ and σ'. Assume that the priority assignment in the schedule σ respect the modified Smith's rule, and not in σ' due only to the interchange of τ_i and τ_j. The values of the criterion in σ_1, σ_2 are the same in σ than in σ'. The only variation in the respective objective functions z and z' can only be due to the interchange of τ_i and τ_j:

$$z' - z = (C_j w_j + (C_i + C_j)w_i)) - (C_i w_i + (C_i + C_j)w_j)) \tag{4}$$
$$z' - z = C_j w_i - C_i w_j \tag{5}$$

Since the tasks respect the modified Smith's rule, then we verify that the criterion cannot be improved in σ' since $C_i/w_i \leq C_j/w_j$: $z' - z \geq 0$. It follows that a lower bound of the criterion has been established.□

2.4 Vertex Elimination Rules

Elimination rules are of prime interest in branch and bound methods because they can drastically prune the search tree. We next detail three conditions to prune a vertex, that are:

- immediate selection,
- a deadline is not met,
- the lower bound is greater than the best known solution (upper bound).

The immediate selection rule detects children that will not lead to a feasible solution, before generating them. The following result leads to such a rule.

Theorem 2 *For all pair τ_i, τ_j of tasks, if:*

$$\left\lceil \frac{T_i}{T_j} \right\rceil \times C_j + C_i > D_i \tag{6}$$

then the priority of τ_i must be higher than the priority of τ_j.

According to this result, we can define a set of constraints that must be satisfied during the branching step. For instance, if we detect that τ_i must have a higher priority than τ_j according to Theorem 2, then a task τ_i will not be generated in the first level of the search tree. Furthermore, τ_i can be assigned to a priority level if, and only if, τ_j has already been assigned one in a predecessor vertex. The constraints are obviously computed and checked in polynomial times.

We now detail the test of deadline constraints for the current vertex. The vertex branching rule generates children of the vertex currently explored while respecting the immediate selection rule. If the vertex of level k is separated, then all its children are assigned to the priority level $n - k$ (remember that priorities are assigned in reverse order). The first step is to verify that the tasks assigned to this priority level meet their deadlines ($\tau_{[n-k+1]}$). Since the vertex is newly generated, then we always know that the tasks assigned to the priority levels $n..n - k + 1$ are feasible. These tasks do not interfere with the execution of $\tau_{[n-k+1]}$. We can check the feasibility of $\tau_{[n-k+1]}$ by solving the equations (2) and (3). Furthermore, its response time depends only on the tasks without assigned priority levels.

Theorem 3 *To prune a vertex, it is unecessary to check the schedulability of the tasks without assigned priority levels.*

Proof: Let S be a set of feasible tasks according to the Deadline Monotonic algorithm, then every $S' \subset S$ is also schedulable according to Deadline Monotonic. Since the initial solution of the branch and bound procedure is obtained by using the Deadline Monotonic priority assignment, then there exists a feasible priority assignment for the tasks without priority in the current vertex. Lemma 1 allows to conclude. □

The second way to prune a vertex is performed when the best solution is lower than the lower bound of the current vertex. Generation of the children can only increase lower bounds. So, when a leaf should be reached, the value of the objective function will not be improved, and it will be greater than or equal to the best known upper bound.

One can remark that checking the feasibility of a child vertex is performed in pseudo-polynomial time. This complexity is only due to the computation of the worst-case response time of the task at the current priority level in the explored vertex (i.e., when equations (2,3) are solved).

3 Experimentation

We shall present a detailed example and numerical results on randomly generated instances of the scheduling problem.

3.1 A Detailed Example

We next consider the task set presented in Figure 3. The utilization factor of the processor (i.e., $\sum_i C_i/T_i$) is $U = 0.792$, and applying the heuristic presented in Section 2.1 leads to a feasible schedule, and the value of the objective function for that schedule is $ub = 254$. The priority assignment and the associated response-times according to the heuristic are also given in Table 3, respectively in columns $H(\pi_i)$ and $H(R_i)$. Figure 4 presents the search tree. The immediate selection rule defines two constraints: τ_4 must have a higher priority than τ_1 and τ_2. The complete search tree has 326 vertices. The optimal value is 174, so the improvement of the initial solution is up to 46 percent. The implicit enumeration performed by the branch and bound generates 15 vertices, so less than one percent of the search tree has been explored to find the optimal priority assignment.

Tasks	C_i	D_i	T_i	w_i	$H(\pi_i)$	$H(R_i)$
τ_0	5	15	30	2	1	5
τ_1	7	50	50	1	4	45
τ_2	8	50	100	3	5	21
τ_3	3	20	25	5	3	12
τ_4	2	7	7	4	2	7

Fig. 3. Task set of the detailed example

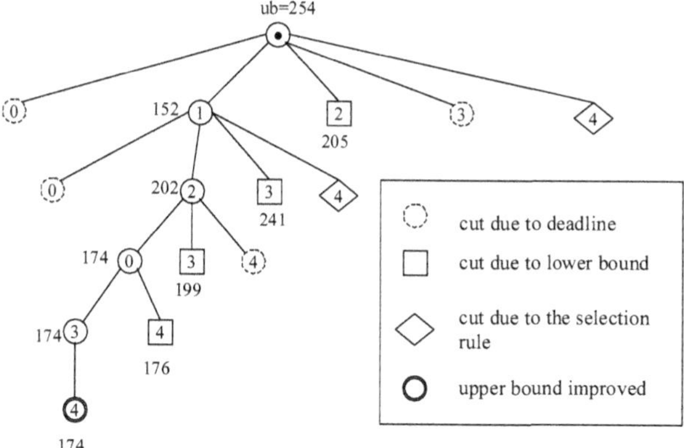

Fig. 4. Search tree of tasks of the detailed example

3.2 Numerical Results

This method has also been experimented with randomly generated problems. For a given number of tasks, we randomly generate 25 instances. Problems have between 6 and 28 tasks, and the utilization factor of the processor is 0.5 for all instances. Uniform law is used by the random generator and the characteristics of the generation are $C_i \in [1..10]$, $D_i = T_i$ are computed in order to have a utilization factor close to 0.5, and $w_i \in [0..20]$. Numerical experimentation has been performed on a Pentium III/450 MHz personal computer. A time limit has been fixed to one hour for every instance.

Figure 5 gives the average resolution time according to the problem size. The best solution indicates at what time the optimal solution has been reached. The elapsed time is the total duration to solve a given problem. The difference between the elapsed time and the time at which the optimal solution has been found, is the delay to prove that the best known solution is an optimal one. As shown in Figure 5, the optimal solution is quickly reached, but proving optimality takes a long time when the size of the problem increases. Figure 5 also presents the number of instances solved versus of unsolved instances for each size of a problem. We can see that no instance with 28 tasks has been solved within the time limit of one hour for each instance.

4 Conlusion

We have presented a method for computing fixed priorities of periodically released tasks so that the weighted sum of their worst-case response times is minimized. These priorities are then used by an on-line scheduler while respecting the hard deadline constraints. Numerical results have been presented to show the efficiency of the method. Perspectives of this work are to extend the existent

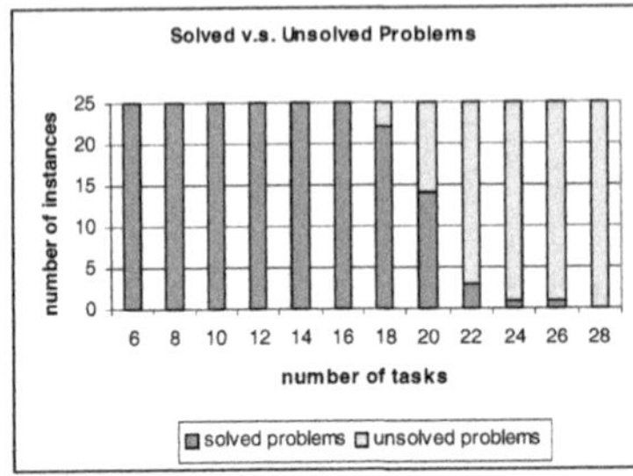

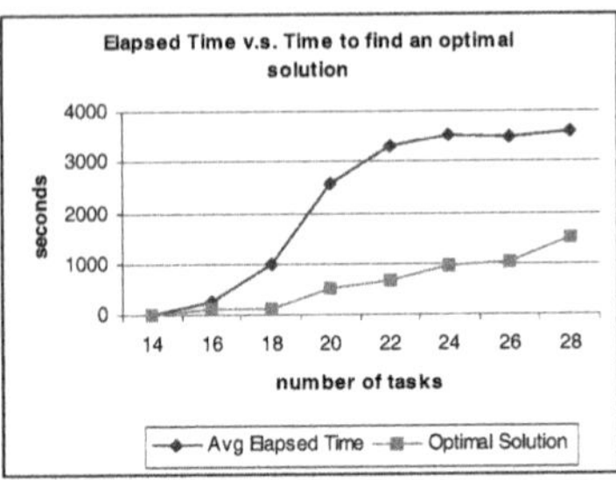

Fig. 5. Solved instances and computation times - Time limit: 1 hour.

tool to other optimization criteria and distributed real-time systems. For that purpose, the priority assignment method presented in [10] will be extended in order to meet QoS requirements.

References

1. Liu, J.: Real-Time Systems. Prentice Hall (2000)
2. Bender, M., Chakrabarti, S., Muthukrishnan, S.: Flow and stretch metrics for scheduling continuous job streams. proc. Symp. on Discrete Algorithms (1998)
3. Kaminsky, P., Simchi-Levi, D.: Asymptotic analysis of an on-line algorithm for single machine completion time problem with release dates. Operations Research Letters **29** (2001) 141–148
4. Du, J., Leung, J.: Minimizing mean flow time with release time and deadline constraints. in: proc. of Real-Time System Symposium (1988) 24–32
5. Muthukrishnan, S., Rajaraman, R., Shaheen, A., Gehrke, J.: Online scheduling to minimize average stretch. proc. IEEE Symp. on Foundations of Computer Science (1999) 433–443
6. Chejuri, C., Khanna, S., Zhu, A.: Algorithms for minimizing weighted flow time. proc. ACM Symp. on Theory of Computing (2001)
7. Joseph, M., Pandya, P.: Finding response-time in a real-time system. BCS Computer Journal **29** (1986) 390–395
8. Audsley, N.: Optimal priority assignment and feasibility of static priority assignment with arbitrary start times. YCS 164, University of York (1991)
9. Smith, W.: Various optimizers for single-stage production. Naval Research Logistic Quaterly **3** (1956) 481–486
10. Richard, M., Richard, P., Cottet, F.: Task and message priority assignment in automotive systems. 4th Int. Conf. on Fieldbus Systems and Their Applications (2001)

Author Index

Lecture Notes in Computer Science

For information about Vols. 1–2238
please contact your bookseller or Springer-Verlag

Vol. 2239: T. Walsh (Ed.), Principles and Practice of Constraint Programming – CP 2001. Proceedings, 2001. XIV, 788 pages. 2001.

Vol. 2240: G.P. Picco (Ed.), Mobile Agents. Proceedings, 2001. XIII, 277 pages. 2001.

Vol. 2241: M. Jünger, D. Naddef (Eds.), Computational Combinatorial Optimization. IX, 305 pages. 2001.

Vol. 2242: C.A. Lee (Ed.), Grid Computing – GRID 2001. Proceedings, 2001. XII, 185 pages. 2001.

Vol. 2243: G. Bertrand, A. Imiya, R. Klette (Eds.), Digital and Image Geometry. VII, 455 pages. 2001.

Vol. 2244: D. Bjørner, M. Broy, A.V. Zamulin (Eds.), Perspectives of System Informatics. Proceedings, 2001. XIII, 548 pages. 2001.

Vol. 2245: R. Hariharan, M. Mukund, V. Vinay (Eds.), FST TCS 2001: Foundations of Software Technology and Theoretical Computer Science. Proceedings, 2001. XI, 347 pages. 2001.

Vol. 2246: R. Falcone, M. Singh, Y.-H. Tan (Eds.), Trust in Cyber-societies. VIII, 195 pages. 2001. (Subseries LNAI).

Vol. 2247: C. P. Rangan, C. Ding (Eds.), Progress in Cryptology – INDOCRYPT 2001. Proceedings, 2001. XIII, 351 pages. 2001.

Vol. 2248: C. Boyd (Ed.), Advances in Cryptology – ASIACRYPT 2001. Proceedings, 2001. XI, 603 pages. 2001.

Vol. 2249: K. Nagi, Transactional Agents. XVI, 205 pages. 2001.

Vol. 2250: R. Nieuwenhuis, A. Voronkov (Eds.), Logic for Programming, Artificial Intelligence, and Reasoning. Proceedings, 2001. XV, 738 pages. 2001. (Subseries LNAI).

Vol. 2251: Y.Y. Tang, V. Wickerhauser, P.C. Yuen, C.Li (Eds.), Wavelet Analysis and Its Applications. Proceedings, 2001. XIII, 450 pages. 2001.

Vol. 2252: J. Liu, P.C. Yuen, C. Li, J. Ng, T. Ishida (Eds.), Active Media Technology. Proceedings, 2001. XII, 402 pages. 2001.

Vol. 2253: T. Terano, T. Nishida, A. Namatame, S. Tsumoto, Y. Ohsawa, T. Washio (Eds.), New Frontiers in Artificial Intelligence. Proceedings, 2001. XXVII, 553 pages. 2001. (Subseries LNAI).

Vol. 2254: M.R. Little, L. Nigay (Eds.), Engineering for Human-Computer Interaction. Proceedings, 2001. XI, 359 pages. 2001.

Vol. 2255: J. Dean, A. Gravel (Eds.), COTS-Based Software Systems. Proceedings, 2002. XIV, 257 pages. 2002.

Vol. 2256: M. Stumptner, D. Corbett, M. Brooks (Eds.), AI 2001: Advances in Artificial Intelligence. Proceedings, 2001. XII, 666 pages. 2001. (Subseries LNAI).

Vol. 2257: S. Krishnamurthi, C.R. Ramakrishnan (Eds.), Practical Aspects of Declarative Languages. Proceedings, 2002. VIII, 351 pages. 2002.

Vol. 2258: P. Brazdil, A. Jorge (Eds.), Progress in Artificial Intelligence. Proceedings, 2001. XII, 418 pages. 2001. (Subseries LNAI).

Vol. 2259: S. Vaudenay, A.M. Youssef (Eds.), Selected Areas in Cryptography. Proceedings, 2001. XI, 359 pages. 2001.

Vol. 2260: B. Honary (Ed.), Cryptography and Coding. Proceedings, 2001. IX, 416 pages. 2001.

Vol. 2261: F. Naumann, Quality-Driven Query Answering for Integrated Information Systems. X, 166 pages. 2002.

Vol. 2262: P. Müller, Modular Specification and Verification of Object-Oriented Programs. XIV, 292 pages. 2002.

Vol. 2263: T. Clark, J. Warmer (Eds.), Object Modeling with the OCL. VIII, 281 pages. 2002.

Vol. 2264: K. Steinhöfel (Ed.), Stochastic Algorithms: Foundations and Applications. Proceedings, 2001. VIII, 203 pages. 2001.

Vol. 2265: P. Mutzel, M. Jünger, S. Leipert (Eds.), Graph Drawing. Proceedings, 2001. XV, 524 pages. 2002.

Vol. 2266: S. Reich, M.T. Tzagarakis, P.M.E. De Bra (Eds.), Hypermedia: Openness, Structural Awareness, and Adaptivity. Proceedings, 2001. X, 335 pages. 2002.

Vol. 2267: M. Cerioli, G. Reggio (Eds.), Recent Trends in Algebraic Development Techniques. Proceedings, 2001. X, 345 pages. 2001.

Vol. 2268: E.F. Deprettere, J. Teich, S. Vassiliadis (Eds.), Embedded Processor Design Challenges. VIII, 327 pages. 2002.

Vol. 2269: S. Diehl (Ed.), Software Visualization. Proceedings, 2001. VIII, 405 pages. 2002.

Vol. 2270: M. Pflanz, On-line Error Detection and Fast Recover Techniques for Dependable Embedded Processors. XII, 126 pages. 2002.

Vol. 2271: B. Preneel (Ed.), Topics in Cryptology – CT-RSA 2002. Proceedings, 2002. X, 311 pages. 2002.

Vol. 2272: D. Bert, J.P. Bowen, M.C. Henson, K. Robinson (Eds.), ZB 2002: Formal Specification and Development in Z and B. Proceedings, 2002. XII, 535 pages. 2002.

Vol. 2273: A.R. Coden, E.W. Brown, S. Srinivasan (Eds.), Information Retrieval Techniques for Speech Applications. XI, 109 pages. 2002.

Vol. 2274: D. Naccache, P. Paillier (Eds.), Public Key Cryptography. Proceedings, 2002. XI, 385 pages. 2002.

Vol. 2275: N.R. Pal, M. Sugeno (Eds.), Advances in Soft Computing – AFSS 2002. Proceedings, 2002. XVI, 536 pages. 2002. (Subseries LNAI).

Vol. 2276: A. Gelbukh (Ed.), Computational Linguistics and Intelligent Text Processing. Proceedings, 2002. XIII, 444 pages. 2002.

Vol. 2277: P. Callaghan, Z. Luo, J. McKinna, R. Pollack (Eds.), Types for Proofs and Programs. Proceedings, 2000. VIII, 243 pages. 2002.

Vol. 2278: J.A. Foster, E. Lutton, J. Miller, C. Ryan, A.G.B. Tettamanzi (Eds.), Genetic Programming. Proceedings, 2002. XI, 337 pages. 2002.

Vol. 2279: S. Cagnoni, J. Gottlieb, E. Hart, M. Middendorf, G.R. Raidl (Eds.), Applications of Evolutionary Computing. Proceedings, 2002. XIII, 344 pages. 2002.

Vol. 2280: J.P. Katoen, P. Stevens (Eds.), Tools and Algorithms for the Construction and Analysis of Systems. Proceedings, 2002. XIII, 482 pages. 2002.

Vol. 2281: S. Arikawa, A. Shinohara (Eds.), Progress in Discovery Science. XIV, 684 pages. 2002. (Subseries LNAI).

Vol. 2282: D. Ursino, Extraction and Exploitation of Intensional Knowledge from Heterogeneous Information Sources. XXVI, 289 pages. 2002.

Vol. 2283: T. Nipkow, L.C. Paulson, M. Wenzel, Isabelle/HOL. XIII, 218 pages. 2002.

Vol. 2284: T. Eiter, K.-D. Schewe (Eds.), Foundations of Information and Knowledge Systems. Proceedings, 2002. X, 289 pages. 2002.

Vol. 2285: H. Alt, A. Ferreira (Eds.), STACS 2002. Proceedings, 2002. XIV, 660 pages. 2002.

Vol. 2286: S. Rajsbaum (Ed.), LATIN 2002: Theoretical Informatics. Proceedings, 2002. XIII, 630 pages. 2002.

Vol. 2287: C.S. Jensen, K.G. Jeffery, J. Pokorny, Saltenis, E. Bertino, K. Böhm, M. Jarke (Eds.), Advances in Database Technology – EDBT 2002. Proceedings, 2002. XVI, 776 pages. 2002.

Vol. 2288: K. Kim (Ed.), Information Security and Cryptology – ICISC 2001. Proceedings, 2001. XIII, 457 pages. 2002.

Vol. 2289: C.J. Tomlin, M.R. Greenstreet (Eds.), Hybrid Systems: Computation and Control. Proceedings, 2002. XIII, 480 pages. 2002.

Vol. 2291: F. Crestani, M. Girolami, C.J. van Rijsbergen (Eds.), Advances in Information Retrieval. Proceedings, 2002. XIII, 363 pages. 2002.

Vol. 2292: G.B. Khosrovshahi, A. Shokoufandeh, A. Shokrollahi (Eds.), Theoretical Aspects of Computer Science. IX, 221 pages. 2002.

Vol. 2293: J. Renz, Qualitative Spatial Reasoning with Topological Information. XVI, 207 pages. 2002. (Subseries LNAI).

Vol. 2295: W. Kuich, G. Rozenberg, A. Salomaa (Eds.), Developments in Language Theory. Proceedings, 2001. IX, 389 pages. 2002.

Vol. 2296: B. Dunin-Keplicz, E. Nawarecki (Eds.), From Theory to Practice in Multi-Agent Systems. Proceedings, 2001. IX, 341 pages. 2002. (Subseries LNAI).

Vol. 2299: H. Schmeck, T. Ungerer, L. Wolf (Eds.), Trends in Network and Pervasive Computing – ARCS 2002. Proceedings, 2002. XIV, 287 pages. 2002.

Vol. 2300: W. Brauer, H. Ehrig, J. Karhumäki, A. Salomaa (Eds.), Formal and Natural Computing. XXXVI, 431 pages. 2002.

Vol. 2301: A. Braquelaire, J.-O. Lachaud, A. Vialard (Eds.), Discrete Geometry for Computer Imagery. Proceedings, 2002. XI, 439 pages. 2002.

Vol. 2302: C. Schulte, Programming Constraint Services. XII, 176 pages. 2002. (Subseries LNAI).

Vol. 2303: M. Nielsen, U. Engberg (Eds.), Foundations of Software Science and Computation Structures. Proceedings, 2002. XIII, 435 pages. 2002.

Vol. 2304: R.N. Horspool (Ed.), Compiler Construction. Proceedings, 2002. XI, 343 pages. 2002.

Vol. 2305: D. Le Métayer (Ed.), Programming Languages and Systems. Proceedings, 2002. XII, 331 pages. 2002.

Vol. 2306: R.-D. Kutsche, H. Weber (Eds.), Fundamental Approaches to Software Engineering. Proceedings, 2002. XIII, 341 pages. 2002.

Vol. 2307: C. Zhang, S. Zhang, Association Rule Mining. XII, 238 pages. 2002. (Subseries LNAI).

Vol. 2308: I.P. Vlahavas, C.D. Spyropoulos (Eds.), Methods and Applications of Artificial Intelligence. Proceedings, 2002. XIV, 514 pages. 2002. (Subseries LNAI).

Vol. 2309: A. Armando (Ed.), Frontiers of Combining Systems. Proceedings, 2002. VIII, 255 pages. 2002. (Subseries LNAI).

Vol. 2310: P. Collet, C. Fonlupt, J.-K. Hao, E. Lutton, M. Schoenauer (Eds.), Artificial Evolution. Proceedings, 2001. XI, 375 pages. 2002.

Vol. 2311: D. Bustard, W. Liu, R. Sterritt (Eds.), Soft-Ware 2002: Computing in an Imperfect World. Proceedings, 2002. XI, 359 pages. 2002.

Vol. 2312: T. Arts, M. Mohnen (Eds.), Implementation of Functional Languages. Proceedings, 2001. VII, 187 pages. 2002.

Vol. 2313: C.A. Coello Coello, A. de Albornoz, L.E. Sucar, O.Cairó Battistutti (Eds.), MICAI 2002: Advances in Artificial Intelligence. Proceedings, 2002. XIII, 548 pages. 2002. (Subseries LNAI).

Vol. 2314: S.-K. Chang, Z. Chen, S.-Y. Lee (Eds.), Recent Advances in Visual Information Systems. Proceedings, 2002. XI, 323 pages. 2002.

Vol. 2315: F. Arhab, C. Talcott (Eds.), Coordination Models and Languages. Proceedings, 2002. XI, 406 pages. 2002.

Vol. 2317: M. Hegarty, B. Meyer, N. Hari Narayanan (Eds.), Diagrammatic Representation and Inference. Proceedings, 2002. XIV, 362 pages. 2002. (Subseries LNAI).

Vol. 2318: D. Bošnački, S. Leue (Eds.), Model Checking Software. Proceedings, 2002. X, 259 pages. 2002.

Vol. 2319: C. Gacek (Ed.), Software Reuse: Methods, Techniques, and Tools. Proceedings, 2002. XI, 353 pages. 2002.

Vol. 2322: V. Mařík, O. Štěpánková, H. Krautwurmová, M. Luck (Eds.), Multi-Agent Systems and Applications II. Proceedings, 2001. XII, 377 pages. 2002. (Subseries LNAI).

Vol. 2324: T. Field, P.G. Harrison, J. Bradley, U. Harder (Eds.), Computer Performance Evaluation. Proceedings, 2002. XI, 349 pages. 2002.